PEARSON
mysoclab™

P9-DFD-313

Save Time.

Improve Results.

More than 3 million students have used a Pearson MyLab product to get a better grade.

MySocLab is an all-in-one learning and testing environment for introductory sociology. The easy-to-navigate site provides a variety of resources including

- An interactive Pearson eText

- Audio and video material to view or listen to, whatever your learning style

- Personalized learning opportunities—YOU choose what, where, and when you want to study

- Self-assessment tests that create a personalized study plan to guide you on making the most efficient use of study time

To take advantage of all that MySocLab has to offer, you will need an access code. If you do not already have an access code, you can buy one online at **www.mysoclab.com**.

PEARSON

Personalized Learning

In MySocLab you are treated as an individual with specific learning needs.

PEARSON

BRUCE RAVELLI   MICHELLE WEBBER   JOHN PATTERSON

SOCIOLOGY FOR EVERYONE

My Course > Study Plan...

To begin, open the Diagnostic Test. After you submit the test, you will return to this screen. If your results indicate that you need to brush up on any learning objectives, you will be assigned remediation content to help with your learning. To complete the study plan, you must meet the pass criteria for the exit test.

Pre Test

Chapter 6 Pre-Test

Your Score   22%

Post Test

Chapter 6 Post-Test

Your Score   70%

Study Material   Show Recommended Study Material   Display Learning Objectives ☑

Our Sensational Senses
Pass criteria: 70.00 %   Your Score 57%

Name	Type	Score	Options
Live!Psych 6.3	Link	--	○
Live!Psych 6.2	Link	--	○
Our Sensational Senses	Link	--	○
Live!Psych 6.1	Link	--	○

Vision
Pass criteria: 70.00 %   Your Score 75%

You have successfully met the pass criteria for this Learning Objective.

The study and assessment resources that come with your textbook allow you to review content and develop what you need to know, on your own time, and at your own pace.

MySocLab provides

- Quizzes with immediate grades

- A personalized study plan that tells you where to study based on your results, and where you can find the key topics you need to review to improve

- A gradebook where you can find your grades see your progress as the term unfolds

- An opportunity for your instructor to see the gradebook, too

- Videos and quizzes to help you learn

SOCIOLOGY**FOR**EVERYONE

BRUCE RAVELLI
Mount Royal University

MICHELLE WEBBER
Brock University

JOHN PATTERSON
Canadore College

Pearson Canada
Toronto

To my students, past, present and future, who continue to inspire
me as a teacher and as a sociologist.—Bruce
To my nearest and dearest, Drew Wallace.—Michelle
To my boys, Liam and Sean—my inspiration.—John

Library and Archives Canada Cataloguing in Publication

Ravelli, Bruce, 1963–

   Sociology for everyone / Bruce Ravelli, Michelle Webber, John Patterson.

Includes index.

ISBN 978-0-13-502607-6

   1. Sociology—Textbooks.   I. Webber, Michelle   II. Patterson, John, 1960—   III. Title.

HM586.R393 2011   301   C2009-905536-8

ISBN 978-0-13-502607-6

Vice President, Editorial Director: Gary Bennett
Editor-in-Chief: Ky Pruesse
Senior Acquisitions Editor: Laura Pratt
Signing Representative: Helene Goulet
Marketing Manager: Arthur Gee
Senior Developmental Editor: Madhu Ranadive
Production Editor: Kevin Leung
Copy Editor: Claudia Forgas
Proofreaders: Maria Jelinek, Susan Broadhurst
Production Coordinator: Sarah Lukaweski
Permissions and Photo Research: Christina Beamish
Composition: Integra
Art Director: Julia Hall
Cover Design: Miguel Acevedo
Cover Image: Getty Images

For permission to reproduce copyrighted material, the publisher gratefully acknowledges the copyright holders listed on pages 430–431, which are considered an extension of this copyright page.

Statistics Canada information is used with the permission of Statistics Canada. Users are forbidden to copy the data and redisseminate them, in an original or modified form, for commercial purposes, without permission from Statistics Canada. Information on the availability of the wide range of data from Statistics Canada can be obtained from Statistics Canada's Regional Offices, its World Wide Web site at http://www.statcan.gc.ca, and its toll-free access number 1-800-263-1136.

1 2 3 4 5   14 13 12 11 10

Printed and bound in the United States of America.

Brief Contents

Contents

Module 2.2   STEPS IN THE RESEARCH PROCESS   44

module 2.3   RESEARCH METHODS IN DETAIL   49

module 2.4   EVALUATING RESEARCH—DEVELOPING A CRITICAL EYE   55

chapter 3   Culture   66

module 3.1   WHAT IS CULTURE?   68

module 3.2   MATERIAL AND NONMATERIAL CULTURE   72

chapter 7   Social Inequality   192

chapter 12   Social Change, Collective Behaviour, Social Movements, and the Future   356

Preface

Dear Students:

Welcome and congratulations! Deciding to attend college is an important and exciting time of your life. You will meet many new people who may become life-long friends, you will explore new ideas, learn new skills, and lay the foundation for your career. Going to college begins a process that in a relatively short time helps transform and prepare you for moving from a student to becoming a police officer, a social worker, a registered practical nurse, or whatever career you find most inspiring.

We know that as a college student your time is precious, you have much to learn, and your primary focus is learning the things that you need to know to work in your chosen profession. As such, students often question the value of taking sociology and request more "practical" courses. However, you should know that the knowledge and skills you learn in sociology are both practical and essential to your career. First, and foremost, sociology is the study of human group life and that the pursuit of sociology is to help us understand why we and others behave in the ways that we do. Anyone who works with people (and most of us do) will benefit from developing the skills to think like a sociologist—to develop their sociological imagination. Second, you should also know that sociological research forms the basis for many of the political and business decisions that affect our lives. Therefore, we would argue that sociology is far more practical to your professional development than you may at first realize.

This textbook provides you with the information you need to begin building a solid foundation in sociology that will allow you to begin to think like a sociologist. We realize, however, that many of you will want information geared specifically to your own career pursuits. We hope that given the input of many of your instructors, we have struck the right balance of content to meet your own educational needs. For example, students in the medical, policing and law, or teaching professions will benefit from our chapters on "Aging, Disabilities and Health", "Deviance, Crime and Regulation", and "Socialization and Social Interaction", respectively. As you can see, our goal was to write a sociology text that is for *everyone*.

We appreciate that college students are a diverse group. Some of you are under 20 and are fresh out of high school while others may be significantly older and have decided to return to school to change careers or just to challenge yourselves. Some of you were born in Canada while others have recently arrived. Many of you have part-time jobs, partners, children, and many other responsibilities and pressures outside school. We understand these challenges and wrote this text with the hope of appealing to all of these diverse audiences. In writing this text, we worked hard to write clearly, provide examples that were relevant to all students, define new terms throughout the text, organize the content in a logical progression of topics, offer frequent and varied forms of evaluation, and provide summaries that are both thorough and, through the addition of the Concept Maps described below, visual. In other words, we have made every effort to write a text that would inspire you and also one that would give you all the tools to succeed in the course.

We hope that as you read through this text, that you take the time to reflect and ponder the concepts and issues that we introduce. By challenging your personal views and by pushing yourself to see the world as sociologists do, you will begin to see the social world in a brand new way. We wish each of you every success in your personal, academic and career pursuits.

Bruce, Michelle, and John

Dear Colleagues:

Do you remember taking your first sociology class? Back then few of us could have predicted the role sociology would play in our lives and the way it would change how we saw ourselves and the world around us. We, the authors of this text, certainly remember our first experiences with sociology, and we regularly returned to them as we wrote this textbook.

Bruce's first Introduction to Sociology class was at Okanagan College in Kelowna, B.C., and the only thing he remembers about it was that the professor memorized all the students' names (about 40) before the end of the very first class! Later, as an undergrad, Bruce took five or six more courses in sociology (his B.A. and Masters are in anthropology), and while he found them interesting, none of them really captivated his attention for very long. All this changed when he began his first full-time teaching position (in anthropology) at Northern Lights College in Dawson Creek, B.C. (his home town). In his second year Bruce was asked to teach a section of Introduction to Sociology in the fall semester, and as he was preparing for the course over the summer he finally read C.W. Mills' *The Promise*. Even 20 years later, he remembers the profound impact the reading had on him, and how it showed him an entirely new way of looking at the social world. For Bruce, reading *The Promise* was the single most important reason that he decided to leave his teaching position the next year and return to school to complete his Ph.D. in sociology.

For Michelle, reading Dorothy Smith's book *The Everyday World as Problematic* in an undergraduate sociological theory course sparked her passion for sociology. Dorothy Smith's work provided a language, a perspective, and a method of inquiry for explaining the social world and the worlds of those close to us. This theory course represented the beginnings of Michelle's academic career. She finished her undergraduate degree at Brock University and then completed her M.A. and Ph.D. at the University of Toronto. As a graduate student, Michelle was privileged to take graduate courses with Dorothy Smith and to complete her MA thesis under Smith's supervision. Michelle has since returned to the scene of the crime, so to speak, as she teaches sociology in the very department that introduced her to a new way of seeing the world.

For as long as John can remember he has been interested in human behaviour. He began his undergraduate studies in sociology at Wilfrid Laurier University (WLU) in Waterloo, Ontario. Among his more memorable experiences while there were courses taught by Juanne Clarke, "The Sociology of Medicine" and Sue Wilson, "Social Stratification". While a student at WLU, John became increasingly interested in social problems. Consequently, his graduate studies took a more applied approach and focused on Human Services Management and Planning. While a graduate student, a new passion emerged—teaching. John had the good fortune to be employed by the Sociology department at York University as a teaching assistant under the direction of Dr. Alice Propper. John credits Dr. Propper for instilling in him the passion and joy of helping others discover sociology.

For us, this text is not intended to be the final word on introductory sociology but instead the beginning of our relationship with you and your students—one that will help us grow as colleagues and authors and allow us to refine and improve the text year after year.

We understand that there are many quality introductory textbooks available for your consideration, but we believe that our passion for sociology, our commitment to introductory students, and over 50 years of combined teaching experience enable us to create a truly unique textbook. We believe that *Sociology for Everyone* offers a number of advantages over other textbooks:

- We are excited to be the first introductory sociology text to present material in a modular format. This approach has been used successfully in other disciplines for years. You will find that the chapters are divided into modules that provide a logical flow to the text. The modular format provides an ideal framework for instructors to create their own lesson plans, assign readings, and develop assignments. Each chapter consists of four modules, breaking down the material into concentrated, manageable parts of information. Organizing the material into meaningful parts helps improve students' working memory capacity—or memory span—allowing for more information to be recalled at one time and gives instructors more options when assigning material. At the end of each chapter flow charts, or Concepts Maps, illustrate how the chapter works as a whole.
- All of our chapters include a discussion of theory. In addition to a discussion of classical theories, you will note that we have included a number of contemporary theories such as

queer theory, post-colonial theory and post-structural theory. We believe that reviewing theory throughout the text, and presenting it in a manner that introductory students will both understand and be challenged by, make for the most comprehensive and contemporary approach on the market.

■ To reflect the evolution of thinking within the discipline, we have included the concept of *racialization* in our discussion of minority populations as well as post-colonial theoretical insights.

■ Our analyses of gender and sexualities represent leading-edge sociological insights and challenge traditional concepts of power and heterosexual privilege.

■ Our review of mass media presents an historical perspective that, although the pace of technological change is increasing, the fundamental nature of mass communication represents a continuation of a process that began thousands of years ago.

■ We include the most recent statistics and sociological literature available. As you will see, the vast majority of our statistical analyses are the most recent available. Moreover, roughly 50% of our references are from 2005 or later, with approximately 10% dating from 2008. While we are the most current resource on the market, we do not diminish the importance of classic contributions from the past.

■ We make extensive use of contemporary Canadian examples during our discussions but never at the expense of poignant international examples whenever they are more salient to the discussion at hand.

■ We believe that the time has come for a completely new textbook written by Canadian sociologists.

When we entitled our text "Sociology for Everyone" the "everyone" we had in mind is your students. But, the "everyone" concept goes deeper than that. It, in fact, became our guiding principle. In writing this text our true objective was to write a sociology text that was student-centred. It was our sincere desire to write a text that was contemporary, interesting, challenging but foremost accessible. We hoped, with your help of course, that through this text we could bring the discipline of sociology to your students.

We realize that as hard as we may try we will not write a book that meets everyone's needs. Through the writing process you quickly learn that when writing a text compromises must be made and so no one person is going to be completely satisfied. However, with the assistance of our reviewers, we believe we have created a text that will exceed the expectations of you and your students. Most importantly, as you read our book, we hope that our passion for sociology and our desire to make it accessible and exciting to your students is evident.

Bruce, Michelle, and John

Text Features

Students often become excited about sociology through their experience in introductory courses. We hope that this text helps bring together professors who are passionate about sociology and students who are willing to learn. Through its distinctive approach to the field, its readability, and its relevance to students' lives, *Sociology for Everyone* helps professors develop the sociological imagination in their students by encouraging them to see sociology from multiple perspectives. Topics are presented in ways that allow students to engage with the material and to exercise their sociological imaginations.

The authors bring over 50 years' experience teaching introductory sociology to a variety of students, in large and small classes, at a variety of schools. This text, therefore, is the culmination of many years of teaching and is an expression of our passion for sociology and our commitment to our students. We believe that the following text features demonstrate this passion as well as our shared experience in how best to inspire students to be as fascinated by sociology as we are.

THEME BOXES

Each chapter features two different theme boxes, each of which are intended to engage you with topical discussions to inspire and challenge your sociological imaginations.

WHY SHOULD WE CARE? Explore many of today's pressing social issues: people who live on the street, using the internet as a research tool, when languages die, feral children, identity theft, the sandwich generation, soup kitchens, feminization of poverty, hate groups in Canada, cyberbullying, obesity and our kids, and reconsidering waste.

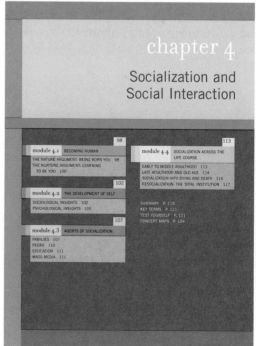

CANADIAN SOCIETY IN FOCUS Highlights issues that are particularly relevant to Canadian society: Raves and Straight Edge, Statistics Canada and Sociology, what constitutes Canadian culture, effects of divorce on children, discrimination in the criminal justice system, child-tax expenses as a tax deduction, Canada's richest people, gender equality, The charter and minority rights, No Logo and You, two-tier health care, and Mothers Against Drunk Driving.

TEACHING AND LEARNING TOOLS

CHAPTER MODULES OVERVIEW Each chapter begins with a brief overview of the chapter modules and key topics to be covered. This feature allows you to focus your reading and helps integrate the material from one chapter to the next. Using the modular format, students and instructors can approach the various topics in a chapter to meet their individual study and teaching needs.

OPENING VIGNETTES Each chapter opens with a vignette designed to engage the student's sociological imagination. The topics, based on events in the news, will generate student discussions and link areas of sociological interest and real world issues.

"THINK ABOUT . . . " QUESTIONS Each module begins with a number of open-ended questions. The questions are designed to have the student reflect on their own knowledge and opinions about the subject matter about to be discussed to focus their reading and maximize their understanding.

Think about Defining Families

1 Think about defining families. Who are the members of your family? Based on those who you chose to include in the list, how might you define family?

2 Think about the relationship we have with our family members. How do we treat them differently from other people?

3 Think about how the word

WHAT DO YOU KNOW ABOUT. . . ? Each module ends with a short multiple choice quiz to help check comprehension and retention of the key concepts and issues discussed in the modules.

What do you know about **Crime: Types and Trends**?

Multiple-choice questions (circle your answer)

1. Crimes that are committed during or as a result of one's employment are called
   a. Street crime
   b. White collar crime
   c. Work crime
   d. Organized crime

2. _____ crime refers to groups involved in the illegal trade of goods and services.
   a. Organized
   b. Corporate
   c. White collar
   d. Political

3. Who is most likely to commit street crimes in Canada?
   a. Women
   b. Men

   c. White people
   d. Torontonians

4. Which ethnic group is most overrepresented in federal correctional institutions in Canada?
   a. Blacks
   b. Aboriginals
   c. Whites
   d. Asians

5. Making offenders pay for their crimes is called
   a. Retribution
   b. Rehabilitation
   c. Deterrence
   d. Incapacitation

Answers: b, a, b, b, a

Summary

module 5.1   CRIME AND DEVIANCE

1. *Criminology* is the study of crime causation, crime prevention, and the punishment and rehabilitation of offenders.
2. *Sociology of law* looks at the social construction of law, the social development of legal institutions, and the relation of law to social change.
3. *Crime* is defined as those behaviours that require legal control and social intervention, codified in law; *deviance* involves actions, beliefs, conditions, and characteristics that depart from social norms and may or may not be against the law.
4. *Social control* describes the methods used by society to discourage deviant behaviour and encourage conformity to social norms.

CHAPTER SUMMARY Each chapter includes a comprehensive summary with information organized by module.

Key Terms

KEY TERMS Key terms are boldfaced within the text and accompanied by brief definitions in the margins that provide a visual and efficient means of building your sociological vocabulary. The key terms are also listed alphabetically at the end of the chapter as a quick reference tool.

Test Yourself

1. A researcher from this theoretical perspective would be interested in interaction patterns within families.
a. Functionalist
b. Conflict theorist
c. Symbolic interactionist
d. Structural functionalist

2. Research that focuses on numerical data is called
a. Quantitative research
b. Qualitative research
c. Numerical research
d. Inductive logic

3. Which approach is likely to have a smaller sample?
a. Quantitative research
b. Qualitative research
c. Numerical research
d. Deductive logic

4. Researchers use two systems of reasoning. Which one moves from data to theory?
a. Inductive logic
b. Deductive logic
c. Quantitative analysis
d. Numerical analysis

5. Which researcher would be most interested in the issue of gender and inequality?
a. Conflict theorist
b. Symbolic interactionist

c. Spurious variable
d. Hypothesis

7. If we make a prediction that married people have more sex than single people, what would be the independent variable?
a. Marital status
b. Frequency of sex
c. Time spent alone
d. Television habits

8. The group selected to be interviewed is called the
a. Population
b. Sample
c. Subject
d. Survey

9. Which step in the research process involves the coding of information?
a. Research design
b. Data collection
c. Data analysis
d. Problem formulation

10. A hypothesis is
a. A tentative statement that you can test empirically about the relationship between two variables
b. A conclusion based on empirical data
c. A statement of fact
d. The first step in the research process

TEST YOURSELF Each chapter ends with a summary multiple choice quiz to allow students to self-test their knowledge of the key concepts and critical issues discussed in the chapter.

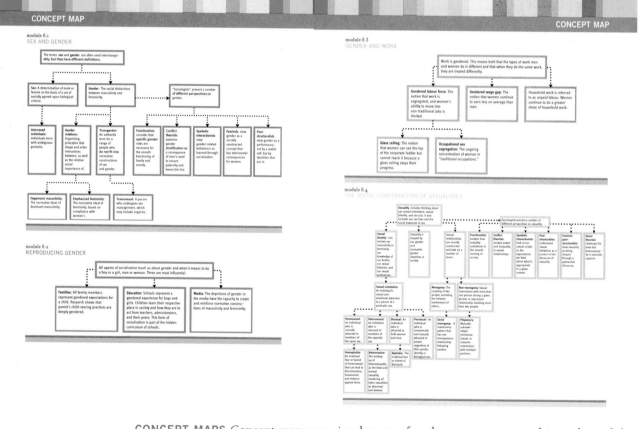

CONCEPT MAPS Concept maps are visual maps of each concept presented in each module. The maps are organized to highlight critical information and provide the links between key concepts. Concept Maps have been created for each module and are grouped together at the end of each chapter, providing an overview of all the modules presented in the chapter and a quick and easy reference for review.

ONLINE RESOURCES

MySocLab—Pearson Canada's online resource, MySocLab, offers instructors and students all of their resources in one place, organized to accompany this text. With MySocLab, you will be able to enliven your lectures with a variety of material. And your students will be able to "study smarter" with an ebook and a diagnostic test that creates a customized study plan to help them prepare for, and perform better on, exams. MySocLab is available for instructors by going to www.mysoclab.com and following the instructions on the page. Students get MySocLab with an access code that is available with the purchase of a new text. Access codes can also be purchased separately at the campus bookstore.

Technology Specialists. Pearson's Technology Specialists work with faculty and campus course designers to ensure that Pearson technology products, assessment tools, and online course materials are tailored to meet your specific needs. This highly qualified team is dedicated to helping schools take full advantage of a wide range of educational resources, by assisting in the integration of a variety of instructional materials and media formats. Your local Pearson Education sales representative can provide you with more details on this service program.

COURSESMART FOR INSTRUCTORS CourseSmart goes beyond traditional expectations—providing instant, online access to the textbooks and course materials you need at a lower cost for students. And even as students save money, you can save time and hassle with a digital eTextbook that allows you to search for the most relevant content at the very moment you need it. Whether it's evaluating textbooks or creating lecture notes to help students with difficult concepts, CourseSmart can make life a little easier. See how when you visit www.coursesmart.com/instructors.

COURSESMART FOR STUDENTS CourseSmart goes beyond traditional expectations—providing instant, online access to the textbooks and course materials you need at an average savings of 50%. With instant access from any computer and the ability to search your text, you'll find the content you need quickly, no matter where you are. And with online tools like highlighting and note-taking, you can save time and study efficiently. See all the benefits at www.coursesmart.com/students.

A student access code card for MySocLab is packaged with every new copy of *Sociology for Everyone*. If a student purchases a used book, access code cards may be purchased at the campus bookstore.

INSTRUCTOR RESOURCES

INSTRUCTOR'S MANUAL This useful teaching aid provides two complementary resources for each chapter: one providing an overview of the key terms and material within the chapter and another moving beyond the text by undertaking an exploration of an issue/case study that accentuates the material. New and experienced instructors will find this resource useful. Some of the features included in the Instructor's Manual are: barriers to effective learning, chapter/issue overviews, student assignments, and MySocLab resources.

POWERPOINT PRESENTATION This PowerPoint Presentation provides graphic and text images for complete multimedia presentations in the classroom.

IMAGE LIBRARY The Image Library provides electronic versions of the figures and tables that appear in the text.

TEST ITEM FILE The Test Item File contains more than 2000 questions in multiple choice, true-false, short answer, and essay formats. The Test Item File is available in both Word and MyTest formats.

MyTest for *Sociology for Everyone* from Pearson Education Canada is a powerful assessment generation program that helps instructors easily create and print quizzes, tests, exams, as well as homework or practice handouts. Questions and tests can all be authored online, allowing instructors ultimate flexibility and the ability to efficiently manage assessments at anytime, from anywhere.

All of these supplements are also available on an Instructor's Resource CD-ROM (ISBN 978-0-13-703797-1) or by accessing the password-protected section of Pearson Education Canada's online catalogue (vig.pearsoned.ca). Navigate to your book's catalogue page to view a list of those supplements that are available. See your local sales representative for details and access.

Acknowledgments

Because of the monumental effort by the editors and staff of Pearson Education Canada, *Sociology for Everyone* reflects the highest standards of textbook publishing in all its phases. Pearson provided us with the peer reviews, editorial comments, and suggestions for reorganizing and updating material that supported our desire to communicate our ideas to students and that nurtured our own creativity as authors. We would like to thank Laura Pratt for her unwavering support and positive outlook, Joel Gladstone and Madhu Ranadive for ongoing support and sage advice throughout the project, and Kevin Leung who pulled it all together. We also appreciate the tremendous efforts of Lorna Kearnes, Sara Cumming, Jennifer Whitten, Amy McGrath and Shannon McHugh, our research assistants, for their willingness to work with tight deadlines without losing their sense of humour. We would like to thank Dr. Edward Thompson for his reflection and input into chapter 11. Finally, we would like to thank our friends and families for their encouragement. In particular, we have deep appreciation for our partners, Sacha, Drew, and Lynda who never complained when we seemed distant or moody because we were overwhelmed or frustrated by our writing—we could not have done this without you.

We would also like to recognize the following colleagues, who took the time and effort to provide thoughtful and meaningful reviews during the development of this textbook:

Michael Del Balso, Dawson College
Marc Belanger, Vanier College
Brenda Bennett, George Brown College
Cynthia Booth, Cambrian College
Deborah Boutilier, Niagara College
Diane Clarke, Lambton College
Jacquie Cottingham, Confederation College
Lidia Dorosz, St Lawrence College
Kelly Henley, St Clair College
Sue Honsberger, Algonquin
Melanie Marchand, Georgian College
John Metcalfe, Humber College
Mary Louise Noce, Sheridan
Daniel S. Popowich, Mohawk College
Pat Reeves, Seneca College
Carolyne Willoughby, Durham College

About the Authors

Bruce Ravelli received his Ph.D. from the University of Victoria in 1997. He has taught introductory sociology for over 20 years, and receives strong teaching evaluations from his students because of his passion for sociology, his dedication to teaching, and his commitment to high academic standards. Bruce has published articles and book chapters on Canadian culture and cross-national value differences as well as students' evaluation of teaching. He is co-author *Exploring Sociology: A* Canadian Perspective with Michelle Webber. He has also co-edited *Seeing Ourselves: Classic, Contemporary, and Cross-Cultural Readings in Sociology*, Third Canadian Edition, with John J. Macionis, Nijole V. Benokraitis and Peter Urmetzer, and edited *Exploring Canadian Sociology: A Reader* as well as co-authored the brief introduction to sociology text entitled *Core Concepts in Sociology*, Second In-Class Canadian Edition, with Linda Lindsey and Stephen Beach. Bruce is the co-developer of award-winning free online software that allows teachers to anonymously assess their teaching/courses at any point during a course (available at: **www.toofast.ca**). He offers workshops and presentations on the software and on anonymous student assessment across North America. Bruce teaches in the Department of Sociology & Anthropology at Mount Royal University in Calgary. If any students or colleagues have questions or comments about the text, please feel free to contact him by email at bravelli@mtroyal.ca.

Michelle Webber received her Ph.D. from the University of Toronto. Her research interests lie in the sociology of education and sociology of gender. She has regularly taught introductory sociology over the last 10 years. Michelle has published articles and book chapters on feminist pedagogies, the regulation of academic work, the work of teaching assistants, the experiences of contingent faculty members, and feminist knowledges. With Bruce Ravelli, she co-authored, *Exploring* Sociology: A Canadian Perspective. She has co-edited *Rethinking Society in the 21st Century: Critical Readings in Sociology* (First and Second Editions) with Kate Bezanson. Her current research project is funded by SSHRC and is an investigation of the tenure system in social sciences faculties in Ontario universities. The research team is headed by Sandra Acker (University of Toronto, Principal Investigator) and also includes Elizabeth Smyth (University of Toronto). Her newest research project (Michelle as Principal Investigator and Sandra Acker as Co-Investigator) examines accountability governance and academic knowledge and subjectivities and is funded by the Social Sciences and Humanities Research Council. Michelle is an Associate Professor in the Department of Sociology and is the Graduate Program Director of the MA in Critical Sociology at Brock University. She can be contacted via email at mwebber@brocku.ca.

John Patterson—has taught introductory sociology at the high school, college and university levels since 1984. John holds an undergraduate degree in sociology (W.LU., 1982), a masters degree in environmental studies (human services planning and management) (York University, 1986) and a Bachelor of Education degree (U of T, 1989). John has been a professor with the Social Sciences department at Canadore College since 1992 where he has been the recipient of both Canadore College's Teaching Excellence Award and the Recognition of Excellence Award for Community Service. In addition to teaching sociology to students in a variety of human services fields, John is also active in the community as a board member with one of the largest social service agencies in North Bay and as a coordinator for an environmental advocacy group. John can be reached by email at john.patterson@canadorec.on.ca.

chapter 1

Understanding the Sociological Imagination

A Day in the Life: Seeing the World Like a Sociologist

To a sociologist, everything people do is fascinating. Have you ever waited in line for a movie and watched the people around you? One night, you notice two people who are obviously smitten with each other holding hands. A few minutes later, you see some young men push through the line in front of the couple and snarl "fags" as they walk by. You think to yourself, "Why are some people so offended by seeing two people show that they care for each other?" Hurtful.

Have you ever driven by homeless people and wondered how they got there and why they do not get jobs? Challenging.

Have you ever walked by an elementary school in the winter and seen a young boy chasing a girl with a handful of snow, yelling that she needs a "face wash"? You cannot help but chuckle as you notice the young girl scream with a huge smile on her face. You remember that boys and girls at that age show who they *like* by acting as though they *don't*. Interesting.

Have you ever wondered whether new communications technology has changed the nature of our relationships? Today, virtually everyone has a cellphone, many have a Facebook site, and perhaps a few even have a cottage at secondlife.com. What influence, if any, do these forms of communication have on today's relationships? Intriguing.

All of these scenarios, and your feelings and emotions about them, are of interest to sociology. These situations illustrate that our entire existence is defined by the reality that we are social beings who live and grow through our interactions with others. Therefore, we cannot hope to understand ourselves, or the world around us, without investigating the interplay between the individual and the social—this is what sociology is all about. Once you can master how sociologists can instantaneously switch their thinking from individual to social, from privileged to non-privileged, and from Western to global, you are well on your way to appreciating the beauty and uniqueness of the sociological endeavour.

module 1.1

Think about the Sociological Imagination

1 Think about sociology. After reading the opening vignette, what do you think sociologists study? How might you define sociology?

2 Look around your classroom. Do you notice anything unique or unusual about the groups of people here? What might you imagine a sociologist would find interesting about this collection of people?

sociology The systematic study of human groups and their interactions.

sociological perspective A view of society based on the dynamic relationship between individuals and the larger social network in which we all live.

Charles Wright Mills

The Sociological Imagination

As an academic discipline, sociology is dedicated to exposing you to a new and unique way of seeing our social world. **Sociology** is the systematic study of human groups and their interactions. To understand the beauty of sociology is to appreciate its distinctive view of the social world, often referred to as the sociological perspective. In essence, the **sociological perspective** is the unique way in which sociologists see our world and can dissect the dynamic relationship between individuals and the larger social network in which we all live. Many people fail to realize how important social forces are in shaping our lives (Babbie, 1994; Bellah et al., 1996). As individuals, we make many decisions every day—for example, what you chose to wear to school or what you decided to eat when you met your friends at the student centre. Even these seemingly mundane choices have rich social significance and reveal a great deal about what sociologists find so fascinating about human behaviour.

CHARLES WRIGHT MILLS AND THE SOCIOLOGICAL IMAGINATION

C.W. Mills suggested that people who do not, or cannot, recognize the social origins and character of their problems may be unable to respond to these problems effectively. In effect, failing to appreciate how individual challenges are influenced by larger social forces diminishes a person's ability to understand and resolve them.

To explore this, Mills highlighted the difference between what he called **personal troubles**, which result from individual challenges, and **social issues**, which are caused by larger social factors. For example, your sociology mid-term can be considered a personal trouble because you have to write it. If you study, you should do well, but if you don't, you might fail. If the exam is fair and other students did well on it, is anyone else responsible for your poor performance? Clearly, your grade would be considered a personal trouble. However, what if the entire class failed the exam? A low class average may occur because no one studied for the test, but this is unlikely. Instead, low scores would suggest that there is more going on—perhaps there was some confusion over what chapters and topics would be tested or perhaps the scores were tabulated incorrectly by the professor. In any event, a student who failed the exam might think that his or her score is a personal trouble, and to some extent it is, but once the class understands that everyone did poorly it may become a social issue—it involves a group of people, and collective action is required for the group's concerns to be acknowledged and potentially acted upon.

According to Mills, many personal troubles never become social issues because people rarely equate what is happening to them with the larger social worlds in which they exist. For example, if you receive back a test that you have failed, chances are that you will feel embarrassed and upset and will probably stuff it into your backpack—you assume that you are one of the only students who failed and do not want to draw attention to yourself. When people face situations of personal failure such as on a mid-term, very few ask for help. For Mills, not seeing such failure as partially, or entirely, the result of social forces is to lack what he called the *quality of mind*. **Quality of mind** has nothing to do with a person's intelligence or level of education; instead, it is the ability to look beyond personal circumstance and into social context. For example, what would happen if no one in the class passed but no one said anything about it? No one would know that everyone else had failed; all of the students in that class would think that they had to deal with their failure on their own, and a possible social issue would never be addressed. Mills (1959/2000, p. 12) reveals the importance of possessing the quality of mind when he writes that, without thinking beyond one's own condition, "much private uneasiness goes unformulated; much public malaise and many decisions of enormous structural relevance never become public issues." Can this concept be applied to the feelings that many students have when they fail a test? Yes, it can.

When a student who has failed does not talk to classmates, family members, friends, or the professor about the test, there is little possibility for a social issue to emerge, even if everyone in the class failed. If no one talks about it, then each student has a *trouble* and the class never realizes that there is an *issue*. Mills would say that these students lack the quality of mind because they did not try to understand their individual circumstance from within the larger social context: How did everyone else do? What could I have done better? How could I have studied more effectively? What have I learned from this experience? None of these questions defer from a student's responsibility to be prepared for all tests, but they recognize that the students are willing to think in social terms, even with regards to a specific situation.

To improve a person's quality of mind, Mills (1959/2000) argued that sociologists need to expose them to what he called the *sociological imagination*. The **sociological imagination** is the ability to understand the dynamic relationship between individual lives and the larger society. It involves stepping outside of your own condition and looking at yourself from a new perspective—seeing yourself as the product of your family, income level, race, and gender. You employ the sociological imagination by asking yourself, "Who am I and why do I think the way I do?" This internal reflection requires us to think about ourselves differently and, by doing so, become more informed about the social forces that have come together to make us who we are. When people can see their own histories in a social context, they cannot help but improve their quality of mind. Mills would suggest that people who judge others without understanding all of the issues involved may lack the quality of mind and thus view the world in black-and-white terms. However, when people understand themselves and others through the sociological imagination, they appreciate that very few things are black and white. The true beauty in the social world is visible only when one can see all shades of grey.

PETER BERGER'S VIEW OF THE SOCIOLOGICAL PERSPECTIVE

American sociologist Peter Berger builds on how sociologists see the world. In his 1963 book *Invitation to Sociology: A Humanistic Perspective*, he defines the sociological perspective as the ability to view the world from two distinct yet complementary perspectives: seeing the general in the particular and seeing the strange in the familiar.

SEEING THE GENERAL IN THE PARTICULAR   According to Berger, seeing the general in the particular is the ability to look at seemingly unique events or circumstances and then recognize the larger (or general) features involved. For example, think about the last time you saw a street person asking people for spare change. Certainly, this is a specific and particular incident; it occurred at a specific time and place. But, to see the general is also to recognize that while you may have only seen one street person, you know that there are many more you do not see. To appreciate an individual circumstance like this and broaden your perspective

personal troubles Personal challenges that require individual solutions.

social issues Challenges caused by larger social factors that require collective solutions.

quality of mind Mills' term for the ability to view personal circumstance within a social context.

sociological imagination C.W. Mills' term for the ability to perceive how dynamic social forces influence individual lives.

To read an excerpt from *The Sociological Imagination*, go to www.lclark.edu/~goldman/socimagination.html.

Peter Berger

to the larger social patterns that create and perpetuate people's living on the streets in one of the richest nations in the world is to employ the sociological perspective. The ability to move from the particular to the general and back again is one of the hallmarks of the sociological perspective. Our experience suggests that some students have difficulty switching from the general to the particular, but if you take your time and work through your own examples of both approaches, you will be able to do so more quickly and accurately over time.

SEEING THE STRANGE IN THE FAMILIAR   According to Berger, sociologists also need to tune their sociological perspective by thinking about what is *familiar* and seeing it as *strange*. For example, as you read this text, everything seems as it should be. Chances are that you are sitting at home, or perhaps at your school's library, doing your best to stay interested and take notes on the text so that you will do well on your exam. However, think for a moment that while all of this seems familiar and normal, if you really think about it, it is truly strange.

Everyone, even those who have never attended a college or university, understands that for students to do well they need to go to class, memorize material, and write tests. But why? Granted, your professor needs you to learn material by memorizing some fundamental concepts and definitions and to demonstrate your command of the material on an exam; after all, he or she must receive something from you to justify your grade. But have you ever considered why students are graded in the first place? Is a student who gets an A in a course smarter than someone who receives a C? Do grades measure intelligence, command of course material, or simply that someone is willing to work hard? (See Preckel, Holling, & Vock, 2006.) Asking these questions suggests that someone is looking at what appears normal and familiar and seeing it as peculiar and strange—evidence of the sociological perspective, having quality of mind, and beginning to develop the sociological imagination.

The ability to see the general in the particular and the strange in the familiar is the cornerstone of the sociological perspective. As you will learn, sociology is less about remembering details and specifics than about seeing the social world from a unique position—one that allows us to understand social context and to appreciate the position of others. Clearly, the work of both C.W. Mills and Peter Berger are complementary and speak to the essence of the sociological perspective.

Our decisions about what and where we study are influenced by a number of social forces such as gender, social class, ethnicity, and family background.

WHY SHOULD WE CARE?

Street People: One Student's View

Lack of affordable housing, reduction in social services spending, mental illness, and substance abuse are just some of the reasons behind homelessness in Canada. Certainly, that first reason is one that hits "home." As a full-time undergraduate student who lives alone and is paying for rent, tuition, and living expenses, I can sympathize with Calgary's current affordable-housing problem. Due to its ever-growing population, the City of Calgary recognizes the significance of the issue and states that "Calgary does not have enough affordable housing to meet demand" (City of Calgary, 2007). It is no wonder, then, that the homeless problem is growing. We should all be concerned.

Statistics on the homeless population are difficult to find. For example, the Government of Canada has acknowledged the lack of accurate data. Human Resources and Social Development Canada states that "to date, no reliable method for counting the number of people who are homeless can be identified" (Government of Canada, 2007d). The federal government has also stated that one of its goals is to provide the homeless with temporary housing, help them locate permanent housing, and assist them in gaining their independence.

The research to date suggests that the homeless population in Canada is growing. In 1998, the Federation of Canadian Municipalities stated that the homeless problem in Canada was a "national disaster" (Halifax Regional Municipality, 2008). More recently, the UN Committee on Economic, Social and Cultural Rights has reprimanded Canada for its failure to address the homeless problem (Pohl, 2001).

Cities across Canada are stepping up to the plate to help their homeless people. For example, the Halifax Regional Municipality has committed itself to help the homeless by supporting community-based initiatives such as Community Action on Homelessness, which provides accommodation and funding for research (Halifax Regional Municipality, 2008). In 2005, the City of Vancouver established the Homeless Action Plan, which attempts to provide financial stability to the homeless as well as to offer the homeless social support services (City of Vancouver, 2005). With so many unique cities spread across the country, it is hard to find a solution that works for all of them. For example, a homeless person in Winnipeg is in a different situation, especially during the winter months, than one living in Vancouver.

With a plethora of social service agencies available to help deal with the problems caused by homelessness, such as mental illness and substance abuse, an equal amount of social programming must exist to assist these agencies. The real problem probably is the reduction in social services spending. Such agencies face a shortage of funding to help them manage and solve such complex issues effectively. Given the shared responsibility between all levels of government, then, I am frustrated and fear that the homeless issue becomes lost in bureaucratic red tape.

As I reflect on the homeless issue in Canada, as well as on my own relationship to it as a full-time student, I find it strange that I feel the need to be worried about how homelessness relates to student life. Like many of my classmates who come from a middle-class background, I need not worry about whether I will have a roof over my head regardless of how much my student loan accumulates. What is strange is why and how the homeless population arrived at their place in life instead of in the chairs next to me in class. Perhaps they are university graduates who have fallen on hard times and do not have the coping mechanisms they need to help themselves. Regardless of the reasons for our respective situations, homelessness is not only a private trouble but also a public issue.

This article is also a peerScholar assignment in MySocLab.

Prepared by Lorna Kearnes, one of our research assistants, who at the time of writing was entering graduate school to complete her master's degree in social work.

WHAT MAKES YOU, YOU? ENGAGING THE SOCIOLOGICAL IMAGINATION

We all understand that we are individuals who think and feel independently of everyone else. Each of us, to some extent at least, has what sociologists refer to as *agency*: the assumption that individuals have the ability to alter their socially constructed lives (Graham & Bruce, 2006). Using some of the ideas and concepts of Mills and Berger, how would you attempt to explain who you are and why you see the world the way you do? Working through this process will help you to understand that while we are all individuals, we are also the culmination of many social forces. Let's investigate you using five social factors and see which ones were the most influential for defining the person you have become.

MINORITY STATUS   Canadian sociological research suggests that people who are members of visible minority groups (Walters, Phythian, & Anisef, 2007), who have a physical disability (Zitzelsberger, 2005) or a mental disability (Tonmyr, Jamieson, Mery, & MacMillan, 2005), or who are lesbian, gay, or bisexual (Lenton, Smith, Fox, & Morra, 1999) face various forms of discrimination. As a budding sociologist, ask yourself whether being a member of any of these groups would influence a person's view of him- or herself or the world in general. If you are a Caucasian person who has never been diagnosed with a mental disability and who is able-bodied and heterosexual, you have experienced social advantage and no doubt have a positive and healthy self-image. However, can you appreciate how it might feel if you were a member of one of these disadvantaged groups? What it must feel like when people treat you as a second-class person, avoid eye contact, or, conversely, stare at you from across a room? Is it possible that these social experiences would influence the person you would become? By thinking about how you would react to these experiences, you are starting to apply your sociological imagination.

GENDER   As we will explore later, society treats men and women differently. Canada, and virtually all human societies, remains patriarchal—a system of rule that translates to "rule by the father" in which men control the political and economic resources of society. For example, Table 1–1 shows earning ratios between 1997 and 2006 and clearly demonstrates that full-time working women earn significantly less than men. Why do you think this is the case? If we think in terms of the general and the particular, you might argue that you know some women who make a lot more than some of the men you know. This may be true, but it does not diminish the importance of the overall trend, which is that men earn about 35 percent more than women. If you also consider that many students probably believe that they live in a more equitable society than these numbers suggest, you might think that this is somewhat *strange*: Why do people believe in something that so clearly is not the case?

SOCIO-ECONOMIC STATUS   As you consider the other students in your sociology class, are you aware of the different socio-economic classes they represent? *Socio-economic status (SES)* is a term used to describe a combination of variables to position or score people on criteria such as income level, level of education achieved, occupation, and area of residence. Would you agree that children from wealthier families whose parents are well educated, have good jobs, and live in a nice part of town have an advantage over children who do not share the same level of prosperity? While wealth and opportunity are certainly *familiar*, isn't it also *strange* how lucky these people were to be born into the families they were? Sociologists use the term **ascribed status** to define a situation in which a person is assigned advantage, or disadvantage, simply through birth. For example, if a child is born to a wealthy family, it has nothing to do with the infant's individual qualities. Being born rich usually means a person will have opportunities for a post-secondary education and material pleasures. However, some people who are born to families with little money also achieve great wealth (for example, Oprah Winfrey had humble beginnings and is now a billionaire). Sociologists refer to this situation as

ascribed status
Attributes (advantages and disadvantages) assigned at birth (e.g., sex).

TABLE 1–1 **Average Earnings by Sex**

Year	Women $ constant 2006	Men $ constant 2006	Earnings Ratio %
1997	24 300	39 300	61.9
1998	25 400	40 400	62.8
1999	25 800	41 200	62.6
2000	26 300	42 500	61.7
2001	26 400	42 400	62.1
2002	26 700	42 500	62.8
2003	26 400	41 900	62.9
2004	26 700	42 100	63.4
2005	27 300	42 700	64.0
2006	27 700	42 900	64.7

Source: Statistics Canada. (2008). *Average earnings by sex and work pattern (All earners)*. Retrieved June 4, 2008, from http://www40.statcan.ca/l01/cst01/labor01a.htm?sdi=earnings.

achieved status, meaning the status a person has been able to gain through personal attributes and qualities. For example, while your parents "assigned" your sex (an ascribed attribute), your grades are the result of your effort and skill (an achieved attribute).

Thinking sociologically is to realize the importance of how one's beginnings influence what people can become. While many people can transcend their low socio-economic status, they are the exception rather than the rule; sociology teaches us that the majority of those born poor remain poor (Keister, 2007).

achieved status
Attributes developed throughout life as a result of effort and skill (e.g., course grades).

FAMILY STRUCTURE   As we have seen, socio-economic status does influence a person's opportunities. The well-being of children appears to be almost always associated with the household income of their families, according to a study recently published by Human Resources and Social Development Canada (Statistics Canada, 2006k). The study found that regardless of a child's age, higher income tends to be related to better physical, social/emotional, cognitive, and behavioural well-being.

Table 1–2 demonstrates that the percentage of all family types at or below poverty level largely declined between 1996 and 2006. However, the incidence of low income for female lone-parent families remains more than four times higher than the incidence for two-parent families with children. As a sociologist, why do you think that higher family income levels are so closely

TABLE 1–2 **Percentage of Persons with Low Income***

	1996	1998	2000	2002	2003	2004	2005	2006
				%				
Persons under 18 years old	18.6	15.5	13.8	12.2	12.5	13.0	11.7	11.3
In two-parent families	12.4	9.9	9.5	7.3	7.9	8.4	7.8	7.7
In female lone-parent families	55.8	46.1	40.1	43.0	41.2	40.4	33.4	32.3
Person 18 to 64 years old	15.7	13.9	12.9	12.1	12.2	11.9	11.4	11.3
Person 65 and over	9.8	8.6	7.6	7.6	6.8	5.6	6.1	5.4

* 1992 Base after-tax income low-income cut-off.
Source: Statistics Canada. (2007). *The daily, Thursday, May 3, 2007. Income of Canadians*. Retrieved June 4, 2008, from http://www.statcan.ca/Daily/English/080505/d080505a.htm.

associated with children's well-being? As you consider your answer, are you reflecting on the structure of your own family and how it may influence your views of yourself and those around you?

Family structure does influence a child's development to the extent that female lone-parent families tend to have lower incomes than two-parent family structures. As we will discuss later, there are many new types of families today and the consistent theme in all of them suggests that loving parents with adequate incomes more often than not raise productive and well-adjusted children.

URBAN–RURAL DIFFERENCES   No doubt some of you reading this text were raised in small towns, while others grew up in cities. Do you think that where you grew up influences you? People who live in small towns report that they are distinct from urban dwellers and that their rural connections are an important defining feature (Mellow, 2005). Bonner (1998) suggests that sociologists have been trying to explain and understand urban–rural differences since the Industrial Revolution. While structural differences between small towns and large cities certainly exist (e.g., access to health care, diversity in entertainment and cultural events), the nature of growing up in either location is more subtle and contextual. For instance, if you grew up in a city, do you ever notice subtle differences when talking to friends who grew up in small towns? Conversely, if you grew up in a small town, do you notice any differences when talking to friends from a city? Is it possible that where you grow up also influences how you view the world?

As you can see from this brief analysis, our perceptions of ourselves and others are the product of many factors. As sociologists, our job is to try to view the world using the sociological perspective—to understand our own biases and investigate the social world by seeing the general, the particular, the strange, and the familiar.

Now that we have considered the sociological perspective and the relationship between social forces and personal social identity, we will explore how the discipline of sociology began and evolved.

What do you know about **the Sociological Imagination**?

Multiple-choice questions (circle your answer)

1. *Sociology* **can best be defined as**
   a. The difference between personal troubles and social issues
   b. The systematic study of human groups and their interactions
   c. The systematic study of society
   d. Seeing the familiar in the strange

2. **Who coined the term** *the sociological imagination*?
   a. Auguste Comte
   b. Peter Berger
   c. Émile Durkheim
   d. C.W. Mills

3. **An attribute (advantage or disadvantage) assigned at birth (e.g., sex) is called**
   a. Ascribed status
   b. Achieved status
   c. Socio-economic status
   d. Sociological status

4. **The incidence of low income for female lone-parent families is _____ times higher than the incidence for two-parent families with children.**
   a. Two
   b. Three
   c. Four
   d. Five

5. **Men on average earn**
   a. 15 percent more than women
   b. 35 percent more than women
   c. Men and women earn the same now
   d. 15 percent less than women

module 1.2

The Origins of Sociology

People have been pondering their place in the universe and our relations with each other for thousands of years. The Chinese philosopher K'ung Fu-tzu (known today as Confucius, 551–479 BCE[1]) and the ancient Greeks engaged in elaborate discussions and writings about society in general and the role of the individual citizen in particular. In ancient Greece (circa 400 BCE), a group of educators called the Sophists (who were the first paid teachers) travelled the country and catered to the rich, who wanted to learn how to live well and be happy (Jones, 1969). The Sophists were the first thinkers to focus their efforts on the human being, in contrast to the earlier tradition that concentrated on understanding the physical world.

Later philosophers, notably Socrates (469–399 BCE) and his student Plato (427–347 BCE), challenged the virtue of being paid for one's knowledge and advocated the necessity of deeper reflection on the human social condition. Plato's *The Republic* is one of the most important works in Western philosophy, as it asks what social justice is and what the characteristics of a just individual are (Jowett, 1892, as cited in Abelson, Friquegnon, & Lockwood, 1977, p. 575).

After the Greeks, Roman emperor Marcus Aurelius (121–180), Muslim philosopher and scientist Al Farabi (870–950), Italian theologian Saint Thomas Aquinas (1224–1274), British playwright William Shakespeare (1564–1616), and English philosopher John Locke (1632–1704) all explored the role of the individual in society.

The ideas that form the foundation of sociology, then, have been around for a long time. Although Ibn Khaldun (1332–1406) is recognized as the first social philosopher working from the sociological perspective (see Zahoor, 1996), it was not until 1838 that the term *sociology* was coined by Auguste Comte (Périer, 1998, p. 343). For his naming of the discipline, Comte is often referred to as the father of sociology.

THREE REVOLUTIONS: THE RISE OF SOCIOLOGY

In general terms, the emergence of sociology was a product of the time. So many striking changes were occurring in eighteenth- and nineteenth-century Europe. The impact of these changes on society and social behaviour led to a desire by some to better understand and manage these changes. The result is the discipline we know as sociology. Three revolutionary events inspired the rise of sociology: the scientific revolution, the political revolution, and the Industrial Revolution.

THE SCIENTIFIC REVOLUTION   With the emergence of the Renaissance in the fourteenth to seventeenth centuries, the insights by thinkers such as Galileo, Newton, and Copernicus began to gain wider acceptance despite resistance from the Church. The development of the scientific method during the Enlightenment period that followed (circa 1650–1800) facilitated the pace of social change.

One of the first thinkers to consider the application of the scientific method to an understanding of the social world was Auguste Comte (1798–1857). Comte believed that if the world was interpreted through a scientific lens then society could be guided by

---

[1] BCE means "before common era" and has become the dating convention to recognize religious diversity. It replaces the previous notation of BC, "before Christ."

Think about the Origins of Sociology

1 Think about a world without science. How do you think the "invention" of science might change the world socially?

2 How do you think society changed as a consequence of the Industrial Revolution? How might those changes have been, in part, responsible for the development of sociology?

3 Think about Canadian history over the past 50 years. How do you think it may have influenced the development of Canadian sociology?

positivism A theoretical approach that considers all understanding to be based on science.

observation, experimentation, and logic. Comte's approach to the world is referred to as *positivism*. **Positivism** is a theoretical approach that considers all understanding to be based on science (Hollinger, 1982). Comte believed that society would be better run if we used positivism to make our decisions on social policy. He also believed that sociologists would make the best leaders because they would be trained in the application of science to society.

THE POLITICAL REVOLUTION   The Renaissance and, later, the Enlightenment inspired a great deal of social and scientific change. With a new view of the world as separate from the teachings of the Church, society evolved to endorse democratic principles.

Renaissance thinkers such as Niccolò Machiavelli (1469–1527), René Descartes (1596–1650), and Thomas Hobbes (1588–1679) challenged social convention and inspired new ways of understanding the social world. For example, Machiavelli challenged the birthright of the nobility and asserted that anyone could become a prince (Zeitland, 1994, p. 224). Descartes in his famous statement "I think therefore I am" confirmed that humans were able to understand their world through rational reflection. Finally, Hobbes influenced thinkers of his time by asserting that humans were driven by two primary passions: fear of death and desire for power. According to Hobbes, the true nature of human kind is self-preservation, which he argued can only be achieved through cooperation (Piirimae, 2006, p. 3).

Many of the philosophical and social trends that began during the Renaissance continued to develop through the Enlightenment. Two of the most influential Enlightenment thinkers in the development of sociology were John Locke (1632–1704) and Jean-Jacques Rousseau (1712–1778). Locke is perhaps most famous for his assertion that ideas are not innate and that all knowledge is the result of experience (Zeitlin, 1994, pp. 4–5). The belief that people are born as blank slates is one of the defining features of the sociological perspective. Locke argued that the only way to increase our knowledge is to gather more information about the material world through science and experimentation.

Jean-Jacques Rousseau's contribution to social theory was his challenge to the true nature of social life. Rousseau suggested that, prior to organized society, human beings existed in a *natural state* whereby an individual's desire was solitary and self-centred. Like Hobbes, Rousseau recognized the benefits that society could achieve if people worked together. He referred to this form of cooperation as the *social contract* (Westby, 1991).

From Machiavelli to Rousseau, from the Renaissance to the Enlightenment, philosophers and social activists promoted novel ideals such as individual rights and social responsibility, equality of opportunity, and the political ideology of democracy. These ideas challenged tradition and nobility, inspired great debate and reflection, and ultimately led to dramatic political changes as witnessed during the American and French revolutions. While we take these ideas for granted today, this transformation of how we saw ourselves, each other, and our entire society led to a restructuring of everything we knew, and it was into this period of tension and re-examination that sociology was born.

THE INDUSTRIAL REVOLUTION   Our human ancestors subsisted through gathering and hunting activities for millions of years, and then, 10 000 years ago, everything changed. Virtually overnight, people decided to settle in one area and raise crops and domesticate animals (O'Neil, 2006). This change must have had extraordinary ramifications for early humans. Only a few thousand years later, everything changed again. Around 1750, the Industrial Revolution replaced agriculture as our dominant means of supporting ourselves and our families (Hooker, 1996).

The Industrial Revolution changed virtually every aspect of life: family structures (Bengston, 2001), how people made a living (Delamotte & Walker, 1976), and even people's thoughts, dreams, and aspirations (Boxer, 2007). While many associate the Industrial Revolution with technological advancements (e.g., steam power, the cotton gin, electricity), what really inspired it were the profound social changes occurring at the time. Moving from an agricultural and rural economy to a capitalist and urban one has left a legacy that some would argue we are still trying to deal with today (Dawley & Faler, 1976; Rosenthal, 1992).

The emergence of the steam engine as a cheap means of power and locomotion was also instrumental in facilitating the rise of the Industrial Revolution. Millions of farmers abandoned traditional village life and moved into the rapidly growing cities in search of factory jobs (Hedley, 2002). The move from a rural to an urban environment led to a new series of social problems, including child labour in factories, crushing poverty, malnourishment, and exploding crime rates. Disturbed by these developments, early sociologists began to try to understand what was causing these conditions and what could be done to address them (Lindsey, Beach, & Ravelli, 2009).

FROM EUROPE TO NORTH AMERICA: THE DEVELOPMENT OF SOCIOLOGY

From Europe to North America, sociology continued to grow and evolve. The scope of sociological investigation from the societal level to the interpersonal level developed as did the perceptions of the role of sociological investigation from scientitfic study to activism.

EUROPE: MACROSOCIOLOGY   Dramatic changes in the social lives of Europeans as a result of the industrial, political, and scientific revolutions became the focus of early European sociologists. They were concerned with issues on a societal level such as poverty, capitalism, war, and political change. Attempting to study and understand society as a whole is referred to as **macrosociology** (i.e., looking at the big picture first and individuals second). In general, early European sociology could be categorized as macrosociology. In the pages to come we will learn more about macrosociology, its perspectives (functionalism and conflict theory), and some of its key theorists (e.g., Émile Durkheim and Karl Marx).

macrosociology   The study of society as a whole.

NORTH AMERICA: MICROSOCIOLOGY   While early American sociology was influenced by the work of Europeans and their macrosociological approach, microsociology was born in the United States. Microsociology focuses on individuals and/or small groups and how they

Many workers, including women and children, worked in deplorable conditions during the Industrial Revolution.

behave in particular face-to-face social networks. Rather than consider system-wide processes and institutions (as noted above), microsociologists look at individual lived realities and then generalize about their social relevance. For example, Charles Horton Cooley (1864–1929) and George Herbert Mead (1863–1931) developed theories on how the self develops. Originating out of the University of Chicago, Herbert Blumer called this new approach to sociological investigation **symbolic interactionism**.

symbolic interactionism
A perspective asserting that people and societies are defined and created through the interactions of individuals.

SOCIOLOGY IN CANADA

CANADIAN SOCIOLOGY   Canadian sociology, at least in the early years, was dominated by American sociology. It developed later (the first American department of sociology was established at the University of Chicago in 1892 whereas the first Canadian department of sociology was established at McGill University in 1924) and on a much smaller scale. Early university faculty tended to be American born and/or trained—many from the University of Chicago. Therefore, an American style of sociology was pervasive in Canada. Not surprisingly, some Canadian sociologists suggest that Canadian sociology is a product of its experiences with, and at times resistance to, the larger and more dominant American sociological tradition (see Brym & Saint-Pierre, 1997; Hiller, 2001; Hiller & Di Luzio, 2001). Yet as Canadian sociology has evolved, it has found its own distinctive style—partly as a response to American dominance but also as a product our own national history. Specifically, five defining features help distinguish Canadian sociology from the American tradition (Lindsey, Beach, & Ravelli, 2009):

1. *Geography*: Canada's size, its climate, and its proximity to the United States have all contributed to its development. Brym and St. Pierre (1997, p. 543) note that a core theme of Canadian sociology is the development and maintenance of a community in the face of hostile elements (e.g., cold winters) and outside forces (e.g., the United States).
2. *Francophone sociology*: Intertwined in the social movement of the time—the Quiet Revolution (1960–1966)—Francophone sociologists focused on the political, religious, and social injustices in Quebec and with Quebec's relationship to the rest of Canada. The work of Quebec sociologists since the 1960s has been highly influential in the development of social policy and the politics we see in Quebec today (Brym and Saint-Pierre, 1997).
3. *Canadianization*: Canadian English-speaking sociology was influenced a great deal by American sociology as practised at the University of Chicago (see Brym & Saint-Pierre, 1997; Eichler, 2001; Hiller, 2001; Hiller & Di Luzio, 2001; S. Langlois, 2000; McKay, 1998). Many early Canadian sociologists were trained in the United States. By the 1950s and 1960s, Canadian sociologists felt a pressing need to hire and train more Canadian sociologists in order to investigate and understand Canadian society from a Canadian perspective.
4. *Political economy*: Wallace Clement, a leading figure in Canadian sociology, believes that a defining element of Canadian sociology is its interest in the political economy. **Political economy** is seen as the interactions of politics, government, and governing, and the social and cultural constitution of markets, institutions, and actors (Clement, 2001, p. 406). One of the first sociologists to study this issue was Harold Innis, who in his Staples Thesis (1930/2001; 1940/1954), accorded that Canadian identity was tied to our subordinate role as a supplier of raw materials to the United States and Europe.
5. *Radical approach*: Margrit Eichler (2001) suggests that the simultaneous emergence of the Canadianization movement and the women's movement led to a politics of knowledge that proved helpful to both. The feminist movement found a new voice on expanding university campuses during the 1960s and 1970s. Coupled with francophone sociology,

political economy   The interactions of politics, government, and governing, and the social and cultural constitution of markets, institutions, and actors.

Canadian sociology took on a far more radical nature than that of the United States (Brym & Saint-Pierre, 1997).

EARLY CANADIAN SOCIOLOGISTS

Annie Marion MacLean (1870–1934) Born in Prince Edward Island, MacLean was the first Canadian woman to receive a Ph.D. in sociology (from the University of Chicago in 1900). MacLean was a forerunner on the subject of working women; her study entitled *Wage-Earning Women* (1910) was one of the first large-scale applications of survey research in Canada (Eichler, 2001, p. 378).

Sir Herbert Brown Ames (1863–1954) Ames is best known for his book *The City below the Hill: A Sociological Study of a Portion of the City of Montreal, Canada* (1897), one of the first Canadian examples of sociology that relied on various statistical analyses to document the slum conditions people experienced living just south of downtown Montreal. Ames was also a Member of Parliament and spent most of his life trying to help improve the plight of the poor.

Carl Dawson (1887–1964) He was the first sociologist to be hired at McGill University (in 1922) and served as chairperson of its Department of Sociology until 1952. He and colleague W. Gettys wrote an introductory sociology textbook that would become one of the most popular and widely used in North America for more than 20 years and contributed greatly to the establishment of the discipline.

Harold Adams Innis (1894–1952) Innis was born in Otterville, Ontario, and received his bachelor's and master's degrees from McMaster University and his Ph.D. from the University of Chicago. Innis is remembered for two primary contributions: his analysis of Canada's political economy through his staples thesis hypothesis and his studies of media theory.

Much of the work of current Canadian sociologists is published in the *Canadian Journal of Sociology*. Check it out at **www.cjsonline.ca**.

Aileen D. Ross (1902–1995) Her work has strong ties to gender roles and includes *Control and Leadership in Women's Groups* (1958), *Changing Aspirations and Roles: Middle and Upper Class Indian Women Enter the Business World* (1976), and *Businesswomen and Business Cliques in Three Cities: Delhi, Sydney, and Montreal* (1979).

Helen Abell

Helen Abell (1919–2003) Born in Medicine Hat, Alberta, Abell is generally regarded as the founder of rural sociology in Canada. Her work focused on farm families and the effects of modernization, contributions by farm women, and the decline of family farming. Her recognition of the efforts of farm wives was an invaluable contribution to both public consciousness and policy-makers (Eichler, 2001).

Kathleen Herman (1920–) She was chair of the Canadian Sociology and Anthropology Association's Canadianization movement and was an active supporter of women's rights through the Royal Commission on the Status of Women.

John Porter

John Porter (1921–1979) *The Vertical Mosaic: An Analysis of Social Class and Power in Canada* (1965) was his most important work. It was an investigation into equality in Canada and the use of power by Canada's bureaucratic, economic, and political elites. Porter challenged the impression that Canada was a classless society with no barriers to opportunity.

Ruth Rittenhouse Morris (1933–2001) Her work focused on the attempt to abolish the penal system in favour of an alternative justice system. She founded several organizations, including Rittenhouse, Toronto Justice Council, St. Stephen's Conflict Resolution Service, and the Toronto Bail Program.

What do you know about **the Origins of Sociology**?

Multiple-choice questions (circle your answer)

1. The term sociology was first described in
a. 1753
b. 1838
c. 1908
d. 1920

2. A theoretical approach that considers all understanding to be based on science is called
a. Negativism
b. Renaissance
c. Enlightenment
d. Positivism

3. Which of the following was not a revolution that inspired sociology?
a. Industrial
b. Scientific
c. Political
d. Military

4. The study of individuals or small group dynamics within a larger society is called
a. Microsociology
b. Macrosociology
c. Formal sociology
d. Molecular sociology

5. Within the context of sociology, Canadianization refers to
a. The selling of raw materials from Canada to Europe
b. The training of Canadian sociologists in Canada
c. The infiltration of Canadian sociologists in American universities
d. The assimilation of immigrant sociologists to Canada

Answers: b, d, d, a, b

module 1.3

Think about Sociology and Its Classical Theoretical Foundations

1 Think about how our society works. Do you see groups of people working together in cooperation or are they in conflict with one another?

2 Think about the post-secondary system. What

Sociology and Its Classical Theoretical Foundations

If there is one area that students new to sociology struggle with, it is their understanding and application of the sociological perspectives. Fear not—once you get it, you will see how much fun it is to see the world in different ways.

A perspective is simply a different way of looking at the world—an angle. Each perspective that we present in this text offers you a different angle by which to look at the world. By looking at the world from different angles, you will gain a new understanding of and appreciation for human behaviour and group life.

Metaphorically speaking, imagine putting on a pair of sunglasses that are tinted with a different colour for each new perspective we discuss below. Notice that with each colour, you see the world in a slightly different way. As you examine each perspective, it is not important that you see one as "right" but rather that you develop the skills to see the world from alternative perspectives. As you progress in your studies, you will no doubt find that each sociological theory has its strengths and weaknesses, and that each of the theorists we present offers unique insights into our social world.

As you begin your reading of theory, consider whether each theorist's insights can be applied to society today. If a theory can help you explain a current issue or event, this strengthens its usefulness; if it cannot, be sure to consider why. By actively engaging with the theories in this way, you will be better able to both synthesize and compare different theoretical perspectives—a skill that all strong sociology students share.

functions do you think it performs for society?

3 Do you think some groups in Canada benefit more from post-secondary institutions than others?

FUNCTIONALISM

Functionalism is a macrosociological perspective. The functionalist view of the social world has two key elements:

1. The social world is a dynamic system of interrelated and interdependent parts.
2. Social structures (e.g., the post-secondary education system) exist to help people fulfill their wants and desires as defined by social values.

To understand how functionalists view society, consider the connection between education and work. An aspect of our value system recognizes and promotes the accumulation of material wealth as an expression of success. One way to be successful is to have a good job. One way to get a good job is to get a good education. Therefore, post-secondary education is functional in the sense that it makes this possible. Universities and colleges are certainly structural (i.e., they have buildings, employees, operating procedures, and enrolment policies), but they are also functional. The focus of analysis then for functionalists is the examination of social structures and their associated functions. This focus has led some to call this theory *structural functionalism*. However, today the preferred term is *functionalism* (Wallace & Wolf, 2006).

One way to understand the functionalist approach better is to think of society as being similar to the human body—a perspective often referred to as the **organic analogy**. Like the human body, society is made up of interrelated and interdependent parts that each has a structure and performs a function for the whole. For example, your skin helps to regulate body temperature, provides surface tension, and protects you from the sun's harmful ultraviolet rays. However, it is also just one part of a much larger system. Your skin is certainly important, but it, in turn, depends on your heart, your lungs, and every other organ in your body that must work together for you to continue living. By suggesting that society is like an organism, functionalists also suggest that the system's natural state of affairs is one of equilibrium, a point at which the system is stable and homeostatic. For example, how does your body react when you sit outside in very hot weather or when you work out at the gym? It sweats. Perspiration helps the body to cool itself so that it can maintain a certain temperature—if you get too hot or too cold, you will die. Your body's response to temperature is one example of how it operates as a homeostatic system, one designed to maintain regularity. When it fails this task, the system—in this case, the human body—will suffer. According to functionalists, the same homeostatic properties are present within social systems.

Like the human body, society is made up of structures that work together for the good of the collective. For a social system to be considered healthy, all individuals that comprise it must feel valued and content. The society must meet the needs of the majority; when it does not, the system is *sick* and must make adjustments to return to a state of equilibrium and harmony. For example, a functionalist would argue that when farmers drove their tractors through the streets of Ottawa in 2004, this action was intended to draw attention to their "rural revolution," which pointed out that the system was not meeting farmers' needs. Much like a fever is a symptom of the flu, their demonstration was a symptom of the changing nature of farming in contemporary society and an indication that the system needed to respond (see Hughes & Roesler, 2004, for a review of the concerns that inspired the farmers' rally). Short-term periods of strife and conflict can occur, but over time these events will be addressed by the system and it will return to a state of homeostasis.

organic analogy   The belief that society is like an organism with interdependent and interrelated parts.

Canadian farmers drove their tractors to Parliament Hill in Ottawa in 2006 to highlight their need for greater government support.

A number of early thinkers helped to build the framework upon which functionalism is built. We will examine the work of Émile Durkheim, Talcott Parsons, and Robert K. Merton.

ÉMILE DURKHEIM (1858–1917)   Émile Durkheim is considered by many to be the founder of modern sociology who committed tremendous energy to establish sociology as a legitimate and serious academic endeavour (Delaney, 2004, p. 93; Garner 2000, p. 64; Ritzer, 2000, p. 73). Durkheim followed Comte's commitment to positivism, and his explanation of human behaviours were always based on his assumption that human actions originate in the collective rather than in the individual.

According to Durkheim, culture and society exist outside the individual, are independent of the individual, and outlive the individual. He referred to this external collective force as the *collective conscience* that drives your behaviours without you even being aware of it.

Durkheim recognized that the social conscience is impossible to observe, but we can observe inaction indirectly by looking at social facts. **Social facts** are general social features that exist on their own and are independent of individual manifestations—for example, laws, beliefs, customs, and morals (see Wallace & Wolf, 2006, p. 20). According to Durkheim, social facts provide the context for our thinking and by so doing constrain and coerce us to behave in established, predictable ways (e.g., they influenced what you had for breakfast this morning and what you decided to wear to school today).

social facts   General social features that exist on their own and are independent of individual manifestations.

TALCOTT PARSONS (1902–1979)   Talcott Parsons was an influential American functionalist who spent virtually his entire academic career teaching and writing at Harvard University. In his book *The Social System* (1951), Parsons describes society as a vast network of interconnected parts (e.g., the family, military, government, economy, religion). Each plays a role in the smooth functioning of a society. If any part is not functioning well, other parts of the system must react to bring society back into equilibrium. According to Parsons, socialization and social control are critical to maintaining social equilibrium.

ROBERT K. MERTON (1910–2003)   Robert K. Merton, a former student of Parsons at Harvard University, furthered our understanding of functionalist theory by stressing that social structures have many functions, some more obvious than others (Macionis & Gerber, 2008, p. 15). Arguably, his most lasting contribution to sociology was his analysis of *manifest* and *latent functions*. According to Merton, **manifest functions** are the intended consequences of an action or social pattern, while **latent functions** are the unintended consequences of an action or social pattern. For example, your intent behind studying for your sociology midterm is to do well on the exam; studying, after all, should improve your grades (an intended consequence). However, what if while you were studying in the library you started up a conversation with someone in the next table and that person eventually became your future spouse? This was certainly not an intended consequence of your studying. While Parsons' work implies that all social institutions are inherently good and functional for society, Merton's analysis suggests that sometimes this is not the case.

Merton also warned sociologists to reflect on what is functional, and for whom (see Wallace & Wolf, 2006). For example, many wealthy people would argue that lowering taxes is always a good thing because it encourages people to spend more money, which helps to create jobs and is therefore functional. However, what if you are on social assistance and the decrease in taxes means that the government cuts some programs for the poor? Clearly, decreasing taxes would not be a good thing for you and may lead to dire circumstances. Thus, to an extent greater than Parsons would acknowledge, the social system may have parts that are dysfunctional. A **dysfunction** is a process or element of society that creates a disruption or instability in a social system. Merton's contribution to sociological theory rests mainly in his analysis of manifest and latent functions and his caution that functionalist theorists need to recognize that what is considered functional often varies by the person or the group (Holton, 2004).

Functionalism was the dominant theoretical paradigm between the late 1920s and the early 1960s, but has lost its prominence over the past 50 years. A refined theoretical application of functionalism, termed *neofunctionalism*, began in the mid-1980s.

CRITIQUING FUNCTIONALISM   Functionalism correctly assumes that changes in one area of society may lead to changes in others; after all, society is an integrated and interrelated system. However, if one argues that society is similar to an organism, one must apply the characteristics of the organism when describing society. How, then, can functionalism account for social change when the organism's natural state is homeostasis?

To be fair, functionalists assert that change is possible when the system faces challenges or dysfunctions. For example, a civil rights demonstration may lead to legislative changes and invoke long periods of stability. However, some critics charge that the functionalist perspective overemphasizes the extent to which harmony and stability actually exist in society. By implying that order is more basic than change (a point entirely consistent with conservative reaction thinking) and maintaining that change is frequently dysfunctional, functionalists seem to be saying that the status quo is almost always desirable. Yet we all understand that change is badly needed at times in order to create a new, more just, and ultimately more effective system. In short, although efforts are now being made to correct this failing (see Alexander, 1998), classic functionalism often overlooked the positive consequences that can result from conflict and struggle (Coser, 1956; Merton, 1968).

manifest functions The intended consequences of an action or social pattern.

latent functions The unintended consequences of an action or social pattern.

dysfunction A process or element of society that creates a disruption or instability in a social system.

CONFLICT THEORY

Conflict theory is a macrosociological perspective. Conflict theory is based on the assumption that society is grounded upon inequality and competition over scarce resources that ultimately result in conflict, which often inspires social change. Two basic principles that all conflict theories share are as follows:

1. Power is the core of all social relationships and is scarce and unequally divided among members of society.
2. Social values and the dominant ideology are vehicles by which the powerful promote their own interests at the expense of the weak (see Wallace & Wolf, 2006, p. 69).

This theory offers a clear alternative to functionalism. To conflict theorists, society is characterized by how power defines and influences virtually all human interactions. Society is not a homeostatic system operating for the benefit of the whole (as it is for functionalists).

ROUSSEAU (1754)   Jean-Jacques Rousseau argued that there are two kinds of inequality among people. First, **natural or physical inequality** is based on physical differences established by nature (e.g., age, physical health, strength, intelligence). Second, **moral or political inequality** is the result of human classification of valuable things (e.g., money, social status, power). Thus, Rousseau believed that society *imposes* some forms of inequality that are not based on natural differences but instead on elements that we decide are important—whether they are or not. For example, is there any justifiable reason why taller people are considered to be more successful and generally make more money than shorter people (see Ingalls, 2006; Judge & Cable, 2004)?

According to Rousseau, inequality is the original evil and explains virtually all forms of conflict between individuals and/or entire societies. Types of inequality that are the result of social definitions and therefore *artificial* demonstrate differences in power between individuals and groups in society. This perspective is one of the defining features of the work of Karl Marx.

MARX AND ENGELS   Karl Marx (1818–1883) was a philosopher and economist. Though not a trained sociologist, he must be considered one given his tremendous contributions to the discipline (Ritzer, 2000, p. 41). Marx and his lifelong collaborator, Friedrich Engels (1820–1895), investigated the nature of the human condition and helped to define an influential sociological theory that offered a clear alternative to functionalism.

To conflict theorists, society is characterized by how power defines and influences virtually all human interactions. Society is not a homeostatic system operating for the benefit of the whole (as it is for functionalists), but rather a system based on tension and struggle.

Of considerable interest to Marx (and Engels) was the way in which work changed under capitalism and, in particular, the relationship between factory owners and their workers. Marx referred to this relationship as the **relations of production**.

Marx explained that there are two main classes: the workers, who do not own land (which he called the **proletariat**), and the rich owners (which he called the **bourgeoisie**). Marx observed that in a capitalist economy, the worker and owner are in diametrically opposed positions: the worker wants to make the most money for the least amount of effort, and the owner wants to obtain the most labour for the least amount of money.

In a capitalist society, Marx argued that two problems emerge. First, **exploitation**—owners do not care about the well-being of their workers; they are only interested in profits. Second, **alienation**—workers become disconnected from their work and each other.

Marx pondered as to why workers would want to live such an existence. He argued that they had been so influenced by the ideology developed by the bourgeoisie that capitalism is good for them that they developed what he called a **false consciousness**—a belief in and support of the system that exploited them. However, Marx believed that the time would come when workers would understand that they are being exploited and would rise up against the

natural or physical inequality According to Rousseau, inequality based on physical differences established by nature (e.g., strength, intelligence).

moral or political inequality According to Rousseau, inequality based on human classification of valuable things (e.g., money, social status).

relations of production The relationship between workers and owners.

proletariat The workers, who do not own land.

bourgeoisie The rich owners.

exploitation The difference between what workers are paid and the wealth they create for the owner.

alienation Marxist concept to describe the process by which workers lack connection to what they produce and become separated from themselves and other workers.

false consciousness Belief in and support of the system that oppresses you.

bourgeoisie. Marx called the proletariat's recognition of domination and oppression and its commitment to do something about it **class consciousness**.

class consciousness
Recognition of domina-
tion and oppression
and collective action
to address it.

CRITIQUING CONFLICT THEORY Conflict theory is almost the mirror image of functionalism because of its focus on conflict and power imbalances to explain social life; issues such as child abuse, terrorism, sexism, and globalization seem well suited to a conflict analysis. However, the conflict approach tends to diminish the many areas of our lives where we experience an uncoerced consensus about things we feel are important—for example, public support for equal access to health care in Canada. Social conflict certainly occurs, but so does cooperation and harmony. Conflict theorists also sometimes fail to acknowledge that much struggle today is not a personal desire for power but instead is institutionalized in such contentious events as political elections and collective bargaining between labour unions and corporate management. In these situations, people compete to win, which may inspire more conflict and tension than exists in everyday life.

In contrast to some functionalists, conflict theorists tend to believe more strongly that they should become actively involved in advocating for those people in society who lack social power (Fay, 1987). However, critics argue that this advocacy may violate scientific objectivity and be interpreted by some as nothing more than social activism. Conflict theorists respond that when social scientists uncover unfair social conditions but do nothing to try to address them, they are no different than bystanders who turn a blind eye to the suffering of others.

Conflict theory is also criticized for its insistence on the primary and driving role of economics and materialist interpretations of social life (Wallace & Wolf, 2006, p. 99). Critics agree that the insights achieved through Marx's analysis of the forces of production and relations of production, while useful, are perhaps too narrow to allow for a complete understanding of social motivation and social organization.

The final criticism of classical conflict theory is that it focuses too much on macro-level issues and fails to investigate individual motivations and reactions to tensions and conflicts in people's lives. The criticism that conflict theory lacked tangible application to everyday lives inspired the emergence of the first microsociological theory: symbolic interactionism.

SYMBOLIC INTERACTIONISM

Symbolic interactionism is a microsociological approach. Originating in the United States it is largely based on the works of George Herbert Mead and Charles Horton Cooley, although it was named by Herbert Blumer (1900–1987).

Functionalists and conflict theorists view society as objectively real and at times exerting a strong, even coercive influence over human behaviour. Symbolic interactionists, on the other hand, emphasize that society and all social structures are nothing more than the creations of interacting people and that they can, therefore, be changed. This point of view was eloquently summed up early in the last century by W.I. Thomas in what has come to be known as the **Thomas theorem**: "If men [*sic*] define situations as real, they are real in their consequences" (Thomas & Thomas, 1928). In other words, if, for example, we as a group define prisons as awful places where criminals are sent to pay for their deeds, and if we build them with that idea in mind, then that is what they will become. However, if we think of them as places where people can be rehabilitated and our prisons reflect that position, then that is what they will be (Lindsey, Beach, & Ravelli, 2009, p. 17).

Thomas theorem The
assertion that what
people define as real
are real in their
consequences.

According to Ritzer (2000, p. 357), symbolic interactionism maintains seven fundamental principles:

1. Unlike other animals, human beings have the capacity for thought.
2. Human thinking is shaped by social interaction.

3. In social settings, people learn meanings and symbols that allow them to exercise their distinctively human capacity for thought.
4. Meanings and symbols enable people to carry on uniquely human actions and interactions.
5. People are able to change meanings and symbols that they use given their interpretation of various social situations.
6. People are able to make these modifications in part because they have the unique ability to interact with themselves. By doing so, they examine different courses of actions and select the one with the most advantages and the least disadvantages.
7. The culmination of patterns of action and interaction make up groups and societies.

These seven principles present a very different view of the individual and his or her relationship to society than does functionalism or conflict theory. Symbolic interactionism is distinct from the other two theories in part because of its microsociological orientation. Instead of focusing on groups, organizations, institutions, and societies, symbolic interactionists study specific cases of how individuals act in small groups and in face-to-face interactions (Brickell, 2006; Denzin, 1992).

Symbolic interactionists highlight the important ways in which meanings are created, constructed, mediated, and changed by members of a group or society (Brickell, 2006, p. 417). Meanings and understandings of our social world are the result of our interactions with others and of how we choose to construct the social world in which we live. What is important here is that our perceptions, values, and meanings are the result of mediated experiences with the people we meet each and every day. For example, as you mature, you are influenced by those around you, not because you depend on them (a functionalist view) or are coerced by them (a conflict view) but because we all look to those around us for insights into our world. These interactions and shifting definitions of the social world are influenced by commonly held rules and definitions that influence how, why, when, and where we interact.

The intellectual roots of symbolic interactionism can be traced to two early sociologists: Max Weber and Georg Simmel (see Delaney, 2004; Wallace & Wolf, 2006). Weber, although classified as a conflict theorist, must be credited for his emphasis on **verstehen**—German for "understanding." By it he meant that students should look for and interpret the subjective meanings of social interactions and integrate this approach to understanding in their research. Simmel, an American sociologist, introduced the idea that society should be viewed as the summation of human experience and its patterned interaction. Together these ideas provide solid roots upon which symbolic interactionism can be developed.

Below we will discuss the work of two influential symbolic interactionists: George Herbert Mead and Charles H. Cooley.

verstehen   Weber's term for a deep understanding and interpretation of subjective social meanings.

GEORGE HERBERT MEAD (1863–1931)   George Herbert Mead's most famous work, *Mind, Self and Society* (1934), consisted of a series of lecture notes compiled by a group of former students after Mead's death. He suggested that the "social organism" is not an organic individual but "a social group of individual organisms" (Mead, 1934, p. 130). The individual therefore exists as a member of a social organism and his or her acts can be understood only in the context of social actions that involve other individuals. Society is not a collection of pre-existing autonomous individuals (as suggested by Hobbes, Locke, and Rousseau) but instead is the result of individuals defining themselves through participation in social acts (Cronk, 2005).

According to Mead, the human mind results from the individual's ability to respond to and engage with the environment. The mind emerges and develops once the individual demonstrates an ability to communicate his or her thoughts to others and to him- or herself (Strauss, 1956, as cited in Delaney, 2004, p. 179). The concept of *self* emerges once an individual actor can reflect on him- or herself as an object and see his or her actions as the result of social processes (Delaney, 2004, p. 179).

CHARLES H. COOLEY (1864–1929) Like Mead, Charles Cooley held that sociology should be the study of social reality, including individual consciousness. Cooley suggested that the best way for a sociologist to examine the social world was through a method he called **sympathetic introspection**. This technique required sociologists to analyze an actor's consciousness by putting themselves in his or her shoes. This process allows sociologists to appreciate the actor's reality and to experience the social reality as he or she would (University of Colorado, 2007). Sympathetic introspection is similar to Mills' concept of the sociological imagination.

While Mead is considered to have had a stronger, more lasting impact on symbolic interactionism, Cooley's contributions remain relevant today (Shaffer, 2005). One of Cooley's most lasting contributions was his concept of the **looking-glass self**, which he outlined in *Human Nature and the Social Order* (1902).

CRITIQUING SYMBOLIC INTERACTIONISM Symbolic interactionism is an excellent vehicle for directing sociologists to study the way in which people define the social situations they find themselves in. It reminds us that social reality is, in the final analysis, a human construct. This theory also adds an important microsociological perspective to classical sociological theory. However, macrosociologists, especially conflict theorists, argue that symbolic interactionists fail to acknowledge how difficult it is to change long-established social arrangements. Critics also point out that symbolic interactionism does not account for the importance of social structures and institutions in defining the world in which we live. The assertion that one can understand and respond to the social world is important, but so is the realization that economic class, education level, minority status, and other structural entities exist and define people's life opportunities. Although people of a lower economic class may understand the importance of a positive self-identity, it may not help them to succeed in the face of institutional racism.

> **sympathetic introspection**
> Cooley's concept of the value of putting yourself into other persons' shoes and seeing the world as they do.

> **looking-glass self**
> Cooley's belief that we develop our self-image through the cues we receive from others.

What do you know about **Sociology and Its Classical Theoretical Foundations**?

Multiple-choice questions (circle your answer)

1. _____ view the world as a dynamic system of interrelated and interdependent parts:
   a. Functionalists
   b. Conflict theorists
   c. Symbolic interactionists
   d. Post-structuralists

2. Durkheim referred to general social features that exist on their own and are independent of individual manifestations as _____.
   a. Social facts
   b. Manifest functions
   c. Latent functions
   d. Social networks

3. In Marx's description of social classes, he referred to the workers as the
   a. Bourgeoisie
   b. Lumpen proletariat
   c. Petite bourgeoisie
   d. Proletariat

4. The belief in and support of the system that oppresses you is called
   a. False consciousness
   b. Class consciousness
   c. Social consciousness
   d. Class conflict

5. Who coined the term the *looking-glass self*?
   a. Mead
   b. Marx
   c. Cooley
   d. Durkheim

Answers: a, a, d, a, c

module 1.4

Contemporary Social Theories

Think about Contemporary Social Theories

1 Can you imagine a different model from those you learned about above to describe the way the world works? What would you call your model?

2 Think about how women might see the world. How would it differ from men?

Contemporary social theories should not be seen as completely separate and different from the classical theories. Social theorists draw on each other's work and, as such, contemporary social theories often build upon elements of other theories.

If we were to look for a common theme among contemporary social theories, it would be that of power. While there are certainly differences in how power is theorized, it is nevertheless a focus in contemporary studies.

Far more theories exist than can be included in this chapter. We discuss additional contemporary social theories in later chapters, including post-colonial theory (Chapter 9) and queer theory (Chapters 6 and 8). Below we consider Western Marxism, feminist theories, post-structuralism, and the dynamic forces of globalization.

WESTERN MARXISM AND GRAMSCI'S CONCEPT OF HEGEMONY

Antonio Gramsci (1891–1937) helped found the Communist Party of Italy in 1921. He was imprisoned in 1926, sentenced to 20 years by Mussolini's regime because of his opposition to fascism. Gramsci continued to think and write, and his sister-in-law smuggled his notebooks out of the prison. Parts of these notebooks were later published as the influential book *Selections from the Prison Notebooks*.

Gramsci accepted Marx's analysis of the struggle between the ruling class and the subordinate working class, but he diverged from Marx in his analysis of *how* the ruling class ruled (Burke, 2005). Marx had explained that the ruling class dominated through both force and coercion, using the strong arm of the state—that is, the police and the military. However, absent from this analysis, according to Gramsci, was a consideration of the ruling class's subtle yet insidious *ideological* control and manipulation.

According to Gramsci, then, there are two different forms of political control: domination and hegemony (Burke, 2005). *Domination*, in this context, refers to the direct physical and violent coercion exerted by the police and the military to maintain social boundaries and enforce social rules (Burke, 2005; Kellner, 2005). **Hegemony** refers to ideological control and consent. According to Marx and Engels (1846, p. 64), "the ideas of the ruling class are in every epoch the ruling ideas." Ideological control, then, means that a society's dominant ideas reflect the interests of the ruling class and help mask social inequalities.

hegemony Domination through ideological control and consent.

Note that hegemony also involves *consent*. Gramsci argued that, regardless of how authoritarian a regime may be, no regime would be able to maintain its rule by relying principally on organized state power and armed force (Burke, 2005). Rather, to enjoy longevity and stability of rule, a regime must have the support of the masses (Sassoon, 1994). Therefore, for a dominant group to stay in power they need the subordinate group to accept their ideas (Burke, 2005; Kellner, 2005).

Marx viewed the economic base of a society as a determining force for the shape of social relations (the superstructure). Gramsci separated the superstructure into the *state* (coercive institutions such as the police, military, government, and system of laws) and *civil society* (schooling, media, religion, trade unions, cultural associations). He focused on the role that civil society plays in establishing hegemony (Kellner, 2005). These institutions are critical for teaching the philosophy, culture, and morality of the ruling class. Through them, the ideology of the ruling class becomes internalized by the population and appears as common sense (Burke, 2005).

For example, if you have grown up in North America (and hence in a capitalist economic society), it is probably difficult for you to imagine that a political economic system such as socialism represents a viable alternative to capitalism. Capitalism, in its longevity, appears as common sense, and thus enjoys hegemonic status. For example, think of some common-sense notions in capitalist societies about the need to work hard. Those who are unemployed are thought of as lazy, unproductive, and without motivation. A prevailing idea is that those who work hard and diligently will be rewarded with financial success. Such ingrained notions sustain the more or less smooth operation of capitalism as well as the hegemony of the bourgeoisie (Palamarek, 2008).

According to Gramsci, hegemony is a process that is constantly negotiated and renegotiated. In other words, hegemony is not static, and as such the ruling class cannot take it for granted. The consent secured by the ruling class is an *active* consent. In order to secure this consent, the ruling class constantly incorporates elements of the subordinate class's culture so that it never feels wholly oppressed by ruling class culture (Sassoon, 1994).

FEMINIST THEORIES

To begin with, to suggest that feminist theories are contemporary theories is misleading. Published works protesting the treatment of women date as far back as the 1630s (Ritzer, 1992, p. 312). Mary Wollenscraft published *A Vindication of the Rights of Women* in 1792, and Harriet Martineau published "Political Non-existence of Women" in *Society in America* in 1837 (Ritzer, 1992, p. 313). However, as feminists point out, sociology, and higher education in general, has been historically male dominated. As such, the contributions to the theoretical foundations of sociology by female scholars such as Martineau have been until recently largely overlooked (Ritzer & Goodman, 2004, p. 271). In fact, Ritzer and Goodman (2004, p. 272) argue that Martineau may be sociology's original founder.

Feminist theories, in general, investigate two basic questions: What about women? and Why is the situation of women as it is? (Ritzer, 1992, p. 356). Based on answers to the first question, feminists have come to three conclusions:

1. Women's location and experience in any given situation differs from men in the same situation.
2. Women experience less privilege than men in any given situation that they share with men.
3. Women are oppressed by men.

Based on answers to the second question, a number of theoretical feminist strands have developed. For instance, liberal feminists view women's position of inequality as a consequence of unequal opportunity structures. Marxist feminists view women's inequality as a consequence of capitalism. Radical feminists view women's oppression as a consequence of patriarchy (male power). Socialist feminists view women's oppression as a consequence of both capitalism and patriarchy (Ritzer, 1992, p. 356). These various approaches differ, for example, in their explanations of women's oppression and the nature of gender as well as in their ideas about women's emancipation. Yet, all of these approaches have at their core a concern for gender oppression.

According to feminist theorists, women and men should be social and political equals. In virtually every society, men (and those things associated with men) are held in higher regard than women (Seidman, 2008). As a group with social power, men thus have an interest in maintaining their social privilege over women. Accordingly, feminist theories offer a view of the world from the position of a socially disadvantaged group.

Here, we focus on two feminist theorists who have made exceptional contributions to social theorizing: Dorothy Smith and bell hooks.

To learn more about Harriet Martineau, check out the Martineau Society at **www.hmc.ox.ac.uk/ MartineauSoc/ martineausoc.html.**

Career options for women in Canada continue to be limited by traditional roles.

DOROTHY SMITH   To gain equality for women, Dorothy Smith's first target was the discipline of sociology. Smith argues that classical sociology (e.g., functionalism, conflict theory) is *androcentric*—male centred. Traditional sociology presents itself as universal and objective, but to Smith it is neither objective nor universal. It does not capture in Smith's words "the everyday/everynight world" of individuals. To Smith (2000b, p. 342), "inquiry starts with the knower who is actually located; she is active; she is at work; she is connected to particular other people in various ways."

Smith uses the term *standpoint* (often referred to as *standpoint theory*) to describe the space created by a researcher for the subject and her or his experiences. She wants sociology to capture the presence of real people and their different experiences. In other words, Smith wants sociologists to understand the world from the standpoint of the subject.

Another focus of Smith's work is understanding the ruling relations that affect our lives. Smith is not solely interested in producing accounts of people's experiences. Experience is a *starting point* of inquiry. Her notion of sociology assumes that we do not really need an account of our experiences—we already know what they are and how we feel about them. What people want to understand is the broader conditions that create these experiences. Ruling relations are abstract, conceptual, and "extra-locally organized relations of state, professions, corporations, academic discourses, mass media, and so on" that affect and shape our lives (Smith, 2004, p. 31).

BELL HOOKS   bell hooks is a critical figure in black feminist thought, also called *anti-racist feminism* and *multicultural feminism*.

hooks argues that race and gender are inseparable. She notes that during the 1960s' civil rights and women's movements, no one paid attention to the lives of black women. hooks (1981) argues that when people talk about blacks, they focus on black men; and when people talk about women, they focus on white women. In such a framework, black women's identities are erased. Although hooks focuses her writing on black women, her goal is the liberation of all people.

POST-STRUCTURALISM

Early theorists argued that scientific knowledge was the path to the truth and the key to human freedom. Post-structuralists challenge this view. They argue that the truth is defined by power relations and that all knowledge is socially constructed. Post-structuralist thinking has influenced feminist thinking, queer theory, post-colonial theory, and anti-racist theory.

MICHEL FOUCAULT French philosopher Michel Foucault (1926–1984) has been instrumental in developing this perspective. Of particular interest to Foucault were the concepts of power, knowledge, and discourse.

Foucault's definition of power is different from that of Marx (Foucault, 1980). To Marx, power comes in the form of oppression. In order to liberate ourselves from oppression we need to seek the truth. As such, Marx sees truth as residing outside of power relations. Foucault counters this argument by noting that the truth is socially constructed and that it is influenced by power relations. Power itself does not reside in one individual. Power relations, he argues, are created in social relationships and can be found everywhere, and are always at work. Foucault also noted that we can resist power (Foucault, 1977).

Power is also related to knowledge. According to Foucault, truths or facts are contextual, meaning that they can be separated from relations of power within which they are produced. To know something (particularly the "truth" about something or someone) is to exercise power. Consider the power medical doctors possess in our society because of their specialized knowledge. They can label us as healthy or sick and can affect our behaviours as they relate to those concepts (McGrath, 2005).

The coming together of truth and facts, according to Foucault, creates systems that he refers to as discourses. **Discourse** is a system of meaning that governs how we think, act, and speak about a particular thing or issue. If we return to the medical example, we can identify the medical discourse as being a system of "facts" that organizes how we think about medicine (e.g., our body, doctors, the environment).

discourse A system of meaning that governs how we think, act, and speak about a particular thing or issue.

Discourses tell us not only what the world *is* but also what the world *ought to* be like (Abbott, Wallace, & Tyler, 2005). For instance, a medical discourse can tell us what it is to be healthy and what we should do to be healthy. This discourse influences our behaviour. If we believe in being healthy then we will use **discipline**, in Foucault's words, to make it so. We will normalize behaviour—marking certain behaviours that we consider healthy as normal and others as abnormal or unacceptable. Further, through *surveillance*—acts of observing, recording, and training—we will produce certain behaviours (e.g., exercising) and discourage others (e.g., overeating). Surveillance functions as a source of power in society that does not require force or coercion (Hunt & Wickham, 1994).

discipline The means by which we become motivated to produce particular realities.

SOCIOLOGY IN GLOBAL PERSPECTIVE

Understanding the historical footprint of sociology is important, as is an appreciation of the contributions of Canadian scholars. However, it is equally, if not more, important to look beyond our own Western boundaries and consider the dynamic forces of **globalization**, a process involving the production, distribution, and consumption of technological, political, economic, and sociocultural goods and services on a global basis (Hedley, 2002). Globalization has made the world seem smaller. In Marshall McLuhan's words (1962) we have, through technology, created a "global village." As such, it is important, as students of sociology, to investigate not only our local individual realities but to consider as well, the effects of an increasingly interconnected world. In the coming chapters we will move from the historical to the modern and from issues that are unique to Canadians to those that affect the world.

globalization A worldwide process involving the production, distribution, and consumption of technological, political, economic, and sociocultural goods and services.

CANADIAN SOCIETY IN FOCUS

Rave and Straight Edge

Sociologists may be interested in how certain groups' social interactions change or are shaped as a result of technological innovations such as the Internet, email, the BlackBerry, iPods, and so forth. Canadian researchers Brian Wilson and Michael Atkinson (2005) have studied youth identities as they relate to both virtual and real spaces. These researchers are critical of past theoretical work that treats young people's offline and online experiences as separate, arguing that instead we need to consider the overlap between online and offline experiences in youth identity formation. The researchers draw from two ethnographic studies of youth subcultures in Canada, one on rave culture and one on straight edge.

Rave is characterized as an all-night dance/drug culture. Wilson and Atkinson (2005, p. 286) looked at ravers' embrace of technology, specifically the use of "Internet technology and communication in the rave subculture." The rave culture under study in southern Ontario is characterized by middle-class youth; amphetamine, ecstasy, and ketamine drug use; techno music; and all-night dance parties. Ravers use listservs, chat rooms, and so forth to advertise the locations and times of parties, to promote rave values, and to post links to articles in mainstream media about rave and drugs. Wilson and Atkinson (2005) also recognize the potential for the global flow of such exchanges and information. They are careful to pay attention to the ways in which the virtual and the real are connected in the lives of these youths, as the youths themselves do not necessarily experience the two modes as separate.

Straight edge has its origins in a 1981 song written by the punk band Minor Threat. The song, "Out of Step," "extolled the virtues of self-restraint, personal responsibility and social awareness" (Wilson & Atkinson, 2005, p. 292). The band encouraged fans to take control of their bodies, which could then lead to enrichment and action. This philosophy, dubbed *straight edge*, was "don't smoke, don't drink, don't fuck. At least I can fucking think" (p. 292). Corporeal (meaning "bodily") control thus leads to social and cultural change. Straight edge, then, is a critique of the excesses associated with North American youth and adult lifestyles (Wilson & Atkinson, 2005).

The straight edge philosophy permeates the everyday lives of its members through their corporeal practices. Wilson and Atkinson (2005) explore how straight edge practitioners in Canada use cyberspace to both endorse and affirm their experiences of bodily purity. Straight edgers rely on the Internet to promote bands and shows; as such, this virtual space creates the condition for meetings in real space. Songs are also posted online and are available for downloading. Straight edge practitioners use the Internet to create and disseminate cultural knowledge about their lifestyles. Their websites, which are publicly accessible, serve as information sites that normalize both the group's resistant lifestyle and their status as social protesters. As a group, they are connected by relationships that are formed both online and offline. Online activities may bring straight edge people together, but their corporeal practices are lived in real spaces.

Both rave and straight edge represent distinct youth subcultures that actively resist mainstream culture (Wilson & Atkinson, 2005). The researchers point to the potential of youths' interactions with new technologies to enhance social cohesion, as members of these groups turn to virtual space to both facilitate their offline gatherings and provide an online environment for discussion and affirmation.

What do you know about **Contemporary Social Theories**?

Multiple-choice questions (circle your answer)

1. **Michel Foucault is most likely to be associated with which of the following perspectives?**
   a. Functionalism
   b. Post-structuralism
   c. Feminism
   d. Western Marxism

2. **Which is false about feminism?**
   a. There are many different feminist perspectives.
   b. Feminists are concerned with gender oppression.
   c. Men and women should be social and political equals.
   d. All feminist perspectives have been united by standpoint theory.

3. **A system that governs how we think, act, and speak about a particular thing or issue is called a**
   a. Discipline
   b. Discourse
   c. Standpoint
   d. Outlook

4. **Which feminist theory sees women's position of inequality as a consequence of capitalism?**
   a. Liberal
   b. Marxist
   c. Radical
   d. Socialist

5. **What woman is considered by some to be the founder of sociology?**
   a. bell hooks
   b. Dorothy Smith
   c. Mary Wollenscraft
   d. Harriet Martineau

Answers: b, d, b, d, d

Summary

1. *Sociology* is the systematic study of human groups and their interactions.
2. The sociological perspective is a view of society based on the dynamic relationship between individuals and the larger social network in which we all live.
3. C.W. Mills defined the sociological imagination as the ability to view yourself as the product of social forces.
4. Mills wanted people to develop a quality of mind so that they would be able to view personal circumstance within a social context.
5. Peter Berger challenged sociologists to recognize general social patterns in particular events and to see the strangeness of behaviours that seem familiar to us.

6. Sociology emerged from the need to understand the striking social changes that occurred in Europe in the form of three revolutions: the scientific revolution, the political revolution, and the Industrial Revolution.
7. Macrosociology, or the study of society as a whole, had its early influence in the work of European theorists such as Karl Marx, Émile Durkheim, and Max Weber.

8. Microsociology, the study of individual or small group dynamics within the larger society, had its early influence in the work of American theorists such as George Herbert Mead, Charles H. Cooley, and Herbert Blumer.

9. Canadian sociology has been influenced by five factors: geography, francophone sociology, Canadianization, political economy, and a radical approach.

module 1.3 SOCIOLOGY AND ITS CLASSICAL THEORETICAL FOUNDATIONS

10. Functionalism encompasses a view of the social world as a dynamic system of interrelated parts.

11. Émile Durkheim described how our behaviour is affected by social facts.

12. Talcott Parsons described society as a social system.

13. Robert Merton introduced the concepts of manifest functions and latent functions. Manifest functions are the intended consequences of an action or social pattern, while latent functions are the unintended consequences of an action or social pattern. Dysfunction refers to a process or structure of society that disrupts or creates instability in the society.

14. Conflict theory holds that power lies at the core of all social relationships and is unequally divided, and that the powerful maintain their control through the dominant ideology.

15. Jean-Jacques Rousseau argued that there are two types of inequality: natural/physical and moral/political.

16. Karl Marx and Friedrich Engels explored the issue of the rise of capitalism and the exploitation of the proletariat (the workers) by the bourgeoisie (the factory owners).

17. Symbolic Interactionists (a microsociological perspective) emphasizes that society and social structures are created by the interactions between people, and that therefore these structures can be changed.

18. Max Weber introduced the term *verstehen*. *Verstehen* means to understand. Weber wanted sociologists to examine subjective social meanings in their research in order to appreciate both the intention and the context of human action.

19. Georg Simmel viewed society as the summation of human experience and its patterned interaction.

20. George Herbert Mead described how the individual exists as a member of a social organism and that his or her acts can be understood only in the context of social actions that involve other individuals.

21. Charles Cooley introduced the concept of the "looking-glass self"—the belief that we develop our self-image through the cues we receive from others.

module 1.4 CONTEMPORARY SOCIAL THEORIES

22. Antonio Gramsci's concept of hegemony holds that the ruling class dominates by the way it promotes its ideology. Because the prevailing ideology appears as common sense by the masses, it is not challenged.

23. Feminists view women as oppressed by men. The goal of feminists is for women and men to be social and political equals. There are several strands of feminism including liberal feminism, Marxist feminism, radical feminism, and socialist feminism.

24. Dorothy Smith's standpoint theory focuses on understanding the world from the subject's point of view.

25. Post-structuralists challenge the view that the path to truth is through science. They argue that truth is defined by power relations and that all knowledge is socially constructed.

Key Terms

achieved status (p. 9)
alienation (p. 20)
ascribed status (p. 8)
bourgeoisie (p. 20)
class consciousness (p. 21)
discipline (p. 27)
discourse (p. 27)
dysfunction (p. 19)
exploitation (p. 20)
false consciousness (p. 20)
globalization (p. 27)
hegemony (p. 24)

latent functions (p. 19)
looking-glass self (p. 23)
macrosociology (p. 13)
manifest functions (p. 19)
moral or political inequality (p. 20)
natural or physical inequality (p. 20)
organic analogy (p. 17)
personal troubles (p. 5)
political economy (p. 14)
positivism (p. 12)
proletariat (p. 20)
quality of mind (p. 5)

relations of production (p. 20)
social facts (p. 18)
social issues (p. 5)
sociological imagination (p. 5)
sociological perspective (p. 4)
sociology (p. 4)
symbolic interactionism (p. 14)
sympathetic introspection (p. 23)
Thomas theorem (p. 21)
verstehen (p. 22)

Test Yourself

1. The ability to perceive how dynamic social forces affect individual lives is called
   a. Sociology
   b. The sociological imagination
   c. Quality of mind
   d. The sociological perspective

2. Who coined the phrase "seeing the general in the particular"?
   a. Auguste Comte
   b. Peter Berger
   c. C.W. Mills
   d. Karl Marx

3. _____ refers to attributes developed throughout life as a result of effort and skill (e.g., course grades).
   a. Ascribed status
   b. Achieved status
   c. Socio-economic status
   d. Personal status

4. Which group is most likely to have persons with low incomes?
   a. Two-parent families
   b. Female lone-parent families
   c. Persons 30 to 50
   d. Persons 65 and older

5. Mills' term for the ability to view personal circumstances within a social context is
   a. The sociological perspective
   b. The sociological imagination
   c. Quality of mind
   d. The sociological view

6. The term *sociology* was coined by
   a. Ibn Khaldun
   b. Auguste Comte
   c. Karl Marx
   d. Plato

7. Who made the famous statement "I think therefore I am"?
   a. Niccolò Machiavelli
   b. René Descartes
   c. Thomas Hobbes
   d. Auguste Comte

8. The Industrial Revolution began around
   a. 1650
   b. 1700
   c. 1750
   d. 1800

9. Which of the following theorists is not considered a functionalist?
   a. Robert Merton
   b. Karl Marx
   c. Émile Durkheim
   d. Talcott Parsons

10. Which perspective compares society as similar to that of an organism like the human body?
    a. Functionalism
    b. Conflict theory
    c. Symbolic interactionism
    d. Feminism

11. The intended consequences of an action or social pattern are called
   a. Manifest functions
   b. Latent functions
   c. Dysfunctions
   d. Social functions

12. Marx is associated with which sociological perspective?
   a. Functionalism
   b. Conflict theory
   c. Symbolic interactionism
   d. Post-structuralism

13. _____ study specific cases of how individuals act in small groups and in face-to-face interactions.
   a. Functionalists
   b. Conflict theorists
   c. Symbolic interactionists
   d. Post-structuralists

14. Which of the following perspectives is a microsociological perspective?
   a. Conflict theory
   b. Functionalism
   c. Symbolic interactionism
   d. Hegemony

15. Hegemony can be described as
   a. Domination through ideological control and consent
   b. Domination through military force
   c. Domination through police force
   d. Subordination through police force

16. What theorist has been most influential in developing the post-structuralist perspective?
   a. Michel Foucault
   b. bell hooks
   c. Dorothy Smith
   d. Antonio Gramsci

17. What philosophy extols the virtues of "self-restraint, personal responsibility and social awareness"?
   a. Queer theory
   b. Standpoint theory
   c. Straight edge
   d. Post-structuralism

18. Which feminist perspective sees patriarchy as the root cause of women's oppression?
   a. Liberal
   b. Socialist
   c. Marxist
   d. Radical

19. Which feminist perspective sees capitalism as the root cause of women's oppression?
   a. Liberal
   b. Socialist
   c. Marxist
   d. Radical

20. Whose name is associated with standpoint feminism?
   a. Dorothy Smith
   b. bell hooks
   c. Antonio Gramsci
   d. Michel Foucault

Answers: b, b, b, b, c, b, a, b, c, c, a, c, d, c, a

Log in to MySocLab for a host of resources that will help you save time and improve your grade. MySocLab contains cutting-edge learning tools such as study plans, practice tests, videos, audio segments, quizzes, and more—all designed to help you better understand the learning objectives for this chapter. Along with your eBook, MySocLab for *Sociology for Everyone* can be found at **www.mysoclab.com**.

module 1.1
THE SOCIOLOGICAL IMAGINATION

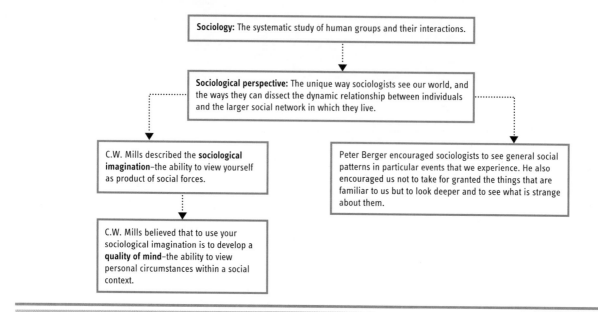

Sociology: The systematic study of human groups and their interactions.

Sociological perspective: The unique way sociologists see our world, and the ways they can dissect the dynamic relationship between individuals and the larger social network in which they live.

C.W. Mills described the **sociological imagination**–the ability to view yourself as product of social forces.

Peter Berger encouraged sociologists to see general social patterns in particular events that we experience. He also encouraged us not to take for granted the things that are familiar to us but to look deeper and to see what is strange about them.

C.W. Mills believed that to use your sociological imagination is to develop a **quality of mind**–the ability to view personal circumstances within a social context.

module 1.2
THE ORIGINS OF SOCIOLOGY

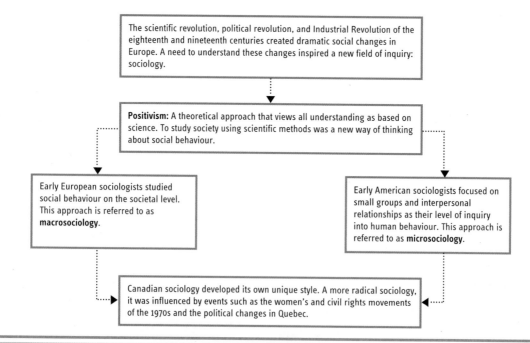

The scientific revolution, political revolution, and Industrial Revolution of the eighteenth and nineteenth centuries created dramatic social changes in Europe. A need to understand these changes inspired a new field of inquiry: sociology.

Positivism: A theoretical approach that views all understanding as based on science. To study society using scientific methods was a new way of thinking about social behaviour.

Early European sociologists studied social behaviour on the societal level. This approach is referred to as **macrosociology**.

Early American sociologists focused on small groups and interpersonal relationships as their level of inquiry into human behaviour. This approach is referred to as **microsociology**.

Canadian sociology developed its own unique style. A more radical sociology, it was influenced by events such as the women's and civil rights movements of the 1970s and the political changes in Quebec.

module 1.3
SOCIOLOGY AND ITS CLASSICAL THEORETICAL FOUNDATIONS

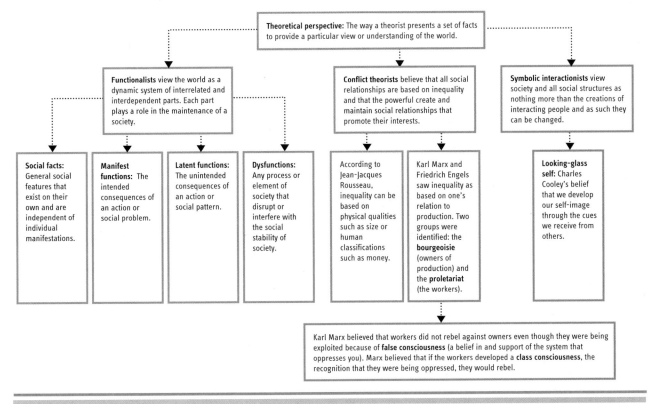

Theoretical perspective: The way a theorist presents a set of facts to provide a particular view or understanding of the world.

Functionalists view the world as a dynamic system of interrelated and interdependent parts. Each part plays a role in the maintenance of a society.

Conflict theorists believe that all social relationships are based on inequality and that the powerful create and maintain social relationships that promote their interests.

Symbolic interactionists view society and all social structures as nothing more than the creations of interacting people and as such they can be changed.

Social facts: General social features that exist on their own and are independent of individual manifestations.

Manifest functions: The intended consequences of an action or social problem.

Latent functions: The unintended consequences of an action or social pattern.

Dysfunctions: Any process or element of society that disrupt or interfere with the social stability of society.

According to Jean-Jacques Rousseau, inequality can be based on physical qualities such as size or human classifications such as money.

Karl Marx and Friedrich Engels saw inequality as based on one's relation to production. Two groups were identified: the **bourgeoisie** (owners of production) and the **proletariat** (the workers).

Looking-glass self: Charles Cooley's belief that we develop our self-image through the cues we receive from others.

Karl Marx believed that workers did not rebel against owners even though they were being exploited because of **false consciousness** (a belief in and support of the system that oppresses you). Marx believed that if the workers developed a **class consciousness**, the recognition that they were being oppressed, they would rebel.

module 1.4
CONTEMPORARY SOCIAL THEORIES

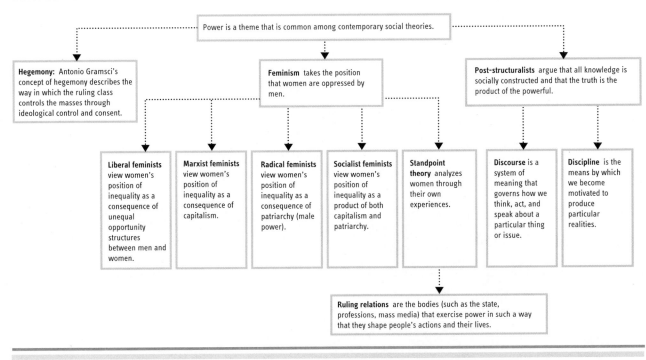

Power is a theme that is common among contemporary social theories.

Hegemony: Antonio Gramsci's concept of hegemony describes the way in which the ruling class controls the masses through ideological control and consent.

Feminism takes the position that women are oppressed by men.

Post-structuralists argue that all knowledge is socially constructed and that the truth is the product of the powerful.

Liberal feminists view women's position of inequality as a consequence of unequal opportunity structures between men and women.

Marxist feminists view women's position of inequality as a consequence of capitalism.

Radical feminists view women's position of inequality as a consequence of patriarchy (male power).

Socialist feminists view women's position of inequality as a product of both capitalism and patriarchy.

Standpoint theory analyzes women through their own experiences.

Discourse is a system of meaning that governs how we think, act, and speak about a particular thing or issue.

Discipline is the means by which we become motivated to produce particular realities.

Ruling relations are the bodies (such as the state, professions, mass media) that exercise power in such a way that they shape people's actions and their lives.

chapter 2

Research, Methodology, and Ethics

Alfred Kinsey

It isn't often that Hollywood profiles the life and work of a social scientist, but it did just that in the 2004 film *Kinsey*. Mind you, the research topic probably had something to do with the making of the film. Sex does sell—so why not research on sex?

The film portrays Alfred Kinsey (played by Liam Neeson), the researcher whose work challenged America's attitudes, beliefs, and values regarding human sexuality. In his efforts to provide counselling to his married students, Kinsey soon discovered that virtually no data existed on the subject of human sexuality and that the average person was extremely naive. Kinsey, a biologist by training, recognized that a scientific study on human sexuality was long overdue. He started his formal research on the subject in 1938 (Kinsey Institute).

As we can see from Kinsey's work, research is not separate from everyday life; in fact, our everyday experiences often drive what we end up researching. For Kinsey, his research was as much a quest for personal insight into his own sexuality as it was a quest to advance scientific knowledge in the area (Kinsey Institute). From 1938 to 1963, Kinsey and his associates conducted almost 18 000 interviews. Kinsey himself interviewed close to 8000 people.

Kinsey produced two books from his data: *Sexual Behaviour in the Human Male* (1948) and *Sexual Behaviour in the Human Female* (1953). His revelations shocked conservative America and forever changed North American attitudes toward human sexuality. Among his findings was the wide range of human sexual experiences; he found that the range of "normal" human sexual behaviour was far greater than he had originally imagined. Based on his findings, Kinsey theorized that few humans are exclusively heterosexual or homosexual. He asserted that most people fit somewhere in a continuum (Kinsey Institute). In other words, he believed that most people are bisexual. For Kinsey, this finding was an affirmation of his own sexual desires and behaviour. While Kinsey's interviewing techniques, his ability to code information, and his efforts at maintaining confidentiality were admired, there were those who criticized the validity of his work. In particular, people criticized the way he gathered his research. Kinsey would interview anyone who was willing to talk to him, and there was a belief that his research focused too much on the fringe of society and did not represent the average person.

A 1994 study by Robert Michael, John Gagnon, Edward Laumann, and Gina Kolata followed up on Kinsey's work. *Sex in America* used sophisticated polling and research techniques, and many believed that its findings revealed a far more accurate picture of the average person. The following true/false questions were included in the 1994 study. What do *you* believe to be true and false?

1. The majority of people are faithful throughout their marriage. T__ F__
2. On average people have sex more than 3 times per week. T__ F__
3. Married people are more likely than single people to have sex. T__ F__
4. Homosexuals make up less than 10% of the population. T__ F__
5. Men have more sexual partners than women in a lifetime. T__ F__
6. Men are more likely than women to masturbate. T__ F__
7. Married people are more likely to have an orgasm than single people. T__ F__

See the answers below. What information did you use to base your answers on—personal experience, opinions, or common knowledge? Sex is one of those topics that people generally believe they know a lot about. In fact, any topic in which we have personal experience will influence our perceptions of it. Based on your answers to the questions above, you have probably discovered that your personal knowledge does not always match the facts. The role of research is to move us beyond our own personal experiences, opinions, and common knowledge—and toward information that we all share, that is verifiable, and that we acknowledge to be the truth.

To learn more about Alfred Kinsey and ongoing research on sex, gender, and reproduction, go to www.kinseyinstitute.org/research/.

Answers:

1. *True*: 75 percent of married men and 85 percent of married women say they have never been unfaithful.
2. *False*: One-third have sex twice a week or more. The rest have less.
3. *True*: 40 percent of married people compared with 25 percent of single people say they have sex at least twice a week.
4. *False*: 2.7 percent of men and 1.3 percent of women reported having homosexual sex in the past year.

module 2.1

Connecting Theory and Research

We all use phrases such as "everybody knows that" or "it just makes sense" when we talk about various aspects of our world. But really, how do we know these things to be "true"? "Everybody knows the earth is round." While this may seem to be common sense now, at one time prevailing wisdom stated that the earth was flat. "Smoking contributes to cancer." Again, this is the current wisdom, but at one point smoking was encouraged. Consider, for example, the popular image of the Marlboro man in the 1950s; at that time, smoking was considered "sexy" and "macho." So how do we come to "know" particular "truths"? Research is conducted in both biomedical and social science disciplines. While

A researcher working from a symbolic interactionist perspective might seek to understand how immigrant families negotiate their sense of identity in their surroundings.

---

[1] Elmer-Dewitt, P. (2002). Now for the truth about Americans and sex. *Sociology: Annual Editions 02/03*. Guilford, CT: McGraw-Hill/Dushkin.

the topics will differ and some intricacies of procedure may vary, for the most part all researchers are pursuing the same outcome: an attempt to create knowledge through a process of discovery.

In the first chapter, we learned about functionalism, conflict theory, feminism, and symbolic interactionism. Each of these perspectives provides the lens by which a sociologist might look at our social world. Because each perspective looks at the world from a different angle and scope, a sociologist's theoretical orientation will influence the type of research questions asked and how they are asked. Simply stated, the conflict theorist will approach a topic differently from a symbolic interactionist or a functionalist. For example, we can take the general topic of families. A researcher working from a functionalist perspective would be interested in the smooth functioning of society. Some of the main concerns of this theoretical perspective are how roles in a family contribute to social stability. Functionalists, then, would be interested in the functions of families within society. For example, they might be concerned with how families teach their children about future roles like parenthood. A functionalist might pose the research question, What are the consequences of changing family forms for the smooth running of society?

Working from a different theoretical perspective, a conflict theorist is generally concerned with the struggle over scarce resources by different groups in society and how elites use power to control the less powerful. So a conflict theorist might be interested in how families cope with the economic strain of our current times. Researchers working from this perspective may be interested in examining government and corporate policies that disadvantage families through the privatization and/or withdrawal of particular social programs. For example, the degree to which a government provides affordable daycare to allow working-class parents to work would be of interest to conflict theorists.

Both functionalism and conflict perspectives are considered macro theories and therefore ask "large" questions. Symbolic interactionism, on the other hand, is a micro perspective, and people working from this approach would therefore ask different kinds of questions. Symbolic interactionists are interested in face-to-face encounters and the meanings that people use to facilitate social life. Researchers working from this perspective might be interested in interaction patterns within families or how labels are used (and impact) family members. A potential research project from a symbolic interactionist perspective might examine how immigrants negotiate identity within the family and how they adapt to their new cultural surroundings. The interplay between immigrant parents and their Canadian-born children as each adapts to Canadian culture would be of particular interest to the symbolic interactionist.

Feminist researchers generally are interested in examining issues pertaining to gender and inequality. Feminist research can take either a micro or a macro approach. Researchers working from a micro approach might wish to examine child-rearing practices used in Canadian families to see whether they promote gender equality or inequality. Researchers working from a macro approach might investigate the incidence of family violence as a gendered issue in Canadian families.

THEORY, RESEARCH, AND METHODS

As outlined above, the theoretical perspective you take will only allow you to pose research questions that make sense within that theoretical paradigm. The same is true for the method or methods that you choose to use to answer your research question. There is no best method for every project. Rather, the method you use will depend on the research question/s you ask. We will return to this relationship in our discussion of research methods.

CANADIAN SOCIETY IN FOCUS

Statistics Canada and Sociology

Statistics Canada is a federally legislated agency. It is responsible for gathering data that enables Canadians to better understand their country (Statistics Canada, n.d.).

The range of research areas that Statistics Canada is responsible for is broad and includes population, resources, the economy, and culture. The agency is involved in over 300 active research projects at any given time (Statistics Canada, n.d.). As well, it conducts the national census, the survey that all Canadians are legally bound to answer, every five years.

The federal government considers that Statistics Canada plays a vital role in our democratic process. By providing easy access to reliable, objective information, our elected officials, business and union leaders, as well as non-governmental agencies can make decisions that best serve the needs of Canadians (Statistics Canada, n.d.). That is why it is essential to participate in the census.

Sociologists play an important role at Statistics Canada. They are directly involved in the research process gathering, analyzing, and publishing information. As well, they serve as consultants to anyone using the data. Most important, their work becomes the foundation for public policy and major business initiatives. Thus, we could argue that many major decisions in Canada, in government or business, have most likely been influenced by the work of sociologists at Statistics Canada.

You will also notice that this book often references Statistics Canada data. That is because sociologists outside of the agency rely on these data for their work. In fact, Statistics Canada is a significant secondary-source resource for sociologists.

For more information on Statistics Canada or if you are looking for information on a social issue, go to **www.statscan.gc.ca**.

METHODOLOGICAL APPROACHES: QUANTITATIVE AND QUALITATIVE RESEARCH

There are two main approaches to social research—quantitative and qualitative. On a basic level, **quantitative** refers to numerical data while **qualitative** refers to non-numerical data. Although some researchers use a combination of both approaches within one study, many researchers are firmly located in one "camp" or the other. We will not enter a debate about whether one approach is superior to the other. Rather, we believe that both approaches are valuable, and that regardless of the approach taken, researchers from both camps are concerned with finding the truth. Which approach you take will depend on your research question or focus and your theoretical orientation.

Let's begin with quantitative approaches. Conducting and analyzing research quantitatively involves converting some aspect(s) of social life to numerical data and testing whether or not there is a significant relationship between sets of data. Each answer, for instance, that you check off on a questionnaire can be converted to numerical form and analyzed. Your answers can then be compared with other people's answers—on the basis of a variety of **variables**. Suppose that a survey is investigating first-year university students' study habits. You might be asked whether you live in residence or off-campus, whether you live alone or with others, whether you pull all-nighters before an exam or ensure you get a full night's sleep, and whether you study with others or by yourself. All of your answers can then be assigned a value. Your answers can be compared on the basis of living arrangements, study habits, gender, age, and

quantitative Regarding numerical data.

qualitative Regarding non-numerical data; the researcher is the research instrument.

variables Characteristics of objects, people, or groups of people that can be measured.

so forth. The researchers might conclude that first-year university students prefer to prepare for an exam with fellow students, studying in a group.

Qualitative approaches do not involve converting aspects of social life to numerical data. Rather, they focus on social behaviours that cannot be easily counted or measured. Because social behaviours are difficult to measure, they need to be described in detail. Quantitative studies tend to have larger samples so that researchers can generalize from their findings. Qualitative studies tend to have smaller samples than quantitative projects because they are more in-depth. Cost is a factor too, as qualitative studies tend to be more expensive to carry out, especially on a large scale. In qualitative studies, the researchers themselves are the research instruments. Qualitative approaches use interviewing and observation as the main techniques of data collection. For example, in interview-based studies, researchers carry out interviews with participants, but they also make observations about feelings, moods, location, body language, and so forth of both the interviewees as well as themselves. These observations are just as valuable as the interview transcripts in terms of being considered viable data. For example, Elizabeth McDermott (2004) noticed that class differences surfaced in how her participants talked about their lives as lesbians. The working-class women were uncomfortable and uncertain during the interviews while the middle-class women seemed to welcome the opportunity to openly discuss their lives. McDermott argues that researchers need to be aware of the subtle ways that social class operates during interview interactions.

A summary of the differences between quantitative and qualitative research is found in Table 2–1. Keep in mind that this summary is a generalization. We may see variations in the two approaches to research. For instance, a quantitative research project involving thousands of respondents could be both time-consuming and expensive.

SYSTEMS OF REASONING: INDUCTIVE AND DEDUCTIVE LOGIC

inductive logic   A way of reasoning that moves from data to the formation of a theory.

deductive logic   A way of reasoning that moves from theory to the formulation of hypotheses for testing.

Researchers use two systems of reasoning—*inductive logic* and *deductive logic*. Those using **inductive logic** move from data to theory, while those using **deductive logic** move from theory to data. See Figure 2–1 for the elements in the inductive and deductive research models.

In inductive logic, what does moving from data to theory actually mean? In this system, a researcher gathers information about topic X before developing theories about how to explain particular aspects of X. For example, a study that is considered a classic in sociology is Paul Willis' (1977) participant-observation study on working-class white males. He was interested in learning how it is that working-class youth settle for working-class jobs rather than aspire to middle-class jobs. What he found is that working-class boys put down middle-class jobs and values. To them, working-class jobs were more masculine. However, in spite of creating a counter–school culture, their efforts resulted in the reproduction of culture rather than the transformation of culture (Gordon, 1984).

Deductive logic uses the same elements of the research cycle as inductive logic, but it begins at the level of theory. Researchers develop a theory or a set of theories to explain or

TABLE 2–1 Differences between Quantitative and Qualitative Research

Quantitative Research	Qualitative Research
Numerical	Non-numerical
Large samples	Small samples
Statistical trends	Behaviours and patterns
Less expensive	More expensive
Less time-consuming	More time-consuming
Survey method	Observation, interviews, surveys

FIGURE 2–1 **Inductive and Deductive Research Models**

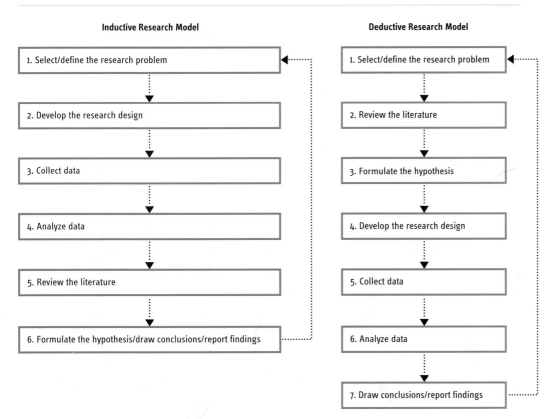

predict a pattern. They then test their theory to see if the expected pattern transpires. For example, Mallie Paschall, Kypros Kypri, and Robert Saltz (2006) were interested in class schedules and the alcohol use of college students. They predicted that based on the students' experiences during their first semester, heavier-drinking students would be less expected to schedule a Friday class in their next semester. Paschall et. al (2006) surveyed 866 New Zealand college students to test this prediction. After analysis of the data, the researchers were able to confirm this prediction: heavier-drinking students were less likely to have a Friday class in their second semester. They were also able to conclude that students who scheduled at least one class on Fridays reduced the probability of heavy alcohol consumption on Thursdays.

Researchers who use a qualitative approach often use inductive reasoning. Likewise, researchers who favour a quantitative approach typically use deductive reasoning. This preference in pairing approaches is not an absolute rule, however.

What do you know about **Connecting Theory and Research**?

Multiple-choice questions (circle your answer)

1. What step comes first in the deductive approach?
a. Collect data
b. Review the literature
c. Formulate the hypothesis
d. Select/define the research problem

2. Which theorists would not take a macro approach?
a. Functionalists
b. Conflict theorists
c. Feminists
d. Symbolic interactionists

3. Which approach is likely to use a large sample?

a.   Quantitative research

b.   Qualitative research

c.   Inductive research

d.   Case studies

4. There are two systems of reasoning that researchers use. Which one moves from theory to data?

a.   Inductive reasoning

b.   Deductive reasoning

c.   Qualitative analysis

d.   The scientific method

5. Which theorists would be interested in examining issues pertaining to gender and inequality?

a.   Functionalists

b.   Symbolic interactionists

c.   Conflict theorists

d.   Feminists

Answers: d, d, a, b, d

module 2.2

Steps in the Research Process

Think about Steps in the Research Process

1 Think back to your high school science classes. Do you remember doing experiments? What were the steps that you followed? How do you think those steps might be different if you were to do sociological research?

Sociology is referred to as a social "science." The term *social* refers to what we study—human group life and their interactions. The term *science* refers to how we study. Sociological research is systematic and based upon specific principles and methods.

Why do sociologists conduct research? Think back to the opening vignette and the true and false questionnaire that you completed regarding your knowledge of human sexuality. How many of your answers were based upon personal experiences or assumptions about human behaviour? How many of those answers proved to be incorrect? Sociologists do not accept common knowledge or common sense answers to explaining human behaviour because, as you have learned, they are not always correct. Rather, sociologists employ research methods that ensure the data they collect has been recorded and tested for accuracy. The aim of sociological research is to provide the most accurate picture of human behaviour possible. The outcome of sociological research is based on the ability of sociologists and others to reliably describe and predict human behaviour within a given context.

THE SCIENTIFIC METHOD

scientific method
A systematic approach researchers follow in their quest for answers to a research problem.

Sociologists, like other scientists, use the scientific method in their research. The **scientific method** is a systematic approach researchers follow in their quest for answers to a research problem. By taking a systematic approach to research, sociologists create an openness to their work that allows others to analyze both their approach to the topic and the merit of their results.

As mentioned above, the research route sociologists take depends upon the topic and their theoretical approach. For the purpose of this discussion, we will follow the steps in the deductive research model.

SELECT/DEFINE THE RESEARCH PROBLEM

How do you decide what to study? There are many forces that drive researchers in a particular direction. Let's refer back to Kinsey. Why study human sexuality? Pushed to provide answers to his students on the topic, Kinsey quickly discovered that there was little literature of scientific merit; in fact, it was more apt to be based on religious beliefs. Thus, to Kinsey the need for a scientific study in the area was clear. Researchers might stumble on a problem as Kinsey did—his actual area of expertise before his work on human sexuality was the gull wasp. Sometimes, researchers are driven by personal experience to seek answers to a question. Other times, they seek to build on the vast knowledge they already have in a particular area. Refining the research problem from a general topic to a specific problem requires more work. This work involves a literature review.

REVIEW THE LITERATURE

A literature review involves an extensive examination of all the reputable research that has been conducted on a subject. By analyzing and cross-referencing this material, researchers can develop a conceptual framework for their own research. At the same time, researchers learn about and from the successes and failures of other research. This knowledge is essential in designing the approach that they will take in their study. Some research actually duplicates another person's work. Human behaviour can vary from time to time, from place to place, and from group to group. Therefore, there is merit in replicating a piece of research. Specifically, we may want to replicate a piece of research to evaluate whether a group's behaviour has changed over time. We may also want to replicate a piece of research to make cross-cultural comparisons. For instance, we may want to compare the sexual behaviour of Americans to Canadians. We can do so by applying the same research method to both groups.

FORMULATE THE HYPOTHESIS

A **hypothesis** is a tentative statement about a particular relationship—whether between objects, people, or groups of people—that can be tested empirically. In a hypothesis, we refer to the variables used to measure this relationship as the independent and dependent variables. The **independent variable** is the variable that researchers can manipulate to create some change in the dependent variable. The independent variable is also called *the cause*. The **dependent variable**'s condition is reliant on the nature of the independent variable. For instance, frequency of sexual intercourse would be a dependent variable; that is, it is reliant on any number of independent variables such as sex, age, marital status, or social class. Researchers would want to discover whether a change in the independent variable has an effect on the dependent variable. That independent variable is often referred to as *the effect*.

A hypothesis would thus make a prediction about the relationship of these two variables. For example, we might predict that married people (independent variable) have more sex (dependent variable) than single people.

In a research project describing the sexual behaviour of Canadians, a hypothesis would not be identified. A hypothesis would be used in instances where the intent is to explain a specific behaviour. In other words, we use hypotheses in quantitative research but not in qualitative research.

MEASUREMENT In order for a variable to be measured, it needs to be defined—this is referred to as the **operational definition**. For instance, in the hypothesis above, what do we mean by more sex? How would we define sex? Does sex include kissing, petting, oral sex, or only sexual intercourse? Without a clear definition of our variables, we would not know what behaviour to include in our study, thus making our research invalid.

The Bill Clinton/Monica Lewinsky case is a good example of how people's definitions of sexual relations differ. When Clinton was asked whether he had sex with Monica Lewinsky,

hypothesis A tentative statement about a particular relationship (between objects, people, or groups of people) that can be tested empirically.

independent variable The variable that researchers manipulate to create some change in the dependent variable.

dependent variable The variable whose condition is reliant on the nature of the independent variable.

operational definition A description of how a variable is measured.

he emphatically stated, "I have never had sexual relations with Monica Lewinsky. I've never had an affair with her." Lewinsky testified that she and Clinton had 10 separate sexual encounters that included fondling and oral sex. When questioned, Clinton testified that an affair required having sexual intercourse, which had not occurred. As well, he testified that Lewinsky performing oral sex on him did not constitute a sexual relationship. In Clinton's mind, that was not sex (Baker, 1998). How many people think like Clinton? Informal polls with several hundred college students over the past few years by this author (John Patterson) would suggest the vast majority. The Clinton case illustrates how people's thinking differs, and when we are studying behaviour we need to be clear about what we plan to measure.

DEVELOP THE RESEARCH DESIGN

Sociologists select research methods based on their theoretical perspective and the question they seek to answer. We will examine six—surveys, interviews, participant observation, secondary analysis, participatory action research, and mixed methods—in greater detail in the next module.

COLLECT DATA

There are four different ways to collect data from a sample. Depending on the research method researchers select, one or more strategies may be used: direct observation, interviewing the sample, having the sample respond in writing to questions, or undertaking an analysis of existing, publically accessible information. In some cases, researchers will use more than one strategy and thus enrich the content of their findings.

Face-to-face interviews are one way that sociologists gather data.

ANALYZE DATA

Data analysis is the stage in the process where researchers sort, sift, and organize data to find the patterns and themes of behaviour upon which their conclusions will be made. The way in which the data is analyzed, however, will differ depending on whether a quantitative or qualitative approach was used.

In quantitative research, researchers look for statistical patterns between variables. Using computer programs, such as the Statistical Package for the Social Sciences, large volumes of coded material can be quickly analyzed. **Coding** in quantitative research involves assigning a numerical value to the answer of a particular question (see Figure 2–2). By cross-referencing variables, patterns of behaviour emerge (Babbie, 2008). For instance, in the example provided in Figure 2–2, we could compare sex to sexual orientation and be able to determine which sex is more likely to be heterosexual, homosexual, or bisexual in a given population.

In qualitative research, such as observation or in-depth interviews, the process of analyzing data can be more difficult. In fact, Babbie (2008, p. 421) states it is "as much art as science." Imagine that you are a researcher who is collecting thousands of pages of notes or hundreds of hours of film while studying a group and its behaviour. In the end, you need to be able to sort through the material and identify themes and patterns of behaviour. Three tools used in the analysis of such data include coding, memoing, and concept mapping (Babbie, 2008).

Coding in qualitative research involves classifying or categorizing data (Babbie, 2008). For instance, suppose you are researching the topic of flirting. You may begin by categorizing male and female behaviours. Then, you may form another category dividing the behaviours into verbal and nonverbal communication, and so forth (see Figure 2–3). After developing various categories, you need a system that allows you to retrieve the material easily.

As researchers code data and begin to develop themes and categories, they should also write brief notes on what they see in the data. This process is referred to as **memoing**. These notes will allow the researcher to cross-reference their ideas and may become the basis for the final report (Babbie, 2008).

Concept mapping is the process of developing a visual diagram of the key concepts discovered and their relationship to each other (Babbie, 2008). Concept mapping has been used throughout this book. Just look at the end of this chapter for examples.

coding (quantitative research) It involves assigning a numerical value to the answer of a particular question.

To learn more about qualitative analysis, go to **http://onlineqda.hud.ac.uk/.**

coding (qualitative research) It involves classifying or categorizing data.

memoing Writing brief notes on arising themes in the data.

concept mapping The process of developing a visual diagram of the key concepts discovered and their relationship to each other.

FIGURE 2–2 Sample Code Sheet—Quantitative Research on Sex and Sexual Orientation

Question #	Variable Name	Variable Label	Value Label	Value*
1	ID	Identification#	Respondent 1	01
			Respondent 2	02
2	Sex	Sex of respondent	Female	01
			Male	02
			Answer missing	09
3	Sexual orientation	Sexual orientation of respondent	Heterosexual	01
			Homosexual	02
			Bisexual	03
			Answer missing	09

* The value is the coded number to the answer for each question.

FIGURE 2–3 Sample Code Sheet—Qualitative Research on Flirting

Theme	Male to Female	Male to Male	Female to Female
Verbal Communication			
Initiator			
Opening line			
Nonverbal Communication			
Body posture			
Proxemics			
Touch			
Eye contact			

DRAW CONCLUSIONS

Research conclusions involve an evaluation of the process itself. The first question researchers must ask themselves is whether the findings support the hypothesis or research problem. Good researchers will identify potential flaws and limitations with the research. Issues that need to be addressed include whether the sample truly represents the population, whether the right questions were asked, and whether there were factors outside of the study that may have influenced the results.

Reporting research findings is also an essential part of this last step. Reported findings give other sociologists the opportunity to critique the research and provide feedback to the colleagues who undertook it.

What do you know about **the Steps in the Research Process**?

Multiple-choice questions (circle your answer)

1. The dependent variable is also referred to as
a. The cause
b. The effect
c. The answer
d. The problem

2. The group that we generalize about is referred to as
a. The population
b. The sample
c. The subject
d. The survey

3. There are four different ways to collect data. Which of the following is not one of them?
a. Direct observation
b. Interviewing the subjects
c. Reviewing secondary sources such as court documents

d. All are methods of data collection that sociologists would use.

4. To have an operational definition of a variable means
a. That we decided which is the independent and which is the dependent variable
b. That we have defined our variables so that they are measureable
c. That we are ready to write our report
d. That we have completed our research

5. Random sampling
a. Is not used by sociologists
b. Is used only in qualitative studies
c. Ensures that everyone in the population has an equal chance of being a subject in the study
d. Both a and c

Answers: b, a, d, b, c

module 2.3

Research Methods in Detail

How do sociologists know which research method to use? As discussed above, the research method used depends on the research question and the sociologist's theoretical orientation. Some research methods are just better suited to researchers' purposes than others. For example, what do you think would be the best way to get information on human sexuality? Factors influencing your decision would include the number of people you hope to study as well as the personal nature of the material you are studying. You would want a large sample size, as Kinsey attempted to achieve, because you are describing human sexuality—that is a lot of people to generalize about. Therefore, you would want to study as wide a range of experiences and people as possible. Because you need a large sample, surveys or interviews are best. You also need to consider ethics and the sensitive nature of the material. Observational techniques—watching people—would probably not be a good idea (we'll talk about ethics later!). Below are the research methods used most often by sociologists.

SURVEYS

Surveys are suited to large-scale research projects. They are useful for asking about *what* people do or think but not as helpful in answering *why* people do particular things or think a certain way. As an example, the *Sex in America* research that we discussed at the beginning of this chapter surveyed 3500 American adults (Elmer-Dewitt, 2006). The researchers discovered *what* people do but not *why* they do it. It is up to researchers to speculate as to why people behave in certain ways.

There are three main types of **surveys**: self-administered questionnaires, telephone surveys, and in-person surveys.

SELF-ADMINISTERED QUESTIONNAIRES   *Self-administered questionnaires* (surveys) can be mailed to prospective participants. The researcher often includes a postage-paid envelope for the respondent to return the completed survey. These questionnaires tend to be used mainly in quantitative research. Questions often list several possible answers (**closed-ended questions**) and the respondent is asked to check off one answer per question. You have probably seen these arrive at your home in the form of market research.

It should be noted that mail-out surveys were considered cost effective at one time for large samples. A more cost effective way to do self-administered surveys (depending on your research topic and access to a sample) is to use emailed surveys. They can be self-administered and returned quickly.

One of the most well-known self-administered surveys in Canada is the Census of Population (known commonly as the census) performed by Statistics Canada every five years. Households are asked to fill in all sorts of information, including the number of people living in the dwelling (and, of course, the type of dwelling), the hours spent on unpaid domestic labour, occupation, education, income, and one's origin or ancestry. All of these questions help to form a statistical representation of Canada. The results of the census are used to help various levels of government (and other policy-makers) develop and/or alter social policies (welfare, daycare, etc.) and/or to assess the needs of particular groups (new immigrants, elderly, etc.). Data are presented in a variety of units with the smallest at the level of neighbourhoods to the largest being the country itself. Questions on the census remain relatively stable, which enables

Think about Research Methods in Detail

1 Think about the following research topics:

■ Human sexuality

■ Classroom behaviour of college or university students

■ Social class and voting patterns

■ Gender stereotyping in television sitcoms

How do you think you would research each of these topics?

survey   A research method in which respondents answer pre-set questions.

closed-ended questions   Questions that list several possible answers.

The organization Egale (Equality for Gays and Lesbians Everywhere) actively lobbied for Canada's 2006 Census to include a question on sexual orientation. The campaign's logo is a play on the Census 2006 logo.

Census 2006:
same-sex couples
deserve equal treatment

researchers and policy-makers to analyze data over time. The census also responds to changing societal contexts and issues and introduces new question areas or makes modifications to existing questions to account for these changes. For example, the definition of a census family now includes partners of the same sex.

TELEPHONE SURVEYS   *Telephone surveys* work in much the same way—questions are asked of respondents by a researcher on the telephone. The researcher then provides the list of possible answers if closed-ended questions are being used. If the questions are open-ended, then the researcher will note the respondent's answers. For example, in a study on whether pets act as a channel for social networks, closed-ended questions such as "Do you talk to other pet owners when walking your dog, yes or no?" were used (Wood, Giles-Corti, & Bulsara, 2005, p. 1163). Other questions can be answered on a scale. Using the pet study again, respondents were asked, "In general, would you say that most of the time people are willing to help each other out?" Respondents then rated their answer on a five-point scale with 1 representing "strongly disagree" and 5 representing "strongly agree" (Wood, Giles-Corti, & Bulsara, 2005, p. 1163). The advantage of a telephone survey over a mail-out survey is that respondents can ask the researcher directly if they have questions or require clarification before answering a question.

IN-PERSON SURVEYS   *In-person, or face-to-face, surveys* are similar to the telephone surveys discussed above in that the respondent has access to the researcher. The advantage is that the researcher can immediately provide clarification or answer questions for the respondent. In-person surveys may be particularly useful with children, people whose first language is not English, people who lack strong literacy skills, or people with visual impairments, all of whom may have difficulty completing a mailed survey.

Kara Chan and James McNeal (2004) used an in-person survey when they explored Chinese children's attitudes toward television advertising. They surveyed 1758 children, ranging in age from 6 to 14, about whether the children liked particular commercials and whether they perceived the information provided in the commercials to be true.

INTERVIEWS

interviews They involve a researcher asking respondents a series of questions; interviews can be unstructured, semi-structured, or structured.

Interviews can be unstructured, semi-structured, or structured. Again, the approach researchers take will depend on the kind of information they are hoping to gather. Qualitative researchers typically use semi-structured or unstructured interviews, although quantitative researchers may use these as well. When researchers use semi-structured interviews, they approach the interview with some set questions but are also open to the interviewees introducing topics that they think are important for the interviewers to know. The idea is that the interview can perhaps unfold in the form of a dialogue between interviewer and interviewee. Similarly, an unstructured interview starts without any predetermined questions being set by the interviewer. Rather, the idea is for the interview to proceed conversationally. When interviews become structured, they fall outside the qualitative range. Structured interviews are typically used in quantitative studies where it is crucial for analysis that each and every respondent is asked the same questions in the same order with no room for deviation.

Power relations is one issue in interviews that may have an impact on the results. At the outset of an interview, there is an unequal relationship between the interviewer and the interviewee. Those who do the interviewing and the eventual analysis and reporting of the data are in a position to select what gets studied (setting the scene for what knowledge is to be produced), who is studied (who is given a voice, which persons or groups in society can we learn about), what data are reported (the researcher ultimately sets the direction of the public presentation of new knowledge), how the data are reported (again, an issue of "voice" concerning whether amalgamated data, summaries of people's experiences in the researcher's words, or interview excerpts in the words of the participants are presented), and so forth. All of these aspects of research involve the exercise of power and ultimately influence what is shared with others.

As Herzog (2005) points out, in the interview relationship, the interviewer is the "taker" and the interviewee is the "giver." Many researchers are aware of the unequal power relations and attempt to work through the complexities of the interview process in as equitable a manner as possible. For example, you might not immediately think that the location of an interview is a major concern in a research project. Rather, you might think of it merely as a logistical decision—can the participant get to the interview site, will nonparticipants be able to hear the interview, will the tape recorder pick up only the voices of the interviewer and interviewee in a public or semi-public location? But as Herzog (2005) argues in her article about her interview-based project with Palestinian citizens of Israel, the interview location can be a far more complex issue than a mere logistical decision. Interview location is crucial to our understanding of what is knowable in that context. Who chooses a particular location and what location is chosen ultimately affects what is revealed in a study and who is able to reveal.

OBSERVATIONAL STUDIES

Participant observation (also referred to as *fieldwork* or *ethnography*) involves a researcher's active participation in the daily life activities of those he or she is observing. The degree of involvement varies from study to study, with some researchers remaining distant observers while others trying to live as much like the people they are researching as possible. Participant observation is a qualitative method that uses processes of induction as opposed to deduction. In other words, researchers do not develop hypotheses but are instead interested in exploring a particular place and people in an in-depth way. For example, Canadian researcher Jane Helleiner decided to conduct her fieldwork among a group of *Travellers* (gypsies and homeless people) in Ireland. She purchased a trailer from one of the Traveller families in a fairly settled "camp" and then lived in this location for nine months (Helleiner, 2000). Living in the camp in this way provided her with the possibility of in-depth interactions with both the Travellers who lived in the camp as well as those who came to visit. Her location also afforded her the opportunity to observe camp life. These interactions and observations enabled Helleiner to understand the production of Traveller culture.

Participant observation is often meant to be informal. That is, researchers want the research to unfold before them rather than have a preconceived, rigid plan in place before "entering the field." As discussed later in this chapter, participant observation can be difficult to explain and justify to a university's research ethics board (REB) that approves, in advance, all research activities of its members. REBs are uncomfortable not knowing ahead of time which people will be included in the study, not seeing what questions will be asked of which participants, and so forth. A cornerstone of modern ethics is informed consent, which usually requires the signature of a prospective research participant on a consent form. Using Helleiner's Travellers study as an example, you can imagine how difficult this requirement may have been to the unfolding of field research. When she met a Traveller, she would have had to whip out a consent form and explain it to that person. What was intended as an informal conversation would have been framed in a formalized, bureaucratic way.

Participant observation can be open, covert, or semi-covert. *Open research* means that the subjects know that you are researching them. *Covert research* means that the people doing the research are undercover. In other words, the people in the research setting are neither informed of the researcher's status nor aware that they are being observed for the purposes of a research project. This kind of deception is uncommon, and REBs (discussed in more detail later in the chapter) require extensive justification as to the benefit of such an approach. *Semi-covert research* involves revealing the nature of your study to only some people. An excellent example is Danielle Egan's (2006) participant observation of exotic dance clubs in New England. Egan described herself as transitioning from full observer to

participant observation Active participation by a researcher in a research setting. It is also known as *fieldwork* or *ethnography*.

Researchers engaged in participant observation research often take part in the practices of the setting under study.

full participant (as an exotic dancer). She called the research *semi-covert* because she did not inform the club owners that she was a researcher, nor did she inform all customers she came into contact with of her researcher status. However, a few of the dancers she worked with knew that she was doing research. She defends her semi-covert approach on the following bases: she did not inform the owners for safety reasons, and she did not disclose her status to all customers because the dancers were the focus of her study, not the customers.

It isn't always possible for sociologists to become a member of the group that they wish to study, so they engage in **nonparticipant observation**. For instance, joining an ethnic group with very different physical traits than the researcher would not be possible. In this case, the researcher observes as an outsider. The advantage of nonparticipant observation is that it may be easier for researchers to stay impartial and more objective. The disadvantage of nonparticipant observation is that researchers never get to feel what it is like to be a member of that group.

nonparticipant observation Direct observation by a researcher in a research setting without interaction with the participants.

SECONDARY ANALYSIS

secondary analysis A research method involving analysis of existing data—archival or current.

Researchers often make use of existing documents for **secondary analysis** (also called *content analysis*). Archival research is well suited not only for studying past events but also for examining trends over time. For example, you could replicate Durkheim's suicide study in different locations and different time periods.

Archives are found not only in university libraries but also in government bodies and churches. You might also find that particular social clubs maintain information records, minutes of meetings, etc. Newspapers, magazines, and other periodicals are also archived.

We discussed Jane Helleiner's (2000) participant observation research about Travellers above. Interestingly, what led her to conduct her fieldwork was her previous archival research. She combed through hundreds of Irish newspaper accounts as well as parliamentary debates in order to find references made about Travellers. Helleiner (1997) was then able to analyze the articles and debates and was able to identify historical discourses of racism and gender operating in Ireland that were used to justify the implementation of a program to settle Travellers in the mid-1960s.

Criminologists often make use of court records in their research. One Canadian researcher, Kirsten Kramar (2005), used legislation, court records, coroner's reports, and various government documents to trace the shifts in thinking about (and action concerning) maternal neonaticide. Kramar shows us how maternal neonaticide was thought of as stemming from socio-economic disadvantage. The thinking then shifted to understanding maternal neonaticide as a psychiatric condition stemming from giving birth and lactation and, finally, to understanding this phenomenon as having no legitimate justification as the "infant-victim has a 'right-to-life' that the courts must protect by punishing fully responsibilized mothers" (p. 16).

The advantage of secondary analysis is that the information is already there—the researcher just has to access the material. It is often a less-expensive form of research than having to collect primary data. The disadvantage is that the researcher is restricted to what information has been collected and recorded. Silences in the data are then important things to note.

PARTICIPATORY ACTION RESEARCH

Participatory action research (PAR) brings together two approaches: action research and participatory research. *Action research* is a research project designed to effect change. This change may take the form of a new social policy, modifications to an existing policy, or other alterations to the lives of disadvantaged people. In action research, though, there is no commitment to involve members of the concerned group or population in the design and implementation of the research project. *Participatory research*, on the other hand, does not necessarily have an

participatory action research (PAR)
Research that combines an action-oriented goal and the participation of research subjects in the project's design and implementation.

WHY SHOULD WE CARE?

Using the Internet as a Research Tool

The Internet is now firmly part of our lives, and today scholars are using online technologies in novel ways. Some scholars discuss online data collection as a way to access people who are geographically diverse (Oringderff, 2004; Turney & Pocknee, 2005). Others point out how these technologies are opening up spaces for methodological innovation (Bampton & Cowton, 2002; Hine, 2005). However, some scholars write cautionary tales about the ethics of conducting online research (Bassett & O'Riordan, 2002; Berry, 2004; Varnhagen et al., 2005).

We focus here on one example of a research project that was conducted online. Jennifer Oringderff (2004) used online focus groups to understand the experiences of international expatriates as they relocated to a different cultural space. She used an asynchronous online focus group (OFG)—which allows participants to access her questions and respond at their leisure. She created this OFG through Yahoo!'s free online group discussion service. Oringderff posted invitations for people to join her group on relevant sites and discussion groups. She posted messages to her group, and then members responded to discussion threads when it suited them.

The benefits of such an approach include a flexible time period for data gathering, since the discussion group can be monitored/maintained as long as the researcher likes. Online research is also an inexpensive method of data collection, assuming that the researcher and participants already have access to the Internet. One can have a large or small research group, depending on the time the researcher has to monitor the group. Also, as we mentioned, online data collection provides access to a wide population, potentially spread across the globe. Oringderff (2004) also noted the possibility of gathering rich detail from participants as they respond to the discussion group on their own time and may be able to write more than they would be able to share verbally in an interview situation.

Oringderff (2004) does point out the limitations of this research method. She identifies that recruitment can be difficult, because people must have access to a computer. Further, creating and moderating a discussion group can be time consuming. Oringderff also notes that group dynamics play out in distinct ways online due to a lack of vocal cues, body movement, etc. Meanings can be misunderstood more easily without these verbal and nonverbal cues.

action component, but it does invite concerned individuals to be part of the project's design process and its execution. Participatory action research puts these two traditions together. PAR projects have an action component and a collaborative component.

An example of participatory action research is found in the work that Michelle Fine and Maria Elena Torre (2006) have done on a college program in a women's maximum security prison. They formed a research collective of both academics and women prisoners and held regular sessions every two to four weeks over a four-year period. They also conducted archival research, focus groups, interviews, and surveys. The goal of their project was to get legislators to restore program funding for college-in-prison programs.

MIXED METHODS

triangulation An approach in which more than one research method is used in an attempt to fully understand an area of study.

You will find that some researchers choose to use more than one research method in order to fully understand what they are researching; this approach is referred to as **triangulation**. Using more than one method often gives researchers a fuller picture. They are able to blend together different ways of understanding or move from generalities to specifics.

For example, the Making Care Visible Project (Bresalier et al., 2002), which investigated how people living with HIV and AIDS take care of their health, used focus group interviews and individual semi-structured interviews. The researchers used the initial focus groups as a way to get a sense of the general issues affecting people with HIV/AIDS in particular life situations (lone mothers, those living in prison, people on social assistance, people newly diagnosed, people on combination therapy, and so forth). After the focus groups, the researchers organized in-depth semi-structured interviews with a few of the focus group participants as well as others from three communities in Ontario. The focus groups allowed the research participants to indicate the important areas that required follow-up in the interviews. The interviews then allowed for a more in-depth examination of the health issues affecting those living with HIV/AIDS than the focus groups.

What do you know about **Research Methods in Detail**?

Multiple-choice questions (circle your answer)

1. **Jane Helleiner joined a gypsy camp to learn about their way of life. What research method did she use?**
   a. Nonparticipant observation
   b. Participant observation
   c. Content analysis
   d. Self-administered questionnaires

2. **Asking every respondent that you interview the exact same question, in the exact same order, and in the exact same way is an example of**
   a. An unstructured interview
   b. A semi-structured interview
   c. A structured interview
   d. Ethnography

3. **Making use of existing documents such as newspapers or magazines is a research method referred to as**
   a. Primary analysis
   b. Non-participant observation
   c. Tertiary analysis
   d. Secondary analysis

4. **A belief that one sex is innately superior to the other sex is called**
   a. Sexism
   b. Androcentricity
   c. Overspecificity
   d. Gender insensitivity

5. **Participant observation is also referred to as**
   a. Mixed method research
   b. Nonsexist research
   c. Ethnography
   d. Secondary analysis

Answers: b, c, d, a, c

module 2.4

Evaluating Research—Developing a Critical Eye

As a student, it is important that you learn to be critical of the things that you read. Not everything that is published in newspapers, magazines, and books is true or accurate. That goes for published research as well. Not all research is equal, and you will need to sort out the bad from the good. Below are some important considerations to keep in mind.

SOURCE

Before you begin to evaluate a piece of research, you need to consider the source. Research conducted by sociologists through universities or research bodies like Statistics Canada would be considered reliable sources. We would have some assurances that all effort was made to follow ethical and scientific guidelines. Once you are satisfied with the source, you would evaluate whether the content meets the criteria that follows.

VALIDITY

The **validity** of a measurement is important to consider. It relates to whether a test really measures what it claims to measure and whether we can safely draw conclusions based on that test. Suppose you wish to study the number of sexual partners a person has had, and your questions ask only about sexual intercourse partners. Could you conclude that your research is valid? Lost would be the person's experiences with partners in oral sex or any form of homosexual relationships.

validity The accuracy of a given measurement.

RELIABILITY

Reliability refers to the consistency of a given result and our ability to duplicate the result. In order for research to be considered reliable, we would need to conclude that following the same process, in the same way, with the same group of people, we would get the same information and, thus, the same results.

reliability The consistency of a given result.

It is possible for research to be reliable and yet invalid. In a study, you could ask the same questions to participants in the same way—duplicating the research—and get the same results; thus, you could argue that the research is reliable. However, if you have not operationalized and defined your variables to measure what you intend to measure, the research will not be valid. For example, in a study on sexuality, you assume that sexual frequency includes only sexual intercourse. You will get consistent results only about sexual intercourse but not about sexual frequency because you have eliminated such behaviours as oral sex. Therefore, the research may be reliable but not valid.

REPRESENTATION

Representation refers to the relationship between a sample and its population. The **population** refers to the target group that a researcher wishes to learn something about.

population The target group that a researcher wishes to learn something about.

Think about Evaluating Research—Developing a Critical Eye

1 Think about bias in research. Do you think it is possible for researchers to be completely objective in their work?

2 Think about the purpose of research. Do you think sociologists should be involved in social change, or should they merely conduct research and leave change to others, such as politicians?

sample A subset of the population that is selected by the researcher to be studied.

Research results will be generalized about this group. The **sample** is a subset of the population that is selected by the researcher to be studied. Samples are chosen when it is impractical to study the entire population because it is too large. It is critical for the sample to be statistically similar to—representative of—the population. That way, the findings from the sample can be used to generalize about the population. In order for a sample to be representative, it must reflect the characteristics of the population. In other words, the sample should have the same mix of people (in terms of sex, age, ethnicity, sexual orientation, etc.) as the population.

SAMPLING   *Sampling* is the method used by researchers to select their sample. There are a number of different methods researchers can use to draw their sample. Random sampling is one method that researchers use to make sure that they get a good cross-section of the population and avoid unwanted biases. In a **random sample**, every person in a population has an equal chance of being selected. Imagine that you want to study the student population at your school. You want to have a sample of 100 students. One way you could draw a random sample is by writing every student's name on a separate piece of paper and placing those pieces of paper into a box. The box would be shaken, and then, without looking, you would draw out 100 pieces of paper. The result would constitute a random sample because every student had an equal chance of being selected.

random sample A sample in which everyone in a population has an equal chance of being selected.

Random samples do not always provide us with a perfect cross-section of the population. For instance, it is possible to get 80 percent males and 20 percent females in a purely random sample. You cannot guarantee that the sample will reflect the population exactly. If it is important to have the same proportions of characteristics (such as gender and age) as the population, then a **quota sample** is preferable. In a quota sample, names would be drawn until "quotas" for each characteristic have been identified.

quota sample A sample that reflects the same proportions of characteristics (such as gender and age) as the population being studied.

In the 1994 study on American sexuality mentioned in this chapter's opening vignette, the researchers drew a random sample, but they only interviewed adults from ages 18 to 59 (Elmer-Dewitt, 2002). Can we generalize about adult sexual behaviour in America based on this sample? Because the research leaves out older adults and teens, the research findings cannot represent them. Therefore, when making conclusions, the researchers must refer only to the age groups that they interviewed.

The sample size is important when considering the representativeness of a study. The greater the number of questions and variables you include in your research, the bigger your sample must be. This is because each question and variable, when cross-referenced, works to create subgroups within the sample. For instance, if you use income as a variable and identify eight income groups, you have now divided your sample into eight subgroups. Add sex to the equation, and you have 16 subgroups. Each time a variable is added, the sample is divided into smaller and smaller subgroups. The smaller the subgroup, the more difficult it is to make generalizations about it. For instance, let's say you wish to study black females in professional occupations, between the ages of 40 and 50, and who are bisexual. How many people are you actually going to have in the sample? In fact, the actual number of people in any ethnic group, profession, or age group is going to be quite small. Thus, if you want to make generalizations about a subgroup within a sample, you need to ensure that you have adequate numbers to do so.

stratified sampling A sampling method that divides the population into categories that are of particular interest to the researcher.

Researchers can use stratified sampling to counteract the issue of having subgroups that are too small to make generalizations from. **Stratified sampling** divides the population into distinct categories (such as geographical areas, age, sexual orientation) that are of particular interest to the researcher; a sample is then taken from each category. This type of sampling achieves sufficient numbers to make generalizations about groups of people that would be relatively small in a given population.

CORRELATION VERSUS CAUSALITY

When evaluating research, it is important to distinguish between *correlation* and *causality*.

A **correlation** is a relationship between two variables; it can range from weak to strong. The stronger a correlation, the greater the connection between two variables. An example of a correlational study examined the connection between women who apply condoms to their male sexual partners, their attitudes toward sexuality, and the frequency of their sexual behaviour (Sanders et al., 2006). The researchers concluded that there is in fact a correlation (relationship) between condom-applying women and positive attitudes toward sexuality. They further concluded that condom-applying women are more likely than non–condom-applying women to have a higher rate of sexual activity (Sanders et al., 2006).

Causality, on the other hand, means that one variable causes a change in another variable. For years, medical researchers have argued that smoking causes cancer. In 1968, the US Surgeon General Advisory Committee issued a report that outlined how cigarette smoking causes bronchitis and chronic non-neoplastic bronchopulmonary disease and lung cancer (Public Health Service, 1969).

A **spurious correlation** occurs when one variable appears to produce a change in another variable, but in fact the correlation is false. For example, one might try to argue that ice cream sales cause sexual assaults because the data may show that when ice cream sales are at their highest (say, from June to August), so too are reported sexual assaults. Does this mean that if we stopped selling ice cream in the summer, we would prevent sexual assaults? Unlikely. The common denominator between the two variables is the warmer weather. Both ice cream sales and the rate of sexual assaults increase during warmer weather, which brings more people out and about. In this example, ice cream sales would be referred to as a spurious variable.

correlation A measure of how strongly two variables are related to each other.

causality A relationship in which one variable causes a change in another variable.

spurious correlation A false correlation between two or more variables, even though it appears to be true.

ETHICAL RESEARCH

Ethical principles (essentially, statements about right and wrong) and policies are in place to guide researchers' actions during all phases of a research project. In the university setting, researchers are subject to scrutiny of a research ethics board (REB) or committee that vets all research enterprises of faculty, staff, and students. Those wishing to conduct research on either animal or human participants must apply for permission and receive clearance from their institution's regulatory body.

In 1998, the *Tri-Council Policy on Ethics Involving Human Subjects* was adopted by the three government research-funding bodies: the Canadian Institutes of Health Research (formerly known as the Medical Research Council of Canada), the Natural Sciences and Engineering Research Council of Canada, and the Social Sciences and Humanities Research Council of Canada. Any research that was to be funded by one of the three bodies was meant to be approved under the guidelines of this policy. However, now *all* research (whether funded or not and whether conducted by faculty or students) is subject to this policy at universities and colleges in Canada (van den Hoonaard, 2001).

One of the main principles of current research ethics is respect for others (Simmerling & Schwegler, 2005). This principle is upheld through current practices of informed consent. Every person who takes part in a research project must understand his or her obligations in the study (how much time is required, what is required—tasks, interview, etc.), the risks or harm that may be faced as a result of participation (emotional trauma, social embarrassment), the benefits that may be realized (a greater understanding of some aspect of his or her life), and his or her rights (freedom to end participation in the study

Laud Humphreys' 1960s research, *Tearoom Trade*, investigated anonymous male–male sexual encounters in public washrooms.

at any time without penalty). In addition, every person must voluntarily agree to such participation.

Ethical guidelines intend to ensure that researchers will balance the risks people are subject to in the course of their involvement in a research study and the benefits of the study to the wider community. In other words, the risks to participants should not outweigh the benefits to the scientific community and wider society.

Laud Humphreys' doctoral dissertation, entitled *Tearoom Trade*, is an example of research that crosses ethical lines and raises questions about people's rights to privacy. In the 1960s, Humphreys wanted to investigate anonymous male–male sexual encounters in public restrooms. He decided that the best way to understand this phenomenon was to gain insider status. He began hanging around public restrooms in parks to watch the goings-on, and even offered to be a "watcher queen," a lookout who would alert the men if police or others were nearby. Humphreys was interested in the home lives of these men as well, so he recorded their licence plate numbers and manipulated his way into obtaining their addresses. He interviewed some of the men in the washrooms without full disclosure of his research interests, and later interviewed other men whom he had tracked to their homes. Humphreys (1975) learned that more than half of these men did not consider themselves homosexual; they were "happily" married and enjoyed sustaining their appearance as "typical" heterosexual men. Humphreys' study was criticized as being unethical since he not only failed to disclose his status as researcher but also invaded the privacy of many of these men.

To learn more about the *Tearoom Trade* research, go to **http://web.missouri.edu/~bondesonw/Laud.html.**

PURE VERSUS APPLIED RESEARCH

An ongoing debate in sociology is how research should be conducted and used. Some sociologists believe that their responsibility is the advancement of knowledge—to gather facts objectively and develop theories that are supported by their findings. They do not believe that their role is to effect social change as a result of their research. To them, that role belongs to others (e.g., politicians). This type of research is called **pure research**.

To learn more about how research is monitored in Canada, go to the Government of Canada–run Panel on Research Ethics at **www.pre.ethics.gc.ca.**

Conversely, a growing number of sociologists believe that they should effect social change through their knowledge, skills, and research. Research targeted toward change is called **applied research**.

Where do you stand on the issue? Should sociologists take a neutral, unbiased approach to their research and work, or should they be active change agents?

pure research
Research whose goal is the advancement of knowledge.

applied research
Research whose goal is to effect social change.

What do you know about Evaluating Research—Developing a Critical Eye?

Multiple-choice questions (circle your answer)

1. **Informing the participants of a research project about their rights and obligations as part of the project is a matter of**
   a. Ethics
   b. Validity
   c. Representation
   d. Reliability

2. **In a situation in which one variable seems to have a relationship with another variable but in fact there is no relationship, we refer to the connection as**
   a. A causation
   b. A correlation
   c. A spurious correlation
   d. An ethical dilemma

3. **When one variable directly affects a change in another variable we refer to this as**
   a. Causation
   b. Correlation

   c. Spurious correlation
   d. Spurious causation

4. **In the case in which a relationship exists between an increase in ice cream sales and an increase in the number of sexual assaults, we would say that ice cream sales represents a**
   a. Dependent variable
   b. Spurious variable
   c. Sample
   d. Causation

5. **Ethical research involves informing participants about all of the following except**
   a. Their obligations
   b. What risks or harm they might face
   c. What benefits they might realize
   d. That the benefits of the research to society outweigh the risks to the participant

Answers: a, c, a, b, d

Summary

module 2.1   CONNECTING THEORY AND RESEARCH

1. The type of research question you ask and how you design your research is dependent on your theoretical orientation. Thus, a conflict theorist will approach a research question differently from a symbolic interactionist.
2. *Quantitative research* involves converting social life into numbers. Qualitative research focuses on explaining social behaviour. Your theoretical orientation will determine whether you use a qualitative or a quantitative approach.
3. *Inductive logic* moves from data to theory while deductive logic moves from theory to data. Those who use a quantitative approach often use deductive logic.

module 2.2   STEPS IN THE RESEARCH PROCESS

4. Sociologists follow the scientific method in their research.
5. The order of the steps that they follow depends on whether they use inductive or deductive logic.

module 2.3   RESEARCH METHODS IN DETAIL

6. Sociologists use a variety of different research methods. The method used depends on the research question asked and the sociologist's theoretical orientation.
7. *Surveys* are favoured for large-scale projects. There are three main types of surveys: self-administered questionnaires, telephone surveys, and in-person surveys.
8. Another research method used by sociologists is interviews. *Interviews* can be structured, semi-structured, and unstructured.
9. Participant observation is also referred to as *fieldwork* or *ethnography*. Researchers can become members of the group they study (participant observation) or observe as outsiders (nonparticipant observation).
10. Researchers also make use of existing documents (e.g., court documents). This is referred to as *secondary analysis* or *content analysis*.
11. Participatory action research combines an action-oriented goal and the participation of research subjects in the project's design and implementation.

module 2.4   EVALUATING RESEARCH—DEVELOPING A CRITICAL EYE

12. As a student, you need to be able to be critical of the things that you read. Not everything is true or accurate. Consider who has done the research, whether they have answered the questions they set out to answer in the research, and whether they can make generalizations based on how they conducted their work.

Key Terms

Test Yourself

1. A researcher from this theoretical perspective would be interested in interaction patterns within families.
a. Functionalist
b. Conflict theorist
c. Symbolic interactionist
d. Structural functionalist

2. Research that focuses on numerical data is called
a. Quantitative research
b. Qualitative research
c. Numerical research
d. Inductive logic

3. Which approach is likely to have a smaller sample?
a. Quantitative research
b. Qualitative research
c. Numerical research
d. Deductive logic

4. Researchers use two systems of reasoning. Which one moves from data to theory?
a. Inductive logic
b. Deductive logic
c. Quantitative analysis
d. Numerical analysis

5. Which researcher would be most interested in the issue of gender and inequality?
a. Conflict theorist
b. Symbolic interactionist
c. Feminist
d. Queer theorist

6. The variable that is referred to as *the cause* is called the
a. Independent variable
b. Dependent variable

c. Spurious variable
d. Hypothesis

7. If we make a prediction that married people have more sex than single people, what would be the independent variable?
a. Marital status
b. Frequency of sex
c. Time spent alone
d. Television habits

8. The group selected to be interviewed is called the
a. Population
b. Sample
c. Subject
d. Survey

9. Which step in the research process involves the coding of information?
a. Research design
b. Data collection
c. Data analysis
d. Problem formulation

10. A hypothesis is
a. A tentative statement that you can test empirically about the relationship between two variables
b. A conclusion based on empirical data
c. A statement of fact
d. The first step in the research process

11. Questions on a questionnaire that have a set answer are
a. Open-ended questions
b. Closed-ended questions
c. Summary questions
d. Reflection questions

12. Questions that allow respondents to elaborate on their answers are called
a. Open-ended questions
b. Closed-ended questions
c. Summary questions
d. Reflection questions

13. Research that involves the researcher actively participating in the daily life activities of those they are observing is called
a. Participant observation
b. Interviewing
c. Secondary analysis
d. Surveying

14. Research projects designed to create some form of social change are called
a. Change research
b. Action research
c. Mixed research
d. Secondary research

15. Research in which the researcher observes a group but does not become part of it is called
a. Nonparticipant observation
b. Participant observation
c. Secondary analysis
d. Survey method

16. _____ refers to the consistency of the research and our ability to duplicate the results.
a. Reliability
b. Validity
c. Representation
d. Ethics

17. We would say that research is _____ if the sample represents the makeup of the population.
a. Reliable
b. Valid
c. Representative
d. Ethical

18. We would say that research is _____ if it accurately measures what it sets out to measure.
a. Valid
b. Representative
c. Reliable
d. Ethical

19. When one variable causes a change in another, we call the process
a. Representation
b. Reliability
c. Validity
d. Causation

20. When there is a relationship between two variables, we refer to the connection as a
a. Correlation
b. Causation
c. Spurious correlation
d. Representation

Answers: c, a, b, a, c, a, b, c, a, b, a, a, c, a, d, a

Log in to MySocLab for a host of resources that will help you save time and improve your grade. MySocLab contains cutting-edge learning tools such as study plans, practice tests, videos, audio segments, quizzes, and more—all designed to help you better understand the learning objectives for this chapter. Along with your eBook, MySocLab for *Sociology for Everyone* can be found at **www.mysoclab.com**.

module 2.1
CONNECTING THEORY AND RESEARCH

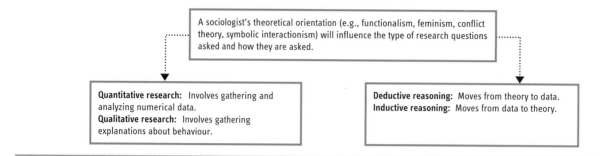

A sociologist's theoretical orientation (e.g., functionalism, feminism, conflict theory, symbolic interactionism) will influence the type of research questions asked and how they are asked.

Quantitative research: Involves gathering and analyzing numerical data.
Qualitative research: Involves gathering explanations about behaviour.

Deductive reasoning: Moves from theory to data.
Inductive reasoning: Moves from data to theory.

module 2.2
STEPS IN THE RESEARCH PROCESS

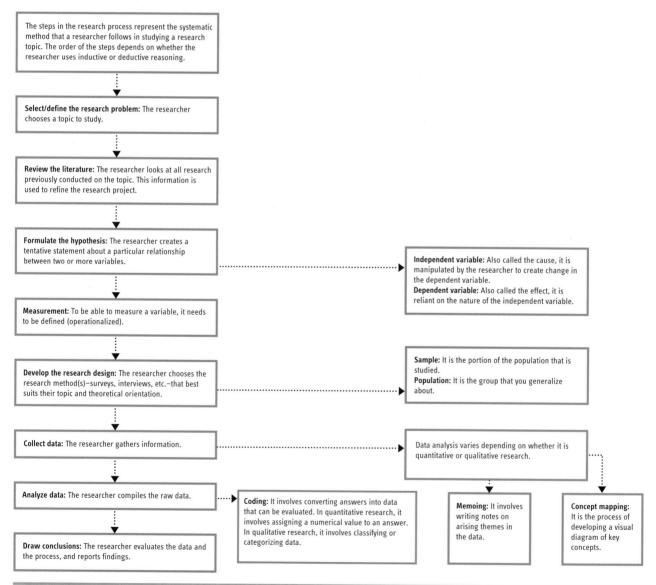

The steps in the research process represent the systematic method that a researcher follows in studying a research topic. The order of the steps depends on whether the researcher uses inductive or deductive reasoning.

Select/define the research problem: The researcher chooses a topic to study.

Review the literature: The researcher looks at all research previously conducted on the topic. This information is used to refine the research project.

Formulate the hypothesis: The researcher creates a tentative statement about a particular relationship between two or more variables.

Independent variable: Also called the cause, it is manipulated by the researcher to create change in the dependent variable.
Dependent variable: Also called the effect, it is reliant on the nature of the independent variable.

Measurement: To be able to measure a variable, it needs to be defined (operationalized).

Develop the research design: The researcher chooses the research method(s)—surveys, interviews, etc.—that best suits their topic and theoretical orientation.

Sample: It is the portion of the population that is studied.
Population: It is the group that you generalize about.

Collect data: The researcher gathers information.

Data analysis varies depending on whether it is quantitative or qualitative research.

Analyze data: The researcher compiles the raw data.

Coding: It involves converting answers into data that can be evaluated. In quantitative research, it involves assigning a numerical value to an answer. In qualitative research, it involves classifying or categorizing data.

Memoing: It involves writing notes on arising themes in the data.

Concept mapping: It is the process of developing a visual diagram of key concepts.

Draw conclusions: The researcher evaluates the data and the process, and reports findings.

module 2.3
RESEARCH METHODS IN DETAIL

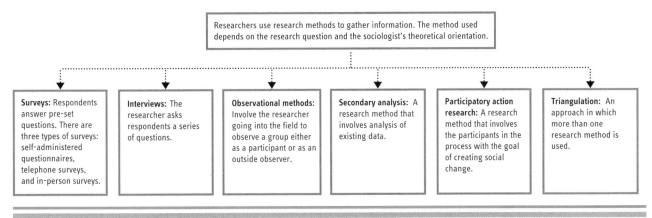

Researchers use research methods to gather information. The method used depends on the research question and the sociologist's theoretical orientation.

Surveys: Respondents answer pre-set questions. There are three types of surveys: self-administered questionnaires, telephone surveys, and in-person surveys.

Interviews: The researcher asks respondents a series of questions.

Observational methods: Involve the researcher going into the field to observe a group either as a participant or as an outside observer.

Secondary analysis: A research method that involves analysis of existing data.

Participatory action research: A research method that involves the participants in the process with the goal of creating social change.

Triangulation: An approach in which more than one research method is used.

module 2.4
EVALUATING RESEARCH—DEVELOPING A CRITICAL EYE

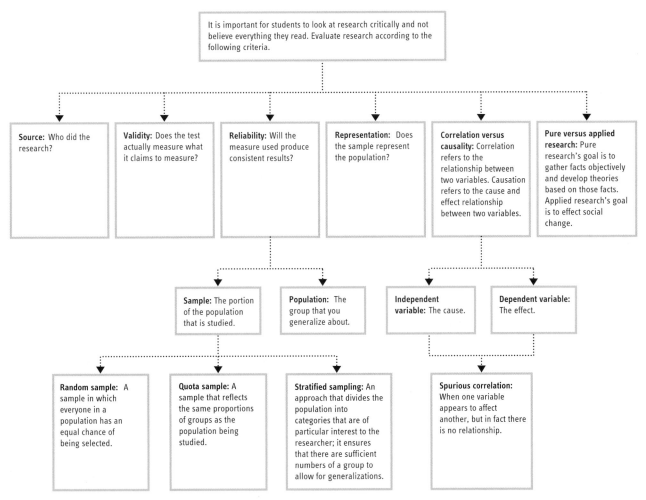

It is important for students to look at research critically and not believe everything they read. Evaluate research according to the following criteria.

Source: Who did the research?

Validity: Does the test actually measure what it claims to measure?

Reliability: Will the measure used produce consistent results?

Representation: Does the sample represent the population?

Correlation versus causality: Correlation refers to the relationship between two variables. Causation refers to the cause and effect relationship between two variables.

Pure versus applied research: Pure research's goal is to gather facts objectively and develop theories based on those facts. Applied research's goal is to effect social change.

Sample: The portion of the population that is studied.

Population: The group that you generalize about.

Independent variable: The cause.

Dependent variable: The effect.

Random sample: A sample in which everyone in a population has an equal chance of being selected.

Quota sample: A sample that reflects the same proportions of groups as the population being studied.

Stratified sampling: An approach that divides the population into categories that are of particular interest to the researcher; it ensures that there are sufficient numbers of a group to allow for generalizations.

Spurious correlation: When one variable appears to affect another, but in fact there is no relationship.

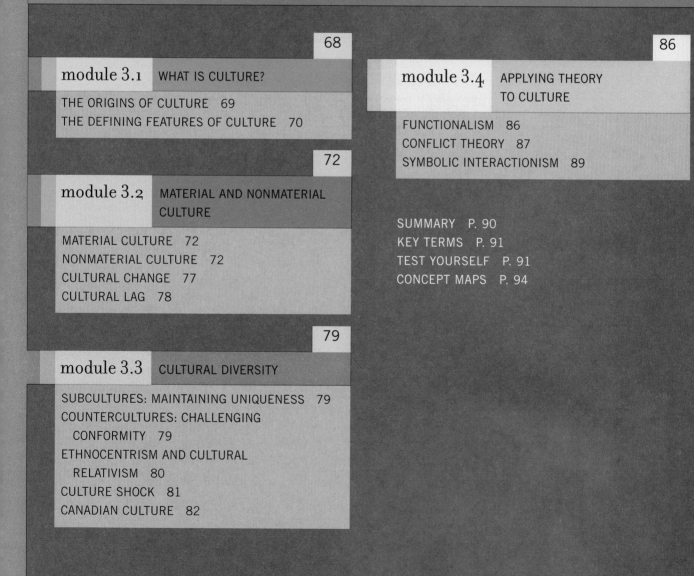

chapter 3

Culture

Sex(ual Assault) on Trial

Is it all right for grown men to have sex with girls who are 11 and 12 years old? Would it be acceptable if everyone in a culture was doing it? Conversely, if we discovered such a culture, would you find it acceptable if we as Canadians made it our business to put a stop to it?

This very scenario played out on Pitcairn Island.

On a tiny speck of rock situated in the Pacific Ocean, halfway between New Zealand and Peru, live the Pitcairn Islanders—arguably, one of the world's tiniest cultures and by far the most isolated.

The island was inhabited in 1790 by 9 mutineers from the British ship *Bounty* along with 12 kidnapped Tahitian women. The two cultures, British and Tahitian, merged to create a set of customs and language (Pitkern) of their own. Today, 47 people call the island home (Dyer, 2004).

The island's history is fascinating in itself and worth study, but it was not what brought the island to global attention. Rather, it was a sensational court case that pitted islander against islander and the Pitcairn culture against the British judicial system.

In the fall of 2004, seven men, half the adult male population of Pitcairn Island, stood trial on 91 charges, including rape and sexual intercourse with girls as young as 11 and 12 (Dyer, 2004; CBS, 2004).

The accused defended their actions based on three key points. First, they asserted that sex with young girls is a cultural behaviour. Pitkerners believe girls to be sexually available at the onset of puberty. Records show that, traditionally, women on the island have their first child between the ages of 12 and 15. Second, they asserted that jailing half the male population of the island would doom the group because the men are critical to the economic livelihood of the island. Some believed that the true agenda of the British government was to destroy the group so that it no longer needed to provide any support to the island. Third, they asserted that the island should not fall under British jurisdiction. The British had largely ignored the island for 200 years, and really only have had a responsibility to the island through default and not desire (Dyer, 2004; CBS, 2004).

Conversely, the British justice system argued that Pitkerners should know British law because the island falls under British rule. Ignorance of the law is not an excuse. Further, it argued that the victims of these "crimes" deserve justice—that the men must be punished. Finally, the British justice system argued that the behaviour must stop so that no other girls are harmed.

Both parties in the case make valid arguments. It is difficult to make an argument that supports sexually assaulting another person. However, as demonstrated by this case, we must recognize that *sexual assault* can be defined differently from one culture to another. If we agree that the Pitkerners constitute a culture, the question we must ask ourselves is, Is it ever right for one culture to pass judgment on the customs of another or to force them to change their ways? This question may or may not be relevant to the sexual assault case on Pitkern Island, but it does lead us to wonder whether the British were simply being ethnocentric in their dealings with Pitkerners.

module 3.1

Think about Culture

1 Think about the word *culture*. What comes to mind?

2 Think about your own culture. What would you say are its defining features?

culture A complex collection of values, beliefs, behaviours, and material objects shared by a group and passed on from one generation to the next.

What Is Culture?

Culture is generally regarded as a complex collection of values, beliefs, behaviours, and material objects shared by a group and passed on from one generation to the next.

The tremendous diversity that human cultures display is fascinating. For example, think about what we eat. All cultures define what is appropriate to eat. What we perceive as appetizing or appropriate for consumption is socially defined. For example, many Canadians eat hamburgers and french fries but some crave prairie oysters, cod cheeks, or peanut butter and pickle sandwiches. In the United States, hot dogs and pizza are popular but so is turducken (a boneless turkey is stuffed with a boneless duck that is stuffed with a boneless chicken and then roasted together). In North America all these foods are acceptable. However, you might feel a little uncomfortable while visiting friends in France if they served you *tête de veau* (calf's head). How would you feel about eating haggis, the Scottish delicacy consisting of a sheep's stomach stuffed with oatmeal and then steamed? In Thailand, water bugs (large, black, hard-shelled insects) are a common cooking ingredient (if you are interested, visit **www.weird-food.com**). The foods that each culture defines as appropriate to eat varies. We may see certain food as disgusting or wrong, but within that culture it is acceptable.

Returning to the case of the Pitcairn Islanders, we realize that sexual expression, like food, varies from one culture to another. The rules guiding the age at which it is acceptable to have sex, who we can have sex with, and the form that sex takes are all socially defined and bound in culture. We may not agree with how a culture conducts itself, but does that make the culture's conduct wrong? We should recognize that another culture may not think much about how we conduct ourselves. When studying culture, the lesson is to keep an open mind.

To learn more about Pitcairn Island, go to **www.onlinepitcairn.com.**

THE ORIGINS OF CULTURE

No one can really determine when culture began for two primary reasons. First, very little material evidence, the things cultures make, survives over a long period of time. Second, much of culture is nonmaterial (e.g., a belief system) and, therefore, cannot be preserved for future consideration.

Paleoanthropologists and archeologists have studied various aspects of the evolution of human culture to determine when in fact human culture may have begun. Consider the following findings (see the Smithsonian Institute, 2006):

1. *Social life*—There is evidence that our early **hominid ancestors** lived in groups as far back as 3.5 million years ago.

   hominid ancestors   Our human ancestors.

2. *Parental care*—Early hominids would have been similar to chimps. Because of their small brain size relative to later hominids, they would have been born in a more advanced developmental stage, thus requiring minimal parental care. As hominids evolved and brain size increased, birthing needed to occur at an earlier stage of development because a large head would not fit through a female's birth canal. Scientists believe that this evolution probably occurred with Homo ergaster 1.9 million years ago.

To learn more about early hominids such as "Lucy," go to **www.stanford.edu/~harryg/protected/evolve3.htm.**

3. *Pair-bonding*—The devotion of a male to a female is believed to have occurred with Homo ergaster. As offspring became more dependent for longer periods of time, the need grew to provide food and protection to both the female and the offspring to ensure their survival.
4. *Home base*—Archeological evidence of a home base, as indicated by remnants of shelters and hearths, dates back at least 500 000 years. There is some indication of home bases emerging 1.7 million years ago.
5. *Subsistence*—The stages in acquiring and distributing food took place over a number of periods. Evidence of tools used for hunting date as far back as 2.5 million years. Evidence of organized hunts dates back 500 000 years. Evidence of fishing dates back 100 000 years, and farming dates back approximately 10 000 years.
6. *Tools*—Evidence of the use of stone tools dates back 2.5 million years.
7. *Environmental adaptation*—The use of caves dates back 800 000 years. The use of fire dates back 450 000 years, and evidence of the sewing of hides for clothing dates back 30 000 years.
8. *Thought, language, art, and religion*—The oldest known piece of art dates back 250 000 years (the figure of a woman carved in stone). Pigments of black and red have been found in caves dating back 400 000 years, with cave paintings dating back over 30 000 years. There is also evidence of Neanderthals performing funerals over 100 000 years ago.

Can we pinpoint the beginning of culture based on these findings? No. But they do suggest that elements of "human" culture predate modern humans. You should realize that evidence of the existence of modern humans, **Homo sapiens sapiens**, dates back only 130 000 years ago. They emerged out of Africa, and began to move to the near east approximately 90 000 years ago. The earliest civilizations, large and complex societies, can be traced back to Sumer

Homo sapiens sapiens   Modern human beings.

(modern day Iraq) a mere 7000 years ago—but a blip in the timeline of human evolution (Smithsonian Institute, 2006).

THE DEFINING FEATURES OF CULTURE

Sociologists suggest that culture has five defining features:

1. *Culture is learned.* No one is born with culture. Rather, as we grow up we are constantly immersed in the cultural traditions of our parents, siblings, and peers. Everything from our language to our attitudes, values, and world views, is learned. This does not mean that your culture defines everything about you, but it does suggest that your culture modifies and influences your perceptions, values, and perspectives. For example, as already discussed, what you define as suitable food is a reflection of what your culture deems appropriate.

2. *Culture is shared.* Culture develops as people interact and share experiences and meanings with each other. Cheering for Team Canada when it plays the Russians is one example of shared cultural values. Shared collective symbols (e.g., the maple leaf, the Royal Canadian Mounted Police) help create and maintain group solidarity and cohesion.

3. *Culture is transmitted.* Cultural beliefs and traditions need to be passed from generation to generation if they are to survive. Communicating cultural traditions and beliefs to the next generation is an important requirement for any culture. For example, many preliterate societies have rich oral traditions in which they tell long and rich stories as a way of communicating the lessons and experiences of their ancestors. By hearing these stories, children learn about what is important to their culture and what separates them from others.

4. *Culture is cumulative.* As members of each generation refine and modify their cultural beliefs to meet their changing needs, they build on the cultural foundation of their ancestors. For example, Canadian students today are exposed to computers from a very early age and are therefore far more computer literate than students from even 10 years ago. This experience with technology will continue and expand with each successive generation.

5. *Culture is human.* Animals are considered to be social (e.g., a lion's pride, an ant colony) but not to be cultural. Animals certainly communicate with each other, but the reasons that they communicate are defined by instinct. Natural hierarchies in the animal world are generally based on physical attributes. In contrast, culture defines how, when, and why humans communicate with each other, and with whom. For example, culture helps to define who is appropriate for you to date and guides how, when, and if you ask these people out. Animals do not possess the capacity to plan and organize their behaviours in this way. Since culture is the product of human interaction, it is a distinctly human endeavour[1] (Ravelli, 2000).

These five defining features of culture are important for understanding both the complexity of culture and its importance for defining how groups maintain their uniqueness over time. Culture influences every area of our lives. From what we choose to wear in the morning to the person we decide to marry, culture is everywhere. If you stop reading for a moment and take a look around you, you will notice that no matter where you are (e.g., your dorm room, at the library, or your favourite coffee shop), everything around you is a reflection of your culture. Even if you are sitting in the park or studying at the library, these environments

---

[1]There is some debate as to the ability of animals to act according to cultural standards. The debate generally involves whether the ability of animals to use tools and to transmit these skills from one generation to the next is evidence of culture (see Davidson & McGrew, 2005).

Musicians, such as The Tragically Hip, often write songs that express the unique features of a society's culture.

are shaped by our culture. For example, many cities design park spaces in the urban core to help people feel more relaxed and comfortable, while your library is intended to be a quiet sanctuary for you to focus on your studies so that you can make a contribution to society once you graduate.

What do you know about **Culture**?

1. **Homo sapiens sapiens emerged out of Africa**
a. 10 000 years ago
b. 30 000 years ago
c. 130 000 years ago
d. 1 million to 3 million years ago

2. **Hominids began using tools for hunting**
a. 10 000 years ago
b. 150 000 years ago
c. 1 million years ago
d. 2.5 million years ago

3. **Each culture refines and modifies its culture. This shows that culture is**
a. Shared
b. Transmitted

c. Cumulative
d. Human

4. **Which of the following is not true of culture?**
a. Animals have culture.
b. Culture is shared.
c. Culture is transmitted.
d. Culture is cumulative.

5. **The common experience of pride when the Canadian flag is flown and the national anthem is played at the Olympics demonstrates that culture is**
a. Innate
b. Shared
c. Non-existent
d. Patriotic

Answers: c, d, c, a, b

module 3.2

Material and Nonmaterial Culture

Think about Material and Nonmaterial Culture

1 Think about the ancient pyramids in Egypt. What do you think we could learn about ancient Egyptian culture by studying them?

2 Think ahead to a thousand years from now. What artifacts from our civilization do you think would say the most about us?

3 Think about your diet. How many of the foods you eat originate from different cultures?

Culture can be divided into two major segments: *material culture* and *nonmaterial culture*. Both components of culture are inextricably bound with each other.

MATERIAL CULTURE

Material culture includes tangible artifacts, physical objects, and items that are found in a society—the physical output of human labour and expression. At the most basic level, our material culture helps us adapt to, and prosper in, diverse and often challenging physical environments. For example, the Inuit of Canada's North must endure long, cold winters, and their material culture has responded by developing exceptionally warm clothing and shelters (Balikci, 1970). Conversely, the material culture of the Yanomamö of South America reflects their adaptation to a hot and humid climate through lack of heavy clothing and open-walled huts (Chagnon, 1997). Canadian material culture, like that of the Inuit or Yanomamö, is everything we build and create. A hockey stick and this textbook are examples of Canadian material culture, as are paintings, snowmobiles, and written music. Canada's material culture is evident in the university or college you attend, the clothes you wear, and the double-double you drink at hockey games.

NONMATERIAL CULTURE

material culture The tangible artifacts and physical objects found in a given culture.

Nonmaterial culture includes society's intangibles—those things we cannot touch but which guide our social interactions—such as values, norms, and language.

nonmaterial culture The intangible and abstract components of a society, such as values, norms, and language.

VALUES For sociologists, values form the foundation for what is considered acceptable. **Values** are the standards by which people define what is desirable or undesirable, good or bad, beautiful or ugly; that is, they are attitudes about the way the world ought to be. Values are general beliefs defining right from wrong or specifying cultural preferences. The beliefs that racial discrimination is wrong and that democracy is right are both values.

values Beliefs about ideal goals and behaviour that serve as standards for social life.

Values guide each decision we make every day. Without values, we would become immobilized—unable to act. Consider how you start your day. The alarm goes off and you wake up. You must decide whether you'll get out of bed or continue to sleep. What values are at play in your decision? The importance of getting good grades may get you out of bed. On the other hand, if you are not feeling well, your health may be a more important factor. Next, you need to decide whether to have breakfast and, if so, what to eat. Your values regarding health and nutrition will direct these decisions.

Values provide the members of society with general guidelines on what their society deems important. For example, in 2007, Canadians viewed government-sponsored health care as one of the most important defining features of their society (Jedwab, 2007; see also Ravelli, 1994, p. 467).

norms Culturally defined rules that outline appropriate behaviours for members of a society.

NORMS **Norms** are culturally defined rules that outline appropriate behaviours for members of a society. Norms help people to know how to act in given social situations. One example of a Canadian norm is our belief that it is rude to speak while your mouth is full. Norms provide general guidelines on how we should act, and because we learn them from an early age, they offer some comfort that we will know how to act in situations we have never faced before (e.g., on your first dinner date, you already know not to eat with your mouth full).

American sociologist W.G. Sumner expanded our understanding of norms in his book *Folkways* (1906/1960). He suggests that there are two different types of norms: *folkways* and *mores*. **Folkways** are behaviours that do not inspire severe moral condemnation when violated—for example, walking on the left side of a busy sidewalk. **Mores**, on the other hand, do inspire strong moral condemnation—for example, extramarital affairs. The important distinction between folkways and mores is not necessarily the act itself, but rather the social reaction that the act inspires. Values, norms, mores, and folkways all help society control those behaviours it deems to be unacceptable.

Laws are formally defined norms that are enacted in legislation. In Canada, it is illegal to steal your neighbour's lawnmower or to cheat on your taxes because there are laws defining this as illegal behaviour. In both cases, the state reserves the right to charge you with a crime because you have broken the law (discussed more fully in Chapter 5).

A **sanction** is anything that rewards appropriate behaviour or penalizes inappropriate behaviour. For example, a reward for appropriate behaviour is getting an A on your sociology exam because you studied and answered all the questions correctly; a penalty for inappropriate behaviour is getting an F on the same test because you never studied and only answered 5 of the 25 questions.

By understanding these various forms of social control, one realizes that there are many informal and formal ways for society to respond to behaviours that are deemed to be unacceptable.

LANGUAGE   All human beings communicate through symbols—a **symbol** is something that stands for or represents something else. A **language** is a shared symbol system of rules and meanings that govern the production and interpretation of speech (Lindsey & Beach, 2003, p. 48). Language is a symbolic form of communication because there is no obvious relationship

folkways   Informal norms that suggest customary ways of behaving.

mores   Norms that carry a strong sense of social importance and necessity.

laws   Norms that are formally defined and enacted in legislation.

sanction   A penalty for norm violation or a reward for norm adherence.

symbol   Something that stands for or represents something else.

language   A shared symbol system of rules and meanings that governs the production and interpretation of speech.

WHY SHOULD WE CARE?

When Languages Die

Places in the world where native languages are in danger of becoming extinct are known as "language hotspots." A language hotspot is defined as an area that has high linguistic diversity and intercultural contact that has not been studied. The Living Tongues Institute for Endangered Languages has identified roughly 20 hotspots in the world today. The top five are Northern Australia, Central South America, Northwest Pacific Plateau, Eastern Siberia, and Oklahoma–Southwest United States (Living Tongues Institute, 2007).

Languages die out when powerful language groups (which are defined by political, economic, or socio-cultural dominance) are adopted by young people. When children are encouraged to speak the dominant language, the traditional language of their parents can be lost in a very short time. For example, in Central Siberia, the language of the Tofa people is spoken by only 30 people, and all of them are elderly. The Tofa were traditionally reindeer herders and hunter-gatherers, and their language was highly specialized (e.g., the term *döngür* means "male domesticated reindeer in its third year and first mating season, but not ready for mating"). Most Tofa are learning to speak Russian, which has no equivalent for terms such as *döngür*.

Harrison (2007, p. 1) states that there are about 7000 languages in the world today and that half are in danger of extinction within the next 100 years. Over 3500 languages are spoken by only 0.2 percent of the world's population, and some are spoken by a single person only. When these people die, so too will their languages. Why should we care?

When a language dies, a little bit of culture dies with it, which is a loss to us all. Harrison suggests that there are at least three reasons why we should be concerned about losing languages. First, as a human collective, each time we lose a language we lose knowledge—each language provides a vast source of information about the past and about how we have adapted to our environments (e.g., the term *döngür* tells us something about what the world is like for a

Tofa). Second, when a language dies, so do its cultural myths, folk songs, legends, poetry, and belief systems. This loss results in what Harrison calls "cultural amnesia" and lessens our ability to live peacefully with diverse populations because our understanding of cultural diversity decreases. Third, the demise of the world's languages hinders our exploration of the mysteries of the human mind. Understanding how people process information from the world around them is only made possible through language—without the ability to convey ideas, we cannot hope to see the world from another's perspective. Harrison (2007, p. 159) writes:

> As languages fall out of use into forgetfulness, entire genres of oral tradition—stories, songs, and epics—rapidly approach extinction. Only a small fraction have ever been recorded or set down in books. And the tales captured in books, when no longer spoken, will exist as mere shadows of a once vibrant tradition. We stand to lose volumes: entire worldviews, religious beliefs, creation myths, observations about life, technologies for how to domesticate animals and cultivate plants, histories of migration and settlement, and collective wisdom. And we will lose insight into how humans fine-tune memory to preserve and transmit epic tales.

The Living Tongues Institute and National Geographic collaborated on a project called Enduring Voices: Saving Disappearing Languages. They visited two of the world's language hotspots (Northern Australia and Central South America) in 2007, and planned three other projects for 2008.

As you can see in Figure 3–1, the Northwest Pacific Plateau (including much of British Columbia) ranks third in the world's language hotspots. As a result of colonization, three native languages in this area are already extinct. Of the 36 remaining languages, 13 are spoken by fewer than 50 people, and 1, the South Tsimshian language, is spoken by a single person (Poser, as cited in Woodward, 2007).

Much of the blame for the extinction of native languages can be traced to the area's residential schools, where Aboriginal children were not allowed to speak their native languages and instead were forced to speak English (Woodward, 2007).

FIGURE 3–1 Top Five Language Hotspots

between the letters H-U-N-G-R-Y and the desire to eat, for example. These letters are symbols that English-speaking people have agreed mean that a person wants to eat. Thus, symbols must have established meanings or no one would understand the thoughts or emotions we were trying to convey. Agreed-upon meanings shared by a group of people are, in essence, what distinguishes one culture from another.

As mentioned in Chapter 1, one of the major principles of symbolic interactionism is that society (and culture) is socially constructed. This principle suggests that every time we interact, we interpret the interaction according to the subjective meanings each of us brings to it. Although shared cultural symbols allow us to interact more smoothly, each of us may bring slightly different meanings to the symbols. For example, some students put much more pressure on themselves to get an A than do others; while the symbol *A* is the same for everyone, students' motivation to get an A varies because of their individual meanings and motivations.

Researchers use a variety of techniques to distinguish cultures, but most consider language as the key identifier of cultural boundaries. For example, Navajo artist Fred Bia states, "My language, to me, . . . that's what makes me unique, that's what makes me Navajo, that's what makes me who I am" (McCarty, 2002, p. 179, as cited in McCarty, Romero, & Zepeda, 2006, p. 28).

Does Language Define Thought?   Two early researchers who investigated the potential for language to influence how we interpret our world were Edward Sapir (1884–1939) and Benjamin Lee Whorf (1897–1941). Their approach, commonly known as the **Sapir-Whorf hypothesis**, suggests that language does in fact determine thought—a position referred to as **linguistic determinism**. According to this hypothesis, what we are able to think, experience, and imagine is influenced by our language, which includes not only vocabulary but grammar (Grelland, 2006). For example, if we lived in an area where it does not snow, we would not have a word for this type of precipitation. Our perception of the world, then, is influenced by the limitations of our language; people who speak different languages comprehend the world differently (Chandler, 1994).

Recent research disputes the Sapir-Whorf hypothesis. One example of such research investigated whether different linguistic groups, given their environmental conditions, have more or fewer terms for colour. Davies et al. (1998) found that while English speakers have 11 basic colour terms, Setswana speakers in Botswana have only 5. This does not mean that they cannot see as many hues on the colour spectrum—colour perception is stable across populations—but rather that culture influences specific terminology.

So, although the Sapir-Whorf hypothesis was popular in the 1940s and 1950s, contemporary research shows very little support for the assertion that language defines how we interpret the world (Lindsey & Beach, 2003, p. 48).

NONVERBAL COMMUNICATION   *Nonverbal communication* is communication without words. Like verbal and written communication, nonverbal communication is learned and is bound in culture. In interpersonal situations, nonverbal communication makes up the majority of our message. The nonverbal element of our interactions becomes highlighted in cross-cultural communication since so much of what we say is in how we say it. The old adage "it's not what you say that is important; it is how you say it" is certainly true. For example, what cues do you use when trying to determine if a person is lying to you? Generally, you rely on a whole spectrum of cues that help you ascertain if you can believe the person (e.g., eye contact, nervous tics, body position).

The main types of nonverbal communication are listed below, along with examples of how their meaning can vary from one culture to another.

- *Body language* uses motions (shrugs, foot tapping, drumming fingers, eye movements such as winking, facial expressions, and gestures) to convey meaning. An example of body

To learn more about the Living Tongues Institute for Endangered Languages, go to **www.livingtongues.org.**

Sapir-Whorf hypothesis (linguistic determinism) **The assertion that language determines thought.**

language is the "OK" gesture. In Japan, it symbolizes money. Meanwhile, in some Latin American countries, this gesture is considered to be obscene.

■ *Proximity* uses personal space (sitting very close to or far away from someone) to convey meaning (privacy, attraction, or fear). When communicating with others, North Americans stand a bit more than an arm's length away. People from the Middle East prefer to stand much closer (Adler et al., 2009, p. 195).

■ *Haptics* uses personal contact (touching) to convey meaning. Latin American cultures would be considered high-touch cultures. In other words, people in these cultures are more likely to touch each other in interpersonal situations. People in Chinese or English cultures, by contrast, are more likely to avoid touch in interpersonal situations (Berko et al., 1994, p. 120).

■ *Oculesics* uses eye contact (staring, looking away when the person you are looking at returns eye contact) to convey meaning (interest or flirting). In a face-to-face discussion, direct gaze is appropriate in Latin America and the Middle East, but it is not in India and Pakistan (Adler & Towne, 2009, p. 196).

Culture is transmitted through verbal and nonverbal communication.

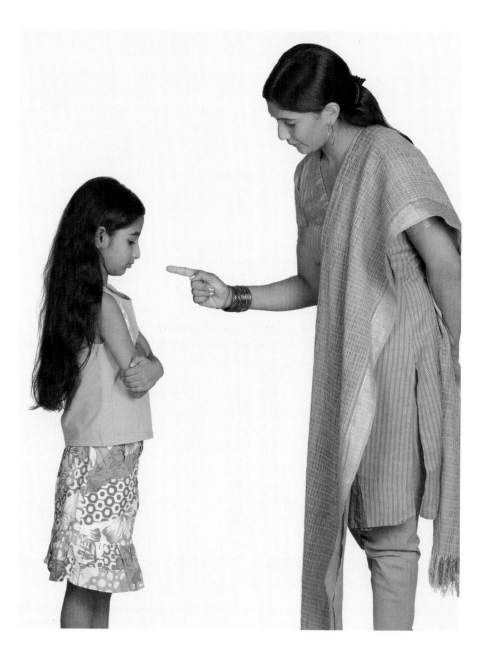

- *Chronemics* uses time (not calling someone back when you said you would, taking long pauses when talking) to convey meaning. In Latin cultures, people would rather be late for an appointment than end a conversation before it has come to a natural conclusion (Devito, 1996, p. 164).
- *Olfactics* uses smell (freshly showered, wearing perfume or cologne) to convey meaning. For instance, in Canada, men may wear cologne to make themselves more sexually attractive.
- *Vocalics* uses voice (volume, tone, speed, accent) to convey meaning. In some cultures, people are soft spoken while in others they speak loudly. For example, Arab cultures tend to speak loudly and with a lot of enthusiasm. To them, loudness is a sign of sincerity and confidence (Berko et al., 1994, p. 126).
- *Sound symbols* use audible cues (grunting, mumbling, sounds such as *mmm, er, ah, uh-huh*) to convey meaning. For instance, in Canada, we may interpret someone grunting a response to us as a sign of disinterest or annoyance.
- *Adornment* uses accessories (types of clothing, jewellery, hairstyles, tattoos) to convey meaning. For instance, the clothing and jewellery people wear indicates their sense of style.
- *Locomotion* uses movement (walking, running, staggering, limping) to convey meaning (see Eryilmaz & Darn, 2005). For instance, in Canada, if we see someone staggering down the street, we might assume that they are inebriated.

Of the different types of nonverbal communication listed above, body language (particularly facial expressions and gestures), eye contact, and proximity are the ones you are probably most familiar with. Given the myriad ways in which people communicate with one another, an analysis of cultural diversity itself should prove useful.

CULTURAL CHANGE

Cultures are always changing to address new social and technological challenges. Consider how Canadian culture was changed by the implementation of the telephone, television, and affordable air travel, or by modifications to the laws allowing divorce and abortion. Social scientists generally consider three different sources for inspiring cultural change: discovery, invention/innovation, and diffusion (Grubler, 1996; see also Ravelli, 2000).

DISCOVERY   **Discovery** occurs when something previously unrecognized or understood is found to have social or cultural applications. Historically, discovery involved findings from the natural world—for example, fire and gravity. Today, discoveries can occur as a result of the scientific process—for example, the ability to split the atom allowed the production of terrible weapons of mass destruction but also the generation of cheap electricity.

discovery   Occurs when something previously unrecognized or understood is found to have social or cultural applications.

INVENTION/INNOVATION   **Invention/innovation** occurs when existing cultural items are manipulated or modified to produce something new and socially valuable. The differences between invention and innovation may appear slight, but the distinction is important. On the one hand, *invention* refers to creating something completely new that has not existed before—for example, Marconi's (1874–1937) device that received the first transatlantic wireless communication at Signal Hill in St. John's, Newfoundland, in 1901. *Innovation* refers to manipulating existing ideas or technologies to create something new, or to apply it to something for which they were not originally intended—for example, the carbon filament in light bulbs was replaced when the much more trustworthy and long-lasting tungsten filament was used (see IN-VSEE, 2007). Innovations emerge almost daily in communication technologies. Recent examples include Voice over Internet Protocol (VoIP) technology (as an alternative to phones), camera cellphones, and text messaging technology.

invention/innovation   Occurs when existing cultural items are manipulated or modified to produce something new and socially valuable.

diffusion Occurs when cultural items or practices are transmitted from one group to another.

DIFFUSION **Diffusion** occurs when cultural items or practices are transmitted from one group to another. Consider, for example, the influence American media have on cultural practices throughout the world. Canadian sociologist Marshall McLuhan understood the power of the media and their ability to transcend geopolitical borders when he coined the phrase *global village* (McLuhan, 1964). While telecommunications have made the world feel like a smaller place, American mass media have also promoted a "culture of thinness" that has diffused throughout popular culture (Media Awareness Network, 2007).

For another good example of diffusion, consider how multiculturalism has changed the Canadian diet. Today, most major grocery stores across Canada carry Italian foods such as pizza and Greek foods such as souvlaki. However, these foods would have been absent from grocery stores in the 1950s and 1960s. In fact, today we can find an incredible array of foods from around the world on the shelves and in the frozen food sections of grocery stores.

CULTURAL LAG

We live in a time of rapid technological change. Just think of how video games, computers, and cellphones have changed in your lifetime.

Technological change has been so rapid that components of our nonmaterial culture cannot keep pace. The time it takes between the introduction of an artifact and its incorporation into a culture's values, norms, and language is referred to as **cultural lag**.

cultural lag The time it takes between the introduction of an artifact and its incorporation into a culture's values, norms, and language.

In 2008, Ryerson University student Chris Avenir faced expulsion over academic dishonesty—cheating—for his role as the administrator of the online group "Dungeons/ Mastering Chemistry Solutions." Many of Avenir's classmates (147) used the site to swap tips and solutions to their chemistry assignments. To Avenir and his classmates, the site was no different than a study group. If the students formed small study groups to discuss assignments, would there have been a problem? The students believe not. The professor, conversely, stated that assignments were to be done independently and thus forced the issue. Ultimately, Avenir was spared expulsion but received zero on the assignments (Jones, Canadian Press, 2008). This case raised the debate over whether web postings of school work constituted cheating. It illustrates that we, as a society, have yet to fully adapt our values and norms as they relate to learning, cheating, and the use of the Internet in education.

What do you know about **Material and Nonmaterial Culture**?

1. The use of touch to convey meaning is called
a. Oculesics
b. Olfactics
c. Haptics
d. Vocalics

2. Informal norms that suggest customary ways of behaving are called
a. Folkways
b. Mores
c. Sanctions
d. Laws

3. The hypothesis that language determines thought is called
a. Linguistic determinism
b. Vocal determinism

c. Haptics
d. Sanctions

4. Manipulating existing ideas or technologies to create something new is called
a. Invention
b. Discovery
c. Innovation
d. Diffusion

5. The mapping of the human genome is an example of
a. Discovery
b. Innovation
c. Invention
d. Diffusion

Answers: c, a, a, c, a

module 3.3

Cultural Diversity

Cultural diversity refers to the range of cultural differences that exists between groups, both within a society and among societies. Canada is a multicultural society, so we could say that it is a culturally diverse country. Other countries, such as Japan, are more culturally homogeneous—they do not have a wide range of ethnic diversity. Ethnicity is only one way to measure diversity. As we discuss in the section that follows, diversity is also a product of such factors as sexuality, age, and occupation.

Cultural diversity is a fact of global life—from new immigrants who bring their traditions with them to new communication technologies that expose us to behaviours from other cultures. In the face of such change, some people try to promote their distinctiveness while others challenge the cultural traditions and value systems of the majority.

Think about Cultural Diversity

1 Think about a time when you were immersed in a different culture. Did you have difficulty adjusting to the culture's customs?

2 Think about groups like gamers, goths, or emos. Would they be considered subcultures?

3 Think about Canada. Do you think there is a Canadian culture?

SUBCULTURES: MAINTAINING UNIQUENESS

A **subculture** is a group within a culture whose values, norms, folkways, or mores distinguish it from the larger culture. You can see this diversity in any one of Canada's many ethnic communities; Toronto's two Little Italy neighbourhoods, Vancouver's Chinatown, Montreal's Jewish Community, or Halifax's black community are all examples of subcultures existing, and prospering, within the larger Canadian culture.

As these examples suggest, subcultures are often based on race, ethnicity, and religion. But they can also be based on age, sexuality, occupation, recreational activities, or any activity, belief system, or special interest that the participants value enough to want to associate with others like themselves (Lindsey & Beach, 2003, p. 56). Subcultures exist largely to promote their members' own interests, but not in a manner that is contrary to the larger culture that surrounds them. For example, the majority of student clubs or groups at your school no doubt focus on single activities or interests (e.g., ski club or Young Liberals club); their members welcome the association with each other, and society as a whole is not worried about membership in this group. Members of subcultures often promote their own rules of behaviour and provide support and guidance for their members, just as the larger society does.

subculture A group within a population whose values, norms, folkways, or mores distinguish it from the larger culture.

COUNTERCULTURES: CHALLENGING CONFORMITY

When members of a subculture become increasingly distinct from the larger society around them, they may become a counterculture. A **counterculture** is a type of subculture that strongly opposes the widely held cultural patterns of the larger population.

The term *counterculture* was popularized by American history professor Theodore Roszak in his book *The Making of a Counterculture* (1969). When the book was published, it captured the minds of young American students who were protesting the Vietnam War, rebelling against traditional society, and experimenting with drugs (Dyck, 2005). Roszak's work investigated the frustrations of many student radicals and hippie dropouts who rejected the goals and aspirations of corporate America. This movement filtered into Canada as an estimated 50 000 young men from the United States fled the draft (Hagen & Hansford-Bowles, 2005). The anti-war movement became associated with rock music, sexual experimentation, and illegal drug use (particularly marijuana)—all of which parents and society as a whole viewed as subversive, dangerous, and immoral (Lindsey & Beach,

counterculture A type of subculture that strongly opposes the widely held cultural patterns of the larger population.

Hippies from the 1960s challenged the dominant definitions of sexuality, appearance, and the need to "sell out" to corporate ideals.

To learn more about the hippie movement in Toronto, including Rochdale College, go to **http://archives.cbc.ca/ society/youth/topics/ 580-3204.**

2003, p. 57). Protesting against a war that many considered unjust also began to inspire young people to challenge what they wanted out of life: Was there not more to happiness than going to school, finding a job, getting married, and having 2.3 children? Members of the counterculture wanted to live differently than their parents and questioned traditional values such as nationalism and patriotism. They also wanted to live for the moment instead of for retirement, and to act as thinking and questioning individuals instead of robots stuck on the conveyor belt of life. The anti-war movement was just one of a number of counter-cultures that have emerged at different times and places.

Other countercultures include religious minorities that find themselves in opposition to the broader society, such as the Puritans in seventeenth-century England. In twentieth-century Canada, the Sons of Freedom Doukhobors blew up property and paraded naked to express their opposition to sending their children to school and serving in the armed forces (Soukeroff, 2007/1959). Criminal subcultures such as the Mafia or the Hell's Angels Motorcycle Club are also examples of countercultures.

A wide variety of countercultures continue to exist today. As was the case in the 1960s, many members of countercultures, though certainly not all, are young. Teenagers and young adults are likely to use appearance to express opposition, with the flowing hair of the 1960s giving way to torn clothing, spiked hair, body piercings, and tattoos. Other groups, such as the Aryan Nation and Heritage Front, have a racist, anti-Semitic agenda, and have been implicated in numerous violent activities. Still others, such as youth street gangs, have no interest in social reform; instead they seek a sense of belonging, often expressed in special clothing, secret signs, and specialized language. What these diverse countercultures have in common is that, like other subcultures and the broader culture in which they exist, they provide feelings of belonging as well as support for their members (Lindsey, Beach, & Ravelli, 2008, p. 73).

ETHNOCENTRISM AND CULTURAL RELATIVISM

Have you ever travelled to a different country? If so, you probably already know that some of the ways Canadians think about the world are not shared everywhere. For instance, Canadians are safety conscious. Driving a motorcycle or a bike without a helmet has become rare in our country, and yet in most of the rest of the world, riding without a helmet is normal. In fact, in many parts of the world adults carry children on motor bikes and neither the driver nor the passengers wear a helmet. Regardless of what we see as right or wrong, the behaviours of each culture tell us important things about a culture's belief system.

Culture is such a powerful influence on our perceptions; it is the lens through which we view the world. Being a member of a particular culture instills a sense of group loyalty and pride that is important when unity is necessary—for example, during wars or natural disasters. It may be this sense of group loyalty that makes most people exhibit **ethnocentrism**—the tendency to view one's own culture as superior to others. But for sociologists, or anyone who wants to understand another culture, ethnocentrism is inconsistent with the sociological perspective because it restricts one's ability to appreciate cultural diversity. How boring would it be if everyone you met while travelling behaved the same way as people at home? The best part of travelling is experiencing how other people live.

An alternative to ethnocentrism is **cultural relativism**—appreciating that all cultures have intrinsic worth and should be evaluated and understood on their own terms. To a certain extent, cultural relativism is an ethical position that assumes no one should judge other people's customs and traditions before truly trying to understand them. To see the world from a culturally relativist position is often easier said than done because other cultural traditions may seriously challenge our own. For example, Canadians generally adore their pets, so how would you feel if you visited another culture where the dog you petted when you arrived was going to be prepared for dinner that night?

> **ethnocentrism** The tendency to view one's own culture as superior to others.

> **cultural relativism** Appreciation that all cultures have intrinsic worth and should be evaluated and understood on their own terms.

CULTURE SHOCK

At times, when people encounter cultures that are vastly different from their own, they experience **culture shock**—a feeling of disorientation, alienation, depression, and loneliness that only subsides once a person becomes acclimated to the new culture (Oberg, 1960). Culture shock can occur when we travel to different countries. Imagine travelling to a country where you do not understand the language. At first, you enjoy the novelty of the different sounds around you; it is exciting to try to learn, to understand, and to communicate with people in this other culture. However, if you are immersed in this culture for a long period, the effort to communicate can become exhausting. Even simple things like going out to dinner can become a trying experience. In North America, we eat at all hours of the day. We like our meals convenient and fast. If you travel to European countries such as Portugal, you will discover a different approach to dining. You would be hard pressed to find a restaurant that opens for an evening meal before 8 p.m., and you should expect to spend a couple of hours while you are there.

> **culture shock** The feeling of disorientation, alienation, depression, and loneliness when entering a culture vastly different from one's own.

Culture shock does not just occur in foreign countries. It can occur right in our own backyard. Imagine moving from the heart of Toronto to a small Northern Ontario town as one of the authors did. At first, the slower pace of life and the friendliness of people in the town created a vacation-like lifestyle. However, adjustment issues quickly began to emerge—the anonymity, stores and restaurants, street lights, and the general hustle and bustle of urban life were missed. Fortunately, over time the yearning for those aspects of urban life decreased as a northern lifestyle was adopted.

As you can see from the examples above, culture shock requires a period of personal adjustment. Oberg listed a four-stage model to understand a person's progression through feelings of culture shock:

1. *Honeymoon*—A feeling of admiration and awe with the new host culture and cordial interactions with locals.
2. *Crisis*—Differences in values, signs, and symbols begin to inspire feelings of confusion and disorientation that lead to feelings of inadequacy, frustration, anger, and despair.

3. *Recovery*—Crisis is gradually resolved with a growing understanding of the host culture and a recognition that its values are consistent with its view of the world.
4. *Adjustment*—An increasing ability to function effectively and enjoy the host culture despite some occasional feelings of anxiety or stress (Oberg, 1960, as cited in Austin, 2005, p. 135).

Oberg's research demonstrates that although people need time to adjust to new cultural standards, they *will* adjust. Many people who have experienced culture shock often feel that they have an enhanced appreciation of diversity they may not have experienced otherwise.

Being aware of ethnocentrism and cultural relativism helps you to become a more informed and critical thinker. Indeed, possessing the sociological imagination requires a conscious effort to appreciate the context of all social behaviour. Anything that makes you question your own values and beliefs, while often a difficult and challenging process, is also an opportunity to explore your own world—a key to being a good sociologist and citizen of the world.

CANADIAN CULTURE

On January 31, 1995, during a television interview, then federal minister of multiculturalism Sheila Finestone declared, "Canada has no national culture." In her view, Canada is a collection of cultures with no single Canadian identity (Coyne, 1995; Wegierski, 2007). There is no disputing the fact that Canada is a nation of many cultures. However, can we conclude, as Finestone did, that there is no Canadian culture?

As we have learned, a culture is defined by a distinct set of norms, language, symbols, and values. Do Canadians share a distinct set of these cultural features? The Canadian Charter of Rights and Freedoms establishes the norms of our country. We have two official languages and a unique history that led to their entrenchment. Within those languages, we have words that are distinctly Canadian. The English version of the *Canadian Oxford Dictionary* identifies 2200 words that are uniquely Canadian—for example, *loonie* and *tuque*. We have symbols that are distinctly Canadian, such as our flag, the beaver, and the Mountie. Finally, we have a shared set of values (see "Canadian Values, 1991," below), some of which are enshrined in our laws. So there does seem to be an argument for the existence of Canadian culture.

Canadian sociologists have long been fascinated by Canadian culture. They argue that our geography, our external relationships with the United States and Britain, and our internal relationships between English and French have all contributed to a unique Canadian identity (Ravelli, 2000).

Defining Canadian culture in a vacuum, by only looking inward, is difficult. Perhaps this is why we are at times challenged by the question, What is Canadian culture? Sociologist Seymour Martin Lipset (1990) addressed this problem in a unique way. Instead of focusing on who we are, he focused on who we are not. And "who we are not" is American. According to Lipset, by understanding how we are different from Americans, we will realize that Canada does have a unique culture.

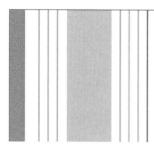

CANADIAN SOCIETY IN FOCUS

What Is Canadian Culture?

To understand Canadian culture, one must first look at the influence of living next door to the largest economic, military, and media presence in the world: the United States of America.

Given our close proximity to the United States, it is inevitable that we would be influenced by its global dominance in virtually every area of contemporary life. In fact, Lipset (1990) suggests that one of the most important defining features of Canadian culture is that Canadians, historically, have defined themselves as what they are not: Americans. Ferguson's (1993) research investigated the national identities of Canada and the United States, and she suggests that each country's national identity is different, but that each is often hard to see. However, she does indicate that there are clear value differences in each country's immigration policies and practices.

The United States maintains a *melting pot* ideology while Canada advocates for *cultural pluralism* as defined by the Multiculturalism Act of 1988 (1993, pp. 48–49). The melting pot ideology asserts that cultural and ethnic differences should be boiled away from immigrant populations and be replaced with the dominant American culture; Americans focus on what makes them the same. Conversely, cultural pluralism advocates that cultural and ethnic differences should be maintained and promoted, as they add to Canadian culture; Canadians focus on what makes them different.

What evidence exists that American and Canadian cultures are distinct? First, Canada has two official languages: French and English. In 2006, about 22 percent of the Canadian population identified French as their mother tongue (Statistics Canada, 2007l). In the United States, 82 percent of the population speaks English only; Spanish is the second most frequently used language, spoken by just over 10 percent of the population (United States Census Bureau, 2006). In other words, the historical, political, and social profile of the francophone population in Canada is far more influential than that of the Spanish-speaking people in America. In large measure, Canadian culture is defined by the often contentious relationship between the French and the English.

Second, each country regulates its media content differently. During the early part of the twentieth century, media content in Canada was largely dominated by the United States. For example, Canadian radio listeners preferred American channels, and the only television channels available in Canada during the first few years of television were American. Given the American media's influence on Canadians, the Canadian Radio-television and Telecommunications Commission (CRTC) was established in 1968 to regulate the content of Canadian media and to promote national values. The CRTC's mandate includes administrative regulation of broadcasters, promotion of the national interest, and advancement of Canadian social and cultural values. The American system of regulation is quite different. It is regulated by the Federal Communications Commission (FCC), which is directed at ensuring fair practices between media companies. While Canadians use the CRTC to promote and support our distinctive culture (an arguably protectionist position), the FCC acts in a more laissez-faire fashion to prevent conflicts and abuse (an arguably expansionist position).

Third, Canadian and American cultures differ in their approach to the military. The United States alone accounts for about 43 percent of the world's expenses on military spending, a percentage that has steadily increased since September 11, 2001. In fact, in 2007, the American budget for military expenses represented about 4 percent of the annual GDP (MIT Center for International Studies, 2008). In Canada, even though we are geographically larger than the United States, we do not come close to its spending levels. In 2007, American military spending came close to $625 billion, while Canada spent around $11 billion in 2005 (around 1 percent of the worldwide total) (Shah, 2007). Arguably, the huge military machine in the United States exists to maintain and preserve American interests worldwide, whereas Canada's military energy is often spent on peacekeeping efforts.

These three arguments provide clear evidence that even though Canada is next door to the United States, Canadians continue to maintain a unique culture.

CANADIAN VALUES, 1991   On November 1, 1990, the federal government announced the creation of the Citizens' Forum on Canada's Future and sent it on a mission to find out how Canadians feel about being Canadian. In his report, commission chair Keith Spicer (formerly chair of the Canadian Radio-television and Telecommunications Commission) highlighted seven core Canadian values (Citizen's Forum on Canadian Unity, 1991):

1. *Belief in equality and fairness in a democratic society.* Forum participants expressed strong support for equality and fairness as guiding principles for Canadian society.
2. *Belief in consultation and dialogue.* Forum participants expressed the view that Canadians attempt to settle their differences peaceably and in a consultative rather than confrontational manner. Only by talking to each other, they said, can we ever hope to resolve our problems.
3. *Importance of accommodation and tolerance.* Forum participants recognized the existence of different groups in our society and their need to sustain their own cultures while joining in the country's society, values, and institutions. As well, they acknowledged the existence of various legitimate competing regional and cultural interests in Canada. Moreover, they explicitly supported the view that Canadians should strive to accommodate and tolerate various groups—as long as they demonstrate their own acceptance of accommodation and tolerance as key values.
4. *Support for diversity.* Forum participants repeatedly emphasized Canada's diversity as one of the things they value most about this country. This diversity has a number of facets: linguistic, regional, ethnic, and cultural differences are all embraced and celebrated by most of the people who spoke to the Forum. Participants expressed appreciation for the linguistic diversity in Canada as well as the contributions of Aboriginal peoples as our original founding nation.
5. *Compassion and generosity.* Forum participants deeply value Canada's compassionate and generous character, as exemplified by our universal and extensive social services, our health care system, our pensions, our willingness to welcome refugees, and our commitment to regional economic equalization.
6. *Attachment to Canada's natural beauty.* Forum participants indicated that Canada's unspoiled natural beauty is a matter of great importance to them and is threatened by inadequate environmental protection.
7. *Our world image: commitment to freedom, peace, and nonviolent change.* Forum participants stressed the importance of our view of ourselves and the world's view of us, as a free, peaceable, nonviolent people. They supported nonviolence and Canada's historical role as an international peacekeeper.

The Citizens' Forum on Canada's Future revealed a great deal about what Canadians felt were the defining features of being Canadian in 1991. But how do these values compare with Canadian values in 2005?

CANADIAN VALUES IN GLOBAL PERSPECTIVE, 2005   The Canadian Values Study, a joint project of the *National Post*, the Dominion Institute, and Innovative Research Group, found that while Canadian values are largely similar to those of other advanced democracies, there are some interesting differences (*National Post*, 2005).

According to the study, 89 percent of Canadians said that they believed in God; in contrast, the World Values Survey found comparable figures of 96 percent in the United States, 95 percent in India, 94 percent in Italy, 72 percent in Britain, and 62 percent in France (**www.worldvaluessurvey.org**). However, when asked whether religious leaders should not try to influence government decisions, 67 percent of Canadians agreed (with similar levels seen in India, Italy, and Britain), compared with only 51 percent of Americans. This is an especially interesting result given that the American Constitution requires a formal separation of church and state.

Another interesting finding was how values relating to welfare systems vary around the world. While Canadians are generally assumed to support a strong social safety net, 60 percent of the study's respondents agreed with the view that "People who don't get ahead should blame themselves, not the system"(*National Post*, 2005, p. 2). Further, when asked to select from a list of 10 qualities they would encourage their children to learn, only 53 percent of Canadians selected "hard work" compared with 86 percent in China, 85 percent in India, 61 percent in the United States, 39 percent in Britain, 36 percent in Italy, and 23 percent in Germany. Clearly, working hard to achieve material comfort at the possible expense of other activities is more important in some areas of the world than it is in others. This trend continues when the value of competition is considered. Sixty-eight percent of Canadian respondents reported that competition was good. This compares quite closely to Americans at 71 percent, Chinese at 70 percent, and Germans at 64 percent, with the British at 57 percent, Italians at 55 percent, Indians at 48 percent, and French at 45 percent.

The survey results indicate that while Canadian values are largely consistent with other industrialized nations, there are some notable cultural differences.

What do you know about **Cultural Diversity**?

1. _____ advocates that cultural and ethnic differences should be maintained and promoted.
   a. Cultural pluralism
   b. Melting pot ideology
   c. Ethnocentrism
   d. Assimilation

2. **Which of the following statements does not belong in the list of core Canadian values as identified by the Citizens' Forum on Canada's Future?**
   a. Support diversity
   b. Compassion and generosity
   c. Importance of assimilating new Canadians
   d. Attachment to Canada's natural beauty

3. **The Canadian Values Study showed that _____ of Canadians believe in God.**

   a. 49 percent
   b. 59 percent
   c. 69 percent
   d. 89 percent

4. **Which of the following is a counterculture?**
   a. Italian Canadians
   b. Ski club members
   c. Card-carrying Conservatives
   d. Hells Angels Motorcycle Club

5. **Which of the following does not belong to Oberg's four-stage model of culture shock?**
   a. Honeymoon
   b. Crisis
   c. Recovery
   d. Abandonment

Answers: a, c, d, d, d

module 3.4

Think about Applying Theory to Culture

1 Think about the knowledge we need to survive in our society. How do you think that knowledge has changed over the past 100 years?

2 Think about how the rules and customs of our society are defined. Do you think the rich have a greater say than the poor in defining our culture?

3 Do you think the television and other forms of mass media play a role in changing culture?

cultural universals
Common features found in all societies.

cultural adaptation
The process by which environmental pressures are addressed through changes in practices, traditions, and behaviours.

Applying Theory to Culture

With our analysis of the many terms and concepts that sociologists used to explore and understand culture, a brief review of how each of the three sociological theories explains culture is necessary.

As you learned in Chapter 1, sociological theory attempts to explain all social phenomena—and culture is certainly of great theoretical interest.

FUNCTIONALISM

Functionalism approaches the value of culture from the knowledge that, since every society must meet basic needs (food, shelter, and water), culture can best be understood in helping society meet those needs. What is fascinating is how differently human societies go about it: Thais eat water beetles and Scots eat haggis; the Inuit live in igloos and the Pueblo live in adobes. Then there's the extent to which we alter our environment to ensure access to water. For example, in North America we dam rivers not only to quench our thirst but also to water our lawns.

Yet within this diversity there are common features that all known societies are believed to share, referred to as **cultural universals**. The first researcher to investigate these universals was anthropologist George Peter Murdock (1897–1985). In *The Common Denominator of Culture* (1945), Murdock compiled a list of more than 70 cultural features common to virtually all known human societies (see Table 3–1).

Table 3–1 highlights that all known human societies treat people differently based on their age (age grading), have rules on who can be considered appropriate sexual partners (incest taboos), use personal names for individuals, and play games (to name only a few cultural universals). Although the particulars may vary (e.g., the specific ages that define age grades, the types of games played), functionalists assert that these universals reinforce the position that social life is best understood by considering what individual practices or beliefs *do* for the collective.

Functionalists argue that unique cultural traditions and customs develop and persist because they are adaptive and improve a people's chances of survival (Lindsey, Beach, & Ravelli, 2006, p. 99). **Cultural adaptation** is the process by which environmental pressures

TABLE 3–1 **Cultural Universals**

Age grading	Body adornment
Division of labour	Courtship
Property rights	Music and dance
Family/kinship groups	Incest taboos
Status differences	Cleanliness training
Cooking	Magic/luck/superstitions
Personal names	Hospitality/greetings
Language	Games
Gestures	Jokes

Source: Based on Murdock (1945). Reprinted with permission of Sociology Central, 2007, Chris Livesey (www.sociology.org.uk) © 1995–2003.

are addressed through changes in practices, traditions, and behaviours as a way of maintaining stability and equilibrium. Because functionalists argue that every social practice leads to some collective benefit, any practice that diminishes a culture's ability to prosper will be unlikely to survive.

For example, Canadians have finally begun to realize the hazards of drinking and driving. In 1982, there were 2501 alcohol-related traffic fatalities (60 percent of all traffic fatalities), whereas in 2004 the number had decreased to 953 (or 34.9 percent). In other words, as Canadians have become more conscious of the costs of drinking and driving as a result of educational programs and increased enforcement, their culture has changed accordingly.

CRITIQUING THE FUNCTIONALIST APPROACH TO CULTURE   One of functionalism's greatest strengths is how it demonstrates that some elements of culture do operate to fulfill human needs. However, by focusing on how cultural elements work together to maintain stability, functionalism does not take into account tension from subcultures or countercultures. For example, while a group of women getting together on the weekend to play recreational hockey (a subculture) may be of no threat to social stability, an outlaw biker gang that challenges the larger society's laws, value system, or beliefs (a counterculture) may warrant concern. Even though a countercultural movement may inspire progressive social change (e.g., student protests of the Vietnam War), the overriding assumption of functionalist theory is stability. To assume that cultural traditions are always useful for the system denies the real pain and suffering they sometimes cause. For example, before the U.S. Civil War, slavery was accepted by many because it was "just the way things were always done." However, the positives for the rich white slave owners do not excuse this morally reprehensible practice. Cultural traditions may help bind people together, but it may also be impossible to justify or defend how they benefit society as a whole (e.g., what were the "benefits" to slavery for the slaves?).

CONFLICT THEORY

Conflict theory views society as based on tension and conflict over scarce resources. Conflict theorists assert that those who hold power define and perpetuate a culture's ideology, and create a value system that defines social inequality as just and proper (Lindsey, Beach, & Ravelli, 2006, p. 100). Conflict theorists would certainly approach the slavery example we used above from a very different perspective: slavery was allowed to exist because it benefited rich white people. Consider our own contemporary views of wealth and success. The culture and the values that support the belief that success requires money are a demonstration of the power of ideology. After all, if people are working hard their whole lives trying to get ahead, how much time do they have to think about how the system exploits them? Conflict theorists view the link between money and success as an expression of the ruling elite's power and influence.

Further exploitation comes in the form of imitation. Having the right car, clothes, and homes, and eating in the right restaurants and drinking the right kind of wine are all attempts to imitate the rich. Cultural patterns that define a society's elite are referred to as **high culture**; examples include the symphony and a wine-tasting party. By contrast, cultural patterns associated with the majority of society are referred to as **popular culture**; examples include a football game and drinking beer. To what extent have Canadians been lured into living the lifestyles of the rich and famous? Does high culture also create a form of social control and the distance that separates rich and poor?

high culture   The cultural patterns that define a society's elite (e.g., polo).

popular culture   Those cultural patterns associated with the majority of society (e.g., a football game).

The rich have a culture of their own.

According to Karl Marx, the dominant culture eventually becomes part of the value system of an oppressed group. Ultimately, the oppressed group begins to view its own culture as inferior and tries to improve its position by adopting the ways of the dominant culture (Lindsey, Beach, & Ravelli, 2006, p. 100).

CRITIQUING THE CONFLICT APPROACH TO CULTURE   The conflict approach suggests that cultural systems perpetuate social inequality. As we learned in Chapter 1, conflict theorists believe that society's elite use ideology to further their own interests and protect themselves from opposition. By defining what the dominant classes perceive as positive, cultural elements promote social inequality through the belief that to be successful you have to be like the elite and perpetuate their control and power.

On the one hand, conflict theory would be supportive of Aboriginal people's efforts at cultural preservation, but, on the other hand, it would recognize that by maintaining their traditions they are isolating and marginalizing themselves from the dominant culture. Overall, the conflict approach favours the notion that cultural change is more beneficial to oppressed people than is cultural continuity (Lindsey, Beach, & Ravelli, 2006, p. 100).

Functionalists view culture as a way of integrating and building on similarities and building a sense of community, while conflict theorists see culture as a vehicle for promoting and maintaining social inequality. Both perspectives would benefit from greater reflection on the other theory's insights. For example, functionalism would benefit by recognizing that culture can be used as a vehicle for oppression, and conflict theory would benefit by acknowledging the potential social benefits gained by uniting people into a common cultural group.

SYMBOLIC INTERACTIONISM

As discussed in Chapter 1, symbolic interactionists argue that social reality is the result of human interaction. In fact, one of the most famous symbolic interactionists Herbert Blumer (1969) suggested that people do not respond directly to the world around them, but instead, to the meanings they collectively apply to it. As a microsociological perspective, symbolic interactionism investigates how culture is actively created and recreated through social interaction. Thus, as people go about their everyday lives, they create and modify culture as they engage in the negotiation of reality based on shared meanings grounded in cultural symbols.

The values and norms that define minority status, for example, are the result of mutual interaction and social definition. People interpret and actively engage with nonmaterial cultural artifacts (symbols) in every social interaction they encounter. Therefore, minority status is a social category created by interacting individuals and manifests itself in society through negotiated social interaction. For example, each time a member of the dominant (i.e., white) culture encounters an Aboriginal person, he or she assigns that person to a category based on predefined cultural meanings that influence how he or she interacts with that person. This serves to reinforce the dominant cultural norms of who minority people are and how they are supposed to act (e.g., be deferential). However, since these meanings are actively negotiated, there is also great potential for resisting and changing dominant cultural meanings, since they are fluid and constantly open to reinterpretation and reflection. According to symbolic interactionists, then, culture is the set of symbols to which we collectively assign values and the result of our active engagement with those around us (Lindsey, Beach, & Ravelli, 2009, p. 72).

CRITIQUING THE SYMBOLIC INTERACTIONIST APPROACH TO CULTURE   Symbolic interactionists rightly point out that culture results from social interaction and collective engagement with our surroundings. However, suggesting that changing cultural definitions requires changing how we define and classify people diminishes the reality that some cultural definitions result from structural oppression and discrimination (e.g., residential school system, Japanese Canadian internment camps during the Second World War). As a microsociological approach, symbolic interactionism, while tremendously insightful about interpersonal definitions of cultural meanings, is less able to explain large cultural manifestations than are functionalist or conflict theories.

Each theoretical approach, then, views culture quite differently; however, as we continue to stress, this diversity is not a sociological weakness but rather a strength.

What do you know about **Applying Theory to Culture**?

1. **Which of the following is not a cultural universal?**
   a. Age grading
   b. Body adornment
   c. Cleanliness training
   d. Eating with utensils

2. _____ **describes the process by which environmental pressures are addressed through changes in practices, traditions, and behaviours as a way of maintaining stability and equilibrium.**
   a. Cultural universals
   b. Cultural lag
   c. Cultural adaptation
   d. Cultural functionalism

3. **The symphony and a polo match are examples of**
   a. High culture
   b. Popular culture
   c. Cultural universals
   d. Cultural adaptations

4. _____ investigate how culture is actively created and recreated through human interaction.
a. Functionalists
b. Conflict theorists
c. Symbolic interactionists
d. Cultural functionalists

5. As a microsociological approach, _____ is tremendously insightful about interpersonal

definitions of cultural meanings but is less able to explain large cultural manifestations.
a. Functionalism
b. Conflict theory
c. Symbolic interactionism
d. Structural functionalism

Answers: d, c, a, c, c

Summary

module 3.1   WHAT IS CULTURE?

1. *Culture* is the complex collection of values, beliefs, behaviours, and material objects shared by a group and passed on from one generation to the next.
2. No one can really determine when culture began, but there is some material evidence that it may date back to 3.5 million years ago.
3. Culture has five defining features: it is learned, shared, transmitted, cumulative, and human.

module 3.2   MATERIAL AND NONMATERIAL CULTURE

4. Culture can be divided into two major segments: (1) *material culture*—the physical output of human labour and expression (2) *nonmaterial culture*—the intangible components of a society, such as values, norms, and language.
5. *Values* are the standards by which people define what is desirable or undesirable.
6. *Norms* are culturally defined rules that outline appropriate behaviours for members of a society. There are two types: folkways and mores.
7. *Language* is a shared symbol system of rules and meanings that governs the production and interpretation of speech. *Nonverbal communication* is also part of a culture's communication system and is unique to the culture.
8. Cultures are always changing to address new social and technological challenges. Social scientists usually consider three different sources for causing social change: discovery, invention/innovation, and diffusion.
9. *Cultural lag* is the time it takes between the introduction of an artifact and its incorporation into a culture's values, norms, and language.

module 3.3   CULTURAL DIVERSITY

10. *Cultural diversity* refers to the range of cultural differences that exists between groups, both within a society and among societies.
11. A *subculture* is a group within a culture whose values, norms, folkways, or mores distinguish it from the larger culture (e.g., Italian Canadians).

12. A *counterculture* is a type of subculture that strongly opposes the widely held cultural patterns of the larger population (e.g., mafia, hippies).
13. We can view different cultures in two ways. We can appreciate and accept the intrinsic worth of another culture (cultural relativism). Or we can see our culture as superior (ethnocentrism).
14. *Culture shock* is a feeling of disorientation, alienation, depression, and loneliness that we experience when we are immersed in a different culture.
15. Canadians are defined by what they are not—Americans. Canadians share a number of values including accommodation and tolerance for different groups in our society.

module 3.4   APPLYING THEORY TO CULTURE

16. Functionalists view the role of culture as instrumental in helping a society meet its basic needs.
17. Conflict theorists view culture as a product of the elite used by them to maintain their position of power.
18. Symbolic interactionists consider that culture is created and recreated through social interaction.

Key Terms

counterculture   79
cultural adaptation   86
cultural lag   78
cultural relativism   81
cultural universals   86
culture   68
culture shock   81
diffusion   78
discovery   77
ethnocentrism   81

folkways   73
high culture   87
Homo sapiens sapiens   69
hominid ancestors   69
invention/innovation   77
language   73
laws   73
material culture   72
mores   73
nonmaterial culture   72

norms   72
popular culture   87
sanction   73
Sapir-Whorf hypothesis
   (linguistic determinism)   75
subculture   79
symbol   73
values   72

Test Yourself

1. The complex collection of values, beliefs, behaviour, and material objects is called
   a. Culture
   b. Cultural universals
   c. Material culture
   d. Nonmaterial culture

2. *Hominid* is a term that refers to
   a. Tools
   b. Our first language
   c. Early human ancestors
   d. An early form of food preparation

3. Which of the following defining features of culture does not belong?
   a. Culture is learned
   b. Culture is shared
   c. Culture is transmitted
   d. Culture is innate

4. Which is true about culture?
   a. Culture is shared
   b. Culture is transmitted
   c. Culture is cumulative
   d. All of the above is true about culture

5. The physical output of human labour and expression is called
a. Material culture
b. Nonmaterial culture
c. Norms
d. Sanctions

6. Standards by which people define what is desirable or undesirable are called
a. Values
b. Sanctions
c. Folkways
d. Material culture

7. Which of the following are components of nonmaterial culture?
a. Values
b. Cars
c. Food
d. Shelter

8. Anything that rewards appropriate behaviour or punishes inappropriate behavior is called
a. A value
b. Material culture
c. A folkway
d. A sanction

9. _____ is a group within a population who share common attributes that distinguish them from the larger population.
a. A subculture
b. Popular culture
c. High culture
d. Mass culture

10. Which of the following is not a counterculture?
a. Doukhobors
b. Aryan nation
c. Mafia
d. Young Liberals club

11. The feeling of disorientation, alienation, depression, and loneliness experienced when entering a culture very different from one's own is called
a. Culture shock
b. Ethnocentrism
c. Linguistic determinism
d. Cultural relativism

12. Who stated that Canadians have defined themselves by what they are not—Americans?
a. Margaret Atwood

b. Seymour Lipset
c. Karl Marx
d. Talcott Parsons

13. The Multiculturalism Act was passed by the Canadian legislature in what year?
a. 1948
b. 1957
c. 1970
d. 1988

14. The Citizens' Forum on Canada's Future identified _____ core Canadian values.
a. Three
b. Five
c. Seven
d. Nine

15. Creating something completely new that has not existed before is called
a. Invention
b. Discovery
c. Innovation
d. Diffusion

16. _____ occurs when something previously unrecognized or understood is found to have social or cultural applications.
a. Discovery
b. Innovation
c. Invention
d. Diffusion

17. _____ occurs when cultural items or practices are transmitted from one group to another.
a. Discovery
b. Innovation
c. Invention
d. Diffusion

18. Common features found in all cultures are called
a. Cultural universals
b. Cultural adaptations
c. Cultural lag
d. Cultural commonalities

19. _____ approaches the value of culture from the knowledge that every society must meet basic needs if it is going to survive.
a. Functionalism
b. Conflict theory
c. Symbolic interactionism
d. The dramaturgical model

20. _____ assert that those who hold the power define and perpetuate a culture's ideology.
   a. Functionalists
   b. Conflict theorists
   c. Symbolic interactionists
   d. Dramaturgical theorists

mysoclab

Log in to MySocLab for a host of resources that will help you save time and improve your grade. MySocLab contains cutting-edge learning tools such as study plans, practice tests, videos, audio segments, quizzes, and more—all designed to help you better understand the learning objectives for this chapter. Along with your eBook, MySocLab for *Sociology for Everyone* can be found at **www.mysoclab.com**.

CONCEPT MAP

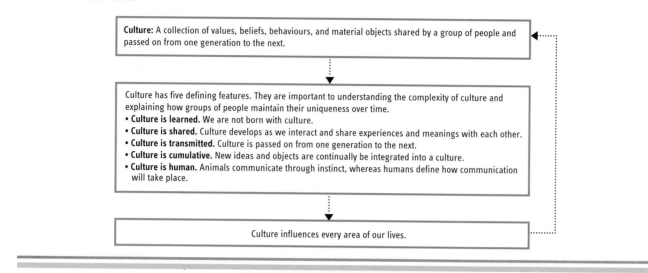

Culture: A collection of values, beliefs, behaviours, and material objects shared by a group of people and passed on from one generation to the next.

Culture has five defining features. They are important to understanding the complexity of culture and explaining how groups of people maintain their uniqueness over time.
- **Culture is learned.** We are not born with culture.
- **Culture is shared.** Culture develops as we interact and share experiences and meanings with each other.
- **Culture is transmitted.** Culture is passed on from one generation to the next.
- **Culture is cumulative.** New ideas and objects are continually be integrated into a culture.
- **Culture is human.** Animals communicate through instinct, whereas humans define how communication will take place.

Culture influences every area of our lives.

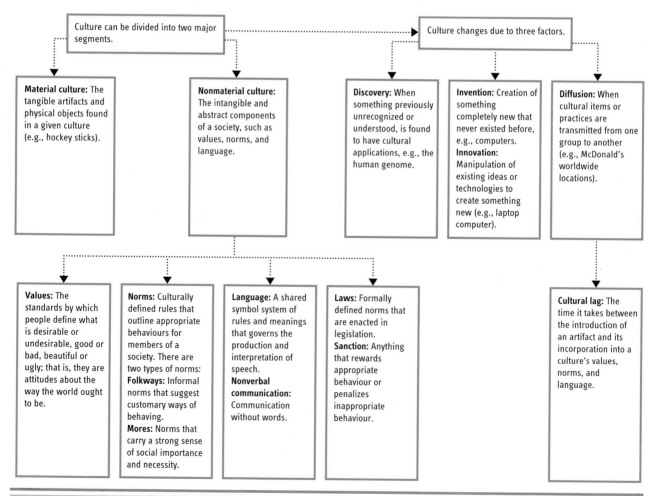

Culture can be divided into two major segments.

Culture changes due to three factors.

Material culture: The tangible artifacts and physical objects found in a given culture (e.g., hockey sticks).

Nonmaterial culture: The intangible and abstract components of a society, such as values, norms, and language.

Discovery: When something previously unrecognized or understood, is found to have cultural applications, e.g., the human genome.

Invention: Creation of something completely new that never existed before, e.g., computers.
Innovation: Manipulation of existing ideas or technologies to create something new (e.g., laptop computer).

Diffusion: When cultural items or practices are transmitted from one group to another (e.g., McDonald's worldwide locations).

Values: The standards by which people define what is desirable or undesirable, good or bad, beautiful or ugly; that is, they are attitudes about the way the world ought to be.

Norms: Culturally defined rules that outline appropriate behaviours for members of a society. There are two types of norms:
Folkways: Informal norms that suggest customary ways of behaving.
Mores: Norms that carry a strong sense of social importance and necessity.

Language: A shared symbol system of rules and meanings that governs the production and interpretation of speech.
Nonverbal communication: Communication without words.

Laws: Formally defined norms that are enacted in legislation.
Sanction: Anything that rewards appropriate behaviour or penalizes inappropriate behaviour.

Cultural lag: The time it takes between the introduction of an artifact and its incorporation into a culture's values, norms, and language.

module 3.3
CULTURAL DIVERSITY

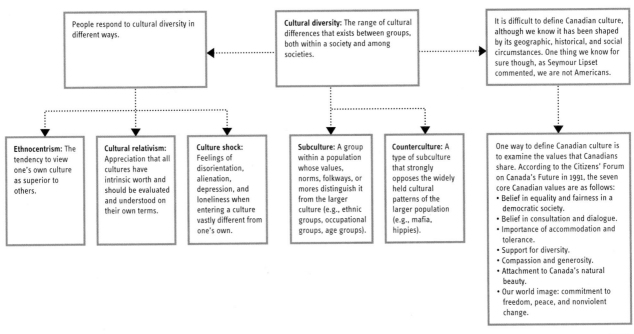

People respond to cultural diversity in different ways.

Cultural diversity: The range of cultural differences that exists between groups, both within a society and among societies.

It is difficult to define Canadian culture, although we know it has been shaped by its geographic, historical, and social circumstances. One thing we know for sure though, as Seymour Lipset commented, we are not Americans.

Ethnocentrism: The tendency to view one's own culture as superior to others.

Cultural relativism: Appreciation that all cultures have intrinsic worth and should be evaluated and understood on their own terms.

Culture shock: Feelings of disorientation, alienation, depression, and loneliness when entering a culture vastly different from one's own.

Subculture: A group within a population whose values, norms, folkways, or mores distinguish it from the larger culture (e.g., ethnic groups, occupational groups, age groups).

Counterculture: A type of subculture that strongly opposes the widely held cultural patterns of the larger population (e.g., mafia, hippies).

One way to define Canadian culture is to examine the values that Canadians share. According to the Citizens' Forum on Canada's Future in 1991, the seven core Canadian values are as follows:
• Belief in equality and fairness in a democratic society.
• Belief in consultation and dialogue.
• Importance of accommodation and tolerance.
• Support for diversity.
• Compassion and generosity.
• Attachment to Canada's natural beauty.
• Our world image: commitment to freedom, peace, and nonviolent change.

module 3.4
APPLYING THEORY TO CULTURE

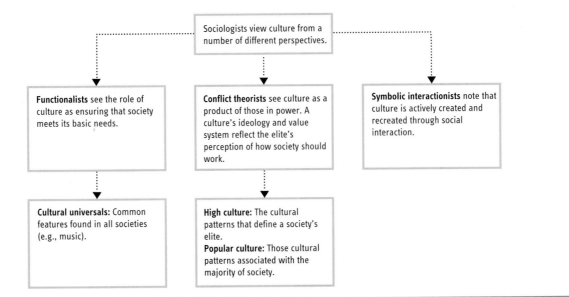

Sociologists view culture from a number of different perspectives.

Functionalists see the role of culture as ensuring that society meets its basic needs.

Conflict theorists see culture as a product of those in power. A culture's ideology and value system reflect the elite's perception of how society should work.

Symbolic interactionists note that culture is actively created and recreated through social interaction.

Cultural universals: Common features found in all societies (e.g., music).

High culture: The cultural patterns that define a society's elite.
Popular culture: Those cultural patterns associated with the majority of society.

chapter 4

Socialization and Social Interaction

Monogamy: Learned or Hard-wired?

What makes us who we are? Do you think we are born with inherent characteristics, or do we develop our personalities as we move through life? Let's consider the differences between the sexes. For example, although certainly an overgeneralization, many would argue that men are more likely to pursue multiple sexual relationships than are women. But why do men and women behave differently? Do these differences stem from biology, whereby genetics defines each sex's responses to the social world, or do they arise from the social environment, whereby our perceptions and behaviours result from how we are raised and inter-act with the social world?

In the simplest terms, the biological argument suggests that because men are capable of impregnating multiple women at the same time, they have an evolved desire for multiple partners, preferably those who are young and physically attractive. Conversely, since women can reproduce through only one pregnancy at a time, they have an evolved desire for someone who can provide for them and their children (Barker, 2006; Kobali, 2004). According to this view, then, genetically based instincts and physical capacities define men's and women's desires and behaviours.

However, sociologists challenge these biologically based assumptions. Instead, they perceive behavioural differences, to the extent that they actually exist, as the result of socialization and social interaction—the subject of this chapter.

Becoming Human

To fully understand what it means to be human is to appreciate that we are the only organisms that can *think about thinking*. How we think about ourselves and the world is an important and dynamic area of research for social scientists.

There are two basic approaches to understanding the development of **personality**—broadly defined as an individual's relatively stable pattern of behaviours and feelings—and how people become members of the larger society: the biological approach and the environmental approach. The traditional debate over which approach defines the person we become is called the **nature versus nurture** debate.

The *nature* side of the debate holds that our actions and feelings stem from our biological roots. Those on the *nurture* side of the debate, on the other hand, argue that we are instead the product of our **socialization**—the lifelong process by which we learn our culture, develop our personalities, and become functioning members of society. Our sense of the world and of ourselves, then, is held to be the result of social interaction. **Social interaction** encompasses all the ways people interact in social settings while recognizing each person's subjective experiences and/or intentions.

Let's consider each side of the nature versus nurture debate in more detail.

THE NATURE ARGUMENT: BEING BORN YOU

The nature argument suggests that most of our behaviour is determined by our genetic makeup. Although sociologists assume that the nurture side is more important in determining the person you become, they also appreciate that biology plays a role in explaining some key aspects of your behaviour, such as athletic ability and intellectual capacity.

Recent medical research demonstrates that evolutionary forces have led to women and men having very different brain structures that influence how each responds to the world around them.

> In the brain centers for language and hearing . . . women have 11 percent more neurons than men. The principal hub of both emotion and memory formation—the hippocampus—is also larger in the female brain, as is the brain circuitry for language and observing emotion in others. This means that women are, on average, better at expressing emotions and remembering the details of emotional events. Men, by contrast, have two and a half times the brain space devoted to sexual drive as well as larger brain centers for action and aggression. Sexual thoughts float through a man's brain many times each day on average, and through a woman's only once a day. Perhaps three to four times on her hottest days. (Brizendine, 2006, p. 5)

The science of **sociobiology** uses evolutionary theory and genetic inheritance to examine the biological roots of social behaviour. Sociobiology began in the early 1960s and is associated with the animal behaviour studies of Nobel Prize winner Konrad Lorenz (1903–1989) and the research into the social behaviour of ants by two-time Pulitzer Prize winner Edward O. Wilson (1929–). Wilson's groundbreaking 1975 book *Sociobiology: The New Synthesis* applies the principles of Darwinian inheritance to show how human behaviours are selected for and passed on from one generation to the next.

Think about Becoming Human

1 Think about how you became who you are. Imagine that you were raised with only the necessities to live but no human interaction. Would you still be the same person you are today?

2 Think about feral children. Feral children are children that have been raised in a wild state—sometimes by animals. Imagine, like Tarzan, that you were raised by gorillas. Would you have grown up to act like a gorilla or a human?

---

personality An individual's relatively stable pattern of behaviours and feelings.

nature versus nurture The debate over whether biological forces or environment define the person we become.

socialization The lifelong process by which we learn our culture, develop our personalities, and become functioning members of society.

social interaction The ways in which people interact in social settings while recognizing each person's subjective experiences and/or intentions.

sociobiology The science that uses evolutionary theory and genetic inheritance to examine the biological roots of social behaviour.

The core assertion of sociobiology is that social behaviour among humans, like all organisms, has evolved over time to secure the survival of the species (Gatherer, 2006). In evolutionary terms, the most important achievement for an organism is to leave as many offspring as possible. Whatever attributes (physical or behavioural) that help an individual produce offspring are selected for, and those attributes that diminish an individual's ability to produce offspring are selected against (Fetchenhauer & Buunk, 2005, p. 98). Sociobiology argues, for example, that the physical and behavioural differences we see in women and men today are the result of millions of years of natural selection.

Sociobiology has gained popularity in recent years under its new name, *evolutionary psychology* (see Driscoll, 2004; Swami, Antonakopoulos, Tovée, & Furnham, 2006). Like sociobiology, **evolutionary psychology** argues that Darwinian inheritance can explain contemporary human behaviour. For example, Victor Nell (1998) suggests that evolutionary psychology can explain why young men are more likely to drive faster than women and older men. Nell argues that when young men reach the "mating and fighting age" (16 to 20 years), their sense of invincibility is at an all time high, and at the very time they are most vulnerable (p. 19). Nell writes:

evolutionary psychology
A relabelled form of sociobiology.

> Our judgments about risky behaviour are often hypocritical. We admire the circus tightrope walker and the young soldier advancing on an enemy position with machine-gun blazing. But when we judge a young driver with his girlfriend snuggled up to him who is driving too fast, or a kid surfing in a violent sea, we say that the soldier and the tightrope walker are brave, but that the surfer and the speeding driver—who are both enjoying the frisson of danger—are stupid. It is important to understand that this mature judgment of risk-taking is irrelevant to injury prevention because it lacks moral weight: the young dismiss these judgments for the hypocrisy they embody, and continue to obey deeper evolutionary urges to take high risks, and thus ensure status and win the most desirable mate. (pp. 20–21)

Evolutionary psychologists, and sociobiologists before them, have had some success in applying evolutionary theory to explain human behaviours. However, empirical support for their overall assertion that human behaviour is determined by genetics remains contentious and has only limited support in the social sciences. Social scientists suggest that

Some evolutionary psychologists suggest that young men's risky behaviours demonstrate their vitality and invincibility—evolved attributes intended to attract women.

biological theories of behaviour disregard the ability of humans to think before they act. Our capacity to reflect on our own behaviour is one that social scientists believe must be fully recognized and appreciated. Even some evolutionary psychologists agree that we can use our intelligence and adaptability to overcome behaviours that our biology influences (Brizendine, 2006).

Sociologists generally acknowledge that some genetic linkages exist and influence human behaviour; however, they remain committed to the belief that the factors influencing the people we become are defined not by nature, but rather nurture.

THE NURTURE ARGUMENT: LEARNING TO BE YOU

Perhaps the most compelling argument to explain why sociologists believe that we become the people we are through social interaction is what happens when young children are isolated from human contact. Children raised in social isolation are referred to as **isolates**.

isolates   Children raised in social isolation.

EFFECTS OF SOCIAL ISOLATION   One of the most famous cases of isolation was that of a five-year-old girl, Anna, who was discovered in 1938 by a social worker visiting a Pennsylvania farmhouse. When she was discovered, Anna was tied to a chair and was so severely undernourished she could barely stand on her own. It was discovered that she had been born out of wedlock to a mentally handicapped mother and kept in the attic by her grandfather because he was embarrassed about her illegitimacy (Lindsey, Beach, & Ravelli, 2009, p. 83). Upon hearing about Anna, sociologist Kinsley Davis immediately travelled to see her and was overwhelmed by what he found. Deprived of normal human contact and receiving only a minimal amount of care to keep her alive, Anna could not talk, walk, or do anything that demonstrated even basic intellectual capacity.

After working with Anna for two years, Davis had been able to teach her how to walk, understand simple commands, and feed herself. After two more years, she had learned basic toilet habits, could use a spoon when eating, and could dress herself. However, at age nine she was less than 1.3 metres tall and weighed only 27 kilograms. When Anna died at age 10 from a blood disorder, she had only progressed to the intellectual capacity of a two-and-a-half-year-old. While she could talk in phrases, she never developed a true capacity for language. Her isolation from other people during the early stage of her life prevented her from developing more than a small fraction of her intellectual potential (adapted from Davis, 1947; Lindsey, Beach, & Ravelli, 2009, p. 83).

Another disturbing example of human isolation is the case of five-year-old Jeffrey Baldwin, who was found dead when Toronto emergency workers arrived at his grandparents' home in 2002. The subsequent investigation revealed that he had been confined to his room for years by his maternal grandparents (CBC, 2007b). At the time of his discovery, Jeffrey weighed only 9.5 kilograms and was less than 1 metre tall. It was obvious from the condition of his body that Jeffrey had died from malnutrition and neglect—an especially horrible outcome in a home with six adults and five other healthy children. Both grandparents were sentenced to life imprisonment in 2006. Although Jeffrey's intellectual and social development at the time of his death is uncertain, research into human isolation suggests that he would never have recovered from such abuse even if he had lived.

The importance of human interaction is obvious in light of such cases of children who have suffered from severe neglect (see www.feralchildren.com). Sociologists argue that social reality is constructed by people every time they interact with others. Our genetic makeup (nature) gives us the capacity to be social beings, but it is the process of social interaction (nurture) that enables us to develop that capacity.

WHY SHOULD WE CARE?

Feral Children: What Can They Teach Us?

Feral (meaning "wild") children are those who have been isolated from human contact from a very young age. They have little or no experience with love or human interaction, nor do they have a grasp of language. They are often confined by a negligent human caregiver or are brought up by animals (Gage Encyclopedia of Childhood and Adolescence, 1998). In the latter case, the children exhibit behaviours we commonly associate with the parenting species—for example, walking on four legs, eating raw meat, being nocturnal, showing fear of or indifference to humans. Over a hundred cases of feral children have been reported from around the world (Ward, 2007). These cases are interesting to sociologists because they offer a unique, albeit disturbing, insight into the necessity of human interaction to make an individual fully human.

In 2002, when Traian Caldarar was discovered in the Transylvanian countryside, he was naked, living in a cardboard box, and was thought to have been raised by stray dogs. Though Traian was estimated to be seven, his body size was that of a three-year-old. When they tried to get Traian to a hospital, his behaviour became that of a wild dog—he became violent and excitable. At the hospital, he preferred to sleep under the bed. Traian now lives with his mother, Lina, who was severely abused by Traian's father and fled from the household when Traian was only three years old. Lina assumed that Traian would do the same as soon as he was able.

When 13-year-old "Genie" (so named by the scientists who studied her) was discovered in Los Angeles in 1970, researchers estimated that she had been locked in her room, alone, for over 10 years. Investigation revealed that during the day Genie was strapped to a potty chair and at night, if her caregivers remembered to put her to bed, she was tied into a sleeping bag. After Genie was hospitalized, caregivers found that she lacked even the most basic language skills, moved in a "bunny-like gait" (she was only rarely allowed to move from her seat or sleeping bag), and held her hands in front of her body like paws. She was not toilet trained, had difficulty focusing her eyes beyond 12 feet, weighed under 27 kilograms, and was less than 1.5 metres tall.

Once she was safe and properly cared for, Genie exhibited a thirst for knowledge. Scientists from around the world (called the "Genie Team") descended upon Los Angeles to study her case, and to investigate the process of human socialization and the effects of long-term isolation and neglect. Though Genie made much progress, she was never able to learn language. The Genie Team was unsure whether her lack of speech was due to her prolonged isolated state or the result of the physical abuse she suffered whenever she made noise while confined to her room (Ward, 2007). Today, Genie is still alive but has been moved from one adult care facility to another as scientific interest and human compassion for her situation have steadily declined. In 2001, a movie was made about Genie's life, entitled *Mockingbird Don't Sing.*

What do you know about **Becoming Human**?

1. **Another term for *sociobiology* is**
   a. Nature versus nurture debate
   b. Sociopsychology
   c. Evolutionary psychology
   d. Evolutionary sociology

2. **The idea that nurture is the most important factor in developing personality is supported by**

   a. Sociologists
   b. Psychologists
   c. Evolutionary psychologists
   d. Biologists

3. **The case of Anna supports**
   a. The importance of nature
   b. The importance of nurture

c. Both the importance of nature and nurture
d. Neither side of the argument

c. Sociobiology
d. Evolutionary psychology

4. The lifelong process by which we learn our culture, develop our personality, and become functioning members of society is called
a. Social interaction
b. Socialization

5. Males reach the "mating and fighting age" at
a. 6 to 10 years
b. 10 to 15 years
c. 16 to 20 years
d. 21 to 25 years

Answers: c, a, b, b, c

module 4.2

The Development of Self

SOCIOLOGICAL INSIGHTS

Think about the Development of Self

1 Think about the games you played when you were a child. What were your favourite games when you were 4 and 5 years of age? What about when you were 10? How did they differ? What do you think we can learn about human development from the types of games we play?

2 Think about when you first became aware of your own abilities and the abilities of others—for example, when you began to compare your academic and athletic abilities with those of others. To whom did you compare yourself? Do you think such comparisons are important and necessary to the development of self-concept?

Every person is unique—just like snowflakes, no two people are completely alike. The self may be defined as "a composite of thoughts and feelings" from which we derive our "conception of who and what" we are (Jersild, 1952, p. 9). The **self**, or one's identity, comprises a set of learned values and attitudes that develops through social interaction and that defines one's self-image. Our **self-image** is an introspective composition of various features and attributes that people see themselves as. The self is a key component of *personality*—defined above as an individual's relatively stable pattern of behaviours and feelings. In healthy individuals, the personality and self join to give an individual the sense that he or she is unique and special.

IMAGINING HOW OTHERS SEE US: C.H. COOLEY   As we discussed in Chapter 1, Charles Horton Cooley introduced the concept of the *looking-glass self*—the idea that what we think of ourselves is influenced by how we imagine other people see us (Cooley, 1902). Indeed, as we have seen with isolated and feral children, self-consciousness cannot develop without social interaction. According to Cooley, to be aware of oneself, one must be aware of society. Self-consciousness and social consciousness are inseparable because people cannot conceive of themselves without reference to others.

Cooley (1902) describes the development of the self as a three-step process:

1. We imagine how we look to others—both physically and socially.
2. We imagine how others look at us and pass judgment on what we present.
3. Based on what we imagine, a self-concept develops.

UNDERSTANDING OURSELVES AND OTHERS: G.H. MEAD   Building upon Cooley's investigation into the development of self, George Herbert Mead argued that the self is composed of two complementary elements. He referred to the first element as the **I**—the part of self that is spontaneous, creative, and impulsive and often unpredictable (Lindsey & Beach, 2003, p. 94). The *I* is the part of consciousness that responds to things emotionally. For example, imagine how you might respond if you just found out that you had won a free trip to Mexico. Chances are you would jump up and down and wave your arms in the air to express your excitement.

However, Mead suggested that while you are jumping up and down, you are also conscious of how others view you. Excitement is one thing, but we have all witnessed instances where someone does not recognize when "enough is enough." Mead termed this second level of consciousness the *me*. According to Mead, the **me** is the socialized element of the self; the part of consciousness that thinks about how to behave so that, for example, you don't embarrass yourself. The *me*, in other words, helps us control the spontaneous impulses of the *I*. The sense of conflict we feel when we are compelled to act one way but discipline ourselves to act in another demonstrates the dynamic relationship between the *I* and the *me* and their influence on our everyday behaviour.

Our understanding of ourselves and our social environment is also influenced by those around us. When we are with our friends, for example, we tend to behave differently than we do when we are with our family. To understand this influence more fully, Mead investigated how we attribute different levels of importance to people around us (Mead, 1934). People whom we want to impress or gain approval from he termed **significant others**. When we are children, our parents are the most important people in our lives, and so are considered significant others. Other family members, close friends, teachers, and coaches would also be considered significant others. As we mature (around age 12), the importance of our family wanes somewhat and we become aware of those in the broader social world who influence our behaviours (Lindsey & Beach, 2003). Mead called these people the **generalized other**—not any one specific person, but rather a compilation of attributes that we associate with the average member of society. This conception of a generalized other represents the recognition that other members of society behave within certain socially accepted guidelines and rules. Understanding the generalized other and how it would feel or behave in certain situations gives the individual a reference point for proper and expected behaviour.

Critical to explaining symbolic interactionists' analysis of how we interpret ourselves, other people, and the social world is the concept of **role-taking**—assuming the position of another to better understand that person's perspective. Role-taking is critical for empathizing with another person's situation. By imagining what it would be like to be homeless, for example, you inevitably become more empathetic to how homeless people must feel and more compassionate about their needs. Similarly, imagining how other people might respond to a given social situation enables you to better anticipate their actions and to respond to them in a manner you have considered in advance.

Mead also contributed to understanding how we develop our sense of self through social interaction by investigating how young children are socialized. He asserted that, as children grow up, they pass through a series of three distinct stages.

Preparatory Stage (birth to age three)   Young children's first experiences when interacting with others are to imitate what they see others doing. Although children don't understand the meanings behind these early interactions, they want to please the significant others in their lives (usually their parents). Through positive and negative reinforcement, children begin to develop the I, but the me is also forming in the background.

self One's identity, comprising a set of learned values and attitudes that develops through social interaction and that defines one's self-image.

self-image An introspective composition of various features and attributes that people see themselves as.

I Mead's term for that element of self that is spontaneous, creative, impulsive, and unpredictable.

me Mead's term for the socialized element of the self.

significant others People we want to impress or gain approval from.

generalized other A compilation of attributes associated with the average member of society; represents an individual's appreciation that other members of society behave within certain socially accepted guidelines and rules.

role-taking Assuming the position of another in order to better understand that person's perspective.

Play Stage (ages three to five)   Children learn a great deal about themselves and the society around them through play. As children begin to assume the roles of others ("I'll be Batman and you be Robin"), they move beyond simple imitation and assume the imagined roles of the characters they are playing. During this stage, the *me* continues to grow because children want to receive positive reinforcement from their significant others. Because language skills are developing throughout this stage, children can more accurately communicate their thoughts and feelings—a skill that must be mastered before a stable sense of self can emerge.

Game Stage (elementary-school years)   As children continue to develop, they become increasingly proficient at taking on multiple roles at once (student, son or daughter, friend) and by doing so begin to identify with the generalized other. Participating in complex games that require them to play a particular role (e.g., playing defence on a field hockey team) teaches them to understand their individual position as well as the needs of the group. The skills developed during the game stage are readily transferred to other real-life situations (Lindsey, Beach, & Ravelli, 2009, p. 90; Mead, 1934).

According to Mead, the game stage marks the period in which primary socialization occurs. **Primary socialization** occurs when people learn the attitudes, values, and appropriate behaviours for individuals in their culture. As language skills are refined throughout the game stage, children begin to gain their first sense of self as a unique individual.

Secondary socialization occurs later, in early adolescence and beyond, through participation in groups that are more specific than the broader society and that have defined roles and expectations. Part-time jobs, city-wide sports teams, and volunteer activities are all examples of secondary groups. Because these groups are more specialized than primary groups, they allow people to develop the skills needed to fit in with various other groups of people throughout their lives (Furseth & Restad, 2006, p. 115).

Considered from a sociological perspective, socialization is a lifelong process: after all, we interact with others throughout our lives, and constantly evolve as a result.

primary socialization
Occurs when people learn the attitudes, values, and appropriate behaviours for individuals in their culture.

secondary socialization
Follows primary socialization and occurs through participation in more specific groups with defined roles and expectations.

Playing in groups helps young people perform multiple roles at one time.

PSYCHOLOGICAL INSIGHTS

Sociologists tend to view socialization as the culmination of a series of predictable stages people undergo that either assist or hinder their adjustment to the society around them. Psychologists, on the other hand, tend to view socialization as a process of internal conflict and tension that people must resolve if they are to have happy and productive lives.

PSYCHOSEXUAL DEVELOPMENT: SIGMUND FREUD (1856–1939) Sigmund Freud believed that people behave according to drives and experiences of which they are not always aware. He suggested that the unconscious mind is full of memories of events, experiences, and traumas from childhood—many of which are sexual in nature (thus the term *psycho*sexual *development*). Freud noted that when these memories are especially painful, people keep them from conscious awareness. He used the term **defence mechanisms** for the ways in which individuals manage painful memories. Freud believed that people use a great deal of mental energy to form and maintain these defence mechanisms, and that not resolving painful memories could limit a person's ability to lead a full and satisfying life (Parker, 2003).

defence mechanisms Freud's term to describe the ways in which individuals manage painful memories.

Freud's model of the composition of the human personality is made up of three unique but interrelated parts. The first and most basic component Freud termed the **id**: the individual's biological needs and impulses. The id is unconscious, selfish, irrational, unsocialized, and focused on instant gratification (Boeree, 2006).

id Freud's term for an individual's biological drives and impulses that strive for instant gratification.

Since the id operates unconsciously and is grounded on instinctual responses, it often conflicts with the second part of one's personality, the superego. The **superego** is Freud's term for all the norms, values, and morals that are learned through socialization. The superego comprises the internalized social standards for a given group and helps form a person's conscience.

superego Freud's term for all the norms, values, and morals that are learned through socialization.

The third part of the personality Freud called the *ego*. The **ego** acts as the intermediary between one's biological drives and the social constraints that would deny them. The ego is largely conscious and reality-based, and therefore provides socially acceptable ways to achieve what a person wants (Freud, 1930/1961). For example, let's say you have gone downtown without your wallet and suddenly find yourself feeling famished. As you walk by an outdoor deli, you spot a sandwich left unattended. Your id tells you to scoop it up, your superego tells you not to because that would be stealing, and your ego reminds you that one of your friends lives close by and might be able to give you something to eat.

ego Freud's term for the intermediary between the id and the superego that provides socially acceptable ways to achieve wants.

You probably noticed that Freud's concepts are similar to Mead's discussion of the *I* and *me*. However, there is a key difference: Mead believed that *I* and *me* worked together as a creative and dynamic force, while Freud focused on the tension between the id and the superego (Lindsey, Beach, & Ravelli, 2009, p. 90; Wallace & Wolf, 1999, pp. 196–199).

PSYCHOSOCIAL DEVELOPMENT: ERIK ERIKSON (1902–1994) Much like Freud, Erik Erikson believed that early childhood experiences are important for personality development and that socialization is marked by crises throughout one's life. However, unlike Freud, Erikson suggested that culture also plays a critical role (Erikson, 1950, 1968). Instead of relying solely on universal drives (e.g., the id) to explain cognitive development and personality, Erikson integrated ideas from anthropology that showed that children from different cultures learn different values and goals and experience vastly different kinds of parenting styles and guidance.

Erikson believed that there are universal development processes as well; he defined eight stages of development that all people must go through from infancy to old age (see

FIGURE 4-1 **Erikson's Stages of Psychosocial Development**

Challenge	Age
Trust vs. mistrust	Birth to 1 year
Autonomy vs. shame and doubt	1 to 3 years
Initiative vs. guilt	3 to 5 years
Industry vs. inferiority	6 to 12
Identity vs. role confusion	Adolescence
Intimacy vs. isolation	Young adulthood
Generativity vs. stagnation	Middle adulthood
Integrity vs. despair	Late adulthood

Source: Erikson, E.H. (1950). *Childhood and society*. New York: Norton.

Figure 4–1). The stages are referred to as psycho*social* because they reflect both individual psychological processes and social challenges that everyone faces during their lives. Each of these stages is marked by the need to overcome a unique crisis. For example, adolescents must deal with rapidly maturing bodies and emerging adult responsibilities that result in a crisis of *identity versus role confusion*. This is the stage during which young people need to resolve the conflict between their desire to engage in experimental behaviours and their desire to be more mature and responsible.

COGNITIVE DEVELOPMENT: JEAN PIAGET (1896–1980)   Jean Piaget was also interested in showing how young people gradually progress through different developmental stages. Piaget discovered that children think and reason differently at different times in their lives. He believed that children pass through four distinct stages; although every healthy child passes through the stages in the same order, there is some variation in the speed at which each child progresses (Turmel, 2004).

During the *sensorimotor stage* (birth to age 2) young children learn about their world through their five senses. The child also forms attachments to parents and/or other close caretakers.

The *preoperational stage* (age 2 to about age 7) is when children begin to use their imagination when playing and continue to develop language skills. Children in this stage are also influenced by fantasy, and the way they would like things to be as opposed to the way they are. Children have difficulty conceptualizing time and assume that everyone else sees the world as they do.

In the *concrete operational stage* (ages 7 to 11) children begin to see causal connections in their environment and to make logical conclusions about the world around them. For example, children can now understand that if they play with matches, they could set the grass on fire, whereas before this stage they would need to observe or manipulate a concept or object directly in order to understand it.

The final stage, the *formal operational stage*, occurs around age 12 and sees the child becoming more comfortable with abstract reasoning. Adolescents at this stage can offer several alternative solutions to a series of problems. For example, when children before this stage are asked, "Do you want to eat the last hot dog?" they respond honestly—"Yes, I do"—and do not think anything more of it. However, children who have achieved abstract reasoning will consider how many hot dogs everyone else has had and how they might be viewed if they eat the last one. Thinking about different ways to handle a situation by envisioning possible scenarios demonstrates abstract reasoning.

Today, sociologists look to both sociological and psychological research to understand how we develop our sense of self as we mature throughout our lives. And central to this understanding of socialization are what sociologists refer to as the *agents of socialization*.

What do you know about **the Development of Self**?

1. **Mead's term for that element of self that is sponta-neous, creative, and impulsive is**
   a. Me
   b. Superego
   c. Id
   d. I

2. **Mead would describe parents as**
   a. Significant others
   b. Generalized others
   c. Specialized others
   d. Socialized others

3. **According to Mead, imitation is typical of the**
   a. Play stage
   b. Game stage
   c. Imitation stage
   d. Preparatory stage

4. **Freud's term for the part of the self that contains norms, values, and morals that are learned through socialization is**
   a. Alter ego
   b. Ego
   c. Id
   d. Superego

5. **According to Piaget, children at the _____ stage believe in magic and fantasy.**
   a. Sensorimotor
   b. Preoperational
   c. Concrete operational
   d. Formal operational

Answers: d, a, d, d, b

module 4.3

Agents of Socialization

Agents of socialization are the individuals, groups, and social institutions that together help people become functioning members of society. Although we are partly defined by our biology as well as our psychological development, according to sociologists we are defined most significantly by the society around us. Today, the four principal agents of socialization are families, peers, education, and mass media.

FAMILIES

Families are by far the most important agents of socialization because they are the centre of children's lives. During this important formative period, families provide the child with nourishment, love, and protection and guide their first experiences with the social world. In the first years of life, families are largely responsible for children's emerging identities, self-esteem, and personalities. In fact, the first values and attitudes a child

Think about Agents of Socialization

1 Think about the influences in your life. At what point in your life were parents the most important influence? At what point in your life were your friends the most important influence?

2 Think about divorce. From your own experience or the experience of your friends, what impact does divorce have on kids? For kids, what

age group do you think is most vulnerable to the divorce of their parents?

3 Think about teenagers today. Do you think they behave better or worse than your cohort?

agents of socialization Individuals, groups, and social institutions that together help people become functioning members of society.

gender stereotyping The assignment of a set of beliefs to men and women, respectively, that are not based on fact.

socio-economic status (SES) Social status as determined by family income, parents' education level, parents' occupations, and the family's social standing within the community.

cultural capital Social assets (values, beliefs, attitudes, competencies) that are gained from one's family and help one succeed in life.

embraces are generally simple reflections of his or her family's values and attitudes. Canadian researchers (Hastings, McShane, Parker, & Ladha, 2007) found that parents teach children how to behave prosocially (i.e., be nice) from a very early age. Families are also responsible for establishing acceptable gender roles, social class, and ethnic identities for children.

Much like symbolic interactionists, social learning theorists emphasize the importance of observing and imitating the behaviours, attitudes, and emotional reactions of others (Bandura, 1977). When parents model what they believe to be acceptable roles for men and women, their child tends to imitate and internalize those patterns. For example, some parents assign different chores for daughters and sons (the daughter may help in the kitchen while the son may mow the lawn), which reinforces **gender stereotyping** that influences what each child considers to be appropriate roles for men and women.

Families are also responsible for assigning the *socio-economic status (SES)* position to its members. **Socio-economic status** is determined by the family's income, parents' education level, parents' occupations, and the family's social standing within the community (e.g., member of local organizations, involved in recreational programs). Growing up rich or poor, knowing whether you are expected to attend university or college, and appreciating how your family is viewed within the local community become part of a person's identity. Affluent parents are better able to provide their children with diverse leisure activities (e.g., music/dance lessons, extra-curricular sports, travel) that tend to contribute to children's *cultural capital*. The term **cultural capital** was coined by French philosopher and sociologist Pierre Bourdieu (1930–2002), who describes how children's social assets (values, beliefs, attitudes, and competencies in language and culture) gained from their families help them in school and prepare them for success, which in turn reproduces ruling class culture (Bourdieu, 1973).

Ethnic and cultural affiliations are also defined within the family. Whether you are Aboriginal, German, or Mexican, your family introduces you to the cultural and ethnic roots of your ancestry. The desire to affiliate with one's heritage varies by family, but it is obvious that one's identity is at least partially defined by familial background. This becomes even more pressing when a person is a visible minority. Canada is considered a multicultural society, but there is much evidence that racism continues to exist. Galabuzi (2006) challenges the claim that Canada is free from the racist policies commonly associated with the United States. She reveals that Canada has its own history of racism, including slavery, head taxes on Chinese immigrants, and the openly acknowledged exploitation of Aboriginal peoples. As we can appreciate, many visible minorities' first experience with racial or ethnic discrimination would have occurred when they were young and with their families; such experiences can drastically modify people's view of themselves and their feelings of social worth.

PEERS

Would you agree that the extent of your family's influence on your life changed when you became a teenager? As we saw in the discussion of developmental stages, the importance of one's friends, or peers, increases during adolescence. During this time, friends are very influential in defining what adolescents think about the world and how they feel about themselves. Part of growing up is leaving the support of your family and putting yourself in situations that can be as frightening as they are invigorating (think, for example, of your first school dance).

peer groups Consist of people who are closely related in age and share similar interests.

Peer groups consist of people who are closely related in age and share similar interests. We first formally meet other young children in school. There, children have to make their own friends for the first time, and they soon find out that not everyone likes them (unlike in their families). This puts a great deal of pressure on children to find peers they can relate to and prefer to

CANADIAN SOCIETY IN FOCUS

Effects of Divorce on Children

Canadian divorce rates saw a rising trend in the late 1960s (after divorce law reform in 1968), reached a peak in 1987, and have since remained relatively stable (Ambert, 2005, p. 5). Given these statistics, several researchers have investigated the influence that divorce has on children.

Research has found that children of divorced parents are more likely to be aggressive, to get into trouble at school, and to become involved in illegal activities. They are also more likely to suffer from low self-esteem and depression and to have a harder time getting along with siblings, peers, and their parents. In adolescence, they are more likely to engage in delinquent behaviour, become sexually active earlier, and experiment with illegal drugs (Ambert, 2005, p. 16). Sociologist Anne-Marie Ambert of York University notes, however, that not all children of divorced parents develop these negative outcomes, but rather are at a greater risk of doing so (p. 17).

Ambert outlines six factors that negatively affect children of divorce: (1) the likelihood that single-parent families have less adequate financial resources than two-parent families; (2) diminished parent–child time after divorce; (3) emotional burdens placed on the divorced parents that are sometimes passed on to the children; (4) ongoing parental conflict, especially when children are used as pawns in the battle between the parents; (5) children's behavioural difficulties prior to their parents' divorce; and (6) genetic inheritance, whereby some children are predisposed to difficult temperaments that are exacerbated by divorce (2005, pp. 18–20).

The age group most negatively affected by divorce are children aged 4 to 10. Ambert notes that these children do not fully understand the changing family dynamics and thus are most likely to blame themselves for what has happened.

Lisa Strohschein, a sociologist from the University of Alberta, has also studied the effects of divorce on children. Her research supports Ambert's results, and includes other interesting findings. For example, children with divorced parents are twice as likely to be prescribed Ritalin (or methylphenidate), a drug used to combat attention deficit hyperactivity disorder (ADHD). Strohschein suggests that this increased likelihood may be related to stress (Strohschein, 2007, p. 1711).

Although the effects of divorce on children can be many and severe, the alternative is at times worse. The Royal College of Psychiatrists asserts that children who witness their parents' domestic violence or are themselves abused by their parents can experience great emotional and physical trauma. Young children suffer from stomach aches, bedwetting, temper tantrums, and sleep difficulties, and often behave more immaturely than other children their age. In older children, boys are more likely to be aggressive, disobedient, and begin to use alcohol and/or drugs earlier. Girls often become withdrawn and depressed, and are more likely to suffer from eating disorders and other forms of self-harm (e.g., cutting behaviour). Children from violent homes tend to perform more poorly in school, and may suffer from post-traumatic stress disorder and have nightmares. Finally, children from violent homes learn the behaviours of their parents and may repeat patterns of abuse in their adult lives (The Royal College of Psychiatrists, 2004, p. 1).

spend time with. Research by Adler (1996) suggests that by as early as grade 3, children have identified with particular groups they want to associate with (Lindsey & Beach, 2003, p. 111).

As children mature, their friends become increasingly important to them. To a young person, belonging to a peer group is vital for establishing a sense of community as well as

During our high school and college years, peer groups are an important agent of socialization.

for achieving and maintaining social influence (Matthews, 2005, p. 42). When you think back to some of the regrettable things you have done, many of them most likely occurred when you were with your friends. Research confirms that teenagers who have friends who are disruptive in school are more likely to become disruptive themselves (Berndt & Keefe, 1995). This finding supports the wealth of research suggesting that peer involvement is the key ingredient in adolescent drug use and other forms of delinquent behaviour (McCarthy, 2007).

To learn more about Reginald Bibby's work and Project Teen Canada, go to **www.ptc08.com/english. html.**

To read Gillis's article "Youth Survey: Generation Tame" in *Maclean's,* go to **www2.macleans.ca/tag/ project-teen-canada/.**

While peer involvement is a key factor in drug use and other delinquent behaviour, we need to ask how pervasive the behaviours are among young people. Ongoing national surveys (called *Project Teen Canada*) by Canadian sociologist Reginald Bibby show that teenagers today are far more "tame" than they were even eight years ago (Gillis, 2009). According to Bibby's research, the percentage of teens who drink, smoke cigarettes, smoke marijuana, or engage in sex has decreased significantly. Teens look forward to settling down and creating a stable family life more than they ever have before.

EDUCATION

Consider how long you have been in school. From daycare to university you were, and are, being socialized. In contrast to the family, school ideally evaluates children on what they do rather than who they are. Children not only acquire necessary knowledge and skills but also learn new social roles by interacting with teachers and peers. In Canadian culture, the socialization function of education emphasizes that children learn academic content, social skills, and important cultural values (Lindsey, Beach, & Ravelli, 2009, p. 84).

hidden curriculum The unconscious, informal, and unwritten norms and rules that reinforce and maintain social conventions.

Another important consideration is the role of the *hidden curriculum*. The **hidden curriculum** is the assertion that beyond schools' conscious, formal obligations to teach course content are the unconscious, informal, and unwritten rules that reinforce and maintain social conventions. For example, sitting in rows, raising one's hand, and lining up to come in from recess are all means of teaching conformity and obedience to authority.

The hidden curriculum also plays an important role in gender role socialization. Teachers, even those who care deeply about their students and believe that they are treating girls and boys equally, are often unaware that they perpetuate gender-based stereotypes (Myhill & Jones, 2006, p. 100). Teachers often perceive that girls work harder and that boys are more likely to be disruptive. While our memories of school may reinforce this perception, it is important to note that if a teacher enters the classroom thinking that girls are more diligent and boys are more difficult to handle, this may become a *self-fulfilling prophecy*—a prediction that, once made, makes the outcome occur.

Research shows that although schools can unintentionally socialize children to perpetuate stereotypes, they also genuinely strive to use their influence to benefit children and society. Sociologists recognize that today's schools are shouldering a bigger share of the socialization function in Canada than ever before (Lindsey, Beach, & Ravelli, 2009, p. 84).

Go to the Toronto District School Board's website at www.tdsb.on.ca and click on About Us > Mission Statement. What is the school board's hidden curriculum?

MASS MEDIA

Mass media are also an influential socializing force. **Mass media** are forms of communication produced by a few people for consumption by the masses (discussed in more detail in Chapter 10). Unlike schools, the socialization function of media is more subtle, with much of it occurring unconsciously.

mass media   Forms of communication produced by a few people for consumption by the masses.

Television is by far the most influential of the mass media. In 2005, 99 percent of all Canadian households had at least one colour TV, and 27.6 percent had three or more (Statistics Canada, 2008r). The number of hours we watch television has remained relatively stable recently: in 2004 men and women over 18 watched 20.9 hours and 25.6 hours per week, respectively (Statistics Canada, 2006l).

People over age 60 are the heaviest viewers, with men watching 31.1 hours per week and women 35.6 (Statistics Canada, 2006k). Research also shows that children from poor homes watch television more than those from affluent homes, minority populations watch more than Caucasians, and working- and lower-class children watch more than those whose parents have higher education and income (Nielsen Media Research, 1994, as cited in Lindsey & Beach, 2003, p. 111). Although television provides some reinforcement for prosocial behaviour (e.g., situations in which people help someone else without the motivation being personal gain), the majority of its content reinforces competition and the desire for financial wealth (consider such reality programs as *Survivor*, *Big Brother*, and *The Bachelor*).

Nielsen Media Research has been a leader in television audience measurement for over 50 years. Their website offers the latest data on the shows people watch as well as a fascinating timeline of the history of television programming. Check out www.nielsenmedia.com/nc/portal/site/Public/.

Television defines and reinforces standards of behaviour, provides role models, and communicates expectations about all aspects of social life. We rely more and more on the mass media, especially television, to filter the enormous amount of information that is available today. When television messages (e.g., definitions of beauty) are reinforced by other mass media (e.g., magazines), the impact on socialization is substantial (Leong, 2006, p. 178).

Internet use from home is another socialization factor that is gaining in importance. In 2005, two-thirds of adult Canadians surfed the Internet, and people in cities were more likely to have done so than those in rural areas or small towns. In 2005, an estimated 16.8 million adult Canadians, or 68 percent, used the Internet for personal nonbusiness reasons (Statistics Canada, 2006d). Statistics Canada's research also reveals some interesting class differences in who accesses the Internet: 88 percent of adults with household incomes of $86 000 or more used the Internet in 2005, while only 61 percent of those with incomes below $86 000 did so. As well, 80 percent of adults with at least some post-secondary education used the Internet, compared with just less than one half (49 percent) of adults with less education (Statistics Canada, 2006d). In other words, those with higher income and education levels may be the first to benefit from using the information highway—perhaps not much of a surprise, but certainly of sociological interest. The Internet today may be what the television was in the 1950s: a new and powerful influence on what we think about and how we define ourselves.

What do you know about **Agents of Socialization**?

1. **The informal, unwritten norms and rules found in the education system intended to maintain social conventions are called the**
   a. Unknown curriculum
   b. Hidden curriculum
   c. Disguised curriculum
   d. Government curriculum

2. **The most influential mass medium is**
   a. TV
   b. Radio
   c. Newspapers
   d. Internet

3. **The age group that watches the most TV is**
   a. Children
   b. Teens

   c. Twentysomethings
   d. Those over 60

4. **Which adult groups are most likely to use the Internet?**
   a. Those with a household income over $86 000
   b. Those with a household income below $86 000
   c. Those with a household income between $40 000 and $60 000
   d. Those without post-secondary education

5. **Which age group is most affected by the divorce of parents?**
   a. 1 to 3 year olds
   b. 4 to 10 year olds
   c. 11 to 16 year olds
   d. 17 to 19 year olds

Answers: b, a, d, a, b

module 4.4

Think about Socialization across the Life Course

1 Think about the issues facing young adults. What life events have the biggest influence on people in their twenties?

Socialization across the Life Course

Sociologists tend to distinguish the socialization that occurs during childhood as *primary socialization* and socialization throughout one's adult life as the **life course** (Hetherington & Baltes, 1988; Kobali, 2004; Salari & Zhang, 2006). One way that sociologists track how events may influence people's lives is by analyzing a **birth cohort**, which encompasses all those who are born during a given period and therefore experience historical events at the same points in their lives. Investigating birth cohorts allows researchers to explain and predict how different groups respond to situations. For example, those who grew up during the Depression are often very concerned with accumulating wealth and "saving for a rainy day." Their cohort's experience of living in poverty became one of the defining features of who they would become as adults.

As we mature and develop, our experience guides us in making the many decisions we face every day. We understand that as we age we change—our personalities are not fixed; instead, they evolve as we experience more challenges and opportunities and learn from the decisions we have made in the past. The ability to change how we see ourselves and the world around us is at the core of adult development (Atchley, 1999).

EARLY TO MIDDLE ADULTHOOD

In Canada, we generally identify people around the age of 20 as young adults. The exception to this rule is when young adults continue their education beyond high school; in those situations, the adult classification generally is not applied until these people have completed their education. Thus, young adults are generally defined as those who have completed school. They may be in a serious romantic relationship, raising young children, and working hard to establish their careers. Women who have children may choose to stay home while they raise them. This can lead to considerable tension if their career aspirations are compromised as a result. To resolve this situation—or *crisis* in Erikson's terminology—a woman may choose to end her career, put it on hold, or work only part-time (Lindsey & Beach, 2003, p. 101; Tomlinson, 2006). Resolving this crisis depends on the woman's long-term self-esteem and the support of the family unit.

Today, of course, many young adults are marrying later or choosing not to marry at all (Kobali, 2004). According to the 2006 Canadian census, for the first time ever there were more unmarried people (aged 15 and over) than legally married people. In fact, 51.5 percent of the population was unmarried (i.e., never married, divorced, separated, or widowed) compared with 49.9 percent five years earlier. This is a significant change from 20 years ago, when 38.6 percent of the population aged 15 and over was unmarried (Statistics Canada, 2007c).

Even so, marriage is one of the most important decisions adults can make, since it is usually the longest lasting and most emotionally charged relationship in one's life. Today, many traditional expectations of marriage have changed (e.g., the majority of mothers working outside the home, greater social acceptance of same-sex marriages), and both married and live-in partners have greater flexibility in how they live their lives than ever before.

Later adulthood, generally between the ages of 40 and 60, is a time of increased focus on career achievement, children leaving home, the birth of grandchildren, and preparation for retirement. This phase of life also includes increased recognition of one's declining health as the first signs of physical aging occur (e.g., loss of hair, need for reading glasses, aches and pains become more common).

During later adulthood, women are said to be more likely than men to become depressed as the last child leaves home—a situation often referred to as the **empty nest syndrome**. However, research suggests that this condition is largely a myth. The majority of women in fact experience an *increase* in life satisfaction and psychological well-being when children leave the home (Harris, Ellicott, & Holmes, 1986). Further, more recent research suggests that retiring from work is a more difficult transition than having children leave home (Crowley, Hayslip, & Hobdy, 2003). Today, most women recognize that once their children leave home, they finally have the time to pursue interests and hobbies that were put off during child-rearing. Reduced work and parental responsibilities help explain increased marital satisfaction in later life for both men and women (Orbuch et al., 1996, as cited in Lindsey & Beach, 2003, p. 101).

Men also face some significant challenges in later adulthood. During what is often referred to as a "mid-life crisis," men may experience both physical and emotional symptoms. Physical

2 Think about the power of groups such as the military in changing the way a person thinks. What process do you think the military uses to change a person from an ordinary citizen into a soldier who is willing to shoot another human being?

life course Socialization that occurs throughout one's adult life.

birth cohort All the people who are born during a given period of time and therefore experience historical events at the same points in their lives.

empty nest syndrome The depression that some mothers experience when their children have left home.

symptoms may include muscle stiffness and sore joints, night sweats, hair loss, and weight gain, while emotional symptoms may include irritability, loss of libido, erectile dysfunction, fatigue, and depression (Malehealth, 2003). Often the psychological and emotional turmoil associated with these symptoms is linked to hormonal changes, including a significant decline in testosterone levels (Brizendine, 2006). Because Western culture associates masculinity with sexual performance, the hormonal changes that may affect a middle-aged man's ability to achieve or maintain an erection can inspire a great deal of fear and anxiety. The popularity of drugs like Viagra and Cialis (whose estimated sales were over $3.2 billion in 2004 [Firn, 2004]) that promise to enhance a men's sexual performance may be linked to this fear.

Still, adulthood is a period where both men and women grow more confident in themselves and focus much of their attention on their family and careers. And as middle adulthood transitions into later adulthood and then old age, many people begin to take stock of their lives and try to enjoy the fruits of their labours.

LATE ADULTHOOD AND OLD AGE

There are many different functional and chronological definitions of old age. A functional definition could, for example, include declining health or mental faculties as a result of the aging process. In Western societies like Canada, the definition of *old* is largely age based and not related to health status or physical abilities. As a result, a fit, healthy 66-year-old who works full-time and a frail 90-year-old living in a nursing home are both called "old" (Thompson, 2006).

In 1951, the federal government defined *old age* by introducing the Old Age Security Act (age 70) and the Old Age Assistance Act (age 65). For many years, mandatory retirement at age 65 was the standard across the country. However, mandatory retirement has recently been

The proportion of Canadians aged 65 and older is expected to rise sharply over the next 50 years.

TABLE 4–1 **Population, Median Age, and Age Distribution, Canada, 1946 to 2056**

Year	Population	Median Age	0 to 19	20 to 64	65 and Over
			%		
1946	12 292 000	27.7	36.6	56.3	7.2
1966	20 014 880	25.4	42.1	50.2	7.7
1986	26 101 155	31.4	28.6	60.9	10.5
2006	32 623 490	38.8	24.0	62.8	13.2
2011 (medium-growth scenarios)	33 909 700	40.1	22.4	63.2	14.4
2031 (medium-growth scenarios)	39 029 400	44.3	19.9	56.7	23.4
2056 (medium-growth scenarios)	42 510 900	46.9	18.4	54.4	27.2

Source: Statistics Canada (2007). *The daily, Thursday, October 26, 2006. Canada's population by age and sex*. Retrieved November 13, 2007, from http://www.statcan.ca/Daily/English/061026/d061026b.htm.

challenged as constituting age discrimination that can no longer be justified since we are living longer and remaining healthier than we did when retirement legislation was first introduced. Today, the majority of provinces and territories do not have mandatory retirement (CBC News, 2006).

Canada's population is getting older (see Table 4–1), as is the case for almost every other developed nation in the world. As of 2006, the median age for a Canadian was a record high of 38.8 years, compared with 38.5 a year before and 37.2 in 2001 (Statistics Canada, 2006c). This increasing median age means that the number of seniors is projected to grow from 4.2 million to 9.8 million between 2005 and 2036. Also, as illustrated in Figure 4–2, seniors' proportion of the population is expected to almost double during the same period, increasing from 13.2 percent to 24.5 percent (Statistics Canada, 2007m).

FIGURE 4–2 **Percentage of Canadian Population Comprising Persons Aged 65 or Older, 1921 to 2005, and Projections to 2056**

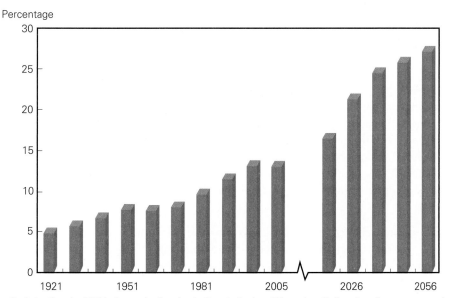

Source: Statistics Canada. (2007). *A portrait of seniors in Canada*. Retrieved November 12, from http://www.statcan.ca/english/freepub/89-519-XIE/2006001/images/chart.gif.

As the proportion of seniors in the Canadian population increases, the common stereotypes of seniors as feeble and vulnerable may well lose currency. Indeed, the Canadian economy needs these older people to continue working. Today, there are six workers for every retired person, but by 2020 this will decline to three workers for every retired person. To address the shortage of workers both now and in the future, some companies are introducing programs such as "retirees on call" and "phased retirement." Such plans are attractive to employers who support mandatory retirement because they can maintain access to the retired workers' expertise but also allow them to unload workers who are at the peak of their earnings. Companies can often hire two young workers for the price of one older worker (CBC News, 2006).

The socialization that occurs during late adulthood and old age is somewhat different from that occurring at earlier stages. The preceding life stages are marked by acquiring new responsibilities and taking on new challenges, whereas retirement and old age can entail a *loss* of identity and satisfaction when people retire from their career and have grown children who no longer need their day-to-day support. Yet, these transitions can also be liberating for aging people, as they are now free to pursue travel and other personal interests they may have deferred in favour of their families and/or careers (Brizendine, 2006). In short, late adulthood and old age requires both the learning of new roles and the unlearning of others, as well as the preparation for the final stage of life.

SOCIALIZATION INTO DYING AND DEATH

The final stage of one's life is associated with old age and the realization of approaching death. The scientific study of old age and aging is called **gerontology**. During late middle age, people usually confront their own declining health and the death of their parents, events that begin their own socialization into death. For the elderly, death becomes a fact of their everyday life.

gerontology   The scientific study of old age and aging.

The process of dying has been studied through the pioneering research of Elisabeth Kübler-Ross (1926–2004). Through interviews with hundreds of terminally ill people, Kübler-Ross (1969) developed a series of stages that people go through as they deal with their own mortality. Just as there is a life course, there is a death course. The general sequence of stages is as follows:

1. *Denial.* People who are told they have a terminal illness experience shock and disbelief. Aside from the personal horror of the news, in a death-denying society this is clearly a logical response.
2. *Anger.* Individuals express hostility and resentment, often toward others who will live on. "Why me?" they ask, with a strong sense of injustice.
3. *Bargaining.* Bargains are made, usually with God. "I will be a better person if only I can live, so please spare me."
4. *Depression.* With the realization that they cannot negotiate their way out of the situation, depression occurs. Sorrow, guilt, and shame are linked with this stage.
5. *Acceptance.* By discussing these feelings openly, the people move into a final stage in which death is accepted. Kübler-Ross believed that only with acceptance can inner peace be reached.

Recent research challenges Kübler-Ross's theory that people move sequentially through each stage, or that in fact there are even identifiable stages (Cassem, 1988; Kastenbaum, 1998). Nonetheless, Kübler-Ross deserves great credit for bringing the analysis of dying to the forefront of social science and to the popular arena.

Socialization into death is similar to other socialization experiences throughout the life course. Indeed, sociologists recognize that our entire lives are the result and expression of socialization and social interaction.

While our analysis of the life course corresponds with the vast majority of people's lives, we turn now to a related but far more extreme and less common phenomenon in which people undergo, a process known as *resocialization*.

RESOCIALIZATION: THE TOTAL INSTITUTION

Resocialization is the profound change or complete transformation of a person's personality as a result of being placed in a situation or an environment dedicated to changing his or her previous identity (Parkinson & Drislane, 2007, p. 136). It generally occurs against one's will and in a location where the person has little or no control over the situation. Classic examples of this type of resocialization occur in prisons or mental institutions, where the desired outcome is to change the way a person behaves. As a rule, resocialization usually occurs within what are called **total institutions**, settings in which people are isolated from society and supervised by an administrative staff.

Erving Goffman was the pioneer in studying the resocialization that occurs in total institutions. In his groundbreaking book *Asylums* (1961), Goffman outlines the five types of total institutions:

1. Institutions that help people who are incapable of taking care of themselves and can be considered harmless (homes for the blind, the aged, the orphaned, and the indigent)
2. Institutions that take care of people who are incapable of looking after themselves and pose a threat to the community, albeit an unintended one (mental hospitals or institutions for those with communicable diseases)
3. Institutions that protect the community from those that would do it harm (prisons or prisoner-of-war camps)
4. Institutions that perform instrumental tasks that require unique work arrangements (army/work camps or boarding schools)
5. Institutions that act as retreats from the rest of the world and serve as locations for religious training (monasteries and convents) (Roberts, 2007)

resocialization The profound change or complete transformation of a person's personality as a result of being placed in a situation or an environment dedicated to changing his or her previous identity.

total institution A setting in which people are isolated from society and supervised by an administrative staff.

Prisons are one type of total institution.

According to Goffman, total institutions are defined by three important characteristics. First, an administrative staff supervises all aspects of the inmates' or residents' life, using electronic surveillance to observe their every move and action. Second, every activity is controlled and standardized so that formal schedules define everything that occurs (e.g., people exercise at the same time each day, and every Tuesday is meatloaf day). Third, formal rules and/or policies define everything about the inmates' or residents' daily lives (Goffman, 1961, as cited in Macionis & Gerber, 2008, p. 126).

mortifications of the self The first stage of the resocialization process, in which a person's existing identity is stripped away.

Resocialization usually occurs in two distinct stages. In the first stage people's existing identity is stripped from them in what Goffman (1961) termed **mortifications of the self**. To accomplish this separation from their past, inmates have all their personal possessions taken away, they lose all control over their daily schedule, they often have to wear uniforms, they have their hair cut, and there is no real way to escape the organizational rules and procedures. In most of these settings the institutional goal is to recreate the individual to fit the demands of the organization (Margolis & Rowe, 2007). During this initial stage, inmates often feel anxious and worthless and have low self-esteem (Walsh, 2001). In the second stage of the resocialization process, the administrative staff builds up inmates through a system of rewards and punishments. By breaking people down in the first stage and then building them up in the second, the resocialization process allows for the formation of a new identity that is clearly distinct from the one that originally entered the total institution. In the case of a prison or a mental institution, one can appreciate why such drastic changes are necessary, but it is less clear why such a process is required by organizations such as the military.

In January 1995, Canadians were shocked to see videotaped scenes of humiliating hazing rituals as practised by 1 Commando, Canadian Airborne Regiment. Anthropologist Donna Winslow (1999) studied the Canadian Airborne Regiment during the mid-1990s as part of an inquiry into Canada's military affairs in Somalia. Her research provided graphic evidence of how initiation rituals were intended to break down the new recruits and build them up to become an elite fighting force. Winslow cites Aronson & Mills (1959), who suggest that the more severe the initiation rituals within an organization, the greater the initiates' bonding to the group will be; this is, in fact, what Winslow found. After initiates completed the various hazing rituals, they were accepted as full members of a group that must trust each other with their lives.

Clearly, this form of socialization is extreme, but it is one that reinforces the point we have been making throughout the chapter—that the development of a sense of self is a dynamic process that influences us each and every day of our lives.

What do you know about **Socialization across the Life Course**?

1. **Which of the following is not a total institution?**
   a. Prison
   b. Military
   c. Convent
   d. College

2. **Which of the following does not belong to Kübler-Ross's stages of dying?**
   a. Denial
   b. Anger
   c. Elation
   d. Depression

3. **The process whereby a person's identity is stripped away is called**
   a. Mortifications of self
   b. Death of self
   c. Identity reassignment
   d. Antisocialization

4. **Which of the following statements is false?**
   a. Canada's population is aging.
   b. The median age for a Canadian is increasing.
   c. The number of seniors is projected to double by 2036.
   d. The majority of Canadian provinces and territories have a mandatory retirement age of 65.

5. Which of the following statements is true?

a. The majority of women experience an increase in life satisfaction when their grown children leave home.

b. The majority of women experience psychological problems when their grown children leave home.

c. The majority of women experience sadness when their grown children leave home.

d. There is no effect on women's life satisfaction when their grown children leave home.

Answers: d, c, a, d, a

Summary

module 4.1   BECOMING HUMAN

1. There are two basic approaches to understanding how we become human and how we develop our personality. These are the biological approach and the environmental approach, traditionally referred to as the nature versus nurture debate.

2. The nature argument suggests that much of our behaviour is determined by our genetic makeup. This argument is made by sociobiologists and evolutionary psychologists.

3. The nurture argument supports the position that we become who we are because of environmental influences. It points to the cases of feral children and children raised in isolation to show that these children cannot meet their potential without human interaction.

module 4.2   THE DEVELOPMENT OF SELF

4. The *self*, or one's identity, comprises a set of learned values and attitudes that develops through social interaction and that defines one's self-image.

5. *Self-image* is an introspective composition of various features and attributes that we see as ourselves.

6. We can gain insight regarding the development of the self from both sociology and psychology.

7. Sociologist Charles Cooley introduced the concept of the looking-glass self—the idea that what we think of ourselves is influenced by how we imagine other people see us.

8. George Herbert Mead built on Cooley's work. He introduced the concepts of *I* and *me*. The *I* is the element of the self that is spontaneous, creative, impulsive, and unpredictable. The *me* is the socialized element of the self.

9. Mead said that children pass through three distinct stages. Passing through these stages the child develops the *me*.

10. According to Mead, the first stage is the preparatory stage. In this stage, children imitate what they see around them, and the reactions of others contribute to the development of the *I*.

11. The second stage is the play stage. Children begin to role play and move from imitation to imagining the roles of the characters that they play. Language skills also develop, which allow a child to move to a higher understanding of themselves in relation to others.

12. The third stage is the game stage. In this stage, children are capable of taking on several roles simultaneously. Playing games teaches children about various roles and the needs of others.

13. In the game stage, children learn *role-taking*—assuming the position of another to better understand that person's perspective.

14. Mead noted that at the game stage, primary socialization occurs. *Primary socialization* occurs when people learn the attitudes, values, and appropriate behaviours for individuals in their culture.

15. *Secondary socialization* occurs later, in early adolescence and beyond, through participation in groups that are more specific than the broader society and that have defined roles and expectations.

16. Mead introduced two other concepts of importance—the specific other and the generalized other.

17. *Significant others* (e.g. family) are essential to the early development of children. In the early years, it is their behaviour that children imitate and learn from.

18. The *generalized other* is not specific people but a compilation of attributes that we associate with the average member of society. Through a comparison to the generalized other, children gain a greater understanding of themselves and who they wish to become.

19. Psychologists tend to view socialization as a process of internal conflict and tension.

20. Sigmund Freud noted that a socialized part of the self—the superego—is developed to counteract the instinctual elements of the self—the id.

21. Erik Erikson viewed the stages of one's life as a series of crises. The way people meet these crises will determine in part their personality. For instance, in the first stage of life, developing trust in others is essential. If a parent is neglectful or abusive, a child grows up to be mistrustful of others.

22. Jean Piaget focused on cognitive development. Piaget discovered that children think and reason differently at different stages of their lives.

module 4.3   AGENTS OF SOCIALIZATION

23. The *agents of socialization* are individuals, groups, and social institutions that together help people become functioning members of society. Included in this group are families, peers, education, and mass media.

24. From our families we get messages regarding gender, class, and race issues.

25. As a teenager, our relationship to our families changes and we become more influenced by our peers.

26. The education system does more than just teach the three *Rs*—it also teaches us how to act in society. The unconscious, informal, and unwritten rules that reinforce and maintain social conventions are referred to as the *hidden curriculum*.

27. Mass media are an influential socializing force. Television still has the greatest influence.

module 4.4   SOCIALIZATION ACROSS THE LIFE COURSE

28. The *life course* is the socialization that occurs throughout one's adult life.

29. People born in a given time are referred to as a *birth cohort*.

30. Early to middle adulthood is marked by the challenges of completing school, establishing careers, building relationships, and parenting.

31. Later adulthood is marked by children moving out of the home. As well, many physical changes associated with aging occur.

32. Late adulthood and old age are marked by the loss of identity/roles, retirement, and an increase in health issues.

33. Elisabeth Kübler-Ross identified the process people go through when they are dying, known as the *death course*. She identifies five stages: denial, anger, bargaining, depression, and acceptance.

34. *Resocialization* is the complete transformation of a person's personality. Sometimes this is seen as necessary by society. Total institutions are charged with the task of resocialization.

35. Examples of total institutions include orphanages, mental hospitals, prisons, and the military.

Key Terms

Test Yourself

1. *Socialization* is defined as
   a. Spending time with friends
   b. An individual's relatively stable pattern of behaviour and feelings
   c. The lifelong process by which we learn our culture, develop our personalities, and become functioning members of society
   d. The ways in which people interact in social settings

2. The debate over whether biological forces or environmental forces define the person we become is called
   a. Socialization
   b. Nature versus nurture
   c. Personality development
   d. Nature versus man

3. A child raised in the wild by wolves is referred to by sociologists as a
   a. Wolf child
   b. Puppy
   c. Feral child
   d. Nature child

4. An individual's relatively stable pattern of behaviours and feelings is the definition of
   a. Personality
   b. Sociability
   c. Genetics
   d. Social interaction

5. The ways in which people interact in social settings while recognizing each person's subjective experiences and/or intentions is called
   a. Social interaction
   b. Socialization

c. Personality development
d. Nature versus nurture

6. One's identity, comprising a set of learned values and attitudes that develops through social interaction and that defines one's self-image is called the
   a. Self
   b. I
   c. Me
   d. Self-image

7. Mead's term for the socialized element of the self is called the
   a. I
   b. Me
   c. Id
   d. Ego

8. Assuming the position of another in order to better understand that person's perspective is called
   a. Socialization
   b. Role-taking
   c. Primary socialization
   d. Secondary socialization

9. Freud's term for an individual's biological drives and impulses that strive for instant gratification is the
   a. Id
   b. Ego
   c. Superego
   d. Alter ego

10. The stage at which children learn through their senses is called the
    a. Sensorimotor stage
    b. Preoperational stage

c. Concrete operational stage

d. Formal operational stage

11. Individuals, groups, and social institutions that together help people become functioning members of society are called

a. Agents of socialization

b. Significant others

c. Generalized others

d. Institutions of socialization

12. The assignment of a set of beliefs to men and women, respectively, that are not based on fact is called

a. Sex stereotyping

b. Gender stereotyping

c. Gender identification

d. Sex identification

13. *Cultural capital* could be defined as

a. Status as determined by a parent's income

b. Status as determined by your own income

c. Social assets that are gained from one's family and help one succeed in life

d. One's social standing in the community

14. Socio-economic status is determined by

a. Income

b. Occupation

c. Education

d. All of the above

15. People who are closely related in age and share similar interests are called

a. Significant others

b. Generalized others

c. Family

d. Peer groups

16. Socialization that occurs throughout one's adult life is called

a. Life course

b. Ongoing socialization

c. Continuing socialization

d. Developmental socialization

17. All the people who are born during a given period of time and therefore experience historical events at the same points in their lives are called

a. Birth cohorts

b. Peer groups

c. Quintiles

d. Birth orders

18. The depression that some mothers experience when their children have left home is called

a. Empty nest syndrome

b. Empty nest depression

c. Postpartum depression

d. Empty house syndrome

19. The scientific study of old age and aging is called

a. Age socialization

b. Ageism

c. Gerontology

d. Sociobiology

20. The complete transformation of a person's personality as a result of being placed in a situation or an environment dedicated to changing his or her previous identity is called

a. Resocialization

b. Total socialization

c. Anticipatory socialization

d. Prison socialization

Answers: c, b, c, a, a, b, b, a, a, b, c, d, d, a, a, c, a

Log in to MySocLab for a host of resources that will help you save time and improve your grade. MySocLab contains cutting-edge learning tools such as study plans, practice tests, videos, audio segments, quizzes, and more—all designed to help you better understand the learning objectives for this chapter. Along with your eBook, MySocLab for *Sociology for Everyone* can be found at **www.mysoclab.com**.

module 4.1
BECOMING HUMAN

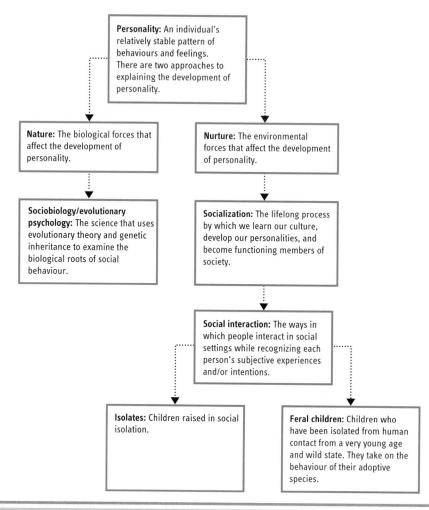

Personality: An individual's relatively stable pattern of behaviours and feelings. There are two approaches to explaining the development of personality.

Nature: The biological forces that affect the development of personality.

Nurture: The environmental forces that affect the development of personality.

Sociobiology/evolutionary psychology: The science that uses evolutionary theory and genetic inheritance to examine the biological roots of social behaviour.

Socialization: The lifelong process by which we learn our culture, develop our personalities, and become functioning members of society.

Social interaction: The ways in which people interact in social settings while recognizing each person's subjective experiences and/or intentions.

Isolates: Children raised in social isolation.

Feral children: Children who have been isolated from human contact from a very young age and wild state. They take on the behaviour of their adoptive species.

module 4.2
THE DEVELOPMENT OF SELF

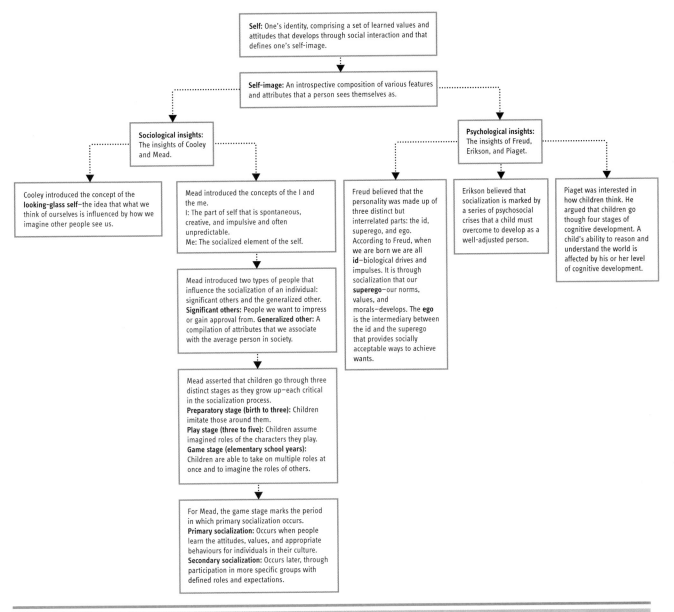

Self: One's identity, comprising a set of learned values and attitudes that develops through social interaction and that defines one's self-image.

Self-image: An introspective composition of various features and attributes that a person sees themselves as.

Sociological insights: The insights of Cooley and Mead.

Psychological insights: The insights of Freud, Erikson, and Piaget.

Cooley introduced the concept of the **looking-glass self**—the idea that what we think of ourselves is influenced by how we imagine other people see us.

Mead introduced the concepts of the I and the me.
I: The part of self that is spontaneous, creative, and impulsive and often unpredictable.
Me: The socialized element of the self.

Freud believed that the personality was made up of three distinct but interrelated parts: the id, superego, and ego. According to Freud, when we are born we are all **id**—biological drives and impulses. It is through socialization that our **superego**—our norms, values, and morals—develops. The **ego** is the intermediary between the id and the superego that provides socially acceptable ways to achieve wants.

Erikson believed that socialization is marked by a series of psychosocial crises that a child must overcome to develop as a well-adjusted person.

Piaget was interested in how children think. He argued that children go though four stages of cognitive development. A child's ability to reason and understand the world is affected by his or her level of cognitive development.

Mead introduced two types of people that influence the socialization of an individual: significant others and the generalized other. **Significant others:** People we want to impress or gain approval from. **Generalized other:** A compilation of attributes that we associate with the average person in society.

Mead asserted that children go through three distinct stages as they grow up—each critical in the socialization process.
Preparatory stage (birth to three): Children imitate those around them.
Play stage (three to five): Children assume imagined roles of the characters they play.
Game stage (elementary school years): Children are able to take on multiple roles at once and to imagine the roles of others.

For Mead, the game stage marks the period in which primary socialization occurs.
Primary socialization: Occurs when people learn the attitudes, values, and appropriate behaviours for individuals in their culture.
Secondary socialization: Occurs later, through participation in more specific groups with defined roles and expectations.

module 4.3
AGENTS OF SOCIALIZATION

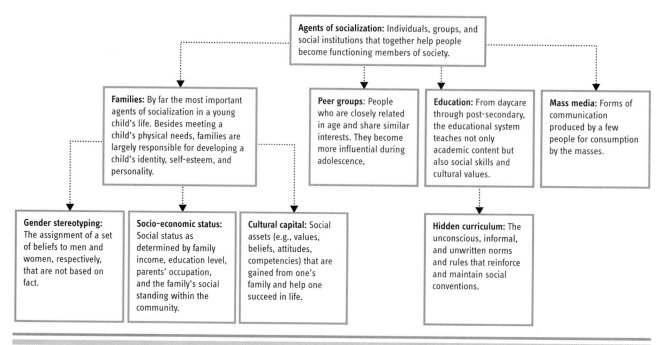

Agents of socialization: Individuals, groups, and social institutions that together help people become functioning members of society.

Families: By far the most important agents of socialization in a young child's life. Besides meeting a child's physical needs, families are largely responsible for developing a child's identity, self-esteem, and personality.

Peer groups: People who are closely related in age and share similar interests. They become more influential during adolescence,

Education: From daycare through post-secondary, the educational system teaches not only academic content but also social skills and cultural values.

Mass media: Forms of communication produced by a few people for consumption by the masses.

Gender stereotyping: The assignment of a set of beliefs to men and women, respectively, that are not based on fact.

Socio-economic status: Social status as determined by family income, education level, parents' occupation, and the family's social standing within the community.

Cultural capital: Social assets (e.g., values, beliefs, attitudes, competencies) that are gained from one's family and help one succeed in life.

Hidden curriculum: The unconscious, informal, and unwritten norms and rules that reinforce and maintain social conventions.

module 4.4
SOCIALIZATION ACROSS THE
LIFE COURSE

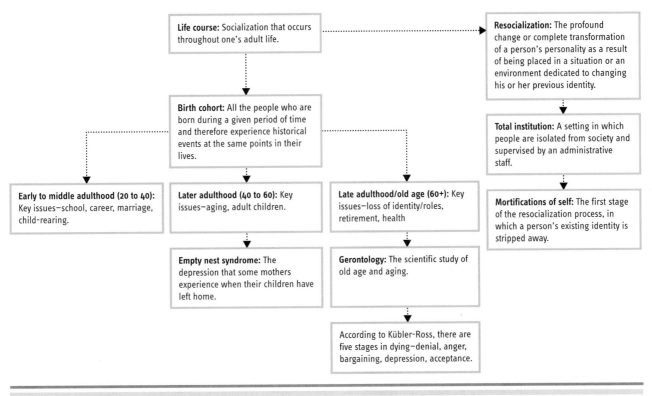

Life course: Socialization that occurs throughout one's adult life.

Resocialization: The profound change or complete transformation of a person's personality as a result of being placed in a situation or an environment dedicated to changing his or her previous identity.

Birth cohort: All the people who are born during a given period of time and therefore experience historical events at the same points in their lives.

Total institution: A setting in which people are isolated from society and supervised by an administrative staff.

Early to middle adulthood (20 to 40): Key issues—school, career, marriage, child-rearing.

Later adulthood (40 to 60): Key issues—aging, adult children.

Late adulthood/old age (60+): Key issues—loss of identity/roles, retirement, health

Mortifications of self: The first stage of the resocialization process, in which a person's existing identity is stripped away.

Empty nest syndrome: The depression that some mothers experience when their children have left home.

Gerontology: The scientific study of old age and aging.

According to Kübler-Ross, there are five stages in dying—denial, anger, bargaining, depression, acceptance.

chapter 5

Deviance, Crime, and Regulation

Canadian Crimes: Murder and Mystery

In 1993, 28-year-old Paul Bernardo was arrested and charged in the sex slayings of Ontario high school girls Leslie Mahaffy and Kristen French. He was subsequently charged with the death of his sister-in-law, Tammy Homolka, as well as many sexual assaults. He and his wife, Karla Homolka, were eventually convicted of the high school girls' murders. However, in a controversial plea bargain, Homolka cooperated with the prosecution and testified against Bernardo. He received a life sentence for the murders and was declared a dangerous offender, while she was sentenced to 12 years in prison.

In 2005, while enjoying a Boxing Day shopping expedition with her sister, Jane Creba was shot and killed on Toronto's Yonge Street. Her death was the result of a shootout between two rival gangs. In December 2008, one man, identified as J.S.R. because he was a youth at the time of the crime, was found guilty of second-degree murder in the shooting. Eight others, one youth and seven adults, are expected to be tried in 2009 on either charges of second-degree murder or manslaughter (CBC, 2008b).

In December 2007, Robert Pickton, a farmer from British Columbia, was convicted of the second-degree murders of six women and sentenced to life in prison with no chance of parole for 25 years. Back in 1983, Rebecca Guno, a sex worker, had disappeared from Vancouver's downtown Eastside. Her name was the first of 61 that would eventually be placed on the list of women (mostly sex trade workers) who disappeared mysteriously from the area over the following years (CBC, 2009b). Pickton was charged but never tried for 20 other counts of first-degree murder. In June 2009, the BC Court of Appeals upheld the guilty verdict on six degrees of second-degree murder. However, two out of three Appeal Court judges agree that Justice James Williams erred in his final instructions to the jury. The Appeal judges ruled that Justice Williams was wrong to split the trial in two, trying six counts of murder separately from the other 20 charges. Should the Supreme Court of Canada rule in favour of the defence, Pickton could be granted a new trial. It has been stated that Pickton confessed to 49 murders to an undercover police officer posing as a cellmate.

Born in Montreal to a wealthy family, Conrad Black enjoyed many of the privileges associated with an upper-class lifestyle. He became a newspaper magnate, managing and controlling Hollinger International Inc., owning and publishing numerous important newspapers across North America. Along with his associates, Black was charged in a large corporate scandal with three counts of fraud and one count of obstruction of justice. In July 2007, he was convicted and later sentenced to serve 78 months in federal prison, to pay Hollinger $6.1 million, and fined $125 000. In May 2009, the Supreme Court of the United States agreed to hear Black's appeal of the conviction (CBC, 2009a).

Why are we so well informed about high-profile murders and yet tend to know very little about the effects of corporate crime? Why do some victims garner more sympathy than others? These are just two of the questions that people interested in the study of crime grapple with. However, what the preceding cases demonstrate is that crime cuts across gender, race, and class lines, touching all aspects of life—from the victims of gang violence to the wealthy to sex workers to the family members of those killed by violent offenders. Crime knows no boundaries—and, as we will see in this chapter, it is often not only about "sick" or "deviant" individuals but is also connected to wider social relations.

module 5.1

Crime and Deviance

Crime and *deviance* are two terms that are often used interchangeably. In this module, we will explain the difference between the two.

CRIMINOLOGY AND THE SOCIOLOGY OF LAW

The theories and research described in this chapter come from two fields of study: criminology and the sociology of law.

Criminology is a multidisciplinary field that draws on sociology, law, psychology, political science, anthropology, history, and geography. It is devoted to the development of information about the causes, patterns, and trends of crime. Criminologists who adopt a sociological approach tend to focus on the societal context within which criminal law is created and applied. They also focus on explanations of crime that consider societal factors such as poverty and discrimination.

Criminology can be defined as the scientific approach to the study of crime causation, crime prevention, and the punishment and rehabilitation of offenders. According to the

Think about Crime and Deviance

1 Think about criminal or deviant behaviour. How do we as a society decide what is or is not criminal?

2 Think about the word *deviant*. Do you imagine behaviour that is "bad"? Do you think it is possible for deviance to have a positive effect on society?

influential definition proposed by Sutherland and Cressey (1960, p. 3), criminology is "the body of knowledge regarding crime as a social phenomenon. It includes within its scope the process of making laws, breaking laws, and reacting towards the breaking of laws." This definition highlights important areas of interest to criminologists: the development of criminal law and its use in defining crime, the causes of breaking the law, and the methods implemented by a society to control criminal behaviour.

The **sociology of law** is a subdiscipline of sociology as well as an approach within the field of legal studies. Sociologists who study law attempt to place laws, regulations, specific legal cases, and the administration of criminal justice into a social context. In other words, they look at how the law and the justice system are socially constructed. As well, they analyze how the criminal justice system influences social values and behaviour (Burtch, 1992).

As a case in point, consider Canada's legal institutions. They have been shaped by a number of principles adopted from Britain. One principle is that of the **rule of law**, meaning that no person, including monarchs, government officials, police officers, and so forth, is above the law, and that there should be no arbitrary exercise of state power (Yates, Yates, & Bain, 2000). The rule of law is meant to ensure that laws are created, administered, and enforced on the basis of acceptable procedures promoting fairness and equality (Goff, 2004, p. 34).

Another adopted principle is that everyone is entitled to equal justice under the law. But is this the case? Sociologists question whether the law is indeed fair and just or whether it in fact serves the interests of particular groups.

Interest in examining the law from a sociological perspective grew after the Second World War. Sociologists looked at the inequalities racialized groups faced and began to understand the law to be a relevant factor (Vago & Nelson, 2004). Although laws are meant to protect all citizens, sociologists recognized that racialized groups were not afforded the same protection as nonracialized groups.

During the social unrest of the late 1960s, many sociologists studied areas of social conflict and social inequality. They argued that a gap existed between the ideals of the law and the reality of the legal system, in which the law was not applied uniformly to all citizens (Vago & Nelson, 2004). We will examine the issues of inequality and justice in Canada in more detail near the end of the chapter.

criminology   The study of crime causation, crime prevention, and the punishment and rehabilitation of offenders.

sociology of law A subdiscipline of sociology as well as an approach within the field of legal studies that looks at how the law and the justice system are socially constructed.

rule of law   The constitutional principle that no person is above the law and that state power should not be exercised arbitrarily.

DEFINING CRIME AND DEVIANCE

Although the terms *crime* and *deviance* are often used interchangeably, they are in fact two distinct phenomena that at times overlap. **Crime** is a concept used to designate certain behaviours and actions (including acts of negligence) that require a formal response through control and that warrant social intervention (Winterdyke, 2006). **Deviance**, on the other hand, involves actions, as well as beliefs, conditions, and characteristics, that violate social norms and that may or may not be against the law (Winterdyke, 2006). *Social norms* are understood here as a given society's accepted standards and social expectations.

The difficulty with this definition of deviance is how these social norms are defined, and by whom. For example, to what degree do your own notions of proper conduct match those of others? Is it possible that some of your behaviours are unacceptable to some people? Are you "deviant"? Behaviours as diverse as committing a violent crime, joining a nudist colony, and acquiring an abundance of body piercings are all seen as deviant acts by a large portion of Canadian society.

Most, but not all, crimes are understood as deviant, but not all deviant acts are considered criminal. For example, assisted suicide is against the law, yet many people do not view it as deviant. In Western cultures, a 50-year-old woman dating an 18-year-old man is seen as deviant by some (and lucky by others), but it is certainly not criminal. We can also ask why some acts are criminalized while others are not. Drinking alcohol is legal, while other forms of ingesting drugs are illegal.

crime   Behaviours and actions requiring social control and social intervention, codified in law.

deviance   Actions, beliefs, conditions, and characteristics that violate social norms, and that may or may not be against the law.

To view the Canadian Addiction Survey, go to **www.ccsa.ca/2005% 20ccsa%20Documents/ ccsa-004028-2005.pdf.**

Over time, some deviant acts come to be deemed criminal and some criminalized acts become legalized. Consider the use and distribution of marijuana. Despite being criminalized in 1923, marijuana still enjoys widespread popularity; in fact, between 1994 and 2004, the number of Canadians using marijuana doubled (CBC, 2004). The Canadian Addiction Survey found that 45 percent of Canadians report having used marijuana at least once in their lives (CBC, 2004). Overall, the proportion of Canadians reporting at least one usage of illicit drugs rose from 28.5 percent in 1994 to 45 percent in 2004 (CBC, 2004). There is currently much debate over whether marijuana use should be decriminalized.

Perceptions of deviance can also change: Acts that were once considered deviant can become an accepted part of society, while acts that were once considered "normal" can become deviant over time. In Canada, women's body modifications, whether in the form of plastic surgeries, piercings, or small tattoos, are not nearly as deviant as they were even just 20 years ago. Whereas smoking, a widespread activity that occurred in university lecture halls, at movie theatres, in bank lineups, and even at your doctor's office 20 years ago, is rapidly becoming understood as a deviant act, thanks in part to government regulations prohibiting smoking in most public settings.

So the distinction between what is, or should be, considered deviant and what is, or should be, considered criminal is not as clear-cut as one might think. Two cases in point are pornography and prostitution. When does sexually expressive material cross the line into pornography? What acts make pornography illegal? Does a woman have the "right" to sell her body for sex? Can prostitution be understood simply as work?

SOCIAL DEVIANCE

social deviance   Any acts that involve the violation of social norms.

Sociologists use the term **social deviance** to refer to any acts, beliefs, conditions, or characteristics that involve the violation of social norms. Deviance is relative; it varies from person to person, from time to time, and from place to place. As Howard Becker (1966) argued, it is not the act itself that is deviant but rather people's interpretation of it and reaction to it that make it deviant. In other words, a given act or behaviour must be viewed from the standpoint

Not all deviant behaviour is criminal behaviour.

of the culture in which it takes place, since what is perfectly acceptable in one culture may be seen as deviant in another. We can see an example of diverging social norms in the widespread media coverage of the polygamous Mormon sect in Bountiful, British Columbia. Within this sect of the Mormon religion, practices such as polygyny, arranged marriages, and young brides are considered socially acceptable. However, within the wider societal context, these acts are viewed as improper and immoral. On January 7, 2009, two of the group's religious leaders, Winston Blackmore and James Oler, were arrested under charges of polygamy. It is alleged that Blackmore has 26 wives and 108 children. The case is bound to test religious freedom under the Canadian Charter of Rights and Freedoms (Hadler, 2009).

WHO DEFINES DEVIANCE?   In Canada, some of the most powerful groups involved in defining deviance are politicians/governments, scientists, religious institutions, and the media (Bereska, 2008). Each of these individuals or institutions may act as **moral entrepreneurs**—those who take action in an attempt to influence or change the development or enforcement of society's moral codes (Becker, 1963). People who act in ways that deviate from what is deemed acceptable behaviour are subject to social controls, both informally and formally.

Forms of Social Control   **Social control** is the term used to describe the methods used by society to discourage deviant behavior and encourage conformity to social norms. Social control can be divided into two groups: informal and formal.

Informal social control occurs through interactions among individuals, and includes the ways in which we try to communicate and enforce standards of appropriate behaviour. How we respond to behaviours makes most people stop and internally question whether their behaviour is appropriate or inappropriate (consider a friend's reaction, such as "You did what?!?" or the dirty look a teacher gives you when you enter late in class). When informal social controls are ineffective, **formal social controls** can be exerted by the state through the criminal justice system, social workers, and psychiatrists. Being gossiped about for being sexually promiscuous is an example of an informal social control, while being imprisoned for having sex with a minor is an example of formal social control.

The rewards and punishments used to gain social control are referred to as *sanctions*. Rewards are referred to as *positive sanctions*, and punishments are referred to as *negative sanctions*. A smile is a *positive informal sanction*, while a scowl is a *negative informal sanction*. A pay raise is a *positive formal sanction*, while dismissal from a job or imprisonment is a *negative* formal sanction.

IS DEVIANCE ALWAYS A BAD THING?   The negative effects of deviant behaviour are perhaps most obvious to us. Deviance can cause disruption to the smooth functioning of social groups. For instance, the child that acts out in class takes the teacher's attention away from other students and the work that needs to be accomplished. Criminal behaviour is not only dangerous to the well-being of others but also costly to society: it requires the ongoing financing of legal institutions that control and regulate it. As well, there is the cost of compensation to the victims of criminal behaviour. For instance, the insurance rates we pay or the price of the products we buy are affected by the losses incurred by criminal behaviour. Deviant behaviour can have social implications if it goes uncontested or is in some way rewarded. Such reactions to deviant behaviour may encourage others to engage in that behaviour (Lindsey, Beach, & Ravelli, 2009). Have you ever bought something privately or had some work done for you "under the table"? We engage in such practices to avoid paying taxes. If such practices become widespread, what impact do you think they might have on Canadian society?

Deviance, according to functionalists, can also have positive outcomes. Our reaction as a group or society to a particular form of deviance can increase group solidarity and clarify group boundaries and norms. Consider our reaction to the 9/11 terrorist attacks in the United States. In Canada, we tightened our border and airline security and changed our laws to deal with terrorist threats. Some may see the outcomes of these changes as negative. For instance,

moral entrepreneur
A person who takes action in an attempt to influence or change the development or enforcement of society's moral codes.

social control   The methods used by society to discourage deviant behaviour and encourage conformity to social norms.

informal social control
Control that occurs through interactions among individuals, and includes the ways in which we try to communicate and enforce standards of appropriate behaviour.

formal social control
Control that is exerted by the state through the criminal justice system, social workers, and psychiatrists.

it has become more difficult to cross the Canada–US border. But, from a functionalist perspective, it does demonstrate how we as a society have strengthened our boundaries. Finally, deviance may signify a need for change (Lindsey, Beach, & Ravelli, 2009). For example, where we see protests and demonstrations we often see evidence of the need for change. Consider gay pride parades, Earth Day marches, and Native blockades as examples of where the public's attention was drawn to areas that needed change.

Criminologists, then, are concerned with shifting definitions of deviant behaviour and their links to our conceptions of crime. Crime—as an instance of deviance that has been formalized into criminal law—is often referred to as "hard" deviance; that is, those acts or behaviours likely to result in arrest and imprisonment (Goode, 2004). We turn next to the theories concerning *why* people commit crimes.

CANADIAN SOCIETY IN FOCUS

Discrimination in the Criminal Justice System?

The Canadian Charter of Rights and Freedoms states that every Canadian citizen is entitled to "equal treatment before and under the law, and equal protection and benefit of the law without discrimination." Today, many criminologists argue that discrimination is embedded in our criminal justice system. For instance, why is it that Aboriginal people, who represent approximately 4 percent of the total population, account for 14 percent of federal prison inmates (Wortley, 1999)? A 2008 coroner's inquiry in the community of Kaschechewan, a reservation on the Ontario James Bay coastline, may provide some answers.

The case involves the deaths of Ricardo Wesley and Jamie Goodwin. The two died in a fire while detained at the Kaschechewan jail. A pre-inquest motion made by lawyers representing the Wesley family asked that at least one member of the five-person jury be from Kaschechewan or at least be Cree. Inquest jurors are selected from the same electoral lists used to select potential jurors for criminal and civil cases (Brown, 2008). However, the family's request could not be granted; there were no people from Kaschechewan on the jury list. An affidavit was then filed with the inquest from the supervisor of court operations in the Kenora judicial district.

According to the affidavit, before 2000, the federal government provided electoral lists for the Kenora district. From 2000 to 2006, the province did not attain the names of First Nation peoples for electoral lists (Brown, 2008). In 2006, the 42 bands residing in the Kenora district were asked by the province to provide names of residents. Only 12 did so (Huber, 2008).

Case law states that a jury should be made up of one's peers. One would assume then that if an Aboriginal person is on trial, at least one Aboriginal person should be on that person's jury. However, the law does not specify what a peer is and, therefore, does not specify that such representation is required. Nonetheless, if Aboriginal people do not appear on a jury list, clearly there is no chance that they would be selected for a jury. Kimberly Murray, executive director of Aboriginal Legal Services and lawyer for the Wesley family, has stated that every Aboriginal person that had a jury trial between 2000 and 2006 in the Kenora district had an illegal jury because the jury lists were not properly prepared (Brown, 2009).

Discussions that Murray has had with Aboriginal leaders in other parts of the province indicate that this problem is widespread. As a result, Aboriginal leaders requested an official government probe into the issue (Brown, 2008; Huber, 2008).

Do you agree with the sociological argument that the disparities noted above are the result of bias? This was certainly the finding of the Commission on Systemic Racism in the Ontario Criminal Justice System in 1995. What other factors might explain these disparities? How would you go about investigating whether disparities exist in Canadian sentencing practices?

What do you know about **Crime and Deviance**?

Multiple-choice questions (circle your answer)

1. _____ refers to behaviours and actions requiring social control and social intervention, codified in law.
   a. Crime
   b. Deviance
   c. Social deviance
   d. Rule of law

2. _____ involves any actions, beliefs, conditions, or characteristics that violate social norms, and that may or may not be against the law.
   a. Deviance
   b. Crime
   c. Norm
   d. Sanction

3. **An example of an informal social control would be**
   a. A smile
   b. A pay raise

   c. A jail term
   d. A traffic ticket

4. **Receiving a pay raise would be an example of**
   a. A positive informal sanction
   b. A positive formal sanction
   c. A principle of law
   d. Social deviance

5. **Crime is often referred to as**
   a. Formalized deviance
   b. Social deviance
   c. Informal social control
   d. "Hard" deviance

Answers: a, a, a, b, d

module 5.2

Explaining Crime and Deviance: Theoretical Perspectives

During the Middle Ages in Europe, supernatural explanations were used to explain crime and deviance. Witchcraft was one explanation of criminal and deviant behaviour. An estimated 10 000 people were accused of witchcraft and burned at the stake during that time (Siegal & McCormick, 2006).

By the mid-eighteenth century, academics began to look for scientific explanations of crime and deviance (Siegal & McCormick, 2006). Below we will examine a number of theoretical perspectives.

CLASSICAL CRIMINOLOGY: RATIONAL CHOICE THEORY

During the mid-eighteenth century, philosophers began to see crime as an act of free will instead of the result of supernatural forces. The most famous of these reformers were Cesare

Think about Explaining Crime and Deviance: Theoretical Perspectives

1 Think about criminal behaviour. Why do you think people commit crimes?

2 Do you think anyone is capable of committing a crime, or do you think only certain people have criminal tendencies?

3 Do you think that your local media portrays crime or criminals in a particular way? If yes, how would you describe that portrayal?

Beccaria (1764), an Italian aristocrat, and Jeremy Bentham (1838), an English philosopher. Beccaria and Bentham argued that if crime results in some form of pleasure for the criminal, then pain must be used to prevent crime. In addition, they argued that sentences must be proportionate to the seriousness of the crime.

Classical criminology was thus developed on the basis of four basic beliefs:

1. People have free will to choose criminal or lawful solutions, and thus crime is a rational choice.
2. Criminal solutions are seen as more attractive than lawful ones if they require less work for a greater payoff.
3. The fear of punishment can control people's choices.
4. When criminality is met with measured severity, certainty of punishment, and swiftness of justice, a society is better able to control criminal behaviour.

Classical criminological approaches believed that before a person commits an offence, he or she engages in a rational evaluation of the pros and cons of the situation. The person evaluates the risk of apprehension, the seriousness of the potential punishment, and the value of the criminal activity. The decision to commit a crime is thus based on the outcome of this rational weighing of gains and risks. While today this classical approach is widely critiqued (as discussed below), many of its principles remain influential in our current criminal justice system. For example, punishment is still based on the principles of proportionality and deterrence.

BIOLOGICAL PERSPECTIVES

positivism   The application of the scientific method to the social world.

biological determinism   The hypothesis that biological factors completely determine a person's behaviour.

The strongest critique of the classical conception of crime came in the nineteenth century from an emerging school of thought that was later identified as **positivism** (Jackson, 1995). Positivists focused on the individual. They believed that biological factors completely determine a person's behaviour, a view that came to be known as **biological determinism**. They assumed that once we could identify the biological features that distinguish criminals from noncriminals, it would be possible to prevent, control, and eliminate criminal behaviour.

Cesare Lombroso (1835–1909), an Italian psychiatrist, was the major proponent of this new approach. While a physician in the army, Lombroso performed a post-mortem on a notorious criminal and found that this man shared skeletal characteristics most commonly associated with animals. Lombroso concluded that some individuals were born to be criminals as a result of congenital factors that compel them to embark on a life of crime (Jackson, 1995). The criminal man, according to Lombroso, could be distinguished by anomalies in the hair and in the shape of the head, eyes, eyebrows, nose, ears, skin, teeth, and chin. Lombroso argued that a born criminal has a low, sloping forehead; high cheekbones; handle-shaped ears; a large, prominent chin; a hawk-like nose; and fleshy lips (see Figure 5–1).

This association of particular physical characteristics with criminality continued with William Sheldon in the 1940s, who argued that behaviours could be predicted by focusing on body types. According to Sheldon, there are three basic body types, as shown in Figure 5–2. *Mesomorphs* are extroverted, aggressive, and muscular; *ectomorphs* are thin, fret a lot, and are introverted; and endomorphs are laid-back, extroverted, and soft and limp. Sheldon argued that most delinquent youths were most likely to be mesomorphs (Jackson, 1995).

These biological theories fail to consider the influences of environmental factors, and as a result are mostly disregarded by contemporary criminologists. However, some biological criminology is still used today by defence lawyers. For example, some researchers argue that nutritional deficiencies can lead to anti-social behaviour (Schoenthaler, 2000), while others

FIGURE 5-1 **Cesare Lombroso's Criminal Man**

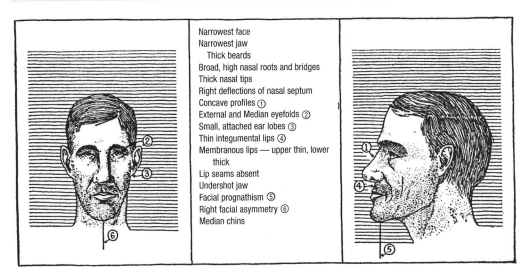

Narrowest face
Narrowest jaw
    Thick beards
Broad, high nasal roots and bridges
Thick nasal tips
Right deflections of nasal septum
Concave profiles ①
External and Median eyefolds ②
Small, attached ear lobes ③
Thin integumental lips ④
Membranous lips — upper thin, lower
    thick
Lip seams absent
Undershot jaw
Facial prognathism ⑤
Right facial asymmetry ⑥
Median chins

Source: Duke University Press, 2006.

argue that diets high in carbohydrates and sugar can influence reasoning processes (Ferguson, 1986; Knox, 1988).

Biosocial theorists are now evaluating the association between violent behaviour and hormone levels. Reiss and Roth (1993) found that female fetuses exposed to elevated androgen levels display high levels of aggression throughout their lives, while male fetuses exposed to steroids that decrease androgens display decreased aggression. Additionally, a link has been proposed between premenstrual syndrome (PMS) and delinquency (Dalton, 1971; Fishbein, 1996). However, debate continues over just such a link, and very few criminal trials have successfully used PMS as a mitigating factor in a woman's defence (Curran & Renzetti, 1994). Fetal alcohol syndrome and attention deficit/hyperactivity disorder have also been associated with delinquent behaviour.

Research by Justin Carré and Cheryl McCormick (2008) of Brock University discovered that hockey players with wider faces tend to be more likely to engage in aggressive behaviour

FIGURE 5-2 **William Sheldon's Body Types**

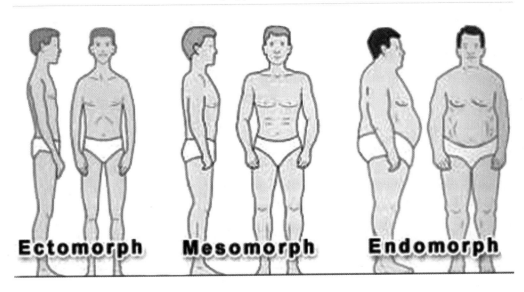

Ectomorph   Mesomorph   Endomorph

To read Carré and McCormick's research article, go to **http://rspb. royalsocietypublishing.org/ content/275/1651/2651. full.pdf+html.**

on the ice. Carré and McCormick argued that the production of higher levels of testosterone during adolescence can result in the development of a wider face. Further, higher levels of testosterone have been linked to aggressive behaviour. To prove their case, they measured the faces of hockey players for the six Canadian NHL teams and correlated their findings with the number of penalty minutes players received for aggressive play such as elbowing and fighting. Facial width was able to predict between 9 percent and 29 percent of the aggressive behaviour (Hall, 2008).

SOCIOLOGICAL APPROACHES TO CRIME

Sociologists argue that crime is not simply the result of genetic disposition, nutritional choices, personal failure, or an individual's free will. Since the beginning of the twentieth century, sociologists have been working to shift the focus of criminology toward the consideration of the environments in which people are located (Messner & Rosenfeld, 1994). After all, explanations of crime at the individual level fail to explain consistent patterns of crime among groups of people. If punishment is handed out uniformly across Canada, why do crime rates differ based on geographic location, ethnicity, gender, and social class? Sociologists emphasize how crime is distributed across different groups. They also emphasize the effect of social change on crime rates. Together, these emphases form the basis of modern criminology (Siegal & McCormick, 2006, p. 190). We now turn to the major theoretical approaches to crime from a sociological perspective.

FUNCTIONALISM   The functionalist approach to criminality has its roots in Émile Durkheim's notion of *anomie*. *Anomie* is a state in which norms are confused, unclear, or not present. Durkheim proposed that anomie can occur during periods of rapid change and uncertainty (he cited the dramatic changes created by the Industrial Revolution as his example). Durkheim felt that such change can create normlessness, which leads to deviant behaviour.

Strain Theory   Following Durkheim's assertion that the structure of society can produce social pressures that result in deviant and/or criminal behaviour, Robert Merton (1938) developed **strain theory**. This theory holds that anomic conditions are produced in society when culturally defined goals cannot be met through socially approved means (Winterdyke, 2006). For instance, a goal in our society is getting a high paying job. Most high paying jobs require a good education. A good education is expensive. Those of low socio-economic status may feel strain due to the fact that legitimate avenues for success (e.g., getting a good education) are less open to them than they are to affluent persons who can afford to go to school.

> strain theory   The assertion that people experience strain when culturally defined goals cannot be met through socially approved means.

Strain theorists argue that most people share similar goals and values, and when legitimate avenues to those goals are not accessible, some will resort to deviant methods (e.g., theft, drug trafficking) to achieve them. Alternatively, they will reject socially accepted goals altogether, substituting more deviant and/or criminal goals. Merton's theory is influential, as it provides an explanation of the existence of high-crime areas and the prevalence of criminal behaviour among the lower class. Merton also asserted, however, that while some people have inadequate means of attaining success, others who do have the means reject societal goals.

Merton (1938) developed a typology to describe five ways in which people react to culturally defined success goals:

1. *Conformity* occurs when individuals both accept social goals and have the means to achieve them.
2. *Innovation* occurs when the goals of society are accepted but the individual is incapable of achieving them through socially approved means. Innovation is most closely associated with criminal behaviour (think of a bank robber or a drug dealer).

3. *Ritualism* occurs when social goals are rejected but the means to those goals are accepted. Ritualists are usually those involved with religious orders; they have abandoned the success goal.

4. *Retreat* involves the rejection of societal goals and the legitimate means of achieving such goals. Retreatists are often found on the fringes of society as they attempt to escape their lack of success by withdrawing (e.g., a dropout, an addict).

5. *Rebellion* involves substituting an alternative set of goals and means for conventional ones. People who want to promote radical change and who call for alternative lifestyles are categorized as rebels (e.g., a political revolutionary or a social activist).

Merton thus suggested that social conditions, not individual personalities, produce crime. Robert Agnew (1985) developed a variation of strain theory. Merton focused on the macro level of strain—societal structures and values. Agnew's strain theory focuses on the micro level, or the individual effect of strain, rather than macro-level (social) effects. For Agnew, criminality is the direct result of negative affective states such as frustration, anger, and any other adverse emotions that come to fruition as a result of negative and destructive social relationships (Siegal & McCormick, 2006).

Illegitimate Opportunity Theory   Richard Cloward and Lloyd Ohlin (1960) sought to extend Merton's strain theory by considering specific environments. While Cloward and Ohlin agreed that the lower classes are more likely to feel goal strain and become frustrated enough to engage in more deviant behaviour, they maintained that while legitimate opportunities for success are more accessible to the middle and upper classes, illegitimate opportunities are not equally accessible to all lower and working-class individuals. They proposed the **illegitimate opportunity theory**, which holds that individuals must be in a deviant "learning environment" that gives them the opportunity to learn and perform the skills and abilities needed to commit crimes (Akers & Sellers, 2004).

> **illegitimate opportunity theory**   The assertion that individuals commit crime as a result of their particular deviant learning environment.

In their study of adolescent boys, Cloward and Ohlin (1960), while recognizing that gangs carry on a variety of illegal activities, found that these gangs develop specialized delinquent sub-cultures according to the illegitimate opportunities in their neighbourhoods (Akers & Sellers, 2004). Cloward and Ohlin (1960) labelled the first type of specialized deviant subculture as "criminal" and characterized them as youth gangs organized around activities that produced income, such as theft, extortion, and fraud. The second type of delinquent subculture, "conflict," consists of violence. These groups earn status by being tough and violent. While the first group is found in lower-class ethnic areas that are organized around adult criminal patterns and values, the "conflict" gangs are found in socially disorganized lower-class neighbourhoods with few illegal opportunities. The third deviant subculture is the "retreatist." Retreatist gang members have given up on both goals and means and are primarily focused on the consumption of drugs and alcohol.

The illegitimate opportunity theory has its critics, however. Goode (2001) argues that Cloward and Ohlin's characterization of young gangs is "largely a fantasy," maintaining that although this "specialization" may have been true in the early 1950s and 1960s, it is not true today. He contends that most present-day gangs, regardless of neighbourhood, are involved in the use and distribution of drugs, theft, and violence.

CONFLICT THEORY   Conflict theorists, as you might expect, primarily view crime as the outcome of class struggle. Their goal, then, is to explain crime within economic and social contexts. In contrast to the functionalist emphasis on the strain that individuals may experience as a result of their socio-economic status, conflict theorists focus on the role government plays in creating a **criminogenic environment** (in which laws that privilege certain groups can be partly blamed for breeding criminal behaviour) and on the relationship of power in controlling and shaping criminal law.

> **criminogenic environment**   An environment that, as a result of laws that privilege certain groups, produces crime or criminality.

Conflict theorists are also interested in the role that bias plays in the criminal justice system. They argue that crimes committed by the wealthy, such as corporate crimes, are punished more leniently than are crimes committed by those in lower classes. One example of this, drawn from the United States, is the disparity in sentencing for possession of crack cocaine versus powder cocaine. Whereas the majority of crack cocaine offenders are black and from the lower classes, powder cocaine is more expensive and thus used primarily by wealthier individuals, the majority of whom are Caucasian (US World News, October 2007). A first-time trafficking offence involving five grams or more of crack cocaine results in a five-year minimum prison sentence; in contrast, the same penalty is meted out for *500* grams or more of powder cocaine.

Conflict theorists argue that criminal law, as a social institution, is merely a tool to protect the interests of the affluent and the powerful. This approach argues that the values and interests of various groups conflict with one another. What is considered normal by one group may be considered deviant by another. The most powerful groups can ensure that their particular views of normality or deviance will be enacted into law, translated into public policy, and protected by the criminal justice system (Ackers & Sellers, 2004). Additionally, when the behaviour of subordinate groups brings them into conflict with the law, they are less able to fight against apprehension, prosecution, conviction, and incarceration.

Yet there is very little empirical research to support this theory (Ackers & Sellers, 2004). While it seems to explain politically motivated crimes, the theory does not fit juvenile delinquency, murder, theft, arson, white-collar crime, and organized crime.

SYMBOLIC INTERACTIONISM   Interactionists who are interested in deviance and crime assert that criminal behaviour is learned in the same way as any other type of behaviour: through interaction with others. Below we consider two symbolic interactionist approaches: differential association theory and labelling theory.

Differential Association Theory   Unconcerned with *why* people become criminals, interactionist theorist Edwin Sutherland sought to explain *how* people come to engage in criminal activity. He maintained that crime, like all other behaviour, is learned behaviour. That is, criminal behaviour is collective in nature and is based on shared experiences and perceptions. Through social interaction with others, people learn the values, norms, motives, rationalizations, and techniques of criminal behaviour. This behaviour is most likely to be learned through intimate personal groups (Sutherland, 1947; Sutherland, Cressey, & Luckenbill, 1992).

Sutherland did not argue that crime is caused by having bad peer groups per se. Rather, in his **differential association theory**, he maintained that the ratio of messages for and against criminal behaviour leads to criminal activity (Hackler, 2006). Our differential associations (the different groups with which we associate) give us contradictory messages about conformity and social deviance. Sutherland argued that in the end, we receive an "excess of definitions" on one side of the spectrum, which leads us either to conform or to deviate. Sutherland contended that differential association is more likely to result in criminal activity when a person has frequent, intense, and long-lasting interaction with others who violate the law.

Differential association remains influential in studying the friendship patterns of delinquent youth. For example, examining data from more than 500 self-administered questionnaires completed by Canadian high school students, Brownfield (2003) explored the relationship between measures of differential association and gang membership. He found that there is a significant relationship between gang membership and normalization of law breaking. Additionally, peer delinquency—that is, having a friendship network that includes individuals who break the law—is a significant and strong correlate of gang membership.

Differential association theory contributes to our understanding of how people come to "normalize" criminal activity; however, it does not adequately consider links between social structures and criminal behaviour. Many critics question why individuals who have far-reaching contact with people who break the law still conform most of the time. Sutherland's conception of differential association is criticized for being vague, complex, and impossible to test. Further, feminists are critical of this theory for its failure to explain why more men than women become criminals (Abbott, Wallace, & Tyler, 2005).

differential association theory   The assertion that the ratio of messages for and against criminal behaviour in one's peer group determines whether one will engage in criminal activity.

Members of conflict gangs earn status through being through and violent.

Labelling Theory Howard S. Becker, one of the early interactionist theorists, first discussed his version of labelling theory in his book *Outsiders: Studies in the Sociology of Deviance* (1963). Influenced by Cooley's looking-glass self, Mead's theories on the internalization of the self, and Edwin Lemert's social constructionism, Becker explains that deviance is based on the reactions of others to an individual's acts; it is this response that leads to the labelling of a person as deviant (Lemert, 1951). Thus, Becker's **labelling theory** holds that deviance is socially produced by making rules whose violation represents deviance and by applying those rules to particular people and labelling them "outsiders." No particular act is inherently deviant until a group with socially powerful statuses or positions label it as such (Becker, 1963).

Labelling theorists focus on understanding what happens to people once they have been singled out and defined as deviant. To be labelled a criminal, a person need commit only a single criminal offence. Once labelled, it is difficult for individuals to shed their labels. The label stigmatizes individuals and leads them to define themselves as deviant; thus, labelling can act as a self-fulfilling prophecy.

Davies and Tanner (2003) test labelling theory by exploring whether contact with school and justice system authorities has long-term and negative effects on individuals' labour market success. Using the National Longitudinal Survey of Youth in Canada, a large and nationally representative sample, they examined whether experiences ranging from school suspension to incarceration from age 15 to 23 can predict occupational status, income, and employment in future years, namely when the youth are aged 29 to 37. Controlling for social background, human capital (meaning properties of individuals: educational background, socio-economic status, and education levels), prior deviant behaviour, family status, and local context, Davies and Tanner's findings support labelling theory. Severe forms of labelling, such as sentencing and incarceration, have the strongest negative effects on career attainment.

Similarly, using data from the Rochester Youth Development Study on the development of drug use and delinquent behaviour among 1000 adolescents and young adults, Bernburg, Kohn, and Rivera (2006) found that juvenile justice intervention positively

labelling theory The assertion that once people have been labelled as deviant, they come to accept the label as part of their identity.

affects subsequent involvement in serious delinquency through association with street gangs and delinquent peers.

Critics argue that labelling theory is unable to specify why some people are labelled and carry that stigma throughout their lives while others remain secret deviants (deviant but not labelled as such). Labelling theory also fails to explain variances in crime rates across time and place.

WHY SHOULD WE CARE?

Identity Theft

Identity theft is a modern crime involving the stealing of a person's identity for financial gain. Perpetrators typically secure credit cards and make purchases in that person's name. Consider the following excerpt:

> I stole a car today. And I used your credit card.
>
> I walked into the car rental shop, and in five minutes drove out with a new minivan. I went shopping, bought a DVD player, a digital camera, some sports equipment, and a computer, which I promptly hawked. On the way to Montreal I stayed in motels, bought meals, and received cash advances, all with your credit card. I sold the car for $5000, which went into a cargo container destined for a foreign country. All told, you're on the hook for $10 000. Your credit rating will be ruined.
>
> This is called identity theft.
>
> The RCMP says that with your name, address, date of birth, and social insurance number, a thief can take over your financial accounts, open new bank accounts, transfer money between accounts, apply for loans or credit cards—all the things that you can do yourself. Except you are no longer yourself . . .
>
> [. . .]
>
> Identity theft is simple . . .
>
> [. . .]
>
> It is unfortunate, but you will spend hundreds of hours and thousands of dollars trying to clear your name, and it will probably never come to trial. The Ontario government is introducing new legislation to deal with what it calls the fastest-growing and most serious consumer crime in North America. We are not yet sure how good that legislation will be. The PhoneBusters organization estimates that the number of identity theft victims grew 8 percent in 2003 over the previous year, and that the losses increased 60 percent. This is definitely the tip of the iceberg. Most victims probably don't realize they've been taken, or they don't report the crime. The three major credit bureaus estimate the problem to be very large, not the 8000 cases reported by PhoneBusters, but at least 20 000 cases a year. This shows a shocking non-report rate of staggering dimensions. All told, identity-theft costs consumers, banks, credit card firms, and business at least $2.5 billion per year.
>
> The cost to society will include money spent by the business community, costs to you for legal assistance from lawyers, costs to the government for judicial and law enforcement, investigation, and prosecution. And we are at an infancy in terms of estimating the costs. . . . There is the cost of the theft

itself, the cost of time to deal with the problem personally, the cost of policing and professional assistance, and most importantly, the cost of the loss of public trust. (McCormick, 2004)

Sociologically, then, how might we investigate identity theft? While the statistics cited above point to the enormous economic cost of such crimes, what are the emotional costs for victims? Which theoretical paradigm might take up such a research query? If you said symbolic interactionists, you would be right. Symbolic interactionists might be interested in interviewing victims of identity theft to explore the meaning such victimization has in their lives and how it has altered their daily existence. And what about larger social effects? If we all fear having our identities stolen, whom do we trust?

FEMINIST THEORY   Traditional sociological theories have been ineffective in describing and analyzing women's deviant and criminal behaviour. Most theories have been written as though they are gender neutral, which completely ignores or overlooks differences in gender. Certain theories have pathologized women's criminal behaviour, arguing that it is a result of psychological problems (Abbot, Wallace, & Tyler, 2005). As a result, traditional sociological theories are largely unable to explain the gendered nature of crime—that is, why men commit the majority of crimes. Additionally, such androcentric (male-centred) theories fail to address the differences in the way women and men are treated within the criminal justice system (Vold, Bernard, & Snipes, 2002). Feminist criminology is concerned with issues of power, distribution of resources, and the position of men and women in society (White & Haines, 2004).

Perceptions of Female Criminals   Historically, women have been considered in need of protection, which has led to the development of laws that regulate women's roles and sexual behaviour (Sangster, 2006). Further, female criminals have been treated differently and more leniently than male offenders. Their criminal behaviour has been deemed to be the result of "illness" and dealt with as such, or it has been overlooked. The **chivalry hypothesis** has been used to explain lower conviction rates for women. This hypothesis presumed that male police officers, prosecutors, and judges have a traditional, chivalrous attitude toward women offenders, and would thus treat women more leniently than they would male offenders (Ackers & Sellers, 2004).

chivalry hypothesis The belief that female offenders are treated more leniently by male law enforcement officials as a result of the latter's traditional, chivalrous attitude toward women.

Feminist theorists propose that the leniency afforded to women was not a consequence of patriarchy but instead a function of *paternalism*. Chesney-Lind (1988) argues that while paternalism may result in more lenient treatment of female offenders, it could and did result in harsher penalties for women in order to maintain their subordinate social status. Chesney-Lind (1989) found that a higher proportion of girls than boys were brought into juvenile court for status offences (offences that permit youth to be arrested for a wider range of behaviours that are in violation of parental authority, such as running away and truancy). Girls were also more likely than boys to be incarcerated for these offences, although less likely to be incarcerated for serious offences. Chesney-Lind and Sheldon (1992) argue that girls were treated more harshly than boys because the criminal justice system sexualized their offences as threats to traditional sex-role expectations.

Other differences in how women and men offenders are perceived are evident in Elizabeth Comack and Salena Brickey's (2007) research, which contends that women who commit violent acts are constructed as "victims," "bad," or "mad." That is, women's violence is seen as falling outside the realm of common sense, and thus in need of explanation. These researchers draw on recent films—for example, those based on Aileen Wuornos, America's first female serial killer (*Monster*), and Karla Homolka, Canada's most notorious female offender (*Karla*)—to illuminate the psychological constructs frequently used to make sense of women who engage in violence.

Female Crime and Victimization   It is important to note that women experience life differently from men and commit different types of crimes, and that most female offenders have been victims of physical and/or sexual abuse themselves (Hackler, 2007; Jackson, 2005; Winterdyke, 2006). Many researchers have found a link between female crime and victimization (see Comack, 2004; Johnson, 1987; Rosenbaum, 1989). For example, women who enter into prostitution are often the victims of abuse and have run away from unstable home environments (Johnson, 1987). The criminal justice system has been built on assumptions about women and has created a system to enforce a version of proper female behaviour (Dodge, 2002). Women are quickly placed in the "sick" role when they do not conform to dominant constructions of femininity (Winterdyke, 2006).

Feminist criminologists characterize crime in terms of gender-*based* acts (the nature of men's violence as it affects both women offenders and women victims) and gender-*related* acts (the ways in which forms of gendered inequality and discrimination are institutionalized) (White & Haines, 2005). Much of the crime against and involving women is seen to be the direct result of social oppression and economic dependency on men or the welfare state.

Feminists view patriarchy (that is, male dominance and male rule) as the underlying condition behind certain crimes, such as sexual assault and domestic violence (McCormick, 1995). Women are more likely to be victims of domestic abuse than men, and are more likely than men to be killed in a domestic assault. In fact, right up until 1983, the Canadian Criminal Code contained a husband-exemption clause stating that a man could not be charged with sexually assaulting his wife.

What do you know about **Explaining Crime and Deviance: Theoretical Perspectives**?

Multiple-choice questions (circle your answer)

1. **Which English philosopher was a proponent of rational choice theory?**
   a. Robert Merton
   b. Émile Durkheim
   c. Richard Cloward
   d. Jeremy Bentham

2. **According to William Sheldon, who was most likely to engage in violent behaviour?**
   a. Ectomorphs
   b. Mesomorphs
   c. Endomorphs
   d. Both mesomorphs and ectomorphs were equally likely to do so.

3. _____ **argue that criminal law, as a social institution, is merely a tool to protect the interests of the affluent and the powerful.**
   a. Conflict theorists
   b. Functionalists

   c. Classical theorists
   d. Symbolic interactionists

4. _____ **is the assertion that once people are considered deviant, they come to accept that description as part of their identity.**
   a. Labelling theory
   b. Strain theory
   c. Differential association theory
   d. Rational choice theory

5. **With what perspective is the labelling theory associated?**
   a. Functionalist
   b. Classical
   c. Conflict
   d. Symbolic interactionist

module 5.3

Crime: Types and Trends

Sociology seeks to understand crime beyond its legal definition. Sociological definitions of crime incorporate how crimes are committed, who commits them, why they commit them, and how society views infractions. They also allow us to consider issues of inequality in the Canadian justice system.

TYPES OF CRIMES

Below, we will examine three types of crime: street crime, white collar crime, and professional crime. As you will see, the type of crime committed and the profile of the criminal differ with each category of crime.

STREET CRIME   When we think about crime, street crime is likely the first type to come to mind because it draws the most attention from the media and the justice system. It is also the form of crime that we fear most.

Street crime involves crime that we would expect to encounter on the street—such as assault, robbery, and auto theft. But street crime is not limited to the street: it can occur in the home, at work, or in any other public or private location. The Canadian Centre for Justice Statistics (CCJS) records incidents of street crime in three broad categories: violent crime, property crime, and other criminal code offences.

Violent crime involves direct violence, threats of violence, and depriving a person of his or her freedom. Offences would include murder, attempted murder, assault (including sexual assault), abduction, confinement, and robbery. According to the CCJS, there were 304 000 violent crime incidents in Canada in 2005 (Gannon, 2005, p. 5).

Property crime is defined as the act or intent of acquiring property without the act or threat of violence. It is far more common than violent crime. According to the CCJS, police reported 1.2 million property crimes in 2005. The most common forms of property crime are theft, auto theft, break and enter, and fraud (Gannon, 2005, p. 8).

Other criminal code offences accounted for 994 000 incidents in Canada in 2005. The most common were mischief (36 percent), counterfeiting (17 percent), and disturbing the peace (12 percent). Also included in this category are moral crimes such as prostitution and drug offences (Gannon, 2005, pp. 10–11).

WHITE COLLAR CRIME   Edwin Sutherland (1940) is credited with bringing our attention to the issue of white collar crime. **White collar crime** refers to illegal activities committed by an individual during or in relation to his or her employment.

White collar crime includes activities such as embezzlement of funds or other forms of employee theft or the acceptance of kickbacks and bribes. The case against Conrad Black provides a good example. Black, in disposing of some of Hollinger Inc. assets, accepted non-competition payments from the owners of the companies he sold. In other words, as part of his deal to the new owners, he agreed not to compete with them in the future. The problem with these payments is that they were not reported to company shareholders or included in company assets. Further, Black was found guilty of using company funds for his own personal benefit, including travel to exotic holiday locations and funding of private parties (CBC, 2007a).

street crime   Crime that we would expect to encounter on the street—such as assault, robbery, and auto theft—but it is not limited to the street.

violent crime   Crime that involves direct violence, threats of violence, and depriving one of their freedom.

property crime   The act or intent of acquiring property without the act or threat of violence.

white collar crime   Crime that involves illegal activities committed by an individual during or in relation to his or her employment.

Some biker gangs are involved in various forms of organized crime.

corporate crime Crime that involves illegal actions by individuals for the benefit of the company with which they are employed.

Corporate crime can also be considered as a white collar crime. **Corporate crime** involves illegal actions by individuals for the benefit of the company with which they are employed. Examples of corporate crime are false advertising; price fixing; copyright, patent, and trademark infringements; and financial fraud.

PROFESSIONAL CRIME   A professional criminal is a person who derives his or her livelihood from criminal activities (e.g., theft, drug trade, prostitution).

organized crime An operation involved in the illegal trade of goods and services.

Organized crime refers to an operation involved in the illegal trade of goods and services. Crimes such as drug trafficking (including the illegal trade of liquor and tobacco), prostitution, trade in stolen goods, and auto theft are good examples. Organizations such as the mafia and biker gangs are examples of organized crime.

CRIME STATISTICS

Official crime statistics in Canada reflect information reported by police services from across the country. Since 1962, these data have been systematically gathered using the Uniform Crime Reporting Survey. The CCJS is responsible for gathering, analyzing, and reporting the data. The data are then used by the criminal justice system to develop appropriate responses to criminal activity (Gannon, 2005).

It is the responsibility of the police to report both the actual criminal incidents as well as those that have come to their attention through police investigation (Gannon, 2005).

It is important to note that data reported by the CCJS reflect, for the most part, street crime. White collar crime is not clearly reflected in the data.

FACTORS INFLUENCING CRIME STATISTICS   As useful as crime statistics are in allowing us to see changes in criminal behaviour over time, they should not be taken at face value. Trends in criminal behaviour can and do reflect actual behaviour, but they can also reflect societal changes. For instance, we can expect certain crime rates to go down as a population ages, and certain crime rates to go up during an economic recession (Gannon, 2005).

The introduction of new laws, changes to old laws, or changes in the enforcement of particular laws also affect trends. For example, the crimes rates for prostitution and drug offences tend to reflect the level of police enforcement more than changes in actual behaviour (Gannon, 2005).

Another important factor influencing crime statistics is the method of data collection by police services across the country. Not all police services collect data in the same way. Some collect data on calls made by victims to police service call centres. Others collect data on reports made by victims who have come in to the station. Thus, we must consider whether the ease of reporting a crime affects reported crime rates in a particular area (Gannon, 2005).

Finally, changes in public opinion regarding a crime and its victims can alter both the level of law enforcement and the willingness of victims to report a crime (Gannon, 2005). For example, if public opinion is decidedly against spousal abuse, law enforcement policies on the matter may become stronger. As well, victims of spousal abuse may be more willing to come forward knowing that they are supported by the public.

CRIME TRENDS—WHO COMMITS CRIME?   Can we develop a profile of a criminal? Sociologists are particularly interested in whether social patterns exist that give us insight into criminal behaviour. Based on information collected by the CCJS, the following factors should be considered: age, gender, ethnicity, social class, and region.

Age   According to the CCJS, age is a significant indicator of one's risk to offend. Findings from the Uniform Crime Reporting Survey in 2003 showed high rates of crime for people between the ages of 15 to 24. That group, representing 14 percent of the total population of Canada, accounted for 45 percent of those accused of property crimes and 32 percent of those accused of violent crimes. Within that group, 15 to 18 year olds had the highest rate of crimes per 100 000 population of any age group in the country. Persons aged 25 to 34, again representing 14 percent of the total population, accounted for 18 percent of property offences and 22 percent of violent offences (Gannon et al., 2005). Figure 5–3 shows the correlation between age and crime rates in Canada. From age 35 on, we see a steady decline in the crime rate. In particular, we see the greatest shift in the decline of property crimes with the increasing age of each cohort (Gannon et al., 2005).

FIGURE 5–3 Rate of Property and Violent Crime Highest among Young People, 2003

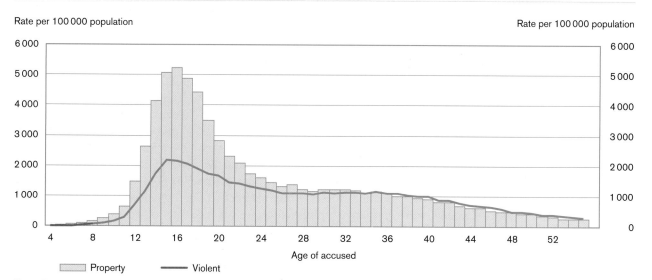

Note: Data are based on a non-representative sample of 122 police services in 9 provinces and represent 61 percent of the national volume reported actual (substantiated) Criminal Code incidents.

Source: Statistics Canada. (2003). Canadian Centre for Justice Statistics, Incident-based Uniform Crime Reporting Survey. Retrieved July 13, 2009, from http://www.statcan.gc.ca/pub/85-227-x/85-227-x2002000-eng.pdf.

Crime rates in Canada have been in decline since the 1990s. Some sociologists reason that this trend can be accounted for by the increasing proportion of older people in Canada (Gannon et al., 2005). As Canada ages, crime rates should drop.

Gender   Gender is also a strong indicator of one's likelihood to offend. In 2003, 81 percent of persons charged by police were males. This number reflects a historical pattern of behaviour (Gannon et al., 2005).

Coupled with age, young males were two times more likely to commit violent crimes and three times more likely to commit property offences than young females (Gannon et al., 2005). Compared with all adults, young males committed twice as many violent crimes and four times as many property crimes in 2003 (Gannon, et al., 2005). Young males are also more likely to be on the receiving end of non-spousal violent crimes (Gannon et al., 2005).

Although females commit far fewer crimes than men, the Elizabeth Fry Society reports that, worldwide, women constitute the fastest-growing prison population and that young women represent a greater proportion of youth sentenced to custodial care than do young males (CAEFS, 2004). The CCJS has not released a gender-specific report since 1990, a fact that has made criminologists question whether a continual lack of interest in female offenders reflects an ideological bias in Canada (Winterdyke, 2006). Of the information gathered by CCJS, the most common forms of crime among women include theft of property, fraud, common assault, and bail violations. Violent crime is not as common. However, trends show that the rate of violent crime among women is on the increase. In 2005, 1 in 5 violent offences was committed by women. In 1986, the ratio was 1 to 9 (Statistics Canada, 2008k).

Compared with males, females were more likely to receive noncustodial care, even when they committed the same crimes. This sentencing trend may reflect the fact that women are less likely than men to be charged with multiple offences and that they are less likely to re-offend (Statistics Canada, 2008k). Interestingly, according to the Elizabeth Fry Society, federally sentenced women are subject to more disadvantaged treatment and more restrictive conditions of confinement than are men (CAEFS, 2008).

Ethnicity   Although statistics on race and crime are not normally released in Canada, the information that is available suggests that certain racial minorities are overrepresented in the correctional system (Wortley, 1999). As previously noted in the Canadian Society in Focus box, data reveal that while Aboriginal people represent approximately 4 percent of the population, they account for 14 percent of federal prison inmates. Similarly, while blacks account for 2 percent of the population, they represent 6 percent of those in federal correctional institutions (Wortley, 1999). There is much debate, however, as to whether this overrepresentation is a result of discrimination in the criminal justice system or of social conditions (from poverty to powerlessness) that put particular groups at greater risk (Fleras, 2006).

When age is coupled with ethnicity, the numbers are more dramatic, especially for Aboriginal youth. According to Canada's Department of Justice, Aboriginal youth across Canada are incarcerated at a rate eight times higher than that of non-Aboriginal youth (Latimer & Foss, 2004). In Saskatchewan, Aboriginal youth were 30 times more likely to be incarcerated than non-Aboriginal youth; in the Yukon, Aboriginal youth were 18 times more likely to be incarcerated than non-Aboriginal youth (Latimer & Foss, 2004).

Researchers point out that these results may reflect Aboriginal peoples' relatively low socio-economic status and lack of education, as well as high rates of victimization, substance abuse, and gang participation (LaPrairie, 1990, 2002; Latimer & Foss, 2004). Researchers also argue that this overrepresentation is in part due to demographics (Latimer & Foss, 2005): because Canada's Aboriginal population is much younger than the non-Aboriginal population, there would likely be a higher percentage of Aboriginal people in prison.

Racism and racial profiling also account for a portion of these trends. This finding was noted in the Commission on Systemic Racism in the Ontario Criminal Justice System in 1995. However, a study by Latimer and Foss (2005) found no evidence that Aboriginal youth were being sentenced to custodial care more than non-Aboriginal youth under the Young Offenders Act. Yet, they did note in their findings that Aboriginal youth were more likely to receive a longer sentence.

Social Class   The link between social class and crime has been the focus of much research and debate among sociologists. However, research has not established a clear correlation between the two areas. Most data on crime are based on street crimes and not white collar crimes. Therefore, data often have a class bias, with lower income classes more likely to be connected to street crime.

However, research does show a correlation between inflation and "financially motivated crimes" such as robbery, motor vehicle theft, and break-and-enter incidents. When inflation increases, making life financially more difficult for the average Canadian, so too do financially motivated crimes (Gannon et al., 2005).

Also, a correlation exists between unemployment and crime. Research shows that young, single, and unemployed people are more likely to commit crime—property crimes, in particular. The unemployment rate for the most at-risk group to offend—males 15 to 24—was double the national average in 2004 (Gannon et al., 2005).

A person's level of education is also an important contributing factor in their risk to offend. According to Gannon et al. (2005, p. 166), the higher a person's education, the greater their employment opportunities and earning potential. The data show that the more likely a person is to be employed and engaged in legitimate activities within society, the lower their risk to offend (Gannon et al., 2005).

Region   Crime rates vary from one province to another and from rural to urban communities. In general, western provinces report higher crime rates. Manitoba, Saskatchewan, Alberta, and British Columbia all reported higher crime rates than any of the eastern provinces. Saskatchewan followed by Manitoba had the highest crime rates in 2007 (Statistics Canada, 2008).

Although crime rates in big cities fell in 2007 (Statistics Canada, 2008), victimization data show that crime rates are higher in cities than in rural Canada (Gannon et al., 2005). The number of criminal incidents is higher overall in large Canadian cities, but western cities have higher crime rates per capita than do eastern cities; for example, Regina, Winnipeg, Edmonton, and Vancouver have higher crime rates than do Montreal and Toronto. Surprisingly, of all the 27 metropolitan areas measured in Canada, Toronto had the second-lowest overall crime rate (Statistics Canada, 2008).

INDIVIDUAL DETERMINANTS OF CRIME   Along with the social factors discussed above, exposure to certain direct experiences can also contribute to a person's risk to offend. Research shows that individuals subjected to violence and/or physical and sexual abuse as children are more likely to abuse or be violent as adults. A person's use and abuse of drugs and alcohol are also linked to higher rates of criminal behaviour (Gannon et al., 2005).

DEALING WITH CRIME

How do we deal with crime and criminals? In Canada, we have developed an elaborate system to identify, catch, prosecute, and punish criminal behaviour. Yet we know that this system is flawed. Not all crimes committed come to the attention of the justice system. Moreover, the crimes that do may or may not result in punishment for the criminal. Finally, sociologists have questioned whether the punishment received by those convicted of crimes is truly effective in reducing crime.

THE FUNNEL EFFECT   The **funnel effect** is a description of the stages followed from the point at which a crime is committed to the point at which a person is institutionalized. There are ten stages in the process (see Figure 5–4). At any of these stages, a crime or criminal can exit the process. Thus, only a small percentage of criminal behaviour results in jail time.

The clearance rate—the point at which at least one person is charged by police—is much higher for violent crimes (approximately 70 percent) than it is for property crimes (approximately

To view a number of current publications by the Canadian Centre for Justice Statistics, go to **www.statcan.gc.ca/bsolc/ olc-cel/olc-cel?catno= 85F0033MWE&lang=eng.**

funnel effect   A description of the stages followed from the point at which a crime is committed to the point at which a person is institutionalized.

FIGURE 5–4 **The Funnel Effect**

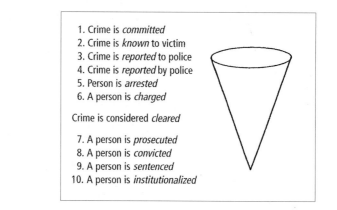

Source: Lindsey, L.L., Beach, S., & Ravelli, B. (2009). *Core concepts in sociology: Second Canadian edition.* (2nd. ed.). Toronto: Pearson Education Canada, p. 235.

20 percent) (Statistics Canada, 2003b). These numbers suggest that police put more energy and effort in solving violent crimes than they do property crimes. It should be noted that although police have laid charges, there is no guarantee that the criminal will be punished. The clearance rate for crimes is much higher than the conviction rate and institutionalization.

THE POLICE   As of 2008, there were 65 000 active police officers across Canada representing federal, provincial, municipal, and Aboriginal governments (Canadian Centre for Justice Statistics, 2008). This figure represents an approximate ratio of 1 police officer for every 517 citizens. The ratio of police officers to citizens has been on the decline since 1991 (Ramcharan et al., 2001, p. 134).

The public sees the police as the front line in crime control. However, the police also provide a number of other services, such as responding to emergencies, assisting victims of accidents and crimes, maintaining peace and order, providing assistance in the prosecution of offenders, and providing education and outreach to the community on issues such as drug abuse and bullying (Li, 2008). In fact, less than 25 percent of an officer's time is spent on crime control (Griffiths & Jones, 1994).

The fact that there are fewer police officers with an expanded role has led some to argue that the workload of police officers has become onerous (Ramcharan et al., 2001, p. 135). It may be surprising to learn that in a big city such as Toronto, only 15 percent of police officers are on patrol between the peak hours of 4 p.m. and 12 p.m. This number drops over-night to 3.2 percent. Given that most crimes occur between 6 p.m. and 2 a.m. (Ramcharan et al., 2001), we must question the effectiveness of the police in crime prevention.

Community policing has been one response to the challenges of crime prevention (Ramcharan et al., 2001; Ramcharan & Ramcharan, 2005). Community policing can be defined as "a return to the principle that policing is accomplished by the community as a whole, rather than one specific agency of government" (Ramcharan et al., 2001, p. 138). This strategy views police officers and citizens as jointly responsible for reducing crime and improving the quality of life in their communities. As police departments modernized over the past few decades, police officers became more detached from the communities they serve. Community policing would see police officers interact more with their communities and return to a role as keepers of the peace (Ramcharan et al., 2001, p. 137).

THE COURTS   Courts are an integral part of the Canadian criminal justice system and the "hallmark" of our democracy (Ramcharan et al., 2001, p. 142). It is through the courts that we decide the innocence or guilt of a person, specify punishment, and maintain social control and order. Further, it is the responsibility of the courts to protect the rights of the accused and in turn monitor other branches of the justice system, such as the police and the prosecution.

The decision to take an accused to trial only occurs if there is a reasonable chance of conviction and that going to trial is in the public interest (Ramcharan et al., 2001, p. 145). This decision is made first by the police, then by the Crown attorney who is responsible for prosecution, and finally by the Justice of the Peace. If the Justice of the Peace agrees to the charges, then a process is put in place to assure that the accused will appear in court.

In Canada, the court process is adversarial, meaning that the prosecution and the defence are at odds. The prosecution attempts to prove guilt while the defence attempts to prove innocence. As such, proceedings in a criminal case can be time consuming and costly. Currently there is a backlog of cases in Canada. To eliminate the backlog, **summary conviction offences** (less serious types of crimes) are dispatched quickly. It is estimated that 75 percent of cases are dealt with through a few short court appearances and that decisions are typically based on a plea bargain. A **plea bargain** is a deal made between the prosecutor and the defence in which the accused agrees to a lesser charge in return for a lighter sentence (Ramcharan et al., 2001, pp. 147–148).

There is concern that justice is circumvented through plea bargaining and the long length of trials that go through the formal process. Yet, to date, no alternatives have been "advocated which can improve upon the peer-based, fact-finding process of our judicial system" (Ramcharan, 2001, p. 157).

summary conviction offences Less serious types of crimes.

plea bargain A deal made between the prosecutor and the defence in which the accused agrees to a lesser charge in return for a lighter sentence

THE PURPOSES OF PUNISHMENT   Punishment has four purposes: retribution, deterrence, rehabilitation, and incapacitation. Sociologists have debated the merits of each in effectively reducing crime (Lindsey, Beach, & Ravelli, 2009, p. 228).

Retribution   The purpose of **retribution** is to make offenders pay for their crimes. The underlying idea is that offenders have made others suffer, so they too should suffer. As a society, we have softened our position on retribution as an effective means of controlling crime. For example, we no longer support capital punishment as a reasonable form of retribution. However, calls for tougher retributive justice tend to emerge when society considers that crime is out of control. For example, in their 2008 election platform the federal Conservative Party proposed longer sentences for violent re-offenders and jail time rather than house arrest for those that commit serious or violent crimes (Conservative Party of Canada, 2008).

retribution Punishment whose purpose is to make an offender pay for his or her crime.

Deterrence   Punishment can also act as a deterrent. If effective, **deterrence** may dissuade an offender from offending again (*specific deterrence*). Further, punishment for a crime can prove to be a lesson to others who have yet to commit a crime (*general deterrence*). The idea of deterrence is rooted in classical theory. It assumes that people who commit crimes are rational and have carefully considered the consequences of their actions (Lindsey, Beach, & Ravelli, 2009, p. 228).

deterrence Punishment whose purpose is to dissuade an offender from offending again or dissuade others who have yet to commit a crime.

Rehabilitation   Another purpose of punishment is **rehabilitation**. If we believe that people commit crimes because of one or a combination of biological, psychological, or social forces, then it stands to reason that we may be able to help them reintegrate into society as productive citizens. Education, job training, life skills training, and addiction counselling are a few of the activities offered to inmates in Canada's correctional institutions. The assumption is that people *can* be rehabilitated. The sad reality is that two-thirds of inmates re-offend within three years of their release from a correctional facility (Lindsey, Beach, & Ravelli, 2009, p. 229).

rehabilitation Punishment whose purpose is to help an offender reintegrate into society as a productive citizen.

Incapacitation   Some people are believed to be a danger to society with no hope for reform or rehabilitation. As such, they are removed from society so that they are unable to commit further offences. In Canada, a person who is identified by the courts as a dangerous offender is locked away for an indeterminate length of time. Serial killer Paul Bernardo is an example of a dangerous offender who has been punished through **incapacitation**.

incapacitation Punishment whose purpose is the removal of an offender from society so that he or she is unable to commit further offences.

What do you know about **Crime: Types and Trends**?

Multiple-choice questions (circle your answer)

1. **Crimes that are committed during or as a result of one's employment are called**
   a. Street crime
   b. White collar crime
   c. Work crime
   d. Organized crime

2. **_____ crime refers to groups involved in the illegal trade of goods and services.**
   a. Organized
   b. Corporate
   c. White collar
   d. Political

3. **Who is most likely to commit street crimes in Canada?**
   a. Women
   b. Men

   c. White people
   d. Torontonians

4. **Which ethnic group is most overrepresented in federal correctional institutions in Canada?**
   a. Blacks
   b. Aboriginals
   c. Whites
   d. Asians

5. **Making offenders pay for their crimes is called**
   a. Retribution
   b. Rehabilitation
   c. Deterrence
   d. Incapacitation

Answers: b, a, b, b, a

module 5.4

Crime, Risk, and Regulation

Think about Crime, Risk, and Regulation

1 Think about crime rates and risk. Do you think crime rates are on the rise? If yes, why do you think so? In what ways do you feel vulnerable to crimes? What crimes do you fear?

2 As a woman, do you think about where you are willing to go at night, and how you are willing to get there? As a man, do you think about this? Does fear of victimization affect your ability to move freely in the world?

So far, we have discussed how criminality and the law have been theorized by criminologists. We now consider the current criminal climate in Canada. Where does our knowledge of crime come from? Is crime really as pervasive as we assume it to be? Canada, like most developed countries, has an elaborate system to ensure that we live in a safe society. In addition to the criminal justice system, discursive practices are used to control the population and prevent deviant and/or criminal behaviour. This section will discuss how victims of crime have been constructed through the media and other agents of socialization as well as how certain groups or individuals are morally regulated.

"AT RISK" FOR CRIME?

Media are governed by a code of conduct that requires them to report the news accurately. Many people assume that this requirement means that media constitute reliable sources of information (Winterdyke, 2006). This affects our knowledge of crime, since much of what we know about it comes from media portrayals, whether through the Internet, TV, radio, newspapers, or magazines.

FIGURE 5–5 Crime Rates, 1962—2006

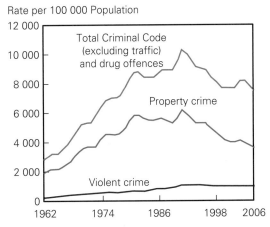

Source: Statistics Canada, *The Daily,* July 2007, http://www.statcan.ca/Daily/English/070718/d070718b.htm.

Yet the media actively construct our sense of who is "at risk" of victimization, as well as who is at risk of becoming a criminal. People consistently rely on media outlets for crime statistics, making them influential in people's perceptions of potential victimization. Media are able to create **moral panic**—the reaction of a group based on the false or exaggerated perception that some group or behaviour threatens the well-being of society—when they sensationalize images of crime (White & Haines, 2006). The most common types of crime, such as property crimes, receive little to no media attention, whereas violent crimes, which are relatively uncommon, receive greater coverage.

Indeed, media convey horrific images and stories that instill fear for our own safety and our children's safety. If you talk about crime and safety with your Canadian-born parents or grandparents, you will surely hear a version of the same story: "It wasn't like this in the old days; it was safe to keep your doors unlocked and you could let your kids play outside without worrying someone was going to kidnap or hurt them." Yet despite the widespread belief that crime is "out of control," the Canadian Centre for Justice Statistics (2006) reports that the national crime rate, defined as the total number of Criminal Code incidents (excluding traffic and drug offences) divided by the population, dropped by 3 percent in 2006.

In fact, since 1991, the crime rate has decreased nearly 30 percent, putting the 2006 crime rate at its lowest level in over 25 years (see Figure 5–5). The drop in 2006 was led by declines in nonviolent crimes. While the overall violent crime rate remained stable in 2006, the homicide rate dropped 10 percent, after increases in the two previous years (Canadian Centre for Justice Statistics, 2006). The crime rates are highest in western Canada and lowest in central Canada (see Figure 5–6). We should note that these statistics are based on reported crimes entered into the Uniform Crime Reporting Survey. As such, they don't account for the "dark figure of crime"—those criminal offences that are never reported to the police.

WOMEN'S FEAR OF CRIME   Government-sponsored national victimization studies in several countries consistently demonstrate that fear of violent crimes is significantly higher than the chances of actually being violently victimized, especially among women (Keane, 1998; Smith, 1988). Fear of crime is measured by one's generalized feeling of vulnerability or a perception of safety in one's neighbourhood, as well as a more specific fear of actually becoming a victim (Keane, 1998). In 2004, Statistics Canada conducted its fourth General Social Survey (GSS) on victimization, asking Canadians aged 15 years and older about their

moral panic A collective reaction based on the false or exaggerated perception that some group or behaviour threatens the well-being of society.

FIGURE 5-6 Crime Rates by Province, 2006

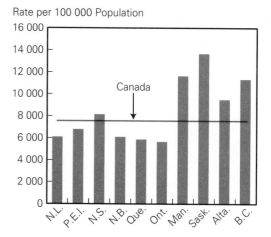

Source: Statistics Canada, *The Daily,* July 2007, http://www.statcan.ca/Daily/English/070718/d070718b.htm.

experiences as victims of crime, about their fear and perceptions of crime, and about the criminal justice system. Not surprisingly, feelings of anxiety about being victimized while waiting for or taking public transportation at night were more prevalent among women than men. Women also expressed higher levels of fear compared with men when home alone at night (Statistics Canada, 2004). Men are more likely than women to be the victims of violent crime perpetrated by strangers. Women are more likely to be victimized by the intimate men in their lives than they are by the "stranger in the bushes."

Public Safety Canada reports that people's fear of criminal victimization remains relatively steady. On average, 31 percent of adult Canadians report feeling fearful of being victimized. However, women are more likely than men to report being fearful (41 percent versus 12 percent) (Roberts, 2001). Fear of crime also varies with geographical location, with the lowest levels of fear in the Atlantic provinces (14 percent) and the highest in British Columbia (39 percent) (Roberts, 2001).

Women's increased fear of victimization is known as the **fear-gender paradox** (Keane, 1998). Although men are at a much higher risk of victimization than women, women continually report higher levels of fear. Non-whites, the elderly, and those of low socio-economic status also report high rates of victimization fear (Keane, 1998).

fear-gender paradox
The phenomenon whereby women experience higher rates of fear of being victimized even though men are more likely to be victims of crime.

There is an increased fear of victimization of crime among women than men—despite the statistical reality that men are more often victims of crime than women.

Many scholars have documented the processes that underlie the popular conceptions of who is at risk. Feminist scholars in particular have challenged the idea that risk is a neutral category (Chan & Rigakos, 2002). Gendered notions about which social groups have legitimate fears of crime and which groups are responsible for these crimes are perpetuated through dominant images of criminals as poor racialized men and victims as white middle-class women (Chan & Rigakos, 2002).

There are significant consequences of women's fear of crime (Stanko, 1997). Several policies have been enacted in the name of addressing women's safety. For example, consider the legislative debates that took place in relation to the Safe Streets Act in 2000. Gender was a salient feature of those debates, as women's fears of victimization, coupled with concerns for women's safety, were deployed as part of a law-and-order agenda aimed at addressing "visible poverty in urban spaces"—that is, "squeegee kids" in Toronto (Glasbeek, 2006a, p. 55). Analyzing media articles and legislative debates, Glasbeek (2006a, p. 75) demonstrates the ways in which fear for women's safety was used to justify the enactment of a "coercive and punitive piece of legislation that aimed to exclude street people from the public."

Many feminists contend that these representations are used to increase women's fear of public spaces and increase their dependency on "protective" men (Chan & Riagakos, 2002; Glasbeek, 2006a). Further, by focusing on risk, responsibility shifts from the state protecting the citizenry to individuals being responsible for avoiding risk and risky situations. Whether fear stems from actual crime or from perceptions of risk, individuals are increasingly encouraged by the state to avoid risk-taking behaviours and to be proactive in crime prevention (Garland, 1996). The threat of becoming a victim encourages women especially to engage in "safe-keeping" acts that include dressing in "appropriate" ways and avoiding certain public spaces (Campbell, 2005). Such a focus on risk aversion "overemphasizes women's risks in the public sphere, and dangerously underestimates women's risks in the private sphere" (Glasbeek, 2006a, p. 61).

Contemporary risk discourses also act as a form of moral regulation (Glasbeek, 2006a; Hunt, 2003). "Risk is not just a condition to be encountered, avoided or managed but is itself, also, productive of moralized subjectivities—that is, the 'good' citizen who avoids 'risky' behaviours" (Glasbeek, 2006a, p. 60). It is to moral regulation that we now turn.

MORAL REGULATION

Within the field of criminology, certain acts are often referred to as **public order crimes**, or **victimless crimes**. These acts are considered crimes on the basis of moral principles, and include such things as prostitution, gambling, pornography, and substance abuse. The primary goal of the law is to protect society by legislating behaviours that are considered immoral and socially harmful; yet in relation to these crimes, there is much debate about who gets to decide what is morally acceptable.

The concept of **moral regulation** is used to describe how some behaviours become constituted as immoral and are thereby regulated (Glasbeek, 2006b). Moral regulation scholars ask why particular groups of people and their behaviours warrant public intervention and action (Glasbeek, 2006b). Let's begin with a look back.

public order crimes (victimless crimes) Crimes such as prostitution, gambling, and pornography that are believed to run contrary to moral principles.

moral regulation The constitution of certain behaviours as immoral and thereby requiring public intervention.

THE SOCIAL PURITY MOVEMENT Beginning in the late nineteenth century, the social purity movement, along with temperance and Sunday observation, helped form a coalition for the moral regeneration of the state, civil society, families, and the individual (Valverde, 2006). This movement included churchgoers, educators, doctors, and social workers who engaged in a campaign to "raise the moral tone" of Canadian society (p. 119). Sexual morality was the movement's main target, although social purists also focused on poverty, crime, and vices such as alcohol and drugs. The criminal, the fallen, and the destitute were increasingly seen as needing treatment, according to a view whereby an "individual without character . . . was a miniature mob, disorganized, immoral and unhealthy, as well as an inefficient member of the collectivity" (p. 128). Instead of solely supplying charity to those who had fallen, the social purity movement focused on training the poor "in habits of thrift, punctuality and hygiene"; lobbied for prohibition of alcohol; and developed pamphlets, books, and lectures regarding the importance of sexual morality (p. 121). Women became rescuers and reformers, or they became the objects of this philanthropic concern.

WELFARE RECIPIENTS   One of the most poignant examples of moral regulatory practices is the welfare recipient. While attempting to meet the economic needs of single parents, for example, the regulations of social assistance historically attempted to also meet the moral needs of society. In *"No Car, No Radio, No Liquor Permit": The Moral Regulation of Single Mothers in Ontario, 1920–1997*, Margaret Little (1998) demonstrates how social assistance policies promote traditional notions of masculinity, femininity, and morality. Through continued surveillance, single mothers' lives are scrutinized to ensure their deservedness (both morally and economically) of financial aid.

In the early years of social assistance, eligibility was based on the untimely death of a woman's husband. However, over time, unwed and deserted mothers became eligible for assistance. The forms of moral regulation also shifted with time. In the early years, caseworkers made surprise home visits to ensure that the women's houses and children were clean and free of alcohol (Little, 1998; Valverde, 2006). Over time, though, the moral terrain shifted to questions of sexuality, fraud, and employment (Little, 1998).

The 1990s witnessed a distinct shift whereby poverty, welfare, and crime became linked. In 1995 the Canadian Assistance Plan was replaced with the Canadian Health and Social Transfer program. Many researchers document the ways in which rhetoric constructing the welfare recipient as "lazy" and "criminal" was used to implement coercive policies (Chunn & Gavigan, 2006; Evans & Swift, 2000; Little, 2003; Mosher, 2000; Swift & Brimingham, 2000). The state, primarily concerned with "welfare cheats," aimed attacks at the poor, women, and/or racialized minorities. In Ontario, there were deep funding cuts to welfare benefits, a broader definition of spouse, restructuring of legislation producing a particular focus on "work," mandatory drug testing, anonymous snitch lines, and zero tolerance for anyone convicted of welfare fraud—resulting in permanent ineligibility (Little & Morrison, 2001; Morrison, 1998). Welfare fraud became welfare *as* fraud (Chunn & Gavigan, 2006, p. 329).

With slashed government budgets in the 1990s, single mothers on welfare experienced increased state scrutiny of their lives (Little, 1998). While the state maintains that such scrutiny is necessary for financial reasons, the scrutiny nonetheless has moral implications. The state is reluctant to financially support single mothers when fathers could do so. As a result, numerous strategies exist to track down or identify potential breadwinning men. A questionnaire, introduced in 1992, must be completed by all single mothers before determining eligibility for social assistance. While the intent of the questionnaire is not explicitly stated, its purpose is to determine whether the prospective welfare recipient is involved in a sexual relationship with anyone who currently, or occasionally, resides with her (Little, 2001). Caseworkers have been known to check for tire tracks in the snow, examine notes on fridges, search bathrooms for shaving cream and razors, and stake out parking lots at night in an effort to confirm that a man is living in the home (Little, 2001). This scrutiny of single mothers' lives suggests that if they are collecting social assistance, then they are not permitted to enjoy a sexual relationship with a man, unless that man is going to assume a breadwinning role.

Moral investigation of single mothers on welfare has intensified in the past decade. This scrutiny is carried out not only by those who administer welfare but also by community members who are encouraged as "paid workers" (and, hence, responsible citizens) to report all suspected cases of welfare "fraud" (Little & Morrison, 2001). Such constant fear of scrutiny leading to a potential loss of assistance results in continual "self-censorship" of women's activities (Chunn & Gavigan, 2006, p. 345). Moral scrutiny is particularly extensive in low-income housing projects and in small communities (Little, 2006). Social assistance policies continue to be intrusive and moralistic, based on discretionary criteria that allow social workers to make judgments about who is "deserving" and "undeserving" (Little, 2006). "These regulations and the relationship between the regulator and the regulated help to reinforce dominant race, class, and gender interests in society at large" (Little, 2006, p. 230).

SEX AND SEXUAL RELATIONSHIPS   Another pervasive area of moral regulation in our society is sex and sexual relationships. Prostitution and homosexuality are two areas in which sexual morality and crime are linked. While we live in a society where sexual norms have changed quite drastically since the 1950s, sexual behaviour between consenting adults is still criminalized at times, as in the case of prostitution.

Focusing on the moral regulation of homosexuals through Canada's anti-homosexual national security campaign in the 1950s and 1960s, Gary Kinsman (2004) argues that homosexuals were constructed as having "immoral," "risky," and "deviant" sexualities. During this period, thousands of homosexuals and suspected homosexuals lost their jobs in the public service and military as a result of their sexuality. Sexual deviance was seen as a threat to the family and thus a threat to national security. As a result, social policing of sexuality focused on the regulation of sexualities through the Criminal Code. Since homosexuality was viewed as immoral, those who partook in homosexual acts were constructed as "untrustworthy" and as "security risks." This rhetoric was then used to legally eliminate the jobs of any known or suspected homosexuals.

Kinsman (2004) argues that the construction of homosexuality as a moral and political problem has been made possible by the construction of homosexuals as different, other, and abnormal. Drawing on the work of Michel Foucault, Kinsman asserts that a key strategy of disciplinary power is normalization. Foucault defined *normalization* as a social process whereby some practices and ways of being are marked as "normal" while others are marked as "abnormal." These idealized norms of conduct are reinforced by truth claims of doctors, psychiatrists, and other "experts." Based on these norms of behaviour, people are either rewarded or punished for conforming to or deviating from the ideal. In North American society, heterosexuality is normalized.

CRIME VICTIMS   Moral regulation also pervades our perceptions of crime victims. Entrenched notions of proper or respectable femininity play into our understandings of who is a "worthy" victim, deserving sympathy. At the beginning of this chapter, we cited the cases of Robert Pickton and Paul Bernardo. When Bernardo's victims, Kristen French and Leslie Mahaffy, went missing, there were search parties, intensive police activity, national media attention, and appeals for the safe return of these two young white girls. School photographs of the two girls accompanied media coverage. In contrast to this sense of urgency, the missing women from Vancouver's downtown Eastside remained faceless and silent, some for as long as two decades. One must question how it is possible that 61 women were missing from one geographic location, yet the story received no media coverage for a long time. Why are there such differences in the levels of attention given to these victims?

Focusing on five years (2001 to 2006) of newspaper coverage of the missing Vancouver women, Jiwani and Young (2006) demonstrate how hegemonic discourses of Aboriginality, drug addiction, and prostitution combined with tropes of geographic morality (that is, particular areas associated with degeneracy) to frame the media coverage of the case. While some stories appeared sympathetic, most underscored stereotypical portrayals of drug-addicted Aboriginal prostitutes. Police described the women as itinerant workers, constantly moving from one location to the next, thus making them responsible for their own disappearances or murders (Jiwani & Young, 2006). When the missing women were actually given media attention, police mug shots were used, thus reinforcing the women's association with criminality.

Additionally, when news first broke about the arrest of Paul Bernardo and followed with information about Karla Homolka's role in the heinous crimes, the couple was portrayed as "Ken and Barbie," the seemingly perfect pairing that appeared to neatly fit dominant constructions of masculinity and femininity. In contrast, Robert Pickton's arrest brought forward a photograph of him with "wild, stringy hair and a blank stare" (Jiwani & Young, 2006, p. 905). It suggested an "aberrant masculinity," making it easy for the public to believe that "only deviant males commit such heinous sexual acts" (p. 905). In this way Pickton's crimes

To learn more about the Bernardo and Homolka case, go to **www.cbc.ca/news/background/bernardo/**.

To learn more about Robert Pickton, go to **www.cbc.ca/news/background/pickton/**.

were viewed as the acts of a "sick" or "pathological" individual rather than seen within a larger framework of the prevalence of men's violence against women (p. 911).

The portrayals of some women as unfortunate victims garnering much sympathy and other women as somehow culpable in their own victimization, alongside depictions of female offenders as "pathological," reinforce dominant hegemonic values. In light of these glaring discrepancies, Jiwani and Young (2006, p. 912) call for the recognition that women are first and foremost "human beings whose material conditions are determined by interlocking legacies of colonialism and a racialized and sexualized economy of representations that privileges some women over others."

What do you know about **Crime, Risk, and Regulation**?

Multiple-choice questions (circle your answer)

1. **Which statement is false?**
   a. Since 1991, the crime rate has increased by 30 percent.
   b. Since 1991, the crime rate has decreased by 30 percent.
   c. Overall, the violent crime rate remained stable.
   d. The homicide rate dropped by 10 percent.

2. **A Public Safety Canada report showed that _____ of women fear criminal victimization.**
   a. 12 percent.
   b. 21 percent.
   c. 41 percent.
   d. 82 percent.

3. **The phenomenon whereby women experience higher rates of being victimized even though men are more likely to be victims of crime is called**
   a. Fear-factor paradox.
   b. Male-female paradox.
   c. Fear-gender paradox.
   d. Victim-gender paradox.

4. **The constitution of certain behaviours as immoral and thereby requiring public intervention is called**
   a. Moral regulation.
   b. Immoral regulation.
   c. Moral intervention.
   d. Immoral control.

5. **The Canadian Assistance Plan was replaced by the Canadian Health and Social Transfer program in _____.**
   a. 1985.
   b. 1995.
   c. 2000.
   d. 2005.

Answers: a, c, c, a, b

Summary

module 5.1   CRIME AND DEVIANCE

1. *Criminology* is the study of crime causation, crime prevention, and the punishment and rehabilitation of offenders.
2. Sociology of law looks at the social construction of law, the social development of legal institutions, and the relation of law to social change.
3. *Crime* is defined as those behaviours that require legal control and social intervention, codified in law; *deviance* involves actions, beliefs, conditions, and characteristics that depart from social norms and may or may not be against the law.
4. *Social control* describes the methods used by society to discourage deviant behaviour and encourage conformity to social norms.

module 5.2   EXPLAINING CRIME AND DEVIANCE: THEORETICAL PERSPECTIVES

5. Classical criminology's basic tenets are (1) crime is a rational choice; (2) if criminal solutions entail less work for greater payoff than legal ones, they are seen as more attractive; (3) fear of punishment can control people's choices; (4) society can better control criminal behaviour if it is met with measured severity, certainty of punishment, and swiftness of justice. Historically, biological approaches posited that some individuals were born to crime as a result of congenital factors, including body type; today, biosocial theorists are evaluating the association between hormonal levels and violent behaviour, among other areas.

6. Functionalists hold that the structure of society can produce social pressures that result in criminal behaviour. Two theories are discussed: strain theory and illegitimate opportunity theory. Strain theory states that people commit crime when they are unable to achieve culturally defined goals through culturally acceptable means. Illegitimate opportunity theory states that people commit crimes as a result of their particular deviant learning environment.

7. Conflict theorists view crime as the outcome of class struggle and focus on how power relationships shape criminal law.

8. Symbolic interactionists assert that criminal behaviour arises from shared experiences and perceptions. Differential association theory asserts that the ratio of messages for and against criminal behaviour in one's peer group determines whether one will engage in criminal activity. Labelling theory asserts that once people have been labelled as deviant they are likely to act that way.

9. Feminist theorists are concerned with issues of power and view patriarchy as the underlying condition behind certain crimes.

module 5.3   CRIME: TYPES AND TRENDS

10. Sociologists have identified a variety of different types of crimes. These definitions give us insight into who commits crimes, and why and how people commit crimes.

11. *Street crime* is crime that we would expect to encounter on the street, but we can encounter it anywhere. This type of crime includes violent crime, property crime, and moral crime.

12. *White collar crime* involves illegal activities committed by an individual during or in relation to his or her employment. *Corporate crime* is a form of white collar crime, but is a crime committed for the benefit of the company.

13. *Professional crime* occurs by people who earn their livelihood through crime. Professional criminals may work for *organized crime*—an operation involved in the illegal trade of goods and services.

14. Crime statistics do not necessarily reflect actual crime rates. A variety of factors—from data collection practices to shifts in demographics and public policy—can affect the data.

15. The police perform many roles, including crime control, responding to emergencies, assisting victims, maintaining peace and order, providing assistance in the prosecution of offenders, and providing education and outreach to the community.

16. The courts decide on the guilt or innocence of the accused. They also protect the rights of the accused and monitor the work of the police and the prosecution.

17. Punishment serves four purposes: retribution, deterrence, rehabilitation, and incapacitation.

module 5.4   CRIME: RISK AND REGULATION

18. Today, the media construct our sense of who is "at risk" of victimization, as well as who is at risk of becoming a criminal. *Public order crimes* are those considered by the state as immoral.
19. *Moral regulation* is the constitution of certain behaviours as immoral and thereby requiring public intervention; targets have included sex and sexual relationships as well as welfare recipients. Moral regulation also affects the perception of crime victims.

Key Terms

biological determinism   136
chivalry hypothesis   143
corporate crime   146
crime   131
criminogenic environment   139
criminology   131
deterrence   151
deviance   131
differential association theory   140
fear-gender paradox   154
formal social control   133
funnel effect   149
illegitimate opportunity theory   139

incapacitation   151
informal social control   133
labelling theory   141
moral entrepreneur   133
moral panic   153
moral regulation   155
organized crime   146
plea bargain   151
positivism   136
property crime   145
public order crimes
    (victimless crimes)   155
rehabilitation   151

retribution   151
rule of law   131
social control   133
social deviance   132
sociology of law   131
strain theory   138
street crime   145
summary conviction offences   151
violent crime   145
white collar crime   145

Test Yourself

1. _____ is the study of crime causation, crime prevention, and the punishment and rehabilitation of offenders.
   a. Criminology
   b. Deviance
   c. Sociology of law
   d. Rule of law

2. The principle that no person should be above the law is called the
   a. Equality principal
   b. Rule of law
   c. Sociology of law
   d. Rule of equality

3. Those that take action in an attempt to influence or change the development or enforcement of society's moral codes are called
   a. Lawyers
   b. Judges
   c. Moral entrepreneurs
   d. Defendants

4. An example of a formal social control would be
   a. A smile
   b. A traffic ticket
   c. A frown
   d. A dirty look

5. The number of Canadians using marijuana _____ between 1994 and 2004.
   a. Decreased
   b. Increased slightly
   c. Stayed the same
   d. Almost doubled

6. Which theory of crime states that people engage in a rational evaluation of the pros and cons of the crime before committing the act?
   a. Biological positivism
   b. Rational choice theory
   c. Illegitimate opportunity theory
   d. Labelling theory

7. Who provided the first illustrations of the criminal man?
   a. Cesare Lombroso
   b. William Sheldon
   c. Jeremy Bentham
   d. Robert Merton

8. According to Merton, drug dealers would belong to which category of deviants?
a. Ritualists
b. Rebels
c. Retreatists
d. Innovators

9. The assertion that the ratio of messages for and against criminal behaviour in one's peer group determines whether one will engage in a criminal activity is called
a. Strain theory
b. Labelling theory
c. Differential association theory
d. Illegitimate opportunity theory

10. The belief that female offenders are treated more leniently by law enforcement officials is called
a. Feminist hypothesis
b. Strain theory
c. Chivalry hypothesis
d. Functionalist hypothesis

11. What forms of crime are most common in Canada?
a. Violent crime
b. Property crime
c. Assault
d. Armed robbery

12. Illegal actions by individuals to benefit the company they are employed by is called
a. Organized crime
b. Corporate crime
c. Work crime
d. Professional crime

13. According to street crime statistics, who is most likely to commit a crime?
a. Young males
b. Young females
c. Middle aged men
d. Middle aged women

14. Crime rates in Canada have _____ since 1990.
a. Declined
b. Increased
c. Stayed the same

d. Doubled

15. What city had the second-lowest crime rate per capita in 2007?
a. Regina
b. Winnipeg
c. Edmonton
d. Toronto

16. A collective reaction based on the false or exaggerated perception that some group or behaviour threatens the well-being of society is called
a. Moral dilemma
b. Moral concern
c. Moral panic
d. Moral issue

17. Which statement is false?
a. Women are more likely than men to be victims of violent crime by a stranger.
b. Men are more likely than women to be victims of violent crime by a stranger.
c. Fear of violent crimes is actually higher than the rate of violent crimes.
d. Women express greater concern about being victims of crime.

18. Which group was the least fearful about being a victim of a crime?
a. Whites
b. Non-whites
c. Elderly
d. The working poor

19. Which of the following would be considered a victimless crime?
a. Prostitution
b. Break and enter
c. Assault
d. Embezzlement

20. When did the social purity movement begin?
a. Late nineteenth century
b. Early nineteenth century
c. 1920s
d. 1970s

Answers: a, b, c, b, d, b, a, c, c, b, a, c, d, c, a, a, a, a

Log in to MySocLab for a host of resources that will help you save time and improve your grade. MySocLab contains cutting-edge learning tools such as study plans, practice tests, videos, audio segments, quizzes, and more—all designed to help you better understand the learning objectives for this chapter. Along with your eBook, MySocLab for *Sociology for Everyone* can be found at **www.mysoclab.com**.

module 5.1
CRIME AND DEVIANCE

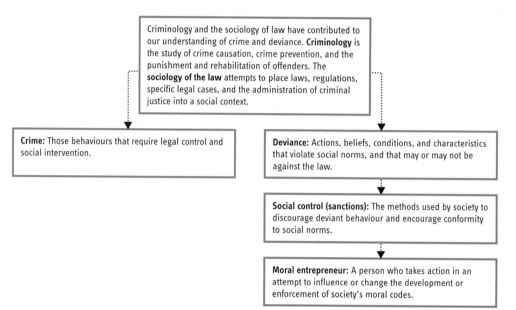

Criminology and the sociology of law have contributed to our understanding of crime and deviance. **Criminology** is the study of crime causation, crime prevention, and the punishment and rehabilitation of offenders. The **sociology of the law** attempts to place laws, regulations, specific legal cases, and the administration of criminal justice into a social context.

Crime: Those behaviours that require legal control and social intervention.

Deviance: Actions, beliefs, conditions, and characteristics that violate social norms, and that may or may not be against the law.

Social control (sanctions): The methods used by society to discourage deviant behaviour and encourage conformity to social norms.

Moral entrepreneur: A person who takes action in an attempt to influence or change the development or enforcement of society's moral codes.

module 5.2
EXPLAINING CRIME AND
DEVIANCE: THEORETICAL
PERSPECTIVES

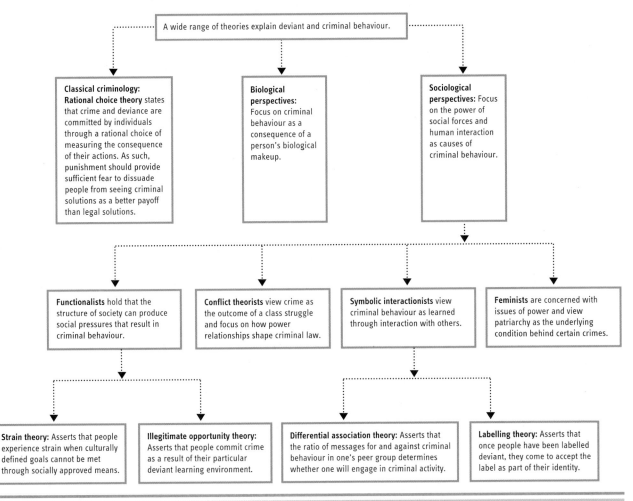

A wide range of theories explain deviant and criminal behaviour.

Classical criminology:
Rational choice theory states that crime and deviance are committed by individuals through a rational choice of measuring the consequence of their actions. As such, punishment should provide sufficient fear to dissuade people from seeing criminal solutions as a better payoff than legal solutions.

Biological perspectives:
Focus on criminal behaviour as a consequence of a person's biological makeup.

Sociological perspectives: Focus on the power of social forces and human interaction as causes of criminal behaviour.

Functionalists hold that the structure of society can produce social pressures that result in criminal behaviour.

Conflict theorists view crime as the outcome of a class struggle and focus on how power relationships shape criminal law.

Symbolic interactionists view criminal behaviour as learned through interaction with others.

Feminists are concerned with issues of power and view patriarchy as the underlying condition behind certain crimes.

Strain theory: Asserts that people experience strain when culturally defined goals cannot be met through socially approved means.

Illegitimate opportunity theory: Asserts that people commit crime as a result of their particular deviant learning environment.

Differential association theory: Asserts that the ratio of messages for and against criminal behaviour in one's peer group determines whether one will engage in criminal activity.

Labelling theory: Asserts that once people have been labelled deviant, they come to accept the label as part of their identity.

module 5.3
CRIME: TYPES AND TRENDS

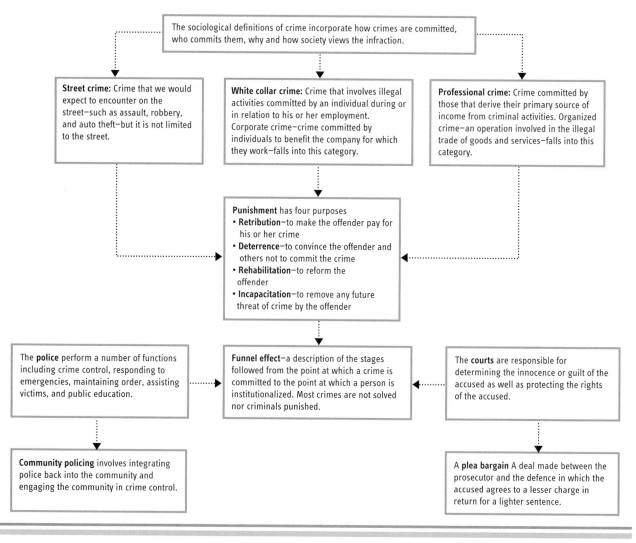

The sociological definitions of crime incorporate how crimes are committed, who commits them, why and how society views the infraction.

Street crime: Crime that we would expect to encounter on the street—such as assault, robbery, and auto theft—but it is not limited to the street.

White collar crime: Crime that involves illegal activities committed by an individual during or in relation to his or her employment. Corporate crime—crime committed by individuals to benefit the company for which they work—falls into this category.

Professional crime: Crime committed by those that derive their primary source of income from criminal activities. Organized crime—an operation involved in the illegal trade of goods and services—falls into this category.

Punishment has four purposes
• **Retribution**—to make the offender pay for his or her crime
• **Deterrence**—to convince the offender and others not to commit the crime
• **Rehabilitation**—to reform the offender
• **Incapacitation**—to remove any future threat of crime by the offender

The **police** perform a number of functions including crime control, responding to emergencies, maintaining order, assisting victims, and public education.

Funnel effect—a description of the stages followed from the point at which a crime is committed to the point at which a person is institutionalized. Most crimes are not solved nor criminals punished.

The **courts** are responsible for determining the innocence or guilt of the accused as well as protecting the rights of the accused.

Community policing involves integrating police back into the community and engaging the community in crime control.

A **plea bargain** A deal made between the prosecutor and the defence in which the accused agrees to a lesser charge in return for a lighter sentence.

module 5.4
CRIME, RISK, AND REGULATION

The media construct our sense of who is "at risk" of victimization, as well as who is at risk of becoming a criminal. They are able to create **moral panic**—a collective reaction based on the false or exaggerated perception that some group or behaviour threatens the well-being of society.

Moral regulation: The constitution of certain behaviours as immoral and thereby requiring public intervention.

Fear-gender paradox: The phenomenon whereby women experience higher rates of fear of being victimized even though men are more likely to be victims of crime.

Public order crimes (victimless crimes): Crimes such as prostitution, gambling, and pornography that are believed to run contrary to moral principles.

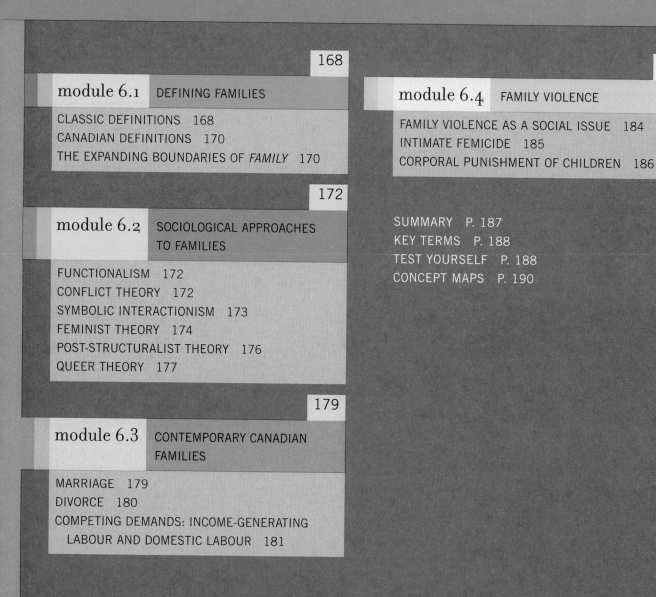

chapter 6

Families

Woody and Soon-Yi

What do you think about a man (62) marrying a woman 35 years his junior (27)? What if that man and woman were of different ethnic backgrounds? Would that trouble you? What if that woman happened to be the adopted daughter of the man's former lover? Such is the case of Woody and Soon-Yi.

"Woody" in this case is the famous director, actor, writer, and musician Woody Allen. Soon-Yi Farrow Previn is the daughter of actor Mia Farrow and conductor André Previn, who adopted her on a trip to Korea when Soon-Yi was eight years old (Lax, 1991).

Mia Farrow and André Previn divorced shortly after Soon-Yi was adopted. In the fall of 1979, a year after the divorce, Woody started a relationship with Mia and entered Soon-Yi's life. At the time, Mia had six children: three were from her relationship with Previn, and three were adopted (Lax, 1991).

Mia and Woody's relationship could be considered unconventional. During their 12 years together, they neither married nor lived together. Their apartments faced each other across Central Park in New York City. However, together they adopted two children (Dylan and Moses) and had one biological son, Satchel (Lax, 1991).

Although Woody did not live with his children, he is reported to have been a dedicated father. He was there in the morning before they woke up, he saw them during the day, and he helped put them to bed (Lax, 1991).

Woody and Mia's relationship ended on January 13, 1992, when Mia discovered nude photos of Soon-Yi, then 19, on the mantelpiece in Woody's den.

Details of the relationship between Woody and Soon-Yi were exposed in the subsequent custody battle over Woody and Mia's children. According to Woody and Soon-Yi, their relationship began when she was 18. Accusations that the relationship started when she was still a minor were denied and not proven in court. Neither Woody nor Soon-Yi believed that their relationship was wrong. Soon-Yi stated that she did not see Woody as her stepfather (Isaacson, 1991) and that he did not see her as his stepdaughter (Hevesi, 1992). However, Woody did admit that dating his previous girlfriend's adoptive daughter was problematic.

On December 24, 1997, Woody and Soon-Yi married. They now have two children.

In response to the marriage, Satchel, Woody's biological son with Mia, was quoted as saying, "He's my father married to my sister. That makes me his son and his brother-in-law. That is such a moral transgression. I cannot see him. I cannot have a relationship with my father and be morally consistent" ("Woody Allen's Son," 2005).

This case raises a number of important questions. What constitutes a family? Who do we consider to be family members? How do family members differ from everyone else in society? What makes them different? How does the concept of family affect the way we interact with members of our family? What are the criteria for a suitable mate? How do we choose a mate? Should we have free choice in choosing a mate?

module 6.1

Think about Defining Families

1 Think about defining families. Who are the members of your family? Based on those who you chose to include in the list, how might you define family?

2 Think about the relationship we have with our family members. How do we treat them differently from other people?

3 Think about how the word *family* is used in Canada. Do you think that when we use that word there is an implied bias of what constitutes a family? In other words, is there a particular model of a family that first comes to mind?

Defining Families

How do we define *family* today? The term is said to be "one of the most misused concepts in the English language," while at the same time it "carries a sense of the best in relationships" (Peters, 1999, pp. 55, 56). As sociologists, why do we care about pinning down a definition of *family*? And do sociological approaches take into consideration "the best" in relationships?

CLASSIC DEFINITIONS

Sociologists have held several long-standing definitions of *family*. Here is one of the most widely cited and influential: "a social group characterized by common residence, economic cooperation, and reproduction. It includes adults of both sexes, at least two of whom maintain a socially approved sexual relationship, and one or more children, own or adopted, of the sexually cohabiting adults" (Murdoch, 1949, p. 1). Can you think of any groups who are not included here?

Another prominent definition holds that family is "a social arrangement based on marriage and the marriage contract, including recognition of the rights and duties of parenthood, common residence for husband, wife and children, and reciprocal economic obligations between husband and wife" (Stephens, 1963). Again, ask yourself who is included and who is excluded from such a definition.

Today's families come in many forms.

A modern recasting of the classic functionalist definition of *family* aims for more precision: "a group manifesting the following organizational attributes: It finds its origin in marriage; it consists of husband, wife, and children born in their wedlock, though other relatives may find their place close to this nuclear group, and the group is united by moral, legal, economic, religious and social rights and obligations (including sexual rights and prohibitions as well as such socially patterned feelings as love, attraction, piety, and awe)" (Coser, 1974, p. xvi). Who is excluded in this instance?

Common approaches to family often refer to two dominant family forms: *nuclear family* and *extended family*. A **nuclear family** includes an adult male, adult female, and their offspring. An **extended family** includes multiple generations of adults living with their spouses and children. In Canada, recent immigrants from both the Middle East and South Asia rely on the extended family as an important living arrangement (Mandell & Duffy, 2005b). As children become adults, they might start to distinguish between their **family of orientation** (the family into which they were born) and their **family of procreation** (the family they create by having children or adopting children). As you can see, these kinds of concepts make it possible to find yourself as a member of multiple families simultaneously.

Notice, however, that the definitions of family we have outlined above all involve an economic relationship, heterosexuality, children, and a common residence (Peters, 1999). But none of them includes either same-sex couples or common-law couples (that is, couples who live together, and who account for 15.5 percent of all Canadian families). Nor do they include lone-parent families (15.9 percent of Canadian families) or couples without children. And today in Canada, these forms *are* considered families—especially by the people in them. In fact, if we used the narrow definition of family as comprising mom and dad (legally married) and their children (who reside with them), less than half (44 percent) of Canadian families would fit it (Statistics Canada, 2003).

nuclear family   An adult male, adult female, and their offspring.

extended family   Multiple generations of adults living with their spouses and children.

family of orientation   The family into which one is born.

family of procreation   The family one creates by having children or adopting children.

CANADIAN DEFINITIONS

Our understanding of what constitutes *family* changes over time. We need only consider the definitions Statistics Canada uses from one census to the next to see the changing nature of family relationships in Canada.

In the 2006 Census, Statistics Canada used two definitions of family. As shown in Figure 6–1, the first is the *census family*, defined as "A married couple (with or without children of either or both spouses), a couple living common-law (with or without children of either or both partners), or a lone parent of any marital status, with at least one child living in the same dwelling. A couple may be of opposite or same sex. 'Children' in a census family include grandchildren living with their grandparent(s) but with no parents present."

The second type of Statistics Canada family is the *economic family*, which is defined as "A group of two or more persons who live in the same dwelling and are related to each other by blood, marriage, common-law or adoption. A couple may be of opposite or same-sex. For 2006, foster children are included." The economic family definition encompasses a wider range of people than does the census family definition. For example, two or more census families (related by blood, marriage, common-law, or adoption) living together in the same dwelling constitute one economic family. Implicit in this definition is the sharing of economic resources.

These census definitions represent two significant changes from the previous census, taken only five years earlier. The 2006 Census represented the first time that same-sex married couples were counted, a development that reflects the legalization of same-sex marriage in Canada with the passing of Bill C-38 (The Civil Marriage Act) in 2005. The 2001 Census did include same-sex common-law couples as family, but not, of course, as "married."

The other significant change concerns the status of children. Prior to the 2001 Census, children living with their parents had to be "never married" to be considered members of the census family. With the change in definition, there is recognition that previously married children may live with their parents and should be included as members of that family.

THE EXPANDING BOUNDARIES OF *FAMILY*

Margrit Eichler (1990) argues that we operate with a bias when we think in terms of "*the* family." Even the concept itself signals that we hold up one ideal type of family as "normal." For example, as students, how do you define your family? If you are living with roommates, are they "family"? If you are renting a room in a family's home, are you part of their family? While you

For a video history of Canadian census families, go to www12.statcan.ca/english/census06/ analysis/famhouse/vignettes/families.html.

FIGURE 6–1 **Distribution of Census Families, Canada, 2006**

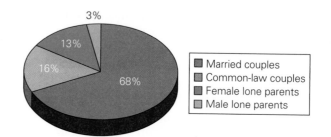

- Married couples
- Common-law couples
- Female lone parents
- Male lone parents

Source: Based on Statistics Canada. (2007). http://www12.statcan.ca/english/census06/analysis/famhouse/tables/table1.htm.

are away from home, are you still considered part of your parents'/parent's family? If you are living alone, who is your family?

To overcome the narrowness of holding up the nuclear family as the ideal to which all should aspire, Eichler (1990) suggests that we expand our understanding of what a family is. She argues that important aspects of families are socialization, emotional relationships, residence, economics, sexuality, and reproduction. Not all of these dimensions need to be present simultaneously, though, for a social arrangement to be understood as a "family" (Peters, 1999). The contemporary focus on human rights and equality, the role of law, and the feminist movement all contribute to the need to re-examine the boundaries of what we consider families to be (Peters, 1999).

Defining *family*, both socially and legally, has important consequences, not only for our individual lives but also for how we are situated in relation to social institutions (Mandell & Duffy, 2005b). For example, the legalization of same-sex marriages has made certain rights and benefits available to married same-sex couples that were at one time available only to married heterosexual couples. Recognized partners can have access to each other's employment benefits, and they are able to apply to adopt or to foster children. In the event of a medical emergency, they are the first persons contacted and are able to make decisions on their partner's behalf. Legalization also affords partners rights and benefits in terms of inheritance in the event of the death of their partner.

Our challenge as sociologists is to research effectively the wide variety of family forms both in Canada and globally. Providing a *universal* definition of family that is relevant in Canada and elsewhere is both highly problematic and undesirable. The term *family* is a "minefield of contested values and power relationships" (Mandell & Duffy, 2005b, p. 4), with some groups lobbying for more inclusive definitions of families and others for tighter restrictions on who can be included in a family. Moreover, different definitions of *family* are invoked in particular circumstances—in law, in government policy, in religious doctrine, and so forth. The reality, then, is that the boundaries of the concept *family* must be understood as fluid.

What do you know about **Defining Families**?

Multiple-choice questions (circle your answer)

1. A(n) _____ family includes multiple generations of adults living with their spouses and children.
   a. Canadian
   b. Nuclear
   c. Extended
   d. American

2. The family we create by having or adopting children is called the
   a. Family of orientation
   b. Family of procreation
   c. Family of origin
   d. Family of extension

3. In Canada, same-sex marriage was legalized in
   a. 2001
   b. 2004
   c. 2005
   d. 2006

4. Which of the following groups would represent the smallest proportion of Canadian families?
   a. Married couples
   b. Common-law couples
   c. Female lone parents
   d. Male lone parents

5. According to Margrit Eichler, which type of family is often held up as the ideal to which all should aspire?
   a. Nuclear family
   b. Extended family
   c. Census family
   d. Economic family

Answers: c, b, c, d, a

module 6.2

Think about Sociological Approaches to Families

1 Think about the role that you play in your family. In what ways do you think it aids in the smooth running of the family? In other words, what do you do for your family?

2 Think about the roles of men and women in families that you know. How do their experiences in families differ?

Sociological Approaches to Families

Sociologists are interested in exploring questions about how families are organized and what their relations are to the wider society and social policies. Sociologists are also concerned about how families work, what challenges they face, and what meanings people hold about them. It is to these questions that we now turn.

FUNCTIONALISM

As we have seen in earlier chapters, the functionalist approach is concerned with order, consensus, equilibrium, and harmony. Societal institutions are understood to be interdependent and existing in harmony with one another. When change occurs in one institution (such as the economy or the education system), change will inevitably take place in other institutions as well. In the functionalist perspective, family is understood to be a major societal institution.

Families accomplish certain social functions:

- They provide individuals with love, and emotional and economic support.
- They regulate sexual expression and reproduction.
- They socialize and discipline children.
- They establish and reproduce social status through the wealth of parents and through inheritance from other family members.

American functionalist Talcott Parsons (1955) argued that with industrialization (1780–1840) families no longer functioned as economic units of production; that is, they no longer produced only the food and goods needed. As a result, the functions associated with families became more specialized, with specific roles developed for men, women, and children alike.

Parsons differentiated adult roles between *instrumental* and *expressive roles*. For groups to run smoothly, both a task leader and an emotional leader are necessary. Parsons argued that women should take on the expressive role while men should fill the instrumental role. The **expressive role** was understood as being concerned with the emotional well-being of family members and the socialization of children, while the **instrumental role** involved men leaving their families to engage in paid labour and deal with the world "out there." A definite split, then, developed between men and women, public and private worlds.

Functionalists have been widely criticized for their conservative approach to gender and for expecting roles in families to be played out on the basis of biology. Functionalists have also been criticized for not adequately dealing with social conflict and social change. While Meg Luxton credits Parsons' approach to the family as "benign in intent" (2001, p. 38), she does assert that his elevation of the nuclear family as "functional" and "natural" allowed for other family forms to be cast as "deviant" or "dysfunctional." As social historians have shown us, the idyllic family (the nuclear family), as presented by functionalists, was just that—a normative construction that does not reflect the reality of multiple family forms (Coontz, 1992).

CONFLICT THEORY

Conflict theorists argue that how people are situated in relation to the means of production, wealth, and power fundamentally shapes the ways in which they both experience and see the world. It follows, then, that when these theorists look at the family, they consider its relationship to the state. They might ask, for example, how a given nation's economy influences the lives of its families.

expressive role
Responsible for the emotional well-being of family members and the socialization of children.

instrumental role
Responsible for engaging in paid labour outside the home.

These theorists perceive that the inequalities inherent in the larger society are perpetuated inside families. So, whereas functionalist theorists argue that the family meets the needs of wider *society*, conflict theorists assert that the family is organized to meet the needs of *capitalism* and, more specifically, to serve ruling class interests (Abbott, Wallace, & Tyler, 2005). People working within this theoretical approach assert that conflict is built into social structures, and is thus a part of social life. Conflict, though, is not always understood as negative; rather, conflict is what drives social change. Through reform or revolution, social conflict can be minimized or even resolved altogether.

INDUSTRIALIZATION AND THE FAMILY   Historically, you will recall, this approach has roots in the work of Karl Marx and Friedrich Engels. In his groundbreaking book *The Origin of the Family, Private Property and the State*, Engels argued that, along with the other vast changes generated by the Industrial Revolution, family forms were radically altered.

With the rise of industrialism, workplaces shifted from homes to factories. Men became workers in these factories, forced to earn a wage for their labour and thus made dependent on business owners for their material survival. Families likewise shifted from being sites of production to sites of consumption. That is, families were no longer organized around producing at home for mainly their own consumption; instead, they purchased goods and services in the marketplace. Essentials such as clothing and food became commodities—articles available for sale or trade in the marketplace.

As a conflict theorist, Engels argued that material conditions determine family life. He pointed out that as societies industrialized, those who were able to provide the necessities of life (i.e., men) amassed social power. Women and children commanded the lowest wages on the earnings ladder, and were thus dependent on male wage earners (Mandell & Duffy, 2005b). Engels demonstrated that with the development of class-based societies, women's social position, relative to men's, declined (Luxton, 2001).

Contrary to popular nostalgia, married women often engaged in waged work. Nonetheless, they were "defined by their domestic roles as private, subservient domestic labourers subject to male control and authority within the home" (Mandell & Duffy, 2005b, p. 10). Not only women, but the family itself was now viewed differently—as a private affair, separate from the public sphere of business and politics.

SOCIAL REPRODUCTION AND THE FAMILY   Marxist-feminist theorists also call attention to the essential work of *social reproduction* done by families. **Social reproduction** ensures the day-to-day, as well as generational, reproduction (and survival) of the population (Luxton & Corman, 2005). Capitalism requires that after a day of work workers be rejuvenated—and this is where families come in. At home, workers are fed, their clothes are laundered, and they are able to rest. In short, their immediate needs are taken care of, thus enabling them to return to work the next day. Nor is this simply a daily cycle; families are also needed to produce the next generation of workers.

> **social reproduction**
> The activities required to ensure the day-to-day and generational reproduction of the population.

Yet Marxist work in the area of families has been criticized for largely taking for granted the division of **domestic labour**—the full range of activities required to maintain a home and care for the people who live in it, including housework, managing money, and caregiving (mainly of children) (Mandell & Duffy, 2005a).

Both functionalist and conflict approaches to families examine the complex relationships that connect families to larger society rather than explore intra-familial relations (Abbott, Wallace, & Tyler, 2005). We now turn to examine the family itself.

> **domestic labour**   The activities required to maintain a home and care for the people who live in it.

SYMBOLIC INTERACTIONISM

Symbolic interactionists take a micro approach to studying family life; that is, they investigate how family members' behaviours are shaped by their definitions and interpretations of particular situations. Context, then, is crucial to symbolic interactionists; they perceive that symbolic meanings vary from one family to the next, and may even vary among members of the same family unit. Researchers working in this area may examine how families contribute to their children's development of self. Overall, symbolic interactionists tend to explore families as cooperative groups with shared interests (Luxton, 2001).

One contemporary example of family research drawing on symbolic interactionism is Suter, Daas, and Bergen's (2008) project on how lesbian mothers negotiate their family identities through symbols and family rituals. The researchers explored how the symbolic use of a child's last name, for instance, concretizes for some lesbian mothers the legitimacy of their family as a family. Some of the mothers in this study gave their child a hyphenated surname made up of both partners' last names. These mothers report that this practice tends to provide them with ease of access on occasions such as emergency room visits. A hyphenated family name also provides them with opportunities to reaffirm the legitimacy of their family, given that people will often ask questions about which woman is the child's mother. Such questions provide an opportunity for the women to proclaim that both of them are the child's mother, symbolically asserting their family as legitimate.

ROLES IN FAMILIES   Symbolic interactionists have used "roles" as one of the basic concepts in their work. Canadian sociologist Erving Goffman (1959) argued that, like actors in the theatre, we play roles in daily life. Symbolic interactionists examine the multiple roles we play on a daily basis and over the course of our lives. You may be a student when you are at school, a roommate when you are eating your breakfast in residence, an employee when you are working, a daughter or son when you go home for a visit, and so forth. In other words, your interactions (and actions) will fluctuate depending on the situation, the setting, and the expectations of those with whom you interact.

Some researchers use this concept to show how our competing roles in families often result in **role strain**—the stress that results when someone does not have sufficient resources to play a role or roles. Some researchers, for example, have studied the strain that mothers experience when they enter the paid labour force—that is, the strain between their responsibilities as mothers and as employees. Since mothers still bear the majority responsibility for child care, they are most satisfied with the balance between home and work when they are able to reduce their time commitments to paid work while their children are still living at home (White, 1999). Role strain, however, is not the exclusive domain of working mothers, as fathers too experience strain as a result of trying to balance their employment and home lives (White & Klein, 2008).

Symbolic interactionists have been criticized for largely accepting the idea of families as sites of harmonious relationships (Luxton, 2001). For instance, some of these theorists view family violence as resulting from the peculiarities of individuals rather than as connected to the larger social issue of the subordination of both women and children. This latter issue is taken up by feminist theory, which we turn to next.

role strain   The stress that results when someone does not have sufficient resources to play a role or roles.

FEMINIST THEORY

Overall, feminist theory holds that families remain primary sites for the continued subordination of women (Abbott, Wallace, & Tyler, 2005). Feminist theorists argue that no one family form is inherently natural or functional, not even the oft-heralded heterosexual nuclear family (Luxton, 2001). Rather, feminist theorists argue that family forms are specific to both time and place. They also argue that even the processes of conception and childbirth are socially constructed and thus vary from one society to another (Luxton, 2001).

One of the most significant contributions of feminist theorizing to the sociology of families is its analysis of familial ideology (Luxton, 2001). Margrit Eichler (1988) and Janet Finch (1989) argue that holding up the nuclear family as the ideal has harmful consequences for women (Luxton, 2001). They stress that imposing one family model that privileges men and subordinates women through its very structure is indeed a political and ideological exercise.

WHY SHOULD WE CARE?

"The Sandwich Generation"

The "sandwich generation" refers to adults "sandwiched" between the potentially conflicting demands of raising children and caring for aging parents or relatives. The phenomenon of adults caring for elderly parents or relatives is not new. However, what is new today is the fact that many of the women who provide such care are also employed in the labour force, which leaves them with less time to care for both dependent children and dependent elders (Williams, 2005).

According to a 2002 Statistics Canada general survey, almost 30 percent of individuals between the ages of 45 and 64 with dependent children under the age of 25 (a total of 712 000 individuals) were involved in caring for an elderly relative. Eighty percent of those sandwiched individuals worked outside the home (Statistics Canada, 2004e).

Sandwiched individuals reported feeling higher rates of stress than their nonsandwiched counterparts. In addition to the increased domestic workload and the strain of meeting the needs of both their children and their elderly dependents, the employment and finances of these individuals were also likely to be affected. To meet their domestic responsibilities, 15 percent of those employed outside the home reported reducing their work hours and 20 percent reported changing their work schedules. As well, 10 percent reported a loss of income, while 40 percent reported increased personal costs to care for the elderly (e.g., the cost of renting medical equipment) (Statistics Canada, 2004e).

Predictably, most eldercare was provided to parents or parents-in-law (75 percent), with most support being provided by women. On average, sandwiched women reported providing 29 hours of support per month to an elderly dependent, while men reported providing 13 hours of support per month on average. The form of support provided also varied by gender; women were most likely to provide personal care such as bathing, feeding, and cleaning, and men were most likely to provide transportation or home maintenance (Statistics Canada, 2004e).

We expect to see more sandwiched individuals in the near future. A couple of key factors will contribute to an increase in this phenomenon. The large and aging baby boom population will soon need care. As well, many young adults today are waiting longer to have children, which increases their chance of having both dependent children and parents to care for at the same time (Statistics Canada, 2004e).

Feminists analyze families at both macro and micro levels.

At a macro level, feminists focus on how our social structures (e.g., laws, social policies, and labour practices) enable and sustain inequality. Marxist feminists in particular argue that the exploitation of women serves capitalist interests (Abbott, Wallace, & Tyler, 2005). For instance, most workplaces do not acknowledge that employees have responsibilities (e.g., children) outside of their paid responsibilities (Luxton, 2001). Because the responsibility of child care, elder care, and housework typically falls on the shoulders of women, women remain disadvantaged at work and economically dependent on men (Baker, 2001; Luxton, 2001).

Feminist research also challenges the assumption that family life is private and separate from public spheres of life (Thorne, 1982). Social and economic policies can (and do) affect family life. Marriage and divorce laws; laws concerning adoption, custody, and child support; as well as tax benefits concerning children and child care all affect family life (Baker, 2001; Beaujot, 2000). For example, in Canada, our taxes are assessed on an individual level except when determining child tax benefits and GST credits, which are calculated on the basis of family income. Such calculations are meant to aid poorer families (Beaujot, 2000).

Through a feminist lens, we are also able to understand the devastating effects of the history of imperialism in Canada on Aboriginal peoples and their established family relationships. Aboriginal familial practices were quite different from European practices. According to accounts written by white settlers, Aboriginal peoples enjoyed spousal relationships without hierarchy, divorces happened with consent, children were clearly loved, there were anti–corporal punishment attitudes in place, and adults enjoyed sexual freedom following marriage (Mandell & Momirov, 2005). However, as the Europeans settled, their marriage practices (in which men's authority was protected through law) were instituted, to women's disadvantage (Luxton, 2001). As a result of colonization, traditional work and family relations were destabilized, resulting in reconstituted gender and family relationships (Anderson, 1991; Bourgeault, 1983; Luxton, 2001).

At a micro level, feminists focus on interpersonal relations—examining everyday interaction as gendered and as perpetuating gender hierarchies. Barrie Thorne (1982) argues that feminist research challenges conventional sociological approaches to studying families since it takes as a basic premise that family members experience family life differently.

Proulx and Helms (2008) explored parent–adult child relationships in a US-based study. The researchers argued that it is problematic simply to use categories such as "parent" and "adult child" to discuss familial relationships, because gender fundamentally shapes such relations. Therefore, it is more appropriate to explore mother–son, mother–daughter, father–son, and father–daughter relationships, since this specificity recognizes that mothers and fathers may have different kinds of relationships with their children (Proulx & Helm, 2008). Ignoring the possibilities of nuance in familial relationships simplifies them as being gender neutral. The researchers also argue that familial relationships are fluid, and thus change over time. One example of this specificity and fluidity is illustrated by a mother who reported a relationship with her son that was increasingly conflict ridden, whereas the father was not experiencing similar conflict with the son (Proulx & Helm, 2008).

Most contemporary feminist research rejects any assertion that men's and women's roles within families are a natural outcome of biological differences. Women are not born knowing how to do laundry, iron clothes, vacuum, or bake, just as men are not born knowing how to work a lawnmower or shovel snow. All of these activities are social practices. This sort of thinking (linking social roles to biology) is most closely aligned with functionalist approaches to understanding families.

One contemporary example of research in this area is Belinda Leach's (2005) work on transformations in steelworker families in Hamilton, Ontario. Leach investigated how economic uncertainty in the steel industry, as a result of global capitalism, affects the lives of working-class families, particularly in terms of the gender politics of family life. Leach documented how these families struggled with the unravelling of the local historical norm of breadwinner-model families. In the face of economic uncertainty, women from these families entered the paid labour force in unprecedented numbers. While many steelworkers' wives had worked for pay in the past during strikes and layoffs, historically they had contributed a low level of income to their families. Having to enter the paid labour force challenged taken-for-granted ideas of masculinity and femininity predicated on a heterosexual family unit—that is, that men work for income and women contribute their labour in the domestic realm (by cleaning, cooking, and caring for children).

POST-STRUCTURALIST THEORY

Post-structuralists are likely to seek to dismantle prevailing discourses about families; for example, the adage that the family serves as "a haven in a heartless world" (Lasch, 1977). Post-structuralists may also question the concept of the "good mother" (one who is married, heterosexual, cares about children, and so forth) or the notion that "good fathers are good breadwinners" (Park, 2006). Post-structuralists argue that such categories operate as *normalizingdiscourses*—they set the boundaries of what is acceptable and appropriate, and work to govern people's behaviour. To demonstrate how such discourses gain currency, post-structuralists look to relations of power.

Sue Peckover (2002) conducted research on how British health visitors (a type of public nurse) exercise disciplinary power when visiting women with young children who have experienced domestic violence. Peckover draws on Foucault's concept of disciplinary power to demonstrate how normalizing discourses of mothering (based on middle-class and patriarchal assumptions) are used to help reproduce and regulate the categories of "good" mothers and "bad" mothers.

One woman reported always having her house clean, food cooking on the stove, and her makeup done for her health visitor appointment—in short, she did not want to display any vulnerability (Peckover, 2002). Concealing incidences of domestic violence was part of producing herself as a good mother. Women who do not fit within this middle-class discourse (e.g., lone mothers, mothers with disabilities, non-white mothers) often experience greater scrutiny than their middle-class counterparts. If women were judged as inadequate, health visitors aimed to reform what they perceived to be inadequate child-care practices.

One of the strengths of Peckover's (2002) work is how she demonstrates that health visitors' work in relation to mothers is neither simple nor straightforward. While health visitors are meant to provide support, there is also a policing role to their visits that leads women to fear moral judgments, which interferes with their ability (or desire) to ask for assistance. For example, some women feared losing custody of their children and/or not being believed about the abuse they experienced from their husbands. In these cases, the women did not want to reach out to the health visitors for fear of potential consequences.

QUEER THEORY

Queer theorists are often influenced by post-structuralist theory. They are interested in questioning normative categories, especially *heteronormativity* (that is, heterosexuality as the norm). In relation to family life, queer theorists might question the assumption that all families are formed through heterosexual unions, and further question expectations of "heterorelationality—of co-residence, romantic love, monogamy and the primacy of the conjugal couple" (Budgeon & Roseneil, 2004, p. 129).

Andrew Gorman-Murray's (2007) Australian-based research illustrates a queer approach to exploring family life and domestic spaces. He demonstrates how the detached suburban house—with its "master bedroom" and smaller bedrooms, presumably for children—is inextricably bound to the heterosexual nuclear family form (p. 195). He also showed how gay men's and lesbians' use of domestic space provides a challenge to the heteronormative assumptions about "home." For example, one respondent, Anthony, used to live with his cousin: "When you're living with someone, they're constantly censoring what you'd hang on the walls. . . . But now she's gone this is the one place where I feel like I don't have to cover anything up" (p. 208). One important domestic practice that Anthony engages in is flying a rainbow flag outside his place as a statement that his is a gay home: "I'm telling you who I am. This is my community too; even though I'm a gay person I don't have to be hidden" (p. 208). Gorman-Murray argues that such a practice is a deliberate challenge to the construction of suburban neighbourhoods as the exclusive domain of heterosexual families.

Another way that lesbians and gays challenge heteronormative domestic spaces is in their frequent use of houses for social gatherings. Using domestic spaces to develop and maintain queer relationships, friendships, and communities—especially where gay/lesbian commercial venues are hard to find—subverts the heterosexual norm of homes as the site of private family relationships (Gorman-Murray, 2007).

Queer communities today may experience a tension between a kind of conservatism that aims for cultural acceptance or assimilation ("We're just like the monogamous heterosexual family, only queer") and an effort to create and practise alternative family forms.

What do you know about **Sociological Approaches to Families**?

Multiple-choice questions (circle your answer)

1. **The _____ role is understood as being concerned with the emotional well-being of family members and the socialization of children.**
   a. Instrumental
   b. Expressive
   c. Nurturing
   d. Essential

2. **The full range of activities required to maintain a home and care for the people who live in it is called**
   a. Domestic labour
   b. Social reproduction
   c. Capitalist labour
   d. Social labour

3. **_____ take a micro approach to studying family life; that is, they investigate how family members' behaviours are shaped by how they define and interpret situations.**
   a. Functionalists
   b. Conflict theorists
   c. Symbolic interactionists
   d. Feminists

4. **_____ would question the assumption that all families are formed through heterosexual unions.**
   a. Functionalists
   b. Queer theorists
   c. Conflict theorists
   d. Feminists

5. **What theorist is most likely to examine and dismantle ideas such as family serves as "a haven in a heartless world"?**
   a. Functionalist
   b. Conflict theorist
   c. Post-structuralist
   d. Queer theorist

Answers: b, a, c, b, c

module 6.3

Contemporary Canadian Families

The composition of Canadian families has changed significantly in the past 40 years. Below we will examine some of the current trends.

MARRIAGE

SAME-SEX MARRIAGE   The most significant shift we have seen in marriages in Canada came with the 2005 passing of Bill C-38, The Civil Marriage Act, which legalized same-sex marriages. This legislation has placed Canada among only a small group of progressive countries—the Netherlands, Belgium, and Spain—that have legalized same-sex unions. Prior to this act, several provinces had already enacted a range of legislative measures enabling a variety of same-sex entitlements. The legalization of same-sex marriages brings both social legitimacy and legal rights and benefits to these partners. It also demonstrates the fluidity of our social categories.

COMMON-LAW COUPLES   Ironically, over the last quarter-century the overall proportion of married couples in Canada has declined. Couples are increasingly choosing to live in common-law relationships, with regional rates highest in Quebec (Statistics Canada, 2007c). This trend is repeated in the United States, Australia, New Zealand, and throughout most of Europe (McDaniel & Tepperman, 2002). In 2006, 68 percent of Canadian families were married couples (with or without children), down from 83 percent in 1981 (see Figure 6–2). And in 2006, common-law relationships (with or without children) represented 16 percent of Canadian families, up from only 5.6 percent in 1981. In the past, common-law unions tended to be associated with the working class; today, however, these unions are prevalent among all social classes (McDaniel & Tepperman, 2002). Women's increased labour force participation and education levels are two factors associated with the rise in cohabitation (McDaniel & Tepperman, 2002).

Despite what appear to be dramatic declines in marriage rates, the majority of Canadian women and men will get married at some point in their lives (McDaniel & Tepperman, 2002).

Think about Contemporary Canadian Families

1 Think about marriage. If you are not married, do you plan to get married? Why or why not? If you are married, why did you get married?

2 Where in Canada would you expect to find the highest levels of common-law unions? On what did you base your answer?

3 Think about divorce. Are you in favour of no-fault divorce?

FIGURE 6–2 Marriages and Common-Law Unions as a Percentage of Canadian Families, 1981–2006

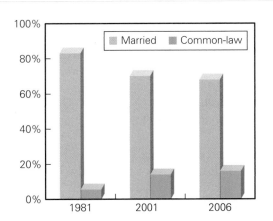

Source: Based on data from Statistics Canada. (2007). http://www12.statcan.ca/english/census06/analysis/famhouse/tables/table1.htm.

To learn more about cohabitation and property rights, go to www.canlii.org/en/on/laws/stat/rso-1990-c-f3/latest/rso-1990-c-f3.html.

The ideals of marriage are still attractive; common-law unions, after all, mimic marriage in its ideals of a monogamous, committed relationship. That is, couples are living together, they are just not "tying the knot" (Mandell & Duffy, 2005b, p. 15).

Common-law unions may be viewed by some people as a less binding, flexible relationship than legal marriage; however, governments are increasingly treating long-term (two years or more) cohabitation as legally binding. If these unions dissolve, the parties are expected to support each other financially, although the degree to which this is required varies from province to province (McDaniel & Tepperman, 2002). One thing is certain, though: the line between legal marriage and cohabitation is no longer clear (McDaniel & Tepperman, 2002).

endogamy Marriage within the same group.

MIXED-RACE COUPLES   Another interesting trend in Canada is the rise in mixed-race couples. In the 2006 Census, 289 420 mixed-race couples were reported—one-third more than in 2001 (Statistics Canada, 2007c). While the numbers are still low relative to the overall population, the upward trend may indicate a changing attitude about potential mates. In the past, mate selection was dictated by the rule of **endogamy**—marriage within the same group—but this practice may become less pervasive in Canada in the future.

polygamy A form of marriage in which an individual has more than one husband or wife at the same time.

polygyny A form of polygamy in which a man has more than one wife.

polyandry A form of polygamy in which a woman has more than one husband.

POLYGAMY   **Polygamy**—a form of marriage in which an individual has more than one husband or wife at the same time—is illegal in Canada. That may soon change.

Attention to polygamy has grown since the RCMP began investigating allegations of child abuse in the openly polygamous community of Bountiful, British Columbia, in 2005. The people of Bountiful are members of the Fundamentalist Church of Jesus Christ of Latter-day Saints. They practise a form of polygamy called **polygyny**, in which a man has more than one wife. (The opposite of polygyny is **polyandry**—a form of polygamy in which a woman has more than one husband.) The concern in Bountiful is that young girls are being married to older men against their will (MacQueen, 2007).

Bountiful is not the only place where polygamy is practised in Canada. Muslim communities in Toronto and Ottawa report that polygyny also occurs in their communities but the unions are rarely discussed outside of their religious communities (MacQueen, 2007).

Legal and constitutional experts acknowledge that Canada's polygamy law is unconstitutional and unenforceable. If challenged in court by either of these groups under the Canadian Charter of Rights and Freedoms' section on religious freedoms, experts argue that polygamy would be legalized in Canada (MacQueen, 2007).

DIVORCE

The most significant changes surrounding divorce in Canada came in 1968 and in 1985. Prior to the 1968 Divorce Act, divorces were granted only on the basis of adultery, desertion, or imprisonment, or if the spouses had lived separately for three years (Gorlick, 2005). The liberalization of divorce laws in 1968 led, unsurprisingly, to an increase in Canadian divorce rates. In 1968 there were 54.8 divorces per 100 000 population; in just one year, that number soared to 124.2 divorces per 100 000 in 1969 (Eichler, 2008). This number continued to climb until levelling off in the early 2000s, when total divorces per year were in the low 70 000s, or 223.6 divorces per 100 000 population (Statistics Canada, 2006e).

In 1985, "no-fault" divorce laws took effect—and in the subsequent two-year period, the numbers and rates of divorces rose significantly. In the peak year of 1987, 96 200 divorces were granted, which represents a rate of 362.3 divorces per 100 000 population (Gentleman & Park, 1997). No-fault divorce reduced the waiting time prior to being able to file for divorce to one year, and uncontested divorces were granted after a separation of three years (Gorlick, 2005).

Other significant changes occurred in 1997 with regard to issues of child support. Changes to the Divorce Act now mean that child support is calculated based on the income of the noncustodial parent and takes into account the cost of living in each province. Judicial discretion in the setting of child support payments was removed, creating uniformity in the way support payments are calculated across Canada. This standardization is meant to ensure that adequate supports are provided for children within the financial means of the supporting parent. The Child Support Guidelines also take into account split custody and shared custody arrangements.

Additionally, changes in the federal Income Tax Act finally halted the practice of noncustodial parents being allowed to deduct monies paid for child support and custodial parents having to pay income tax on child support payments received (Gorlick, 2005; Philipps, 2004).

For more information on family legal issues, including divorce and child custody, go to **www.attorneygeneral.jus. gov.on.ca/english/family/**.

COMPETING DEMANDS: INCOME-GENERATING LABOUR AND DOMESTIC LABOUR

The question "Who makes up a family?" is perhaps not the most useful one we can ask. What happens when we shift the question to "What does a family do?" Further, we could ask: "How do you recognize and support the people who do what families do?" These questions enable us to investigate the relationship between larger social relations (including economic and political ones) and what families "do."

Typically, families are units that cooperate economically. Families depend on two kinds of labour: (1) income-generating work and (2) unpaid domestic labour. In capitalist societies such as Canada's, the demands of domestic labour and the demands of income-generating work are organized in conflict with one another. The state negotiates between these two spheres only partially, through schools and health care (Luxton and Corman, 2005).

Two big changes in recent decades have affected how families negotiate the competing demands of income generation and managing households. The first is a change in the number of hours of income-generating work required to support a household. Today, the standard of living for an average family of two adults and two children requires more paid hours than it did 30 years ago. In the 1970s only 44 hours of income-generating work per week were required to sustain such a household, whereas by the 1990s, 65 to 80 hours per week were required (Wolff, 1994).

The need for more paid labour hours to maintain the average standard of living has translated into a higher proportion of women working in the paid labour force, and families with two income earners are now the statistical norm among Canadian families. Seventy-two percent of two-parent families with children under 12 years of age have both parents engaged in the paid labour force (Lapierre-Adamcyk, Marcil-Gratton, & Le Bourdais, 2006). In 45 percent of these families, both parents are working full-time (30 hours or more per week).

Of course, women have entered the paid labour force increasingly since the 1950s. Participating in paid labour began mainly with single women and childless women; mothers of school-aged children followed soon after, and then mothers of small children (Lapierre-Adamcyk, Marcil-Gratton, & Le Bourdais, 2006). In 2002, 61 percent of women aged 15 to 65 were in the formal labour force, compared with 14 percent in 1901 (Luxton & Corman, 2005). Labour force participation of men aged 15 to 65 stands at 73 percent (Luxton & Corman, 2005).

The second big change affecting contemporary families is the major cutbacks in government support to schools, health care, and social service agencies that Canadians have seen over the last 20 years (Luxton & Corman, 2005). These spending cuts have resulted in caregiving responsibilities falling increasingly to families, and most often to women. In other

Families depend on both income-generating work and unpaid domestic labour to survive. Some women attempt to combine income-generation work with domestic responsibilities (e.g., child care).

CANADIAN SOCIETY IN FOCUS

Child-Care Expenses as a Tax Deduction?

From 1982 to 1985, Beth Symes, a full-time practising lawyer, employed a nanny to care for her children. In her personal tax returns for those years, Symes claimed the wages she paid to the nanny as a business expense. Revenue Canada (now called Canada Revenue Agency) allowed the deductions in 1982 and 1983. However, through notices of reassessment, Revenue Canada subsequently disallowed the deductions for the entire period of 1982 to 1985. Revenue Canada's position was that "the expenses were not outlays or expenses incurred for the purpose of gaining or producing income from business, as required under s. 18(1)(a) of the Income Tax Act, but were personal or living expenses, deduction of which was prohibited by s. 18(1)(h)" (*Symes v. Canada*, 1993). Symes took her case to trial, and the Federal Court "held that the appellant could deduct the payments to the nanny as business expenses." However, the Federal Court of Appeal reversed the lower court's decision. The case was then appealed to the Supreme Court of Canada.

In 1993 the Supreme Court ruled against Symes in a majority decision. The court was split along gender lines—with seven male justices ruling against Symes and the two female justices providing dissenting judgments. Neither the Federal Court of Appeal nor the Supreme Court of Canada "was prepared to see the costs associated with child care as ones incurred in the public domain—that is, the public market (or business) in contrast to the private family" (Young, 2003, p. 1926).

Such a decision communicates that the responsibility (and cost) of children remains with the family. Also, Young (2003) argues that the discourse of "choice" runs through the majority decision of the Supreme Court. That is, an underlying perception on the part of the court is that it is women's personal choice to have children.

Even though Symes "lost" the argument that child-care costs are a legitimate business expense, legislative changes that expanded allowable child-care deductions following *Symes v. Canada* can be considered a small victory.

The dissenting judgment in *Symes v. Canada* showed promise of understanding the gendered nature of the case—that since women overwhelmingly bear the primary responsibility for child care in Canada, they are disproportionately affected in terms of possible or actual labour force participation. The dissent drew on feminist research and gender equity principles.

> Child care expenses should not be disallowed as a business expense under s. 18(1)(h) as being personal in nature. While for most men the responsibility of children does not impact on the number of hours they work or affect their ability to work, a woman's ability even to participate in the work force may be completely contingent on her ability to acquire child care. Many business deductions have been permitted in the past even though these expenditures have a personal element. The real costs incurred by businesswomen with children are no less real, no less worthy of consideration and no less incurred in order to gain or produce income from business. (*Symes v. Canada* [1993] 4 S.C.R. 695)

words, the cutbacks mean that more unpaid work is required for households to survive. For example, cuts in health care lead to people being sent home from hospital while they still require care.

How are people negotiating the competing demands of more hours required in the paid labour force and more hours required for domestic labour? One strategy is to increase the hours of paid labour in order to be able to purchase more services. For example, individual family members might find themselves combining more than one paid job in order to pay for a housecleaning service. Another strategy is to decrease the hours engaged in paid labour in order to have more time available for domestic labour, including child care (Luxton & Corman, 2005).

Yet even when all family members (including men and children) participate in domestic labour and child care, there is still not enough time in a day or week to get everything done to a satisfactory level (Luxton & Corman, 2005). In heterosexual families, as we have seen, mothers more often than fathers are the ones to adjust their work lives to take care of home responsibilities, with women frequently taking on part-time rather than full-time employment (Baker, 2001; Cheal, 2002; Ravanera & McQuillan, 2006).

This problem of the competing demands of paid labour and domestic labour is not easily solved at the level of individual families and households. Critical sociologists point to the need for broader state supports for families. Such state supports might include a national, state-funded child-care program, increased state-legislated provisions for family leaves, sufficient levels of education funding such that parents are not relied on for school fundraising, and quality affordable elder care (Luxton & Corman, 2005).

DOMESTIC LABOUR   One of feminists' achievements in the area of families is their recognition of the importance and value of domestic labour. Society as a whole, not just individual family members, benefits from the enormous contributions of unpaid domestic labour (Luxton, 2001). In her book *If Women Counted*, Marilyn Waring (1990) argues that unpaid domestic labour should be calculated and valued such that women could be compensated and have their work socially recognized. Statistics Canada has valued unpaid domestic labour at $297 billion a year, which represents 33 percent of the gross domestic product (Hamdad, 2003).

The pattern of women's dual responsibility holds regardless of race, class, and culture (Canadian Council on Social Development, 1996). Sociologist Arlie Hochschild (1989; 2003) coined the term **second shift** to refer to the domestic labour performed by employed women at home after finishing their paid workdays.

second shift   The domestic labour performed by women at home after finishing their paid workdays.

Couples who attempt to divide household responsibilities more equitably nonetheless exhibit persistent gendered patterns. Repetitive, regular indoor household tasks such as cooking, cleaning, and bathing children are more likely to be performed by women. Men, on the other hand, are more likely to engage in outdoor tasks and tasks where completion times are not as rigid—such as mowing the lawn and completing repair jobs around the home (Baker, 2001; Daly, 2000; Hochschild, 1997).

Signalling a change in attitudes, we do see attempts to more equitably share household tasks associated with young, well-educated couples who have a small number of children or no children (Baker, 2001).

What do you know about **Contemporary Canadian Families**?

Multiple-choice questions (circle your answer)

1. **Which of the following statements is false?**
   a. Overall, the proportion of married couples in Canada has been declining.
   b. The highest rates of common-law relationships in Canada is in British Columbia.
   c. Common-law relationships have risen since 1981.
   d. The majority of Canadian men and women will get married at some point in their lives.

2. **A form of marriage in which an individual has more than one husband or wife at the same time is called**
   a. Endogamy
   b. Polygyny
   c. Polygamy
   d. Exogamy

3. No-fault divorce laws took effect in
a. 1968
b. 1976
c. 1985
d. 1989

4. Which of the following statements is false?
a. An average standard of living for an average family of two adults and two children requires more paid hours of work than it did 30 years ago.
b. More women are in the paid labour force than 30 years ago.

c   There are now more women than men in the paid labour force.
d. The majority of two-parent families with children under 12 years of age has both parents in the paid labour force.

5. Which of the following statements is false?
a. Polygamy is legal in Canada.
b. The number of mixed-race couples is increasing in Canada.
c. Common-law unions tend to be monogamous.
d. The divorce rate peaked in 1987.

Answers: b, c, c, a

module 6.4

Think about Family Violence

1 Think about family violence. Do you think it is on the rise in Canada? Who do you think is most likely to be victimized by such crimes? On what did you base your answers?

2 Think about spanking and corporal punishment. Do you think that spanking is a reasonable way to discipline children?

Family Violence

Family violence as a concept brings up a paradox. On the surface of things, "family" and "violence" are often taken up as opposites. As mentioned earlier, family is construed as a "haven in a heartless world." Many of us understand our families to be (or should be) sites of intimacy, love, caring, and safety.

Those who are uncomfortable recognizing families as sites of violence often say that it occurs only in exceptional cases, perpetrated by sick individuals. However, this approach is not a useful one for understanding family violence from a sociological perspective.

FAMILY VIOLENCE AS A SOCIAL ISSUE

We tend to internalize messages that state that violence lurks out in the world rather than at home, and yet women are in fact at greater danger in and near their homes than in the public arena (Canadian Centre for Justice Statistics, 2003). Women are more than twice as likely to be assaulted by someone known to them than by a stranger. In Canada in 2002, 27 percent of all reported violent crimes involved instances of family violence, and 62 percent of these were committed by a spouse or ex-spouse (Brzozowski, 2004). Women account for 85 percent of victims of family violence, with young women (aged 25 to 34) experiencing the highest rates of violence committed by a spouse (Brzozowski, 2004).

Sadly, these numbers tell us that violence is pervasive in Canadian families. When we take into account the amount of money spent in Canada in connection with family violence through social services, the criminal justice system, absenteeism from work, and health care costs (estimated to be over $4 billion per year; Prevent Family Violence, 2006), we are able to see that family violence is not an issue that merely affects a few, unfortunate people. Family violence is a social issue, not a private trouble. Sociologists investigate family violence from this premise.

Feminist analyses have contributed greatly to our understanding of family violence. Such analyses demonstrate that mainstream approaches to understanding family violence merely total individual episodes of violence (hitting, slapping, shouting, throwing objects, and so forth) and lead people to conclude that family violence is gender neutral—in other words, that both men and women engage in violence. However, feminists note that the quality of violence is affected by gender and, thus, must be considered (Duffy & Momirov, 2005).

For example, while women are more likely than men to use weapons, their weapons are household objects that are immediately at hand—things like scissors, wooden spoons, hair brushes, or television remotes. When men use weapons, they use objects like firearms, baseball bats, hammers, and metal pipes (Glasbeek, 2005). Further, women are more likely than men to be severely assaulted, to suffer injury and require medical attention, and to live in fear for their lives (Glasbeek, 2005). Feminist analyses highlight the significance of patriarchal social arrangements and men's social power over women (Duffy & Momirov, 2005).

INTIMATE FEMICIDE

Intimate femicide—the killing of women by their intimate male partners—accounted for the majority of women killed in Ontario (63 percent to 76 percent) from 1974 to 1994 (Gartner, Dawson, & Crawford, 1998). Gartner, Dawson, and Crawford's 1998 research is the only recent work that includes "killings of women by their estranged common-law partners and current and former boyfriends" in the calculation of intimate femicides; most research includes only current common-law partners and current and ex-spouses.

Who are the victims of intimate femicide? The answer may surprise you: they are women from across all social classes, age groups, and cultural and ethnic origins. The average age at death was 37. Half of the women were employed (51 percent), most had children (80 percent), and most were born in Canada (76 percent) (Gartner, Dawson, & Crawford, 1998).

However, the researchers point to some "risk markers" that identify certain women as having a higher risk of victimization (Gartner, Dawson, & Crawford, 1998). Statistics from Canada, the United States, Australia, and Great Britain all demonstrate that estrangement from the intimate partner and common-law status are both linked to a greater possibility of spousal killings of women. Canadian data demonstrate that women's risk of femicide increased sixfold when they were estranged from their male partners (DeKeseredy, 2001; Wilson & Daly, 1994).

Another risk marker is ethnicity. For instance, whereas in the United States African-American women face a disproportionate risk of intimate femicide, in Canada Aboriginal women are at increased risk. During the 21-year period under study, Gartner, Dawson, and Crawford (1998) discovered that at least 6 percent of all victims of intimate femicide in Ontario were Aboriginal women. Given that only 1 percent of women in Ontario during this time frame identified as Aboriginal, Aboriginal women were overrepresented as intimate femicide victims.

A further risk marker is the partner's violent history. Much research demonstrates that men who murder their spouses (or estranged spouses) have a long history of violent behaviour—one that is not restricted to marital relationships (Gartner, Dawson, & Crawford, 1998; Johnson, 1996).

Further undermining the notion that our homes are our refuge, 75 percent of intimate femicides take place in the victim's home, with almost half of these killings occurring in the victim's bedroom (Gartner, Dawson, & Crawford, 1998). Offenders used firearms in one-third of these killings, and in the remaining two-thirds "stabbed, bludgeoned, beat, strangled, or slashed the throats of their victims" (p. 151).

How can we understand intimate femicide? Gartner, Dawson, and Crawford (and many others) argue that it is best understood as a "manifestation of extreme (if ultimately self-defeating) controlling and proprietary attitudes and behaviours by men toward their female partners" (1998, p. 151). That women are the victims of spousal homicides is not incidental. Intimate femicide "is violence that occurs and takes particular forms because its target is a woman, a woman who has been intimately involved with her killer" (p. 151). As feminists

Violence is pervasive in Canadian families, with women representing 85 percent of victims.

intimate femicide   The killing of women by their intimate male partners.

For current research on family violence in Canada, go to www.statcan.gc.ca/pub/85-224-x/85-224-x2008000-eng.htm.

argue, we can understand this violence as an extension of men's proprietary attitudes toward the intimate women in their lives.

As demonstrated, women are more likely than men to be killed by the intimate partners. Researchers argue that such gendered patterns are reflective of larger social relations of masculinity and femininity, in which men occupy more dominant positions in our social hierarchy (Duffy & Momirov, 2005).

CORPORAL PUNISHMENT OF CHILDREN

Where and how do we draw the line between abuse and discipline in the use of physical force on children? We have clear rules about the use of physical force against adults, but what about children?

corporal punishment In relation to children, any physical force with the intent of causing a child to experience pain in the hope of changing that child's behaviour.

Corporal punishment of children can be defined as any physical force with the intent of causing a child to experience pain in the hope of changing that child's behaviour (Gagne, Tourigny, Joly, & Pouliot-Lapointe, 2007). At present, corporal punishment of children is legal in Canada, but it has been outlawed in 19 countries around the globe.

Section 43 of the Criminal Code of Canada stipulates that parents, teachers, and others who act in the place of a parent can use force to correct a child's behaviour. A challenge to this law was made in 2004. The challenge argued that section 43 is unconstitutional according to section 15 of the Canadian Charter of Rights and Freedoms because it discriminates against children on the basis of age (Watkinson, 2006, p. 531). In a Supreme Court ruling, the court concluded, 6 to 3, that section 43 does not violate children's rights. However, it did provide guidelines for corporal punishment, noting that it should be used only with children between the ages of 2 and 12, only with the hand, and blows to the head were not permitted.

Since that ruling, Bill S-209 was introduced to Parliament. Bill S-209 proposes to eliminate section 43 of the Criminal Code. Should it pass into law, the spanking of children will become illegal in Canada (CBC, 2008c).

What do you know about **Family Violence**?

Multiple-choice questions (circle your answer)

1. Victims of family violence are most likely to be
a. Teenage girls (14 to 19)
b. Young women (25 to 34)
c. Young men (25 to 34)
d. Middle-aged women (35 to 44)

2. Which of the following statements is false?
a. In cases of domestic violence, women are more likely to use household items as weapons.
b. In cases of domestic violence, women are more likely to use weapons.
c. In cases of domestic violence, men are more likely to use firearms.
d. In cases of domestic violence, women are most likely to use hammers or baseball bats.

3. The killing of women by their intimate male partners is called
a. Intimate homicide
b. Intimate femicide

c. Intimate murder
d. Intimate domicide

4. According to a 2004 Supreme Court ruling, children between what ages can be spanked?
a. 1 to 5
b. 2 to 18
c 2 to 12
d. 13 to 18

5. What document would outlaw corporal punishment of children in Canada?
a. Section 43 of the Criminal Code
b. Section 15 of the Canadian Charter of Rights and Freedoms
c. Bill S-209
d. The Canadian Constitution

Answers: b, d, b, c, c

Summary

module 6.1   DEFINING FAMILIES

1. Classic definitions of *family* as comprising husband, wife, and children have been expanded to include same-sex and common-law couples, lone parents, and childless couples in recognition of the many forms that families take today.
2. Common approaches to family often refer to the *nuclear family* (an adult male, adult female, and their offspring) and *extended families* (multiple generations of adults living with their spouses and children).
3. Another way to distinguish families is to identify the *family of orientation* (the family in which you were born) and the *family of procreation* (the family that you have created through procreation or adoption).
4. In the 2006 Census, Statistics Canada used two definitions of *family* for data-gathering purposes: the "census family" and the "economic family."
5. The *census family* is defined as a married couple (with or without children of either or both spouses), a couple living common-law (with or without children of either or both partners), or a lone parent of any marital status, with at least one child living in the same dwelling. A couple may be of the opposite or same sex. Children in a census family include grandchildren living with their grandparent(s) but with no parents present.
6. The *economic family* is defined as a group of two or more persons who live in the same dwelling and are related to each other by blood, marriage, common-law, or adoption. A couple may be of opposite or same sex. Foster children are included.

module 6.2   SOCIOLOGICAL APPROACHES TO FAMILIES

7. Functionalists state that families accomplish certain social functions, such as providing individuals with love, and emotional and economic support. Families also maintain and stabilize society by regulating reproduction and socializing children.
8. Conflict theorists argue that inequalities inherent in the larger society exist in families. Further, families are organized to meet the needs of a capitalist society.
9. Symbolic interactionists take a micro approach to studying family life; that is, they investigate how family members' behaviours are shaped by how they define and interpret situations.
10. Feminists argue that families are structured to benefit men and maintain women's subordinate role.
11. Post-structuralists challenge the way we think and talk about families. For instance, they may question the concept of the "good mother."
12. Queer theorists examine how families and family life are structured around the norm of heterosexuality.

module 6.3   CONTEMPORARY CANADIAN FAMILIES

13. Overall marriage rates are on the decline, but common-law unions are increasing.
14. Canada is seeing a rise in mixed-race marriages.
15. Same-sex marriage was legalized in Canada in 2005.
16. Polygamy may become legalized in Canada if the legality of polygamy law is challenged in court under the Canadian Charter of Rights and Freedoms' section on religious freedoms.

17. Divorce rates increased dramatically first in 1968 when the divorce laws were changed and again in 1985 when no-fault divorce was legislated.
18. Demands to balance home and work life have increased as the need for more than one income has increased. Women still feel the weight of domestic labour in spite of the fact that many now work outside the home as well.

module 6.4   FAMILY VIOLENCE

19. In Canada in 2002, 27 percent of all reported violent crimes involved instances of family violence.
20. From 1974 to 1994, the majority of women killed in Ontario died at the hands of intimate male partners.
21. In 2004, the Supreme Court of Canada ruled that corporal punishment of children is constitutional and does not violate children's rights. Currently, Bill S-209 is before Parliament. Should it pass into law, the spanking of children will become illegal in Canada.

Key Terms

corporal punishment   186
domestic labour   173
endogamy   180
expressive role   172
extended family   169
family of orientation   169

family of procreation   169
instrumental role   172
intimate femicide   185
nuclear family   169
polyandry   180
polygamy   180

polygyny   180
role strain   174
second shift   183
social reproduction   173

Test Yourself

1. A(n) _____ family includes an adult male, adult female, and their offspring.
   a. Canadian
   b. Nuclear
   c. Extended
   d. American

2. The family of _____ is the family into which we are born.
   a. Orientation
   b. Procreation
   c. Origin
   d. Extension

3. Which family group is the largest in Canada?
   a. Same-sex couples
   b. Common-law couples
   c. Lone-parent families
   d. Legally married couples with children

4. Statistics Canada created two definitions of *family* in the 2006 Census. Who is not included in the definition?
   a. Common-law couples without children
   b. Never-married lone parent living with children
   c. A single person living alone
   d. Grandchildren living with their grandparents but not their parents

5. The legalization of same-sex marriage has made certain rights and benefits available to married same-sex couples. Which of the following rights and benefits are available to same-sex married couples?
   a. Access to each other's employment benefits
   b. Ability to adopt children
   c. Inheritance rights
   d. All of the above

6. _____ are concerned with how families contribute to order, consensus, equilibrium, and order in society.
   a. Functionalists
   b. Conflict theorists
   c. Symbolic interactionists
   d. Feminists

7. _____ perceive that inequalities inherent in the larger society are perpetuated inside families.
   a. Functionalists
   b. Conflict theorists
   c. Symbolic interactionists
   d. Post-structuralists

8. The stress that results when someone does not have sufficient resources to play a role or roles is called
   a. Role strain

b. Role stress

c. Work overload

d. Domestic stress

9 _____ approaches hold that families remain the primary sites for the subordination of women.

a. Functionalist

b. Conflict theorist

c. Symbolic interactionist

d. Feminist

10. *Heteronormativity* describes a view that considers

a. Heterosexuality as the norm

b. Homosexuality as the norm

c. Bisexuality as the norm

d. Transsexuality as the norm

11. Which of the following countries has not legalized same-sex marriage?

a. Canada

b. United States

c. Belgium

d. The Netherlands

12. The term used to describe marriage within one's group is

a. Endogamy

b. Polygamy

c. Exogamy

d. Polygyny

13. The Divorce Act was passed in

a. 1960

b. 1968

c. 1974

d. 1986

14. The domestic labour that women engage in after returning home from paid labour is called the

a. Double shift

b. End shift

c. Extra shift

d. Second shift

15. The act that legalized same-sex marriage is called

a. The Gay Marriage Act

b. The Civil Marriage Act

c. The Same-Sex Marriage Act

d. The Same-Sex Union Act

16. In Canada in 2002, _____ of all reported violent crimes involved instances of family violence.

a. 8 percent

b. 20 percent

c. 27 percent

d. 39 percent

17. The majority of reported violent crimes within a family are committed by a

a. Spouse or ex-spouse

b. Parent

c. Sibling

d. Grandparent

18. Which of the following statements is false?

a. Women are more likely to be severely assaulted than men.

b. Men are more likely to suffer an injury.

c. Women are more likely to require medical attention.

d. Women are more likely than men to live in fear for their lives.

19. Who is allowed to spank children according to the Criminal Code of Canada?

a. Teachers

b. Grandparents

c. Daycare workers

d. All of the above, as long as they are acting in the place of parents.

20. Which of the following statements is true?

a. Most countries in the world have outlawed spanking.

b. Canada will be the first country to outlaw spanking.

c. According to the law, parents can hit children as long as they don't hit them in the head.

d. The use of straps and rulers to punish children at school is deemed acceptable by the Supreme Court of Canada.

Answers: b, a, d, c, d, a, b, a, b, d, b, c, a, b, d, c

Log in to MySocLab for a host of resources that will help you save time and improve your grade. MySocLab contains cutting-edge learning tools such as study plans, practice tests, videos, audio segments, quizzes, and more—all designed to help you better understand the learning objectives for this chapter. Along with your eBook, MySocLab for *Sociology for Everyone* can be found at **www.mysoclab.com**.

module 6.1
DEFINING FAMILIES

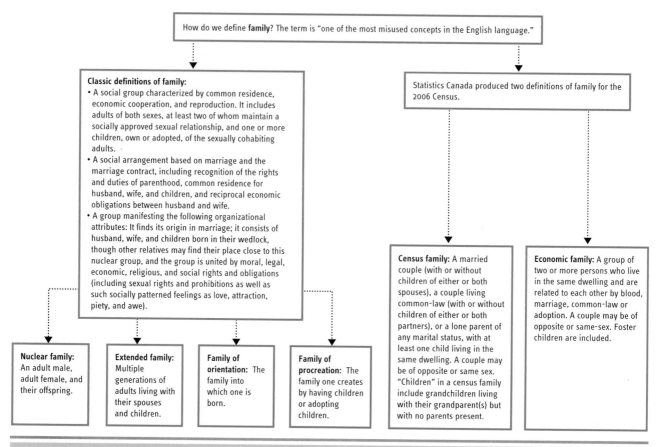

How do we define **family**? The term is "one of the most misused concepts in the English language."

Classic definitions of family:
- A social group characterized by common residence, economic cooperation, and reproduction. It includes adults of both sexes, at least two of whom maintain a socially approved sexual relationship, and one or more children, own or adopted, of the sexually cohabiting adults.
- A social arrangement based on marriage and the marriage contract, including recognition of the rights and duties of parenthood, common residence for husband, wife, and children, and reciprocal economic obligations between husband and wife.
- A group manifesting the following organizational attributes: It finds its origin in marriage; it consists of husband, wife, and children born in their wedlock, though other relatives may find their place close to this nuclear group, and the group is united by moral, legal, economic, religious, and social rights and obligations (including sexual rights and prohibitions as well as such socially patterned feelings as love, attraction, piety, and awe).

Statistics Canada produced two definitions of family for the 2006 Census.

Census family: A married couple (with or without children of either or both spouses), a couple living common-law (with or without children of either or both partners), or a lone parent of any marital status, with at least one child living in the same dwelling. A couple may be of opposite or same sex. "Children" in a census family include grandchildren living with their grandparent(s) but with no parents present.

Economic family: A group of two or more persons who live in the same dwelling and are related to each other by blood, marriage, common-law or adoption. A couple may be of opposite or same-sex. Foster children are included.

Nuclear family: An adult male, adult female, and their offspring.

Extended family: Multiple generations of adults living with their spouses and children.

Family of orientation: The family into which one is born.

Family of procreation: The family one creates by having children or adopting children.

module 6.2
SOCIOLOGICAL APPROACHES TO FAMILIES

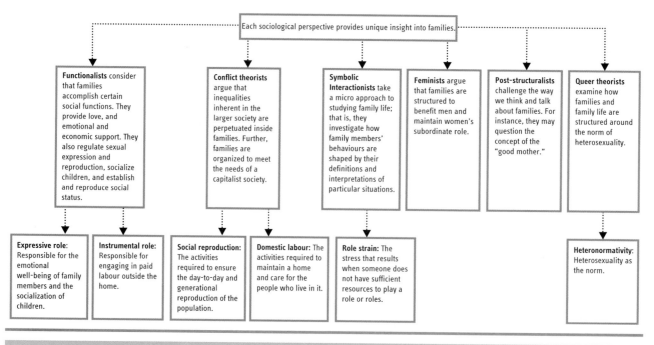

Each sociological perspective provides unique insight into families.

Functionalists consider that families accomplish certain social functions. They provide love, and emotional and economic support. They also regulate sexual expression and reproduction, socialize children, and establish and reproduce social status.

Conflict theorists argue that inequalities inherent in the larger society are perpetuated inside families. Further, families are organized to meet the needs of a capitalist society.

Symbolic Interactionists take a micro approach to studying family life; that is, they investigate how family members' behaviours are shaped by their definitions and interpretations of particular situations.

Feminists argue that families are structured to benefit men and maintain women's subordinate role.

Post-structuralists challenge the way we think and talk about families. For instance, they may question the concept of the "good mother."

Queer theorists examine how families and family life are structured around the norm of heterosexuality.

Expressive role: Responsible for the emotional well-being of family members and the socialization of children.

Instrumental role: Responsible for engaging in paid labour outside the home.

Social reproduction: The activities required to ensure the day-to-day and generational reproduction of the population.

Domestic labour: The activities required to maintain a home and care for the people who live in it.

Role strain: The stress that results when someone does not have sufficient resources to play a role or roles.

Heteronormativity: Heterosexuality as the norm.

module 6.3
CONTEMPORARY CANADIAN FAMILIES

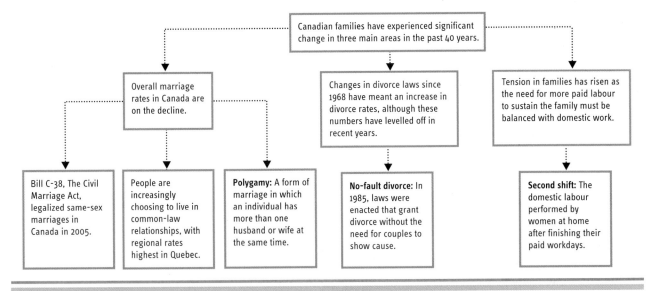

Canadian families have experienced significant change in three main areas in the past 40 years.

Overall marriage rates in Canada are on the decline.

Changes in divorce laws since 1968 have meant an increase in divorce rates, although these numbers have levelled off in recent years.

Tension in families has risen as the need for more paid labour to sustain the family must be balanced with domestic work.

Bill C-38, The Civil Marriage Act, legalized same-sex marriages in Canada in 2005.

People are increasingly choosing to live in common-law relationships, with regional rates highest in Quebec.

Polygamy: A form of marriage in which an individual has more than one husband or wife at the same time.

No-fault divorce: In 1985, laws were enacted that grant divorce without the need for couples to show cause.

Second shift: The domestic labour performed by women at home after finishing their paid workdays.

module 6.4
FAMILY VIOLENCE

Family violence: In Canada in 2007, 27 percent of all reported violent crimes involved instances of family violence.

Intimate femicide: The killing of women by their intimate male partners. The killing of women by their intimate male partners accounted for the majority of women killed in Ontario from 1974 to 1994.

Corporal punishment: In relation to children, any physical force with the intent of causing a child to experience pain in the hope of changing that child's behaviour.

Social Inequality

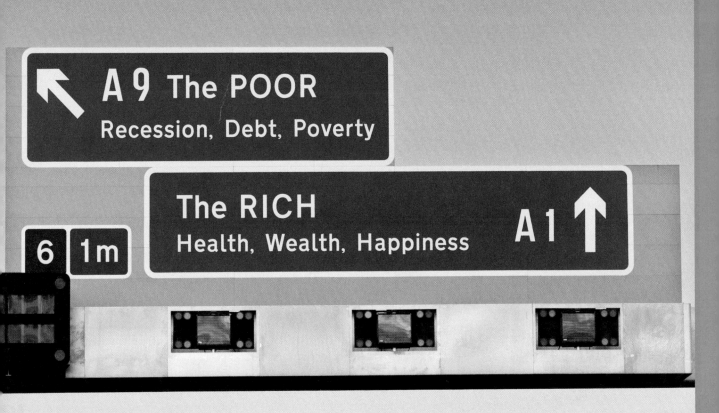

What Are You Worth?

Have you ever thought about the value of work? If you have a job, how much do you earn? Do you think you are paid a fair wage for the work that you do? What criteria do you think was used to determine your wage?

In 2005, the average Canadian earned a salary of $38 010. Those working at a full-time minimum-wage job earned less than half that amount at around $16 000. Meanwhile, the average pay of the top 100 Canadian CEOs according to *Report on Business Magazine* was $9 million in 2005 (Nugget, 2007).

Does the gap in wages seem significant to you? It should. Based on these numbers, the average CEO from that list earns the equivalent of $16 000 by the time we roll out of bed on January 1. By the time we hit the shower, that same CEO will have earned more than a minimum-wage worker would earn in an entire year. By 9:47 a.m. on January 2, that CEO will have earned more than the average Canadian (Nugget, 2007).

We debate the earnings of CEOs, movie stars, and sports heroes without really considering how those earnings relate to the wages of everyday people. For example, we might ask, How much is Sidney Crosby worth? Should he earn more than Mats Sundin? Should he earn less than Alexander Ovechkin? Our discussion surrounds hockey players who earn multi-millions of dollars a year. However, do we ask whether hockey players truly deserve to earn more than police officers, firefighters, social workers, and teachers?

The Canadian class system is based on inequality. We reward individuals differently for the things they do, and as a society we accept, at least implicitly, this unequal distribution of wealth as fair. Criteria used to determine one's income include the effort they expend, the contribution they make to society and/or the economy, their skills and their achievements, and the level of need society has for the work they perform.

Now back to you. How much is your labour worth?

module 7.1

What Is Social Stratification?

Think about Social Stratification

1 Think about class and discrimination. People discriminate against others based on a number of criteria (e.g., gender, ethnicity, and age). Describe ways in which people are discriminated against based on their social class.

2 Think about your opportunities for advancement in Canada. Do you believe that if you work hard, Canada is a good place to move up the social ladder? Why or why not?

social stratification
A society's hierarchical ranking of people into social classes.

social class A group of individuals sharing a common position in a social hierarchy, based on both birth and achievement.

social status An individual's position within the class structure.

meritocracy A system of rewards based on personal attributes and demonstrated abilities.

social mobility Movement between social classes.

intergenerational mobility Status as defined by parents' social class.

intragenerational mobility Status movement throughout one's life.

Social stratification is a society's hierarchical ranking of people into social classes (see Nayebi & Abdollahyan, 2006). An individual's **social class** is based on both birth and achievements in life. A person's position within the class structure is called his or her **social status**.

While we may want to believe that everyone in Canada is equal, the fact is that we are not. We put different values on assets such as special talents and education, and we compensate people differently based on those assets. The question to ask yourself is, Why are all complex human societies (i.e., those with specialized tasks and occupational separation) stratified (see Service, 1962)?

Social stratification is based on a few key principles. First, all societies redistribute materials and social rewards to individuals (e.g., food, money, social prestige). A stratified system ensures that those individuals who do more or are more capable receive more material wealth and social recognition (Nayebi & Abdollahyan, 2006, p. 250). By rewarding deserving individuals, society allocates its limited resources to those who offer the greatest benefit to the whole. For example, Canadians recognize the tremendous dedication and talent physicians and surgeons possess and therefore grant them relatively high material rewards (i.e., money) as well as social recognition and profile (i.e., being a doctor is a high-status position in Canadian society). In this sense, then, social stratification makes sense—it allows people who offer more to society to have more. For this system to work, people in the society must believe that they can achieve wealth and status through individual attributes, a system of rewards called a *meritocracy*. A **meritocracy** is a system based on the principle that people achieve what they deserve (Applebaum, 2005). For example, the grades you obtain in college or university should be based on how well you do on your tests and assignments and not on your age, gender, or physical appearance; grades are granted on your demonstrated command of the material.

Second, since social stratification transcends any single generation (with social position largely granted by one's parents), the system is relatively stable over time. Although there is some movement between social levels—which sociologists refer to as **social mobility**—the reality is that very few people are able to move out of the social class to which they were born (Western & Wright, 1994). Social mobility is typically measured by comparing adult children's status to that of their parents (called **intergenerational mobility**), but it can also be measured by comparing a person's status position over his or her lifetime (called **intragenerational mobility**); for example, a young woman who grows up in a poor family may achieve a scholarship to university and ultimately become a successful lawyer. Sociologists use social mobility to measure a society's equality of opportunity (Mookherjee & Napel, 2007). As a rule, social stratification has little relationship to skills or abilities. High-status people, even those who lack intelligence or talent, generally find it far easier to obtain property, prestige, and power than do those who are more capable but reside in the lower classes.

Third, social stratification is present in all known human societies, but varies in how it expresses itself. For example, in some societies like our own, some status is granted by how much money one has, while in others status is granted by how much wealth one gives away (as in Northwest Coast potlatch ceremonies; see Godelier, 1999; Roth, 2002). Further, even in our own society, which values material wealth, we are quick to judge someone who achieves material wealth in a manner we do not condone or respect. For example, a drug dealer and a surgeon may both make the same annual income, but we would certainly grant the drug dealer lower social status and prestige than the surgeon.

Fourth, while all societies recognize differences in wealth and prestige, the criteria by which they are granted are nonetheless considered fair and just by the majority of the population—even those in the lower classes. This acceptance of often unjust criteria is grounded on the dominant ideology—the set of beliefs and values that support and justify a society's ruling class.

WHAT IS SOCIAL INEQUALITY?

Social inequality results from collective decisions about what is important in evaluating a person or a group. This inequality takes various forms: women may be paid less than men for the same job; members of visible minority groups may be less likely to be hired than members of the majority; those with more education tend to make more money than those with less education. Inequality, then, results from a system that ranks people from high (better) to low (worse) on such subjective criteria as gender and minority status. These criteria are considered *subjective* because they have no material influence on whether a person can actually perform a particular job. In other words, there is no inherent necessity for the majority of truck drivers or lawyers to be men, or for most elementary school teachers to be women. These subjective assessments of people's worth are supported not by individual capability but by the dominant ideology.

CLASSISM

Most Canadians are aware of the biases inherent in the ideologies that have traditionally supported racial, gender, and age inequality (called *racism*, *sexism*, and *ageism*, respectively). Yet, the same ideological support for discrimination exists for social class as well. **Classism** is the belief that people's relative worth is at least partially determined by their social and economic status (Shpungin & Lyubansky, 2006, p. 231). Classism legitimates economic inequality and has been called "the ideology of competitive individualism" (Lewis, 1978, as cited in Lindsey, Beach, & Ravelli, 2008, p. 239).

classism An ideology that suggests that people's relative worth is at least partially determined by their social and economic status.

Classisism is based on the idea that everyone has an equal chance of getting ahead if they just work hard. This idea, sometimes referred to as the "American Dream," is fundamental to the smooth operation of capitalist society. However right or wrong, classism results in the belief that the wealthy deserve what they have and that the poor are responsible for their failure.

In a classic work, sociologists Huber and Form (1973) found that wealthy and middle-class Americans saw themselves as deserving of their wealth and status. They believed their success was the result of their own abilities, skills, and effort. The poor, however, were more likely to see their economic plight as the result of structural factors such as high unemployment rates, lack of opportunity, and the failure of society to provide adequate schooling (Newman & Smith, 1999).

Newman and Smith (1999) argue that these perceptions of why people succeed or fail have important policy implications for government. If decision-makers believe that poor people lack motivation, then government should focus on reducing people's dependence on subsidy programs such as welfare. The Mike Harris Conservative government in Ontario in the 1990s followed this type of thinking. It believed that those on welfare should work for their money. As a result, it replaced welfare with its work-fare program (CBC, 1995). Implicit in the Conservative government's thinking was the idea that the poor are simply lazy and should not look for government handouts. However, if poverty is viewed as the result of structural barriers for the poor, then policy-makers should focus on increasing educational and occupational opportunities for everyone. Both perspectives lead to vastly different ways of trying to help the poor. Not surprisingly, after a lifetime of living with the idea that people ultimately get what they deserve (i.e., classist thinking), most Canadians are not interested in changing our welfare or educational programs.

Classist thinking can lead people to reject policies that would help the disadvantaged overcome the structural factors that limit their opportunities to improve their chances of upward mobility. However, some suggest that classism is being challenged more frequently today, and that awareness of class discrimination is improving (Nakhaie, 1997; Simpson, Stark, & Jackson, 1988). Not only are educational levels rising in Canada, but communication technology is making it easier for marginalized groups to spread their message and join collective efforts to promote social change.

CLOSED AND OPEN SOCIAL SYSTEMS

closed system A social system in which status is based on ascribed attributes at birth.

open system A social system in which status is based on achieved attributes.

caste system An ascribed system of hereditary class designation.

Sociologists define two major ways that social systems rank people: *closed systems* and *open systems*. **Closed systems** are those based on *ascribed status*—that is, the status associated with attributes that people are born with. These systems are "closed" because innate attributes (e.g., race, ethnicity) cannot change, and thus allow for very little social mobility. An example of a closed system is the caste system of India. Conversely, an **open system** is based on a person's achieved status where social mobility is more likely because movement between social classes is the result of personal attributes. An example of an open system is the class system in Canada.

CLOSED SYSTEMS   **Caste systems**—ascribed systems of hereditary class designation—allow virtually no social mobility. Given the tremendous disparities between the wealth, social status, and occupational prestige among castes, these systems usually emphasize a legitimating ideology, nearly always religious in character, to support and justify such differences. The very idea of social mobility is foreign within caste societies. A person's caste is a central component of who they are and determines virtually everything in their lives, including what they can wear, what jobs they can perform, and who they can marry (Lindsey & Beach, 2003, p. 198).

One of the more infamous examples of a caste society is India. The Indian caste system is thought to date from as early as 350 BCE, when the varna system (a Sanskrit word meaning "colour") divided Indian society into four primary groups (Lahiri, 2005). Each caste was broadly associated with the types of work its members performed:

Although India's caste system was outlawed in 1950, caste continues to shape the lives of many Indians.

Brahmin: teachers, doctors, and other scholars
Kshatriya: warriors and politicians
Vaishya: merchants and artists
Shudra: workers in the service occupations (Howard, 2006)

Beneath these four main castes are *Dalit*, "untouchables" who literally have no caste and whose name translates as "oppressed, downtrodden, and exploited." Dalits are believed to pollute people of higher caste. In fact, if a higher-caste Hindu is touched by a Dalit or crosses into a Dalit's shadow, he or she is considered polluted and must go through a series of rigorous cleaning rituals (Dalit Freedom Network, 2007). Today, there are about 240 million Dalits living in India.

As in all caste systems, membership in a caste is hereditary. Therefore, even when a person of low caste becomes wealthy or a high-caste person loses all of his or her money, their castes remain the same. Moreover, a person is expected to work and marry within his or her caste. The only way people in this system can change their caste is through **reincarnation**. Depending on the life a person leads, he or she will move to a higher or lower caste in their next life.

Although the Indian Constitution of 1950 abolished the caste system, discrimination toward lower castes persists, particularly in rural areas. To counter discrimination based on caste, the Indian government has instituted various affirmative action policies to provide the lower castes with access to government jobs, higher education, and politics. The aim of these policies is to improve the plight of historically stigmatized populations and promote them into positions that would strengthen their representation and preserve their rights (Raman, 1999). Some movement toward equality has occurred in larger centres, but because the caste system is so deeply entrenched in Indian culture, it may take generations to disappear.

OPEN SYSTEMS   In theory, in open systems, where you end up is where you deserve to be. For example, the **class system**, an open system, is based on achieved status—people can change their status or social rank based on their own abilities and efforts.

Open systems comprise a **class structure**—the overall economic hierarchy that categorizes groups of people based on their socio-economic status. **Socio-economic status (SES)** is made up of three loosely related indicators (or measures) of social position: income, occupational prestige, and education (Veenstra, 2006). It is important to analyze each of these indicators in coordination with the other two, because looking only at one can be misleading. For example, based solely on income, a drug dealer and a lawyer (both of whom live in nice houses and drive Porsches) are comparable. But clearly they are not. The drug dealer, while financially successful, is involved in illegal activities, does not participate in what the larger society considers a prestigious career, and may not have completed high school. Conversely, the lawyer has a prestigious occupation and an extensive post-secondary education. As you can see, looking at one SES indicator in isolation may leave out a great deal.

PROPERTY AND OCCUPATIONAL PRESTIGE: TWO COMPONENTS OF INEQUALITY

PROPERTY   Property is an important indicator of where one resides in the class structure. Sociologists generally divide property into two general categories: income and wealth. **Income** is defined as the money one receives annually from all sources, such as salaries, fees paid for services, rents, grants, support payments, government assistance, and interest and dividends paid from stocks, bond holdings, and other investments. **Wealth** is defined as one's net accumulated assets including homes, land, automobiles, jewellery, factories, savings, and stocks and bonds. Income, then, is what you earn, and wealth is what you have.

To view an excellent CBC documentary series on modern-day India, go to **www.cbc.ca/documentaries/indiareborn/watchepisodes.shtml.**

reincarnation   The belief, associated with Eastern religions, that one's essence does not die and instead is reborn in another form.

class system   Social stratification based on achieved status.

class structure   A society's economic structure that categorizes groups of people based on their socio-economic status.

socio-economic status (SES)   Social status as determined by family income, parents' education level, parents' occupations, and the family's social standing within the community.

income   Money received annually from all sources.

wealth   Net accumulated assets, including homes, land, and stocks.

TABLE 7–1 Median Wealth of Families (Including Unattached Individuals), by Quintile, 1984 to 2005*

Quintile	1984	1999	2005	1999 to 2005	1984 to 2005
	(2005 dollars)			*% change*	
Bottom	0	–700	–1 000	–43	. . .
Second	14 100	14 400	12 500	–13	–11
Third	67 300	74 400	84 800	14	26
Fourth	143 400	181 400	212 600	17	48
Top	335 500	464 900	551 000	19	64

. . . not applicable

* Excluding the value of registered pension plans.

Source: Statistics Canada. 2006. *The Daily, Wednesday, December 13, 2006. Study: Inequality in wealth.* Retrieved June 12, 2007, from http://www.statcan.ca/Daily/English/061213/d061213c.htm (December 6, 2007).

quintile A measure that divides population into five categories, each representing 20 percent.

The distribution of Canadian wealth between 1984 and 2005 is presented in Table 7–1. In the table, the Canadian population is divided into **quintiles**—five categories, each representing 20 percent of the total population. Between 1999 and 2005, the median net worth of Canada's richest families increased by 19 percent, while the net worth of the poorest Canadians fell by 43 percent. In 2005, the richest 20 percent of Canadians had a median net worth (excluding the value of employer-sponsored pension plans) estimated at $551 000 (in 2005 dollars). This net worth grew from $335 500 in 1984 and $464 900 in 1999 (an increase of 64 percent between 1984 and 2005). In contrast, the median net worth of the poorest 20 percent of Canadians fell between 1984 and 2005. In fact, the two lowest groups in the table (accounting for 40 percent of Canadians) had their real wealth decline between 1984 and 2005.

The concentration of wealth in the top quintile is staggering. For example, the Thomson family had a family fortune estimated at more than $22 billion in 2007. Although this wealth pales in comparison to that of the richest man in the world (Microsoft CEO Bill Gates, who has a personal wealth estimated at around $56 billion [see www.forbes.com]), it demonstrates that the world's wealthiest people live in a very different world than the rest of us.

occupational prestige The social value of a particular occupation.

OCCUPATIONAL PRESTIGE   When we meet someone for the first time, one of the most common questions we ask is, "What do you do?" Their answers help us classify their class position, and for many of us, influence how we interact with them (e.g., consider how you react when a person introduces himself or herself as a student or as a doctor). We do this, in part, because people generally agree on the prestige, and therefore the social value, of various occupations (Goyder, 2005; Goyder & Frank, 2007; Lindsey & Beach, 2003, p. 212). The fact that you are in school is probably an indication that you want to pursue a career that will be both emotionally and financially rewarding. Table 7–2 lists a number of occupations and their ranking on an **occupational prestige** scale.

Is there anything about these rankings that you find interesting? For example, while income is generally correlated to occupational prestige (i.e., the higher the salary, the higher the prestige) there are some exceptions. For example, bartenders may make more per year (when you include tips) than some carpenters or social workers. Do you think gender plays a role in which occupations score highly on the prestige scale? Why do you think this may be the case? Researchers have found that occupations dominated by women or visible minorities tend to be poorly paid and less prestigious (Denton & Boos, 2007; Kazemipur & Halli, 2001; Preibisch & Binford, 2007; Reid, Adelman, & Jaret, 2007). However, some

CANADIAN SOCIETY IN FOCUS

Canada's Wealthiest People

Canada's largest media conglomerate, the Thomson Corporation, began in 1934 when its founder, Roy Thomson, acquired his first newspaper in Canada—the *Timmins Press*. Thomson later acquired more newspapers in Canada, Scotland, and the United Kingdom through Thomson Newspapers Ltd. Thomson Publications (UK) was formed in 1961 with the intent of acquiring business and consumer magazines and book publishing companies. Thomson Travel emerged with the purchase of Britannia Airways in 1965. When Roy Thomson died in 1976, his son, Kenneth Thomson, took over the family business. Throughout the 1970s and 1980s, Kenneth Thomson acquired interests in oil and gas in the United Kingdom and the North Sea. The Thomson Corporation was formed in 1989 with the merger of Thomson Newspapers and the International Thomson Organization. In 2006, Kenneth Thomson died and his eldest son, David Thomson, assumed control of the corporation (Canadian Business, 2007). Today, the Thomson Corporation owns the *Globe and Mail*, various holdings in health-care products, legal services, financial services, tax and accounting software and services, educational publishing, and hundreds of associated products and international interests. In less than 100 years, the organization has grown to include more than 32 000 employees worldwide and is emerging as a global player in mass media and e-information (www.thomson.com, 2007).

George Weston Bakeries Ltd. is currently run by Galen Weston, but was founded by his grandfather in 1882. The company is currently one of the largest food processing and distribution groups in North America. The two operating segments of the Weston Corporation include Weston Foods and Loblaw Companies Limited. Weston Foods is involved in the baking and dairy industry in North America, while Loblaw Companies Limited is Canada's largest food distributor and a leading provider of general merchandise, drugstore, and financial products and services (www.weston.ca, 2007). Galen Weston's other retail interests include department stores Holt Renfrew (in Canada), Brown Thomas (in Ireland), and Selfridges (in England).

Founded in 1824 by K.C. Irving, Irving Oil is a family-run corporation run by K.C. Irving's grandsons and brothers, James (J.K.), Arthur, and John (Jack) Irving. Irving Oil is Canada's largest refinery headquartered in Saint John, New Brunswick (it produces over 300 000 barrels per day). Irving Oil originally began as a garage and service station in K.C. Irving's hometown of Bouctouche, New Brunswick. In the 1930s, Irving Oil expanded the company to include various lubricating products. In 1931, K.C. Irving opened a Ford franchise in Saint John. In the 1960s, Irving Oil entered the propane business by acquiring Speedy Propane and Burma Propane. In 1992, K.C. Irving passed away at the age of 93 and left his three grandsons to run the business. Today, family-owned Irving Oil continues to provide products and services to customers across eastern Canada and in New England (www.irvingoil.com, 2007).

Are you surprised that all of these examples are men? That they are all white? As a sociologist, what does this tell us about our society?

researchers suggest that gender differences in Canadian occupational prestige are declining over time (Goyder, Guppy, & Thompson, 2003). Finally, if you look at the occupations that are rated highly, you will notice that they generally require university education, provide a great deal of independence and autonomy, and depend on sound decision-making and abstract reasoning skills.

TABLE 7–2 **Occupational Prestige Scores**

Occupation	Prestige Score
Physician	86
Lawyer	75
University professor	74
Architect	73
Dentist	72
Pharmacist	68
Registered nurse	66
High school teacher	66
Accountant	65
Elementary school teacher	64
Computer programmer	61
Police officer	60
Librarian	54
Social worker	52
Realtor	49
Mail carrier	47
Secretary	46
Welder	42
Farmer	40
Carpenter	39
Child-care worker	36
Truck driver	30
Cashier	29
Garbage collector	28
Bartender	25
Farm labourer	23
Janitor	22
Shoe shiner	9

Source: NORC General Social Surveys, 1972–1996: Cumulative Codebook. Chicago: NORC, 1996. Reprinted by permission of NORC, Chicago, IL.

What do you know about **Social Stratification**?

Multiple-choice questions (circle your answer)

1. **An individual's position within the class structure is called**
   a. Social group
   b. Social stratification
   c. Social status
   d. Meritocracy

2. **Social mobility that is measured by comparing adult children's social class to that of their parents is called**
   a. Intergenerational mobility
   b. Intragenerational mobility
   c. Meritocracy
   d. Parental mobility

3. **An ideology that suggests that people's relative worth is at least partially determined by their social and economic status is called**
   a. Social mobility
   b. Classism
   c. Meritocracy
   d. Horizontal mobility

4. **Social stratification based on achieved status is called**
   a. Class system
   b. Class structure
   c. Caste system
   d. Closed system

5. **Wealth is**
   a. Money received annually from all sources
   b. Net accumulated assets, including homes, land, and stocks
   c. Stocks and bonds only
   d. Both a and b

Answers: c, a, b, a, b

module 7.2

Sociological Approaches to Social Inequality

Social inequality affects our lives and our behaviour in a number of ways—from the life choices we make to how we treat each other. Each sociological perspective gives us insight into how social inequality affects us.

FUNCTIONALISM

Functionalists argue that all social practices and structures must perform some useful service to society. Therefore, they would conclude that if social stratification exists, it must serve some purpose in society.

Functionalists note that all societies have important jobs that need to be filled. Some jobs require a lot of education or training and a special set of skills (e.g., a doctor). Other jobs are unpleasant tasks that, if given a choice, some people would not want to do (e.g., garbage collector). Still other jobs are dangerous (e.g., firefighter). According to functionalists, to attract the most capable and skilled people into such important and demanding jobs, the rewards must be high enough to compensate them for their time and effort.

Kingsley Davis (1908–1997) and Wilbert Moore (1941–1987) developed one of the most influential theories of social stratification. The **Davis-Moore thesis** holds that social inequality serves two important social functions: first, it motivates people to fill certain social positions, and second, it motivates people to fulfill their duties and responsibilities (Davis & Moore, 1945, p. 242; Nayebi & Abdollahyan, 2006).

Most Canadians believe that doctors and firefighters should be rewarded accordingly for what they give to society. Prestige and financial rewards are good motivators. However, critics of functionalism recognize that the system does not work quite as fairly as it sounds. For instance, family connections and inheritance may be the basis for getting a high-paying job and have nothing to do with merit. A lack of financial support may inhibit talented people from acquiring the education they need to have prestigious careers. Discrimination on the basis of gender or ethnicity may limit access to elite positions (Gyimah, Walters & Phythian, 2005; McMullin, 2004; Preibisch & Binford, 2007), even by highly skilled and talented people—a fact clearly in opposition to the Davis-Moore thesis (Lindsey & Beach, 2003, p. 201). Further, the comparatively low salaries of socially important occupations such as daycare workers, public school teachers, and social workers clearly demonstrates the extent to which gender bias may influence salary levels. Finally, the salary of an occupation can have more to do with market forces than the work's value in society.

In its recognition of the need to reward those willing to contribute to collective social benefit, the Davis-Moore thesis offers an important insight into the functional benefits of social stratification. However, the theory largely ignores the power of the social elite and the negative impact on the poor and the lower classes (Porter, 1965).

CONFLICT THEORY

According to conflict theorists, a society that contains social classes is simply a manifestation of competition between those who have social power and those who do not. While Karl Marx and Max Weber would agree that competition exists between classes, they differ on why social stratification occurs and whether it is inevitable.

KARL MARX Marx believed that all of social life was influenced by how people interact during the process of economic production. There were those that owned the production—the bourgeoisie—and those that provided the labour—the proletariat. This new social structure

Think about Sociological Approaches to Social Inequality

1 Think about social inequality. Do you think it is fair to pay people different amounts of money for different jobs? Why? Could you imagine a world in which everyone earned the same amount of money, regardless of the job they did? Why or why not?

2 Think about the ways people show their social status. What objects do you possess that tell others about your social rank?

Davis-Moore thesis
The theory that social stratification is functional for society because it ensures that key social positions are held by the most capable people.

came as a consequence of industrialization. Marx argued that the interests of these two social classes are incompatible. The bourgeoisie are motivated to maintain their control over society so that they can accumulate as much profit as possible, while the proletariat tries to get as much money for their labour as possible. The bourgeoisie maintain their position of power by using the "state machinery" (e.g., police, prisons, the military) to protect their class interests (Lindsey & Beach, 2003, p. 202). According to Marx, only by recognizing their "false consciousness"—that they are indeed being exploited and controlled—can the proletariat hope to challenge the bourgeoisie. By developing a "class consciousness"—a sense of their own needs and collective power—the proletariat could challenge the bourgeoisie for a greater share of the resources. Thus, according to Marx, social stratification is the embodiment of class conflict and is inevitable in capitalist economies that require the exploitation of the working classes. But Marx believed that a classless society could exist. This was the basis for Marx's *Communist Manifesto*.

Marx's analysis of social inequality continues to influence sociologists today. However, while much contemporary sociology is undertaken from a conflict perspective, Marx's focus on revolutionary ideas advocating for the overthrow of capitalism remains controversial and somewhat outdated. While capitalism continues to exploit many workers around the world, it has also led to a rising standard of living. Further, workers have created extensive labour organizations, and in many areas of the world enjoy more protection under the law than ever before (Shalla, 2004). Finally, in publicly traded companies, the line between owner and worker has become blurred. It is possible to work for a company and also be part owner through shareholding.

MAX WEBER   Weber (1864–1920) agreed with Marx's conclusion that capitalism led to class conflict, but he also suggested that Marx's single-minded focus on economic production was overly simplistic and failed to appreciate the multi-dimensional nature of social class, inequality, and the role of cultural values (Inglehart & Baker, 2000, p. 19). Thus, for Weber, Marx's desire for a classless society was not inevitable; in fact, Weber thought that social stratification was, at some level at least, unavoidable and necessary.

Weber agreed with Marx that modern society was divided into economic classes and that the ownership of property was important for gaining influence. However, he also argued that there were other sources of influence: class, status groups, and party (Weber, 1946).

According to Marx and Weber, conflicts between workers and owners are grounded in economic inequality.

Class   For Weber (and Marx), class differences are largely based on economic inequality—some people have more wealth than others. For example, the amount of wealth and property one has defines one's class position. The rich landowners are in the higher echelons of society, while the poor workers are in the lower echelons of society. Weber thought economic class was relatively unimportant, given that most people lack class consciousness (Lindsey & Beach, 2003, p. 203) and are therefore unlikely to challenge the status quo.

Status Groups   People rarely consider themselves as members of a particular status group. According to Weber, **status groups** are composed of people who share similar social status, common lifestyles, world views, occupations, and standards of living (Nayebi & Abdollahyan, 2006, p. 252). Status groups based on ethnicity include First Nations, Asians, blacks, and Ukrainians. Status groups based on religious beliefs include Jews, Muslims, and Catholics. Other groupings are based on occupation: manual labourers, academics, dentists, drug dealers.

status group   A group of people who share similar social status, lifestyles, world views, occupations, and standards of living.

According to Lindsey & Beach (2003), people are more likely to act collectively as part of a status group (e.g., as a member of a First Nation band) than they are as part of an economic class (see also Turner, 1986). This is not surprising when we consider that beyond family and friends, we usually feel more connected to those with whom we share common interests and experiences than to those in the same economic class.

Party   According to Weber, "parties" are organizations that attempt to achieve certain goals in a planned and logical manner. Parties are associations of people that have the power to influence social action and change (for example, non-governmental organizations [NGOs] such as the Canadian Red Cross or the Alberta Council for Global Justice). For sociologists, **power** is defined as the ability to make others do something they would not otherwise do. According to Marx, power generally originates with the possession of wealth and privilege, but Weber went beyond this to investigate alternative types of power in developed societies.

power   The ability to make others do something they would not otherwise do.

Weber's analysis of bureaucracy revealed that there are workers who do not have a lot of economic power or status but can still exert a tremendous amount of power because they have the authority to make important decisions (Zeitlin, 1994, p. 217). For example, if your college or university application failed to include what you might consider a fairly minor piece of information (e.g., your final grade in high school English) the admissions manager has the authority to withhold your registration until you have provided it—a delay that could affect your ability to register for courses.

Weber also suggested that because three distinct systems of stratification are at work (class, status, and power), there exists the possibility of status inconsistency. **Status inconsistency** occurs when an individual occupies several differently ranked statuses at the same time. For example, as we saw earlier, a drug dealer may have a great deal of money and live in a big house but have little social prestige.

status inconsistency   Occurs when an individual occupies several differently ranked statuses at the same time.

Weber's contribution to the sociological analysis of stratification is his recognition that social stratification and inequality are not the same thing, but instead a combination of many factors.

SYMBOLIC INTERACTIONISM

Symbolic interactionists are less interested in trying to explain why stratification exists than they are in looking at how people interpret and construct their responses to class inequality. Instead of speculating about the function or inevitability of stratification, inter-actionists are principally interested in how class affects patterns of everyday social life. In particular, they consider how people use and respond to status symbols (Hartl, Novak, Rao, & Sethi, 2003).

status symbols   Material indicators that demonstrate a person's social and economic position.

Status symbols are material indicators that demonstrate a person's social and economic position. One of the pioneers in the study of status symbols was Thorstein Veblen (1857–1929), with his concept of conspicuous consumption. **Conspicuous consumption** is

conspicuous consumption   The purchase of expensive goods simply because they are valuable, not because there is any innate satisfaction in them.

the purchase of expensive goods simply because they are valuable, not because there is any innate satisfaction in them—for example, paying $100 for a designer T-shirt. Veblen would argue that people are willing to pay $100 for the T-shirt because they want to be seen by others as being able to pay such an amount. The $100 T-shirt does the same thing as a $15 one (i.e., it covers you up), so the satisfaction is not in the product's functionality, but instead in the status it implies (Mukherjee, 2006).

In *The Theory of the Leisure Class* (1899/1979), Veblen also developed two other key concepts to show how people communicate their social wealth to others: *conspicuous leisure* and *conspicuous waste*. According to Veblen, **conspicuous leisure** is the demonstration of one's high social status through forms of leisure that include taking long vacations in exotic locales. **Conspicuous waste** is the disposal of valuable goods to demonstrate wealth. For example, giving a $100 tip to a valet for parking your car.

Veblen suggested that people want to be seen as living one class stratum above where they actually live. Until recently, households were largely trapped in their class stratum because they had limited means by which to reach the next level. However, Scott (2007) argues that credit cards have changed people's ability to reach, or at least appear to reach, that next higher level. He suggests that conspicuous consumption is more prevalent than at any other point in history. Easy access to credit allows people to purchase items that they may not be able to afford or justify if they had to pay cash: large homes, expensive clothes, winter vacations, and dining at expensive restaurants. Today, easy credit allows people to appear wealthier than they really are (Scott, 2007, p. 570).

There are other nonmaterial indicators of social class as well. For example, in some countries (e.g., England) a person's accent is a powerful indicator of their social position. Some research suggests that the lower a person's social status when compared with the status of someone that person is waiting to see, the longer the wait (Levine, 1987 as cited in Lindsey & Beach, 2003, p. 205). How long would you spend waiting in a doctor's office before you would leave?

Veblen's contribution to the study of stratification, then, was his analysis of how we seek to appear as belonging to a higher social class than our actual one. This approach is entirely consistent with symbolic interactionism and its belief that we constantly define and reconstruct our impressions of ourselves and others.

FEMINIST THEORY

In general, feminism is interested in how the dominant (i.e., male) perspective has determined society's evaluation of what is deemed valuable and important. Feminist insight into social inequality generally follows two lines of investigation: (1) recognizing the working lives of women within capitalism (Armstrong & Armstrong, 1994), and (2) investigating the role of class position in determining one's view of the world (Harding, 2006; Sangster, 2007).

The feminist investigation of the working lives of women focuses on how gender influences what Canadian sociologists Pat and Hugh Armstrong (1994) have termed, "the double ghetto." The **double ghetto** is the situation in which women who have full-time jobs outside the home often work another "shift" when they get home. The additional responsibilities of home life limit women's full participation in the workforce. The consequence is a subordinate role for women at work and at home.

Feminists also consider that a woman's social class defines who she is and how she sees the world. For example, Lichterman's (1995) research into the environmental movement found that women's class position (and their resulting life experiences) leads low-income women to prefer more collective, egalitarian, and participatory approaches to life than women from higher classes, who tended to favour more hierarchical, bureaucratic organizations that support individual effort to achieve goals (as cited in Statham, 2000). Thus, feminist sociology assumes that the production of social reality is influenced by one's class (Ritzer, 2000, p. 479).

conspicuous leisure
The demonstration of one's high social status through forms of leisure.

conspicuous waste
The disposal of valuable goods to demonstrate wealth.

double ghetto
Recognition that women who work full-time often have another "shift" when they get home.

"A Woman's Place: Programming for the Modern Homemaker" is a series of radio and television broadcasts produced by CBC from 1945 to 1969 that describes the role of women and work in Canada during that time. To view this documentary series, go to http://archives.cbc.ca/lifestyles/etiquette/topics/1192/.

What do you know about **Sociological Approaches to Social Inequality**?

Multiple-choice questions (circle your answer)

1. **Which theorists argued that social stratification is functional for society because it ensures that key social positions are held by the most capable people?**
   a. Karl Marx and Friedrich Engels
   b. Max Weber and Karl Marx
   c. Kingsley Davis and Wilbert Moore
   d. Kingsley Davis and Karl Marx

2. **Those that own the means of production are referred to by Marx as the**
   a. Proletariat
   b. Bourgeoisie
   c. Working class
   d. Union bosses

3. **What occurs when an individual occupies several differently ranked statuses at the same time?**
   a. Status inconsistency
   b. Rank inconsistency
   c. Rank order
   d. Primary rank

4. **_____ are associations of people that have the power to influence social action and change.**
   a. Parties
   b. Ranks
   c. Statuses
   d. Classes

5. **The situation in which women who have full-time jobs outside the home often work another "shift" when they get home is referred to as**
   a. Overtime
   b. Extra duty
   c. Double duty
   d. Double ghetto

Answers: c, b, a, d

module 7.3

The Canadian Class System

Sociologists have presented a number of models to describe social class. Marx's model identified two classes—the bourgeoisie and the proletariat. To Marx's model, Erik Olin Wright (1996) added *managers* and the *petite bourgeoisie*—small business owners. Most sociologists prefer to follow a simpler scheme of class as described by Dennis Gilbert and Joseph Kahl (1993). The following discussion of the Canadian class system is based on this interpretation. As you will see, social class in Canada is based on one's wealth, income, education, occupation, and the social standing of one's family.

THE UPPER CLASS

Although relatively few Canadians reside in the upper class, their influence is hard to overestimate. Though members of this class earn at least several hundred thousand dollars a year, their chief economic resource is accumulated wealth rather than income. Most upper-class

---

Think about the Canadian Class System

1 Think about the Canadian class system. To what social class do you think you belong? What criteria did use to arrive at your answer?

2 Think about the rich. How would you define "rich" in Canada? What criteria did you use to arrive at your answer?

To learn more about Canada's 100 richest people, go to www.canadianbusiness. com/after_hours/ lifestyle_activities/article. jsp?content=20071131_1 98701_198701.

families inherited the bulk of their money (Morck, Stangeland, & Yeung, 1998; Thurow, 1987), and some estimates suggest that about 40 percent inherited all of it (Lindsey & Beach, 2003, p. 213; Queenan, 1989).

Members of the very rich are often viewed as being comprised of two different populations (Allen, 1989). At the extreme top are the "old rich," families like the Thomsons, Westons, and Irvings, who have been wealthy for generations. But another group is the "new rich" and includes people like Jeffrey Skoll, eBay's first employee and president; Michael Lee-Chin, who immigrated from Trinidad with very little and who now has over $10 billion in assets under management with his investment services firm (AIC); and Lino Saputo, the son of an Italian cheese maker who now continues the tradition on an international scale. This group also includes a few highly paid athletes and actors as well as some top professionals (e.g., plastic surgeons, defence lawyers).

Male members of the old rich may work, but many simply manage their investments. Meanwhile, many of the "new rich" occupy top executive positions in the largest corporations. For this reason, the latter group is sometimes called the "corporate class." Women in both groups sometimes work but often focus on civic and charitable activities (Lindsey & Beach, 2003; Ostrander, 1984). In some cases, the new rich may be wealthier than the old, but members of both groups generally acknowledge the higher social status of the old rich.

Traditionally, members of the upper class were almost entirely white Protestants of British descent, but today the class appears to be opening up to people of other religions and ethnic backgrounds. However, there are still comparatively few members of visible minorities in the upper class. Upper-class people tend to live in a small number of elite communities, marry within their class, send their children to the same schools, join the same clubs, and vacation in the same exclusive resorts (Newman, 1998). More than any other class, members of the elite form insulated social networks out of the public eye (Lindsey & Beach, 2003, p. 214).

THE UPPER-MIDDLE CLASS

Few people have much contact with the upper class because its members tend to use their wealth to maintain their privacy (Kingston & Köhler, 2006). Not so the upper-middle class, whose members tend to be highly visible. Lacking significant power at the national level, these are often the "movers and shakers" within local communities (Trounstine & Christensen, 1982).

The upper-middle class generally consists of people working in professional careers (e.g., doctors and lawyers). People in the upper-middle class are not enormously wealthy, but they are financially secure and tend to drive new cars, take international holidays, and live in very nice homes. Much of the success of this class is the result of having a good education; virtually everyone in the upper-middle class has a university degree, and a significant number have graduate degrees. Upper-middle class families usually live in the suburbs, and are often active in municipal politics and volunteer organizations. Although mostly white, they are more ethnically diverse than the upper class (Lindsey & Beach, 2003, p. 214; Marger, 1998).

THE LOWER-MIDDLE CLASS

The Canadian lower-middle class is made up of managers, small business operators, senior executive assistants, and some of the minor professions, such as school teachers and social workers. The majority of people in this class have at least some college or university education, but only a few have completed their degrees. In most lower-middle-class families, both spouses work so they can support a moderately comfortable lifestyle, albeit one more tenuous than the higher economic levels, given that this class does not have substantial investment income or

Expensive homes and lavish lifestyles are public demonstrations of social class.

sizeable cash savings. However, most people in this class take occasional vacations, eat out fairly regularly, drive later-model cars, and send their children to university or community colleges. Historically, most families in the lower-middle class own their homes, but they also have a sense of insecurity and vulnerability to market forces, particularly interest rates on home mortgages (Lochhead & Shalla, 1996).

People in the lower-middle class typically encourage their children to continue their education in the hope that they can achieve a profession, more financial security, and independence in their chosen careers. The majority of this class rarely participate in local, provincial, or national politics because they feel powerless and do not believe they could make substantial change. In general, this class quietly follows the rules as defined by their managers and superiors (i.e., members of the upper-middle class).

THE WORKING CLASS

Roughly 30 percent of the Canadian population can be considered working class. However, as you have no doubt already noticed, the criteria separating these classes are somewhat vague. Most members of the working class are skilled and semi-skilled manual workers. The skilled working class includes such occupations as carpenters, plumbers, and electricians. The semi-skilled working class includes low-level clerical workers, salespeople, and machine operators. This class also includes unskilled labour found in factories, construction, and the service sector. Most jobs in this class are highly routine and closely supervised. Typically, both members of a couple within this class must work outside the home to pay their bills (Lindsey & Beach, 2003, p. 215; Rubin, 1976).

Working-class people usually complete high school, but few go on to college or university. While many will own their own homes, the majority have no other significant assets and are vulnerable to a financial crisis resulting from illness or unexpected and long-term unemployment (Rubin, 1994). Most working-class people drive used cars, take holidays that are close to home, and live in modest neighbourhoods.

While upward mobility is encouraged in the working class, many people in this stratum emphasize the importance of being respected by their community as a means of underscoring their superiority over the lower classes.

THE "UNDERCLASS"

Some Canadians face long-term, chronic poverty in which they have little ability to realize their potential since they are in a constant struggle to meet their immediate needs. Sociologists disagree about what to call this group (Bagguley & Mann, 1992). Some use the term *underclass* (Auletta, 1982), but others argue that this word is stigmatizing (Gans, 1995). Others have suggested *welfare class* or *lower-lower class*, but these are also harmful and derogatory terms. Whatever term is used, the members of this class generally lack marketable skills and have little or no experience with full-time work (Welshman, 2006). Unless given extensive training and educational upgrading, many are virtually unemployable. Their annual household income is typically below $15 000, so for many, the only legitimate source of income is social assistance. Many survive only through an elaborate network of sharing based largely on kinship ties (Stack, 1975).

What do you know about **the Canadian Class System**?

Multiple-choice questions (circle your answer)

1. **People with professional careers belong to which group?**
   a. Upper class
   b. Upper-middle class
   c. Lower-middle class
   d. Working class

2. **Which group is most likely to have a university degree?**
   a. Upper class
   b. Upper-middle class
   c. Lower-middle class
   d. Working class

3. **This group generally lacks marketable skills and has no experience with full-time work.**
   a. Lower-middle class
   b. Working class
   c. Upper class
   d. Underclass

4. **Which group is made up of minor professions such as school teachers and social workers?**
   a. Upper-middle class
   b. Lower-middle class
   c. Working class
   d. Underclass

5. **The underclass is also called**
   a. Working class
   b. Lower-lower class
   c. Welfare class
   d. Both b and c

Answers: b, b, d, b, d

module 7.4

Poverty

DEFINING POVERTY

Although **poverty** can be defined as a state in which a person has no money, goods, or means of support, sociologists make a distinction between *absolute poverty* and *relative poverty*. **Absolute poverty** is defined as the failure to meet the basic needs of life, such as adequate food, clean water, and shelter. In Canada, the homeless are considered to be absolutely poor. **Relative poverty** is defined as the inability to secure goods and services required to live a life equal to working-class standards. In a state of relative poverty, a person may have their basic needs met but, compared with others in their community, they fall far short of the average standard of living. In general, the millions of people sociologists and anti-poverty activists describe as poor live in relative poverty.

There is no official definition of *poverty* or an official poverty line in Canada. Canadian sociologists use three approaches to measure and analyze poverty. The **Market Basket Measure (MBM)** estimates the cost of an established set of goods and services and, from that, estimates the income a family needs to get by. To allow for variances in cost for different geographic regions, the MBM is based on 45 thresholds in 35 geographic regions across Canada. The **low income measure (LIM)** calculates the number of families that have incomes which are less than half the median income in Canada. This measure is most often used to make international comparisons. Finally, the **low income cut-off (LICO)** represents the level of income at which a household in a particular location must spend 20 percentage points more of their gross income on food, shelter, and clothing than does the average Canadian household. Currently, this means spending about 55 percent of gross income on these necessities. But, as Statistics Canada regularly points out, this is a measure of income inequality (Fellegi, 1997) and such relative definitions don't really tell us about poverty, but rather about inequality. Of the three measures, the LICO is used most often to measure poverty in Canada. Currently, different LICOs have been established for 35 regions in Canada (Goldberg, 2008).

Table 7–3 outlines LICO scores according to various social criteria. One of the more notable results is that women, young adults, people without a high school diploma, and visible minorities who are not working are the most likely to be poor in Canada. While none of these findings are necessarily surprising, they do demonstrate various factors that are associated with poverty.

FACTORS INFLUENCING POVERTY

GENDER   As shown in Figure 7–1, Canadian women continue to earn less than men—a situation that exists in virtually all contemporary societies (Jurajda & Harmgart, 2007; United Nations, 2006, p. 54) and one that many Canadians perceive as "natural" (Gazso, 2004).

Sociologists, however, use the phrase **feminization of poverty** (coined by Diana Pearce in the 1970s) to recognize the universality of women's wage discrimination (Thibos, Lavin-Loucks, & Martin, 2007). In fact, even though the Pay Equity Act of 1987 makes it illegal to pay someone less, or more, for their work on the basis of gender, women continue to be paid less for the same work as men (Kovach, 1996; Phillips & Phillips, 2000). As well, women are outnumbered by men in the highest-paying jobs and dominate in the lowest-paying jobs. Clearly, then, being female is an important factor when we consider who is likely to be poor in Canada.

poverty   A state in which a person has no money, goods, or means of support.

absolute poverty   The failure to meet the basic needs of life, including adequate food, clean water, and shelter.

relative poverty   The inability to secure goods and services required to live a life equal to working-class standards.

Market Basket Measure (MBM)   Estimates the cost of an established set of goods and services and, from that, estimates the income a family needs to get by.

low income measure (LIM)   Calculates the number of families that have incomes which are less than half the median income in Canada.

low income cut-off
(LICO) The level of
income at which a
household spends 55
percent or more of its
gross income on basic
necessities.

feminization of poverty
The universal phenome-
non whereby women are
more susceptible to
poverty than are men.

TABLE 7–3 **Low-Income Rates of Unattached Individuals Aged 18 to 64, 2005**

Characteristic	Low Income Rate
Gender	
Male	31.2
Female	35.9
Age	
18 to 24	58.1
25 to 34	21.8
35 to 44	26.9
45 to 54	31.6
55 to 64	39.9
65 and over	
Education	
Less than high school	55.0
High school completed	31.4
Post-secondary	33.3
University	17.6
Minority Status	
Visible minority	43.8
Not a visible minority	31.8
Work Status	
Employed	20.7
Self-employed	39.7
Not employed	68.2

Source: Statistics Canada. (2007). *Persistence of low income among non-elderly unat-tached individuals*. Retrieved December, 9, 2007, from http://www.statcan.ca/english/research/75F0002MIE/75F0002MIE2007005.pdf.

WORK STATUS   One of the most obvious factors in whether a person lives in poverty is whether they have jobs. Table 7–3 demonstrates that only 20.7 percent of people who work live in poverty compared with 68.2 percent of people who do not have a job. You can predict that while periods of economic growth give rise to more jobs, when the economy suffers a downturn, people who lack savings and support networks can wind up living in poverty very quickly.

FAMILY STRUCTURE   As shown in Table 7–4, in 2005, two-parent families (6.7 percent) were much less likely to live below the LICO threshold than were female lone parent-families (29.1 percent), which accords with the pay inequality between men and women. However, since 1996, the trends for both types of families seem to have been moving in the right direction. Overall, virtually all family types in Canada are showing declining poverty rates—no doubt a function of a strong Canadian economy over the past decade. Yet Table 7–4 also reveals that female-headed lone-parent families have the second-highest poverty rates in the country, second only to single persons, who are generally more likely to have higher proportional living costs than others.

AGE   Between 1996 and 2005, the number of children living in low-income families fell from 1.3 million to 788 000, or 18.6 percent to 11.7 percent of all children. In 2005, just less than half of all children in low-income families lived with their mothers in lone-parent families. The chance of a child living in a low-income family was four times higher in a female headed lone-parent family than it is in a two-parent family (Statistics Canada, 2007g).

FIGURE 7–1 **Average Income of Women and Men, 1993, 1997, and 2003***

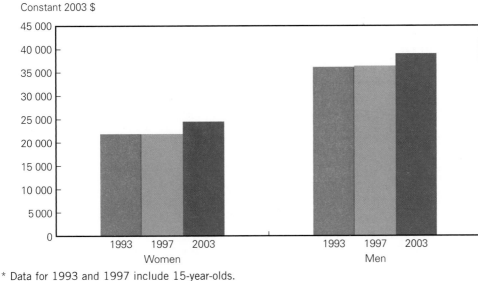

Constant 2003 $

* Data for 1993 and 1997 include 15-year-olds.
Source: Statistics Canada, Survey of Labour and Income Dynamics.

Further, Table 7–3 shows that people in their late teens and early twenties are most likely to live in poverty in Canada. This should not come as a surprise either, because this age group is just entering the labour market and beginning to develop their marketable skills. However, after age 34 there is a steady rise in the incidence of people living in poverty.

EDUCATION   In 2004, the unemployment rate for 25- to 29-year-olds with less than a high school education was 15 percent, compared with 9 percent for those who had completed high school, 6 percent for college or trade school graduates, and 7 percent for university

TABLE 7–4 **Low-Income Rates by Main Family Types (1982 Base After-Tax Income Low Income Cut-Off)**

	1996	1998	2000	2002	2003	2004	2005
				%			
Economic families, two persons or more*	12.1	10.1	9.0	8.6	8.5	8.0	7.4
Senior families**	3.3	3.9	3.1	2.9	2.7	2.1	1.6
Non-senior couples without children	8.4	6.7	6.9	7.1	6.6	6.4	6.4
Two-parent families with children	10.9	8.6	8.3	6.6	6.8	6.9	6.7
Female lone-parent families	52.7	42.9	36.3	39.4	38.8	36.0	29.1
Single persons	37.3	35.1	32.9	29.5	29.6	30.1	30.4

*Economic family refers to a group of two or more persons who live in the same dwelling and are related to each other by blood, marriage, common law, or adoption. A couple may be of opposite or same sex. Foster children are included.
**Families in which the main income earner is age 65 or over.
Source: Statistics Canada. (2007). *Income of Canadians*, The Daily, May 3. Retrieved from http://www.statcan.ca/Daily/English/070503/d070503a.htm.

WHY SHOULD WE CARE?

Soup Kitchens in Canada

During the Depression of the 1930s, when millions of Canadians lived hand-to-mouth and missing meals was an everyday occurrence (Struthers, 2007), soup kitchens flourished. How did they begin? The notorious gangster Al Capone established the first soup kitchens in the United States in the late 1920s in an effort to improve his public image.

Since then, soup kitchens have sprung up all across North America. Today, most soup kitchens are affiliated with non-profit or religious organizations (U.S. History, 2007). The largest soup kitchens in Canada include the Union Gospel Mission in Vancouver, the Yonge Street Mission in Toronto, Romero House in Saint John, the Union Mission in Ottawa, and the Hope Mission in Edmonton (www.soupkitchen.ca, 2005).

During a downturn in the Canadian economy in the 1980s, food banks emerged to help feed the poor. The Canadian Association of Food Banks (CAFB) was established in 1985 to advocate for food banks across the country. Originally intended to be only a short-term solution to help those in need, food banks have become a necessary feature of Canadian society. In 2007, 673 food banks were operating in Canada along with 2867 affiliated agencies providing resources to the poor (Canadian Association of Food Banks, 2007a).

Food banks exist in every province and territory, and they account for about 90 percent of all emergency food programming nationwide. In March 2007 over 720 000 different people accessed these food banks, about 39 percent (around 280 000) of them children (Canadian Association of Food Banks, 2007b, p. 2).

In 2006, the CAFB distributed over 8.5 million pounds of food donated by companies to its members through the National Food Sharing System. Nationwide, private donations account for approximately 150 million pounds of food per year. While the CAFB provides food to those in need, its ultimate goal is a hunger-free Canada. It tries to achieve this goal by raising public awareness through educational initiatives and by lobbying provincial and federal governments on the need for new and expanded social welfare programming (Canadian Association of Food Banks, 2007a).

Those who receive food bank donations include people on welfare (50.7 percent of total food bank users), the working poor (13.5 percent), people with disabilities (12.5 percent), and seniors (6.1 percent). In 2006, children made up 38.7 percent of food bank users and lone parents (usually single mothers, some of whom are on welfare) made up 30.4 percent (Canadian Association of Food Banks, 2007b, p. 2). Between 1989 and 2006, the number of people using food banks increased 99.3 percent (Canadian Association of Food Banks, 2007a).

These statistics confirm that poverty is a significant concern in Canada and that the number of people who need to use soup kitchens and food banks is growing. Even though Canada is one of the richest countries in the world, some Canadians still fall through the cracks. As a sociologist, how would you explain the growing need for these social services?

graduates (Statistics Canada, 2006g). Clearly, the more education people have, the less likely they are to be unemployed and hence, on average, to be poor (refer back to Table 7–3).

As shown in Figure 7–2, in 2000, the average annual earnings (among those who had work income) for people between 20 and 24 years of age who had not completed high school was the same as for those who had a university degree, around $14 000. Keep in mind, though, that those who left school had been working for a few years while the university graduates were just beginning their careers. Between the ages of 30 and 34, university

FIGURE 7–2 **Average Employment Income, by Age Group and Education Level, Canada, 2000**

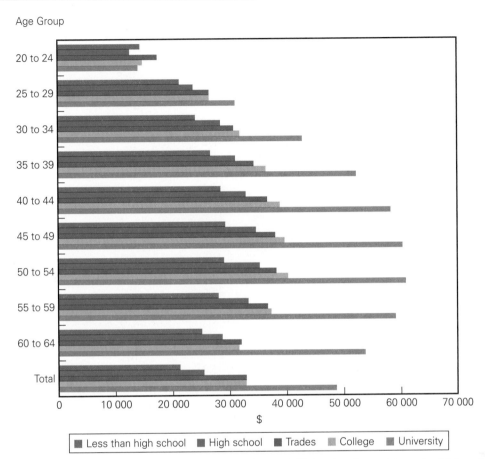

Source: Statistics Canada. (2006). Education matters. Retrieved July 31, 2008, from http://www.statcan.ca/english/freepub/81-004-XIE/2006003/backto.htm.

graduates were earning $19 000 more per year than those with less than a high school education. This difference increased to its widest margin in the 50 to 54 age group, where university graduates earned $32 000 more per year, on average, than those who had not completed high school. Staying in school, then, has a lasting benefit in terms of a person's overall lifetime earnings.

VISIBLE MINORITY STATUS   There are several Canadian studies of ethnic and racial discrimination in labour markets and hiring practices (Driedger, 2003; Hatfield, 2004; Palameta, 2004; Pendakur & Pendakur, 1996; Walks & Bourne, 2006). One common finding is that a significant proportion of the existing wage gap between white and non-white workers is not directly attributable to the demographic, educational, or occupational characteristics of workers. Instead, the wage gap appears to be the result of racial discrimination practised by employers in the hiring and promotion of visible minority workers (Canadian Heritage, 1998). Table 7–3 shows that 43.8 percent of visible minorities live in poverty, compared with 31.8 percent of nonvisible minorities.

LOCATION: URBAN VERSUS RURAL, AND PROVINCE   Another factor we rarely consider but that influences the likelihood of being poor is whether a person lives in the country or in

TABLE 7–5 **Poverty Statistics for Canada, Rural and Urban Regions, 1980–2000**

	1980	2000	Increase or Decrease	20-Year Average	Above Canadian Rural Average?
Rural					
Canada	16.2	13.6	−2.6	15.4	
Nfld and Labrador	22.0	19.3	−2.7	21.0	Yes
PEI	17.7	12.6	−5.1	14.8	No
Nova Scotia	17.3	17.3	0	17.4	Yes
New Brunswick	19.3	15.0	−4.3	17.6	Yes
Quebec	17.1	14.3	−2.8	16.8	Yes
Ontario	14.4	10.9	−3.5	12.5	No
Manitoba	19.1	13.6	−5.5	16.3	Yes
Saskatchewan	18.3	15.2	−3.1	17.7	Yes
Alberta	14.5	11.6	−2.9	14.3	No
British Columbia	12.4	14.5	+2.1	14.6	No
Urban					Above Canadian Urban Average?
Canada	15.6	17.3	+1.7	17.5	
Nfld and Labrador	20.1	18.3	−1.8	19.5	Yes
PEI	N/A	N/A	N/A	N/A	N/A
Nova Scotia	15.5	15.5	0	15.5	No
New Brunswick	17.6	18.1	+0.5	18.8	Yes
Quebec	18.9	20.5	+1.6	21.1	Yes
Ontario	13.9	15.2	+1.3	15.0	No
Manitoba	17.9	20.2	+2.3	20.5	Yes
Saskatchewan	15.8	16.5	+0.7	17.4	No
Alberta	13.1	14.8	+1.7	16.5	No
British Columbia	14.2	19.9	+5.7	18.3	Yes

Source: Compiled from National Anti-Poverty Organization. (2003). *The face of poverty in Canada: An overview.* Retrieved July 31, 2008, from http://oafb.ca/portal/images/pdfs/Poverty_Canada/Face%20of%20Poverty%20in%20Canada%202003.pdf.

the city, and in which province. Table 7–5 provides a breakdown of people living in poverty by province and by urban and rural regions. Note that in just 20 years, Canadians moved from being slightly more likely to be poor in rural areas to being more likely to be poor in urban areas. The national trend over these 20 years saw rural poverty rates fall by 2.6 percent and urban rates increase by 1.7 percent.

GLOBAL POVERTY

The picture of poverty around the globe is very different from that of poverty in Canada. In Canada, as in most wealthy nations, poverty focuses on relative poverty. While absolute poverty exists in Canada, it is somewhat limited to groups such as the homeless. Globally, the focus of analysis is on absolute poverty.

The World Bank defines *absolute poverty* as not being able to afford the most basic necessities to ensure survival. According to this definition, anyone living on less than US$1 per day is poor. Based on this definition, 1 billion people or 1 in 6 on the planet are living in absolute poverty (NetAid, 2008; Sachs, 2005).

The World Bank has also defined another category—*moderate poverty*—which lies somewhere between relative and absolute poverty. Moderately poor households are just barely able to meet their basic needs, and they must forgo many things (such as education and health care) that we take for granted in Canada. The World Bank measures moderate poverty as anyone living on an income of between US$1 and US$2 per day. Based on this definition, 1.6 billion people live in moderate poverty.

If we total the number of people living in relative poverty, moderate poverty, and absolute poverty, half of the world's population is considered to be poor.

WHERE DO THE POOR LIVE?   There is a clear north–south divide in the world when it comes to the issue of poverty. Most sociologists refer to this divide as the Global North and the Global South. The **Global North** includes the wealthy industrialized countries of Western Europe, Canada, the United States, Australia, and Japan. In general, states in the Global North are democratic and technologically advanced, have a high standard of living, and experience very low population growth. While some states in the Global South share some of these characteristics (e.g., Saudi Arabia is rich but not democratic), no single country in the Global South shares them all (Kegley & Wittkopf, 2006, p. 135). Citizens in the Global North are well educated, have access to health care and clean water, and exist within stable political structures. Given their economic, political, and social clout, it should come as no surprise that people who live in the Global North generally enjoy long, happy, and productive lives.

The **Global South** includes the poor countries of the world that are largely located in Asia, South America, and Africa. A full 93 percent of the world's extreme poor live in three regions: Sub-Saharan Africa, Southern Asia, and Eastern and South-Eastern Asia (see Table 7–6). Further, 87 percent of the world's moderately poor live in the same regions. These regions are home to well over 2 billion of the poorest people on the planet (Sachs, 2005). All Global South countries are less powerful both economically and politically than those in the Global North.

CONSEQUENCES OF POVERTY   The consequences of extreme poverty are many. Below are just a few:

- According to UNICEF, 26 000 to 30 000 children die each day due to poverty.
- 1.8 million child deaths each year are a result of diarrhea.
- More than 800 million people go hungry each day.
- 100 million children do not go to school.
- Nearly 1 billion people entered the twenty-first century unable to read or sign their names.
- 1.1 billion people do not have access to water.
- 2.6 billion people lack basic sanitation.
- 1.6 billion people live without electricity. (Shah, 2008)

WHY ARE SOME COUNTRIES SO POOR?   The reasons why some countries are so much poorer than others are numerous: lack of natural resources, war, unstable and corrupt governments, population growth, and environmental disasters are but some of the causes (Sachs, 2005b). Some suggest that foreign aid policies and debt repayment policies have

Global North Wealthy industrialized countries in the Northern Hemisphere (previously referred to as the First World).

Global South Poor countries in the Southern Hemisphere (previously referred to as the Third World).

For more interesting statistics and facts on global poverty go to **http://www.globalissues.org/article/26/poverty-facts-and-stats.**

TABLE 7–6 **Percentage of Population Living below $1 per Person per Day[1,2]**

Percentage of people living on less than $1 purchasing power parity (PPP) per day			
	1990	1999	2005
Northern Africa and Western Asia	3.5	3.8	3.8
Sub-Saharan Africa	55.7	56.3	50.3
Latin America/Caribbean	9.7	10.8	8.0
Eastern and South-Eastern Asia	56.0	35.5	17.8
Southern Asia	48.9	42.2	38.6
Commonwealth of Independent States	1.9	6.8	5.4
Transition countries of South-Eastern Europe	0.1	1.7	0.5

[1] High-income economies, as defined by the World Bank, were excluded.

[2] Estimates by the World Bank, September 2008.

Source: United Nations. (2008). *The millennium development goals report.* Retrieved from http://mdgs.un.org/unsd/mdg/Resources/Static/Data/Stat%20Annex.pdf.

Over 1 billion people live in absolute poverty worldwide.

made it particularly difficult for poor countries to raise their standards of living (Juhasz, 2006). Historically, two factors stand out as having had an impact on the world order of have and have-not nations—*colonization* and *industrialization*.

Colonization   *Colonialism* is a process whereby one country lays claim to another and controls their political, economic, and cultural systems. Beginning in the fifteenth century, the armed forces of several powerful Western European countries (e.g., Portugal, Spain, England, and France) conquered many parts of the world and colonized their territories. Canada's history is of course linked to both British and French colonization. Colonization continued into the twentieth century (Chirot, 1977).

The purpose of colonization is quite simple—to expand the wealth of the colonizer. Colonial powers became rich by taking raw materials from the colonies. Paul Barans (1957) argued that European colonial expansion promoted the "outright plunder or in plunder thinly veiled as trade, seizing and removing tremendous wealth from the place of penetration" (pp. 141–142). The result was a transfer of raw materials from the poor countries to the wealthy, where these materials were used to fuel economic growth. Over time, colonies became dependent on the colonial powers. The colonies no longer had self-sustaining economies. They became reliant on the colonial powers for their income and for goods that they could not provide for themselves. For instance, colonies that converted all of their farming to a single cash crop (e.g., sugar cane) were no longer able to produce enough food for themselves; thus, they needed to import food. Colonies that supplied natural resources to colonial powers did not develop their own manufacturing sector; thus, they needed to import finished goods. Of course, all of these imported goods cost more than the colonized people could afford (Chirot, 1977). This relationship of dependence by the colony on the colonizer is referred to as **dependency theory**.

dependency theory The economic dependence that many Global South countries experience as a consequence of colonialism and neo-colonialism.

By the 1960s and 1970s, most of the world's colonies had gained political independence (Chirot, 1977, p. 174). However, they did not gain economic independence. After years of economic exploitation, former colonies did not have the financial, industrial, and technological infrastructure necessary to develop their own vibrant and competitive economies. What they could offer to the rest of the world was cheap labour and raw materials. As such, wealthy, industrialized nations, including their former rulers, took advantage. This continued economic relationship in which Global North countries exploit and control the economies of Global South countries is referred to as *neo-colonialism*.

transnational corporation (TNC) A large company based in one country with overseas operations in two or more countries.

An examination of transnational corporations illustrates this ongoing relationship. A **transnational corporation (TNC)** is a large company based in one country with overseas operations in two or more countries. The defining feature of TNCs is that their strategic decision making is based entirely on economic goals, with little or no regard for national boundaries (Gershon, 2005, p. 17). Because of their sheer size and influence, TNCs have become some of the most powerful economic and political entities in the world today. Many TNCs are richer and more powerful than the countries in which they operate.

The largest transnational corporation is retail giant Wal-Mart. Wal-Mart had sales of $378 billion dollars in 2008, and it employs 1.5 million workers globally. In 2003, Wal-Mart imported more than $15 billion of goods from China alone (Global Economy, 2005). In fact, if Wal-Mart were a state, it would be China's eighth-largest trading partner (Valladão, 2006, p. 247). Because of its purchasing power, Wal-Mart is able to pressure suppliers to lower their prices in order to gain access to Wal-Mart's consumers. This, in turn, forces suppliers to move their production facilities to countries in the Global South, where they can save money by paying their workers lower wages (Collins, 2006, p. 16; Morrison, 2008).

In 2002, there were 64 592 TNCs operating, along with a network of 851 167 foreign affiliates (Ietto-Gilles, 2003). While they are global in their reach, 90 percent of these companies are based in the Global North countries, and more than half are from just five nations: France, Germany, the Netherlands, Japan, and the United States (Karliner, 1997, p. 6).

You may question why Global South countries willingly trade cheap labour to the TNCs of the Global North. The answer is simple—competition. The economies of many of these countries are dependent on the business that transnationals provide. If they are unwilling to provide what the company wants, the company will relocate to another country.

Industrialization   Industrialization is another important factor determining the relative economic wealth of a country. The countries that were the first to industrialize were able to accumulate wealth and power. This world dominance continues to this day.

Chirot (1977, pp. 24–25) notes that by 1900, the relationship between industrialized and non-industrialized countries was well established. In that year, four countries, Great Britain, the United States, Germany, and France produced 74 percent of the total manufactured product in the world while comprising only 13 percent of the world's population. You will note that all are Global North countries.

Industrialization allowed for the mass production of food, which meant that few people needed to be involved in agriculture. Freedom from the production of food allowed industrial countries to focus on education and manufacturing. As a consequence, industrial societies became much wealthier (Chirot, 1977, p. 27). Wealth, technological knowledge, and a philosophy that encourages capital accumulation led to the economic and political domination of industrialized nations over non-industrialized nations.

Immanuel Wallerstein (1976, 2004) described the relationship between industrialized nations and non-industrialized nations in his **world system theory**. According to Wallerstein, an unequal relationship has developed between industrialized countries (the **core**) and non-industrialized countries (the **periphery**). Historically, industrialized countries and their TNCs have exploited and controlled the economies of non-industrialized countries through unequal trade agreements, the exploitation of a cheap labour force, and the extraction of raw materials necessary for industrial growth. This exploitation has maintained poverty and a level of dependence, no different than colonial times, which has made it difficult if not impossible for non-industrialized countries to overcome.

It is critical to note that a strong correlation exists between colonialism and industrialization. Many of the colonial powers are also industrialized powers. Further, the relative economic power of these nations (which are located primarily in the Global North) has remained stable for over 100 years. Meanwhile, the nations of the periphery (which are located primarily in the Global South) continue in a relationship of economic dependence and vulnerability.

world system theory Wallerstein's view of the world economic system in which industrialized nations control global wealth and exploit non-industrialized nations.

core Wealthy countries with developed economies.

periphery Poor countries that are exploited for their raw materials by core countries.

GLOBAL POVERTY AND THE FUTURE   According to the International Monetary Fund (2002) and the World Bank (2005), poverty rates worldwide have been declining. In 1981, the extreme poverty rate worldwide was 1.6 billion, and in 2002 it had dropped to 1.2 billion, in spite of the fact that world populations have increased (World Bank, 2005).

Much of this change can be attributed to the burgeoning economies in India and China. The rapid modernization of the economies of India and China has led to a rise in each country's affluence and had a tremendous positive impact on internal poverty issues. In turn, China and India's economic growth has had a tremendous impact on world poverty numbers. For example, China was among the poorest countries in 1981, with 60 percent (well over 0.5 billion) of its population living in extreme poverty. That number was cut in half by 1990, and by half again by 2001 (World Bank, 2005). This outcome supports the theory that by modernizing and industrializing an economy, poverty can be drastically reduced.

The World Bank (2005) has projected that by 2015, extreme poverty worldwide could be reduced to 600 million if economic growth rates in developing countries are sustained.

The picture is not so rosy for all, however. While there has been significant economic growth in Southeastern Asia, economies in Latin America and the Caribbean have stagnated or shown little growth. Sub-Saharan Africa has not improved at all. On the contrary, extreme poverty rates in this area of the world doubled from 1981 to 2001 (World Bank, 2005).

Recently, we have seen a shift in the world economy. The war in Iraq, drought, and natural disasters, such as the hurricanes in the Gulf of Mexico, have led food and fuel prices to skyrocket. West Africans have been among those hardest hit. Mexicans have also faced a rise in the cost of corn, which threatened to put their staple food source out of reach. Ironically, the booming economies of Southeastern Asia threaten to increase the number of poor worldwide. How? Consider the fact that about 1 billion new middle-class people can now afford meat and cars. Then, consider the impact that this will have on the cost of food and fuel. Grain, a staple of the world's poor, is being diverted to feed animals raised for their meat and to produce biofuels to run cars. The demand for meat and cars affects not only food and fuel prices but also global warming—consider the impact on the environment of all the new cars being purchased in India and China. Global warming compounds the world food shortage as droughts hit areas that were once our best grain producers (Gillis, 2008). Given these events, we must wonder whether poverty rates will yet again rise and whether industrialization is in fact the answer to the issue of poverty.

What do you know about **Poverty**?

Multiple-choice questions (circle your answer)

1. **This measure of poverty identifies a family as poor if its income is less than half the median income in Canada:**
   a. Market Basket Measure (MBM)
   b. Low income cut-off (LICO)
   c. Low income measure (LIM)
   d. Median income measure (MIM)

2. **According to Statistics Canada, which group had the lowest unemployment rate in 2004 among the 25 to 29 age group?**
   a. High school dropouts
   b. High school graduates
   c. College or trade school graduates
   d. University graduates

3. **According to Statistics Canada, which group had the highest average income between the ages of 25 and 64 in Canada?**

   a. High school graduates
   b. Trade school graduates
   c. College graduates
   d. University graduates

4. **Among the following groups, who is most likely to have a low income?**
   a. A male
   b. A person aged 25 to 34
   c. A visible minority
   d. A university graduate

5. **According to the World Bank, absolute poverty is measured as those living on less than**
   a. US $1 per day
   b. US $2 per day
   c. US $10 per day
   d. US $20 per day

Answers: c, c, d, c, a

Summary

module 7.1   WHAT IS SOCIAL STRATIFICATION?

1. *Social stratification* is a society's hierarchical ranking of people into social classes.
2. Canada is stratified. In Canada, we distribute goods and other rewards based on a system of merit. This system is referred to as a *meritocracy*.
3. There are two aspects to our dominant ideology that affect how we relate to social inequality. Our system of meritocracy states that if we work hard we will be rewarded. Further, a person's social worth will be measured by his or her social and economic status. *Classism* is the belief that people's relative worth is at least partially determined by their social and economic status.
4. Canadian society is based on an open system. Many believe that by working hard, they can get ahead. Those in the middle class have stronger faith in this notion. Those who are poor tend to see the system as closed and unfair. They recognize that there are many barriers to advancement in their way.
5. Two components of inequality are property and prestige. A person's social worth is measured by his or her income and assets (property), and by the social value of the positions he or she holds (prestige).

module 7.2   SOCIOLOGICAL APPROACHES TO SOCIAL INEQUALITY

6. Functionalists believe that a system of stratification is necessary because it ensures that people will fill the jobs that keep a society running smoothly.
7. Conflict theorists consider that social stratification was created to benefit those in power. Karl Marx did not believe that stratification needed to exist.
8. Marx described social class as the consequence of one's relationship to the means of production—owner and worker.
9. Weber recognized that social class was multi-dimensional. Besides one's relationship to the means of production, associations with a class, a status group, and a party also gave individuals influence over others.
10. Feminists look at how the dominant male perspective has determined society's perceptions of what is valuable and important.
11. Symbolic interactionists are interested in how people interpret and construct their responses to class inequality. For instance, they would examine how we use and respond to status symbols.

module 7.3   THE CANADIAN CLASS SYSTEM

12. The Canadian class system as described by Dennis Gilbert and Joseph Kahl can be divided into five groups: the upper class (rich), the upper-middle class (professionals), the lower-middle class (lower professionals), the working class (skilled and semi-skilled workers), and the underclass (the poor).

module 7.4   POVERTY

13. There is no official definition of poverty in Canada. When we discuss poverty in Canada, we are mostly focused on relative poverty which is more of a discussion of inequality.
14. A variety of factors correlate with a person's socio-economic status. These include age, work status, education, ethnicity, gender, where one lives, and family type.
15. Discussions of global poverty are focused more on the issue of absolute poverty. Half of the world's population cannot meet their basic needs on a daily basis.
16. Two critical factors have created global inequality, with countries in the Global North dominating countries in the Global South: colonization and industrialization.

Key Terms

absolute poverty 209
caste system 196
class structure 197
class system 197
classism 195
closed system 196
conspicuous consumption 203
conspicuous leisure 204
conspicuous waste 204
core 217
Davis-Moore thesis 201
dependency theory 216
double ghetto 204
feminization of poverty 210

Global North 215
Global South 215
income 197
intergenerational mobility 194
intragenerational mobility 194
low income cut-off (LICO) 210
low income measure (LIM) 209
Market Basket Measure (MBM) 209
meritocracy 194
occupational prestige 199
open system 196
periphery 217
poverty 209
power 203

quintile 198
reincarnation 197
relative poverty 209
social class 194
social mobility 194
social status 194
social stratification 194
socio-economic status (SES) 197
status group 203
status inconsistency 203
status symbols 203
transnational corporation (TNC) 216
wealth 197
world system theory 217

Test Yourself

1. A group of individuals sharing a common position in a social hierarchy, based on both birth and achievement is called
a. Social class
b. Social stratification
c. Social status
d. Meritocracy

2. A system of rewards based on personal attributes and demonstrated abilities is called
a. Social class
b. Social status
c. Meritocracy
d. Classism

3. Social mobility measured by comparing a person's status position over his or her lifetime is called
a. Intergenerational mobility
b. Intragenerational mobility
c. Childhood mobility

d. Horizontal mobility

4. SES stands for:
a. Socio-economic status
b. Social equality status
c. Social equality standards
d. Social equity standards

5. A caste system is an example of a(n)
a. Open system
b. Closed system
c. Meritocracy
d. Neutral system

6. Which perspective sees stratification as an important system that ensures all necessary social positions will be filled?
a. Functionalism
b. Conflict theory
c. Symbolic interactionism
d. Feminist theory

7. Who believed that all social life was influenced by one's relationship to the process of economic production?
a. Karl Marx
b. Kingsley Davis
c. Wilbert Moore
d. Erving Goffman

8. People that share similar status, common lifestyles, world views, standards of living, and occupations are called
a. Classes
b. Status groups
c. Parties
d. Power groups

9. A drug dealer may live in a big house and have a lot of money but little social prestige. This is an example of
a. Status inconsistency
b. Status consistency
c. Role confusion
d. Role strain

10. Giving a $100 tip to a valet to park your car is an example of
a. A status symbol
b. Conspicuous consumption
c. Conspicuous waste
d. Foolishness

11. The corporate class belong to which group?
a. Upper class
b. Upper-middle class
c. Lower-middle class
d. Working class

12. Which group has the greatest impact on local politics?
a. Upper class
b. Upper-middle class
c. Lower-middle class
d. Working class

13. Skilled and semi-skilled workers belong to which class?
a. Upper class
b. Upper-middle class
c. Lower-middle class
d. Working class

14. The difference between old rich and new rich is
a. The old rich have more money than the new rich
b. The old rich are more likely to work
c. The new rich are made up mostly of celebrities
d. The old rich are more likely to have inherited their money

15. This group generally own their own homes but is vulnerable to market forces:
a. Upper class
b. Upper-middle class
c. Lower-middle class
d. Working class

16. LICO is the acronym for
a. Low income community organizations
b. Limited income calculations for Ontario
c. Low income cut-off
d. Low income calculations for Ontario

17. When a person's basic needs are met but their standard of living falls far short of the average standard of living, we refer to this situation as
a. Relative poverty
b. Absolute poverty
c. Extreme poverty
d. Objective poverty

18. The phrase used to recognize that women are more susceptible to poverty than men is
a. Gender poverty gap
b. Pay equity gap
c. Feminization of poverty
d. Masculinization of wealth

19. What type of family has the highest poverty rate?
a. Two-parent family
b. Couples without children
c. Female lone-parent family
d. Male lone-parent family

20. We are most likely to find absolute poverty in what part of the world?
a. Europe
b. Southern Europe
c. North America
d. Africa

Answers: a, c, b, a, b, a, c, a, b, d, d, c, c, a, c, d

Log in to MySocLab for a host of resources that will help you save time and improve your grade. MySocLab contains cutting-edge learning tools such as study plans, practice tests, videos, audio segments, quizzes, and more—all designed to help you better understand the learning objectives for this chapter. Along with your eBook, MySocLab for *Sociology for Everyone* can be found at **www.mysoclab.com**.

module 7.1
WHAT IS SOCIAL STRATIFICATION

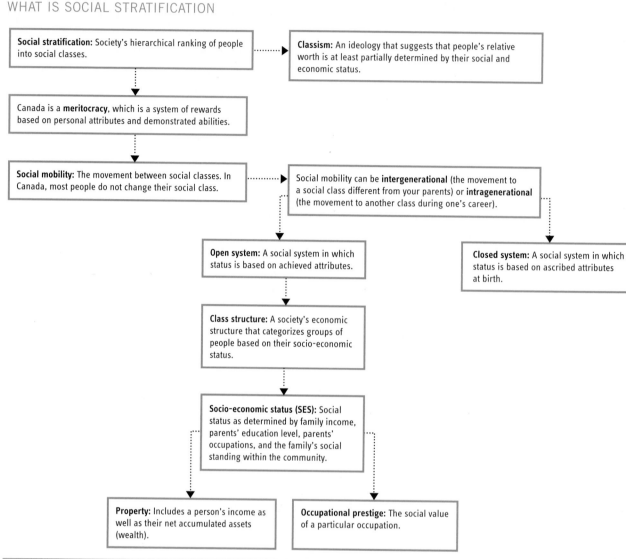

Social stratification: Society's hierarchical ranking of people into social classes.

Classism: An ideology that suggests that people's relative worth is at least partially determined by their social and economic status.

Canada is a **meritocracy**, which is a system of rewards based on personal attributes and demonstrated abilities.

Social mobility: The movement between social classes. In Canada, most people do not change their social class.

Social mobility can be **intergenerational** (the movement to a social class different from your parents) or **intragenerational** (the movement to another class during one's career).

Open system: A social system in which status is based on achieved attributes.

Closed system: A social system in which status is based on ascribed attributes at birth.

Class structure: A society's economic structure that categorizes groups of people based on their socio-economic status.

Socio-economic status (SES): Social status as determined by family income, parents' education level, parents' occupations, and the family's social standing within the community.

Property: Includes a person's income as well as their net accumulated assets (wealth).

Occupational prestige: The social value of a particular occupation.

module 7.2
SOCIOLOGICAL APPROACHES TO
SOCIAL INEQUALITY

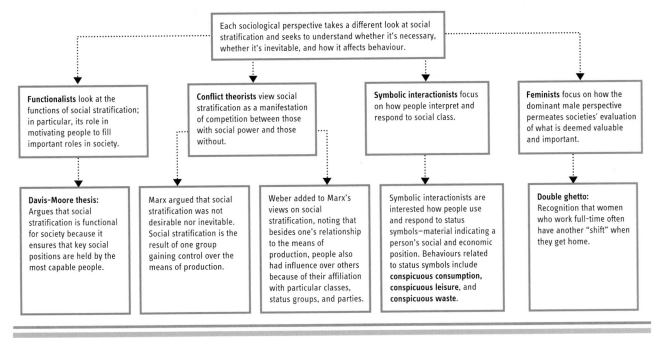

Each sociological perspective takes a different look at social stratification and seeks to understand whether it's necessary, whether it's inevitable, and how it affects behaviour.

Functionalists look at the functions of social stratification; in particular, its role in motivating people to fill important roles in society.

Conflict theorists view social stratification as a manifestation of competition between those with social power and those without.

Symbolic interactionists focus on how people interpret and respond to social class.

Feminists focus on how the dominant male perspective permeates societies' evaluation of what is deemed valuable and important.

Davis-Moore thesis: Argues that social stratification is functional for society because it ensures that key social positions are held by the most capable people.

Marx argued that social stratification was not desirable nor inevitable. Social stratification is the result of one group gaining control over the means of production.

Weber added to Marx's views on social stratification, noting that besides one's relationship to the means of production, people also had influence over others because of their affiliation with particular classes, status groups, and parties.

Symbolic interactionists are interested how people use and respond to status symbols—material indicating a person's social and economic position. Behaviours related to status symbols include **conspicuous consumption, conspicuous leisure,** and **conspicuous waste**.

Double ghetto: Recognition that women who work full-time often have another "shift" when they get home.

module 7.3
THE CANADIAN CLASS SYSTEM

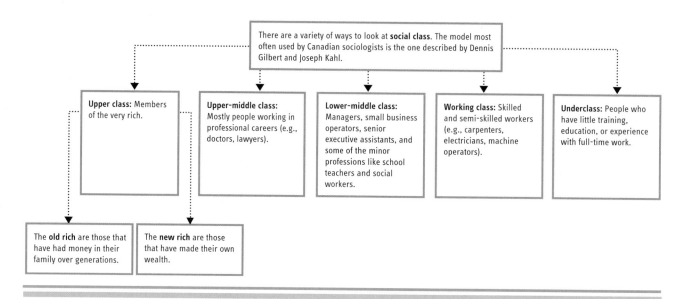

There are a variety of ways to look at **social class**. The model most often used by Canadian sociologists is the one described by Dennis Gilbert and Joseph Kahl.

Upper class: Members of the very rich.

Upper-middle class: Mostly people working in professional careers (e.g., doctors, lawyers).

Lower-middle class: Managers, small business operators, senior executive assistants, and some of the minor professions like school teachers and social workers.

Working class: Skilled and semi-skilled workers (e.g., carpenters, electricians, machine operators).

Underclass: People who have little training, education, or experience with full-time work.

The **old rich** are those that have had money in their family over generations.

The **new rich** are those that have made their own wealth.

module 7.4
POVERTY

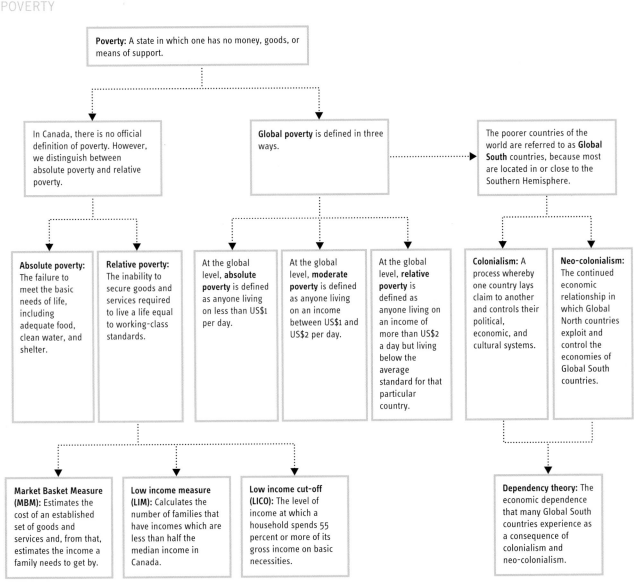

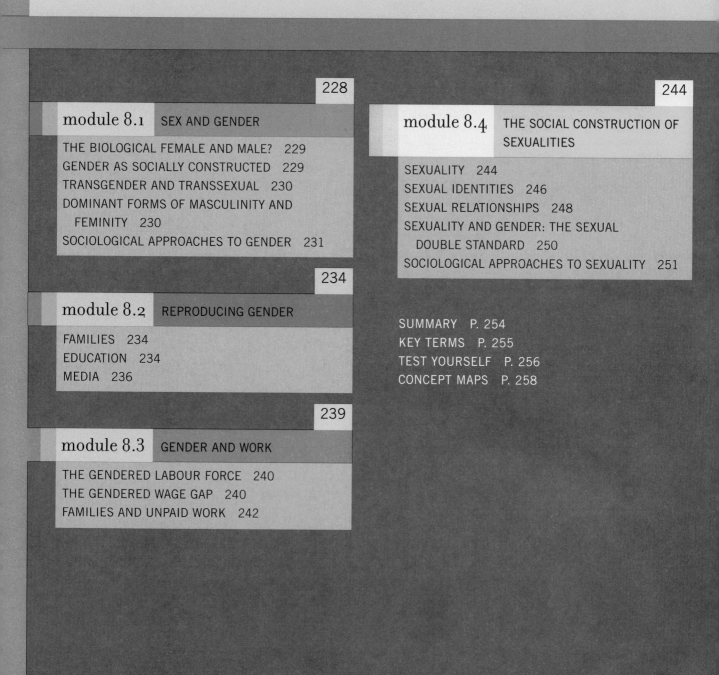

chapter 8

Gender and Sexualities

Guyland or Wasteland?

Sometime before age 16 and lasting well into their late twenties, after adolescence but before manhood, North American males become "guys."

What is a guy? According to Dr. Michael Kimmel, sociologist and author of the book *Guyland* (2008), a guy is typically, but not always, white and middle class. He is college bound, in college, or a recent college graduate. He is unmarried. He drifts from "hookup to hookup." He shares housing with other "guys," or he lives with his parents. He is typically unemployed or underemployed. When employed, he works at jobs with minimal hours and responsibilities so that he has more time to party, and if the job gets too serious, he moves on.

Kimmel (2008) remarks that in some respects, "Guyland can be defined by what guys do for fun. It's the 'boyhood' side of the continuum they're so reluctant to leave. It's drinking, sex, and video games. It's watching sports, reading about sports, listening to sports on the radio. It's television—cartoons, reality shows, music videos, shoot-em up movies, sports and porn—pizza and beer." Guyland is the place where "guys gather to be with guys . . . not hassled by the demands of parents, girlfriends, jobs, kids and the other nuisances of adult life."

If you are trying to picture a "guy," think of actor Seth Rogan's role in the hit movie *Knocked Up*. In fact, a slew of movies in recent years have depicted "guys." Seth Rogan in *The 40 Year Old Virgin* or Adam Sandler in *Billy Madison* are good examples as well.

Although some may view guy behaviour as delayed adolescence, Kimmel (2008) insists that it is not. Rather, he sees it as a new stage of life in the development of most North American males, and he believes that it has become the norm. Kimmel points out, however, that this new behaviour is not restricted to North America—Australia, Britain, Italy, and France have seen similar developments among their young males.

Why have "guys" emerged? Are they a product of a far too affluent society—which affords "guys" the luxury of not having to take care of themselves or others? Are they a consequence of "helicopter parenting"—parenting that is intensive and doting up until "guys" leave home for college and completely uninvolved afterwards (Kimmel, 2008)? Or are they, as Kimmel suggests, a backlash to feminism?

Certainly, when we consider the attitudes of "guys" toward women, we could theorize that "guys" may have emerged in part as a result of the shifting roles of men and women. Over the past 15 years, the number of women who have attended post-secondary programs outnumbered the number of men. Kimmel (2008) found in his research that "guys" tend to resent women who are career oriented and goal focused.

According to Kimmel, "guys" put women into two groups: babes and bitches (Pearce, 2008). *Babes* are women willing to enter Guyland. *Bitches*, on the other hand, are not and focus on their education and careers. We see these images of women portrayed in the media. As Kimmel notes, women may be progressing in the economic world, but "guys" still control the social realm (Pearce, 2008).

To what extent do you think Kimmel is correct? Does Guyland exist on your campus? If so, is there reason to be concerned?

module 8.1

Sex and Gender

Think about Sex and Gender

1 Think about the differences between men and women. How many of these differences are socially constructed?

2 If you were to change your gender, what would you need to learn about masculinity or femininity to function well in Canadian society?

sex   A determination of male or female on the basis of a set of socially agreed-upon biological criteria.

People often use the terms *sex* and *gender* interchangeably. Yet each term has a significantly different connotation, so it is important to distinguish between them. We will consider each one in turn.

Those who make a distinction between sex and gender tend to refer to **sex** as being rooted in biology—that is, the term refers to the way in which we distinguish between male and female based on a set of socially agreed upon biological criteria. In the 1970s, feminist theorists argued that we needed a way to distinguish between biology and the social effects of biological differences. As a result, theorists began using the term *gender* as a way of directing attention to the social realm. **Gender**, then, refers to the socially constructed characteristics associated with girls and boys, women and men—what we call *masculinity* and *femininity*.

Notice that the definitions of sex and gender suggest only two possible categories for each concept. In other words, *sex* is divided into the categories of male and female, while *gender* is divided into the categories of masculine and feminine. This form of categorization, based on two mutually exclusive and diametrically opposite groups, is known as *binary construction* (Nelson, 2006). We have examples of binary constructions everywhere: yes and no, black and white, right and wrong (or as we saw from the "guy"'s view of women, "babes" and "bitches"). Binary constructions help us simplify the world. However, in most cases, they are oversimplifications and can be problematic. For instance, people cannot simply be divided into two categories—good or bad. Our behaviour can vary from one situation to the next and from one day to the next. Sociologists note that likewise, definitions of sex and gender based on binary constructions are oversimplifications. In this chapter, we will discuss the range of possible definitions of gender and sex.

gender Social distinctions between masculinity and femininity.

THE BIOLOGICAL FEMALE AND MALE?

In the sex/gender distinction, the assertion that our bodies are either absolutely male or absolutely female is problematic. Consider the issue of intersexed individuals. **Intersexed individuals**—those born with ambiguous genitalia—do not fit into either of these categories. Also referred to as *hermaphrodites*, these people tend to have some combination of male and female genitalia and/or chromosomes (Kessler, 1990).

intersexed individuals Individuals born with ambiguous genitalia.

Consider the case of Maria Patiño, a top woman hurdler who was set to compete for Spain in the 1988 Olympics. The International Olympic Committee (IOC) requires proof of femininity in the form of a doctor's certificate. Patiño forgot her certificate and reported to what researchers refer to as the "femininity control head office" (Fausto-Sterling, 2009, p. 6) to have her cheek scraped for cells that were then tested to prove her female status. A few hours later, she was asked to submit to further examination. Later that day, officials told Patiño that she had failed the test; despite looking like a woman and living as a woman, Patiño was informed that she had a Y chromosome and internal testes and had neither ovaries nor a uterus (Fausto-Sterling, 2009). Patiño was not allowed to compete in the Olympics, as the IOC deemed that she was not a woman.

As a result of the IOC testing and subsequent media coverage, Patiño was banned from all future competition, stripped of her past athletic titles, and evicted from Spain's athletic housing (Fausto-Sterling, 2009). Doctors eventually explained to her that while she had a Y chromosome and testes (and her testes did produce testosterone), her cells did not respond to the testosterone in her body and thus she developed a female shape (breasts, narrow waist, wide hips) (Fausto-Sterling, 2009).

This example illustrates the social process involved in determining who is a man and who is a woman, and how our social categories of gender render particular bodies as "unintelligible" (Fausto-Sterling, 2009). "A body's sex is too complex. There is no either/or. Rather, there are shades of difference. . . . Our beliefs about gender affect what kinds of knowledge scientists produce about sex in the first place" (Fausto-Sterling, 2009, p. 7).

GENDER AS SOCIALLY CONSTRUCTED

Gender is socially constructed. This means that any given culture or society defines what it means to be a man or a woman, boy or girl, masculine or feminine. To understand this concept, consider how ideas about appropriate gender vary across cultures and across time. For example, in seventeenth-century France, to be masculine meant wearing frilly shirts, wigs, and powdered makeup—a view that obviously differs radically from current Western notions of masculinity.

Moreover, **gender relations** act as organizing principles in society—they shape and order interactions between women and men. They also shape the relative social importance and worth of women and men (Cook, 2007). Throughout most of the world, that which is associated with masculinity and men is more highly valued than that which is associated with femininity and women (Cook, 2007; Kimmel, 2004).

gender relations Organizing principles that shape and order interactions between, as well as the relative social importance of, women and men.

Gender also intersects with other organizing principles in society. Women and men are not homogeneous groups; we are also shaped by characteristics such as ethnicity, social class, and sexuality. As a result, while there may be *dominant constructions* (definitions created by the dominant groups in society) of masculinity and femininity in a given society, in reality there are multiple masculinities and femininities.

TRANSGENDER AND TRANSSEXUAL

transgender An umbrella term for a range of people who do not fit into normative constructions of sex and gender.

Transgender is often used as an umbrella term for a range of people who do not fit into normative constructions of sex and gender. It refers to people who live as the gender they identify themselves as being, with or without sex reassignment procedures. Transgendered individuals include transsexuals, transvestites (including drag queens and drag kings), intersexed individuals, and those who do not identify themselves as either male or female (Hines, 2004; Namaste, 2005; Nash, 2008). Some present themselves as deliberately gender incoherent, which, as Bobby Noble (2006) argues, is a form of resistance to dominant constructions (and expectations) of gender.

The 1970s and 1980s gave rise to the concept of *transsexualism*, which in the early 1970s became a diagnostic term—meaning that it appears in medical discourse as a pathology, or something in need of treatment (Devor, 2005). The term **transsexual** is often used as a more precise category to encompass those individuals who undergo sex reassignment (some use the term *sex realignment*), which can include facial reconstruction surgeries, genital reassignment surgery, and hormone treatments (Hines, 2004). The terms *pre-operative*, *post-operative*, and *non-operative* refer to whether an individual has undergone or is waiting to undergo sex reassignment surgery. Some people reject the transsexual label because of its connection to medical discourse; these people instead prefer the terms *transman* or *transwoman* (Hines, 2004). *Transvestites*, in contrast, engage in cross-dressing (publicly, privately, or both), but unlike transsexuals, they do not necessarily identify as another gender.

transsexual A person who undergoes sex reassignment, which may include surgeries.

For resources on sexual orientation and gender identity, go to **www.pflagcanada.ca/en/index-e.asp.**

DOMINANT FORMS OF MASCULINITY AND FEMININITY

While there is no *single* form of masculinity or femininity in Western societies, there are, nonetheless, *culturally dominant* forms—and these are known, respectively, as *hegemonic masculinity* and *emphasized femininity* (Connell, 1987).

hegemonic masculinity The normative ideal of dominant masculinity.

HEGEMONIC MASCULINITY   Our views of masculinity are constructed through our relationships with ourselves, with each other, and with our world (Kimmel, 2001). **Hegemonic masculinity** is the normative ideal (the concept of what we consider as normal and acceptable) of masculinity that men are supposed to strive to achieve. Although it is not necessarily the most prominent form of masculinity, it is the one that is most socially endorsed. That means that both men and women participate in sustaining this particular image of ideal masculinity (Connell, 2002).

What is this image of ideal masculinity? In North American culture, hegemonic masculinity is associated with the traits of aggressiveness, strength, drive, and ambition; in other words, it is constructed as the opposite of everything that is feminine. Hegemonic masculinity is also associated with whiteness, heterosexuality, and the middle class (Connell, 1987).

This prevailing notion of manhood requires men to be successful, capable, and reliable—a man *in* power, *with* power, and *of* power (Kimmel, 2001). The very definition of such manhood, or masculinity, helps to maintain the power that some men have over other men and that men have over women.

Hegemonic masculinity is irrevocably tied to heterosexuality (Connell, 2002; Kimmel, 2001). In Western societies, the ideal man is heterosexual. Indeed, *homophobia* is a central organizing principle of our cultural definition of manhood. Homophobia is much more than the irrational fear of gay men; it is also the fear that men will unmask other men, emasculate them, and reveal to the world that they do not measure up to the ideal construction of masculinity (Kimmel, 2001).

The character of James Bond (played by Daniel Craig) is an example of hegemonic masculinity—the normative ideal of masculinity that men strive to achieve. In North American culture, hegemonic masculinity is associated with aggressiveness, strength, drive, and ambition.

This fear of being unmasked leads to shame and silence. In turn, men become complicit in the subordination of women and of other men (Kimmel, 2001). This occurs, for example, in the failure to intervene when other men make sexist or racist jokes, the turning of a blind eye when a woman is harassed on the street by men, and the laughter that follows gay-bashing jokes. In these ways, men's fear of being discovered as frauds ("not man enough") results in the perpetuation of gendered behaviour and stereotypes (Kimmel, 2001).

EMPHASIZED FEMININITY   Connell (1987) uses the term *emphasized femininity* to contrast with hegemonic masculinity. **Emphasized femininity** is the normative ideal of femininity, or what we believe to be normal and acceptable feminine behaviour. It is based on women's compliance with their subordination to men and is oriented to obliging men's interests and desires (Connell, 1987). Stiletto heels, for example, are an enduring signifier of emphasized femininity (Kelly, Pomerantz, & Currie, 2005). Defined at the level of social relations, emphasized femininity is the most culturally valued form of femininity. Like hegemonic masculinity, emphasized femininity need not be the most prevalent form of femininity; rather, it is understood as the ideal that women should try to achieve.

emphasized femininity
The normative ideal of femininity, based on compliance with women's subordination to men.

Characteristics associated with emphasized femininity include "supportiveness, enthusiasm and sexual attractiveness" (Grindstaff & West, 2006, p. 500). For example, in their research on cheerleading, Laura Grindstaff and Emily West demonstrate how femininity is "performed" in concert with athleticism. Female cheerleaders are expected to dress in ways that emphasize their femininity—they wear short skirts and form-fitting tops (often with stomachs bared) and tie up their long hair with ribbons, all of which suggests a blend of "youthfulness and sexual availability" (p. 509). One cheerleader commented that the coaches police appearances: "We're told to be in full makeup, to do our hair. Because we're performing. If you're not wearing lipstick, that's the first thing [the coach] will say to you, ‘why isn't your lipstick on?'" (p. 509). Cheerleading is an excellent example of a "performative" emphasized femininity—one that is performed particularly for heterosexual men (Grindstaff & West, 2006).

SOCIOLOGICAL APPROACHES TO GENDER

FUNCTIONALISM   Functionalists maintain that human societies are composed of interrelated parts, with each part serving a function that helps maintain equilibrium in the whole. Consequently, functionalists argue that women and men perform separate, specialized, and complementary roles to maintain cohesiveness within families and in the wider society.

According to functionalists, men fulfill an instrumental role. Through their paid labour in the public sphere, they provide the money for food, shelter, and other necessities as well as make decisions for the family unit. Women are positioned as fulfilling the expressive role, in that they provide emotional support and nurturance for all members of the family unit (Parsons & Bales, 1995). According to this perspective, these well-defined roles reduce confusion and conflict regarding gender expectations and also ensure that societal tasks are fulfilled.

Women, being responsible for rearing society's next generation, are seen as key in reproducing the moral fabric of society. Therefore, this conservative approach also holds women responsible for any changes in gender relations (such as women entering the paid labour force or fighting for social equality with men) that may disrupt the smooth functioning of family life. According to the functionalist perspective, upsetting the supposed natural order in this way may result in higher crime rates, illicit drug use, and incidents of violence—all because women are not at home to provide care (Gilder, 1986).

CONFLICT THEORY   Conflict theorists tend to focus on examining gender differences in access to and control of scarce resources. For example, Friedrich Engels argued that gender stratification in capitalist societies was a direct result of the accumulation of private property (Kimmel, 2004). He argued that because the development of a capitalist economy gave rise to private property, lines of inheritance became important. If a man was to be able to leave his wealth to his heir (that is, his son), he needed a way to ensure that his heir was indeed *his*. The institution of monogamous marriage, then, has little to do with notions of romantic love, but rather with ensuring paternity to determine inheritance lines.

SYMBOLIC INTERACTIONISM   Symbolic interactionists are interested in the *meanings* of male and female and of masculinity and femininity. They argue that gender is created through social interaction, mainly through the mechanism of role-taking. In this way, people learn contrasting expectations about gender on the basis of their perceived sex.

According to this perspective, children learn gender-related behaviours through social institutions such as families, schools, peers, and mass media.

This approach has been criticized for not accounting for social change and for presenting individuals as passive recipients of socialization rather than as active beings (Francis, 2006). Responding to these critics, Candace West and Don Zimmerman (1991) introduced the idea of gender being an accomplishment—something we "do." "Doing gender," as they put it, means that we actively create the differences between girls and boys—and that any differences we see are not natural, essential, or biological. We "do" gender through social interaction—when we display ourselves as a member of a gender.

Once gender differences are socially constructed, they become so taken for granted that we no longer see them that way; rather, we assume that they are based in biology (Nelson, 2006). These gender constructions are then institutionalized in such a way that makes them appear normal and natural. Consider, for example, sex-segregated public washrooms. Such washrooms are furnished with different equipment and different accessories, reinforcing the differences between genders. Yet in the privacy of one's home, men and women use the same equipment (West & Zimmerman, 2002).

FEMINIST THEORY   Feminists argue that many women live under conditions of subordination and oppression, conditions that are neither natural nor inevitable (Nelson, 2006). They view gender as a socially constructed concept that has important and at times detrimental consequences in the lives of both men and women. Feminists, then, endeavour to identify the ways in which institutionalized and internalized norms limit women's behaviours and opportunities. Feminist theorizing is typified by the statement "Biology is not destiny." Since women's oppression is socially produced, it follows that there is hope for social change.

Contemporary feminist theorists take an intersectional approach in their analysis of how gender, race, class, and so forth simultaneously produce relations of privilege and relations of subordination. They also seek to explore the multiplicity of femininities and masculinities.

For example, skater girls studied by Kelly, Pomerantz, and Currie (2005) saw themselves as enacting an alternative femininity. Engaging in skateboarding includes taking physical risks and persevering through injuries, while engaging in skateboarding culture includes wearing clothes associated with skater culture as well as shunning "girly" practices.

POST-STRUCTURALIST THEORY   Drawing on the work of Michel Foucault, post-structuralists understand people as positioned within, and produced by, *discourse* (Francis, 2006). Gender discourses position all people as either men or women—and these categories are relational (Francis, 2007). In this view, masculinity and femininity, and even sex itself, are socially and discursively constructed.

Post-structuralists contend that gender cannot be thought of as having some essential basis, and that there is no authentic masculinity and femininity rooted in male and female bodies. Rather, they view gender as something that we *do* as a performance (Butler, 1997).

You may be asking yourself what the difference is between West and Zimmerman's symbolic interactionist approach of "doing gender" and Butler's approach of gender as performance. The major difference between them is their treatment of the self (also called the *subject* in post-structuralist theorizing). While symbolic interactionists argue that a relatively coherent, stable self (your sense of who you are, the *real* you) underlies social interactions, post-structuralists argue that there is no coherent or essential self behind our performances—our identities are fragmented, contradictory, and always in flux. According to post-structuralists, our "performances" are driven by discourses of power that shape the limits and possibilities for the construction of our identities. Gender is but one of these performances.

What do you know about **Sex and Gender**?

Multiple-choice questions (circle your answer)

1. _____ is the determination of male or female on the basis of a set of socially agreed-upon biological criteria.
   a. Sex
   b. Gender
   c. Sexuality
   d. Sexual orientation

2. The concept of gender was developed by feminists during the
   a. 1940s
   b. 1950s
   c. 1960s
   d. 1970s

3. Transvestites, drag queens, drag kings, and intersexed individuals can be included in the broad category of
   a. Homosexuals
   b. Transsexuals
   c. Transgendered individuals
   d. Bisexuals

4. Which perspective argues that men and women perform separate, specialized, and complementary roles to maintain cohesiveness within families and the wider society?
   a. Feminist
   b. Functionalist
   c. Symbolic interactionist
   d. Conflict theorist

5. The normative ideal of dominant masculinity is called
   a. Emphasized masculinity
   b. Western masculinity
   c. Dominant masculinity
   d. Hegemonic masculinity

Answers: a, d, c, b, d

module 8.2

Reproducing Gender

Think about Reproducing Gender

1 Think about how boys and girls are socialized through the toys with which they play. If you were to go to a local toy store, what would you notice about the colours used on toys for boys and toys for girls?

2 Think about television characters. How would you describe the difference between how men and women are portrayed in lead roles?

3 Think about your experiences in the school system? Who do you think received more positive attention in class—boys or girls? Who was most likely to be punished?

Our understanding of gender and gender relations is taught to us implicitly and explicitly by all agents of socialization. In this section, we will examine three of the most influential agents of socialization: families, education, and the media.

FAMILIES

Gendered expectations begin at birth, after the proclamation of whether a baby is a girl or a boy. Family, friends, and co-workers who flock to see a new baby girl are often loaded down by pink balloons, pink flowers, and teddy bears wearing pink ribbons and pink frilly dresses. Within hours of giving birth to a girl, a hospital room can be transformed to such an extent that one wonders if a bottle of Pepto Bismol has exploded. The same thing is found after the birth of boys, except that people bring blue balloons and blue clothes, with nary a dress in sight.

Such gendered interactions do not stop there. Parents' child-rearing practices are deeply gendered. For instance, research finds that mothers respond more quickly to the cries of their baby girls than they do to the cries of their baby boys (Kimmel, 2004). This speed of response is most likely connected to our ideas about gender and emotion—that girls are more emotional and so it is okay for them to cry, whereas boys should not cry (think of the phrase "big boys don't cry"). In the first six months of life, boys are more likely than girls to be held, rocked, and kissed, but this situation reverses after six months, when girls receive more physical touch (Kimmel, 2004). From a sociological perspective, we can theorize that this practice has to do with normative constructions of gender—the idea that boys and men are to be more independent than girls and women.

Studies also show that parents tend to spend more time talking to little girls, while leaving boys alone (Armstrong, 2004). Parents punish their sons more often than they do their daughters (Armstrong, 2004). Girls often receive toys that reinforce the stereotypical role of caretaker (dolls to dress and care for, nursing kits, and so forth). Barbie dolls and kitchen sets, complete with accessories, adorn girls' rooms, while boys are more likely to have toy cars, video games, and sports equipment. Interestingly, research documents that at an early age (around 2 to 2.5 years), boys are just as interested in playing with dolls and dollhouses as are girls. Yet parents' negative reactions and redirections to more *masculine* toys communicates to boys that it is gender inappropriate for them to be interested in such toys (Kimmel, 2004). These very toys, and parents' practices, encourage the reproduction of hegemonic masculinity and emphasized femininity—boys as active and girls as passive.

Later, boys and girls take on gendered household tasks at the behest of their parents; boys take out the garbage and shovel the snow while girls do dishes and wash floors (Armstrong, 2004). These child-rearing practices work to reinforce notions that there are gender-appropriate behaviours for girls and boys.

EDUCATION

Schools remain a gendered space and experience for children (Webber). The hierarchical structure of schools, interactions between teacher and students, and curricular materials all contribute to normative constructions of masculinity and femininity.

Today, children in Canada are far more likely to have a female teacher than a male teacher (Statistics Canada, 2007a). According to one report, male teachers in Ontario number less than

Girls often receive toys that reinforce caretaking actions such as dolls or kitchen sets. Boys, on the other hand, tend to receive video games and sports equipment.

1 in 3. In elementary schools, 1 in 10 teachers are male teachers under the age of 30, which is strikingly low. The report states that the number of male teachers across Canada has dropped from 41 percent in 1990 to 35 percent in 2000 (Canadian Council on Learning, 2009). Jon Bradley, an education professor at McGill University, reported that the number of males enrolled at the Faculty of Education has continued to decline. In 2003, Bradley found that only 19 percent of Faculty of Education students at McGill University were male (Reynolds, 2003). Bradley also found that in some elementary schools in the Montreal area, there were no male teachers.

Low salaries, negative stereotypes, and the fear of being accused of sexual misconduct were reported as key barriers to men participating in the profession (CBC, 2004).

The proportion of male and female principals in Canadian schools is also changing. Although male principals are overrepresented in both elementary and secondary schools, the number of female principals in these schools is growing. Today, 53 percent of principals in elementary schools are female, while 42 percent of principals in secondary schools are female (Statistics Canada, 2006h).

Since 2001, school boards across Ontario have become concerned about the academic achievement of boys (discussed in more detail below). This concern has prompted educators in the province to evaluate their curriculum. Some believe that what we teach and how we teach favours boys over girls (Fine, 2001; see Leonard Sax in Fillion, 2008). In response, in 2001 the Durham School Board proposed buying more books and magazines geared toward male interests to encourage reading, and a more active classroom for boys. In recent years, some educators and psychologists have suggested that single-sex schools may be the best learning environments for boys. In their report "Single-sex Classrooms," Demers and Bennett do not recommend single-sex schools (2007). However, they do acknowledge the need for a more diversified approach to teaching that recognizes boys' and girls' different interests, tastes, and learning needs.

STUDENT ACHIEVEMENT   Both male and female teachers tend to interact more with boys than they do with girls (Abbott, Wallace, & Tyler, 2005; deMarrais & LeCompte, 1999; Renzetti & Curran, 1999; Skelton, 1997). For example, boys are praised more by their teachers when they successfully complete a task, whereas girls tend to be applauded for presenting an attractive appearance or for being quiet (Nelson, 2006). Teachers also tend to praise girls for being "congenial" and "neat," while they more often praise boys' work for its intellectual quality (Renzetti & Curran, 1999). These types of gendered interactions may contribute to the promotion of girls' dependence and boys' independence (Webber).

In spite of this additional praise, boys continue to be outperformed by girls academically. Ontario student achievement testing (in which all students are tested in grades 3, 6, and 9 in the subjects of reading, writing, and math) has consistently shown a gender gap. Girls outperform boys in each subject, but especially in reading and writing (Education Quality and Accountability Office, 2008). In Ontario, in language-based programming, such as French immersion, more girls than boys are enrolled (Page, 2008). Further, research on French immersion programs has shown that a far greater number of boys than girls move out of French immersion and into English programming (Arnett & Fortune, 2004).

Post-secondary institutions have also seen a decline in the enrolment of male students. In 1990, an equal number of men and women enrolled in Canadian universities (Canadian Council on Learning, 2007a). Currently, women outnumber men in universities by a wide margin: 604 920 to 442 419 (Statistics Canada, 2008). In Ontario, women represent 53 percent of the community college population (Colleges Ontario, 2008).

MEDIA

Gender divisions are reflected in and reinforced by all forms of media. From children's books and movies to programming directed at teens and adults; from advertisements for cars to those for the hottest new clothing trends; and from country ballads to rap and hip hop, we are continually bombarded with masculine and feminine imagery.

For many years, researchers have understood that depictions of gender in the media have the capacity to create and reinforce normative constructions of femininity and masculinity (Armstrong, 2004; Nelson, 2006). Historically, hegemonic masculinity and emphasized femininity have been embodied by portrayals of white men as aggressive, physically competent leading characters and white women as beautiful, nurturing, and docile. Current depictions do little to alleviate such gender-typing.

TELEVISION SHOWS   Even though women are increasingly portrayed in leading roles on prime-time television, with shows focusing completely on their lives (e.g., *Desperate Housewives*), female characters can at times remain manipulative, using helplessness or seduction to get their way (Basow, 1992; Kramar, 2005). In fact, media critics have debated whether strong female characters (as seen in *Xena: Warrior Princess* or *Buffy the Vampire Slayer*) actually represent progressive roles (Kramar, 2005). Buffy is a vampire slayer—she is strong, has many skills, and relies on her friends when she needs help—yet is still a young, beautiful, heterosexual woman.

While there are many examples of current television shows in which women play strong leading characters (*Medium, In Plain Sight, The Closer, Saving Grace, Ghost Whisperer,* and *Grey's Anatomy,* among others), the actors who star in these shows are beautiful, the characters are mostly heterosexual, and, with a few exceptions, the leading women are white. Gender and race intersect in media depictions of women and men. While white men tend to be portrayed as heroes, black men tend to be portrayed as frightening, scary characters (Kramar, 2005; Matthews & Beaman, 2007). White women are beautiful and docile, while black women are constructed as welfare queens or aggressive with bad attitudes (Kramar, 2005; Matthews & Beaman, 2007). Even on shows that are heralded as progressive, like *Buffy the Vampire Slayer*, the main characters remain steadfastly white. In Candra Gill's (2007) exploration of race in that series, she finds that despite its positive portrayal of a female heroine, the show was conventional in its treatment of race. However, in its seventh and final season, the writers finally took up the issue of race and racism. After one non-white woman is mock-killed during training, her character, responding to a question about why she died, replies ironically, "Cuz the black chick always gets it first" (Gill, 2007, p. 249).

The reality television trend, which has pervaded our airwaves for close to a decade, is but one example of the ways in which media shower us with normative images of men and women and masculinity and femininity. One need only watch one or two episodes of *America's Next Top Model, Big Brother, The Biggest Loser, The Bachelor* and/or *The Bachelorette, Survivor,* or *The Amazing Race* to see how reality television reinforces gender stereotypes; glorifies competitive, cutthroat behaviour; and effectively deceives audiences into thinking that what they are watching is unfiltered, real, and unedited, while in reality these shows are heavily edited (Waddle, 2006). The women in these shows tend to be depicted as whiny, emotional, and backstabbing, whereas the men tend to be portrayed as tough and interested in women, sex, and drinking.

TELEVISION COMMERCIALS   Commercials also contribute to the reproduction of particular forms of masculinity and femininity. Consider the ads aired during the Super Bowl, one of television's most-watched events. Researchers studying these ads found four dominant gender themes:

1. Advertisements for alcohol primarily construct men as "losers" who hang out with their male buddies, self-mock, and are ironic about their loser status.
2. Male friendships are the centre of most of the ads.
3. Men in these ads are not in committed relationships and are always ready to engage in sexual activity with fantasy (and, hence, unattainable) women.
4. The women in these ads are dichotomously depicted either as "hotties" (sexualized fantasy objects who often humiliate the men) or as "bitches" (wives or girlfriends who undermine men's freedom to enjoy male bonding) (Messner & Montez de Oca, 2005).

Commercials such as these reinforce the notion that average men cannot pursue beautiful women, and that if they attempt such pursuits, the women will embarrass them (Messner & Montez de Oca, 2005). In contrast, the non-fantasy women (the wives or girlfriends) are depicted as wanting to capture men for a commitment and limit their freedom.

TALK SHOWS   "Trashy" talk shows (think Jerry Springer) have come under much scrutiny for their portrayals of lower-class masculinities and femininities (that is, linked to being loud and crass and behaving badly according to middle-class standards). Yet while we do not see many transgendered characters in mainstream television shows or movies, we may see real transgendered people on talk shows. Producers parade these gender nonconformists for high ratings, of course, but agreeing to be on such shows actually increases the visibility of trans people (Gamson, 2007). Their presence on television talk shows challenges the previous silence around what is and is not acceptable content. In this way, the boundaries of normality are challenged.

Despite some progressive movement in media characters (with strong heroines and such unlikely heroes as Homer Simpson), gender depictions in the media continue to reproduce normative constructions of gender (Armstrong, 2004; Nelson, 2006).

MEDIA AND THE BEAUTY IDEAL   Much of the programming of television networks is aimed at helping individuals achieve beauty ideals. For example programs such as *What Not to Wear, 10 Years Younger, Makeover Train,* and *Big Medicine* are all geared to improving one's physical appearance. These programs convey the message that moulding one's appearance to resemble dominant constructions of femininity and masculinity will lead to a better sense of self. In other words, these shows do not just make the participants look better, they make them feel better.

Both men and women are submitting themselves to popular notions of what constitutes a perfect body based on narrowing conceptions of ideal physiques depicted in television, film, and the music industry (Turner, 2006). One way in which men and women attempt to achieve the ideal physique is through plastic surgery.

In Canada, women undergo 85 percent of all cosmetic procedures (Medicard, 2003). In 2003, Canadian women and men underwent 302 000 cosmetic procedures at a total cost of

FIGURE 8–1 **Surgical Cosmetic Procedures in Canada, 2002 and 2003**

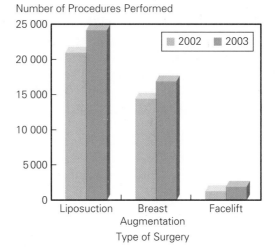

Source: Based on data from Medicard Finance. (2003). http://www.plasticsurgerystatistics.com/number_performed_canada.html.

$665 400 000 (Medicard, 2003). This number represents a 24 percent increase in procedures from 2002—quite a difference in only one year (Medicard, 2003).

The top cosmetic surgeries in Canada are liposuction (surgical removal of excess body fat), rhinoplasty (nose reshaping), and breast augmentation (Medicard, 2003). The most common surgeries among women are liposuction, breast augmentation, and surgical facelifts, while men's most popular surgeries are liposuction, rhinoplasty, and eye lifts (Medicard, 2003). These gendered patterns tell us that both women and men feel pressure to conform to norms of thinness and beauty. Both sexes also access nonsurgical cosmetic procedures: injections (to smooth or fill wrinkles) and nonsurgical facelifts (Medicard, 2003). Figures 8–1 and 8–2 illustrate the surgical and nonsurgical procedures carried out in 2002 and 2003 in Canada.

In summary, then, our bodies do not sit outside social relations. Rather, our daily practices with regard to how we present our bodies, how we wish our bodies to look, and how we evaluate others' bodies are embedded in social constructions of masculinity and femininity and thus embedded in relations of power.

To learn more about plastic surgery and various cosmetic procedures, go to **www.plasticsurgery.ca.**

FIGURE 8–2 **Nonsurgical Cosmetic Procedures in Canada, 2002 and 2003**

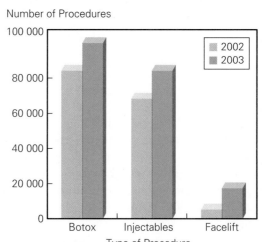

Source: Based on data from Medicard Finance. (2003). http://www.plasticsurgerystatistics.com/number_performed_canada.html.

What do you know about **Reproducing Gender**?

Multiple-choice questions (circle your answer)

1. **Which of the following statements is true?**
   a. Mothers respond more quickly to the cries of their baby boys than their baby girls.
   b. In the first six months of life, boys are more likely than girls to be held, rocked, and kissed.
   c. Parents spend more time talking to little boys.
   d. Parents punish their daughters more than they do their sons.

2. **Which of the following statements is false?**
   a. Girls outperform boys on Ontario school testing.
   b. Men outnumber women in post-secondary institutions.
   c. Girls outnumber boys in French immersion programs.
   d. Girls are most likely to outperform boys in language skills.

3. **Which of the following is false regarding gender themes in television commercials?**
   a. Alcohol advertisements typically depict men as losers.
   b. Female friendships are the centre of most advertisements.
   c. Men in ads tend to be single.
   d. Women in ads tend to be depicted either as "babes" or "bitches."

4. **What is the most common cosmetic procedure in Canada?**
   a. Liposuction
   b. Rhinoplasty
   c Breast augmentation
   d. Facelift

5. **In which subject do boys perform at a level close to girls, according to results from Ontario's student achievement testing?**
   a. Reading
   b. Writing
   c. Math
   d. French

Answers: b, b, b, a, c

module 8.3

Gender and Work

The greatest change in Canada's labour force since the 1960s has been the dramatic increase in the number of employed women, in particular married women with children (Nelson, 2006). This enormous growth in women's labour force participation is a result of and has resulted in inflationary pressures that require higher family incomes, the growth of the service sector, and changing gender expectations.

As we examine the relationship between gender and work and the current trends in Canadian society, keep in mind that not all women share the same levels of inequality. Factors

**Think about
Gender and Work**

1 Think about your work experience. Who was most often in charge in the places you have worked—men or women? Do you think your experience reflects reality in Canada?

2 Think about housework. In heterosexual relationships, who do you think does more housework—men or women?

3 Think about how housework is divided in your home. What do you think affects the decisions around who does what?

such as race, ethnicity, and social class combine with gender to create very different experiences for different groups of women (Fleras, 2009).

THE GENDERED LABOUR FORCE

Women are playing an increasingly stronger role in the Canadian workforce. Women today are more educated, and their profile is rising in many professional fields (Statistics Canada, Daily, 2006n). In 2004, 58 percent of women aged 15 and over were in the paid labour force (up from 42 percent in 1976). In the same year, 68 percent of men aged 15 and over were in the paid labour force (down from 73 percent in 1976) (Statistics Canada, 2006n). Women now make up over half of all people employed in medicine, other related health professions, and business.

In spite of these positive gains, significant segregation in the workforce remains. Women continue to be underrepresented in managerial positions. This form of segregation has been referred to as the **glass ceiling**—the notion that women can see the top of the corporate ladder but cannot reach it because a glass ceiling stops their progress. In 2004, 37 percent of all managerial positions in Canada were held by women. However, this figure represents an upward trend when we consider that 30 percent of managerial positions were held by women in 1987 (Statistics Canada, 2006n).

Another area of concern is the ongoing concentration of women in "traditional occupations." This pattern is referred to as **occupational sex segregation** (Mooney et al., 2004). In spite of the fact that many women are branching out into other fields, for the most part it appears that women continue to select traditional occupations. As of 2004, two-thirds of all women worked in four fields: teaching, nursing and health related occupations, clerical and administration, and sales and service (Statistics Canada, 2006n).

Finally, the number of women in part-time jobs is also troubling. Women represent 70 percent of part-time workers. While many women *choose* to work part-time, as much as one-third of women working part-time do so because they cannot find full-time work (McMullin, 2004). In a 2003 labour force survey, 39 percent of women reported that they work part-time due to family obligations, compared with less than 5 percent of men (Nelson, 2006). Moreover, women who work part-time are nearly twice as likely as their male counterparts to have completed university or college (Comfort, Johnson, & Wallace, 2003). Women tend to work part-time throughout the life cycle, whereas for men, part-time work is associated with their youth and initial entry into the labour market (Comfort, Johnson, & Wallace, 2003).

Child-rearing and other family responsibilities are most often cited as reasons for women's part-time work (Comfort, Johnson, & Wallace, 2003). Generally, women leave work for at least short periods of time to bear children, and often for longer periods to rear their children full-time. This discontinuity in employment is one of the greatest barriers faced by professional and nonprofessional women alike. Impressions about one's commitment to work, current earnings, lifetime earnings, opportunities for advancement, and future employability are all greatly influenced by interruptions in one's career (Nelson, 2006). Women who work in male-dominated industries (e.g., manufacturing, construction, engineering, finance) are more likely than women in other occupations to never marry or to remain childless (Marshall, 1987; Mason & Goulden, 2004). These women find that their co-workers and bosses are quite intolerant of the difficulties women face in trying to combine full-time paid work and child-rearing responsibilities (Wolf-Wendel & Ward, 2003).

THE GENDERED WAGE GAP

Paid work influences gender relations and is implicated in many tensions associated with them (Nelson, 2006). The employment conditions that most women face, as well as the structural barriers to obtaining and maintaining careers, have the potential to make participation in the workplace less appealing and less rewarding for them than for men.

glass ceiling   The notion that women can see the top of the corporate ladder but cannot reach it because a glass ceiling stops their progress.

occupational sex segregation   The ongoing concentration of women in "traditional occupations."

WHY SHOULD WE CARE?

The Feminization of Poverty

Statistics Canada uses a measure called the *low income cut-off (LICO)* to determine poverty levels. Falling below this cut-off point means that a family is spending a larger proportion of its income on the basic necessities of life (food, shelter, and clothing) than an average family spends (see Chapter 7). When calculating the LICO, Statistics Canada takes into account both family size and geographic location (community size). For example, in 2007, the LICO for a family of four living in an urban setting (population between 30 000 and 99 999) was $28 352 (Statistics Canada, 2008o).

Sociologists note that poverty is a gendered phenomenon. More women than men live in poverty in Canada (Canadian Council on Social Development, 2004). Because women disproportionately live in poverty, sociologists call this the *feminization of poverty*. As you can see in Figure 8–3, when we consider poverty by family composition, women younger than 65 living on their own and female-headed lone-parent families are the two groups with the highest poverty rates in Canada (Canadian Council on Social Development, 2004).

Figure 8–3 shows that two of the top five groups living in poverty are female-headed and male-headed lone-parent families. This means that many Canadian children also live in poverty. Poverty, then, is not just a women's issue; it is a social issue. In 2004, 865 000 Canadian children lived in poverty, which is equivalent to one in eight children (Canadian Council on Social Development, 2004). Some of the consequences of living in poverty are poor-quality food and health (less expensive foods tend to be lower in nutritional value), reliance on social assistance (welfare), and homelessness (Harman, 2005).

This article is also a peerScholar assignment in MySocLab.

FIGURE 8–3 Family Composition and Poverty, 2004

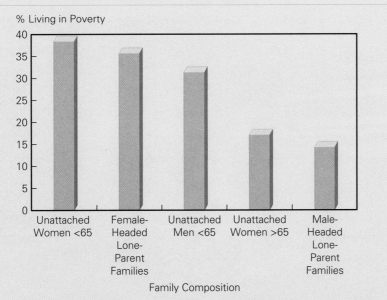

Source: Based on data from Canadian Council on Social Development. (2004). *A profile of economic security in Canada.* Retrieved July 10, 2008, from http://www.ccsd.ca.factsheets/economic_security/poverty/index.htm.

The gendered wage gap has been found to exist in all occupational categories (Nelson, 2006). Statistics Canada (2003c) reports that despite substantial gains in earning during the past two decades, women still earn much less than men. In 2002, women working in full-time, full-year positions earned an average of $36 000, while employed men working the same schedule earned $50 500 (Statistics Canada, 2003c). According to the Canadian Labour Congress, by 2008, women working full-time in full-year employment earned on average 70.5 percent of what men earned ($39 200 for women versus $55 700 for men). This wage gap is even greater for university-educated women, who earned only 68 percent of what all men earned in 2005 (Fleras, 2009). As well, Aboriginal women and minority women earn less money than white women (Luxton & Corman, 2005).

The wage gap can be explained by such factors as occupational segregation (women and men being employed in different employment sectors), undervaluing of women's work (paying women less than men for working in the same positions), restructuring of women's work by privatization and outsourcing, and lack of affordable child care (limiting women's choices for employment) (Fleras, 2009).

FAMILIES AND UNPAID WORK

Our families represent one of the key environments in which gender relations are produced and sustained. In Canada, by the age of 45, 97 percent of women and 96 percent of men have lived in a union or raised children (Beaujot, 2000).

Over the past 20 years, the gap between men and women in the realm of domestic labour has decreased. Today, there is greater equality between heterosexual couples "in the sharing of financial, childcare and household responsibilities" (Marshall, 2006). If we compare the number of hours a man spends on paid and unpaid work per day with that spent by a woman, the totals are almost the same. On average, men spend 8.8 hours on paid and unpaid work per day, while women spend 8.7 hours. The difference is that women do more work inside the home, while men do more work outside the home. In 2005, women's unpaid work in the home averaged 4.3 hours per day, while men's averaged 2.5 hours per day. Further,

Gender relations are produced and sustained within families where women remain primarily responsible for domestic labour. Although men are closing the gap, they are still less likely to engage in the daily routines of child care.

women are more apt to do repetitive types of household chores than are men (Baker, 2005, p. 112). Notably, over the past 20 years, women's unpaid work has dropped 4.8 hours per day while men's has increased 2.1 hours per day (Lindsay, 2008).

Given that on average, women make about 70 percent of what men make, one argument as to why housework remains primarily women's work concerns the imbalance in their economic contribution to the household. This argument is the basis for the exchange theory, which suggests that power flows from bringing resources to a relationship. Thus, economically based bargaining power determines who does what chores around the house. Researchers testing this theory found that women do indeed decrease their housework as their earnings increase, right up to the point where both spouses contribute equally to a household's income (Bittman et al., 2003).

exchange theory The assertion that power flows from the resources that a member brings to a relationship.

After that point, women who earn *more* money than their male partners appear to compensate by taking on more of the household labour and child-rearing responsibilities than their partners. So, between the point at which women contribute half of the family income and the point at which they provide all of it, money does not necessarily translate into reduced household work for women (Bittman et al., 2003). As women provide more income than their male partners, their hours of unpaid work in the home *increase* by five to six hours per week (Bittman et al., 2003). Thus, gendered expectations come into play regardless of paid employment. Yet, further research shows that women with high incomes (over $100,000 per year) experience greater parity with their male partners and do less housework on average (Marshall, 2006).

Whether a couple has children also affects the balance of work in the home. Research shows that when couples have children, men, on average, do an extra 0.4 hours of paid work and 0.3 hours of unpaid work per day. Women do not increase the amount of paid work they do but do increase the amount of unpaid work by 0.6 hours per day on average (Marshall, 2006).

Men who remain at home to do the majority of child-rearing, or who take an active part in domestic work, risk having their masculinity jeopardized, by themselves and by others. Fathers who raise their children are scrutinized by their communities for being primary caregivers rather than primary breadwinners (Doucet, 2004). In a qualitative study of 70 stay-at-home fathers in Canada, Andrea Doucet (2004) found that each father she interviewed felt the weight of peer disapproval and felt social pressure to be earning rather than caring. Most of the men in Doucet's study engaged in some type of part-time work so that they had something to talk about with other men. In addition to feeling a loss of masculinity due to their caretaking role, many of these fathers indicated that the community cast a suspicious eye toward them. Even when there appears to be some resistance to preconceived gendered expectations, men and women tend to work hard to maintain notions of masculinity and femininity.

In sum, women who earn more money than their male partners attempt to address this seemingly upset gender relationship by taking on more domestic duties, while men who stay at home to parent tend to take on more part-time work and home renovations to assert their masculinity (Bittman et al., 2003; Doucet, 2004).

To learn more about how domestic work has changed, go to **www.statcan.gc.ca/pub/75-001-x/10706/9268-eng.htm.**

What do you know about **Gender and Work**?

Multiple-choice questions (circle your answer)

1. In 2004, _____ of women aged 15 and over were in the paid labour force.
   a. 14 percent
   b. 48 percent
   c. 58 percent
   d. 72 percent

2. The concentration of women in traditional occupations is called
   a. Occupational sex segregation
   b. Occupational gender segregation
   c. Traditional career selection
   d. Normative career selection

3. Women working in full-time positions earn
a. As much as men
b. Slightly less than men
c. More than men
d. Much less than men

4. Which of the following statements is false?
a. Today, there is greater equality in the sharing of household duties between heterosexual couples than there was 20 years ago.
b. If we combine unpaid and paid work, women work slightly more than men.

c. Women do more unpaid work than men.
d. Over the past 20 years, women's unpaid work has dropped by 0.5 hours per day.

5. Which of the following occupational fields would not be considered traditional for women?
a. Teaching
b. Nursing
c. Sales and service
d. Engineering

Answers: c, a, d, b, d

module 8.4

The Social Construction of Sexualities

Think about the Social Construction of Sexualities

1 Think about all of the kinds of kisses that you give in a week. How many types of kisses are there? Whom do you kiss? When? What social rules about kissing do you follow?

2 Think about the sex education that you received in school. What were the topics that were covered? Do you think that you were adequately educated? How might politics and social power influence what is taught in school?

Did you think about why this chapter is entitled Gender and "Sexualities" as opposed to Gender and "Sexuality"? We are beginning from the premise that there are multiple sexualities, and that we need to recognize such multiplicity. But what is sexuality? And why are sociologists interested in this private matter? We challenge you to consider whether your sexuality is really all that private.

SEXUALITY

Sexuality includes your sexual orientation (who you are attracted to sexually), your sexual identity (butch, femme, heteroflexible, queer, straight, genderqueer), and sex acts (masturbation, bondage, kissing, oral sex, barebacking, penetration). Sexuality also includes our sex lives (polyamory, monogamy, infidelity, age of consent) and the commodification of sex (prostitution, pornography). Sexual politics (activism, family values, homophobia, heteronormativity) are also a part of sexuality, as are reproductive politics (abortion, adoption) and sexual violence. Our bodies are also part of sexuality (orgasm, erection, circumcision, sexually transmitted infections, Viagra).

As sociologists, we are interested in all of the above, particularly in examining how our understanding of these aspects of sexuality is socially constructed (Steele, 2005). These meanings are embedded in our language, laws, popular culture, social rituals, and even medical definitions (Weeks, 2003). We learn what is deemed socially appropriate and inappropriate through our interactions with others and our culture. Understanding sexuality as a social construction, then, means understanding that the meanings of sexual desires and sexual acts, as well as which sexual expressions have social approval and which are disavowed, are all socially organized

CANADIAN SOCIETY IN FOCUS

Gender Equality

According to the World Economic Forum's 2007 report on global gender equality, Canada ranked 18th out of 128 countries (more than 90 percent of the global population), down from 14th in 2006. Sweden (first), Norway (second), Finland (third), and Iceland (fourth) were the highest-ranking countries, with Nepal (125th), Pakistan (126th), Chad (127th), and Yemen (128th) comprising the lowest-ranked countries (WEF, 2008). The World Economic Forum (WEF) argues that women's position vis-à-vis men's within a nation influences the growth or development of that nation. The WEF report examined the gap between women and men in the following areas: educational attainment, economic participation and opportunity, political empowerment, and health and survival.

Canada ranked 13th in terms of economic participation and opportunity. This category examines the labour force participation rates of men and women; women's incomes as a ratio of men's earnings; the proportion of women who are legislators, senior officials, and managers; and the proportion of women who are either professionals or technical workers (WEF, 2008).

Canada ranked 26th in terms of educational attainment, scoring 0.9987 out of a possible 1.0 (indicating that there is very little meaningful separation among the highest-ranking countries on this measure). This category measures the literacy of women compared to men, as well as women's access to all levels of education (WEF, 2008).

Canada ranked 36th in terms of political empowerment. Important here is the fact that Canada's score out of a possible 1.0 was only 0.1592. So, while Canada did rank 36th, this is actually our country's poorest score on all of the measures. This category examines the gap between women and men in political decision-making positions. The length of time that women have served as prime minister over the past 50 years is also factored in (WEF, 2008).

Canada ranked 51st in terms of health and survival, but it is important to note that the score was 0.9787 out of a possible 1.0, so again there is very little meaningful separation between many countries. Men's and women's life expectancies and years of expected good health, as well as the sex ratio at birth, are captured in this category (WEF, 2008).

Among these global rankings, gender equality is positively correlated with economic development. That is, richer countries are more gender equitable than are poorer countries. As a result of these types of rankings, countries are encouraged to be aware of the continuing challenges posed by gender inequality and to enact social change to eradicate gender disparities (WEF, 2007).

(Seidman, 2003). Moreover, these meanings are fluid; they change over time and from culture to culture.

Consider the kiss. Do you think that kissing is a natural act? In North American society, we associate kissing with romance and sex, as well as with affection. We also use the kiss for nonsexual purposes, including "greeting and farewell, affection, religious or ceremonial symbolism, deference to a person of high status" (Tieffer, 2005, p. 25). We grow up watching a range of kissing practices in television shows and movies (the peck, the French kiss). So would it surprise you to learn that anthropological researchers have found several societies in which sexual kissing is unknown? These societies include several from Oceania (Balinese, Chamorro, Manus, Tinguian), Africa (Chewa, Thonga), South America (Siriono), and Eurasia (Lepcha) (Tieffer, 2005). In these cultures, mouth-to-mouth kissing is deemed disgusting, unsafe, and unhealthy (Tieffer, 2005). According to anthropologists, Thonga individuals in Africa laughed when they first witnessed Europeans kissing, and said, "Look at them—they eat each other's saliva and dirt" (Tieffer, 2005, p. 24). Therefore, while kissing involves parts of our bodies, its meaning and practice is shaped by our culture.

SEXUAL IDENTITIES

sexual identity A broad term that can include our masculinity or femininity, our knowledge of our bodies, our sexual histories, and our sexual preferences.

Sexuality is basic to our identity, and hence to our way of life. **Sexual identity** is a broad term that can include our sense of self as masculine or feminine (our society recognizes only these two alternatives), our knowledge of our bodies (function, pleasure, pain), our sexual histories, and our sexual preferences (or orientation). We convey our sexual identity through, for example, how we speak about our sexual attractions and how we interact with others. Identities, then, are what Michel Foucault called *disciplinary*: they are not biological realities but rather are produced socially and maintained through continuous performance. Only some identities are socially recognized, yet many exist nonetheless, which demonstrates that some people actively resist disciplinary power.

sexual orientation An individual's sexual and emotional attraction to a person of a particular sex.

Part of our identity is, of course, our **sexual orientation**, which refers to an individual's sexual and emotional attraction to a person of a particular sex. We now look at four sexual identities: homosexuality, heterosexuality, bisexuality, and pansexuality.

homosexual An individual who is sexually attracted to members of the same sex.

HOMOSEXUALITY   People with a **homosexual** identity are sexually attracted to, and engage in sexual activities with, members of the same sex. Acceptance of homosexuality has varied from time to time and place to place. In Canada, homosexuality has been viewed as unacceptable since the beginning of European settlement. As such, homosexuals have been closeted and subjected to systemic oppression. Despite significant shifts in both social attitudes and legal status, heterosexism and homophobia still exist in our society. **Heterosexism** is the practice of holding up heterosexuality as the ideal and normal sexuality, rendering all other sexualities as abnormal and deviant.

heterosexism The holding up of heterosexuality as the ideal and normal sexuality, rendering all other sexualities as abnormal and deviant.

Homophobia is an irrational fear or hatred of homosexuals. It works to declare homosexuality as deviant, abnormal, and thereby punishable. Homophobia can lead to discrimination, harassment, and violence against homosexuals. Homophobic attitudes are often expressed through language that constructs gay men as promiscuous, oversexed, and effeminate, and lesbians as manly or butch. Homophobia also has the effect of asserting heterosexuality in public spaces. For example, in research on homophobic harassment in American schools, the words *faggot* and *dyke* are found to be used routinely against lesbian, gay, bisexual, transgendered, and questioning (LGBTQ) students as well as heterosexual students (Pettett, 2007). Such harassment can lead to anxiety, depression, isolation, and even suicide (Pettett, 2007).

homophobia An irrational fear or hatred of homosexuals that can lead to discrimination, harassment, and violence against them.

The Emergence of Homosexual Identities As discussed earlier, lesbian and gay identities are, like any other sexual identity, socially produced. In countering what he sees as the myth of the "eternal homosexual," social historian John D'Emilio (2005) emphasizes the distinction between homosexual *behaviour* and the development of homosexual *identities*. He argues that lesbian and gay identities are a product of the social changes that came about first during the Industrial Revolution and later in the early part of the twentieth century.

Prior to industrialization, the family was a unit of both production and consumption—men, women, and children all farmed, and women used the materials produced by the farm for the family's consumption. Everyone worked interdependently to ensure the family's survival (D'Emilio, 2005). However, with the advent of the Industrial Revolution—and the wage labour to which it gave rise—the family was no longer needed as a self-sufficient household economy and instead became primarily responsible for the emotional satisfaction of its members separate from the "public world of work and production" (D'Emilio, 2005, p. 217). Moreover, as rates of wage labour increased, children were no longer required to work on family lands.

Taken together, these changes in the family paved the way for sexuality to become dissociated from a procreative imperative (D'Emilio, 2005). By helping to separate sexuality from procreation, capitalism helped to create conditions that allowed some women and men to arrange private lives around their erotic and emotional attractions to members of their own sex. As a result of these changes, it became possible for lesbians and gay men to establish gay communities (mainly in urban spaces) and, later, to establish a sexual identity–based politic through the gay liberation movement.

However, initially, there were no public social spaces in which to take such attractions and preferences and carve out a way of life for one's self—in other words, to create an identity (D'Emilio, 2005). It was only in the early part of the twentieth century that this sexual identity truly began to emerge.

The Gay Liberation Movement   In North America, gay men and lesbians began to congregate in social spaces in the 1920s and 1930s as gay and lesbian bars opened in large cities. By the 1950s and 1960s, a gay subculture had developed (D'Emilio, 2005). The publishing world took notice of the emergent gay and lesbian world and produced newspaper and magazine articles and novels depicting lesbian and gay male life (D'Emilio, 2005).

Gays and lesbians were nonetheless subjected to oppression, much of it state sanctioned—including the criminalization of homosexual acts, a ban in the United States against employing lesbians and gay men in the federal government (implemented by President Eisenhower), and increased police surveillance in the name of morality (D'Emilio, 2005). This oppression led to the gay liberation movement of the 1960s.

The 1969 Stonewall riots in New York City are considered to be the pivotal point marking the start of the gay liberation movement. On June 27 of that year, New York City detectives raided the Stonewall Inn, a gay bar in Greenwich Village. The raid set off a riot as patrons resisted the police. Publicity of the event sent a shock wave through lesbian and gay communities across the country. "Overnight, this unprecedented surge of organizing transformed what had been a largely underground vanguard movement into a highly public mass movement for gay pride, power, and community" (Marotta, 2006, p. 35).

In Canada, the first gay rights demonstration took place in Ottawa in August 1971, when demonstrators from across the country demanded civil rights from Parliament (Smith, 1998). Until only two years earlier, homosexual sex acts had been included in the Criminal Code (D'Emilio, 2005, p. 216), and the demonstration was part of an organized attempt to further legitimize gay and lesbian identities. While the achievement of equality rights was of prime importance, the gay social movement also helped to create both gay communities and gay political identities (Smith, 1998).

Today, gays and lesbians can claim many victories; for example, gay marriages are now legal in Canada as well as in the Netherlands, Belgium, and Spain. In Toronto, the Toronto District School Board has developed the first alternative school in Canada for lesbians, gays, bisexual, transgender, queer, and questioning students (Toronto District School Board, 2009).

HETEROSEXUALITY   **Heterosexuals** are individuals who are attracted to and/or engage in sexual activities with members of the opposite sex. As the dominant (accepted) sexuality in Canadian society, heterosexuality is more than an individual identity—it also represents a norm and a socially approved role (Katz, 2005). As a social construct, heterosexuality is reinforced coercively through what Michel Foucault termed *surveillance*; that is, we police our own and others' sexualities, granting approval to some while disparaging others. for example, how many times have you heard homophobic remarks like "you fag" or "you queer"? Heterosexuality is also reinforced through the organization of society and through the messages we receive from the various agents of socialization (Renold, 2006).

As with any identity, heterosexuality comes in multiple forms and means different things to different people. You can practise heterosexual monogamy or heterosexual non-monogamy. You may be very "girlie" in your heterosexuality or may be a "manly man." The meaning and social organization of heterosexuality vary across time and location.

heterosexual   An individual who is attracted to members of the opposite sex.

In Western societies, heterosexual desires tend to be organized around marriage or other long-term relationships and monogamy. Heterosexuals enjoy social privilege because heterosexuality is constructed as *the* normal sexuality (Allen, 2007). It is privileged as both normal and natural, and is simultaneously prevalent and invisible. Social interactions, language, and social institutions are all organized according to heterosexual norms (Renold, 2006). Heterosexuality also acts as the dominant standard against which all other sexualities are measured and compared.

Many feminist sociologists argue that sexuality and gender are inextricably linked. That is, those who assume a heterosexual identity are often understood as having simultaneously established a so-called normal gender identity (Seidman, 2003). Gender deviance or variance is thus assumed to be a sign of homosexuality. Such an assumption leads people to cultivate identities of *masculine* men and *feminine* women to avoid being mislabelled as homosexual (Seidman, 2003).

bisexual An individual who is attracted to both women and men.

BISEXUALITY   As a sexual identity, **bisexuality** includes individuals who are attracted romantically and/or sexually to both men and women; it also tends to be linked with non-monogamy (Klesse, 2005; Rodríquez Rust, 2000). Bisexuals tend not to be equally attracted to both sexes simultaneously, and those identifying as bisexual may shift between heterosexual and homosexual relationships over their lives. Bisexuality challenges the notion that heterosexuality and homosexuality are mutually exclusive and oppositional categories (Klesse, 2005). As such, there is a perception that bisexual individuals are in a perpetual conflict.

When a bisexual individual is in a monogamous relationship, his or her sexual identity as bisexual is perceived by some to be destabilized (Klesse, 2005). The perception is that "authentic bisexuality" can only occur within a non-monogamous context (Klesse, 2005, p. 448).

biphobia The irrational fear or hatred of bisexuals.

This perception can lead to **biphobia**—the irrational fear or hatred of bisexuals. Biphobia can result in discrimination, marginalization, and even violence (Klesse, 2005). Such stereotypes include assuming that bisexuals have heightened levels of sexuality and are promiscuous and, therefore, constitute risky and untrustworthy partners (Klesse, 2005). Discrimination can come from both heterosexual and homosexual contexts.

Within lesbian circles in particular, bisexuality is marked as especially problematic (Klesse, 2005; Matheson & Endicott, 1998; Rust, 1995). In this context, bisexuality is constructed as an act of disloyalty to lesbian and gay politics (Matheson & Endicott, 1998; Rust, 1995). Women who identify as bisexual are perceived as giving in to compulsory (normative) heterosexuality; in short, they are considered to be "sleeping with the enemy" (Rodríguez Rust, 2000). Such marginalization can contribute to the erasure of bisexuality as an identity, especially within lesbian cultural and political spaces (Klesse, 2005).

pansexuality Romantic and sexual desire for people regardless of their gender identity or biological sex.

PANSEXUALITY   The term **pansexuality** refers to romantic and sexual desire for people regardless of their gender identity or biological sex (*pan* is a Greek word meaning "all" or "every"). In other words, it means sexual attraction to all genders. Pansexuality is distinct from bisexuality in that it includes attraction to transsexuals and transgendered individuals (Hird, 2004). However, it does not entail sexual attraction to all people or acceptance of all sexual practices. Pansexuality favours more fluid notions of sexual pleasure without categorizations such as homosexuality or heterosexuality.

SEXUAL RELATIONSHIPS

All sexual relationships, whether they are monogamous or take one of the several forms of non-monogamy, are socially shaped. Of interest to sociologists is how monogamous relationships have come to be privileged in society while non-monogamous relationships have been rendered problematic. We explore this question by looking at each form of relationship in turn.

MONOGAMY   **Monogamy** refers to the coupling of two people, excluding the intimate involvement of others. It is commonly contrasted with *polygyny,* which refers to the coupling of one man and more than one woman (Loue, 2006).

In Canada, heterosexual monogamous relationships are dominant (84 percent of census families include a husband and wife). Because of the pervasiveness of this type of relationship, many believe that an individual should have only one sexual relationship at a time. Attached to the idea of monogamy are assumptions about fidelity, love, mutual respect, mutual sexual satisfaction, and exclusivity (Loue, 2006). For some, monogamy implies lifelong coupling. For others, there is no guarantee that either partner will remain sexually or emotionally faithful.

Monogamy can mean different things to different people at different times. For example, some people would not consider cyber-sex with another person as cheating on their primary partner. Thus, our commonly held assumptions about monogamous sexual relationships can be problematic (Loue, 2006).

Serial Monogamy   Sexuality scholars such as Anapol (1997) and Loue (2006) refer to successions of monogamous partnerships as *serial monogamy.* **Serial monogamy** refers to a relationship pattern that has one monogamous relationship (whether long-term or short-term) following another (Loue, 2006).

Of course, when the intervals between these exclusive relationships are short, the distinction between serial monogamy and monogamy is not always clear-cut (Loue, 2006). In fact, serial monogamists tend to have a series of short-term relationships, one after the other. Serial monogamy usually occurs when individuals do not have any overriding economic, legal, or moral reasons (including child dependants) to stay together in a single lifelong monogamous relationship (Anapol, 1997).

Many sexuality scholars therefore identify serial monogamy as a form of, or replacement for, multiple-partner sexuality. In this sense, it could be considered a form of non-monogamy (Loue, 2006). If the serial monogamist has multiple sexual partners, with each partner separated merely by linear time, we may even understand serial monogamy to be a kind of fictional monogamy (Anapol, 1997).

NON-MONOGAMY   **Non-monogamy** refers to sexual interactions with more than one person during a given period, or to any sexual relationship involving more than two people (Anapol, 1997). Although popular perceptions of those engaging in non-monogamy are as having deviant sexualities—and even as engaging in frequent public sex environments such as parks, parking lots, clubs, parties, and other subcultural contexts—their social activities in fact differ little from those who practise monogamy (Anapol, 1997). Non-monogamous relationships vary according to the number of partners, arrangements, legal status, genders, and sexualities. They also vary according to degrees of intimacy, closeness, and commitment (Klesse, 2005).

Polyamory   **Polyamory** is a distinct form of non-monogamous relationship that involves mutually acknowledged emotional, sexual, or romantic connections with multiple partners. The term *polyamory,* deriving from the Latin word for "love" and the Greek word for "many," translates to "many loves" or "more than one love" (Klesse, 2006, p. 568). Polyamory emphasizes long-term, emotionally intimate relationships that transcend sexual intimacy. As one participant in Klesse's (2006) UK research on polyamory remarked, "People who identify as polyamorous believe in the idea of more than one relationship, meaning more than one love relationship. And they don't even have to be sexual" (p. 567).

Polyamory is not about having many sexual relationships. Indeed, people in polyamorous relationships often invoke a moral distinction between their relationships and those involving casual sex or "swinging" (associated with couples who have casual sex with others or "swap" partners) (Klesse, 2006). Polyamory, then, is understood as "responsible non-monogamy" that excludes sexual experiences that do not involve love (Klesse, 2006). People in polyamorous

monogamy The coupling of two people, excluding the intimate involvement of others.

serial monogamy A relationship pattern that has one monogamous relationship following another.

non-monogamy Sexual interactions with more than one person during a given period, or any sexual relationship involving more than two people.

polyamory Mutually acknowledged emotional, sexual, or romantic connections with multiple partners.

relationships are consensual, and open and honest with their partners (Bloomquist, 2000; Klesse, 2006; Lano & Parry, 1995).

In summary, just as we demonstrated that sexual identities are socially organized, so too are sexual relationships. As such, judgment of acceptable and unacceptable sexual relationships are socially defined. Despite many people's assumption that monogamy is natural, the privilege accorded to monogamous relationships in Western societies is a social process.

SEXUALITY AND GENDER: THE SEXUAL DOUBLE STANDARD

Sexuality is socially embedded within a matrix of power relations that are shaped by our gender as well as by our social class, race, ethnicity, age, ability, and so forth (Abbott, Wallace, & Tyler, 2005). We "perform" our gender every day, through what we choose to wear, how we style (or do not style) our hair, how we speak, and how we interact with others. All of these acts contribute to our presentation of our selves as feminine or masculine (or other) beings. Yet contrary to dominant discourse, a natural (biological) or fixed (stable) gender is in fact an illusion (Renold, 2006). That is, our gendered selves are socially produced and can change over time. Consider how your own presentation of masculinity or femininity has changed from one year ago, five years ago, and so forth.

Still, Western culture demands that we choose which gender to identify with, masculine or feminine. These normative gender identities tie into heterosexuality as the dominant presumption; in other words, a "correct" gender includes heterosexuality. "Abnormal" gender performances are subject to policing and shaming, which helps to reproduce gender inequality (Renold, 2006).

You are probably very familiar with the sexual double standard, whereby those who have many sexual relations experience gendered consequences; men are heralded as "studs," while women are marked as "sluts." In this way, the double standard divides men and women into two opposing groups: active and passive. Let's look at how masculine and feminine identities are constructed.

THE CONSTRUCTION OF "MASCULINITY"   Hegemonic masculinity (meaning the dominant cultural form of masculinity) depicts *real* men as always being interested in sex (with women); being in physical and emotional control; being strong, aggressive, and physically dominant; and not needing help from others (Courtenay, 2000; Kumar, Larkin, & Mitchell, 2002). Dominant discourses of masculinity also position men as being somewhat sexually irresponsible, which can undermine their sexual health (Larkin, Andrews, & Mitchell, 2006). Masculine sexuality is constructed as uncontrolled and uncontrollable, with women often positioned as the gatekeepers of sex (Larkin, Andrews, & Mitchell, 2006). Such thinking may result in pressuring women for sex and committing sexual assaults against both women and men (Kumar, Larkin, & Mitchell, 2002).

Sexual competency also defines masculinity (Tieffer, 2005). Since they are always interested in sex, masculine men are encouraged to deny the emotional and interpersonal factors of sexual relationships and to see that as the domain of femininity (Tieffer, 2005). In North America, having sex with multiple women is a cultural ideal that men are pressured to achieve (Kumar, Larkin, & Mitchell, 2002). By exchanging sexual stories (bragging about their conquests), men use sex as a means of bonding and achieving social status with other men (Tieffer, 2005). Indeed, men are congratulated for engaging in sex (Tanenbaum, 2005).

THE CONSTRUCTION OF "FEMININITY"   In dominant constructions of femininity, women are largely positioned as being subordinate to men's sexual desire. They are constructed as the passive objects of men's sexual desire, with limited sexual agency (Cram & Jackson, 2003). When young women do talk about sex, they tend to frame their discussions in terms of men's needs, desires, and bodies (Cram & Jackson, 2003; Holland et al., 1996). Given that the dominant construction of sex is understood as vaginal penetration, with women as passive recipients of men's sexual action, young women may find it difficult to talk about sex in terms of their own sexual needs (Kumar, Larkin, & Mitchell, 2002, p. 37).

Moreover, women are divided into one of two categories: "good" girls and "bad" girls, Madonnas and whores. Within this construction, bad girls are disposable and good girls are to be treated well (Tanenbaum, 2005). The sexual double standard is enforced through the social power of reputation; as noted above, men who engage in sexual relations with more than one woman are *studs* whereas women who behave in similar ways are *sluts* (Cram & Jackson, 2003). Women experience tension between feeling pressure to have sex and needing to preserve their reputations as good girls for fear of being labelled promiscuous. As a result, women are often less comfortable with sexual interaction than men (Tanenbaum, 2005). Women's fear of damaged reputations as a result of their sexual behaviour works to constrain their behaviour, since men (and sometimes women) may use labels such as "slut" and "whore" to describe women they perceive as promiscuous (Cram & Jackson, 2003).

Use of the Term *Slut*   The term *slut* is used to mark and shame women who are perceived as promiscuous or who have a casual attitude toward sex (Tanenbaum, 2005). These types of negative labels denigrate and censure active and desiring female sexualities.

The threat of being labelled a slut ensures that many young women come to believe that sex is bad and will lead to a bad reputation (Tanenbaum, 2005). In fact, Tanenbaum's research with women who had been labelled sluts in either middle school or high school found that the threat of being cast as a slut actually decreased the likelihood of using contraceptives or carrying condoms. Being called a slut can also follow a girl into adulthood. It may cause her to shut down her sexuality or become a target for further forms of harassment (Tanenbaum, 2005).

Slut-bashing affects not only girls. The culture that is created through this practice also teaches boys that there are two kinds of girls—good girls and bad girls—and hence that there are two ways to treat girls, depending on within which category a girl is located. Good girls are treated well; bad girls are expendable (Tanenbaum, 2005).

Use of the Term *Promiscuous*   The use of the term *promiscuous* works in the same way as that of the term *slut*. **Promiscuous** is a derogatory term used to describe anyone who is assumed to have had sex with an "unreasonable" number of sexual partners (Klesse, 2006). Of course, as sociologists, we should ask, Who gets to decide what constitutes unreasonable numbers? Promiscuity discourses are used to constrain women's sexuality (Klesse, 2006). The very fact of "promiscuous" women challenges dominant discourses of female sexuality that position women as naturally passive and submissive. Calling a woman promiscuous, then, is a means of regulating her sexuality and encouraging her to remain firmly located within the boundaries of the sexual double standard.

promiscuous A derogatory term used to describe anyone who is assumed to have had sex with an "unreasonable" number of sexual partners.

SOCIOLOGICAL APPROACHES TO SEXUALITY

Sociological approaches to sexuality examine issues such as the function of sexuality, the influence of the social world, and the ways in which our sexual identity and sexual relationships are defined.

FUNCTIONALISM   Functionalists may be interested in analyzing how sexuality is functional to the smooth running of society. As an example, can you think through how prostitution might be functional for society? Kingsley Davis (1937), an American sociologist, argued that prostitution actually helps to keep families together (at the time Davis was writing, he would have assumed families to be heterosexual and nuclear). According to Davis, if the husband is not having his sexual needs and wants fulfilled, prostitution provides an avenue to meet those needs. Therefore, prostitution serves a function. (Notice the sexist assumption that it is always husbands whose needs are unfulfilled.)

CONFLICT THEORY Conflict theorists, as you know, tend to explore how various social groups compete over scarce resources; they study the exercise of power and relations of inequality. They are also interested in the commodification of goods and services. Conflict theorists may be interested in exploring how various aspects linked to our sexualities become **commodified** (that is, available for purchase in the market). Services such as prostitution and pornography are good examples of such commodification.

Capitalist consumerism has the ability to shape contemporary sexualities as new sexual products and services emerge to meet an ever-expanding range of sexual desires (Seidman, 2003). Diversification of sexual practices and subcultures expands the market and helps to produce new consumer markets (Seidman, 2003). However, some Marxists are concerned about the narrowing of the range of sexual possibilities, since commodification may halt the expansion of desire by offering fixed, repetitive, identical images, activities, and services for purchase (Evans, 1993).

SYMBOLIC INTERACTIONISM Since symbolic interactionists study the meanings attributed to aspects of social life, they are interested in the social meanings that a society attributes to sexuality, including sexual behaviour. Of course, symbolic interactionists are also concerned with the everyday micro interactions people have with other members of a society.

John Gagnon and William Simon (1986) are credited with developing the important concept of **sexual scripts**—the cultural expectations we hold about what constitutes appropriate sexuality, as manifested in language, practices, and social rules. Through social interaction, then, we learn the sexual scripts of our culture. These scripts are flexible, in that different situations and contexts require different behaviours and attitudes. For instance, we have scripts

commodification The process whereby goods and services become available for purchase in the market.

sexual scripts Cultural expectations about appropriate sexuality that are learned through social interaction.

The couple pictured here is acting out a sexual script—culturally accepted forms of sexual behaviour.

that vary from culture to culture, outlining what sexual behaviours are permitted in public and what sexual behaviours should be private.

POST-STRUCTURALIST THEORY   Post-structuralists argue that sexual behaviour and sexual identity are products of *discourses* (that is, the ways we speak, think, and write about the world). Discourses describe how the world is and shape our views about how the world *should* be (Abbott, Wallace, & Tyler, 2005).

Michel Foucault is one of the most prominent sexuality scholars (his work was introduced in Chapter 1). Foucault argued that what we understand today as sex is a product of the *discourse of sexuality*. Challenging the idea that sex is natural and biological, he contended that we are not born sexual beings; instead, we *learn* to be sexual. This process of becoming sexual can occur only in a society that has created the idea of "sexuality" (Seidman, 2003). Of course, Foucault is not arguing that erotic feelings, pleasures, and behaviours were *created* by discourses, but rather that these feelings, pleasures, and behaviours came to be *categorized* as expressions of human sexuality (Seidman, 2003). In turn, discourses of sexuality constitute individuals as particular sexual subjects—as having either a normal sexuality or a pathological sexuality (Green, 2007).

FEMINIST POST-STRUCTURALISM   Feminist post-structuralists, influenced by Foucault's work, argue that sexuality is fashioned and refashioned through discourse (Abbott, Wallace, & Tyler, 2005).

Feminist post-structuralists argue that there is no one true sexuality. Sexuality is not defined by biology. We currently live in a world in which sexuality has been defined by patriarchal discourses. These discourses place masculinity above femininity and heterosexuality above homosexuality (Butler 1990, p. 151). However, feminists argue that because sexuality and sexual relations are socially defined, they can be redefined (Butler, 1990).

QUEER THEORY   Queer theory emerged in the late 1980s. Queer theory challenges *heterosexism*, which is the belief that heterosexuality is naturally superior to all other sexual identities. Queer theorists seek to deconstruct and dissolve normalizing sexuality discourses that are used to control and constrain people (Green, 2007). By exposing how identity is constructed through discourses, queer theorists dismiss binary (either/or) constructions of gender and sexual identities—male/female, masculine/feminine, and heterosexual/homosexual (Reynolds, 2004). Instead, queer theorists propose an ever-changing range of possibilities (Reynolds, 2004).

What do you know about **the Social Construction of Sexualities**?

Multiple-choice questions (circle your answer)

1. _____ is a broad term that can include our masculinity or femininity, our knowledge of our bodies, our sexual histories, and our sexual preferences.
   a. Sexual history
   b. Sexual identity
   c. Sexual experience
   d. Sexual orientation

2. **An irrational fear or hatred of homosexuals is called**
   a. Racism
   b. Sexism
   c. Heterosexism
   d. Homophobia

3. **An individual who is attracted romantically and/or sexually to both men and women is called**
   a. Heterosexual
   b. Homosexual
   c. Bisexual
   d. Pansexual

4. A relationship pattern that has one monogamous relationship following another is called
a. Monogamy
b. Serial monogamy
c Non-monogamy
d. Polygamy

5. _____ understand sexual behaviours as a product of the discourse of sexuality.
a. Feminists
b. Post-structuralists
c Conflict theorists
d. Symbolic interactionists

Answers: b, d, c, b, b

Summary

module 8.1   SEX AND GENDER

1. *Sex* refers to the way in which we distinguish between male and female based on a set of socially agreed upon biological criteria.
2. *Gender* refers to the socially constructed characteristics of masculine and feminine.
3. *Intersexed individuals*: Individuals born with ambiguous genitalia; they challenge our notion of male and female, and thus our definition of *sex*.
4. *Transgendered individuals*: An umbrella term for a range of people who do not fit into normative constructions of sex and gender; they challenge our notions of masculinity and femininity.
5. Sociologists note that male/female and masculine/feminine are examples of binary constructions. Intersexed and transsexual people show us that the world cannot be simplified into either/or terms.
6. The dominant forms of masculinity and femininity are called, respectively, *hegemonic masculinity* and *emphasized femininity*. Both represent the ideals to which men and women are supposed to aspire.
7. Functionalists see set gender roles as necessary for the smooth functioning of the family and society.
8. Conflict theorists see gender as a way for men to subordinate women to ensure paternity and the line of inheritance.
9. Symbolic interactionists view gender-related behaviours as learned through socialization.
10. Feminists view gender as a socially constructed concept that has negative consequences for women.
11. Post-structuralists view gender as a performance.

module 8.2   REPRODUCING GENDER

12. Gender divisions are reproduced through families at birth and are sustained through child-rearing practices that differ according to the sex of the child.
13. In schools, curricular materials and student–teacher interactions tend to underline traditional gendered expectations of girls and boys.
14. All forms of media reinforce normative construction of masculinity and femininity.

module 8.3   GENDER AND WORK

15. Gender segregation in the labour force is evident in the large percentage of women still employed in traditional, low-paying occupations. This pattern is referred to as *occupational sex segregation*.

16. Women continue to be underrepresented in managerial positions. This underrepresentation is referred to as the *glass ceiling*.

17. Women continue to earn less than men. This is attributed to such factors as the under-valuing of women's work and the responsibilities of child care.

18. Women continue to do more domestic/unpaid labour. This is partly attributable to their lower economic contribution to the household and partly due to gendered expectations.

module 8.4   THE SOCIAL CONSTRUCTION OF SEXUALITIES

19. The meanings people attribute to sex are socially constructed; they differ from culture to culture and change over time as a result of economic, social, and cultural shifts.

20. Sexuality includes our sexual orientation, our sexual identity, sex acts, our sex lives, and the commodification of sex.

21. *Sexual identity* is a broad term that includes our sense of self as masculine and feminine, our knowledge of our bodies, our sexual histories, and our sex preferences.

22. A *homosexual* is a person who is sexually attracted to people of the same sex.

23. A *heterosexual* is a person who is sexually attracted to people of the opposite sex.

24. A *bisexual* is a person who is sexually attracted to people of both sexes.

25. A *pansexual* is a person who has romantic and sexual desire for people regardless of gender or biological sex.

26. All sexual relationships are socially constructed.

27. *Monogamy* refers to the coupling of two people, excluding intimate involvement of others.

28. *Serial monogamy* refers to a relationship pattern that has one monogamous relationship following another.

29. *Non-monogamy* refers to sexual interactions with more than one person during a given period, or any sexual relationship involving more than two people.

30. *Polyamory* refers to mutually acknowledged emotional, sexual, or romantic connections with multiple partners.

31. Masculinity and femininity intertwined with heterosexuality produce sexual double standards for men and women.

32. Functionalists analyze how sexuality contributes to the smooth running of society.

33. Conflict theorists analyze power and inequality in sexual relationships.

34. Symbolic interactionists examine our sexual scripts.

35. Post-structuralists examine our discourses of sexuality.

36. Feminists argue that sexuality is based on a patriarchal discourse.

37. Queer theorists challenge the view that heterosexuality is naturally superior.

Key Terms

biphobia   248
bisexual   248
commodification   252
emphasized femininity   231

exchange theory   243
gender   229
gender relations   229
glass ceiling   240

hegemonic masculinity   230
heterosexism   246
heterosexual   247
homophobia   246

Test Yourself

1. _____ refers to socially constructed characteristics associated with girls and boys, women and men.
   a. Sex
   b. Gender
   c. Sexuality
   d. Sexual orientation

2. Intersexed individuals are
   a. Those born with ambiguous genitalia
   b. Those born with external genitalia
   c. Hyper-sexual individuals
   d. Those who engage in bisexual behaviour

3. _____ see gender as a way for men to subordinate women to ensure paternity and the line of inheritance.
   a. Functionalists
   b. Conflict theorists
   c. Symbolic interactionists
   d. Post-Structuralists

4 Organizing principles that shape and order interactions between women and men are called
   a. Gender relations
   b. Gender groups
   c. Gender patterns
   d. Gender concepts

5. The normative ideal of femininity is called
   a. Hegemonic femininity
   b. Emphasized femininity
   c. Western femininity
   d. Dominant femininity

6. Which of the following statements is true?
   a. Children are more likely to have a male teacher than a female teacher.
   b. Most elementary school principals in Canada are male.
   c. Male principals are overrepresented in elementary and secondary schools.
   d. There are now more female principals in secondary schools.

7. Which of the following statements is false?
   a. Women in lead television roles are typically beautiful, heterosexual, and white.

b. White men tend to be portrayed as heroes in the media.
   c. Black men tend to be portrayed as frightening, scary characters.
   d. White women tend to be portrayed as aggressive while black women tend to be portrayed as docile.

8. Which of the following statements is false?
   a. Women are far more likely than men to undergo cosmetic surgery.
   b. The most popular cosmetic surgery for men and women is liposuction.
   c. Most people who seek cosmetic procedures are over 50.
   d. For women, liposuction is a cosmetic surgery that is more popular than breast augmentation.

9. Which of the following nonsurgical procedures is most popular in Canada?
   a. Botox
   b. Injectables
   c. Facelift
   d. Liposuction

10. Which of the following statements is false about children's toys?
    a. Girls tend to receive toys that reinforce the caretaker role.
    b. Boys are just as interested in playing with dolls as girls are at an early age.
    c. Boys tend to focus on action.
    d. Recent research shows that toys today do not reproduce gender stereotypes.

11. In 2004, 37 percent of all managerial positions in Canada were held by women. This fact supports the concept of the
    a. Corporate ladder
    b. Glass ladder
    c. Glass ceiling
    d. Glass floor

12. Women who work in male-dominated industries are
    a. More likely to never marry or to remain childless than women in other occupations
    b. Just as likely to marry as other women

c. More likely to have children

d. Experience no differences in their personal lives than women who select traditional occupations

13. In 2008, women working full-time earned on average _____ of what men earned.

a. 61.5 percent

b. 65 percent

c. 70.5 percent

d. 75 percent

14. The assertion that power flows from the resources that a member brings to a relationship is called

a. Exchange theory

b. Trade theory

c. Household labour theory

d. Gender-gap theory

15. What statement is false?

a. One-third of women work part-time because they cannot find full-time work.

b. 39 percent of women work part-time because of family obligations.

c. Men tend to experience part-time work throughout their lives, while for women it is only during the early child-bearing years.

d. Women's time away from work to raise children is one of the greatest barriers to career advancement.

16. An individual's sexual and emotional attraction to a person of a particular sex is called

a. Sexual knowledge

b. Sexual identity

c. Sexual experience

d. Sexual orientation

17. In Canada, the first gay rights demonstration took place in Ottawa in

a. 1929

b. 1959

c. 1971

d. 1981

18. Romantic and sexual desire for people regardless of their gender identity or biological sex is called

a. Transsexuality

b. Bisexuality

c. Pansexuality

d. Homosexuality

19. Mutually acknowledged emotional, sexual, or romantic connections with multiple partners is called

a. Serial monogamy

b. Polyamory

c. Polyandry

d. Pansexuality

20. _____ challenge the view that heterosexuality is naturally superior.

a. Functionalists

b. Conflict theorists

c. Feminists

d. Queer theorists

Answers: b, a, b, c, d, c, a, d, c, a, c, d, c, b, d

Log in to MySocLab for a host of resources that will help you save time and improve your grade. MySocLab contains cutting-edge learning tools such as study plans, practice tests, videos, audio segments, quizzes, and more—all designed to help you better understand the learning objectives for this chapter. Along with your eBook, MySocLab for *Sociology for Everyone* can be found at **www.mysoclab.com**.

CONCEPT MAP

module 8.1
SEX AND GENDER

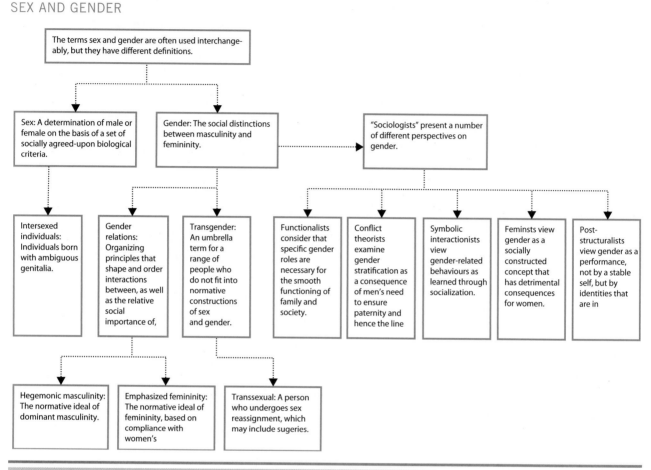

The terms sex and gender are often used interchangeably, but they have different definitions.

Sex: A determination of male or female on the basis of a set of socially agreed-upon biological criteria.

Gender: The social distinctions between masculinity and femininity.

"Sociologists" present a number of different perspectives on gender.

Intersexed individuals: Individuals born with ambiguous genitalia.

Gender relations: Organizing principles that shape and order interactions between, as well as the relative social importance of,

Transgender: An umbrella term for a range of people who do not fit into normative constructions of sex and gender.

Functionalists consider that specific gender roles are necessary for the smooth functioning of family and society.

Conflict theorists examine gender stratification as a consequence of men's need to ensure paternity and hence the line

Symbolic interactionists view gender-related behaviours as learned through socialization.

Feminsts view gender as a socially constructed concept that has detrimental consequences for women.

Post-structuralists view gender as a performance, not by a stable self, but by identities that are in

Hegemonic masculinity: The normative ideal of dominant masculinity.

Emphasized femininity: The normative ideal of femininity, based on compliance with women's

Transsexual: A person who undergoes sex reassignment, which may include sugeries.

module 8.2
REPRODUCING GENDER

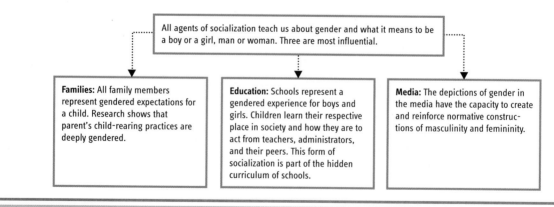

All agents of socialization teach us about gender and what it means to be a boy or a girl, man or woman. Three are most influential.

Families: All family members represent gendered expectations for a child. Research shows that parent's child-rearing practices are deeply gendered.

Education: Schools represent a gendered experience for boys and girls. Children learn their respective place in society and how they are to act from teachers, administrators, and their peers. This form of socialization is part of the hidden curriculum of schools.

Media: The depictions of gender in the media have the capacity to create and reinforce normative constructions of masculinity and femininity.

module 8.3
GENDER AND WORK

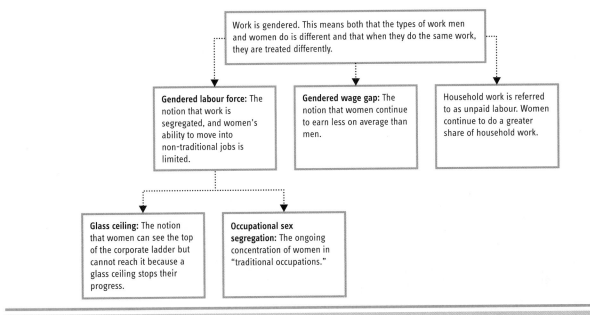

Work is gendered. This means both that the types of work men and women do is different and that when they do the same work, they are treated differently.

Gendered labour force: The notion that work is segregated, and women's ability to move into non-traditional jobs is limited.

Gendered wage gap: The notion that women continue to earn less on average than men.

Household work is referred to as unpaid labour. Women continue to do a greater share of household work.

Glass ceiling: The notion that women can see the top of the corporate ladder but cannot reach it because a glass ceiling stops their progress.

Occupational sex segregation: The ongoing concentration of women in "traditional occupations."

module 8.4
THE SOCIAL CONSTRUCTION OF SEXUALITIES

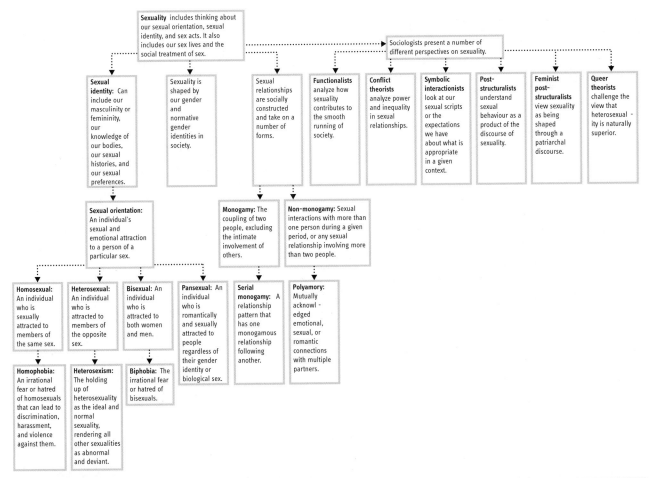

Sexuality includes thinking about our sexual orientation, sexual identity, and sex acts. It also includes our sex lives and the social treatment of sex.

Sociologists present a number of different perspectives on sexuality.

Sexual identity: Can include our masculinity or femininity, our knowledge of our bodies, our sexual histories, and our sexual preferences.

Sexuality is shaped by our gender and normative gender identities in society.

Sexual relationships are socially constructed and take on a number of forms.

Functionalists analyze how sexuality contributes to the smooth running of society.

Conflict theorists analyze power and inequality in sexual relationships.

Symbolic interactionists look at our sexual scripts or the expectations we have about what is appropriate in a given context.

Post-structuralists understand sexual behaviour as a product of the discourse of sexuality.

Feminist post-structuralists view sexuality as being shaped through a patriarchal discourse.

Queer theorists challenge the view that heterosexual - ity is naturally superior.

Sexual orientation: An individual's sexual and emotional attraction to a person of a particular sex.

Monogamy: The coupling of two people, excluding the intimate involvement of others.

Non-monogamy: Sexual interactions with more than one person during a given period, or any sexual relationship involving more than two people.

Homosexual: An individual who is sexually attracted to members of the same sex.

Heterosexual: An individual who is attracted to members of the opposite sex.

Bisexual: An individual who is attracted to both women and men.

Pansexual: An individual who is romantically and sexually attracted to people regardless of their gender identity or biological sex.

Serial monogamy: A relationship pattern that has one monogamous relationship following another.

Polyamory: Mutually acknowl - edged emotional, sexual, or romantic connections with multiple partners.

Homophobia: An irrational fear or hatred of homosexuals that can lead to discrimination, harassment, and violence against them.

Heterosexism: The holding up of heterosexuality as the ideal and normal sexuality, rendering all other sexualities as abnormal and deviant.

Biphobia: The irrational fear or hatred of bisexuals.

chapter 9

Race and Racialization

Testing Tolerance: The Story of Hérouxville

On January 25, 2007, the tiny town of Hérouxville, Quebec, created an international controversy when its town council adopted a five-page document that listed community standards for new immigrants (Aubin & Gatehouse, 2007).

The list, based on an opinion poll of 196 area residents, managed to offend a variety of people. It prohibited people from covering their faces except on Halloween; stoning; live burning; and disfiguring women with acid (standards directed at Muslims). It also prohibited children from carrying weapons to school, regardless of whether they are symbolic or not. This standard was directed at Sikhs in response to a high-profile Montreal court case that gave a Sikh boy the right to carry his kirpan to school. The list also included a response to the creation–evolution debate, stating that biology will be taught in local schools (Aubin & Gatehouse, 2007). Other topics were covered in the list, including standards on health care, families, and festivities.

Hérouxville's initiative fired up the simmering debate over the integration of new immigrants into Quebec society, an issue highlighted during the 2007 provincial election campaign. As a result, the Consultation Commission on Accommodation Practices Related to Cultural Differences (co-chaired by Gérard Bouchard and Charles Taylor) was created to give citizens across Quebec the opportunity to express their opinions on reasonable accommodation to new immigrants. The commission wanted to know (1) to what degree new immigrants should be accommodated and (2) to what degree new immigrants should accommodate Quebec society. Quebecers are clearly split on the issue, but there seems to be greater support for limiting accommodation (Patriquin, 2007).

Canadians in other parts of the country tend to share a similar point of view. A poll conducted by the Institute for Research on Public Policy found that a significant majority of Canadians favour limits on the accommodation made to immigrants on cultural and religious grounds (MacDonald, 2007).

Since multiculturalism became an official policy in Canada in 1971, Canadians have been proud to support and accommodate newcomers. Yet, it appears that Canadians may be becoming less tolerant than we once liked to believe we were.

Where do you stand on the issue of reasonable accommodation? To what degree do you think cultural and religious minorities should be accommodated by public institutions (such as schools and hospitals), private organizations (such as companies), and the neighbourhoods in which they live?

module 9.1

What Is a Minority?

Think about Minorities

1 Think about your ethnicity. Do you consider yourself as belonging to a minority group?

2 Think about Canadian immigration. Do you think today's immigrants are different from those who came to Canada 50 years ago? If yes, how?

minority A definable category of people who are socially disadvantaged.

To view the Bouchard/ Taylor commission's final report, *Building the Future: A Time for Reconciliation*, go to www.accommodements. qc.ca/documentation/ rapports/rapport-final-integral-en.pdf.

For sociologists, a **minority** is any definable category of people who are socially disadvantaged. Membership in a minority group has two components: the group lacks social power, and it is definable from the majority. The "majority" is not defined by any inherent characteristics, but rather those characteristics that define the dominant group.

The first component of minority group membership accentuates the sociological principle that, despite what the term implies, it's not the size of any given group that makes it a minority but rather its lack of power. A classic example of this principle is the South African system of apartheid (from the Afrikaans word for "apartness"); although the number of whites in the population was a small fraction of the number of blacks, the whites still dominated. Apartheid was legal in South Africa from 1948 until the early 1990s.

Because of their powerlessness, minorities often experience both prejudice and discrimination. Members of minority groups are often stigmatized by members of the dominant group and assigned attributes that do not in fact exist. In other words, stigmatizing is based on perceived attributes (Nelson, 2004, pp. 317–318). For example, the simple act of wearing a turban can lead to active or passive avoidance of a Sikh man based on a person's or group's perceived associations with turbans. To be stigmatized, then, is to be socially excluded and diminished because of one's minority status. For this reason, most minorities develop a strong sense of in-group solidarity (Bernd & Brown, 2000, p. 328).

The second component of minority groups is that they are definable—that is, they are recognizably different from the majority. Race is often considered the key differentiating feature of a given minority group; however, as we discuss below, race is a socially constructed concept.

Around the world, minority groups are defined by various cultural and physical characteristics. Canadians might think first of language (French or English), Americans of skin colour

Many Canadian cities offer vibrant and diverse ethnic communities.

(black or white), and the Northern Irish of religion (Catholic or Protestant). As a general rule, the more obvious the defining characteristic (language, skin colour, religious belief), the more severe the stigma, or negative social labels, that are assigned to the minority (Lindsey, Beach, & Ravelli, 2009, p. 175). The case for some gets even more challenging if they happen to be members of more than one minority group—think of Aboriginal people who speak only their native language and adhere to traditional spiritual practices. The cumulative effect of visible difference, language, and religion heightens their exclusion and increases their chances of experiencing prejudice and discrimination.

RACE: THE SOCIAL CONSTRUCTION OF DIFFERENCE

Race and race relations have been central concerns for sociologists for many years. The assignment of individuals to racial categories can determine people's quality of life and even how long they live (Reif, Whetten, & Thielman, 2007). Historically, **race** was defined as a group of people who were physically and genetically distinguished from other groups. These differences were largely evident in skin colour, hair texture, and facial features. For European and American researchers, the differences resulted from various groups of people becoming isolated from each other and having to adapt to their unique environments. For these researchers, the fact that European populations were generally white (Caucasoid), people from Africa black (Negroid), and Asia "yellow" (Mongoloid) confirmed that people developed differently and could therefore be compared with each other on various criteria (including intelligence).

However, since genetic differences do not determine significant behavioural or substantive biological differences, early researchers can be understood as having invented the "myth" of race (Gibel Azoulay, 2006, p. 354). The assignment of people to racial categories is, therefore, a function of social construction. Indeed, social scientists today assert that what most people call *race* is little more than a historical legacy of Western colonialism and ethnocentrism. While there are certainly variations in how people look around the world, these differences are only

race   Historically, a group of people who were physically and genetically distinguished from other groups.

cosmetic. And given worldwide travel and interracial unions, whatever differences there were historically have certainly been diminished (Smedley, 2007).

Some estimates suggest that about 75 percent of all genes in a human being are identical to those in every other human being. With regards to the 25 percent of genes that do vary between people, about 85 percent of that variation would still occur even if those people were related to each other. Another 9 percent of that variation would result from membership within a particular nation or tribe within a race—for example, both Swedes and Germans are part of the traditional Caucasoid classification. Only the final 6 percent of genetic variation results from what has been called *race*. Researchers suggest that a person's race accounts for a tiny 0.24 percent of his or her genetic makeup. One might think of it this way: it's entirely possible that Céline Dion shares more genetic material with Queen Latifah than she does with Nelly Furtado (see Gardner, 2000).

Moreover, there does not appear to be any credible evidence to substantiate the claim that people of different "races" are innately superior or inferior in temperament or in mental or physical abilities (Kenny, 2004, p. 410; Shanklin, 2000, 1994).

Yet the fact that the term *race* is biologically meaningless does not mean it is unimportant—especially to sociologists. As the Thomas theorem (see Chapter 1) tells us, what people believe to be real is real in its consequences. Since members of minority groups are perceived as different, they may over time *feel* different and begin to assume the attributes that others credit them with—in effect, a self-fulfilling prophecy. In other words, if the majority constantly looks upon minority group members as failures, then some will indeed become failures.

racialization The process of attributing complex characteristics (e.g., intelligence) to racial categories.

Sometimes sociologists also use the term **racialization** to describe the process of attributing complex characteristics (e.g., intelligence, athletic abilities) to racial categories. A related concept, **internalized racism**, occurs when members of a racial group assume the attributes associated with that racial classification and incorporate them into their identities (Lindsey, Beach, & Ravelli, 2009, pp. 173–174; Rajiva, 2006). This can result in identity confusion, whereby people are torn between wanting to belong on the one hand and wanting to embrace their differences from the majority on the other (Masko, 2005).

internalized racism The internalization of racial categorizations into a person's identity.

Today's sociologists prefer not to use the term *race*, then, because it is socially constructed, because there is a lack of evidence that meaningful genetic differences exist between groups, and perhaps most importantly, because the term has colonial and ethnocentric biases (Omi & Winant, 2008). Wherever possible, the term *race* should be replaced with *minority population*, since the latter term de-emphasizes biology and accentuates the importance of a group's lack of social power.

Race, then, is an important concept for sociologists to understand, by appreciating not only its colonial past but also how it continues to influence visible minorities and their integration into contemporary society.

ETHNICITY: THE SOCIAL CONSTRUCTION OF GROUP IDENTITY

ethnicity A multi-dimensional concept that includes one's minority or majority status, ancestry, language, and often religious affiliation.

Sociologists suggest that, like race, one's ethnic identity is socially constructed (Doane, 1997, p. 376) and significant in defining one's perception of self. **Ethnicity** is a multi-dimensional concept that includes one's minority or majority status, ancestry, language, and often religious affiliation. For example, identifying with your family's Greek, Chinese, or German heritage and customs is part of your ethnicity and helps define your self-concept. An **ethnic group** is a collection of people who identify with each other and share a common culture, art forms, language, music, traditions, and beliefs (Breton, 2005; Fischer, 2007).

ethnic group A collection of people who identify with each other and share a common culture.

Canada is home to many different ethnic minorities, which we often associate with their country of origin or ancestry (e.g., Irish Canadians, Italian Canadians, Chinese Canadians, Vietnamese Canadians). As these terms suggest, ethnicity is closely linked to migration (Bathum & Bauman, 2007). This makes sense, because people naturally gravitate to others like themselves when they relocate to a new country. This is especially true when the new immigrants are quite different culturally or physically from the dominant group and may face open prejudice and discrimination (Sharma, 2005, p. 105). However, the longer the immigrants have been in Canada and the more friends they have, the more likely they are to associate themselves with being Canadian (Walters, Phythian, & Anisef, 2007, pp. 59–60). Research confirms that with each subsequent generation, the immigrant population becomes more like the dominant culture (Rumbaut, 2004, p. 1162). However, this does not mean to suggest that the ties with the country of origin do not remain an important link for individuals, families, or ethnic communities.

IMMIGRATION

Many minority groups gain their inferior social status only once they migrate to other countries. Others, such as Aboriginal peoples in Canada or Catholics in Northern Ireland, became minorities when more dominant outsiders came to their land and settled.

Immigration levels are the result of many forces: displacement of people caused by war and political upheaval, economic growth or collapse, changes in immigration policies and procedures, and changes in global communication and transportation networks. Figure 9–1 shows that immigration levels in Canada spiked during the 1910s, 1950s, and early 1990s, and continued to rise through 2006.

During the beginning of the twentieth century, new immigrants to Canada were instrumental not only in developing the West but also in setting up various industrial plants throughout the country. Not surprisingly, the First World War and the Great Depression led to lower immigration levels. The 1950s saw vast post-war economic growth as well as global recognition that Canada was a safe and stable place in which to settle and raise a family. The economic problems through the 1970s and 1980s saw immigration rates fall once again, only to recover somewhat with the economic prosperity of the mid-1990s.

More recently, changes to federal immigration policy have made it easier to come to Canada— a situation that many believe is in the best long-term interests of the country, since immigration promotes diversity and facilitates population growth. Indeed, without immigration, Canada's population growth would slow—an unhealthy condition for any country (Wayland, 1997).

In 2006, over 6 million foreign-born people lived in Canada, representing 19.8 percent of the total population—the highest proportion in the last 75 years (the United States, in contrast, has 12.5 percent foreign-born people, and Australia has 22.2 percent). The largest group of recent immigrants is from Asia (including the Middle East) at 58.3 percent, followed by Europe at 16.1 percent, and Central and South America and the Caribbean at 10.8 percent (Statistics Canada, 2007f). Table 9–1 outlines the changing distribution of the top 10 countries of origin between 1981 and 2006.

FIGURE 9–1 **Canadian Immigration Levels between 1901 and 2006**

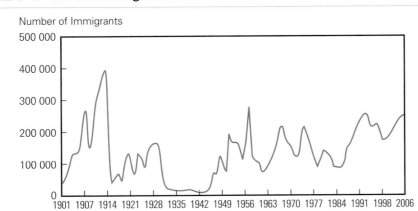

Source: Citizenship and Immigration Canada, *Facts and figures 1998: Immigration overview.*

TABLE 9–1 **Top 10 Countries of Birth of Recent Immigrants to Canada, 1981 to 2006**

Rank	2006 Census	2001 Census	1996 Census	1991 Census	1981 Census
1	People's Republic of China	People's Republic of China	Hong Kong	Hong Kong	United Kingdom
2	India	India	People's Republic of China	Poland	Vietnam
3	Philippines	Philippines	India	People's Republic of China	United States of America
4	Pakistan	Pakistan	Philippines	India	India
5	United States of America	Hong Kong	Sri Lanka	Philippines	Philippines
6	South Korea	Iran	Poland	United Kingdom	Jamaica
7	Romania	Taiwan	Taiwan	Vietnam	Hong Kong
8	Iran	United States of America	Vietnam	United States of America	Portugal
9	United Kingdom	South Korea	United States of America	Lebanon	Taiwan
10	Colombia	Sri Lanka	United Kingdom	Portugal	People's Republic of China

Note: *Recent immigrants* refers to landed immigrants who arrived in Canada within five years prior to a given census.

Source: Statistics Canada. *Censuses of population, 1981 to 2006*. Retrieved January 26, 2008, from http://www12.statcan.ca/Framework/Images/scheme-v101/fipstc01-en.gif.

Table 9–1 shows that over the last 25 years, the People's Republic of China has become the largest country of origin for Canadian immigrants (up from tenth place in 1981), while India, the Philippines, and the United States remain important sources of immigrants. Conversely, the United Kingdom, Canada's largest source of immigrants in 1981, fell to sixth place in 1991 and has not scored in the top 10 since.

According to the 2006 Census, immigrants tend to settle in the more populous provinces—Ontario, Quebec, and British Columbia—and are least likely to settle in the northern regions. They are attracted to urban centres, which offer better employment potential and tend to provide more services for immigrant populations. However, Statistics Canada suggests that when immigrants choose to live in small urban centres or in rural areas, they tend to achieve economic integration much faster than immigrants who choose to live in large urban areas. For example, in large urban areas, the initial income gap between immigrants and other Canadians is 37 percent, after 4 years decreases to 22 percent, and after 12 years falls below 10 percent. In contrast, in small urban or rural areas, the initial income gap is 14 percent; however, after 4 years these immigrants earn 2 percent more than other Canadians, and after 11 years, they earn on average 18 percent more.

Nonetheless, according to the 2006 Census, immigrants are still more likely to settle in urban centres, with 75 percent of recent immigrants choosing to live in Toronto, Montreal, and Vancouver (compared with 34 percent of the general population) and less than 3 percent settling in a small town or rural area (compared with 22 percent of the general population). An interesting exception to this rule occurs with immigrants from the United States, who integrate more quickly in larger centres than they do in smaller ones. All other immigrants, especially those from Asia, integrated more rapidly (in economic terms, at least) in smaller cities.

To fully appreciate how minority groups in Canada and around the world are treated, we turn next to the concepts of *prejudice*, *racism*, and *discrimination*.

What do you know about **Minorities**?

Multiple-choice questions (circle your answer)

1. **Sikhs in Canada represent members of a(n)**
   a. Ethnic group but not a minority group
   b. Racial group but not a minority group
   c. Both an ethnic and a minority group
   d. A minority group but not a racial or ethnic group

2. **The process of attributing complex characteristics (e.g., intelligence, athletic abilities) to racial categories is called**
   a. Racialization
   b. Minority classification
   c. Racial identification
   d. Race relations

3. **Ethnicity**
   a. Is an achieved status
   b. Is an ascribed status

   c. Is defined by others
   d. Applies only to minority groups

4. **A collection of people who identify with each other and share a common culture are called a(n)**
   a. Race
   b. Ethnic group
   c. Minority group
   d. Dominant group

5. **Between 1981 and 2006, Canada received most of its immigrants from**
   a. China
   b. India
   c. Pakistan
   d. South Korea

Answers: c, a, b, b, a

module 9.2

Prejudice, Racism, and Discrimination

Prejudice, *racism*, and *discrimination* are terms we use to describe the ways in which we view or treat members of groups other than our own. Although these words are commonly used interchangeably, they are not the same. Below we will explore the meaning of each concept. We will also explore how prejudice develops.

PREJUDICE

Prejudice is a prejudgment; a negative assessment about what a person or group is like before you actually meet them. Prejudice is also irrational, long-lasting, and not based on fact.

When people draw conclusions about individual attributes from data gathered from an entire group, they make a mistake researchers call an **ecological fallacy**. For example, to assert that all white people are hard working is just as absurd as suggesting that all Asian

Think about Prejudice, Racism, and Discrimination

1 Think about Hérouxville's list of community standards for new immigrants. Do you think this list is racist?

2 Think about discrimination. Do you think that you have ever been a victim of discrimination?

prejudice A negative judgment about a person or group that is irrational, long-lasting, and not based on fact.

ecological fallacy Drawing conclusions about individual attributes from data gathered from an entire group.

exception fallacy Drawing conclusions about an entire group based on observations of individuals.

stereotype A stable and sweeping generalization about a category of people.

racism An ideology that maintains that one "race" is inherently superior to another.

democratic racism A system that advocates equality but in fact perpetuates minority differentiation and oppression.

discrimination Actions that deny or grant advantages to members of a particular group.

people are good at math. Conversely, when people draw conclusions about an entire group based on observations of individuals, they make a mistake called an **exception fallacy** (Trochim, 2006). That is, if a black student in your class is highly intelligent, you cannot correctly conclude that all black people are just as intelligent.

Sociologists generally view prejudiced attitudes as being the result of dominant group members' classifications because they are the ones who have the power to impose their views on others. These views also often result in the most harm. While minority group members may themselves have prejudiced views of the dominant group or other minorities, they are generally not in a position to systematically impose their views on others. One particular type of a prejudice (again, a prejudgment about a person or group) is called a *stereotype*.

Stereotypes are stable and sweeping generalizations about a category of people that are applied to all members of that category (e.g., all blond-haired people are slow-witted) (Millard & Grant, 2006, p. 659). Stereotypes may be accurate for some members of a group, but assuming that all members of a group adhere to that generalization is inaccurate. Yet it may nonetheless influence some people's interaction with those people. Even when stereotypes appear favourable (e.g., the common belief that Asian Canadians are good at math), they still influence some people to pigeonhole others, thus distorting their perceptions of them.

RACISM

Another type of prejudice is, of course, racism. As we have seen, people are often treated differently because of the belief that there is such a thing as "race" and that these biological differences are directly related to ability or character. Sociologists view racism as an ideology that justifies treating people differently because of their racial category. More formally, **racism** is an ideology that maintains that one race is inherently superior to another (Miles & Brown, 2003).

Today, some sociologists suggest that a racist ideology is an invaluable tool in helping a group feel better about itself (Tredoux & Finchilescu, 2007, p. 675). By defining others as inferior, the majority group reinforces its own collective identity and sense of superiority. Further, other sociologists point out that even belief systems that promote equality for all (the belief that "we're all just people" and should treat everyone equally) in fact perpetuate minority differentiation and oppression. That is because, without real change, dominant groups will simply continue to maintain their positions of privilege (Henry & Tator, 1994; Walker, 2006). The result is a form of **democratic racism**.

Stereotypes and racism are the result of social processes, and to some extent everyone has some stereotypical views of other people and groups. But when a person or group does something to another person or group based on those views, it is a cause for more serious concern.

DISCRIMINATION

Discrimination occurs when a person or group either denies or grants advantages to members of a particular group (Feagin & Feagin, 2008; Giddens, 1997, p. 582). For example, if you decide not to hire particular people (or decide *to* hire them) based on your preconceived ideas about what you could expect from the group to which they belong, you are guilty of discrimination. In most modern societies it is illegal to discriminate. Teachers and employers, for example, cannot let factors such as minority status, ethnicity, and gender influence how they treat their students or their employees. Anyone who violates these norms is guilty of discrimination as defined by the *Charter of Rights and Freedoms*. Sociologists also acknowledge that discrimination is not a single entity but instead operates on a number of levels in society.

WHY SHOULD WE CARE?

Hate Groups in Canada

Canadians generally picture themselves as a peaceful, tolerant people who support multiculturalism. Does this picture fit reality?

The Canadian public became concerned over hate groups with the 1965 *Report to the Minister of Justice of the Special Committee on Hate Propaganda in Canada* (commonly referred to as the Cohen Committee). The committee found that although hate propaganda was limited to a small number of individuals, the very presence of this material compromised Canadian values. As a result of the report, in 1970 Parliament amended the *Criminal Code* by making hate propaganda a punishable offence (Statistics Canada, 2001b).

According to the *Criminal Code,* hate propaganda includes advocating genocide and public incitement of hatred. Yet it can be difficult to define what constitutes a hate crime. For example, threatening violence against someone because he or she is a minority is clearly illegal, but what about wearing racist symbols (e.g., a swastika)? Although this symbol does not target any specific group, some might argue that given its unique history, wearing a swastika should qualify as a hate crime (even though, taken alone, wearing symbols is unlikely to qualify as such).

The Canadian *Charter of Rights and Freedoms* confirms that everyone is equal and should not be discriminated against because of their ethnicity, race, gender, or sexual orientation. Other legislation responsible for preserving equality within Canada includes the *Criminal Code,* the *Canadian Human Rights Act;* the *Canadian Bill of Rights;* the *Employment Equity Act;* the *Official Languages Act;* the *Canadian Multiculturalism Act;* the *Immigration* and *Refugee Protection Act;* and the *Citizenship Act* (Canadian Heritage, 2005). Unfortunately, these have had little impact on stopping the activities of hate groups in Canada.

Many Canadians would be surprised to learn just how many hate groups exist in their country, and why they continue to exist. These groups include the Northern Alliance, the Heritage Front, London-area Tri-City Skinheads, the Canadian Heritage Alliance, Freedomsite.org, Western Canada For Us, Stormfront Canada, the Canadian Association for Free Expression (CAFÉ), and the recently defunct Canadian Ethnic Cleansing Team (League for Human Rights of Canada, 2006). Hate groups often attract members who are young, vulnerable, and socially isolated. These groups understand that young people today are both Internet savvy and very busy; thus the groups' messaging is distributed through various mechanisms including Internet sites, spam email, viral marketing, printed pamphlets, and the promotion of rock concerts featuring racist performers and the selling of their CDs. One popular avenue for delivering hate messages is through video games such as *Ethnic Cleansing* (League for Human Rights of Canada, 2006).

Why do you think some people are drawn to the racist messages and activities of hate groups? What should we be doing to help confront these groups?

To find out how one group combats anti-Semitism, racism, and bigotry in Canada, visit the League For Human Rights of B'nai Brith Canada website at **www.bnaibrith.ca/league/league.htm.**

Discrimination can be classified as *individual* (Booker, 2007), *direct institutional* (Owens, 2000), or *indirect institutional* (Hemphill & Haines, 1997). **Individual discrimination** is just what the term implies—individuals advantage or disadvantage someone because of their group membership. For example, deciding not to hire a tutor for your sociology class because she is Italian would constitute individual discrimination—no one told you to not hire the

individual discrimination
Occurs when an individual advantages or disadvantages someone because of that person's group membership.

person; you made this decision on your own. In contemporary society, few people would try to justify such actions, even though they happen each and every day.

Direct institutional discrimination occurs when an institution employs policies or practices that are discriminatory against a person or group in that they deny them a right or a freedom (Hally, 2004). For example, a restaurant that won't hire Aboriginal women is guilty of institutional discrimination. With many people today becoming more informed about their rights, the instances of direct institutional discrimination are declining, although they do continue to exist (Feagin & Feagin, 2008).

Indirect institutional discrimination occurs when an action produces uneven results on a group or a person because of an unlawful criterion (physical characteristics, cultural origin, age, gender, religion, handicap), but lacks the intent of being discriminatory. One of the most common examples of this form of discrimination is the weight or size requirements necessary to become a police officer or a firefighter. While not intended to exclude certain individuals (e.g., women are, on average, physically smaller than men), these requirements effectively limit some people's ability to pursue those careers (Hally, 2004). And while Canadian law requires that people performing the same work receive the same pay, a study by Pendakur (2000) shows that people from non-European origins experience a clear disadvantage in the Canadian job market even after age and education levels are controlled for (as cited in Helly, 2004). This finding reinforces the fact that Canadian minority populations continue to face discrimination.

According to a Statistics Canada survey (2003d), 20 percent of visible minority respondents (and 32 percent of blacks, 21 percent of South Asians, and 15 percent of Chinese) reported that they were victims of discrimination (see Figure 9–2 for a graphical representation of these results). As well, 24 percent of visible minorities felt uncomfortable or out of place most or some of the time. The most frequently reported types of discrimination were being passed over for jobs, being treated differently than other employees who were members of the dominant group, and being passed over for promotions.

direct institutional discrimination Occurs when an institution employs policies or practices that are discriminatory against a person or group.

indirect institutional discrimination Occurs when an action produces uneven results on a group or person because of an unlawful criterion, but lacks the intent of being discriminatory.

FIGURE 9–2 **Percentage of People Reporting Discrimination or Unfair Treatment "Sometimes" or "Often" in the Past Five Years, by Visible Minority Status, 2002**

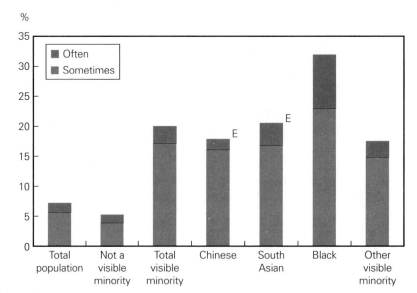

E Use with caution.
Note: Refers to Canada's non-Aboriginal population aged 15 and older reporting discrimination or unfair treatment in Canada because of ethnocultural characteristics.
Source: Statistics Canada. (2003). *Ethnic diversity survey: Portrait of a multicultural society.*

IS PREJUDICE THE SAME AS DISCRIMINATION?

This is a good question. What do you think? Most people assume that how people act reflects how they feel, but this is not necessarily the case. Consider an unprejudiced white man living in Toronto in the nineteenth century. If he was a university engineering professor, do you think you would have advocated for the right of women to attend his classes? Probably not. During this time, very few women attended university, and he may have not wanted to challenge the status quo (Miller-Bernal & Poulson, 2007). Consider the same male teacher today who believes strongly that his female students are not as good at engineering as his male students. (Female engineering students appear to be as good, if not better, than male engineering students; see Chen et al., 2003.) Is he likely to restrict women's access to his courses? Again, probably not. As well, he may not even believe that he is discriminating against women.

Even when we don't intend to discriminate it is sometimes hard not to; we are social be ings who are often influenced by those around us. As a rule, we generally spend time around people who are like us; the adage "Like attracts like" does have some merit (Mazzarella, 2004). However, by interacting with people from our own racial, ethnic, or professional organizations, we may be discriminating against others and not even know it. For example, if you hire someone who went to the same university as you (but whom you don't know), are you guilty of discrimination? Are you discriminating against graduates from other schools?

The point is that we cannot always predict what a person is thinking or what motivates their actions. Sociologists have known for a long time that what people think, say, and do is not always consistent (LaPiere, 1934).[1] As Robert Merton (1938) illustrated over 70 years ago, the relationship between being prejudiced, or not, and discriminating, or not, is a complex one. He pointed out that people can be prejudiced discriminators and nonprejudiced nondiscriminators, but also prejudiced non-discriminators or non-prejudiced discriminators. A review of Figure 9–3 will help you visualize Merton's typology.

FIGURE 9–3 **Relationship between Prejudice and Discrimination**

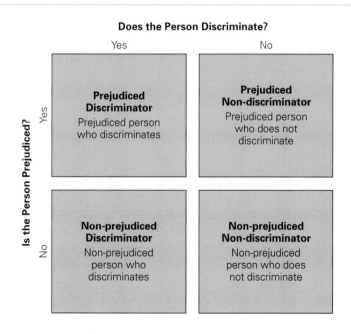

---

[1] For a critique of LaPiere's classic study, see Dockery & Bedeian, 1989.

EXPLAINING PREJUDICE AND DISCRIMINATION

If you were to sit back and think to yourself why prejudice exists and why some people discriminate against others, how would you explain it? Both social psychologists and sociologists have offered several theories to explain prejudice and discrimination.

PSYCHOLOGICAL THEORIES

Scapegoat Theory   **Scapegoat theory** asserts that prejudice and discrimination originate in the frustrations of people who want to blame someone else for their problems. The theory originated with the work of American psychologist John Dollard (Dollard et. al., 1939), who suggested that people displace their frustrations about virtually anything onto other identifiable people whom they can target as being responsible for their problems (Weatherley, 1988, p. 88). As stated by Babad, Birnbaum, and Benne (1983, p. 83), "when there is tension and social problems seem insurmountable, find an innocent, weak and distinctive group to blame and victimize" (as cited in Gibson & Howard, 2007, p. 193). This is the approach Hitler took in blaming the Jews for Germany's economic problems.

Authoritarian Personality Theory   Theodor Adorno (1950) was integral in developing the **authoritarian personality theory**. According to the authoritarian personality theory, extreme prejudice is a personality trait linked to people who believe strongly in following cultural norms, traditions, and values. People with an authoritarian personality are generally conformists, faithfully follow instructions from their superiors, and reject those whom they consider to be inferior to them.

SOCIO-CULTURAL THEORIES

Culture Theory   **Culture theory** suggests that some prejudice is found in people all over the world; it is a part of culture. It occurs because some belief in the benefits of one's own culture over others (called *ethnocentricism*) is healthy, since it unifies the group.

In one of the earliest attempts to understand intercultural diversity, Emory Bogardus (1925) examined the issue of social distance—the degree to which people feel comfortable in different social situations with people from different racial or ethnic groups. Bogardus found that people were able to rank different ethnic groups based on how close or distant they felt to them, a concept he referred to as **social distance** (Bogardus, 1925, 1967).

In 1993, Kleg and Yamamato replicated Bogardus's research. The findings after almost 70 years were remarkably consistent. Canadian research in the 1970s (Mackie, 1974) found similar results, suggesting that not only is there consistency within cultures but across them as well (as cited in Macionis & Gerber, 2008, p. 357).

Bogardus's research challenges the assumption of the authoritarian personality theorists by demonstrating that prejudice is not simply the result of an individual's personality but rather part of a culture's social fabric. It may be the case that there really is a **culture of prejudice**.

Functionalist Theory   Functionalist theory examines the role of prejudice and discrimination. Limited prejudice, they would argue, acts to draw groups closer together. Thus, racist ideologies and the prejudice and discrimination that they breed often promote social cohesion and, in turn, social stability. Moreover, some suggest that minority groups have been socialized to accept racist belief systems, and that this makes them less likely to challenge existing social convention (Levin & Levin, 1982).

Conflict Theory   Conflict theory assumes that people naturally compete over limited resources; of course, prejudice and discrimination are logical outcomes of that competition. Two key approaches to prejudice and discrimination are discussed below.

The first approach is called the **dual labour market theory** (also called *split labour theory*), which argues that modern societies have two distinct types of labour markets. The *primary labour*

---

scapegoat theory Asserts that prejudice and discrimination originate in the frustrations of people who want to blame someone else for their problems.

authoritarian personality theory Asserts that extreme prejudice is a personality trait of people who strongly believe in following cultural norms, traditions, and values.

culture theory Asserts that some prejudice is healthy and part of all cultures.

social distance Bogardus's concept of the relative distance people feel between themselves and other racial/ethnic groups.

culture of prejudice A value system that promotes prejudice, discrimination, and oppression.

dual labour market theory Asserts that modern societies have two distinct labour markets (called the primary and secondary labour markets).

market includes secure positions that are paid a healthy salary (instead of an hourly wage), offer attractive fringe benefits (such as vacation time and bonus structures), and have the potential for upward mobility within an organization. The *secondary labour market* includes jobs that offer none of these advantages; they are often insecure and temporary, paid hourly wages, provide only legally required benefits, and rarely offer any training to advance one's position. Members of minority groups are disproportionately found in the secondary labour market (Salaff, Greve, & Ping, 2002; Schaefer, 2008). Cheap, transitory labour benefits the entire dominant class because people in this labour pool do the jobs that members of the majority would find demeaning and/or distasteful. Members of the dominant group defend their advantage by keeping visible minorities out of their unions and opposing equal rights initiatives (Lindsey, Beach, & Ravelli, 2009, p. 180).

The second approach is commonly referred to as the **Marxist exploitation theory**, which views the powerful economic elite, rather than the entire dominant group, as benefiting the most from discrimination (Cox, 1948). Exploitation theory maintains that the ruling class deliberately promotes prejudice and discrimination in order to divide the workers so that they cannot present the rich with a united front of opposition. Minority groups are taught to view each other, instead of the ruling class, as the enemy. As a result, workers around the world are unlikely to join together to demand fair treatment and better wages (Olzak, 2006). Due to this lack of coordinated opposition, the economic elites continue to oppress the workers and maintain their control over the society that clearly benefits them.

Marxist exploitation theory Asserts that the powerful economic elite promotes and benefits from prejudice and discrimination.

Symbolic Interactionist Theory   Symbolic interactionists are keenly aware of the social environment when constructing their insights into prejudice and discrimination. They believe that a person's attitudes and perceptions about minority groups are not innate, but rather learned as a required component of culture or an expression of class conflict. It follows that because prejudice is learned, it can be unlearned.

Research shows that negative racial and ethnic attitudes are developed between the ages of four and seven and are often greatly influenced by media images portrayed on television (Al-Shehab, 2008, p. 49; Ou & McAdoo, 1999, p. 258). As we grow older, if prejudiced attitudes and discriminatory behaviour are consistently reinforced, we learn to limit our perception of the positive attributes of minority groups and accentuate our perceptions of the negative—a process commonly referred to as **selective perception** (Fendler & Tuckey, 2006, p. 591). For example, selective perception is at work when you complain every time you witness a woman or a member of a visible minority group being a bad driver; do you also make a mental note every time you see them driving well? Prejudiced people focus on the negative, and this reinforces—to them, at least—the accuracy of their judgment of the person or group.

selective perception The process whereby people see only those things that reinforce their preconceived perceptions.

Symbolic interactionists also point out the powerful role that language plays in covertly reinforcing prejudiced attitudes and values. As just one example, consider the use of the term *boy* by slave owners in the American South when referring to their adult male slave labourers.

These theorists note that prejudice attitudes can decline if inter-group contact is initiated and nurtured. This position is referred to as the **contact hypothesis**.

contact hypothesis The proposal that prejudiced attitudes can decline with inter-group contact.

Post-Colonial Theory   Post-colonial theory investigates countries around the world that have achieved political independence from a colonial empire; examples include India, Jamaica, and Nigeria (to name only a few). **Post-colonial theory** examines the ways in which the colonial past has shaped the social, political, and economic experiences of a colonized country (Bhambra, 2007). The theory integrates an analysis of both the past and the present to help understand the effects of the historical legacy of the colonial experience and its impact on social institutions and structures as well as the formation of people's identities.

post-colonial theory An approach that examines the ways in which the colonial past has shaped the social, political, and economic experiences of a colonized country.

A country's colonial experience has a tremendous impact on the social fabric of its society. The long-term effects of imperialism and dependence on the colonial empire often translate into feelings of exclusion, and at times result in people rejecting the ideas and attitudes of the dominant culture—for example, challenging perceptions of race and ethnicity and promoting a desire for autonomy and independence.

The contact hypothesis suggests that in most situations, the more time a person spends with members of a minority group, the less likely they are to be prejudiced.

What do you know about **Prejudice, Racism, and Discrimination**?

Multiple-choice questions (circle your answer)

1. **To draw conclusions about individual attributes from data gathered from an entire group is called**
   a. Prejudice
   b. Ecological fallacy
   c. Exception fallacy
   d. Discrimination

2. **Which of the following statements is false?**
   a. Racism is a type of prejudice.
   b. Racism is an ideology which holds that one race is inherently superior to another.
   c. Racism is an ideology that justifies treating people differently because of their racial category.
   d. Racism is a form of discrimination.

3. **_____ occurs when individuals advantage or disadvantage someone because of that person's group membership.**
   a. Individual discrimination
   b. Direct institutional discrimination
   c. Indirect institutional discrimination
   d. Nondirect institutional discrimination

4. **_____ theory states that prejudice and discrimination originate in the frustrations of people who want to blame someone else for their problems.**
   a. Scapegoat
   b. Authoritarian
   c Conflict
   d. Postcolonial

5. **Research shows that negative racial and ethnic attitudes are developed between the ages of**
   a. 2 and 4
   b. 4 and 7
   c. 7 and 10
   d. 10 and 13

Answers: b, d, a, a, b

module 9.3

The Five Categories of Minority Relations

All nations need to integrate diverse minority populations, which include indigenous peoples (Canada's Aboriginal peoples, Australia's Aborigines), linguistic groups (Canada's French-speaking people, Estonia's Russian-speaking people), groups arranged by sexual orientation (heterosexual, homosexual, bisexual), and ethnic communities (Ukrainians living in Winnipeg, New York's Chinatown), to name only a few. Since no nation today can completely control who comes in or moves outside of its borders, a national strategy is usually developed to manage inter-group relations, whether between minority groups or between the dominant group and minority groups. These relations can be either positive and mutually beneficial or fraught with conflict and struggle.

Sociologists put forth five general categories to help define how dominant groups interact with minority groups, from the most exclusionary to the most inclusive: genocide, expulsion or population transfer, segregation and separatism, assimilation, and cultural pluralism or multiculturalism.

GENOCIDE

Genocide is the intentional extermination of all members of a category of people (such as those belonging to a particular religion, ethnicity, or nationality) by another group of people. Typically, but not necessarily, the group that is exterminated is a minority group. Genocide of a minority group is most likely to occur when three conditions are met: (1) the dominant group is much larger than the minority, (2) the minority is of little or no economic value to the dominant group, and (3) the dominant group needs a scapegoat to blame for economic or military setbacks (duPreez, 1994; Lindsey, Beach, & Ravelli, 2009, p. 182).

Perhaps the most infamous example of genocide in the last 100 years is the Holocaust. Hitler and his Nazi regime exterminated 6 million Jewish men, women, and children as well as hundreds of thousands of Roma (Gypsies), homosexuals, Jehovah's Witnesses, physically and mentally disabled people, communists, political opponents, prisoners of war, and many others (Bauman, 1989; Chirot & McCauley, 2006; Gerlach, 2006). During the late 1970s, the Khmer Rouge in Cambodia killed at least 2 million of its own people in an effort to wipe out all Western influence—even going so far as to attempt to kill everyone who could read and write (Shawcross, 1979, as cited in Lindsey, Beach, & Ravelli, 2009, p. 182). The Hutu massacred the Tutsi in 1994 (Kuperman, 2000, p. 117). And, in the 1995 Srebrenica massacre, Bosnian Serbs executed and bulldozed into mass graves 7000 Muslim men and boys in an act of "ethnic cleansing" (Evans, 2006, p. 388).

In Canada, genocide was perpetrated against the indigenous Beothuk, who lived in what is now Newfoundland. Their population at the time of European contact is thought to have been between 500 and 1000, but shortly after the Europeans settled, the Beothuk (and many other Aboriginal groups) faced disease, malnutrition, and armed conflict with settlers and other Aboriginal groups that ultimately resulted in their extinction in 1829 (Pastore, 1997). Many other Aboriginal populations in Canada were also decimated by disease and malnutrition resulting from contact with explorers and settlers.

EXPULSION OR POPULATION TRANSFER

Sometimes, under the same circumstances that can lead to genocide, the dominant group forces a minority group to leave the country or confines them to a particular location. The

Think about the Five Categories of Minority Relations

1 Think about multiculturalism. Do you think multiculturalism is working as intended in Canada?

2 Think about the treatment of First Nation peoples in Canada. Consider, in particular, the reserve system. Do you think it reflects the values of a multicultural society?

3 Have minorities in Canada ever been faced with genocide or expulsion?

genocide The intentional extermination of all members of a category of people (such as those belonging to a particular religion, ethnicity, or nationality) by another group of people.

During the Second World War, 22 000 Japanese Canadians were sent to forced-labour camps.

decision to expel or transfer the minority group instead of exterminating them is partly due to a mix of morality and political practicality, but the goal is essentially the same: to remove the minority group from society (Lindsey, Beach, & Ravelli, 2009, p. 183).

An early Canadian example of a population transfer occurred between 1755 and 1763, when French-speaking Acadians were exiled by the British from what is now Nova Scotia. Over 12 000 people were exiled and many died from illness, drowning, misery, and starvation (Canadiana, 2008; Doucet, 2000; Historica, 2008). And, of course, in the nineteenth century, the Canadian and American governments forced many Aboriginal people onto reserves.

Two other examples from Canadian history clearly demonstrate the challenges faced by minorities during times of war. During both world wars, descendants and immigrants from countries that were considered enemies of the Canadian government were sent to internment (prison) camps and put into forced labour. The "enemy aliens" placed in internment camps were Ukrainians (during the First World War), Japanese, Germans, and Italians (during the Second World War). Roughly 30 000 people were sent to internment camps in Canada during the two wars.

More recent global examples of large-scale forced migration include Serbia's expulsion of as many Muslims as possible beginning in the late 1990s (Carmichael, 2006, p. 383). Today, more than 2 million people in the Darfur region of Sudan are living in refugee camps after fleeing their country's pro-government Arab militias, which are accused of war crimes against the region's black African population (BBC World, 2007).

SEGREGATION AND SEPARATISM

segregation The formal physical or social separation of dominant and minority groups.

Segregation is the formal physical or social separation of dominant and minority groups. It often allows the dominant group to benefit from the exploited labour of minority groups while maintaining its superior social position.

The Canadian Aboriginal reserve system is one example of segregation. Today, there are approximately 600 occupied land reserves for First Nation peoples in Canada (Indian and

Northern Affairs Canada, 2004). In most cases, these reserves are isolated from urban centres and lack many of the social services and municipal infrastructures common in Canadian cities and towns. Registered Indians living on reserves remain some of the poorest people in Canada.

Another example is the segregation of blacks in the United States, where slave labour was essential to the plantations of the American South and where, prior to 1865, African Americans were subjected to the ultimate degradation of being "owned." Finally, under apartheid, although South African blacks were technically free, their rights to live, work, and travel where they wished were restricted (Sparks, 1990). In these latter two cases, blacks were regarded as less than fully human, denied most or all civil rights, and frequently treated with great brutality (Lindsey, Beach, & Ravelli, 2009, p. 184).

A concept related to segregation is separatism. **Separatism**, also called *ethnic nationalism*, occurs when minority groups believe the dominant group will never allow them to assimilate or to exist within a truly pluralistic society. While segregation is imposed by the majority to separate them from the minorities, separatism is pursued by the minority as a means of preserving their cultural integrity. Separatism may take the form of seeking to establish an independent state, as in the Quebec sovereignty movement and the Kurds in central Asia. It may also take the form of seeking to live a largely separate life within a country dominated by a different group—for example, those living in Vancouver's Chinatown who preserve their traditions and choose to live in close proximity to other Chinese Canadians. The classic Canadian example of separatism, the Quebec sovereignty movement, is discussed later in the chapter.

ASSIMILATION

Over time, some dominant group–minority group relationships reach the point where assimilation occurs. **Assimilation** is a one-way process that occurs when a minority group sheds its differences and assumes the traits of the dominant group. This transition is made easier when five conditions are met:

1. Members of the minority groups migrated to the area voluntarily.
2. Minorities arrived during a period of economic prosperity.
3. Members of the minority group are physically similar to the dominant group.
4. Minority group is culturally similar to the dominant group.
5. The number of members in the minority group is relatively small (Blauner, 1972; Brown & Bean, 2006; Simpson & Yinger, 1985).

Not one of these conditions applies to Canada's Aboriginal peoples. Nonetheless, the federal government's 1969 White Paper advocated total assimilation of First Nation peoples. All legislation pertaining to them was to be repealed, thereby denying their unique and special status in Canada. The report also rejected existing treaties and land claims and was an obvious attempt to sever all ties between the First Nation peoples and the federal government (Lazar, 2003).

In the face of strong opposition, the federal government never enacted any of the contentious policies proposed in the White Paper. Yet the legacy of the residential school system, along with the poor living conditions on reserves and Aboriginal peoples' ongoing economic plight, demonstrates that new strategies for helping Aboriginal peoples prosper must be pursued.

While complete assimilation holds the promise of full acceptance of the minority group, it comes at a significant cost (Snipp & Hirschman, 2004; Viruell-Fuentes, 2006, p. 338). The minority group loses its unique identity and risks never being fully accepted. Is it possible that some members of the majority would never view visible minorities as equals (Zweigenhaft & Domhoff, 1998)? Some minorities assume that assimilation is little more than abandoning one's cultural identity in the pursuit of material gain (Nagel, 1994).

To learn more about issues facing Canada's First Nation peoples, go to **http://ainc-inac.gc.ca/index-eng.asp.**

separatism Voluntary structural and cultural isolation by minority groups from the dominant group.

assimilation A one-way process that occurs when a minority group sheds its differences and assumes the traits of the dominant group.

CULTURAL PLURALISM, OR MULTICULTURALISM

**cultural pluralism
(multiculturalism)** The
retention of minority
groups' cultural identities
and the promotion of
cultural, ethnic, and
racial diversity by the
larger society.

The final pattern of minority group–dominant group relations is **cultural pluralism**, commonly referred to as **multiculturalism**. This situation exists when minority groups retain their cultural identity and the larger society promotes cultural, ethnic, and racial diversity—arguably the Canadian approach to minority integration. In 1971 Canada became the first country in the world to adopt multiculturalism as official policy—an interesting turnaround just two years after the notorious White Paper (Canadian Heritage, 2007a). The 1971 policy also confirmed the rights of Aboriginal peoples and the status of Canada's two official languages. Later, in 1985, Canada's *Multiculturalism Act* confirmed the federal government's intention of preserving and enhancing the spectrum of human diversity in Canada, be it racial, cultural, or linguistic. By so doing, Canada affirmed the value and dignity of all Canadian citizens regardless of their racial or ethnic origins, language, and religious affiliation.

Canadian multiculturalism is grounded on the belief that, while all citizens must be treated equally, we should not overlook how our differences enrich our society. Multiculturalism confirms that all citizens can retain their unique cultural and ethnic identities and be proud of their ancestry, yet still feel a sense of belonging as Canadians. However, skeptics might question whether the dominant white majority follows through on its commitment to multiculturalism in light of how many react during times of economic hardship or during international conflicts. Some critics perceive multiculturalism as merely the superficial encouragement of ethnic dancing and traditional foods; immigrants are still expected to adopt the values and attitudes of the dominant society. Others complain that multiculturalism tends to freeze cultures in a fixed state and not allow them to evolve (Lindsey, Beach, & Ravelli, 2009, p. 186).

melting pot The
blending of new
immigrants' traditions
and cultural identity into
the dominant American
culture.

The contrasting American approach to integrating minority populations is commonly referred to as the **melting pot**, a metaphor for an approach to minority integration whereby new immigrants willingly blend their traditions and cultural identity into the dominant American culture (Newman, 2006). In fact, during the nineteenth century, many influential Americans believed that the "American race" could effectively absorb and permanently improve the less desirable traits of all immigrant groups (Mason, 2007, p. 102).

What do you know about **the Five Categories of Minority Relations?**

Multiple-choice questions (circle your answer)

1. **The extermination of Jewish men, women, and children by Hitler and his Nazi regime is an example of**
   a. Genocide
   b. Expulsion
   c. Segregation
   d. Assimilation

2. **The formal physical or social separation of dominant and minority groups is called**
   a. Pluralism
   b. Separatism
   c. Assimilation
   d. Segregation

3. **The Canadian Aboriginal reserve system is an example of**
   a. Assimilation
   b. Separatism
   c. Segregation
   d. Pluralism

4. **A one-way process that occurs when a minority group sheds its differences and assumes the traits of the dominant group is called**
   a. Assimilation
   b. Pluralism
   c. Separatism
   d. Segregation

5. **Another term for *multiculturalism* is**
   a. Assimilation
   b. Segregation
   c. Separatism
   d. Cultural pluralism

Answers: a, d, c, a, d

module 9.4

Minority Groups in Canada

As Canadians, we take pride in our multiculturalism and consider that our country treats all of its citizens without prejudice. Yet, the existence of minority groups (groups that are socially disadvantaged) in Canada is an undeniable fact. Below we explore four minority groups in Canada: Aboriginal peoples and the Québécois (special-status groups in Canada according to the Constitution), and Chinese Canadians and black Canadians (the second- and third-largest visible minority groups in Canada, respectively). It's important to recognize, however, that the number of minority groups in this country is far greater.

Think about Minority Groups in Canada

1 Think about minority groups. Can you name any minority groups that exist in Canada?

2 Think about the Québécois. Do you see them as a minority group?

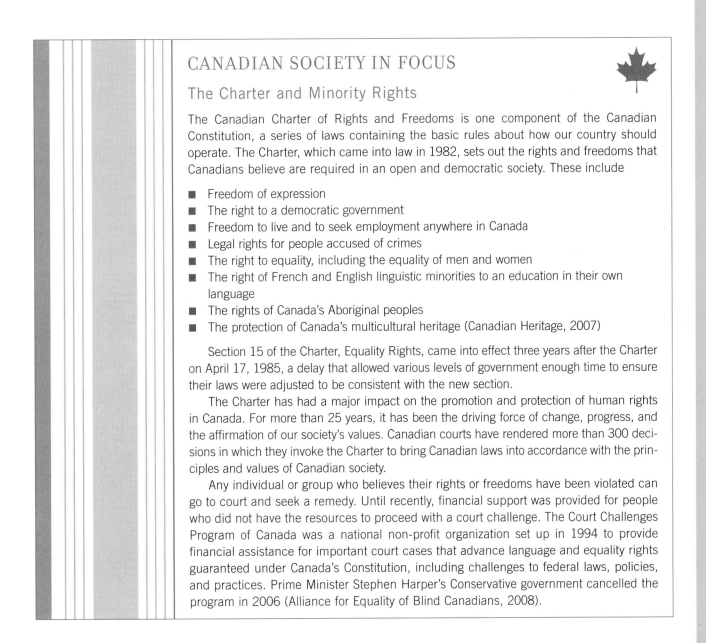

CANADIAN SOCIETY IN FOCUS

The Charter and Minority Rights

The Canadian Charter of Rights and Freedoms is one component of the Canadian Constitution, a series of laws containing the basic rules about how our country should operate. The Charter, which came into law in 1982, sets out the rights and freedoms that Canadians believe are required in an open and democratic society. These include

- Freedom of expression
- The right to a democratic government
- Freedom to live and to seek employment anywhere in Canada
- Legal rights for people accused of crimes
- The right to equality, including the equality of men and women
- The right of French and English linguistic minorities to an education in their own language
- The rights of Canada's Aboriginal peoples
- The protection of Canada's multicultural heritage (Canadian Heritage, 2007)

Section 15 of the Charter, Equality Rights, came into effect three years after the Charter on April 17, 1985, a delay that allowed various levels of government enough time to ensure their laws were adjusted to be consistent with the new section.

The Charter has had a major impact on the promotion and protection of human rights in Canada. For more than 25 years, it has been the driving force of change, progress, and the affirmation of our society's values. Canadian courts have rendered more than 300 decisions in which they invoke the Charter to bring Canadian laws into accordance with the principles and values of Canadian society.

Any individual or group who believes their rights or freedoms have been violated can go to court and seek a remedy. Until recently, financial support was provided for people who did not have the resources to proceed with a court challenge. The Court Challenges Program of Canada was a national non-profit organization set up in 1994 to provide financial assistance for important court cases that advance language and equality rights guaranteed under Canada's Constitution, including challenges to federal laws, policies, and practices. Prime Minister Stephen Harper's Conservative government cancelled the program in 2006 (Alliance for Equality of Blind Canadians, 2008).

ABORIGINAL PEOPLES

In 2006, Aboriginal peoples accounted for 3.8 percent of Canada's total population, an increase from 3.3 percent in 2001 and 2.8 percent in 1996 (in comparison, Aborigines in Australia account for 2 percent of the population, and in the United States, indigenous peoples constitute around 1.5 percent of the population). The Canadian Aboriginal population has grown much faster than the non-Aboriginal population. For example, between 1996 and 2006, the Aboriginal population's rate of growth was 45 percent, while the rest of the Canadian population was around 8 percent for the same period. Further, of the three Aboriginal groups, the Métis showed the fastest growth between 1996 and 2006, at 91 percent (Statistics Canada, 2008b). Table 9–2 shows the Aboriginal population in Canada by group as well as by province and territory.

Many Aboriginal communities have made impressive strides to increase education levels, decrease infant mortality rates, and address substance use issues. Despite these successes, Aboriginal people remain at higher risk for illness and die younger than the Canadian population as a whole. They also suffer from more chronic diseases such as diabetes and heart disease than the general population, and there is evidence that these illnesses are getting worse (Health Canada, 2005).

Inadequate housing and crowded living conditions are factors in the higher rates of respiratory problems and other infectious diseases among Aboriginal children. Children in Aboriginal families also have higher rates of unintentional injuries and accidental deaths. Young men (particularly in Inuit communities) are far more likely to commit suicide than their peers in Canada as a whole (Health Canada, 2005). Aboriginal children in some communities are more likely than children in the general population to smoke, drink, and use illegal drugs.

Aboriginal families are also more likely than the general population to have inadequate food and housing. In 2005, Aboriginal people faced higher unemployment rates (18 percent) than non-Aboriginal people (6.5 percent), and when they do find work, they are paid less for it. Aboriginal employees earned less on average than their non-Aboriginal counterparts ($14.20 per hour versus $15.50 per hour). These average hourly earnings mask important distributional differences, however. For example, one in four Aboriginal employees earned less than $10 per hour, compared with only one in six non-Aboriginal employees; and only

Canadian Aboriginal peoples are considered a minority because they often lack social power and are visually unique.

TABLE 9-2 **Aboriginal Identity Population for Canada, Provinces and Territories, 2006**

Geographic Area	Total Population	Aboriginal Identity Population*	North American Indian	Métis	Inuit
Canada	31 241 030	1 172 785	698 025	389 780	50 480
Ontario	12 028 895	242 495	158 395	73 605	2 035
Quebec	7 435 905	108 425	65 085	27 980	10 950
British Columbia	4 074 385	196 075	129 580	59 445	795
Alberta	3 256 355	188 365	97 275	85 495	1 610
Manitoba	1 133 515	175 395	100 640	71 805	565
Saskatchewan	953 850	141 890	91 400	48 120	215
Nova Scotia	903 090	24 175	15 240	7 680	325
New Brunswick	719 650	17 650	12 385	4 270	185
Newfoundland & Labrador	500 610	23 455	7 765	6 470	4 715
Prince Edward Island	134 205	1 730	1 225	385	30
Northwest Territories	41 060	20 635	12 640	3 580	4 160
Yukon Territory	30 190	7 580	6 280	800	255
Nunavut	29 325	24 915	100	130	24 635

* The total Aboriginal identity population includes the Aboriginal groups (North American Indian, Métis, and Inuit), multiple Aboriginal responses, and Aboriginal responses not included elsewhere.

Source: Statistics Canada. (2008). Aboriginal identity population by age groups, median age and sex, 2006 counts, for Canada, provinces and territories—20 percent sample data (table).
Aboriginal Peoples Highlight Tables. 2006 Census. Statistics Canada Catalogue no. 97-558-XWE2006002. Ottawa. Released January 15, 2008. Retrieved January 27, 2008, from http://www12.statcan.ca/english/census06/data/highlights/aboriginal/index.cfm?Lang=E.

29 percent of Aboriginal employees earned $20 or more per hour, compared with 40 percent of non-Aboriginal employees (Luffman & Sussman, 2007).

QUÉBÉCOIS

From the earliest contact between European explorers and Aboriginal peoples, it became clear that Canada would develop according to the needs and practices of the French and English—two groups that sociologist John Porter (1965) termed Canada's **charter groups**. Porter argued that French and English settlers quickly became the social, economic, and political elite of the new country, a situation that remains largely unchanged today. While the dominance of the English linguistic group in Canada is unquestioned, the unique influence of French-speaking Canadians cannot be overestimated. The French have always seen themselves as a distinct society; when Prime Minister Stephen Harper suggested in 2006 that the "Québécois form a nation within a united Canada" (Sheppard, 2006), it was only the latest demonstration of the central role that the tension between French and English Canada continues to play in setting the national political agenda.

Quebec separatism has been a contentious issue throughout much of Canadian history. Since the eighteenth century, when England defeated France in the battle for control of North America, the relationship between English Canadians and French Canadians has been strained. The English–French relationship has been defined as "one country, two histories" and as "two solitudes" (MacLennan, 1945). Even before Canada's birth in 1867, there were French Canadians who believed that their province must become an independent state or the French would face the loss of their language and culture. Throughout much of the nation's history, the Québécois have felt that they are an oppressed minority. Even in Quebec, where the French are the majority, political and economic life has often been dominated by the English.

This situation began to change during the 1960s when Quebec underwent the **Quiet Revolution**, during which Quebec moved into a more modern phase of its development and challenged the traditional power of the Catholic Church while advocating for greater economic, political, and cultural equality with the rest of Canada (Juteau, 2002, p. 450).

charter groups The French and the English in Canada; Porter recognized the important role these groups played in Canadian history and contemporary social and political development.

Quiet Revolution A movement in Quebec during the 1960s, when political and religious traditions were challenged and the French struggled for greater economic, political, and cultural equality with the rest of Canada.

In 1976, the first separatist government came to power in the province. The Parti Québécois (PQ) held a referendum on separatism in 1980, but 60 percent of Quebecers voted against the idea. In 1995, a second referendum on "sovereignty association" resulted in a "no" vote, but the narrow margin in votes nonetheless emphasized the strength of separatist feelings. While the movement has since retreated, many Québécois still feel strongly about the need to protect their distinct culture and their language (CBC, 2005).

Language laws have also been a point of tension on the national stage for well over 400 years. In 1974, Quebec Liberals passed Bill 22, which made French the province's official language and restricted enrolment in English schools. Three years later, the newly elected Parti Québécois, under the leadership of René Lévesque, introduced the Charter of the French Language, or Bill 101 as it became known. Within that bill was the declaration that, with few exceptions, French was to be the only language allowed on commercial signs in the province. In 1988, the Supreme Court of Canada ruled that English could not be prohibited altogether, but that requiring the predominance of French on commercial signs was a reasonable limit on freedom of expression. In response, premier Robert Bourassa invoked the "notwithstanding" clause that overrode the *Charter of Rights and Freedoms*, and later introduced Bill 178, which decreed that only French could be used on exterior signs while English would be allowed inside commercial establishments.

After nearly 100 years of fiery debate and highly controversial language legislation—and despite the massive English presence surrounding Quebec, the pervasive influence of English television, and the burgeoning borderless use of the Internet—79.6 percent of Quebecers still speak French at home (CBC News in Depth, 2005; Statistics Canada, 2007b).

CHINESE CANADIANS

Chinese Canadians are currently the second-largest visible minority group in Canada. Unfortunately, their history in this country has been fraught with hardship.

The Chinese first began settling in the United States after slavery was abolished. Wealthy American farmers and businessmen found that poor, landless Chinese men from Guangdong and Fujian provinces would do the back-breaking work that used to be done by African slave labourers. Some of these Chinese men ultimately immigrated to Canada when gold was found in British Columbia's Fraser River Valley in 1858 (CBC News in Review, 1999). Once here, the Chinese found that they were allowed access to the mines only after white prospectors had extracted virtually all of the gold. By 1860, other Chinese had begun arriving in British Columbia directly from China. Between 1881 and 1884, over 15 000 Chinese came to Canada to work.

About 17 000 Chinese immigrants became labourers on the Canadian Pacific Railway—very difficult and dangerous work. In all, over 700 Chinese men lost their lives helping Canadians build their national railway. Chinese workers were paid half as much as white workers who did the same job. The only other work that the Chinese were able to get was as cooks and launderers—two occupations that did not threaten white male workers, since these jobs were considered "women's work" (CBC News in Review, 1999).

Although the Chinese were tolerated when their labour was needed, once the railway was completed in 1885, they were no longer welcome. Thousands of labourers were laid off from the railway, and the Canadian government imposed a "head tax" on any Chinese person wanting to enter Canada. The head tax was initially set at $50, but in 1900 it was increased to $100, and in 1903 it was increased again—this time to $500, the equivalent of two years' salary for the Chinese labourers at the time. The Chinese were the only ethnic group that had to pay such a tax. On July 1, 1923, the Canadian government passed the *Chinese Immigration Act* (also known as the *Chinese Exclusion Act*), which prevented any further Chinese immigration to Canada. The act remained in effect until 1947.

The act meant that Chinese men already in Canada could not bring their wives and children from China, and therefore had to face their hardships alone. For the women and children left in China, this meant hardship as well: the families who were left behind experienced starvation and extreme economic hardships. Many families were separated for long periods of time, and some never reunited again. For many years, Chinese Canadians protested against the *Chinese Exclusion Act* by closing their businesses on July 1 and boycotting celebrations on Dominion Day (now known as Canada Day), which they referred to as "Humiliation Day" (Chinese Canadian National Council, 2005).

It was also not until 1947 that Canada finally granted Chinese Canadians full status rights as Canadian citizens and the right to vote in federal elections (CBC News in Review, 1999). However, as a highly visible group with cultural traditions very different from those of the European majority, they continued to face prejudice and discrimination.

In 2006, Stephen Harper apologized in the House of Commons for the Canadian government's implementation of the head tax. The government also announced that it would make symbolic payments of $20 000 to living head-tax payers and to persons in a conjugal relationship with a now deceased head-tax payer.

The Canadian government is undertaking further historical recognition initiatives. In 2006, it launched a $24 million Community Historical Recognition Program and the $10 million National Historical Recognition Program. The purpose of these programs is to "commemorate and educate Canadians about the historical experiences and contributions of ethnocultural communities impacted by wartime measures and immigration restrictions" (Government of Canada, 2007b).

From a sociological perspective, Chinese Canadians are remarkable for how resilient and successful they are, and for the tremendous contributions they have made to Canadian society.

BLACK CANADIANS

Black Canadians, the third-largest visible minority group in Canada, have also had a long and troubled history.

The history of black Canadians really began in the United States with the slave trade. In the seventeenth and eighteenth centuries, tens of millions of Africans were shipped in deplorable conditions to the United States to work on sugar plantations. Some estimate that only 15 million survived the journey. In their new homeland, harsh living conditions and cruelty led to many more deaths from disease and exhaustion. Thus began their quest for freedom—the international clandestine uprising which has come to be known as the underground railroad (Owen Sound's Black History, 2004), a loosely constructed network of escape routes that began in the Deep South, continued through the northern free states, and eventually led to Canada. In Canada, as in Mexico and the Caribbean, blacks could live as free citizens.

The network was so secretive that very little is known about its actual operation. However, historians estimate that between 40 000 and 100 000 freedom seekers made it to Canada. Ultimately, a substantial black population established itself in Upper Canada (now known as Ontario). When peace and civil rights returned to the United States, many former slaves travelled south to reconnect with family and friends (Owen Sound's Black History, 2004).

Although slavery was never a significant part of Canada's social structure, we should not believe that slavery never happened here. It was not until 1793 that Lieutenant-Governor John Graves Simcoe banned the importation of slaves to Upper Canada. However, because a number of United Empire Loyalists had brought enslaved people with them, those already in the colony would remain enslaved under the law; the children of enslaved women would be freed at age 25. In 1833, the *Emancipation Act* abolished slavery in all British holdings, including Canada.

The black population in Canada is growing quickly, and currently stands at over 1 million. This number represents a steady increase over the last few decades, owing in part to increasing overall immigration levels and to the elimination of immigration policies that were preferential to European immigrants.

Immigration decisions are now largely based on a point system that rewards immigrants with high employability potential. Applicants are assigned points for specific occupational skills, education level, knowledge of English and French, and other similar criteria. Black

To learn more about the history of Canada's black community, go to **http://blackhistory canada.ca.**

immigrants have competed very successfully under these new immigration procedures. The majority of black immigrants come not from the United States but from the Caribbean and, more recently, from Africa, including refugees from Ethiopia and Somalia.

Black Canadians are just as likely to attend university as non-blacks. As such, their prosperity and political power is increasing within the broader social context. However, blacks on average earn less and are unemployed more often than other Canadians. As well, black children are more likely to live in lone-parent families than are non-black children (Statistics Canada, 2004a).

What do you know about **Minority Groups in Canada**?

Multiple-choice questions (circle your answer)

1. **Which of the following statements is false?**
   a. Aboriginal people die younger than the general population.
   b. Aboriginal people suffer from more chronic illnesses than the general population.
   c. The Canadian Aboriginal population has grown much slower than the rest of the Canadian population.
   d. The Aboriginal population suffers from inadequate food and housing.

2. **The Parti Québécois held its first referendum on separatism in**
   a. 1970
   b. 1980
   c. 1995
   d. 1996

3. _____ **Canadians are the second-largest visible minority group in Canada.**

   a. Chinese
   b. Japanese
   c. Black
   d. Korean

4. **Once the railway was completed, Chinese people that wanted to enter Canada were required to pay a**
   a. Landed immigrant tax
   b. Land tax
   c Head tax
   d. Railway tax

5. **Which of the following is not in the Canadian Charter of Rights and Freedoms?**
   a. Freedom of expression
   b. Freedom to live anywhere in Canada
   c. Legal rights for people accused of crimes
   d. All are in the Charter of Rights and Freedoms.

Answers: c, b, a, c, d

Summary

module 9.1   WHAT IS A MINORITY?

1. There are a number of minority groups in Canada. A *minority* is any definable category of people who are socially disadvantaged; minority groups lack power and are recognizably different from the majority.

2. Race and ethnicity are two ways that minority groups are defined. *Race* is considered a socially constructed concept because actual genetic differences between what are called races are tiny and determine neither behavioural nor biological differences. *Ethnicity* is socially constructed to the extent to which it encompasses minority or majority status, ancestry, language, and often religious affiliation.

3. New immigrants often find themselves in minority group situations. In 2006, the percentage of foreign-born people living in Canada was at an all-time high, with the largest group of recent immigrants coming from China. The highest number of immigrants live in Ontario, Quebec, and British Columbia, and in urban centres more so than rural areas.

module 9.2   PREJUDICE, RACISM, AND DISCRIMINATION

4. *Prejudice* is a negative judgment about a person or group that is irrational, long-lasting, and not based on fact.
5. One type of prejudice is a stereotype. A *stereotype* is a stable and sweeping generalization about a category of people.
6. Another type of prejudice is racism. *Racism* is an ideology that maintains that one race is inherently superior to another.
7. While prejudice and racism are belief systems, *discrimination* represents the actions of such beliefs. There are three levels of discrimination.
8. *Individual discrimination* occurs when a person advantages or disadvantages someone because of that person's group membership.
9. *Direct institutional discrimination* occurs when an institution employs policies or practices that are discriminatory against a person or group.
10. *Indirect institutional discrimination* occurs when an action produces uneven results on a group or person because of an unlawful criterion, but lacks the intent of being discriminatory.
11. Psychological theories on prejudice and discrimination include scapegoat theory and authoritarian personality theory.
12. Socio-cultural theories on prejudice and discrimination include culture theory, functionalist theory, conflict theory, symbolic interactionist theory, and post-colonial theory.

module 9.3   THE FIVE CATEGORIES OF MINORITY RELATIONS

13. *Genocide* is the intentional extermination of all members of a category of people (such as those belonging to a particular religion, ethnicity, or nationality) by another group of people (e.g., the Holocaust).
14. *Segregation* is the formal physical or social separation of dominant and minority groups.
15. *Separatism* is the voluntary structural and cultural isolation by minority groups from the dominant group.
16. *Assimilation* is a one-way process that occurs when a minority group sheds its differences and assumes the traits of the dominant group.
17. *Cultural pluralism* or *multiculturalism* is the retention of minority groups' cultural identities and the promotion of cultural, ethnic, and racial diversity by the larger society.
18. Canada practises multiculturalism. The United States practises assimilation—often referred to as the melting pot.

module 9.4   MINORITY GROUPS IN CANADA

19. Canada's two special-status groups are Aboriginal peoples and the Québécois. Today, Chinese Canadians are the second-largest visible minority group, and blacks are the third-largest minority group.
20. The Canadian *Charter of Rights and Freedoms* upholds the right to equality for all peoples, including Aboriginal rights and the protection of the country's multicultural heritage.

Key Terms

Test Yourself

1. A definable category of people who are socially disadvantaged is called a(n)
   a. Ethnic group
   b. Race
   c. Minority group
   d. Ethnic population

2. _____ has been defined as a group of people who are physically and genetically distinguished from other groups.
   a. Minority group
   b. Ethnic group
   c. Race
   d. Cultural group

3. In the past, whites were classified into what race?
   a. Caucasoid
   b. Mongoloid
   c. Negroid
   d. Europoid

4. Which of the following statements is false?
   a. Almost 20 percent of Canadians are foreign born.
   b. The United States has a slightly higher foreign-born population than Canada.
   c. The proportion of foreign-born Canadians has risen over the past 75 years.
   d. Today, most new immigrants to Canada come from Asia.

5. Which of the following statements is false?
   a. Immigrants to Canada tend to settle in British Columbia, Ontario, and Quebec.
   b. Immigrants to Canada tend to settle in small urban centres.

   c. Immigrants to Canada tend to achieve economic integration faster if they settle in small urban centres.
   d. Immigrants to Canada tend to settle in large urban centres.

6. A negative judgment about a person or group that is irrational, long-lasting, and not based on fact is called
   a. Prejudice
   b. Ecological fallacy
   c. Exception fallacy
   d. Discrimination

7. A stereotype is
   a. A stable and sweeping generalization about a category of people
   b. An accurate portrayal of ethnic groups
   c. A form of discrimination
   d. Always negative

8. Actions that deny or grant advantages to members of a particular group are called
   a. Discrimination
   b. Racism
   c. Stereotyping
   d. Prejudice

9. _____ occurs when an action produces uneven results on a group or person because of an unlawful criterion, but lacks the intent of being discriminatory.
   a. Individual discrimination
   b. Direct institutional discrimination
   c. Indirect institutional discrimination
   d. Nondirect discrimination

10. _____ theory assumes that people naturally compete over limited resources and prejudice and discrimination are logical outcomes of that discrimination.
    a. Scapegoat
    b. Functionalist
    c. Symbolic interactionist
    d. Conflict

11. The intentional extermination of all members of a category of people is called
    a. Genocide
    b. Segregation
    c. Separatism
    d. Assimilation

12. Voluntary structural and cultural isolation from the dominant group is called
    a. Pluralism
    b. Separatism
    c. Assimilation
    d. Segregation

13. The retention of minority groups' cultural identities and the promotion of cultural, ethnic, and racial diversity by the larger society is called
    a. Cultural pluralism
    b. Assimilation
    c. Separatism
    d. Segregation

14. The American approach to integrating minority groups is commonly called
    a. Accommodation
    b. Segregation
    c. Cultural pluralism
    d. The melting pot

15. The confinement of Japanese Canadians to internment camps during the Second World War is an example of
    a. Genocide
    b. Segregation
    c. Expulsion
    d. Cultural pluralism

16. In 2006, Aboriginal peoples accounted for _____ of Canada's total population.
    a. 3.8 percent
    b. 7.8 percent
    c. 10 percent
    d. 17.3 percent

17. John Porter named the following two groups Canada's charter groups:
    a. French and Aboriginal
    b. Métis and Inuit
    c. English and Aboriginal
    d. English and French

18. In all, Quebec has held _____ referendums on Quebec separation and sovereignty.
    a. Two
    b. Three
    c. Four
    d. Five

19. _____ Chinese immigrants worked to build the Canadian Pacific Railway.
    a. 2000
    b. 10 000
    c. 17 000
    d. 27 000

20. _____ Canadians are the third-largest visible minority group in Canada.
    a. Chinese
    b. Black
    c. Indo-
    d. Pakistani

Answers: c, c, a, b, b, a, a, c, d, a, b, a, c, a, a, c, b

Log in to MySocLab for a host of resources that will help you save time and improve your grade. MySocLab contains cutting-edge learning tools such as study plans, practice tests, videos, audio segments, quizzes, and more—all designed to help you better understand the learning objectives for this chapter. Along with your eBook, MySocLab for *Sociology for Everyone* can be found at **www.mysoclab.com**.

CONCEPT MAP

module 9.1
WHAT IS A MINORITY?

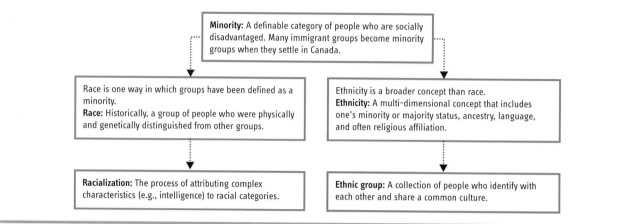

Minority: A definable category of people who are socially disadvantaged. Many immigrant groups become minority groups when they settle in Canada.

Race is one way in which groups have been defined as a minority.
Race: Historically, a group of people who were physically and genetically distinguished from other groups.

Ethnicity is a broader concept than race.
Ethnicity: A multi-dimensional concept that includes one's minority or majority status, ancestry, language, and often religious affiliation.

Racialization: The process of attributing complex characteristics (e.g., intelligence) to racial categories.

Ethnic group: A collection of people who identify with each other and share a common culture.

module 9.2
PREJUDICE, RACISM, AND DISCRIMINATION

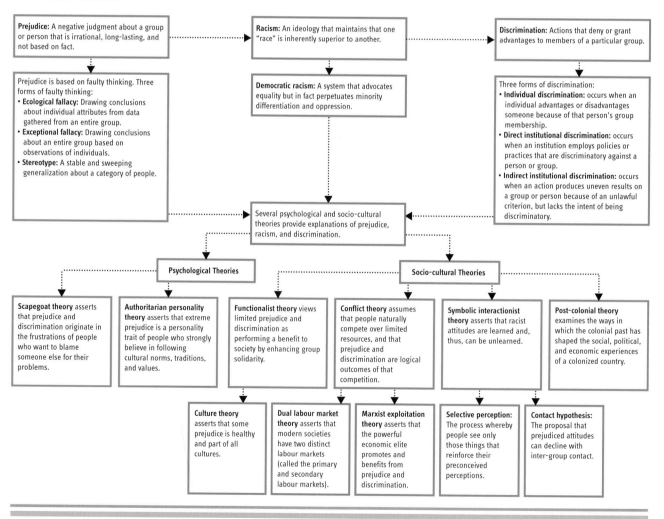

Prejudice: A negative judgment about a group or person that is irrational, long-lasting, and not based on fact.

Racism: An ideology that maintains that one "race" is inherently superior to another.

Discrimination: Actions that deny or grant advantages to members of a particular group.

Prejudice is based on faulty thinking. Three forms of faulty thinking:
• **Ecological fallacy:** Drawing conclusions about individual attributes from data gathered from an entire group.
• **Exceptional fallacy:** Drawing conclusions about an entire group based on observations of individuals.
• **Stereotype:** A stable and sweeping generalization about a category of people.

Democratic racism: A system that advocates equality but in fact perpetuates minority differentiation and oppression.

Three forms of discrimination:
• **Individual discrimination:** occurs when an individual advantages or disadvantages someone because of that person's group membership.
• **Direct institutional discrimination:** occurs when an institution employs policies or practices that are discriminatory against a person or group.
• **Indirect institutional discrimination:** occurs when an action produces uneven results on a group or person because of an unlawful criterion, but lacks the intent of being discriminatory.

Several psychological and socio-cultural theories provide explanations of prejudice, racism, and discrimination.

Psychological Theories

Socio-cultural Theories

Scapegoat theory asserts that prejudice and discrimination originate in the frustrations of people who want to blame someone else for their problems.

Authoritarian personality theory asserts that extreme prejudice is a personality trait of people who strongly believe in following cultural norms, traditions, and values.

Functionalist theory views limited prejudice and discrimination as performing a benefit to society by enhancing group solidarity.

Conflict theory assumes that people naturally compete over limited resources, and that prejudice and discrimination are logical outcomes of that competition.

Symbolic interactionist theory asserts that racist attitudes are learned and, thus, can be unlearned.

Post-colonial theory examines the ways in which the colonial past has shaped the social, political, and economic experiences of a colonized country.

Culture theory asserts that some prejudice is healthy and part of all cultures.

Dual labour market theory asserts that modern societies have two distinct labour markets (called the primary and secondary labour markets).

Marxist exploitation theory asserts that the powerful economic elite promotes and benefits from prejudice and discrimination.

Selective perception: The process whereby people see only those things that reinforce their preconceived perceptions.

Contact hypothesis: The proposal that prejudiced attitudes can decline with inter-group contact.

module 9.3
THE FIVE CATEGORIES
OF MINORITY RELATIONS

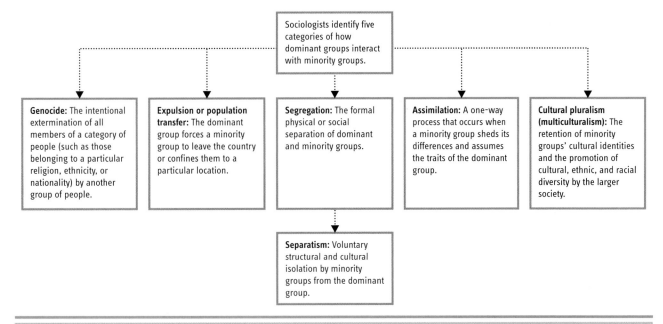

Sociologists identify five categories of how dominant groups interact with minority groups.

Genocide: The intentional extermination of all members of a category of people (such as those belonging to a particular religion, ethnicity, or nationality) by another group of people.

Expulsion or population transfer: The dominant group forces a minority group to leave the country or confines them to a particular location.

Segregation: The formal physical or social separation of dominant and minority groups.

Assimilation: A one-way process that occurs when a minority group sheds its differences and assumes the traits of the dominant group.

Cultural pluralism (multiculturalism): The retention of minority groups' cultural identities and the promotion of cultural, ethnic, and racial diversity by the larger society.

Separatism: Voluntary structural and cultural isolation by minority groups from the dominant group.

module 9.4
MINORITY GROUPS IN CANADA

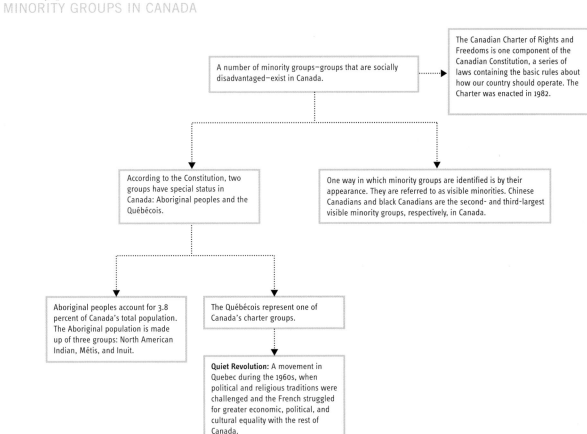

A number of minority groups—groups that are socially disadvantaged—exist in Canada.

The Canadian Charter of Rights and Freedoms is one component of the Canadian Constitution, a series of laws containing the basic rules about how our country should operate. The Charter was enacted in 1982.

According to the Constitution, two groups have special status in Canada: Aboriginal peoples and the Québécois.

One way in which minority groups are identified is by their appearance. They are referred to as visible minorities. Chinese Canadians and black Canadians are the second- and third-largest visible minority groups, respectively, in Canada.

Aboriginal peoples account for 3.8 percent of Canada's total population. The Aboriginal population is made up of three groups: North American Indian, Métis, and Inuit.

The Québécois represent one of Canada's charter groups.

Quiet Revolution: A movement in Quebec during the 1960s, when political and religious traditions were challenged and the French struggled for greater economic, political, and cultural equality with the rest of Canada.

chapter 10

Mass Media

Information Highway to Hell

"The Internet sucks," according to the front cover of the October 30, 2006, issue of *Maclean's* magazine.

Steve Maich (2006), the author of the issue's feature story, argues that "[a]fter 15 years and a trillion dollars of investment, just about everything that we've been told about the Internet and what the information age would mean has come up short" (Maich, 2006, p. 44). Maich points out that the proponents of the Web claimed that it would bring us to an age of enlightenment; all knowledge would be free and accessible to anyone with access to the Internet. Globally, this would lead us to a level of shared understanding. Instead of a utopia, however, Maich says that the Internet has created a "virtual Wild West."

Pornography, gambling, infidelity, plagiarism, misinformation, scams, and theft are but a few of the Internet practices that have left many disenchanted. Maich (2006, p. 44) states that the Internet has become a place where "the masses indulge their darkest vices."

But is the Internet *all* bad? Certainly, we can list a few of its benefits: for example, it has provided people with greater mobility and access to information, increased the speed and range of communication, fostered online communities, and enhanced democracy. Although the Internet is not perfect, these benefits certainly reflect the kind of world idealists envisioned at the birth of the World Wide Web.

It is safe to say that the Internet is here to stay. There is no turning back. As Maich (2006, p. 49) states:

It is so deeply entrenched in our culture—in the way we speak and work and create and think—that the only thing to do is to try and make it better, and hope that maybe we might somehow realize some of the dreams the idealists had when they invented the thing.

So, what do you think? Does the Internet suck?

module 10.1

Think about Mass Media through Time

1 Think about communication. List all of the ways in which humans communicate with each other. How many ways of communicating involve communication to large groups of people at once. What do these forms of communication have in common?

2 Tink about radio and television. From your own experience, how have radio and television changed in your lifetime?

mass communication
The transmission of messages by a person or group through a device to a large audience.

Cave art could be considered one of the first forms of mass media.

Mass Media through Time

Everyone realizes how important media are for people today. From radio and television to text messaging and Internet searches, these technologies influence how individuals interact with the world around them. To begin our discussion, we distinguish between the terms *mass communication* and *mass media*. **Mass communication** is the transmission of messages by a person or group through a device to a large audience. Printing flyers about an upcoming political protest and posting them around campus constitutes mass communication; that is, printed flyers (the device) are used to communicate about the protest (the message) to everyone on campus (the audience). **Mass media**, on the other hand, include any medium designed to communicate messages to a mass audience.

To appreciate contemporary mass media and the role they play in society today, we begin with a review of communication media through time. Historically, our human ancestors first began using paintings and engravings on cave walls to communicate ideas during the Upper Paleolithic era (40 000 to 10 000 years before the present). Much later, between 4000 and 3000 BCE, the Egyptians developed **hieroglyphics** and introduced a form of writing paper called **papyrus**. Around 1500 BCE, the Greeks developed a phonetic alphabet, which was written from left to right and represented the sounds of the spoken language (Couch, 1996, p. 103). All of these innovations contributed to written forms of communication.

FROM BLOCK PRINTING TO MOVABLE TYPE

With the diffusion of written language throughout the world, people began to appreciate the potential uses of making exact copies of written text to allow more than one person access

to the materials at one time. The earliest printing process, called **block printing**, was developed during the T'ang dynasty (618–907 BCE) (Yao, 2002). This process involved engraving text and illustrations onto wooden blocks that were then inked and pressed onto paper (Avery, 2003). The process was used to print cards, calendars, and early notices by merchants to promote their wares—an early form of advertisements. While this process allowed the production of virtually identical copies, it was a relatively labour-intensive process. The blocks had to be engraved (and if a mistake was made, one would have to start over), and if any changes were required, a new block would have to be produced. Around 1450, however, all of this changed.

Johannes Gutenberg's printing press had a tremendous influence on human social development. The revolutionary element of his invention was the implementation of **movable type**. In contrast to block printing, movable type used small metal shafts whose ends took the form of letters or images, which could be moved into sentences and patterns and then transferred to paper. If a mistake was made or a revision to the text was desired, only that which needed to be corrected had to be changed, and not the entire printing surface. Further, because the metal letters and images could be re-used, the process was very economical.

Gutenberg's printing press would go on to transform human society. Not only was it one of the first major applications of mass production, but its interchangeable parts constituted one of the earliest instances of a technique that would become instrumental to the Industrial Revolution three centuries later. Moreover, by making copies of Bibles and other documents affordable, people outside the upper class were motivated to learn to read. In fact, because Gutenberg's printing press allowed inexpensive copies to be made available to the masses, it inspired a rapid increase in literacy levels across Europe (Eisenstein, 1979, p. xii).

NEWSPAPERS

After the printing press made books (beginning with the Bible) and pamphlets accessible to the masses, newspapers also began to emerge across Europe. The oldest newspaper still in publication is Sweden's *Post-och Inrikes Tidningar*, which began printing in 1645. In 2007, after more than 350 years in existence, and perhaps a signal of change for all newspapers, its publisher announced that it would stop producing a paper copy and instead move completely online (Associated Press, 2007). The first Canadian newspaper was the *Halifax Gazette*, which began printing in 1752 (Province of Nova Scotia, 2003). Table 10–1 demonstrates that the world's largest newspapers remain a popular medium.

THE TELEGRAPH

After the newspaper, the next important medium of mass communication was Samuel Morse's telegraph, patented in 1843. The Morse telegraph used a keypad to send short and long electrical pulses—called Morse code—through telegraph lines to be received and translated at the other end (The Alberta Pioneer Railway Association, 2007).

As railroad companies built railway lines throughout the world, they would run telegraph lines along the tracks that allowed messages to be sent from one place to another with the tap of a telegraph key. Telegraph messages were far more efficient and timely than sending printed documents across the country by train. In fact, the telegraph became Canada's primary means of sending messages over long distances until the widespread use of the telephone almost 100 years later. Even after the telephone became popular, the railways continued to use the telegraph to transmit train orders and other communications. The last official telegraph transmitted in Canada was sent by Canadian Pacific Operator Rene Chevalier on May 30, 1972. It read: "This is the last

mass media Devices designed to communicate messages to a mass audience.

hieroglyphics An early form of visual communication developed by the Egyptians.

papyrus An early form of writing paper developed by the Egyptians.

block printing A process in which wooden blocks are engraved with images and text, inked, and then pressed onto paper.

movable type Gutenberg's invention that allowed individual letters or images to be moved without influencing the surrounding text.

TABLE 10–1 **World's Largest Newspapers by Circulation, 2005**

Rank	Title	Country	Daily Circulation
1	*Yomiuri Shimbun*	Japan	14 067 000
2	*The Asahi Shimbun*	Japan	12 121 000
3	*Mainichi Shimbun*	Japan	5 587 000
4	*Nihon Keizai Shimbun*	Japan	4 635 000
5	*Chunichi Shimbun*	Japan	4 512 000
6	*Bild*	Germany	3 867 000
7	*Sankei Shimbun*	Japan	2 757 000
8	*Canako Xiaoxi* (Beijing)	China	2 627 000
9	*People's Daily*	China	2 509 000
10	*Tokyo Sports*	Japan	2 425 000
13	*USA Today*	United States	2 310 000
14	*The Wall Street Journal*	United States	2 107 000
37	*The New York Times*	United States	1 121 000
*	*The Toronto Star*	Canada	**3 258 000
*	*The Globe and Mail*	Canada	**2 014 000
*	*Le Journal de Montréal*	Canada	**1 910 000
*	*La Presse*	Canada	**1 514 000
*	*National Post*	Canada	**1 387 000
*	*Toronto Sun*	Canada	**1 351 000

* not in the top 100

** weekly circulation

Source: World Association of Newspapers. (2005). *World's 100 largest newspapers*. Retrieved May 2, 2008, from http://www.wan-press.org/article2825.html; Canadian Newspaper Association. (2006). *Canadian newspaper circulation data, 2006*.

telegram via Morse Code in Canada. What hath God wrought?" (The Alberta Pioneer Railway Association, 2007).[1]

THE PHONOGRAPH

Until the middle of the nineteenth century, mass communication was largely limited to printed text and fixed images. Then, in 1877, Thomas Edison's invention of the phonograph ushered in sound. Edison's phonograph used a spinning cylinder (made from paper, wax, and, ultimately, metal) and a needle that would scratch the surface (making grooves) as vibrations of sound were passed through a mouthpiece. Once the grooves were made on the cylinder, another needle was used to replay the recording (Library of Congress, n.d.).

While Edison is generally credited with inventing the first machine to capture and replay sound, recent research suggests that Parisian typesetter Édouard-Léon Scott de Martinville developed a similar device in 1860—17 years before Edison's. His machine, which he called a *phonautograph*, was intended to record sounds visually, not to play them back. Scott's device had a barrel-shaped horn attached to a stylus (similar to Edison's), which etched sound waves onto sheets of paper blackened by smoke from an oil lamp.

These recordings were never intended for listening, but rather as a visual representation of sound waves. However, American researchers at Stanford University discovered that they could use a "virtual stylus" to scan the images and then play them back. This finding challenges Edison's historical claim of being the first to invent a machine that captured and replayed sound (Rosen, 2008).

---

[1] Although Alexander Graham Bell's invention of the telephone in 1876 was a technological marvel, the telephone does not qualify as a medium of mass communication. By definition, mass communication is sending a message from an individual or group to a mass audience; telephones (at least until recently) were unable to send a single message to large groups of people at one time.

MOVING PICTURES

It seems almost inevitable that if mass media were able to transmit text, static images, and sound (through the printing press, telegraph, and phonograph), the next development would be moving pictures. The first scientist to successfully provide the impression of visual movement was a Belgian named Joseph Antoine Ferdinand Plateau. In 1832, Plateau developed what he called the *phenakistoscope*, which consisted of two spinning disks that gave the impression of movement (the same process used when flipping through individual scenes in a comic book—the technique tricks the mind to infer movement where none exists).

In 1877, Eadweard Muybridge used a process that linked 24 still cameras alongside a racetrack so that as a horse and rider went by, a string tripped each camera's shutter and made consecutive still photographs of the running horse. These images were then strung together and similarly tricked the mind to infer movement. The first invention to truly capture full-motion imagery was made by the prolific American inventor Thomas Edison.

Beginning in 1888, Edison developed a technique whereby photographic film could be run rapidly across a camera's shutter, which would expose the film in frames. Since the exposures were shown very quickly, one after the other, when they were played back, the impression of fluid movement was finally achieved. In the following decade, motion pictures would become a successful entertainment industry. Projector systems were used to play short films for large audiences, who were amazed by the moving pictures (Library of Congress, n.d.).

The first movie theatre in the United States, the Nickelodeon, opened on June 19, 1905, in Pittsburgh (Mondello, 2005); less than six months later, on January 1, 1906, the Ouimetoscope opened in Montreal. The Ouimetoscope offered two screenings a day with as many as 20 short films per show, each with accompanying live musical performances. Tickets cost between 10 and 35 cents (Stastna, 2006). Most of the early shows were about famous people, current events, and scenic tours of exotic destinations and other leisure activities. Over time, these documentaries declined in popularity and production companies began to cater to the public's growing desire for comedies and dramas.

RADIO

The development of radio technology began in the 1860s when Scottish physicist James Clerk Maxwell predicted the existence of radio waves. In 1886, German physicist Heinrich Rudolph Hertz showed that fluctuations of electric current could be projected into space as radio waves, and that they operated in a fashion similar to light and heat waves. However, the real breakthrough came when Guglielmo Marconi sent and received his first radio signal in Italy in 1895 (Bellis, 2008). Later, in December 1901, he transmitted the first transatlantic message (which was simply the letter *S* in Morse code) between Poldhu, England, and Signal Hill, Newfoundland, located just outside St. John's. A few weeks later Marconi received another transmission, this one from a colleague in England, 1700 miles away, saying the words "pip, pip, pip" (Webb, 2001).

Over the next decade, the technology improved to such an extent that commercial broadcasters became interested in radio's ability to reach a mass audience. The key development of radio over earlier technology was that it did not require wires and allowed a single signal to be transmitted to anyone with a receiver. Radio was capable of providing millions of people with news, public service announcements, and entertainment. Canada's first radio station—XWA, now CFCF—began broadcasting in 1919 (Nolan, 2001, p. 72), and one year later KDKA in Pittsburgh became the first radio station in the United States (Winston, 1998, p. 77). In 1936, the Canadian Broadcasting Act established the Canadian Broadcasting Corporation (CBC Radio-Canada, n.d.).

Radio's prominence as a mass medium has lessened over time. In fact, since 1999, the number of hours people listen to the radio has steadily declined, particularly among young people aged 12 to 24, who appear to be switching to digital music players and online music

FIGURE 10–1 **Radio Listening in Canada, 1999–2006**

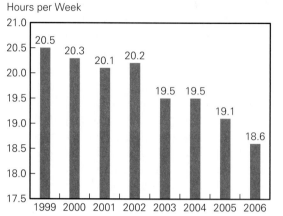

Gradual decline in radio listening

Hours per Week

Source: Statistics Canada. (2007). *Radio listening. The daily, June 26, 2007.* Retrieved June 5, 2008, from http://www.statcan.ca/Daily/English/070626/d070626b.htm.

services (Statistics Canada, 2007d). As you can see in Figure 10–1, if current trends continue, the future of traditional radio may be in jeopardy.

TELEVISION

Television has become an integral part of the world's social, political, and economic landscape; indeed, few technological developments have had such a profound influence on the social fabric of our lives.

The first person to build a working mechanical television was German student Paul Gottlieb Nipkow. In the late 1880s, Nipkow was able to send images through wires and a rotating metal disk. The technology was called the "electric telescope" and had 18 lines of resolution (compare that to today's high-definition televisions, which have 1080) (Jezek, 2006; Metzger, 2007). Then, in the early 1900s, two inventors—A.A. Campbell-Swinton from England and Boris Rosing from Russia—were experimenting with two different approaches to television: mechanical scanner systems and cathode ray electronic systems. Although the former had some early success, today's televisions are based on electronic technologies. The first working model of an electronic television was invented by Philo Taylor Farnsworth in 1927 (Jezek, 2006; McGee, 1977).

Television really began in 1927, when General Electric inventor Ernst Alexanderson demonstrated that he could broadcast pictures and sound through the air and receive them on a television. Shortly thereafter, television broadcasting was born when station WRGB in Schenectady, New York, began offering short programs on January 13, 1928. A few months later, on May 10, the station began regular programming (twice a day, three days per week) that included local weather and farm reports (CBS, n.d.). Although Canadians received television signals from the United States as early as the 1940s, the country's first television station was Montreal's CBFT, which began broadcasting on September 6, 1952. By the mid-1950s, virtually all Canadian cities had television stations, and by 1958 the CBC network had stations from Victoria to Halifax (Vivian & Maurin, 2009, p. 114).

What are our television viewing habits today? In 2004, Statistics Canada found that Canadians preferred to watch dramas and comedies (37 percent of viewing hours), more than 80 percent of which were foreign programs. The second most popular programming was news and public affairs (24 percent), of which 75 percent was of Canadian origin. Figure 10–2

FIGURE 10–2 **Television Viewing in Canada, 1995–2004**

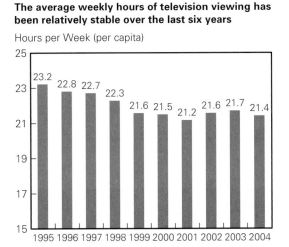

The average weekly hours of television viewing has been relatively stable over the last six years

Hours per Week (per capita)

Source: Statistics Canada. (2006). *Television viewing, by age and sex, by province.* Retrieved September 11, 2007, from http://www40.statcan.ca/l01/cst01/arts23.htm.

demonstrates that television viewing has remained relatively stable. Recently, however, teenagers' viewing has been declining sharply, with those aged 12 to 17 watching 16 hours per week in 2003 and only 13 hours per week in 2004 (Statistics Canada, 2006k). This decline is undoubtedly a result of the emerging dominance of the Internet.

For more information on the major milestones in radio and television broadcasting in Canada, go to **www.cbc.radio-canada.ca/history/index.shtml**.

THE INTERNET

The Internet had its beginnings in 1967 as a $19 000 American Department of Defense contract to design a computer network to act as a vehicle for communication that would be impervious to a nuclear strike (Federal Communications Commission, 2005). As the technology developed, its early adopters comprised not only military personnel but also researchers and academics, who quickly grasped how the technology could facilitate a new and virtually instantaneous form of communication. What began as a military need, then, led to a technological revolution that has transformed how, and how quickly, we communicate with one another. We turn next to a discussion of the myriad forms this revolution takes today.

What do you know about **Mass Media through Time**?

Multiple-choice questions (circle your answer)

1. *Mass communication* is defined as
   a. The transmission of messages by a person or group through a device to a large audience
   b. Devices designed to communicate messages to a mass audience
   c. Any medium designed to communicate to a mass audience
   d. Both b and c above

2. **The printing press was invented by**
   a. Thomas Edison
   b. Samuel Morse
   c. Johannes Gutenberg
   d. Eadweard Muybridge

3. **The world's largest newspaper by circulation is located in**
   a. United States
   b. Canada
   c. Russia
   d. Japan

4. **The phenakistoscope is associated with which medium?**
   a. Radio
   b. Newspapers
   c. Phonographs
   d. Moving pictures

5. **Television broadcasting began in**
   a. 1928
   b. 1938
   c. 1948
   d. 1958

Answers: a, c, d, d, a

module 10.2

Think about the Mass Media Today

1 Think about cellphones, email, and instant messaging. Do you think our ability to be constantly in touch with others has improved our relationships?

2 Think about the use of the Internet as a research tool. Do you consider all information on the Internet reliable? Are there any sites that you think you should not use?

Web 2.0 Interactive online tools dedicated to promoting a greater sense of community.

Mass Media Today

In 2006, 75.4 percent of Canadian homes had a personal computer (up from 55.2 percent in 2000), and 68.1 percent had Internet access (up from 42.6 percent in 2000) (Statistics Canada, 2008e). In 2007, 73 percent of Canadians aged 16 and older went online, a 5 percent increase from 2005 (Statistics Canada, 2008e).

In recent years, people have been making use of technologies that give them greater control over their own entertainment and their ways of staying in touch with each other. While traditional mass communication technologies (radio, newspapers, television) *push* content to their audiences, new technologies enable consumers to *pull* content that reflects their particular and unique interests whenever they want. People are no longer confined to the narrow media streams that existed only a few short years ago.

The enabling technology for many new online media forms is often referred to as Web 2.0. **Web 2.0** represents a significant evolution over earlier technologies in that it encourages more interactivity among users and, as some argue, results in both a deeper learning and a better potential to build online communities (Beer & Burrows, 2007; Kamel Boulos & Wheeler, 2007, pp. 3–4).

Today's media landscape is marked by a number of communication avenues, ranging from advances in satellite television and radio stations to the burgeoning use of cellphones, text messaging, music file sharing, blogs, wikis, podcasts, YouTube, and social networking sites. Let's look at each of these technologies in turn.

SATELLITE TELEVISION AND RADIO

Canadian satellite television programming—through Bell's ExpressVu and Shaw's StarChoice, for example—is an expanding and flourishing industry (Doyle, 2008). Satellite stations target a broad audience and offer hundreds of channels, an increasing number of which are in high definition formats. With channels dedicated to such diverse pursuits as golf, cooking, and NASCAR, it seems that everyone can find something that appeals to them. Further, the advent of personal video recorders (PVRs) means that viewers can "pause" live programming, automatically record shows for later viewing, and even remove commercials. Television has come a long way since traditional networks "pushed" a limited selection of programs into homes. Today, people can watch what they want, when they want.

A significant number of people spend time in their cars and appreciate hearing diverse music selections during their work commutes or while on vacation. Compared with traditional broadcast services, satellite radio stations are available anywhere a car's satellite antenna can pick up a signal (which is just about anywhere, except for mountainous regions or during severe weather conditions). With dozens of stations catering to all musical tastes and without the distractions of ads, satellite radio has become a popular choice for many Canadians since it was introduced in 2005.

CELLPHONES

In 2002, the number of people with cellphones worldwide surpassed the number with fixed phone lines, confirming that cellphones had become the dominant form of voice technology (Srivastava, 2005). Indeed, "the mobile phone has now moved beyond being a mere technical device to becoming a key 'social object' present in every aspect of a user's life" (Srivastava, 2005, p. 111). Users are increasingly attached to their cellphones, often using them as a calendar, an alarm clock, a camera, and even a calorie counter. In this way, the mobile phone has become part of a user's "personal sphere of objects," much like a wallet and keys. Srivastava suggests that "it gives users the impression that they are constantly connected to the world outside, and therefore less alone" (2005, p. 113). In fact, a study by Harkin (2003) revealed that 46 percent of mobile phone users interviewed in the United Kingdom described the feeling of losing their cellphones as a "form of bereavement" (as cited in Srivastava, 2005, p. 113). Devices such as the iPhone or BlackBerry, in addition to being a

Today, cellphones are changing the way people communicate.

phone, allow users to take a few quick "bites" of information or entertainment as part of their "mobile snacking" as they walk to work or wait for a bus (Persaud, 2008, p. 45).

Cellphones have been criticized for contributing to poor spelling and grammar (due to text messaging), for being a distraction from tasks that require concentration, for promoting the demise of intimate face-to-face relationships, and even for causing brain cancer. Nonetheless, their use is becoming ubiquitous within a social landscape that Thompson and Cupples (2008) refer to as **digital sociality**. They argue that this sociality in fact promotes human interaction and contact. For example, as a result cellphones' mobility and efficiency, young people are now more likely to call friends throughout the day than were their parents' generation. Even when you miss a call, you are still "connected"—you can always send a text message.

digital sociality A social landscape in which new communication technologies are promoting human interaction and contact.

TEXT MESSAGING

Text messaging is becoming the most common form of mobile communication among young people. Estimates suggest that more than 1 trillion instant messages were sent worldwide in 2006 (World Association of Newspapers, 2007, p. 3). While some question the negative influence that text messaging has on writing ability (see Gray, 2008; Jones, 2008), others see it as an opportunity for artistic expression. For example, Miyake's (2007) research into text messaging among Japanese youth found that they often expressed their individuality by creating new and artistic forms of written language that deviated from the largely conservative Japanese culture and its distaste for individuality. Japanese youth appear to enjoy the intimacy and creativity of sending visual messages to each other. They also appreciate that text messaging maintains some distance, which they feel helps to alleviate social anxiety (e.g., the embarrassment that comes with "losing face"; see Malley-Morrison & Hines, 2004, p. 202).

How does text messaging qualify as a medium of mass communication? Certainly, the majority of text messaging occurs between two people; however, recent software developments make it possible for an individual or business to convey a message through virtually any text messaging device. For example, TXTlaunchpad (www.txtlaunchpad.com) urges potential buyers of its software to "Reach Your Audience Anytime, Any Place, Anywhere," while Omnilert (www.omnilert.com) says that its service allows "content providers to quickly offer their own private-branded mass communications system."

The April 2007 tragedy at Virginia Tech, in which 32 students were shot and killed by a fellow student, was one of the first instances in which text messaging played a key role in informing the police, other students, and the media as events unfolded. After these killings, police and civic leaders tried to develop a system that could be used to inform citizens if a similar event occurred in the future. During their deliberations, they heard from Bryan Crum, an Omnilert spokesperson, who said, "Nothing is faster and more effective than mass text messaging" (Swartz & Hopkins, 2007). Omnilert already had 30 American schools using its technology to send messages to students regarding weather closures, hazardous waste spills, power outages, and anything else that school administrators deemed appropriate.

MUSIC FILE SHARING

A significant challenge to radio is, of course, the emergence of online music sites that allow users to download portable digital media files and listen to their favourite songs where and when they want.

The revolution began in 1999, when student Shawn Fanning, working out of his dorm room at Northeastern University, created Napster. Fanning was the first to use peer-to-peer (P2P) software that allowed Internet users—millions of them—to share digital music files for free (Van Hoorebeek, 2004, p. 219). Napster's success was extraordinary. Don Dodge, a former Napster vice-president, has said that in 2000 the company went from 1 million to more than 50 million users in just 7 months, making it the fastest-growing application in the history of the Internet.

Napster also represented the biggest threat the recording industry had ever faced. Neither record companies nor artists were receiving any royalty payments for these shared files, an issue that continues to plague the music industry. The recording industry took Napster to court for copyright infringement and ultimately forced it into bankruptcy on June 3, 2002. Today, music file sharing continues to be an important feature of the musical landscape (through companies such as BitTorrent, Blubster, Kazaa, iMesh, iTunes, LimeWire, Morpheus, Puretracks, and Soulseek, to name only a few).

The Canadian Recording Industry Association (www.cria.ca) estimates that file sharing has cost more than $465 million in retail sales and resulted in employee layoffs and lost opportunities for artists. In late 2007, the federal government announced that it would proceed with new copyright legislation, which would make music file sharing illegal within the next few years (CBC News, 2007b).

BLOGS

Estimates from 2007 suggest that the number of blogs had reached more than 70 million; roughly 120 000 new ones were being created every day, with approximately 1.4 million postings per day (Sifry, 2007). A **blog** (a shortened form of *Web log*) is essentially an online diary in which an individual regularly reflects on events, specific topics, and/or personal experiences. Bloggers post their insights in a manner that may, for example, inform others or act as an opportunity to voice dissenting opinions or perspectives.

blog An online diary in which an individual posts personal reflections on events, specific topics, and/or experiences.

Many blogs go unnoticed and are little more than a series of thoughts that few people see; however, some become very popular and may even win a Bloggie (an annual award for the best blog in various categories; see www.bloggies.com). Regular readers of particular blogs can be informed by the Web feed format known as **RSS (Really Simple Syndication)**, which provides either a summary of a new entry or its entire text, thus eliminating the need to continually revisit sites to check for updates.

RSS (Really Simple Syndication) A web feed format that informs subscribers of new information posted on online services.

The blog's principal attraction—the ability to present one's ideas to a global audience and invite a dialogue—means that, over time, these dialogues may take on the characteristics of an online global community (Vandegriend, 2006). Indeed, some of the Web's best-known blogs (e.g., Go Fug Yourself, The Smoking Gun, boingboing) can have tens of thousands of visitors per day and hundreds of posts.

WIKIS

A **wiki** is an online body of information that is designed to allow anyone access to add or modify its content. Arguably, the best-known wiki today is the online encyclopedia Wikipedia. The greatest advantage of wikis over blogs is that wikis allow everyone to participate as a community that is nonhierarchical and nonregulated. Information posted on a wiki is available right away and is open for review and discussion (Cernohous, 2007, p. 2). Wikis, then, are an important resource for people who want to work openly and collaboratively. However, wikis—and Wikipedia in particular, which many students rely on for information—do not necessarily provide reliable information. There is no guarantee that entries are accurate precisely because they can be created and edited at any time and by anyone.

wiki An online body of information to which anyone can add or modify content.

PODCASTS

Podcasts are a technology that allows the automatic downloading of audio and video files that are produced in a series. These files can then be played back on personal computers or loaded onto portable players such as iPods, meaning that people can then listen to or watch

podcast A technology that allows automatic downloading of audio and video files that can then be played back on personal computers or loaded onto portable players.

the programs whenever they like. Podcasting emerged in 2005 and quickly became a popular means by which to stay up to date on news events and areas of personal interest.

Although a number of large companies produce podcasts (which are usually simply captures of existing radio or television programming), many podcasters are amateurs who produce their own material from home studios. So, just as blogging allows anyone with a computer to become a social commentator, podcasting allows people to go beyond text interaction and become disc jockeys, talk show hosts, or recording artists (Watson, 2008). Since most amateur podcasters are not in it to make money, the subject matter, much like that of blogs, ranges from the insightful to the silly. Podcasters generally focus on a niche audience that shares similar interests.

Podcasting is considered a **narrowcast**, in contrast to the *broad*cast of, say, radio signals that are sent over large areas and that anyone with a radio can pick up for free. Individuals subscribe to narrowcasts because these programs target their individual interests. (For a directory of podcasts by topic or interest, see www.podcastpickle.com or www.podcast.com.)

The mass media's targeting of a smaller segment of the audience is a process known as demassification. **Demassification** occurs when an audience is fragmented into small groups or niches that mass media use as a basis to develop specific content. This is not to say, however, that mass media are not still motivated by commercial interests to maximize profits (Wimmer & Dominick, 2006, p. 9). Subscribing to any number of podcasts (or magazines, or satellite channels, or websites) may give an individual the impression of being outside mainstream mass media, and while some certainly are, big business is still responsible for most media content in all of its forms. For example, even YouTube, an apparent alternative to mainstream media, is a vehicle for corporate interests.

narrowcast   A transmission of data to specialized audiences who subscribe to the service.

demassification
A process by which the mass audience is fragmented into small groups or niches to appeal to unique interests.

WHY SHOULD WE CARE?

Cyberbullying

Today's rapid developments in online technologies have engendered myriad changes in how we communicate—yet not all of these changes have been beneficial. Consider classroom bullies, who now have the ability to inflict their pain and suffering well beyond the playground. *Cyberbullying* involves sending or posting harmful or cruel text or images through electronic devices with the intent and purpose of hurting another (Willard, 2005, as cited in Beale & Hall, 2007, p. 9). Cyberbullies can use email, instant messaging, chat rooms (or *bash boards*), websites, and online polls to harass and threaten their victims (Beale & Hall, 2007, p. 9; Chibbaro, 2007).

Although email messages can be traced to a unique mail account, it is virtually impossible to prove who actually sent the note, since anyone with access to a person's passwords may have been responsible. While most email software can block messages from a particular address, bullies can simply set up new accounts or use aliases to bypass any names being blocked by the victim. Bullies can also use chat rooms to initiate real-time forums in which they, and others, can gang up on an individual, usually under the cover of anonymity. Websites can also be constructed to mock and harass others as well as to post unauthorized and often embarrassing pictures of the victim. Finally, online voting tools can rank people and post the results for all to see (Beale & Hall, 2007, p. 9). It is not difficult to imagine how painful these constant attacks must be—and how they have even driven some victims to commit suicide.

While new technologies facilitate more efficient and convenient communication, it is important to realize that for every intended outcome of a given development, there are unintended consequences.

YOUTUBE

YouTube was created in February 2005 by Steve Chen, Chad Hurley, and Jawed Karim, who perceived a need for an easy-to-use website that would allow users to share personal videos. Within the year, registered users were downloading 2 million videos per day, and by July 2006, that number had increased to 100 million. In October 2006, YouTube was purchased by Google for $1.65 billion (Hinderliter, 2007). Today, YouTube is the third-most-visited website in the world (after Yahoo! and Google).

YouTube has also played an important role in challenging oppressive political regimes by making available video clips that show abusive or repressive actions by government representatives (Bentley, 2008, p. 41), military soldiers, or police officers. It appears that the days of conventional mass media controlling all of the information that the world sees may be over.

YouTube's tremendous growth and popularity provide an excellent example of how young people are attracted to new media forms that allow them to control their media experience. YouTube's tag line—Broadcast Yourself—encapsulates users' desire to present themselves to a global audience. It constitutes a fascinating example of how technology is transforming the individual's relationship to the social—which is, after all, the defining interest of sociology.

For the top 500 sites on the Web, go to **www.alexa.com/topsites.**

SOCIAL NETWORKING SITES

Perhaps the best examples of how Web 2.0 technology can link people are the social networking sites MySpace and Facebook. Both sites are designed to provide users with a series of tools to help them connect with friends or to join groups with common interests (e.g., fringe music, sports teams, etc.).

MySpace was launched on August 15, 2003, by Brad Greenspan, who believed that social networking was the future of the Internet. Less than two years later, MySpace was purchased for $580 million by News Corporation, part of Rupert Murdoch's media empire, which also owns Fox Network (Scott-Joynt, 2005). Today, MySpace is the Web's largest social networking site, with more than 117 million users worldwide (Nakashima, 2008).

Facebook was founded by Harvard University psychology student Mark Zuckerberg (then aged 23) in February 2004 (Phillips, 2007). Today, Facebook remains a privately held company and claims to have more than 70 million active users (Facebook, 2008).

MySpace was the first site to make it easy for the common computer user to create a webpage, write a blog, or post photos online. Yet MySpace's appeal to both tech-savvy users and novices is why some prefer Facebook. Until late 2006, Facebook targeted only university and college students, meaning that it had a relatively well-educated and affluent audience. Facebook is both less customizable and more orderly than MySpace, and the graphics look more technical, less commercial, and more "high brow" (Falls, 2008). The class divisions between users on MySpace and Facebook have been demonstrated by other researchers as well (Boyd, 2007).

What do you know about **Mass Media Today**?

Multiple-choice questions (circle your answer)

1. **The percentage of Canadian homes with a personal computer is**
   a. Over 75 percent
   b. 60 percent
   c. 55 percent
   d. Under 50 percent

2. **In 2006, it was estimated that _____ instant messages were sent worldwide.**
   a. 10 million
   b. 100 million
   c. 100 billion
   d. More than 1 trillion

3. As of 2007, the number of blogs had reached _____ worldwide.
a. 10 million
b. 20 million
c. 50 million
d. More than 70 million

4. A transmission of data to specialized audiences who subscribe to the service is called a
a. Podcast
b. Broadcast

c Narrowcast
d. Procast

5. YouTube was created in _____.
a. 1999
b. 2001
c. 2003
d. 2005

Answers: a, d, d, c, d

module 10.3

Think about Sociological Approaches to Mass Media

1 Think about the impact of mass media on society. Do you think that mass media contribute positively to society? If yes, how?

2 Think about mass media and the truth. Do you believe that mass media present you with the truth? What forms of mass media do you believe? Why?

3 Do you think mass media ownership affects the news we receive?

Sociological Approaches to Mass Media

We will now examine how each sociological perspective considers the importance and social impact of mass media.

FUNCTIONALISM

Functionalists view mass media as providing a unique and powerful ability to promote common values and beliefs. Generally, functionalists see four primary areas in which mass media contribute to society: socialization, surveillance, correlation, and entertainment (Perse, 2001, p. 54).

The **socialization function** is achieved by mass media as they transmit values, beliefs, and traditions from one generation to the next. By reinforcing certain messages (e.g., the benefits of democracy and a free market economy), mass media effectively promote social integration and the formation of a common cultural identity (Perse, 2001, p. 56). However, targeting messages to a mass audience often oversimplifies issues. As well, since mass media messages reflect the views of the dominant groups in society, these messages fail to promote alternative perspectives and largely ignore the voice of minority groups.

The **surveillance function** can be understood as the need for society to have a mechanism in place that gathers information for the population (e.g., weather reports, news items) and allows members of society to focus on their own activities and interests. Traditionally, this function was fulfilled by mass media (e.g., newspapers, radio, and television), but, as discussed earlier, research suggests that more and more people are turning to alternative media (amateur podcasts, blogs, and other online resources) to get news and information (World Association of Newspapers, 2007).

socialization function
Mass media's role in transmitting beliefs, values, and traditions from one generation to the next.

Mass media carry out the **correlation function** when they present difficult and complex issues in a way that most people can understand. This filtering is necessary, given not only the sheer number of newsworthy events that occur every day but also the need to present stories as concisely as possible to maintain audience interest. In some respects, the correlation function is a check on the surveillance function, in that there must be some filter through which vast amounts of information pass before reaching us—otherwise, the populace would be overwhelmed by such volume (Perse, 2001, p. 55). Over time, however, the audience may lose its ability to evaluate critically what mass media portrays and simply assume it to be true—which, of course, is not always the case (Bronfen, 2006, p. 22).

The **entertainment function** allows people to rest, relax, and escape the pressures of everyday life (Dyer, 2002, p. 178). The popularity of comedy shows such as *Seinfeld* and *The Simpsons* is a testament to the fact that people enjoy losing themselves in a program. However, the entertainment function may distract people from important events that require action (Perse, 2001, p. 56). For example, spending an entire evening watching television or surfing the Web when you have a term paper to write is probably not the most effective use of your time.

Functionalists, then, view mass media as filling some important needs in society. While some find merit in using functionalist theories to understand the media landscape in contemporary society, others argue that these theories of media are outdated (see Couldry, 2004, p. 124).

CONFLICT THEORY

According to conflict theorists, mass media are vehicles used by the rich and powerful to control the masses and to reinforce their false consciousness.

Consider, for example, daily news broadcasts. Media scholar Michael Parenti argues that in capitalist societies, the corporate news media faithfully reflect the dominant class's ideology in what they choose to cover and in the words they use to describe it—while at the same time giving the impression that they are being fair and objective (Parenti, 1993, 2001, 2007). That is, it is not so much that mainstream media define how we think; rather, it is that they grant legitimacy and exposure to certain views over others. The media also influence our perceptions of events through their use of negative and positive labelling. For example, words and phrases like *stability*, *the prime minister's firm leadership*, and *the healthy economy* all attribute positive slants to the story at hand, while terms like *terrorist*, *gang*, and *civil disturbance* provide a negative spin (Parenti, 2001).

Advertising similarly moulds our opinions through the images it presents. For example, marketing certain products to children in a school setting (Molnar, 2006, p. 623) and casting thin actors on television shows (Venturini, Castelli, & Tomelleri, 2006, p. 391) reinforce, respectively, the positive cultural value of consumerism and the negative perception of people, particularly women, who are overweight (Rasberry, 2008, p. 423).

Conflict theorists argue that taken collectively, media messages influence our perception of our social environment to promote corporate interests and perpetuate class differences. In their book *Manufacturing Consent* (1988), Edward Herman and Noam Chomsky assert that the media intentionally create a social environment favourable to the dominant classes. Indeed, since most mainstream media are owned by large corporations (see Table 10–2), information presented to the public may be slanted to protect the interests of those corporations.

For example, if General Electric was charged with an environmental crime, NBC (which is owned by GE) may choose to not cover the story, or to cover it differently than another network would. According to this reasoning, news stories that endanger the financial interests of the parent company would present the greatest bias and potential for censorship. By manipulating the stories that are covered and the manner in which they are presented, mass media effectively "manufacture" consent through their filtering (Herman & Chomsky, 1988, pp. xi, 2). This filtering generally takes two forms: (1) deciding not to cover a story or (2) presenting a

surveillance function Mass media's role in gathering and disseminating information to the population.

correlation function Mass media's role in filtering and making comprehensible the huge daily volume of news stories and issues.

entertainment function Mass media's role in helping people rest, relax, and escape the pressures of everyday life.

TABLE 10–2 **Key North American Media Corporations**

Corporation	Country of Origin	Key Media Holdings	Market Value
General Electric	US	NBC; History Channel; Universal Pictures; Little, Brown & Co.; Vivendi Universal Entertainment	$390.6 billion
Microsoft	US	WebTV, OnFolio, Massive	$306.8 billion
Google	US	Blogger, Picasa, Dodgeball, YouTube	$154.6 billion
Time Warner	US	AOL, Time Inc., HBO, TBS, Warner Brothers, CNN, Cinemax	$90.7 billion
The Walt Disney Company	US	ABC, ESPN, Pixar, A&E, *US Weekly*, Discover	$72.8 billion
News Corporation	US	Fox TV, *New York Post*, 20th Century Fox, *TV Guide*, MySpace, HarperCollins	$56.7 billion
Viacom	US	CBS, Blockbuster, Comedy Central, Showtime, Dreamworks, Paramount, Simon & Schuster	$53.9 billion
Yahoo!	US	GeoCities, Musicmatch, eGroups, Online Anywhere, LAUNCH Media, del.icio.us, Blo.gs, flickr	$40.1 billion
Thomson	Canada	CTV Globemedia, Reuters, *Globe and Mail*, CHUM	$32 billion*
Rogers Communications	Canada	CityTV, The Shopping Channel, Rogers Sportsnet	$15.3 billion*
CanWest Global	Canada	Alliance Atlantis, Global Communications, *National Post*	$672 million*

* In Canadian dollars

Source: Shah, A. (2007). *Media conglomerates, mergers, concentration of ownership—global issues.* Retrieved August 30, 2008, from http://www.globalissues.org/HumanRights/Media/Corporations/Owners.asp#MediaConglomeratesMegaMergersConcentrationof Ownership; Shecter, B. (2008). *Canwest jumps at universal TV shows.* Retrieved May 14, 2008, from http://www.nationalpost.com/ related/topics/story.html?id=498627; Surridge, G. (2008). *Doubts on Thomson.* Retrieved May 14, 2008, from http://www. financialpost.com/story.html?id=477503; http://your.rogers.com/investorrelations/investor_overview.asp; Hugh Harley, personal communication, May 27, 2008.

story in such a way as to diffuse or bias its content. As you can imagine, such filtering influences how people see and interpret the social world; it helps to define their reality.

Herman and Chomsky (1988, p. 298) suggest, then, that the primary role of mainstream media is to ensure popular support for the economic, social, and political agenda of the privileged classes. This perspective is commonly referred to as the **propaganda model** (Herman, 2003), which asserts that, since the dominant media are commercial enterprises, their content will reflect the interests of the rich and powerful. *Propaganda* can be defined as the large-scale use of messages or images designed to influence the opinions and/or behaviours of the majority of the population. Propaganda isn't simply the provision of information but rather the active creation of content that appears to be truthful and accurate but is instead an intentional manipulation of the facts to promote a particular position or world view.

Let's take the American tobacco industry as one example. In 1979, it created the Social Costs/Social Values Project to construct an alternative cultural repertoire of smoking by using social scientists to create and disseminate non-health-related, pro-tobacco opinions without disclosing their financial relationship with the tobacco industry (Landman, Cortese, & Glantz, 2008). After the Surgeon General reported in 1988 that nicotine was in fact an addictive substance, the tobacco industry formed Associates for Research in the Science of Enjoyment, whose members travelled the world speaking about the health

propaganda model
The assertion that mainstream media companies, as businesses, will transmit content that reflects their commercial interests.

benefits of using legal substances such as tobacco to relieve stress, without ever revealing that the group was formed and funded by the tobacco industry. Landman, Cortese, and Glantz's work (2008) documents how the tobacco industry employed social scientists (including sociologists) to create and disseminate research that presented tobacco in a positive light through reputable scholarly channels (including scholarly articles, books, conference presentations, and interviews in newspapers). This research influenced both public opinion and academic research on the social acceptability of smoking (Landman, Cortese, & Glantz, 2008).

Although the propaganda model is an important contribution to our understanding of media, some contemporary researchers (see Britt, 2003) challenge the assumption that audiences are passive, credulous recipients of media content. These researchers assert that audiences are critical of what they see and hear through the media; they understand that some media bias is inevitable, and thus control for it.

SYMBOLIC INTERACTIONISM

Symbolic interactionists view mass media as an important part of contemporary life, but one that is no more important than any other. This approach rejects all forms of determinism and therefore views media as part of a complex and multi-faceted process in which meaning is defined and granted by those involved in the interaction (Hodson & Vannini, 2007, p. 263).

Symbolic interactionists are interested in exploring how media influence our perceptions of our social world. Rather than separating media from other aspects of social life, they prefer to see it as part of a multi-faceted and complex process (Hodson & Vannini, 2007, p. 263; Saettler, 2004, p. 264). Our engagement with mass media is no different from any other form of human communication in which meaning is actively constructed. Indeed, symbolic interactionists believe that people do not internalize media images passively but rather are actively involved in a dynamic process that views media images and messages, reshapes them, and stores them when they reinforce cultural beliefs (Baran & Davis, 2009; Pascali, 2006, p. 685). In this way, media help to form identities by presenting images and situations that reinforce our cultural ideals of what makes people happy or successful.

One of the clearest examples of how media messages influence our views is our definition of ideal body types. A great deal of sociological and psychological research has found a relationship between media depictions of the thin ideal and body dissatisfaction (Bessenoff, 2006, p. 239; Jung & Peterson, 2007, p. 40) and eating disorders (Derenne & Beresin, 2006, p. 258). In short, people compare their bodies to those they see in the media, a comparison that often leads them to be overly critical of how they look (Bessenoff, 2006, p. 239). With constant exposure to media images of what one is "supposed" to look like, many begin to define themselves by their perceived shortfalls rather than appreciating their own beauty and vitality.

For a very good overview of the effects of media advertising, go to **www.media-awareness.ca** and www.jeankilbourne. com.

Altheide (2003) investigates the effect of electronic communication technologies on what he calls the **e-audience**, which comprises all those who spend time in cyberspace answering email and surfing or talking on their cellphones (which is to say, most of us). According to Altheide, the defining feature of this audience is the perception of control and sense of entitlement that comes from being able to communicate whenever they want (p. 664).

e-audience   Those who use electronic communication technologies.

FEMINIST THEORY

The feminist critique of mass media investigates media's patriarchal nature by highlighting the use of images of women in advertising, the exploitation of women in the pornography industry, and the tendency to present a solely masculine view of the world. For example, Gaye Tuchman (1978) refers to the "symbolic annihilation of women" in her discussion of the way in which media ignore, exclude, and marginalize women and their interests (as cited in Strinati, 2004, p. 162).

Media advertising often portrays women as sex objects in order to sell their product.

Feminist researchers also critique media portrayals of women as they relate to the reality of women's lived experiences. Television shows such as *The Bachelor* and *America's Next Top Model*, for example, not only have little to do with women's actual lives, but also reinforce the view that women need to compete with each other to "catch" a man or must be so beautiful that they could have their pick of men. Such portrayals devalue both women and men. Sexist imagery permeates television shows, Hollywood movies, the Internet, magazines, and, of course, advertising, which includes the multi-billion-dollar cosmetic industry.

Today, online pornography provides an accessible and efficient means for even greater exploitation of women. Feminists argue that pornography is a tool used by men to control, objectify, and suppress women (Lubey, 2006). They have proposed two strategies to diminish the effects of pornography on society.

First, in the 1980s, early anti-pornography feminists rejected the idea of state censorship in favour of adopting a human rights approach that would allow those negatively affected by pornography access to the courts to seek damages (Jensen, 2007). In fact, two noted feminists, Catherine MacKinnon and Andrea Dworkin, helped to draft a Minnesota law that allowed victims of sexual assault and other sex crimes to sue pornographers for damages, reasoning that the culture created by pornography supported sexual violence against women (Brest & Vandenberg, 1987). Feminists appreciate the importance of preserving the right of free expression, but argue that the harm resulting from the exploitation of women requires some legal remedy (Martinson, 2005).

Second, contemporary feminists point to the importance of educating the public about the effects of pornography, not just its effect on those involved in its production but on society as a whole. The intent of these education programs is to inspire a discussion about how mainstream pornography (the vast majority of which targets heterosexual men) is becoming increasingly cruel and degrading to women and is more openly racist than ever (Jensen, 2007). Confronting the pornography industry challenges us to acknowledge the deep misogyny and white supremacy that continue to exist in our society.

CANADIAN SOCIETY IN FOCUS

No Logo and You

Estimates suggest that people receive between 3000 and 5000 product impressions per day (CBS News, 2006; IPC Media, 2006). Naomi Klein, Canadian author of the bestselling book *No Logo* (2000), reveals a great deal about the inner workings of the advertising industry and our increasingly branded society (Marshall, 2008).

Klein demonstrates that brands are much more than just symbols used to market products; they invoke associations with products, but also, by extension, provide information about what the people who purchase them are like. Do you have preconceived ideas about how Tim Hortons customers differ from Starbucks habitués? Do you associate different attributes with each (i.e., working class versus middle class)? If so, you have internalized the brands' images. As Klein argues, brands today represent a lifestyle, a look, and a culture. For example, what does it mean to be a "Tommy Boy" or a "GAP Kid"?

Moreover, corporate sponsorship is changing our perception of public spaces. Klein cites as an example the banning of York University students from campus after they were "caught" distributing no-smoking pamphlets during the du Maurier Open tennis tournament being hosted by the university. In effect, a public university had been branded by a cigarette company. People are even agreeing to become walking billboards for products—for example, in 2002, a young man sold advertising space on his forehead through eBay (Paulson, 2002, p. 361).

Klein also points out the power of Wal-Mart in determining what North American consumers get to see, read, and listen to. As the world's largest retailer, Wal-Mart exerts tremendous influence on magazine, book, movie, and music companies that need their products to be sold in Wal-Mart stores. The chain has been known to refuse media content if it does not comply with the retailer's family-oriented standards (Marshall, 2008).

POST-STRUCTURALISM

One of the most important post-structuralist writers on mass media was French philosopher Jean Baudrillard (1929–2007). Baudrillard perceived that while modern societies focus on the production and consumption of commodities, postmodern societies focus on simulation and the creation and interplay of images and signs. In a world of simulation, identities are constructed by the internalization of images that ultimately determine how people see themselves and others (Kellner, 2007). Baudrillard's analysis of media, then, centred on his concepts of simulation and hyperreality.

Simulation is Baudrillard's term for how media create what we consider real through the reinforcement of certain images and signs. Media convey to us the fashions we should like, the music we should listen to, and the art we should find appealing. According to Baudrillard, the **hyperreal** is the phenomenon that results when people define their experiences based on a perception of the world that has been simulated and constructed by the media (Redhead, 2007, p. 102). Media do not represent social life as it truly exists but rather as it is manufactured. The news media in particular present stories as theatre, whereby glorified, manipulated, and censored events are packaged and displayed.

Baudrillard argued that, dominated as we are by simulated experience and feelings, we have lost the ability to comprehend reality as it truly exists. What we see as "real" on television, for example, is the result of editing and simplification for distribution to the masses. Media content is produced with the lowest common denominator in mind and, as a result, softens rather than challenges our intellect. According to Dominic Strinati (1993), for example, the postmodern view of contemporary television reveals how the medium has become preoccupied with elementary, juvenile themes in place of a deeper understanding of the realities of the human condition.

simulation Baudrillard's assertion that media create a "simulated" world through the reinforcement of certain images and signs.

hyperreal Baudrillard's belief that people's perceptions, as defined by media, lead to the sense of a simulated reality.

Baudrillard did not suggest that what we perceive as reality is simply an illusion; instead, he argued that the illusion has *become* the reality. The line between what is real and what is simulated is blurred, and it becomes increasingly difficult to distinguish between the two (Baudrillard, 1983; Fox & Miller, 2005, pp. 650–654).

CANADIAN INSIGHTS INTO MASS MEDIA: MARSHALL MCLUHAN

One of Canada's most famous scholars in the field of mass media was Marshall McLuhan (1911–1980). McLuhan believed that media influence the ways in which individuals, societies, and cultures perceive and understand their environments (Skinner, 2000, p. 56). According to McLuhan (1964), the reason for studying media was to make visible what was invisible—to go beyond the actual material being transmitted by media and uncover the underlying message. McLuhan thought that to study media content only was to miss the point, since the medium itself was most important. This belief is encapsulated in McLuhan's famous phrase: "The medium is the message."

According to McLuhan, each medium influences the mind in largely unconscious ways. Thus, it is not the simple message (which appeals to the conscious mind) that is important but rather the manner in which it is conveyed (which appeals to the unconscious mind) (Soules, 2007). McLuhan never suggested that the message content was unimportant per se, just that to truly understand the social significance of media, one needed to understand the primary importance of the medium over the message.

McLuhan was concerned about the fact that we often focus on the obvious, and that when we do, we miss important and subtle changes that occur over time. For example, individual messages about murders contained in newscasts are not as significant as the resulting change in the public attitude toward crime, or the creation of a climate of fear (Federman, 2004). McLuhan writes of how a medium's message influences human change:

> The message of any medium or technology is the change of scale or pace or pattern that it introduces into human affairs. The railway did not introduce movement or transportation or wheel or road into human society, but it accelerated and enlarged the scale of previous human functions, creating totally new kinds of cities and new kinds of work and leisure. (McLuhan, 1964, p. 8)

McLuhan's insight into the need to look beyond the simple message to the social influence of the medium itself has important sociological ramifications. The manner in which people communicate shapes not only the society in which they live but how they interact within it. Today, our ability to communicate instantaneously both locally and globally has changed how we perceive our world.

To learn more about Marshall McLuhan, go to **www.marshallmcluhan. com.**

What do you know about Sociological Approaches to Mass Media?

Multiple-choice questions (circle your answer)

1. **Mass media's role in filtering and making comprehensible the huge daily volume of news stories and issues is called the**
   a. Socialization function
   b. Surveillance function
   c. Correlation function
   d. Entertainment function

2. **Which perspective views mass media as fulfilling important needs for society?**
   a. Functionalism
   b. Conflict theory
   c. Feminist theory
   d. Post-structuralism

3. _____ is interested in how mass media influences our perceptions of the social world.
a. Functionalism
b. Conflict theory
c. Symbolic Interactionism
d. Feminist theory

4. _____ argue that pornography is a tool used by men to control, objectify, and suppress women.
a. Feminists
b. Conflict theorists

c. Functionalists
d. Symbolic interactionists

5. Jean Baudrillard used the term _____ to describe how media create what we consider real through the reinforcement of certain images and signs.
a. Simulation
b. Hyperreal
c. Surreal
d. Propaganda

Answers: c, a, c, a, b

module 10.4

The Future of Mass Media

As sociologists, we see the future of mass media as challenging and changing society in a number of ways.

HOMOGENIZATION OF CULTURE

Western media, and in particular American media, are consumed throughout the world. As Croteau and Hoynes note, "Like sand castles on a beach, local cultures are being eroded and flattened by the gradual impact of the endless tide of U.S. and other Western media products" (2003, p. 358). The effect of the proliferation of American culture is that cultures around the world are becoming more alike—homogeneous. For example, shopping malls around the world contain the same megastores catering to increasingly similar consumers.

Canadian media and culture are greatly influenced by their close proximity to the United States; as a result, the federal government has implemented policies and programs to protect media companies and promote Canadian artists in the hope of preserving Canadian culture.

To this end, the Canadian Radio-television and Telecommunications Commission (CRTC) licenses, regulates, and administers the broadcasting industry in Canada. It has put forward strict Canadian content guidelines (popularly known as **CanCon**) that require Canadian radio and television stations to broadcast content written and performed by Canadian artists (CRTC, 2007). These regulations are contained in the Canadian Broadcasting Act, which aims to promote Canadian culture by

1. providing a wide range of programming that reflects Canadian attitudes, opinions, ideas, values, and artistic creativity

Think about the Future of Mass Media

1 Think about the Internet and education. Do you think the Internet has made you a better student? If yes, how? If no, why not?

2 Think about the Internet and cybercrime. Do you think that children need to be protected from the Internet? Why or why not?

CanCon (Canadian content) Federal regulations that stipulate the required percentage of Canadian content in television and radio broadcasts.

2. displaying Canadian talent in entertainment programming
3. offering information and analysis concerning Canada and other countries from a Canadian point of view (CRTC, 2007)

For a piece of music to qualify as Canadian content, it must fulfill at least two of the four criteria of the **MAPL system**:

MAPL system CRTC requirements used to determine whether a piece of music qualifies as Canadian content.

1. the music (M) is composed by a Canadian
2. the artist (A) who performs the music is Canadian
3. the production (P) of the music occurred in Canada (that is, the music was recorded in Canada) or the music is performed in Canada and broadcast in Canada
4. the lyrics (L) are written by a Canadian (CRTC, 2001)

According to the CRTC guidelines, commercial radio stations must ensure that at least 35 percent of the popular music they play is Canadian, as defined by the MAPL system. French radio stations have a higher threshold in that they must play 55 percent Canadian content; if the music includes French-language vocals, the required percentage is 65 percent. Both English and French stations must meet these requirements over the broadcast week and between 6 a.m. and 6 p.m., Monday through Friday (this ensures that Canadian content is not only broadcast late at night). The regulations also stipulate that qualifying musical selections be played in their entirety (CRTC, 1998).

Television content is treated in much the same way. For the CRTC to certify a television program as Canadian, the program must meet all three of the following criteria:

1. the producer is Canadian
2. key creative personnel are Canadian
3. 75 percent of service costs and post-production lab costs are paid to Canadians

Television stations and networks (e.g., CTV, Global, TVA) and ethnic television stations (e.g., CFMT) must achieve an annual Canadian content level of

1. 60 percent overall, measured during the day (between 6 a.m. and midnight)
2. 50 percent, measured during the evening broadcast period (between 6 p.m. and midnight) (CRTC, 2004)

As a government-owned broadcaster, the CBC must ensure that at least 60 percent of its programming, including the evening broadcast period, is Canadian. If broadcasters present Canadian dramas during peak viewing hours (7 p.m. to 11 p.m.), they are eligible for a 125 percent to 150 percent time credit (CRTC, 2004). These credits are intended not only to promote Canadian dramas, but also to encourage that they be shown during prime time. Consistent with the intent of the Broadcasting Act, the CRTC licensed the Aboriginal Peoples Television Network (APTN) in 1999 to promote Aboriginal issues on the national stage; the channel is available to all Canadians.

Not everyone approves of the CanCon regulations. Some claim that they take away the rights of consumers to make their own entertainment choices. Others claim that it is difficult for the CRTC to monitor Canadian content effectively on satellite radio stations, which allow people to select programming from around the world. Finally, still others argue that attempts at cultural nationalism are devoid of any real consequence in our electronic world, because global media content is controlled by a handful of multinational corporations (Fotopoulos, 1999, p. 43).

THE EFFECTS OF MEDIA VIOLENCE

Mass media, as noted in Chapter 4, play a powerful role in our socialization. They teach us about roles, values, and norms, and although we may believe that we are immune to the influence of these messages, research overwhelming suggests that we are not.

Numerous studies have demonstrated a strong correlation between the degree of exposure to television/video game violence and aggressive behaviour (Brady & Matthews, 2006;

Bushman & Huesmann, 2006; Huesmann et al., 2003). A 2003 longitudinal study of 329 youths over a 15 year span reported the following:

> Childhood exposure to media violence predicts young adult aggressive behaviour for both males and females. Identification with aggressive TV characters and perceived realism of TV violence also predict later aggression. These relations persist even when the effects of socio-economic status, intellectual ability and a variety of parenting factors are controlled. (Huesmann et al., 2003)

INTERNET ADDICTION

People are becoming addicted to the Internet (Block, 2008; Chou, Condron, & Belland, 2005). Heavy Internet users (the majority of whom send text messages, surf pornography, or play online games) can suffer from withdrawal symptoms when they do not have Internet access; they lie to friends, family, and partners about their use; and they suffer from poor achievement, depression, fatigue, and social isolation (Block, 2008; Meenan, 2007, p. 1117).

While the Internet can provide a wonderful opportunity to share with others, there is concern that with this openness comes risk (Whitlock, Lader, & Conterio, 2007). For example, recent research found that the more time adolescents spend on the Internet, the less satisfied they are with their lives (Wang, Chen, Lin, & Wang, 2008) and the more likely they are to be overweight (Fontaine & Allison, 2002, p. 611). According to recent estimates, the average North American teenager spends between five and six hours daily in front of a screen—on the Internet, playing video games, watching television or DVDs, etc. (Bauerlein, 2008; Ottawa Citizen, 2008).

Email addiction is a concern for teens and adults alike. In Japan, government officials have become so concerned about the addiction to Internet-linking cellphones that they are encouraging parents to limit a child's access to the devices (Toronto Star, 2008). A survey of 1300 business people by Reuters news agency found that two-thirds of respondents reported checking email after hours, on weekends, and on holidays. Executives at a large, multinational pharmaceutical company, Pfizer Inc., instituted a "Freedom Six to Six" ban that disallowed the sending of work-related email messages between 6 p.m. and 6 a.m. and on weekends (Maclem, 2006). The degree to which working adults have become reliant on and perhaps addicted to email communication was highlighted during the BlackBerry outage in April 2007. BlackBerry, developed by Canadian company Research In Motion, is a wireless smart phone with email capability. Many users reported that during the outage they felt lost and isolated. Others reported feeling liberated. In general, users have reported the addictive effects of the device that has been nicknamed "Crackberry" (a reference to the highly addictive drug crack). As of 2007, 8 million people used BlackBerries (Mayerowitz, 2007).

Online gaming is another form of Internet addiction. Massively Multiplayer Online Role-Playing Games (MMORPGs) that allow players to create virtual identities and become immersed in an online fantasy world have been proven to be very addictive. Estimates suggest that there are 12.5 million MMORPG players worldwide (Meenan, 2007). MMORPGs are designed so that gamers can access higher levels, and more money, weapons, skills, and power through increased playing time. At the game's highest levels, players must band together to go on raids that can require 10 or more hours of continuous play; some players have reported playing for more than 70 hours per week (Meenan, 2007).

In the fall of 2008, Brandon Crisp, a 15-year-old Barrie, Ontario, boy was found dead after a three-week search for his whereabouts. The boy, a runaway, was alleged to have been addicted to online gaming (Doolittle & Wilkes, 2008). According to Crisp's parents, the boy was addicted to the online game "Call of Duty: Modern Warfare." The countless hours he had spent on the game had affected his social relationships, school work, and extracurricular activities. Concerned about the boy's changing behaviour, his parents took away his game console. In response to his parent's actions, Crisp ran away from home. Three weeks later he was found

Internet gaming addiction is becoming a growing concern.

dead from apparent injuries caused after falling from a tree. Although his death was accidental, Crisp's parents see his death as a direct consequence of his addiction (Doolittle & Wilkes, 2008).

Online gaming addiction is a problem that did not exist a decade ago and as of yet has not been recognized as a condition by the medical community. Nonetheless, it is estimated that worldwide there are 16 million gaming addicts. Canada's first support group for gaming addicts, Online Gamers Anonymous, was started in London, Ontario, on November 5, 2008, to provide support to those with a gaming addiction (Pedro, 2008). Coincidentally, it was the same day that Brandon Crisp's body was found.

INTERNET PORNOGRAPHY

> The way you know if your technology is good and solid is if it's doing well in the porn world. (Susan Struble, Sun Microsystems spokesperson, as cited in Bedell, 2001)

Internet pornography is big business. Forbes estimated in 2001 that the online porn industry was worth over US$1 billion per year (Ackman, 2001). The question remains, however, whether this is an issue of concern.

Tony Tremblay (1999) would agree with Susan Struble's quotation in that all new media forms are initially pushed to their limits in their ability to convey sexual imagery and to titillate a new audience. He points out, for example, that some of the earliest movies produced were peep shows: *Serpentine Dance* (1895) and *Pull Down the Curtains, Suzie* (1904) (Tremblay, 1999, p. 168). Consistent with our approach to mass media in this chapter, Tremblay's investigation teaches us that Internet pornography should be understood in a historical context.

He argues that all new media begin by pushing the social boundaries of morality because they offer new avenues for people to explore their sexuality. Through his concept of **cybriety** (a neologism that combines *cyber* and *sobriety*), he captures the social response to these challenges of morality, which generally involve attempts to censor new media content (Tremblay, 1999, p. 168). His historical analysis shows that as a new technology matures and becomes

cybriety Tremblay's term describing attempts to censor new media content that pushes the boundaries of morality.

more commonplace, society adjusts and moral boundaries are broadened accordingly. Each medium is doomed to fail when the next new technology that promises more erotic potential emerges; that is, from written letters and stories to still pictures, movies, videos, cable, and the Internet, each new technology surpassed its predecessor. Yet Tremblay argues that despite the pervasiveness of online pornography, all technology ultimately fails because it cannot fulfill the human need for companionship and physical contact: "Internet censorship, or cybriety, is not new; it is a re-run of our favorite drama, the psychoanalytic morality play that teeters between our desires and our fears of their fulfillment" (Tremblay, 1999, p. 181).

CYBERCRIMES

Internet users are vulnerable to a number of online crimes. Consumer Reports conducts an annual survey of Internet users in the United States. Based on its research, American Internet users lost $8.5 billion over the past two years because of viruses, spyware, and email scams. One in seven Internet users reported problems with viruses, which cost an estimated $2.9 billion in repairs and computer replacements. One in 14 Internet users reported serious problems with spyware; and 566 000 computers were replaced because of spyware issues at an approximate cost of $3.6 billion. One in 13 Internet users gave personal information to online scammers, with 14 percent reporting that they had lost money. **Phishing**, sending authentic-looking but fraudulent email designed to steal personal information, resulted in $2 billion in personal losses (Consumer Reports, 2008).

The vulnerability of people—especially young people—to sexual predators is also a significant issue. The University of New Hampshire's Crimes Against Children Research Center estimated that 13 percent of children between the ages of 10 and 17 had received unwanted sexual solicitations while online (Maich, 2006). In 2007, MySpace found 29 000 sex offenders on its site, and that figure included only those that used their real names (CBC, 2007d).

To learn more about how the RCMP deals with cybercrime, go to **www.rcmp-grc.gc.ca/on/prog-serv/support-soutien/itcu-gict-eng.htm.**

phishing Sending authentic-looking but fraudulent email designed to steal personal information.

INCREASED MOBILITY AND ACCESS TO INFORMATION

The technology of the future will provide people with even greater ability to move wherever they like and remain connected to their friends, family, work, and school in ways that will continue to break down geographic barriers. Further, barriers to information will continue to fall as more and more people seek to be able to find out what they want when they want it. For example, online courses are now provided by most Canadian colleges and universities to address student access issues (e.g., people in very small communities without a campus, or those who require greater flexibility due to health issues, child-care responsibilities, or work schedules). Further, as cellphone technology continues to expand, the separation between the information people can gather from their computers and their phones will decline.

FOSTERING ONLINE COMMUNITIES

Web 2.0 technologies and social software have a tremendous potential to bring people together. Wikis, blogs, and podcasts are just the tip of the social-software iceberg that could emerge in the coming months and years (Kamel Boulos & Wheeler, 2007). A Statistics Canada (2008e) study found that 20 percent of home Internet users had contributed content to the Internet by posting images, writing blogs, or participating in discussion groups. Over 50 percent of these contributors were under the age of 30.

DEMOCRATIC POTENTIAL

The power of media to transform society and to challenge repressive regimes was first demonstrated in the 1950s with the civil rights movement and then in the 1960s when the American public rallied against its own government to oppose the war in Vietnam. Television ushered in an age in which people could watch the world's events unfold in their living rooms, and what they saw often inspired them to rise up and seek change. From the young man in Tiananmen Square who stood in front of Chinese tanks to amateur videos of the aftermath of Hurricane Katrina, new media technologies enable people to capture and post images to the Internet that could challenge existing power structures and lead to progressive social change.

In a Statistics Canada (2008l) study entitled "Internet Use and Social and Civic Participation," researchers found that 40 percent of Internet users went online in the past year to research community events. Over 50 percent of Internet users stated that they had used the Internet to research social and political issues in the past year.

What do you know about **the Future of Mass Media**?

Multiple-choice questions (circle your answer)

1. **Canadian content guidelines that require Canadian radio and television stations to broadcast content written and performed by Canadian artists is popularly known as**
   a. CanCon
   b. ConCan
   c. CRTC
   d. CBA

2. **In what Canadian city did Canada's first support group for gaming addicts appear?**
   a. Toronto
   b. Montreal
   c. London
   d. Barrie

3. **The _____ represents CRTC requirements used to determine whether a piece of music qualifies as Canadian content.**
   a. MAPL system
   b. CRTC system

   c. APTN system
   d. CANC system

4. **Sending authentic-looking but fraudulent email designed to steal personal information is called**
   a. Phishing
   b. Fishing
   c Scamming
   d. Spying

5. **A study conducted by Statistics Canada found that _____ of home Internet users had contributed content to the Internet by posting images, writing blogs, or participating in discussion groups.**
   a. A small fraction
   b. 20 percent
   c. 50 percent
   d. A majority

Answers: a, c, a, a, b

Summary

| module 10.1 | MASS MEDIA THROUGH TIME |

1. The earliest communication technology took the form of prehistoric cave art, followed much later by Egyptian hieroglyphics (an early form of visual communication) and later still by the phonetic alphabet developed by the Greeks.
2. Block printing gave way to movable type, which resulted in the dissemination of books and newspapers.
3. The inventions of the telegraph, phonograph, radio, moving pictures, television, and the Internet have resulted in communication systems today that allow users simultaneous, ongoing contact.

module 10.2   MASS MEDIA TODAY

4. Today's communication technologies include music file sharing, text messaging, blogs, wikis, podcasts, and social networking sites—all of which are changing the way people interact online.
5. A *blog* is an online diary in which an individual posts personal reflections on events, specific topics, and/or experiences.
6. A *wiki* is an online body of information to which anyone can add or modify content.
7. A *podcast* is a technology that allows automatic downloading of audio and video files that can then be played back on personal computers or loaded onto portable players.

module 10.3   SOCIOLOGICAL APPROACHES TO MASS MEDIA

8. Functionalists view mass media as contributing to society in four primary areas: socialization, surveillance, correlation, and entertainment.
9. Conflict theorists, in contrast, view mass media as a mechanism by which to uphold the ideology of the dominant class.
10. Symbolic interactionists are primarily interested in how mass media influence our definitions of ourselves and others.
11. Feminist theory targets mass media as an expression of patriarchy in its dissemination of sexualized imagery of women.
12. Post-structuralists focus on how media create an imaginary world in which simulated experiences are perceived as real.
13. Marshall McLuhan argued that we need to recognize the primacy of the medium in understanding content ("The medium is the message").

module 10.4   THE FUTURE OF MASS MEDIA

14. The future of mass media is likely to entail a continuation of current trends—both negative and positive.
15. Homogenization, the erosion of global cultural diversity by Western mass media, is one concern.
16. One way that Canada has reacted to the onslaught of American mass media is to establish Canadian Content (CanCon) regulations.
17. There is a strong correlation between watching violence on screen and acting aggressively.
18. Internet and gaming addictions are a new and growing problem. Support groups have emerged and the medical community is beginning to react to this increasing trend.
19. Internet crimes, spying, viruses, phishing, and pornography are but some of the new crimes related to this technology.
20. In terms of positive effects, increasingly the Internet is being used as a tool to foster online communities and enhance democracy.

Key Terms

block printing 293
blog 301
CanCon (Canadian content) 311
correlation function 305
cybriety 314
demassification 302
digital sociality 300
e-audience 307
entertainment function 305

hieroglyphics 293
hyperreal 309
MAPL system 312
mass communication 292
mass media 293
movable type 293
narrowcast 302
papyrus 293
phishing 315

podcast 301
propaganda model 306
RSS (Really Simple Syndication) 301
simulation 309
socialization function 304
surveillance function 305
Web 2.0 298
wiki 301

Test Yourself

1. *Mass media* is defined as
   a. The transmission of messages by a person or group through a device to a large audience
   b. Devices designed to communicate messages to a mass audience
   c. Any medium designed to communicate to a mass audience
   d. Both b and c

2. Television was invented by
   a. Thomas Edison
   b. Paul Gottlieb Nipkow
   c. Samuel Morse
   d. Heinrich Rudolph Hertz

3. The printing press was developed around
   a. 1250
   b. 1450
   c. 1670
   d. 1740

4. The first Canadian newspaper published in 1752 was the
   a. *Halifax Gazette*
   b. *Montreal Gazette*
   c. *Toronto Telegram*
   d. *Globe and* Mail

5. Canada's first television station began broadcasting from Montreal in
   a. 1928
   b. 1932
   c. 1948
   d. 1952

6. Some researchers argue that cellphone use promotes human interaction and contact. This form of behaviour has been referred to as
   a. Digital sociality
   b. Push technology

   c. Digital socialization
   d. Digital enhancement

7. Music file sharing started with which of the following companies?
   a. LimeWire
   b. BitTorrent
   c. Morpheus
   d. Napster

8. An online body of information to which anyone can add or modify content is called a
   a. Blog
   b. Wiki
   c. Podcast
   d. Web log

9. A process by which the mass audience is fragmented into small groups or niches to appeal to unique interests is called
   a. Narrowcasting
   b. Podcasting
   c. Demassification
   d. Broadcasting

10. Less than two years after its creation, YouTube was purchased by _____ for $1.65 billion.
    a. Yahoo!
    b. Google
    c. LimeWire
    d. News Corporation

11. Mass media's role in gathering and disseminating information is called the _____ function.
    a. Socialization
    b. Surveillance
    c. Correlation
    d. Entertainment

12. Which perspective would argue that mass media are vehicles used by the rich and powerful to control the masses?
    a. Functionalism
    b. Conflict theory
    c. Symbolic Interactionism
    d. Feminist theory

13. The phenomenon that results when people define their experiences based on a perception of the world that has been simulated and constructed by the media is called
    a. Simulation
    b. Hyperreal
    c. Simulated reality
    d. Illusion

14. Who said "the medium is the message"?
    a. Harold Innis
    b. Marshall McLuhan
    c. Jean Baudrillard
    d. Naomi Klein

15. Which perspective is most likely to investigate the exploitation of women's images in advertising?
    a. Feminist theory
    b. Conflict theory
    c. Functionalism
    d. Symbolic Interactionism

16. Between 6 a.m. and midnight, Canadian television broadcasters must have a minimum of _____ Canadian content.
    a. 20 percent
    b. 40 percent

    c. 60 percent
    d. 80 percent

17. MMORPG stands for
    a. Massively Multiplayer Organized Role-Playing Games
    b. Maximum Multiplayer Organized Role-Playing Games
    c. Many Multiplayer Online Role-Playing Games
    d. Massively Multiplayer Online Role-Playing Games

18. Tony Tremblay's term for attempts to censor new media content that pushes the boundaries of morality is
    a. Pornography
    b. Cybriety
    c. Sobriety
    d. Anti-sobriety

19. The University of New Hampshire's Crimes Against Children Research Center estimated that _____ of children between the ages of 10 and 17 had received unwanted sexual solicitation while online.
    a. 10 percent
    b. 13 percent
    c. 20 percent
    d. 22 percent

20. _____ of Internet users stated that they had used the Internet to research social and political issues in the past year.
    a. 10 percent
    b. 25 percent
    c. 40 percent
    d. A majority

Answers: d, b, b, d, a, d, b, c, b, b, b, d, a, c, d, b, b, c

Log in to MySocLab for a host of resources that will help you save time and improve your grade. MySocLab contains cutting-edge learning tools such as study plans, practice tests, videos, audio segments, quizzes, and more—all designed to help you better understand the learning objectives for this chapter. Along with your eBook, MySocLab for *Sociology for Everyone* can be found at **www.mysoclab.com**.

module 10.1
MASS MEDIA THROUGH TIME

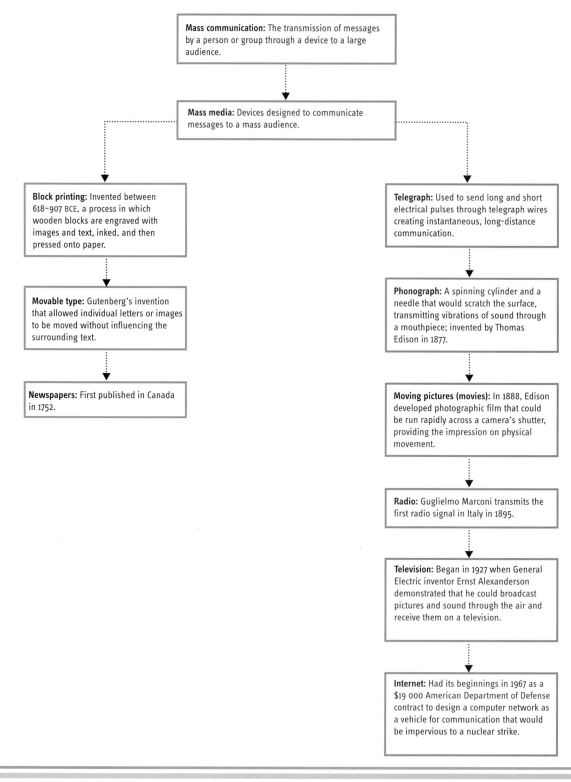

Mass communication: The transmission of messages by a person or group through a device to a large audience.

Mass media: Devices designed to communicate messages to a mass audience.

Block printing: Invented between 618–907 BCE, a process in which wooden blocks are engraved with images and text, inked, and then pressed onto paper.

Movable type: Gutenberg's invention that allowed individual letters or images to be moved without influencing the surrounding text.

Newspapers: First published in Canada in 1752.

Telegraph: Used to send long and short electrical pulses through telegraph wires creating instantaneous, long-distance communication.

Phonograph: A spinning cylinder and a needle that would scratch the surface, transmitting vibrations of sound through a mouthpiece; invented by Thomas Edison in 1877.

Moving pictures (movies): In 1888, Edison developed photographic film that could be run rapidly across a camera's shutter, providing the impression on physical movement.

Radio: Guglielmo Marconi transmits the first radio signal in Italy in 1895.

Television: Began in 1927 when General Electric inventor Ernst Alexanderson demonstrated that he could broadcast pictures and sound through the air and receive them on a television.

Internet: Had its beginnings in 1967 as a $19 000 American Department of Defense contract to design a computer network as a vehicle for communication that would be impervious to a nuclear strike.

module 10.2
MASS MEDIA TODAY

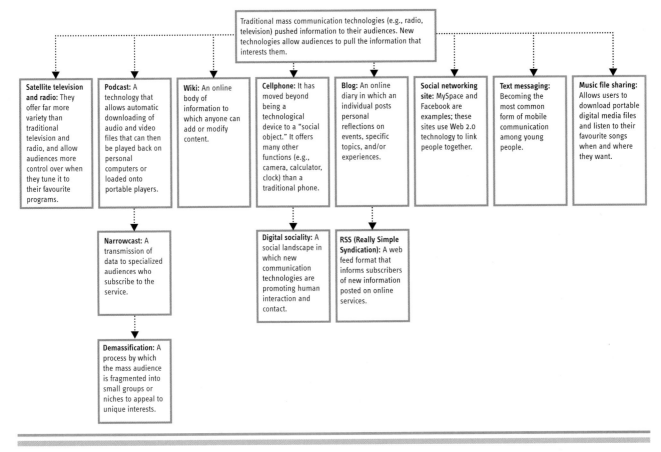

Traditional mass communication technologies (e.g., radio, television) pushed information to their audiences. New technologies allow audiences to pull the information that interests them.

Satellite television and radio: They offer far more variety than traditional television and radio, and allow audiences more control over when they tune it to their favourite programs.

Podcast: A technology that allows automatic downloading of audio and video files that can then be played back on personal computers or loaded onto portable players.

Wiki: An online body of information to which anyone can add or modify content.

Cellphone: It has moved beyond being a technological device to a "social object." It offers many other functions (e.g., camera, calculator, clock) than a traditional phone.

Blog: An online diary in which an individual posts personal reflections on events, specific topics, and/or experiences.

Social networking site: MySpace and Facebook are examples; these sites use Web 2.0 technology to link people together.

Text messaging: Becoming the most common form of mobile communication among young people.

Music file sharing: Allows users to download portable digital media files and listen to their favourite songs when and where they want.

Narrowcast: A transmission of data to specialized audiences who subscribe to the service.

Digital sociality: A social landscape in which new communication technologies are promoting human interaction and contact.

RSS (Really Simple Syndication): A web feed format that informs subscribers of new information posted on online services.

Demassification: A process by which the mass audience is fragmented into small groups or niches to appeal to unique interests.

module 10.3
SOCIOLOGICAL APPROACHES
TO MASS MEDIA

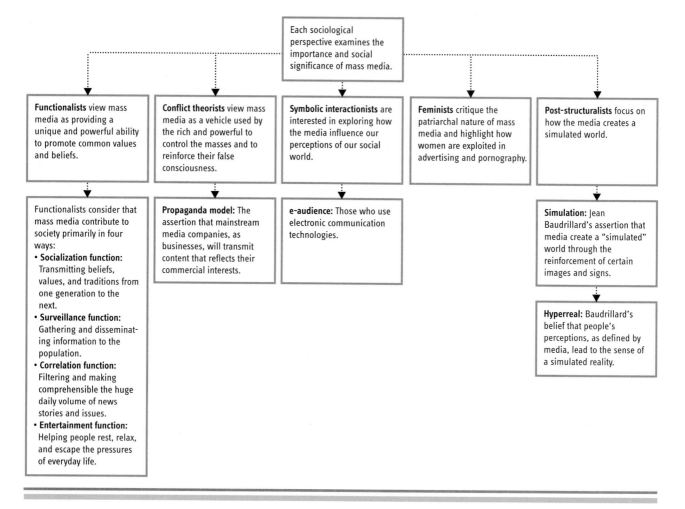

Each sociological perspective examines the importance and social significance of mass media.

Functionalists view mass media as providing a unique and powerful ability to promote common values and beliefs.

Conflict theorists view mass media as a vehicle used by the rich and powerful to control the masses and to reinforce their false consciousness.

Symbolic interactionists are interested in exploring how the media influence our perceptions of our social world.

Feminists critique the patriarchal nature of mass media and highlight how women are exploited in advertising and pornography.

Post-structuralists focus on how the media creates a simulated world.

Functionalists consider that mass media contribute to society primarily in four ways:
• **Socialization function:** Transmitting beliefs, values, and traditions from one generation to the next.
• **Surveillance function:** Gathering and disseminating information to the population.
• **Correlation function:** Filtering and making comprehensible the huge daily volume of news stories and issues.
• **Entertainment function:** Helping people rest, relax, and escape the pressures of everyday life.

Propaganda model: The assertion that mainstream media companies, as businesses, will transmit content that reflects their commercial interests.

e-audience: Those who use electronic communication technologies.

Simulation: Jean Baudrillard's assertion that media create a "simulated" world through the reinforcement of certain images and signs.

Hyperreal: Baudrillard's belief that people's perceptions, as defined by media, lead to the sense of a simulated reality.

module 10.4
THE FUTURE OF MASS MEDIA

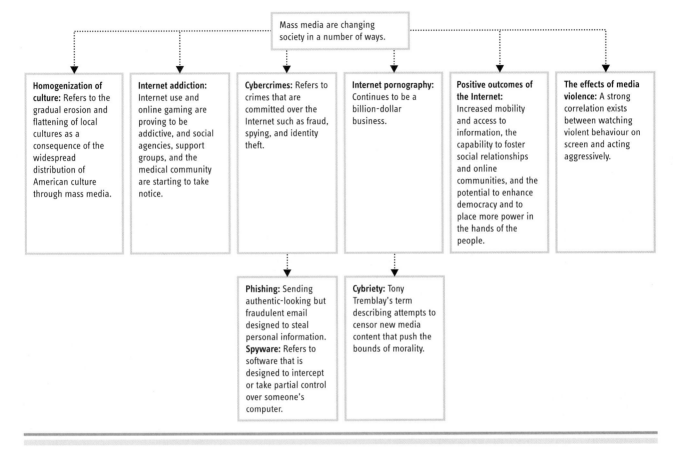

Mass media are changing society in a number of ways.

Homogenization of culture: Refers to the gradual erosion and flattening of local cultures as a consequence of the widespread distribution of American culture through mass media.

Internet addiction: Internet use and online gaming are proving to be addictive, and social agencies, support groups, and the medical community are starting to take notice.

Cybercrimes: Refers to crimes that are committed over the Internet such as fraud, spying, and identity theft.

Internet pornography: Continues to be a billion-dollar business.

Positive outcomes of the Internet: Increased mobility and access to information, the capability to foster social relationships and online communities, and the potential to enhance democracy and to place more power in the hands of the people.

The effects of media violence: A strong correlation exists between watching violent behaviour on screen and acting aggressively.

Phishing: Sending authentic-looking but fraudulent email designed to steal personal information. **Spyware:** Refers to software that is designed to intercept or take partial control over someone's computer.

Cybriety: Tony Tremblay's term describing attempts to censor new media content that push the bounds of morality.

chapter 11

Aging, Disabilities, and Health Policy

Challenging Stereotypes: The Stories of Shirley and Oscar

Below are the stories of two people, a 73-year-old woman and a man who lost his legs at a young age. What makes these stories interesting is that they challenge our perceptions about two groups of people: the elderly and the disabled.

Shirley Lewis, age 73, is an excellent example of someone who has not stopped being active simply because she has retired. She continues to work part-time, reviewing children's books for libraries and schools across Canada. She has also travelled to Ethiopia four times with Volunteer Service Overseas (VSO) to help set up and maintain university libraries, and founded and serves as executive director of the Children of Ethiopia Education Fund. She is also an editor of *Contact*, the newsletter of the Older Women's Network, and she sings with an award-winning barbershop quartet. Shirley's story is typical of a growing number of seniors, particularly those who are university educated, who continue to work and volunteer, and who report being healthy and happy.

Oscar Pistorius, a South African, had both legs amputated when he was very young. Later in life, he was fitted with carbon-fibre limbs, trained hard, and today is able to run almost as fast as the finest Olympic sprinters. In fact, in January 2008, the International Association of Athletics Federations declared Pistorius ineligible for the Olympics because his prosthetic limbs were deemed better than human legs and thus gave him an unfair advantage. In 2008, the Court of Arbitration for Sport overturned this decision, but in July 2008 he was unable to make his country's relay team. Nonetheless, given Pistorius's athletic ability, would you still consider him disabled?

While we may see Shirley Lewis and Oscar Pistorius as exceptional examples of the groups they represent, they remind us that people may be limited more by the perceptions and expectations of others than their own abilities.

module 11.1

Think about Aging in Canada

1 Think about the concept of "old." How would you define "old"? How do you think we discriminate against those that are elderly?

2 Think about retirement. Do you think we should require people to retire at a certain age or do you think people should be able to work at a job for as long as they wish?

Aging in Canada

Shirley Lewis is one of a growing number of seniors who are as active in retirement as they were when they worked full-time. We need to appreciate that a new kind of older adult is emerging today—one who is healthier, better educated, and more financially secure than ever before (Arsenault, Anderson, & Swedburg, 1998, p. 101).

The proportion of seniors (65 years and older) in the Canadian population increased from just over 7 percent in 1946 to more than 13 percent in 2006, and is projected to exceed 27 percent by 2056. If these predictions are correct, the importance of the elderly in society will continue to grow. And the elderly population will become more diverse; according to Statistics Canada, the proportion of seniors who are visible minorities and of Aboriginal descent will also continue to rise (Turcotte & Schellenberg, 2007).

SENIORS' WELL-BEING AND HEALTH STATUS

Most Canadian seniors today are happy and healthy. Figure 11–1 shows that men and women between the ages of 65 and 74 report the highest scores on measures of well-being. We can infer from these results that people between the ages of 25 and 54 (most of whom are hard at work building careers and starting families) are not yet experiencing the freedom one enjoys upon retirement—nor, it must be added, the wisdom that often comes with age.

These feelings of well-being among seniors are no doubt influenced by their physical health. Figure 11–2 illustrates that seniors with a university degree are more likely to report excellent or very good health than are those with less than a high school education. You can see that more than half of the seniors with a university degree reported excellent or very good health, a level similar to those aged 25 to 54 who had not completed high school.

Why might seniors with a university degree enjoy better health? Research has shown that people with higher education have a greater awareness of health risks and are more likely to make use of medical services (Statistics Canada, 2005e). Educated seniors are also more likely to have a higher income (Statistics Canada, 2006f), which is linked to better health (Statistics Canada, 2007i). As well, they are more likely to engage in physical exercise (Statistics Canada, 2007k), which is another important factor contributing to healthy aging (Statistics Canada, 2005e).

Since more people are completing post-secondary education today, and indications are that this trend will continue (Statistics Canada, 2008i), it is possible that society as a whole, including seniors, will report being increasingly healthy in the future.

To read "A New Vision of Aging for Canada" by the Canadian Association of Retired Persons, go to **www.carp.ca/About/index. cfm.**

FIGURE 11–1 **Canadians' Scores on the Well-Being Scale, by Age Group and Sex, 2002**

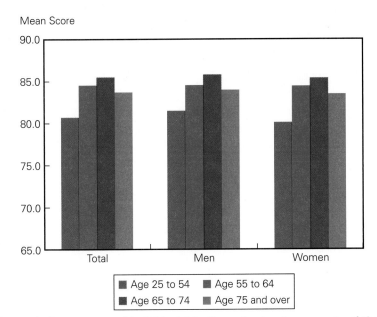

The well-being scale is a measure of individuals' feelings about various aspects of their lives, such as the frequency with which they feel self-confident, satisfied with their accomplishments, and loved and appreciated; and have goals and ambitions. The scale ranges from a minimum of 3 to a maximum of 100.

Source: Turcotte, M., & Schellenberg, G. (2007). *A portrait of seniors in Canada.* Retrieved June 24, 2008, from http://www.statcan.ca/english/freepub/89-519-XIE/89-519-XIE2006001.htm.

FIGURE 11–2 **Percentage of Canadians Reporting Excellent or Very Good Health, by Age Group and Level of Education, 2003**

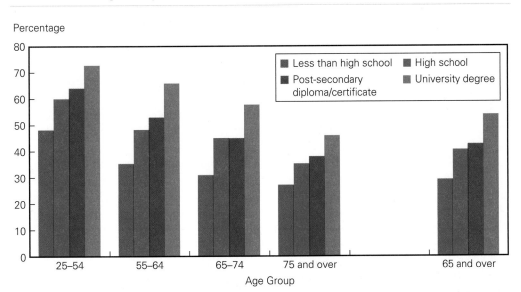

Source: Turcotte, M., & Schellenberg, G. (2007). *A portrait of seniors in Canada.* Retrieved June 24, 2008, from http://www.statcan.ca/english/freepub/89-519-XIE/89-519-XIE2006001.htm.

ISSUES FACED BY SENIORS

Despite the good news discussed above, six issues stand out for seniors as areas of concern: transition to retirement, financial pressures, age discrimination, vulnerability to crime, chronic pain and the need for long-term care, and preparing to die.

TRANSITION TO RETIREMENT   In Canada, labour laws do not specify a retirement age for employees. However, some laws or government policies governing specific occupations set an age limit for persons employed in those occupations (Human Resources and Social Development Canada, 2007). Forcing employees to retire due to their age is considered by many to be a human rights issue, since it discriminates against people on the basis of age. For this reason, virtually all Canadian provinces have done away with mandatory retirement legislation.

For many, leaving a career is difficult; after all, so much of who we are is defined by what we do. While most people retire voluntarily, others are forced to do so as a result of corporate downsizing (Turcotte & Schellenberg, 2007, p. 123). Unsurprisingly, those who choose to retire are likelier to report that they enjoy life more. However, a small percentage of people who retire enjoy life less; these people have fair to poor health, do not have much financial support, and did not plan adequately for retirement (Turcotte & Schellenberg, 2007).

FINANCIAL PRESSURES   In general, income declines after retirement. Among Canadian workers with average incomes, family income falls after age 60, continues to decline until age 68, and then stabilizes at about 80 percent of the income level they had at age 55 (LaRochelle-Côté, Myles, & Picot, 2008, p. 4). In contrast, low-income individuals (those in the poorest 20 percent) experience little change in income throughout their retirement, largely due to the income-maintenance effects of the Canadian pension system. After periods of income instability in their late fifties and early sixties, their income tends to stabilize after retirement. Wealthy individuals experience a substantial loss of income; however, they often have significant personal wealth upon which to draw.

More recent groups of retirees are experiencing higher income levels than earlier cohorts, largely because of higher private pensions (LaRochelle-Côté, Myles, & Picot, 2008, p. 4). In fact, the relatively greater financial resources of today's seniors challenge an earlier concern that an aging population would place undue pressure on younger workers to support it.

elderly dependency ratio
The ratio of seniors to workers.

The **elderly dependency ratio** measures the proportion of seniors (aged 65 and older) to workers (aged about 20 to 64) (Wu & Li, 2003, p. 24). As the proportion of seniors in the population increases, the number of workers supporting them falls. According to some, given our aging society, the number of seniors being supported will ultimately outweigh society's ability to provide for them (Huber & Hennessy, 2005, p. 100).

The elderly dependency ratio in Canada was 14.7 seniors per 100 workers in 1960 and 20.3 in 2000, and it is projected to increase to 43.7 in 2040.

Although Canada's rising elderly dependency ratio is reason for some concern, the Canadian government has taken measures to ensure that the Old Age Security system remains stable. As well, legislative changes to the Canada Pension Plan in 1998 increased payments from workers to ensure that the fund would meet future obligations (Chappell, McDonald, & Stones, 2008, p. 376). Further, Canadians are using the tax benefits of Registered Retirement Savings Plans (RRSPs) as well as employer-sponsored retirement plans to save money for their retirement. The growth of retirement plans across all sectors suggests a certain level of financial security for the vast majority of Canadian seniors. This is further confirmed by the fact that compared with other age groups, seniors have had the most substantial decline in those living with low incomes over the past 25 years (as shown in Figure 11–3).

As you can see, in 1980 more than 20 percent of seniors were living under the low income cut-off, but by 2003 this had declined to just over 5 percent. The decline was largely due to government transfer programs, employer plans, and RRSP savings (Human Resources and Social Development Canada, 2006b; Statistics Canada, 2007p). Over the past 25 years, retirement

FIGURE 11–3 **Incidence of Low Income*, by Age Group, Canada, 1980 to 2003**

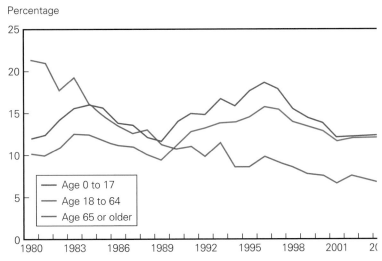

* Low income cut-off after tax, 1992 base.

Source: Turcotte, M., & Schellenberg, G. (2007). *A portrait of seniors in Canada*. Retrieved June 24, 2008, from http://www.statcan.ca/english/freepub/89-519-XIE/89-519-XIE2006001.htm.

income has grown faster than any other income source for seniors. In 1980, retirement income made up less than 15 percent of total income for senior couples, but by 2005 it had increased to more than 30 percent. Over the past 25 years, in constant 2005 dollars, average retirement income more than tripled (Statistics Canada, 2008g). In fact, some seniors continue to support their children and grandchildren financially (Galt, 2008, p. B5). Of course, some seniors do live with low incomes and, as might be predicted from our earlier discussions, they tend to be women and recent immigrants.

AGE DISCRIMINATION   While seniors may face many forms of discrimination, the most obvious is ageism. **Ageism** is a system of inequality based on age that privileges the young at the expense of the old (Calasanti, Slevin, & King, 2006, p. 13). In contrast to other serious "isms" such as racism (Chapter 9) and sexism (Chapter 8), ageism may touch everyone if they live long enough. After all, as we learned in Chapter 4, much of our society is grounded in our social infatuation with youth. Consider how media portray the young in contrast to how they present the elderly—for example, how often are senior citizens the stars of television shows? Yet in many societies around the world, the elderly are not diminished and dismissed as ours are, but instead are considered to be knowledgeable and deserving of honour and respect (Palmore, 2004, p. 41).

Seniors in our society are routinely subjected to negative stereotypes regarding their physical and mental abilities. The power and prevalence of these cultural stereotypes affect not only how seniors are treated but also how they see themselves (Horton, Baker, & Deakin, 2007, p. 1021).

VULNERABILITY TO CRIME   Although older people are less likely than younger people to be victims of violent crime (see Figure 11–4), they experience more fear of it and feel vulnerable when they leave their homes (Public Health Agency of Canada, 2005; Smolej & Kivivuori, 2006).

However, older people are more likely than younger people to be the targets of other types of crime. For example, seniors make up 60 percent of victims who lose money in telemarketing scams. Some estimates suggest that investment schemes and home improvement and telemarketing scams cost Canadians $3 billion—and that people over age 60 lose 84 percent of

ageism A system of inequality based on age that privileges the young at the expense of the old.

FIGURE 11-4 Self-Reported Incidents of Violent Victimization[1], 2004

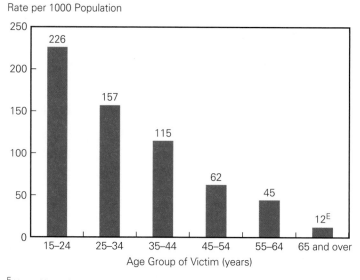

Rate per 1000 Population

Age Group of Victim (years)

[E] Use with caution.

1. Violent offences include sexual assault, physical assault, and robbery.

Source: Statistics Canada. (2007). *Seniors as victims of crime*. Retrieved August 30, 2008, from http://www.statcan.ca/Daily/English/070306/d070306b.htm.

this total dollar amount, or about $2.5 billion (CARP, 2005). In 1998, the Canadian Association of Retired Persons (www.carp.ca) created a National Forum on Scams and Frauds, whose recommendations included providing more information to seniors, instituting cooling-off periods for contracts, and freezing the assets of scam artists.

elder abuse Any form of mistreatment that results in harm or loss to an older person.

Another form of victimization particular to seniors is **elder abuse**, defined as any form of mistreatment that results in harm or loss to an older person. E.K. Podnieks and her colleagues found that in the late 1980s, 4 percent of Canadian seniors (about 98 000) suffered from some form of abuse (as cited in Novak & Campbell, 2006, p. 310). In 2005, close to half (44 percent) of the homicides of seniors were committed by a family member. Of seniors killed by a family member, 37 percent of female victims were killed by a spouse and 37 percent were killed by an adult son or stepson. Among male victims, 57 percent were killed by an adult son or stepson. More than half of family violence incidents against seniors do not cause physical injury, and where injuries are sustained, they are generally minor (Statistics Canada, 2007d).

Victims of elder abuse may be vulnerable to complications resulting from physical violence, since physical injuries may worsen pre-existing health problems or inhibit an older person's ability to function independently. Many analysts believe that elder abuse is underreported because victims, due to fear or shame, are often unwilling to report it to the police. Although some analysts initially believed that younger people were likely to exploit older people who were psychologically and economically dependent on them, just the opposite has often proven true: younger people are more likely to exploit elders upon whom they themselves are dependent (Novak & Campbell, 2006. p. 311).

CHRONIC PAIN AND THE NEED FOR LONG-TERM CARE According to the 2001 Census, 93 percent of seniors live in private households, while the remaining 7 percent reside in collective dwellings (primarily health care institutions such as nursing homes and hospitals). Institutional residency is related to age, increasing from 2 percent among young seniors (aged 65 to 74) to 32 percent among old seniors (aged 85 and older) (Turcotte & Schellenberg, 2007). When seniors can no longer take care of themselves, they often make use of long-term care resources either in their home or in an institutional setting.

Long-term care is defined as the provision of any services required by persons who are dependent on others to meet their basic daily needs (e.g., bathing, dressing, eating, using the toilet, and moving around the home). Long-term care is often provided in combination with such basic medical services as changing wound dressings, pain management, provision of medications, rehabilitation, and palliative care (Huber & Hennessy, 2005, p. 17).

long-term care The provision of any services required by persons who are dependent on others to meet their daily needs.

In Canada, health care, including long-term care, is under the jurisdiction of the provinces and territories (Health Canada, 2004). Although health care plans vary across the country, all jurisdictions provide some support for long-term care institutions, palliative care, respite care, home-care nursing, rehabilitation services such as physiotherapy and occupational therapy, and personal care services (Huber & Hennessy, 2005, p. 116). According to the Organisation for Economic Co-operation and Development (OECD), Canada spends 1.23 percent of its GDP on long-term care (of which 0.99 percent is public funding and 0.24 percent is private). This compares favourably with the average 1.25 percent of GDP for the 19 OECD countries that have similar public/private health care systems. Among these countries, Sweden spent the highest percentage of GDP on long-term care (2.89 percent) and Mexico spent the lowest (less than 0.20 percent) (Huber & Hennessy, 2005, p. 26).

One of the primary objectives of long-term care providers is to help their patients deal with chronic pain, a debilitating condition that affects many aspects of people's lives. **Chronic pain** is generally defined as ongoing pain that lasts longer than three months after the usual recovery period for an injury or ailment (Geertzen, Van Wilgen, Schrier, & Dijkstra, 2006, p. 364). Constant pain is a significant concern for seniors who already may be coping with various changes as they age, including disease, cognitive impairment, and side effects from various medications.

chronic pain Ongoing pain that lasts longer than three months after the usual recovery period for an injury or ailment.

Chronic pain is common among Canadian seniors, affecting 27 percent who live at home and 38 percent who live in health care institutions. Its incidence is likely to grow as Canada's population ages. Many seniors no doubt understand that some of the diseases they face cannot be cured, but they certainly experience a better quality of life if their pain can be adequately assessed and controlled (Ramage-Morin, 2008).

PREPARING TO DIE   As people age they inevitably begin to ponder their own death. Some go to great lengths to ensure that they are well prepared (e.g., by putting their wills and estates in order), while others deny their own mortality. No matter how a person prepares or fails to prepare for death, many worry about *how* and *when* they are going to die.

As Canada's population ages, one issue that may see more political pressure is the right to die. In Canada, euthanasia and physician-assisted suicide are both illegal (Pereira, 2003, p. 167). **Euthanasia** (a Greek word whose roots mean "good death") is generally defined as the deliberate ending of the life of a person who has an incurable or painful disease (see Keown, 2000, p. 390). For many, the idea of planning for their own death, on their own terms, is both comforting and empowering. Support for the legalization of euthanasia and physician-assisted suicide is strong in some parts of Canada. Recent polls in Quebec show 80 percent of the people of that province in support of legalizing euthanasia (Friesen & Seguin, 2009). The Quebec College of Physicians also supports the legalization of euthanasia. In a recently drafted report, it argues that euthanasia could be considered an appropriate form of care in certain circumstances (Freisen & Seguin, 2009).

euthanasia The deliberate ending of the life of a person who has an incurable or painful disease.

Some countries around the world have decided to make euthanasia legal. In April 2001, the Netherlands became the first country in the world to legalize euthanasia; a year later, Belgium did the same. In 2005, the number of reported euthanasia cases in the Netherlands was 1933 (*Time*, 2006, p. 12). Whether Canadians will follow the lead of these countries is impossible to say. However, as our population ages, increased political pressure to legalize euthanasia may emerge.

SOCIOLOGICAL APPROACHES TO AGING

disengagement theory
The assertion that successful aging requires the gradual withdrawal from social activity.

FUNCTIONALISM   Functionalists stress harmony between society's institutions and the need for smooth transitions from one generation to the next. One functionalist approach concerned with aging is **disengagement theory**, which proposes that successful aging requires the gradual withdrawal from social activity (Cumming & Henry, 1961; Duay & Bryan, 2006, p. 423). This theory suggests that older people want to be released from roles that require hard work and responsibility; consider, for example, the London Life Insurance Company's ad campaigns touting "Freedom 55." According to functionalists, the transition to retirement is a welcome one, and not only for those who relinquish the pressure of stressful roles. Retirement also ensures that jobs are made available to younger people just starting their working careers.

One criticism of disengagement theory is that just like Shirley Lewis, many older people enjoy becoming more involved with friends and family as well as social and political issues (Carstensen, 1995, p. 152). Given the declining birth rate and rising elderly dependency ratio, as well as the increased number of jobs that depend on brain power rather than muscle power, it is likely and perhaps necessary that people will continue to work after age 65. Accordingly, as discussed, most provincial governments have eliminated mandatory retirement.

CONFLICT THEORY   The conflict perspective highlights the roots of institutional ageism in that it focuses on the constant tension between the old and the young. For example, as workers age, they are slowly removed from positions of power and influence to make way for younger "up and comers," creating economic competition between different age categories (Moody, 2006, p. 249). Conflict theory also suggests that the pressure either to exclude or to embrace the elderly is a direct consequence of labour market conditions. That is, during times of economic prosperity, older workers are enticed to stay on, but during a downturn, when fewer jobs are available, these workers become much less attractive (Morrow-Howell, Hinterlong, & Sherraden, 2001, p. 55).

Some ads challenge the negative view of the elderly and promote images demonstrating their health and vitality.

SYMBOLIC INTERACTIONISM   Symbolic interactionists stress that one's identity is constructed by performing many interacting roles. In contrast to disengagement theory, **activity theory** holds that people should remain engaged and active for as long as possible (Wicks, 2006, p. 263). Indeed, this theory, which rests on the assumption that remaining active and engaged has important positive benefits and leads to happier lives, has been influential in designing programs and services for older people (Duay & Bryan, 2006, p. 423; Neugarten, Havighurst, & Tobin, 1968).

activity theory   The belief that people should remain engaged and active for as long as possible.

Activity theory asserts that people construct perceptions about themselves through the activities they do and the roles they play. As we remarked at the beginning of this chapter, since so much of who we are is defined by what we do, the transition from a full-time job to retirement challenges many people's perceptions of themselves. The retiree is no longer a manager, doctor, or engineer, but instead a *retired* manager, doctor, or engineer. Thus, it is very important for aging people to maintain activities, and to take on new ones, that reinforce their sense of self as valuable and important. Of course, all activities are not considered equal; joining a lawn bowling club, for example, may not be as rewarding as volunteering as chair of a community association.

An obvious limitation of this theory, and one that it cannot be expected to address, is that over time everyone becomes less able to remain active as a result of the inevitable physical degeneration that occurs in very old age.

FEMINIST THEORY   The feminist perspective on aging explores, for example, how women respond to an aging body in a society fixated on appearance and youth. While much feminist literature accentuates the cultural preference granted to the masculine, we should appreciate that young, attractive women also possess social power. As women age, they lose this power; as well, as they reach menopause, they are devalued because they can no longer bear children. Contemporary feminist scholars explore what this transition means to women's perceptions of self as they age (Winterich, 2007, p. 54). Many feminists assert the value of "agelessness," in that all perceptions of age are socially constructed and therefore open to change (Calasanti, Slevin, & King, 2006, p. 16).

POST-STRUCTURALISM   Post-structuralist thinkers approach the concept of aging as embedded in a framework of truth and knowledge that develops through circulating power relations within society. One of these "truths" about aging is that older people consume more of society's health care resources, which to some suggests that older people should remain in the labour force to help pay their way (Carroll, 2007, p. 73). Since so many seniors do so well into their eighties and beyond, post-structuralist theorists question how transitions such as growing old are defined, and if they are changing. Some contemporary researchers (Carroll, 2007) challenge negative stereotypes about the elderly; indeed, the fact that they are a dynamic and engaged population may represent a deconstruction of the entire category of what it means to be old (Holstein, 2005, p. 38; Morris, 1998, p. 236).

What do you know about **Aging in Canada**?

Multiple-choice questions (circle your answer)

1. In 2006, the proportion of seniors (65 and older) in Canada reached more than	2. Any form of mistreatment that results in harm or loss to an older person is called
a. 7 percent	a. Elder abuse
b. 10 percent	b. Geriatric abuse
c. 13 percent	c. Elder harm
d. 27 percent	d. Senior abuse

3. **One theory of aging asserts that successful aging requires the gradual withdrawal from social activity. This theory is called**
a. Activity theory
b. Engagement theory
c. Conflict theory
d. Disengagement theory

4. **The belief that people should remain engaged and active for as long as possible is called**
a. Engagement theory
b. Disengagement theory
c. Activity theory
d. Involvement theory

5. **Which of the following statements is false?**
a. Seniors with university degrees reported very good or excellent health.
b. People are required to retire at 65 in Canada.
c. Recent groups of retirees are experiencing higher income levels than groups of retirees before them.
d. Over the past 25 years, retirement income has grown faster than other income sources for seniors.

Answers: c, a, d, c, b

module 11.2

Think about Disabilities in Canada

1 Think about the term *disabled*. What do you consider to be a disability? Do you think people who are obese fit that definition?

2 Think about the discrimination received by people with mental illnesses. In what ways do you think people with mental illnesses are discriminated against at work or school?

people first philosophy
An approach that focuses on the individual and his or her abilities rather than limitations.

disability A mental or physical condition that limits people's everyday activities and restricts what they can do.

Disabilities in Canada

As sociologists, we understand better than most how the society around us influences how we see ourselves. So far, we have reviewed how people are influenced by factors such as culture, socio-economic status, families, gender, sexuality, race, and mass media. However, we cannot neglect to appreciate how some in society react to people with disabilities, nor how this interaction must in part define how people with disabilities see themselves. In approaching disability studies, we introduce the concept of the **people first philosophy**. To operate from a people first perspective is to place the individual before the disability, to focus on a person's abilities rather than limitations, and to use the phrase "people with disabilities" rather than refer to people as "disabled" (Russell, 2008, p. 40).

WHAT IS A DISABILITY?

While aging affects everyone, disabilities are commonly thought to affect relatively few people. Only a small percentage of those with a disability were born with it; accidents, disease, and violence account for most disabilities in Canada. What is a disability, and how many Canadians have one?

A **disability** is defined as a mental or physical condition that limits people's everyday activities and restricts what they can do (Statistics Canada, 2008p). The Participation and Activity Limitation Survey (PALS) found that among Canadians aged 15 and older,

- 3 million reported problems with pain, mobility, and agility
- 1.26 million reported problems with hearing
- 815 000 reported problems seeing
- 480 000 reported problems with speaking or communicating (Statistics Canada, 2008p)

FIGURE 11–5 **Disability Rates in Canada, by Age and Sex, 2006**

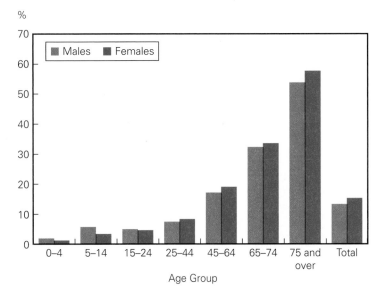

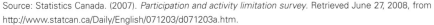

Source: Statistics Canada. (2007). *Participation and activity limitation survey.* Retrieved June 27, 2008, from http://www.statcan.ca/Daily/English/071203/d071203a.htm.

Research has also found that virtually all disability rates are increasing. Between 2001 and 2006, the overall disability rate for Canadian adults (aged 15 and older) rose from 14.6 percent to 16.5 percent (Statistics Canada, 2007j). This increase is no doubt a result of two main factors. First, with advances in medical technology, many children born with a serious disability or many people injured in accidents are more likely to survive today than they were in the past. Second, as the population ages, a higher percentage of people are more likely to experience chronic diseases (such as arthritis) that may have disabling consequences (see Figure 11–5) (Albrecht, 1992).

For people between ages 15 and 64, the most common disability that limited daily living was pain, affecting about three-quarters of all respondents. Among those 65 and older, the most common disability was limited mobility (i.e., cannot walk without pain, difficulty standing for long periods or going up or down stairs) (Statistics Canada, 2007n). About 60 percent of those with disabilities used or needed technical aids or specialized equipment to assist them with daily living. Of those needing assistive aids, about 30 percent did not have all of the aids they needed. The most frequently cited reason (about 56 percent of respondents) was cost, since these aids are not covered by health care insurance (Statistics Canada, 2008p).

MENTAL ILLNESS According to the Canadian Community Health Survey (CCHS), 4.5 percent of people interviewed reported having experienced symptoms or feelings associated with major depression, almost 5 percent had experienced anxiety, and when substance dependence was included, 1 in 10 Canadians aged 15 and older had experienced mental problems at some time within 12 months of the interview (Statistics Canada, 2003a). (See Table 11–1.)

Table 11–1 indicates that women have higher rates of mood and anxiety disorders, while men are more than twice as likely to have a substance dependency. When mental disorders and substance dependence are combined, however, there is very little difference between women (11.1 percent) and men (9.7 percent) (Statistics Canada, 2003a). The same study found that seniors aged 65 and older suffered much less than did youth aged 15 to 24. Whereas 3 percent of seniors experienced mental disorder or substance abuse problems,

TABLE 11–1 Measured Mental Disorders or Substance Dependence in the Past 12 Months

Disorders or Substance Dependence	Total		Males		Females	
	Number	%	Number	%	Number	%
Major depression	1 120 000	4.5	420 000	3.4	700 000	5.5
Mania disorder	190 000	0.8	90 000	0.7	100 000	0.8
Any mood disorder	1 210 000	4.9	460 000	3.8	750 000	5.9
Panic disorder	400 000	1.6	130 000	1.1	270 000	2.1
Agoraphobia	180 000	0.7	40 000	0.4	140 000	1.1
Social anxiety disorder (Social phobia)	750 000	3.0	310 000	2.6	430 000	3.4
Any anxiety	1 180 000	4.7	440 000	3.6	740 000	5.8
Alcohol dependence	640 000	2.6	470 000	3.8	170 000	1.3
Illicit drug dependence	170 000	0.7	120 000	1.0	50 000	0.4
Substance dependence	740 000	3.0	540 000	4.4	200 000	1.6
Total—Any measured disorder or substance dependence	2 600 000	10.4	1 190 000	9.7	1 410 000	11.1

Source: Statistics Canada. (2003). *Canadian community health survey: Mental health and well-being.* Retrieved June 27, 2008, from http://www.statcan.ca/Daily/English/030903/d030903a.htm.

downward drift hypothesis The assertion that those with mental illnesses, unable to finish their education or secure a job, tend to drift into low-income groups.

obesity A state characterized by a BMI of 30 percent or more in an adult.

BMI (body mass index) Calculated by dividing an individual's weight (kg) by height (m²).

about 18 percent of youth did (which supports the finding that seniors experience a high level of well-being). As well, people in low-income groups are found to have higher rates of mental disorders than those in high-income groups. However, this relationship could be explained by the **downward drift hypothesis**, which asserts that because people with mental illnesses are unable to function properly, complete their education, or keep a job, they tend to drift into the low-income groups.

OBESITY A relatively new disability is affecting almost half of the Canadian population, and is considered by some to be a worldwide epidemic (see Dumme, 2008, p. 1177): obesity. **Obesity** is defined as a state characterized by a body mass index (BMI) of 30 percent or more in an adult (Barness, 2007, p. 78). **BMI** is calculated by dividing an individual's weight in kilograms (kg) by his or her height in metres squared (m²). A person with a BMI of 18.5 or less is considered to be underweight; someone with a BMI of 18.6 to 24.9 is considered to be of normal weight; someone with a BMI of 25.0 to 29.9 is considered to be overweight; and someone with a BMI of 30.0 or more is considered to be obese. Being overweight has been linked to heart disease, Type 2 diabetes, certain forms of cancer, and stroke (Agarwal, 2007, p. 65; Zohrabian, 2005, p. 104).

In 2004, 2.7 percent of Canadians aged 15 and older were found to be underweight, 46.7 percent normal weight, one-third overweight, and 14.9 percent obese. Whereas 15.9 percent of men were obese, 13.9 percent of women were obese (Statistics Canada, 2004b). In 2005, the CCHS released figures obtained with actual measurements and found not only higher rates of obesity (23 percent for Canadian adults) but also significant increases in some age groups in comparison with figures obtained in 1978–79. Figure 11–6 shows the increases in obesity for those aged 12 to 17 (from 3 to 9 percent), 25 to 34 (from 9 to 21 percent), and 75 and older (from 11 to 24 percent) over the past 25 years (Statistics Canada, 2005a).

The figures from the CCHS in 2007 show no change in the percentages of those overweight (32 percent) and obese (16 percent) among Canadians aged 18 and older (Statistics Canada, 2008d). And obesity is not just a problem in Canada; it is found in all high-income countries. Between 30 and 80 percent of the European population also suffers from obesity. This creates a major economic burden and consumes 2 to 8 percent of overall health care budgets (World Health Organization, 2006).

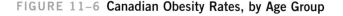

FIGURE 11–6 **Canadian Obesity Rates, by Age Group**

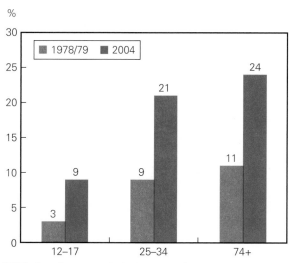

Obesity rate more than doubled for some age groups

Source: Statistics Canada. (2005). *Canadian community health survey: Obesity among children and adults.* Retrieved June 28, 2008, from http://www.statcan.ca/Daily/English/050706/d050706a.htm.

DISCRIMINATION AGAINST PEOPLE WITH DISABILITIES

As discussed in Chapter 9, discrimination occurs when a person or group either denies or grants advantages to members of a particular group (Feagin & Feagin, 2008; Giddens, 1997, p. 582). Section 15 of the Canadian Charter of Rights and Freedoms protects anyone who has a physical or mental disability from being discriminated against (Canadian Heritage, 2007). Although federal and provincial laws have been enacted to protect the rights of people with disabilities, they are extremely difficult to enforce. Often, victims of discrimination are too embarrassed to report it (Woodcock, Rohan, & Campbell, 2007, p. 372). In Canada, 36 percent of people without disabilities reported witnessing discrimination against those with disabilities, and 52 percent of Canadians with disabilities reported that they have personally experienced regular or occasional forms of discrimination (Canadian Council on Learning, 2007).

The term **ableism** refers to discrimination against those who have a mental or physical disability on the basis of preconceived, stereotypical notions about their limitations (Castañeto & Willemsen, 2006, p. 1229). People with a disability may indeed have certain limitations, but the belief that one form of disability means that a person is therefore incapable of other tasks is often unfounded (e.g., in addition to many other occupations, blind people can become medical doctors[1], psychologists,[2] and sociologists[3]). The emotional impact of being discriminated against helps to explain why people with physical disabilities are more likely to report feeling lonely than are those from the general population (Rokach, Lechcier-Kimel, & Safarov, 2006, p. 681).

In 2001, 10.7 percent of people with disabilities between ages 25 and 64 were unemployed, compared with 5.9 percent for those without disabilities. Among people 25 to 54 years

ableism Discrimination against those who have disabilities on the basis of preconceived notions about their limitations.

---

[1] Tim Cordes graduated with a medical degree from the University of Wisconsin-Madison in 2005.
[2] Paul Gabias holds a Ph.D. in psychology as well as an LL.D. and teaches at the University of British Columbia, Okanagan.
[3] Rod Michalko holds a Ph.D. in sociology and teaches at St. Francis Xavier University.

WHY SHOULD WE CARE?

Life Expectancy, Obesity, and Our Kids

Life expectancy (the average lifespan of a newborn) has increased since we began to keep birth and death records. In 1920, the average life expectancy in Canada was 60 years (Statistics Canada, 2005d). By 2008, that number jumped to 80.4 years (CBC, 2008a). Reasons for this increase include better sanitation and nutrition, and advancements in medicine and medical technology (Conference Board of Canada, 2009). However, we may be at a crossroads in the health history of our nation. The expectation that our children will live longer, healthier lives than ours may no longer be realistic. The health of our children has become threatened by obesity.

To read the *Healthy Weight for Healthy Kids* report, go to **www.ccfn.ca/pdfs/ HealthyWeightsForHealthy Kids.pdf.**

Rob Merrifield, chair of the House of Commons Standing Committee on Health, stated that "For the first time in our recorded history, our younger generations are expected to live shorter lives than their parents" (CBC, 2007c). In his report *Healthy Weight for Healthy Kids*, Merrifield declared that the number of obese children in Canada has reached epidemic proportions.

In 1978, 12 percent of children and adolescents (ages 2 to 17) were overweight, and 3 percent of the age group were obese (a combined overweight/obesity prevalence of 15 percent). In 2004, 18 percent of children in this age group were overweight, and 8 percent were obese (a combined overweight/obesity prevalence of 26 percent). Among First Nation peoples, the numbers are much higher: 55 percent of children living on reserves were either overweight or obese (Merrifield, 2007).

The report noted that overweight children become overweight adults, and that the costs of obesity to the health care system are heavy. Obesity triggers a variety of chronic but preventable illnesses such as diabetes, heart attack, stroke, and mental illness. According to the report, obesity currently costs Canadian taxpayers $1.6 billion annually in direct health costs and an additional $2.7 billion in indirect costs (such as lost productivity, disability insurance, and mental health problems) (Merrifield, 2007).

According to the report, the rise in obesity rates among children is attributed to poor diets, namely those high in sugar, fat, and calories. Moreover, children are not getting enough exercise and are spending too much time watching television and playing video games. Other determinants of healthy weight include socio-economic factors such as income, neighbourhood, and the level of education of parents. The higher the income and education level of a child's parents, the lower the obesity rate (Merrifield, 2007).

The report made several recommendations to the federal government to tackle the problem, including

- A comprehensive public awareness campaign
- Mandatory, standardized, simple front-of-package labelling
- The removal of trans fats from the Canadian diet

The House of Commons Standing Committee on Health called for an end to the rise in childhood obesity by 2010, and a reduction in the rate of childhood obesity to 6 percent from 8 percent by 2020.

From what you have seen in food labelling and public awareness campaigns, do you believe that the federal government is doing enough to deal with the epidemic of childhood obesity?

of age in 2001, 47 percent of those with disabilities had incomes below $15 000, compared with 25 percent of those without disabilities (Statistics Canada, 2004d, p. 18). A Human Resources and Social Development Canada report entitled *Advancing the Inclusion of People with Disabilities 2006* investigated the opportunities available to people with disabilities. The report

People with a disability continue to face discrimination. However, there are some positive signs that employers are beginning to realize the tremendous contributions they can, and do, make to their organizations.

shows that while the percentage of people with disabilities is increasing in the workplace and other social venues, it is still lower than for those without disabilities. For example, in 2004,

- Compared to 65.3 percent of people without disabilities, only 46.4 percent of those with disabilities were employed.
- People with disabilities were underrepresented in the labour market, based on all employers covered by the Employment Equity Act (e.g., federal government ministries, chartered banks, First Nations, airlines, television and radio stations) (see Canadian Human Rights Commission, 2007).
- The number of people with disabilities working in the private sector increased from 1.6 percent in 1987 to 2.5 percent in 2004.
- People with disabilities who were employed worked in a variety of occupations; for example, 41.9 percent were in clerical positions, 22.4 percent in manual labour and trades, and 16.2 percent in professional designations (e.g., doctor, lawyer, engineer) (Human Resources and Social Development Canada, 2006a).

These results show that while progress has been made, there is still some way to go before people with disabilities are treated equally within the labour market.

SOCIOLOGICAL APPROACHES TO DISABILITIES

FUNCTIONALISM   The functionalist perspective on disabilities is typified by Talcott Parsons' concept of the sick role. The **sick role** is a patterned social role that defines the behaviour that is appropriate for and expected of those who are sick. In this way, it is similar to all other social roles (e.g., student, mother) that include certain rights and responsibilities (Parsons, 1951). Those who are sick are temporarily exempt from usual role expectations (e.g., they can miss shifts at work) and generally are not seen as being responsible for being ill. Conversely, those who are sick are expected to want to get better, to seek out competent experts to help them recover, and to comply with these experts' recommendations (Parsons, 1951, p. 436). Functionalists would assert, then, that the sick role reinforces society's desire to give people time to recover while accentuating the need to seek professional help and to return to the roles they possessed before they became ill.

Critics of this perspective suggest that this concept is not adequate for people with disabilities, since it does not apply very well to those with lifelong physical or mental conditions (Wade, 2007, p. 295).

sick role   A patterned social role that defines the behaviour that is appropriate for and expected of those who are sick.

CONFLICT THEORY   As discussed, people with disabilities have higher rates of unemployment and low income than do people without disabilities. Moreover, many people with disabilities need specialized equipment (e.g., wheelchairs, hearing aids) that they may not be able to afford (Statistics Canada, 2008p). For conflict theorists, these facts underscore the fact that economic inequality affects people with disabilities differently.

The conflict perspective also stresses the work of disability advocacy groups. For example, many spokespersons for people living with disabilities objected to Richard Latimer's so-called mercy killing of his daughter (discussed earlier) by emphasizing that having cerebral palsy does not mean that a person cannot enjoy life and certainly does not justify taking the life of that person (see Council of Canadians with Disabilities, 1998).

SYMBOLIC INTERACTIONISM   Reflecting symbolic interactionists' emphasis on development of the self, Segall and Chappell expanded Parsons' concept of the sick role to include those with long-term disabilities. They emphasize not only the use of diverse mechanisms of social support (e.g., outpatient services), but also the assumption of more self-health responsibilities for people with disabilities (Segall & Chappell, 2000, p. 25). Self-health management includes such practices as maintaining a balanced diet, exercising, getting regular checkups, and seeking help from others when necessary in order to promote one's own health and happiness.

Symbolic interactionists also focus on how labelling can affect how people with disabilities are viewed and how they view themselves. Consider the use of disabilities in a metaphorical, and usually disparaging, way. For example, to say that someone is deaf or blind to the facts, or that a strike has crippled production, is to use a disability as a negative stereotype. As you may have thought, this approach has been criticized as constructing a problem; after all, people generally do not intend to be offensive when they use physical metaphors such as "spineless," "stiff-necked," and "weak-kneed."

FEMINIST THEORY   The feminist perspective on disability emphasizes that our perceptions of what constitutes a disability are socially constructed in the same way that gender is. Feminists believe that we need to look beyond a narrow definition of disability. For instance, feminists point to the way we categorize people into the binary opposites of abled/disabled or ill/healthy. Feminists would assert that definitions of disability are a form of oppression that results from society's being ill-equipped to deal with anyone who is different, in whatever form that difference may take (McHugh, 2007, p. 28). In Canada, the Disabled Women's Network Ontario (http://dawn.thot.net) provides a wealth of information on contemporary feminist theory and disability studies. DAWN Ontario states, "As feminists, we are concerned with exclusion and inequality based on gender, as well as other factors such as class, race, education, or *ability* that limit women's full participation in the legal, social, political, economic and cultural benefits of society" (DAWN, 2003; emphasis added).

One criticism of the feminist approach to people with disabilities is that it may be overly theoretical, and as such may not lead to the kinds of practical changes that would improve the lives of those living with disabilities.

POST-STRUCTURALISM   Post-structuralist theory has been instrumental in critiquing the notion of disability in that it challenges normative definitions of social order and individual identity (Prendergast, 2008, p. 55). Post-structuralists investigate how the concept of the body is constructed and deconstructed through individual and social interactions (O'Brien, 2005, p. 54). By reinforcing what is considered "normal," society develops a more narrow definition of what is acceptable. People with physical or mental disabilities are seen as even further from the ideal and therefore as less worthy of attention or concern.

One criticism of the post-structuralist approach is similar to that levelled at feminist theory—that theorizing issues of disability within the context of the postmodern economy, while potentially accurate, has little concrete application.

What do you know about **Disabilities in Canada**?

Multiple-choice questions (circle your answer)

1. **An approach that focuses on the individual and his or her abilities rather than limitations is called a**
   a. Disability first approach
   b. People first philosophy
   c. Disabled person's philosophy
   d. Disabled person's approach

2. **The Participation and Activity Limitation Survey (PALS) found that among Canadians aged 15 and older, most reported problems with**
   a. Pain, mobility, and agility
   b. Hearing
   c. Vision
   d. Speaking or communication

3. **According to the Canadian Community Health Survey, _____ Canadians aged 15 and older had experienced mental problems at some time within the past 12 months.**
   a. 1 in 5
   b. 15 percent

c. 1 in 10
d. 1 in 20

4. **BMI stands for**
   a. Body mass index
   b. Body mass indicator
   c. Body measurement index
   d. Body measurement indicator

5. **Which of the following statements is false?**
   a. People with disabilities are underrepresented in the labour market.
   b. People with disabilities have incomes comparable to those without disabilities.
   c. People with disabilities are more likely to feel lonely than those without.
   d. The number of people working in the private sector has increased since 1987.

Answers: b, a, c, a, b

module 11.3

Health Policy

Exploring Canadian health policy is important if we want to understand the parameters within which society helps the aged and people with disabilities, and the myriad illnesses we all face from time to time. The policies that governments use to operate our health care system provide important information about Canadians' social values and priorities. From long wait times for surgery to our aging population and the SARS outbreak, media emphasize the many challenges facing our health care system. To begin our analysis, we must first ask: What does *health* mean?

Think about Health Policy

1 Think about Canada's health care system. Do you think that people should have access to better and/or quicker medical services if they are willing to pay for them?

2 Think about the cost of health care in Canada. Can you think of ways in which Canadians could make health care less expensive?

health A state of complete physical, mental, and social well-being.

life expectancy The average lifespan of a newborn.

WHAT IS HEALTH?

The World Health Organization (WHO) defines **health** as a "state of complete physical, mental and social well-being and not merely the absence of disease or infirmity" (World Health Organization, 2008). This definition suggests that health is a social issue that is influenced by such factors as income and gender (Ahmad & Bradby, 2008, p. 47; Link, Phelan, Miech, & Leckman Westin, 2008, p. 72; Neckerman & Torche, 2007, p. 335).

Sociologists use a diversity of measures to determine whether a population can be considered healthy. The most common measure is to assess how long the average citizen will live in a given society. **Life expectancy** represents the average lifespan of a newborn, and is an indicator of the overall health of a country. Life expectancy rates can fall because of famine, war, disease, and overall poor health, and can rise when health and welfare programs are initiated. As a rule, the higher the life expectancy, the healthier is a given population. Life expectancy rates for Canadians are generally high, with women, on average, outliving men. In 2005, Canadian men had a life expectancy of 78 years and Canadian women of 83 years.

In Canada, individuals who live in households with combined incomes of less than $20 000 are almost three times more likely to experience self-reported poor health than are people with the highest incomes (see Figure 11–7). A study published in the *International Journal of Behavioral Medicine* investigated the relationship between income and self-rated health over a two-year period and what role, if any, stressors (e.g., problems at work, financial pressures) have in helping to explain the relationship. The report found that compared with those in the highest income group, people in the lowest and second-lowest income groups had significantly higher odds of experiencing a decline in health. The study concluded that a small but important portion of the relationship between lower income and the decline in self-rated health was associated with these stressors (Statistics Canada, 2007i).

FIGURE 11–7 **Fair/Poor Health by Household Income Quintile, Canada and the United States, 2002/03**

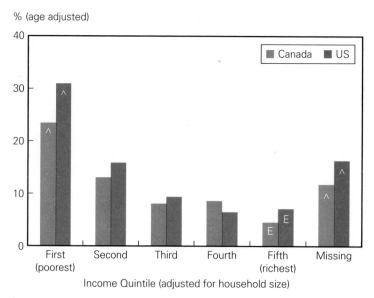

^ Statistically significant difference between Canada and the United States (p<0.05).
E Interpret with caution (high sampling variability).

Source: Statistics Canada (2004). *Joint Canada/United States survey of health. The daily, June 2.* Catalogue no. 11-001. Retrieved June 29, 2008, from http://www.statcan.ca/Daily/English/040602/c040602b.gif.

FIGURE 11–8 **Life Expectancy at Birth, by Sex, 1991 and 2001, Canada**

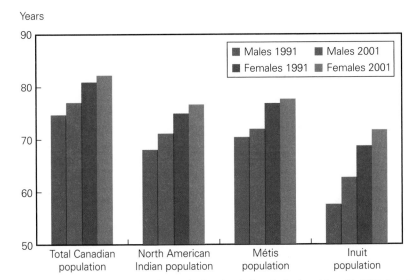

Source: Turcotte, M., & Schellenberg, G. (2007). *A portrait of seniors in Canada.* Retrieved June 24, 2008, from http://www. statcan.ca/english/freepub/89-519-XIE/89-519-XIE2006001.htm.

Life expectancy is also related to minority status. For example, a gap of six years has been found to exist between the life expectancies of Aboriginal peoples and the rest of the Canadian population (Frideres, 2002, p. 155). The rates are improving, however. Figure 11–8 shows that from 1991 to 2001, men and women in all three Aboriginal groups (Indian, Métis, and Inuit) experienced rising life expectancy rates.

The social factors that help to explain these differences include Aboriginal people's level of poverty, access to health care facilities, and diet. Cultural factors also play a role; according to Frideres (2002), while many Aboriginal peoples use the health care system, some prefer traditional healing techniques and others report that they experience negative stereotyping when dealing with some health care professionals. However, Frideres (2002, p. 162) also notes that over time, Aboriginal peoples have been experiencing a better quality of life, particularly in the area of health.

Table 11–2 compares key health care statistics for a number of countries. As you can see, Canada compares fairly well on a number of criteria (e.g., life expectancy, number of adults who smoke, per capita health spending) but falls behind on some others (e.g., obesity rate, number of MRI machines per million persons). Note how much the United States spends per capita on health care ($6401 compared with Canada's $3326); despite this relatively high rate, almost 44 million Americans (or 14.8 percent of the population) have no insurance coverage (Ginsburg, Doherty, Ralston Jr., & Senkeeto, 2008, p. 55). For proportionately less, Canada provides health care coverage for all of its citizens.

PRINCIPLES OF THE CANADIAN HEALTH CARE SYSTEM

Canadians have a health care system that is often, though mistakenly, referred to as *socialized medicine*. In socialized medicine, the government owns and operates most medical facilities and employs most physicians; Sweden is one example of this type of system. Canada, in contrast, has *socialized insurance*, whereby the government pays doctors and hospitals for the services they provide according to a schedule of fees set annually by governments in consultation with professional medical associations. While the federal government provides some funding to the provinces to manage health care, the provinces are responsible for its administration.

TABLE 11-2 International Comparisons of Key Health Care Statistics*

Variable	United States	Australia	Belgium	Canada	Denmark	France	Germany	Japan
Infant mortality per 1000 births (2004)	6.8†	5	3.7	5.3†	4.4	3.6	3.9	2.8
Life expectancy at birth (2004)	77.8†	80.9	79.4†	80.2†	77.9	80.3	79	82
Population age 65 y (2007), %‡	12.5	13.1	17.4	13.3	15.2	16.4	19.4	20.0
Obesity rate	32.2†	20.4†	12.7†	18	11.4	9.5†	13.6	3†
Adult smoking rate	16.9	17.7†	20	17.3	26†	23†	24.3§	26.3 (2006)
Practicing physicians per 1000 persons	2.4	2.7†	4	2.2†	3.6	3.4	3.4†	2
Generalists of practicing physicians (2000), %¶	43.6	51.9	NA	47.5	19.1**	48.8	32.7	NA
Inpatient beds per 1000 persons	2.7	3.6†	4.4	2.9†	3.1†	3.7	6.4	8.2
MRI units per 1 million persons	26.6†	4.2	6.8	5.5	10.2†	3.2	7.1	40.1
Per capita health spending, $	6401	3128†	3389	3326	3108	3374	3287	2358†
Prescription drug spending per capita, $	792	383	344	559	270	NA	438	425
Drug spending as % of total health, $	12.4	13.3	11.3	17.8 (2006)	8.9	16.4	15.2	19†

* Data are for 2005 (unless otherwise noted) from: World Health Organization. World Health Statistics 2007. Accessed at www.who.int/whosis/ whostat2007.pdf on 22 May 2007 and Organization for Economic Co-operation and Development (OECD). OECD Health Data 2007. Accessed at www.oecd.org/document/30/0,3343,cn_2649 _37407_12968734_1_1_1_37407,00.html on 23 July 2007. MRI = magnetic resonance imaging; NA = not available.

† Latest available data: 2004.

‡ CIA World Factbook. Age Structure 65 Years and Over (%) 2007. Accessed at www.photius.com/rankings/population/age_structure_65_years_and_over_2007_0.html on 10 May 2007.

§ Latest available data: 2003.

‖ Latest available data: 2002.

¶ Colombo F. Tapay N. Private Health Insurance in OECD Countries: The Benefits and Costs for Individual and Health Systems. OECD, 2006.

** The low percentages of generalist physicians reported for Denmark and the Netherlands compared with other countries may be due to different methods for collecting and reporting workforce data. Further research is needed to better understand these apparent discrepancies.

Source: Ginsburg, J.A., Doherty, R.B., Ralston Jr., F., & Senkeeto, N. (2008). Achieving a high-performance health care system with universal access: What the United States can learn from other countries. *Annals of Internal Medicine, 148*(1), 55–75.

Through the Hospital Insurance and Diagnostic Services Act of 1957, the Medical Care Act of 1966, and the Canada Health Act of 1984, five universal principles of health care have been enshrined in Canadian law:

- *Universality*: The system must cover all Canadians.
- *Accessibility*: The system must provide reasonable access for everyone and must be unimpeded by financial or other barriers so that no one can be discriminated against on the basis of age, income, or health status.
- *Comprehensiveness*: The system must cover all medically necessary services.
- *Portability*: The system must provide coverage between provinces should a person move.
- *Public administration*: The system must be operated by a public body on a not-for-profit basis (Government of Canada, 2003).

The site Canadian Medicine: Doctors and Discoveries presents key figures and events in the history of Canadian medicine. To learn more, go to **www.mta.ca/about_ canada/study_guide/ doctors/index.html.**

In 2003, the federal and provincial governments developed a 10-year plan to strengthen health care in Canada. One of the outcomes was the creation of a Health Care Council that would monitor progress toward reducing wait times, enhancing primary care (including more support for home care and catastrophic drug coverage), improving diagnostic and medical equipment, and investigating electronic medical file technologies (www.healthcouncilcanada. ca) (Health Canada, 2006a).

HEALTH CARE ISSUES

In this section, we discuss three salient issues related to health care in Canada today: access, costs, and the expansion of alternative health care.

ACCESS   Many Canadians are concerned about unequal access to health care. For some, this means that they do not have a regular family doctor, they live in rural areas without health care facilities, or they have to wait in a long queue for particular non–life threatening services (e.g., hip replacement surgeries).

Although wait times are a barrier for some procedures in some provinces, there are signs that they are improving (Health Council of Canada, 2008) but remain a significant cost to the Canadian economy (The Centre for Spatial Economics, 2008). For example, in Ontario, wait times have dropped substantially over the past four years for cataract surgery (from 311 to 118 days), knee replacements (from 440 to 253 days), hip replacements (from 351 to 198 days), and cancer surgeries (from 81 to 57 days) (Ontario Health Quality Council, 2008). As one way to improve access and efficiency, Ontario has instituted a Web service (www.health. gov.on.ca/transformation/wait_times/wait_mn.html) that allows patients to view wait times at specific hospitals for specific procedures.

Yet "access" means more than just wait times; it also means that everyone who needs health care is treated equally, which is not always the case. For example, the rich can choose to skip the line in Canada and pay for medical services in another country, an option not available to the poor. As well, members of the military, members of the RCMP, prisoners, and workers' compensation claimants all receive more timely health services because they are not covered by the Canada Health Act (Jacobs, 2005).

A significant challenge to Canada's public health care system came in 2005 with the Supreme Court of Canada's decision in the Chaoulli case (Carpay, 2006). The case was brought to the Court by a physician, Jacques Chaoulli, and his patient, George Zeliotis. Over a number of years, Zeliotis

Many Canadians face long waiting lines when attempting to access the public health care system in Canada.

experienced various health problems for which he received treatment, including heart surgery and a number of operations on his hip, within the public health care system. However, he had experienced significant waits before obtaining treatment. Dr. Chaoulli, a long-time advocate of greater private sector involvement in Canadian health care, challenged the prohibition against private insurance because, he argued, it effectively violates the rights to "life, liberty, personal security" as defined in the Quebec Charter of Human Rights and Freedoms and the Canadian Charter of Rights and Freedoms. In its decision, the Supreme Court concluded that when the government fails to deliver health care in a reasonable manner and increases the risk of complications and death, it interferes with life and security of the person as defined in the Charter (Lundell, 2005).

These concerns notwithstanding, according to Health Canada, most people are satisfied with their access to health care. For example, of the 2.8 million people aged 15 or older who visited a medical specialist in 2005, only 19 percent reported that they faced difficulties accessing care. Of the 1.6 million people who reported that they had non-emergency surgery, only 13 percent had difficulty accessing care (Statistics Canada, 2006b).

COSTS   Today, almost 10 percent of Canada's GDP is spent on health care (see Table 11–3), a level of spending that is similar to that of most high-income countries. The exception is the United States, which devotes just over 15 percent of its GDP to health care while providing only 45.1 percent of funding (compared with Canada's 70.3 percent and Japan's 81.7 percent). This apparent paradox is largely a result of administrative costs: some estimates suggest that 24 percent of all health care spending in the United States is for administration, which includes the paperwork associated with hundreds of private health care companies (Le Goff, 2005).

While Canada's numbers seem reasonable at first glance, health care is one of the single largest expenses in provincial budgets. For example, it comprised 41.7 percent of Ontario's 2008–09 budget (Conference Board of Canada, 2008), 40 percent of British Columbia's 2007 budget (Smith, 2007), 44 percent of Quebec's 2008 budget (Conference Board of Canada, 2008), and 36.4 percent of Alberta's 2008 budget (Government of Alberta, 2008). As the population ages, these numbers are expected to rise.

alternative medicine
Those treatments not normally taught in medical schools, used in hospitals, or included in health care plans (e.g., acupuncture).

ALTERNATIVE HEALTH CARE   In Canada, **alternative medicine** (also known as complementary medicine) is defined as "those treatments and health care practices not widely taught in medical schools, nor routinely used in hospitals, and not typically reimbursed by health benefit plans" (Millar, 2001, p. 9). In 2006, nearly three-quarters of Canadians had used at least one form of alternative therapy at least once in their life. The most popular forms of alternative medicine are chiropractics (40 percent of Canadians have tried it), massage therapy (35 percent), relaxation techniques (20 percent), prayer (18 percent), and acupuncture (17 percent) (Esmail, 2007, p. 4).

The fact that Canadians are increasingly turning to alternative health care presents a challenge on two fronts. First, alternative health care workers may not undergo the same type of training as the university-educated practitioners in our existing medical model of health care

TABLE 11–3 Health Expenditures across Eight Countries

Country	Percentage of GDP to Health Care	Percentage of Government-Supported Health Care
Canada	9.8	70.3
France	11.1	79.8
Japan	8.0 (2004)	81.7 (2004)
Mexico	6.4	45.5
Poland	6.2	69.3
Sweden	9.1	84.6
United Kingdom	8.3	87.1
United States	15.3	45.1

Source: OECD. (2008). *Health data 2008*. Retrieved June 30, 2008, from http://www.oecd.org/dataoecd/46/36/38979632.xls.

(Haigh, 1999, p. 146). Second, alternative health care systems have hidden costs (e.g., testing herbal remedies for safety) that could overwhelm the system's ability to pay (Danzon, 1992).

Esmail (2007, p. 5) estimates that Canadians spend about $8 billion annually on alternative health care; yet despite this significant outlay, fully 60 percent of Canadians believe that these procedures should not be covered under provincial health plans. Alternative health care is used by

- Women more than men
- Middle-aged people more than the young or elderly
- People with higher educational levels more than those with lower educational levels
- People with higher incomes more than those with lower incomes
- People with a diagnosed chronic condition more than others (Statistics Canada, 2005g)

In addition, an earlier study found that those who were more proactive about their own health care were more likely to consult alternative providers (Millar, 2001, p. 17). Millar (2001, pp. 19–20) concluded that these people were generally "supplementing, not rejecting, conventional health care," and that as the population ages, "the demand for alternate therapies could increase even further."

SOCIOLOGICAL APPROACHES TO HEALTH CARE

FUNCTIONALISM   Functionalists view health care as an important mechanism through which society administers the care and treatment of its citizens. By providing hospitals and trained staff, the health care system is able to treat the ill and, in doing so, maintain a more stable and harmonious society. Critics point out, however, that while the health care system treats many people effectively and efficiently, it has also been responsible for harming some people's health. For example, a study of hospital records from 2000 to 2001 found that mistakes (e.g., wrong medication or dose given, catching an infection) or accidents (e.g., falling while in hospital) occurred in 7.5 percent of hospital admissions; of these, 36.9 percent were preventable and 20.8 percent resulted in death (Baker et al., 2004).

CONFLICT THEORY   Conflict theorists would argue that Canada already has a two-tier health care system in that the rich can get treatment faster than the poor simply by going to another country. Conflict theorists would assert that the poor must instead wait their turn in an overburdened health care system, at times dying before they can be treated (Peat, 2008). Further evidence of inequality in Canadian health care is seen in the problems that Aboriginal people face when they try to access the system from remote locations.

Conflict theorists would also argue that the medical profession legitimates and sanctions its control over people's health in a process known as **medicalization**. Medicalization is a concept first conceived by Ivan Illich (1926–2002). One of Illich's central insights was how health care professionals, drug companies, medical equipment companies, and indeed the entire medical establishment have a vested interest in sponsoring sickness to promote unrealistic health expectations that require more treatments and resources (Hammond, 2005, p. 13). For example, nervousness, attention deficit disorder, and shyness can all be classified as medical problems worthy of medications, treatment, and therapy. The point is not that these conditions may not be helped by these treatments, but that we need to recognize that the boundaries of what is considered acceptable have narrowed over time. Similarly, Michel Foucault described the spread of the medical profession's influence in defining what is normal and abnormal (Reznick, 2006, p. 85). According to conflict theorists, these definitions reflect the needs of the rich and powerful.

medicalization   The increasing influence of the medical profession in defining what is normal/healthy and abnormal/ill.

SYMBOLIC INTERACTIONISM   The symbolic interactionist perspective on health rests on two central insights. The first is the influence of labelling. People use the labels *health* and *illness* as fixed, binary opposites, whereas in reality what can be considered healthy falls

CANADIAN SOCIETY IN FOCUS

Two-Tier Health Care?

Universal health care is regarded by many Canadians as an essential Canadian value (Cukier & Thomlinson, 2005, p. 94). However, rapidly rising costs have inspired much discussion about allowing more private agencies to help with existing and future economic challenges to the health care system.

Much of the concern about privatizing aspects of the health care system centres on two of Canada's five universal health care principles: accessibility and public administration. Some argue that if private, for-profit companies are allowed greater access to the system, what will emerge is one health care system for the rich and one for the rest of society—commonly referred to as a *two-tier system*. Those who support public health care argue that more private health care facilities will allow the wealthy to get better and timelier treatment than those in the publicly administered system. Conversely, proponents argue that the private sector can deliver higher-quality health care more efficiently than the public sector, since the private sector is driven by competition that will invariably lower costs.

The BC Health Coalition, an advocacy group dedicated to maintaining the public system, outlines the following threats from privatization:

1. The rich will be able to access health services more quickly than those relying on the public system.
2. Private health clinics will attract doctors away from the public system, potentially leading to doctor shortages.
3. There is a loss of control and lack of public accountability for private health care providers.
4. Existing salaries for contract workers (including cleaning staff and administrative positions) will decline.
5. Standards of patient care will fall, since services for patients may be supplied by the lowest-cost, and not necessarily best-qualified, suppliers. (BC Health Coalition, 2005)

As health care costs continue to rise, governments will likely encounter increasing pressure to implement changes to the existing system—whether or not these changes involve privatization.

This article is also a peerScholar assignment in MySocLab.

within a wide spectrum. Once labelled as being ill, people often assume a set of expectations that are based on both the diagnosis and the individual. Symbolic interactionists would point out that these labels (e.g., sick, healthy, cancer survivor) are social constructions that can be changed (Lindsey & Beach, 2003, p. 342).

The second symbolic interactionist insight is the influence of the self-fulfilling prophecy (Buunk, Zurriaga, & González, 2006, p. 793). For example, the growth of alternative medicine suggests that it works for many people and cannot be dismissed simply as a medical fluke. The power of the mind to influence one's health or illness is in part explained by the self-fulfilling prophecy—if a person thinks a remedy might work, it may have a greater chance of doing so. On the other hand, patients who believe that they are beyond healing and thus do not seek help are more likely to suffer the most negative effects of their illness.

FEMINIST THEORY   Feminists are critical of how the medical profession treats women. For example, medical research is often androcentric, in that findings from research conducted on men are inferred as also applying to women. Feminists also point out that combining *medical* and *science* into *medical science* confirms a strong male-centred bias in that it seeks to find universal truths. This approach suggests that when knowledge is gained through impersonal, objective methods, it can have the effect of diminishing the value of the individual human experience. Thus, the attributes that define women's reality—intuition, subjectivity, and emotions—are generally dismissed by the medical establishment (Williams & Mackey, 1999, p. 31). This system therefore attributes childbirth, for example, as a purely biological process and not the culmination of emotional and subjective realities. Thus, our dominant cultural categories that influence science and medicine (e.g., male, white, upper-middle class) make it difficult for anyone (patients or medical professionals) to re-evaluate and alter the dominant patriarchal categories that typify traditional health care (Kinser & Lewis, 2005, p. 423).

POST-STRUCTURALISM　Modernists believe that an underlying, unified truth can be found through objectivity, causality, and the pursuit of impartial observation. In contrast, post-structuralists attempt to suspend all preconceived judgments and to deconstruct conventional wisdom (Newbold, 2005, p. 440). According to post-structuralists, then, health care must become more responsive to the needs of the individual patient and become less about the need of health professionals to "fix" the problem. For example, people today are more likely to take ownership of their own health (as seen in the rise of alternative medicine) and to actively critique their own clinical treatment to determine if it is what they believe they need. If it isn't, they are more likely to terminate the treatment independent of what doctors may recommend. In this way, empowerment flows to the patient and turns the traditional modernist hospital on its head. "When patients enter the 'postmodern hospital,' they come neither to be disciplined into a morally improved state, nor to be 'operated upon' by the medicine machine: they come to comparison shop. In this world of consumer medicine, the very categories of disease and health alter, along with the shifting, ever reconstructed identity of patients who purchase and doctors who provide" (Galison, 1999, as cited in Newbold, 2005, p. 445).

What do you know about **Health Policy**?

Multiple-choice questions (circle your answer)

1. *Health* can be defined as
   a. A state of complete physical well-being
   b. A state of complete physical and social well-being
   c. A state of complete physical and mental well-being
   d. A state of complete physical, mental, and social well-being

2. **Which of the following statements is false?**
   a. In 2005, Canadian men had a life expectancy of 78 years.
   b. In Canada, women on average outlive men.
   c. People in lower income groups report poorer health than people in higher income groups.
   d. Canada spends more on health care per capita than does the United States.

3. **Which province spent the greatest portion of its 2008 budget on health care?**
   a. Ontario
   b. British Columbia
   c. Quebec
   d. Alberta

4. **The increasing influence of the medical profession in defining what is normal/healthy and abnormal/ill is called**
   a. Medicalization
   b. Medical domination
   c. Demedicalization
   d. Pro-medicalization

5. _____ **argue that there is economic inequality in the health care system.**
   a. Functionalists
   b. Symbolic interactionists
   c. Conflict theorists
   d. Post-structuralists

Answers: d, d, c, a, c

Summary

module 11.1   AGING IN CANADA

1. In 2006, seniors made up 13 percent of the Canadian population. In 2056, seniors are expected to exceed 27 percent of the Canadian population.
2. Most Canadian seniors today report being happy and healthy.
3. Canadian seniors face challenges in six areas: transition to retirement, financial pressures, age discrimination, vulnerability to crime, chronic pain and the need for long-term care, and preparing to die.
4. Canadian labour laws no longer identify a retirement age because such laws were determined to be discriminatory.
5. On average, seniors' incomes decline after retirement. Nonetheless, today seniors are enjoying greater wealth than previous cohorts.
6. The Canadian government has prepared well for an increase in the number of seniors in relation to the number of workers. Shortfalls in Canada's pension plans are no longer a major concern.
7. *Ageism* is the term used to describe a system of inequality based on age that privileges the young at the expense of the old. Seniors are routinely subjected to negative stereotypes regarding their physical and mental abilities.
8. Older people are more likely to be victims of fraud. *Elder abuse* refers to any form of mistreatment that results in harm or loss to an older person.
9. A total of 7 percent of the elderly reside in collective dwellings (primary health care institutions such as nursing homes and hospitals).
10. Chronic pain affects 27 percent of seniors who live at home and 38 percent who live in health care institutions.
11. *Euthanasia* is the deliberate ending of the life of a person who has an incurable or painful disease. Although illegal in Canada, there is considerable support among Canadians to legalize the act.
12. Functionalists support the idea that older people should disengage from their roles to allow younger people to assume those roles.
13. Conflict theorists point to economic competition between the old and the young.
14. Symbolic interactionists stress the importance of seniors' continuing engagement and activity.
15. Feminists stress the extended disadvantage for senior women in a culture of youth.
16. Post-structuralists critique the prevailing definitions associated with aging.

module 11.2   DISABILITIES IN CANADA

17. Disability affects about 15 percent of Canadians; pain is the most common disability for those between ages 15 and 64, whereas those age 65 and older most commonly suffer from limited mobility.
18. 1 in 10 Canadians aged 15 and older experienced mental problems at some time in the past 12 months, according to the Canadian Community Health Survey.
19. Factors that influence rates of particular mental illnesses include gender, income, and age.
20. People with disabilities are often discriminated against. *Ableism* can be seen in the labour market where people with disabilities are underrepresented.
21. Functionalists hold that the sick role defines the expected behaviour of those who are sick.

22. Conflict theorists focus on the types of inequality experienced by people with disabilities.
23. Symbolic interactionists stress the importance of self-management for those with disabilities, as well as the negative consequences of labelling.
24. Feminists critique the narrowly defined, binary opposition of abled/disabled as contributing to the oppression of people with disabilities.
25. Post-structuralists likewise challenge normative definitions of the body and instead investigate it as socially constructed.

module 11.3   HEALTH POLICY

26. *Health* is defined as a state of complete physical, mental, and social well-being.
27. While Canadians have a relatively high life expectancy, overall health is affected by income level, with those in the lowest income groups more likely to experience poor health.
28. The five universal principles of Canada's health care system are universality, accessibility, comprehensiveness, portability, and public administration.
29. Health care issues in Canada include unequal access, the high percentage of provincial budgets devoted to health care, and the growth of alternative medicine.
30. Functionalists view the health care system as contributing to a stable society.
31. Conflict theorists highlight the economic inequality in Canada's (virtual) two-tier health care system and how increasing medicalization has served the interests of the rich and powerful.
32. Symbolic interactionists look at how labelling and the self-fulfilling prophecy affect the conception of one's own health.
33. Feminists point out the androcentric nature of health care and the devaluation of subjective information.
34. Post-structuralists highlight the changing nature of health care whereby patients assume more responsibility and control over their health and so diminish the control traditionally exercised by doctors and the health care system.

Key Terms

ableism   337
activity theory   333
ageism   329
alternative medicine   346
BMI (body mass index)   336
chronic pain   331
disability   334

disengagement theory   332
downward drift hypothesis   336
elder abuse   330
elderly dependency ratio   328
euthanasia   331
health   342
life expectancy   342

long-term care   331
medicalization   347
obesity   336
people first philosophy   334
sick role   339

Test Yourself

1. The ratio of seniors to workers is called
   a. Worker/pension ratio
   b. Elderly dependency ratio
   c. Senior dependency ratio
   d. Senior/worker ratio

2. Which of the following statements is false?
   a. Seniors make up 60 percent of victims who lose money in telemarketing scams.
   b. In 2005, 445 of the homicides of seniors were committed by a family member.

c. Male seniors were most likely to be killed by a son or stepson.

d. Younger people are more likely to exploit older people who are psychologically and economically dependent on them.

3. What percentage of people in Quebec support euthanasia?
a. 20 percent
b. 40 percent
c. 60 percent
d. 80 percent

4. Disengagement theory is linked to which of the sociological perspectives?
a. Functionalism
b. Conflict theory
c. Symbolic interactionism
d. Post-structuralism

5. Activity theory is linked to which of the sociological perspectives?
a. Functionalism
b. Conflict theory
c. Symbolic interactionism
d. Feminism

6. What percentage of those with disabilities require some form of technical aids or specialized equipment?
a. 20 percent
b. 40 percent
c. 50 percent
d. 60 percent

7. Which of the following statements is false?
a. Disability rates are increasing.
b. Advances in medical technology may be responsible for an increase in the number of people living with disabilities in Canada.
c. The number of disabled people is increasing as our population ages.
d. Medical technology is decreasing the number of people living with disabilities in Canada.

8. The assertion that those with mental illnesses, unable to finish their education or secure a job, tend to drift into low-income groups is called
a. Downward drift hypothesis
b. Low-income drift hypothesis
c. Vertical mobility theory
d. Downward mobility theory

9. Discrimination against those with disabilities on the basis of preconceived notions about their limitations is called

a. Sociologists do not have a term for such discrimination.
b. Ableism
c. Disableism
d. Handiableism

10. Behaviour that defines the behaviour that is appropriate for and expected of those who are sick is called
a. Ableism
b. Disableism
c. Disengagement theory
d. The sick role

11. _____ hold that the sick role defines expected behaviour of those that are sick.
a. Functionalists
b. Conflict theorists
c. Feminists
d. Post- structuralists

12. _____ examine the negative consequences of labelling someone as sick.
a. Functionalists
b. Conflict theorists
c. Symbolic Interactionists
d. Post-structuralists

13. _____ critique the narrowly defined, binary opposition of abled/disabled as contributing to the oppression of people with disabilities.
a. Functionalists
b. Conflict theorists
c. Feminists
d. Symbolic Interactionists

14. _____ investigate how the definitions of the body are socially constructed.
a. Functionalists
b. Post-structuralists
c. Feminists
d. Conflict theorists

15. The average lifespan of a newborn is called
a. Life expectancy
b. Life measurement scale
c. Health determinant measure
d. Health determinant scale

16. Which principle of the Canadian health care system states that "the system must provide coverage between provinces should a person move"?
a. Accessibility
b. Comprehensiveness
c. Portability
d. Public administration

17. Which of the following statements is false? Alternative health care is used more by
a. Men
b. Middle-aged people
c. People with higher education levels
d. People with higher incomes

18. The term *medicalization* was coined by
a. Karl Marx
b. Talcott Parsons
c. Ivan Illich
d. R.K. Merton

19. _____ view the health care system as contributing to a stable society.

a. Functionalists
b. Conflict theorists
c. Feminists
d. Symbolic interactionists

20. _____ note health care has changed as patients are assuming more control and responsibility for their own health.
a. Functionalists
b. Symbolic Interactionists
c. Feminists
d. Post-structuralists

Answers: b, d, d, a, c, d, a, b, d, a, c, b, a, c, b, a, c, a, d

Log in to MySocLab for a host of resources that will help you save time and improve your grade. MySocLab contains cutting-edge learning tools such as study plans, practice tests, videos, audio segments, quizzes, and more—all designed to help you better understand the learning ob-jectives for this chapter. Along with your eBook, MySocLab for *Sociology for Everyone* can be found at **www.mysoclab.com**.

CONCEPT MAP

module 11.1
AGING IN CANADA

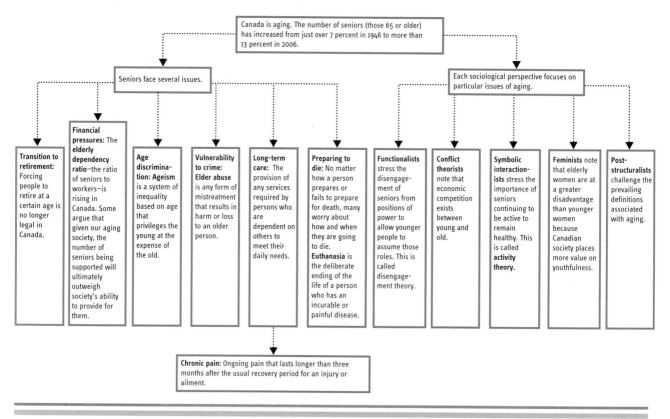

Canada is aging. The number of seniors (those 65 or older) has increased from just over 7 percent in 1946 to more than 13 percent in 2006.

Seniors face several issues.

Each sociological perspective focuses on particular issues of aging.

Transition to retirement: Forcing people to retire at a certain age is no longer legal in Canada.

Financial pressures: The elderly dependency ratio—the ratio of seniors to workers—is rising in Canada. Some argue that given our aging society, the number of seniors being supported will ultimately outweigh society's ability to provide for them.

Age discrimination: Ageism is a system of inequality based on age that privileges the young at the expense of the old.

Vulnerability to crime: Elder abuse is any form of mistreatment that results in harm or loss to an older person.

Long-term care: The provision of any services required by persons who are dependent on others to meet their daily needs.

Preparing to die: No matter how a person prepares or fails to prepare for death, many worry about how and when they are going to die. **Euthanasia** is the deliberate ending of the life of a person who has an incurable or painful disease.

Functionalists stress the disengagement of seniors from positions of power to allow younger people to assume those roles. This is called disengagement theory.

Conflict theorists note that economic competition exists between young and old.

Symbolic interactionists stress the importance of seniors continuing to be active to remain healthy. This is called **activity theory.**

Feminists note that elderly women are at a greater disadvantage than younger women because Canadian society places more value on youthfulness.

Post-structuralists challenge the prevailing definitions associated with aging.

Chronic pain: Ongoing pain that lasts longer than three months after the usual recovery period for an injury or ailment.

module 11.2
DISABILITIES IN CANADA

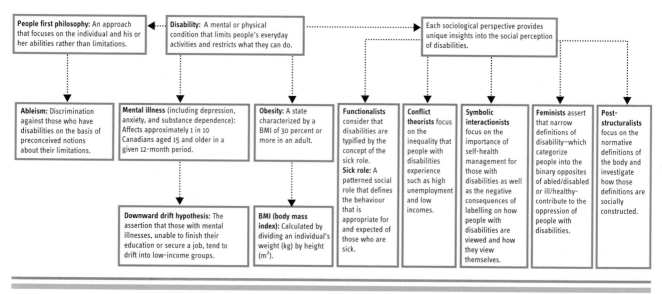

People first philosophy: An approach that focuses on the individual and his or her abilities rather than limitations.

Disability: A mental or physical condition that limits people's everyday activities and restricts what they can do.

Each sociological perspective provides unique insights into the social perception of disabilities.

Ableism: Discrimination against those who have disabilities on the basis of preconceived notions about their limitations.

Mental illness (including depression, anxiety, and substance dependence): Affects approximately 1 in 10 Canadians aged 15 and older in a given 12-month period.

Obesity: A state characterized by a BMI of 30 percent or more in an adult.

Functionalists consider that disabilities are typified by the concept of the sick role. **Sick role:** A patterned social role that defines the behaviour that is appropriate for and expected of those who are sick.

Conflict theorists focus on the inequality that people with disabilities experience such as high unemployment and low incomes.

Symbolic interactionists focus on the importance of self-health management for those with disabilities as well as the negative consequences of labelling on how people with disabilities are viewed and how they view themselves.

Feminists assert that narrow definitions of disability—which categorize people into the binary opposites of abled/disabled or ill/healthy—contribute to the oppression of people with disabilities.

Post-structuralists focus on the normative definitions of the body and investigate how those definitions are socially constructed.

Downward drift hypothesis: The assertion that those with mental illnesses, unable to finish their education or secure a job, tend to drift into low-income groups.

BMI (body mass index): Calculated by dividing an individual's weight (kg) by height (m²).

module 11.3
HEALTH POLICY

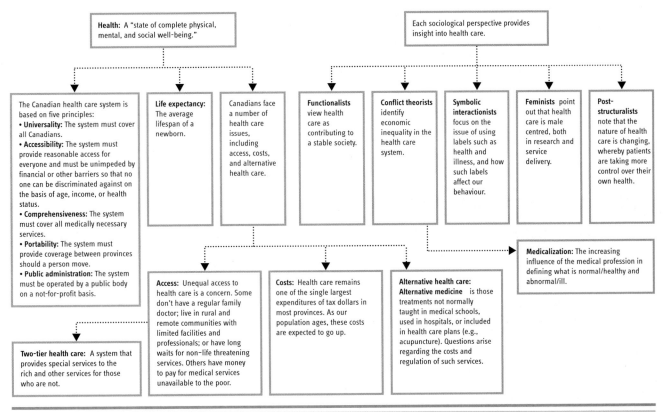

Health: A "state of complete physical, mental, and social well-being."

Each sociological perspective provides insight into health care.

The Canadian health care system is based on five principles:
• **Universality:** The system must cover all Canadians.
• **Accessibility:** The system must provide reasonable access for everyone and must be unimpeded by financial or other barriers so that no one can be discriminated against on the basis of age, income, or health status.
• **Comprehensiveness:** The system must cover all medically necessary services.
• **Portability:** The system must provide coverage between provinces should a person move.
• **Public administration:** The system must be operated by a public body on a not-for-profit basis.

Life expectancy: The average lifespan of a newborn.

Canadians face a number of health care issues, including access, costs, and alternative health care.

Functionalists view health care as contributing to a stable society.

Conflict theorists identify economic inequality in the health care system.

Symbolic interactionists focus on the issue of using labels such as health and illness, and how such labels affect our behaviour.

Feminists point out that health care is male centred, both in research and service delivery.

Post-structuralists note that the nature of health care is changing, whereby patients are taking more control over their own health.

Medicalization: The increasing influence of the medical profession in defining what is normal/healthy and abnormal/ill.

Two-tier health care: A system that provides special services to the rich and other services for those who are not.

Access: Unequal access to health care is a concern. Some don't have a regular family doctor; live in rural and remote communities with limited facilities and professionals; or have long waits for non-life threatening services. Others have money to pay for medical services unavailable to the poor.

Costs: Health care remains one of the single largest expenditures of tax dollars in most provinces. As our population ages, these costs are expected to go up.

Alternative health care: Alternative medicine is those treatments not normally taught in medical schools, used in hospitals, or included in health care plans (e.g., acupuncture). Questions arise regarding the costs and regulation of such services.

chapter 12

Social Change, Collective Behaviour, Social Movements, and the Future

Making Peace

The Raging Grannies, Code Pink, and the Missile Dick Chicks are just three examples of groups of people rallying together for a common cause.

The Raging Grannies emerged in Victoria, British Columbia, in 1987 when a group of women tried to draw attention to American warships with nuclear capability that were passing through our waters just off the West Coast (Roy, 2002). Since then, the organization has grown to more than 80 chapters across North America (Kutz-Flamenbaum, 2007, p. 93). Each chapter (known as a "gaggle") comprises performance-based protest troops who sing satirical songs and wear old-fashioned clothes to draw attention to the issue at hand. The Raging Grannies challenge dominant gender norms that construct grandmothers as nice old ladies who should be content with baking cookies and spoiling their grandchildren rather than participating in political protests (Kutz-Flamenbaum, 2007, p. 97).

Code Pink is an American movement that began in 2002 in response to the war in Iraq. Today, there are more than 250 chapters operating across the United States. Their intent is to stop the war in Iraq, prevent future wars, and reallocate their country's wealth into such life-affirming activities as education, health care, veterans' benefits, and social services (www.codepink4peace.org). They believe that women have the moral authority to contest the war in Iraq—after all, women didn't start it, and women are naturally caregivers and nurturers—and call on all women to join them in their pursuit of peace (Kutz-Flamenbaum, 2007, p. 93).

Based in New York, the Missile Dick Chicks formed in early 2003 to protest the war in Iraq and the policies of the Bush administration. Wearing blue costumes with protruding "missile dicks," they present themselves ironically as rich, conservative housewives who are drug-using, greedy, and play on the masculine attitude expressed in military conquest (Kutz-Flamenbaum, 2007, p. 99).

These performance-based activist groups all work to inspire reflection and promote social change. This chapter explores how sociologists explain groups like these, as well as the general phenomena of collective behaviour and social movements. It also examines how sociologists make predictions about the future.

module 12.1

Think about Social Change

1 Think about new technologies. Do you rush out to buy the latest technology or do you resist technological change? Do you think that the technologies you use today make you see the world differently from your parents?

2 Think about social change. What change do you think has had the greatest impact on Canadian society in your lifetime?

social change Changes in the typical features of a society (e.g., norms and values) over time.

collective behaviour Occurs when people come together to achieve a meaningful short-term goal that may result in social change.

social movements Collections of people who are organized to bring about or resist social change.

What Is Social Change?

For sociologists, **social change** can be defined as changes in the typical features of a society (e.g., norms and values) over time (Boehnke, Kindervater, Baier, & Rippl, 2007, p. 67). We can see evidence of social change everywhere in society, from what is considered deviant over time to the clothes we wear; social change is ongoing and inevitable. It occurs when there are modifications or adjustments to public policy, cultural traditions, or social institutions that at times are inspired by collective behaviours. **Collective behaviour** occurs when people come together to achieve a single and meaningful short-term goal that may result in social change (Kurzman, 2008). Social scientists typically suggest that collective behaviours are not regulated by the everyday rules and expectations that normally shape people's actions—for example, during riots after hockey games.

One type of collective behaviour is the social movement. **Social movements** comprise groups and individuals that provide largely continuous and organized efforts to bring about—or resist—social change (see Caroll & Ratner, 2007). These movements generally emerge from grassroots organizations that operate outside existing social power structures, including established political parties and the legal system (Corbett, 2006, p. 286; Johnston & Almeida, 2006, p. 62). Social change is a broad concept used to explore the changes that take place in interpersonal relations as well as in society's social organization (e.g., the influence of computers on communication between friends as well as on the education system). Sometimes, social change is predictable, as when a society is defeated in a war, but usually it is not (consider the unintended consequences of computers). However, the one unmistakable global trend today is the accelerating pace at which social change occurs (Ginsberg & Gekonge, 2004, p. 354; Rudel & Hooper, 2005, p. 275). As a rule, social change is most likely to occur when

1. The change originates within what are seen as cutting-edge sources (e.g., fashion shows, academic research findings).
2. The change addresses a strongly felt need among the public (e.g., legislation to restrict access to questionable content on the Internet).
3. The change is material rather than nonmaterial (e.g., subsidizing the costs of alternative fuels versus brochures promoting the benefits of mass transit).
4. The change is broadly compatible with people's existing values (e.g., recycling programs succeed because people's environmental awareness is rising). (Etzkowitz, 1992, as cited in Lindsey, Beach, & Ravelli, 2009, p. 286)

Code Pink protestors in the United States believe that because women are more nurturing than men, they are uniquely qualified to challenge the war in Iraq.

THE LIFE CYCLE OF SOCIAL CHANGE

Social change moves through a type of life cycle. In the first stage of **innovation**—something new that inspires a change—a few "early adopters" adapt to the change. During this stage, change is very slow, but when it is adopted by 10 percent to 25 percent of the population, the rate of change accelerates very quickly—an idea consistent with Malcolm Gladwell's (2000) concept of the "tipping point." Most of the people who become early adopters are young, tend to live in cities, and are middle class (or higher) with good educations. Generally, early adopters enjoy distinguishing themselves from the crowd by setting trends, not following them.

The second stage of change is a time of **exponential growth**, when the majority of the population adopts the technology or behaviour. The final stage is referred to as **saturation**, whereby the change enters a society's traditions and normal daily practices (Orum, Johnstone, & Riger, 1999, p. 87).

Another way of understanding how technology can spread through society is found in the work of Marc Prensky (2001) and his concepts of **digital natives** (people who grew up with digital technology) and **digital immigrants** (people who grew up before digital technology became commonplace). As you can see in Table 12–1, digital natives and digital immigrants respond to technology differently.

OPPOSITION TO SOCIAL CHANGE

Of course, not everyone supports change—for example, the rich and powerful generally resist social change, given that it often occurs at their expense. In his book *Vested Interests and the Common Man* (2004 [1919]), sociologist Thorstein Veblen coined the term **vested interests** to describe why privileged members of society resist change. Veblen argued that since many in the leisure class gain their wealth and social position not by personal actions or attributes

innovation Something new that inspires social change (e.g., cellphones).

exponential growth The adoption of a new technology or behaviour by the majority of the population.

saturation The point at which a new technology or behaviour becomes a part of everyday living.

digital natives Prensky's term for people who grew up with digital technologies.

digital immigrants Prensky's term for people who grew up before digital technologies became commonplace.

vested interests Veblen's term to describe why privileged members of society resist change.

TABLE 12-1 **Digital Natives and Digital Immigrants**

Digital Native	Digital Immigrant
Studies or reads with music and/or television on	Studies or reads in silence
Frustrated when email is not replied to immediately	Calls to see if you have received email
Ignores email forwards	Replies to and sends email forwards
Uses text messaging	Does not see the point of text messaging or is confused by it
Reads text and emails from computer screen	Prints out texts and emails to read from paper
Embraces new technology	Is nervous of new technology
Buys music online	Buys music from a store
Reads online newspapers	Reads paper newspapers
Engages in instant chats	Communicates through phone calls
Keeps cellphone turned on at all times	Turns off cellphone
Has latest video games	Prefers older video games
Programs television so as not to miss an episode	Alters schedule around a television show or misses the episode
Uses Google maps	Uses paper maps
Multitasks	Does one thing at a time

Source: Adapted from www.theramartens.com/thesis_website/appendix.html (accessed July 3, 2008). Used with permission of the author.

but through inheritance, these people would resist any change, as it might cost them their lives of privilege (O'Hara, 2002, p. 87). This was certainly true when owners in the music industry went to court against those who were sharing music files over the Internet for free. However, perhaps the most famous example of people resisting social change is the case of the Luddites in the early nineteenth century.

The **Luddites** were a loosely bound group of displaced textile workers who destroyed the new machines that put them out of work (Kivisto, 2004, p. 12). The Luddite movement was well organized, but lasted just over a year before the British army quashed it. It is important to understand that the Luddites were not against all technology, just those technologies that presented a direct threat to their way of life. (Today, the term *Luddite* is used to refer to someone who is resistant to new technology.) The lesson to take away from the Luddite uprising is their belief that technological advancement is neither inevitable nor uncontrollable—ideally, technology makes our lives better, not worse (Petch, 2002).

INSPIRATIONS FOR SOCIAL CHANGE

Sociologists understand that social changes do not happen in a vacuum; instead, they are often inspired by the world around us. In this section, we review some of the inspirations for social change.

TECHNOLOGY   **Technology** is broadly defined as the application of knowledge to achieve practical purposes; in effect, it is anything that provides an artificial means to achieve a given end or result. For example, technology is the tractor that allows one farmer to seed hundreds of acres in a single day, or the microwave oven that can heat up a bowl of soup in less than a minute.

Both tractors and microwave ovens have become more powerful and efficient through the years; technology, then, builds on past discoveries. As well, technological developments can inspire a great deal of social change that similarly accumulates over time. The farmer's ability to seed, spray, fertilize, and harvest many more hectares than in the past has been one factor that has contributed to the decline in the number of small family farms. Microwaveable foods

Luddites   A loosely bound group of displaced textile workers who destroyed the new machines that put them out of work in the early nineteenth century.

technology   Anything that provides an artificial means to achieve a given end or result.

have contributed to our contemporary "drive-through" lifestyle, wherein we rarely sit down with our families to talk about what is going on in our lives.

PHYSICAL ENVIRONMENT   Living through a cold Canadian winter is proof that people are able to adapt to a harsh physical environment. In order to survive, the ancestors of Aboriginal peoples needed to alter their material culture (e.g., through the development of warm winter clothing) as well as their social behaviour (e.g., the sharing of food between families to protect against starvation) (Moran, 1981). Living in hot climates, or any other type of climate, requires similar novel adaptations.

DEMOGRAPHIC SHIFTS   Population changes due to events such as immigration, increased or decreased birth rates, or the migration of people can create social change. Another inspiration for social change is the growing population of healthy seniors. Consider Canada's aging population, for example. The proportion of Canadians over age 65 is increasing—from just over 7 percent in 1946 to more than 13 percent today—and is projected to exceed 37 percent by 2056. The growing population of healthy seniors who are living well into their eighties has resulted in changes to mandatory retirement legislation as well as greater public awareness of such issues as long-term care requirements.

ECONOMIC COMPETITION   The emergence of China and India as industrial powerhouses has led to a reordering of global capitalism. While the world's dominant national economy continues to be the United States, the fact that China holds about 20 percent of all American foreign debt concerns many economists, in that the United States' primary political, military, and economic adversary holding that much debt weakens its ability to compete (Barrera, 2008, p. 295; Hubbard, 2008).

WAR   Warfare has always been a prime inspiration for technological development—from gunpowder to nuclear weapons. At times, the technologies developed for military application (consider nuclear fission and the Internet) find their way into the larger society and can result in social change.

IDEAS   While we can readily perceive how technology, economic competition, and war can lead to social change, we cannot underestimate the power of ideas to inspire change as well. Consider how such ideas as free will, evolution, democracy, and freedom each played an important role in social change.

GOVERNMENTS   Governments with strong political leadership can mobilize large-scale efforts to alter the character of a society. In Canada, for example, the federal government has contributed to significant changes in human rights legislation, health care reform, and environmental protection.

INDIVIDUALS   From time to time, certain people inspire social change through their personality, charisma, and conviction. While there are many examples of leaders who diminish the value of human life—Adolf Hitler, Saddam Hussein, and, more recently, Robert Mugabe—there are others—Mahatma Gandhi, Martin Luther King Jr., and Nelson Mandela, to name only three—whose actions have helped to make the world a better place.

SOCIAL MOVEMENTS   The emergence of grassroots movements such as Greenpeace proves that when ordinary people come together to fight for or against something, tremendous social changes can occur (Anheier, 2005, p. 286). Characteristics common to all successful social movements include a strong organizational capacity, a clear position on their grievances and goals, and active engagement with existing political power structures to facilitate the achievement of these goals (Pellow, 2007, p. 54).

To learn how one Canadian, Craig Kielburger, is changing the world, go to **www.freethechildren.com.**

SOCIOLOGICAL APPROACHES TO SOCIAL CHANGE

Sociologists provide four theoretical perspectives on social change: functionalist, conflict, evolutionary, and cyclical.

FUNCTIONALISM   As a rule, functionalists are more interested in the forces that keep a society stable than in those that change it. Yet Talcott Parsons, while perceiving society in its natural state as stable and balanced, saw that change did occur through a process of differentiation (Gerhardt, 2001, p. 192). According to Parsons (1951), the emergence of a social problem indicates that the social system needs to change in order to regain a state of equilibrium. This functionalist approach to change is called the **equilibrium theory**, which holds that changes in one part of society require changes in another part in order for society to return to a natural state of balance and harmony (Trevino & Smelser, 2001, p. xxxv). For example, the civil rights demonstrations in the 1960s were an expression of the need for American society to become more accepting of racial diversity. The demonstrations motivated politicians and lawmakers to begin changing the laws of segregation to reflect the new social values of the time.

Critics of functionalist theory point out that at times, social changes amount to far more than a simple adjustment. The two World Wars, for example, fundamentally changed international relations, and the eradication of apartheid in South Africa represented nothing less than a complete reordering of that country's entire society. To argue that societies can be understood as organic entities that maintain equilibrium is also problematic in that it confers intent and conscious action to the conceptual notion of society.

CONFLICT THEORY   Conflict theorists argue that since the rich and powerful maintain their control over society to benefit their interests, anything that challenges the status quo will be resisted. While Marx accepted a broad evolutionary path along which societies develop—from Asiatic to ancient to feudal to modern modes of production (Botttomore, Harris, & Miliband, 1991, p. 23)—he did not believe that each was necessarily an improvement over the earlier form. According to Marx, history is full of examples of societies that moved through stages defined by the exploitation of the poor. True equality was possible only in the final stage of social development: communism (Slattery, 2003, p. 43). To achieve equality, Marx viewed social change as coming about through active revolt against oppression and exploitation. Unlike the functionalists' focus on stability, then, conflict theorists consider conflict as inevitable and necessary to inspire social changes that will ultimately rid the world of inequality.

Although conflict theory is well suited to explain changes that occur as a result of tension and confrontation (including union strikes and government overthrows), it is less able to explain long-term stability and change that can occur without conflict (see Mayer, 1960).

EVOLUTIONARY THEORY   Sociologists as far back as Auguste Comte have used evolutionary principles to explain social change. Comte believed that societies move through three stages of evolution—what he called the *Law of Three Stages*. Comte referred to the first stage as the theological stage. During this stage, people use religion, and the acts of gods or spirits, to explain the world and human behaviour. As societies evolve, they move into the *metaphysical stage*. During this stage, societies begin to question the teachings of religion. This stage is characterized by the assumption that people can understand and explain their universe through their own insight and reflection (Ritzer, 2008). During the final stage, referred to as the *positive stage*, societies use science to gain an understanding of their world. Émile Durkheim similarly proposed that over time, societies inevitably become more complex. Both Comte and Durkheim set forth what are referred to as evolutionary theories.

Unilinear evolutionary theories hold that there is one path through which an organism or society can evolve (e.g., Comte's Law of Three Stages contended that no theological society could skip the metaphysical stage on its way to the positive stage). **Universal evolutionary theories** argue that all societies must progress in the same manner; no society can stay at the

---

equilibrium theory The assertion that a system's natural state is one of balance and harmony.

unilinear evolutionary theory The assertion that there is only one path through which an organism or society can evolve.

universal evolutionary theory The assertion that all societies must progress in the same manner.

theological stage or evolve into any form other than the three stages. While these views of social development have been discounted, a new form of evolutionary theory has been proposed by Gerhard Lenski (Barnett, 2004).

Neoevolutionary theory highlights the role of technology in assisting human beings with their subsistence needs. Lenski (1966, 1996) agued that evolution is not unilinear or universal. Rather, he believed that evolution is multilinear, continuous, and fluid (Kennedy, 2004, p. 316). Despite their differences, all evolutionists would agree that all societies have some internal drive that inspires them to adapt to the environment so that they can compete more effectively for survival—this applies not just to individuals, but to entire societies as well.

Evolutionary theory has been influential in the past, but continues to face criticism. First, there is no evidence to suggest that all traditional societies were alike, and when societies do change, there does not appear to be a fixed set of stages through which they pass. Another criticism of evolutionary theory is the underlying assumption that societies progress over time After all, in terms of social development, defining *progress* is difficult. For example, while the standard of living in wealthy countries has been rising over the past 50 years, environmental degradation, warfare, global terrorism, poverty, and human rights abuses around the world challenge the assumption that societies inevitably make positive social "progress" (Becker, 2007).

neoevolutionary theory
Lenski's analysis of the role that technology plays in people's adjustment to the physical world.

CYCLICAL THEORY The idea behind cyclical theory is that social change occurs in a cycle much like the changing seasons of the year. Cyclical theory does not argue that social change occurs in a defined direction, but instead that there is an ebb and flow through time according to a series of endless cycles.

The earliest sociologist to apply cyclical theory to social change was Pitirim Sorokin (1889–1968). Sorokin held that social change occurred over time by moving back and forth between these two opposites: ideational culture and sensate culture. An **ideational culture** is driven to seek and achieve spiritual goals. Ideational cultures are religious. Over time, people's faith begins to falter and they transition into what Sorokin described as a **sensate culture**—a society that interprets the physical and social world through the senses (in other words, a science-based culture). According to Sorokin, as a society moves in one direction, the attraction of the opposing force becomes stronger until the society reverses course (Bainbridge, 2007, p. 207).

Cyclical theory is certainly compelling, given that some things really do appear to change in cycles (consider economic boom and bust cycles; see Broadway, 2007, p. 565). However, other changes, such as technological innovations, appear to build on each other, and thus imply a direction of increasing complexity. Furthermore, cyclical theory is far more descriptive than analytic. It is possible that it was more applicable in the past than it is today (Lindsey & Beach, 2003, p. 428).

ideational culture
Sorokin's term for a society driven to seek and achieve spiritual goals.

sensate culture
Sorokin's term for a society that interprets the social and physical world through the senses.

What do you know about **Social Change**?

Multiple-choice questions (circle your answer)

1. **Behaviours that occur when people come together to achieve a meaningful short-term goal are called**
   a. Social change
   b. Collective behaviours
   c. Social movements
   d. Innovation

2. **The last stage in the life cycle of social change is**
   a. Innovation
   b. Saturation
   c. Exponential growth
   d. Over-development

3. **Prensky's term for people who grew up with digital technologies is**
   a. Digital natives
   b. Digital immigrants
   c. Digital children
   d. Digital emigrants

4. **Technology can be defined as**
   a. Anything that provides an artificial means to achieve a given end or result
   b. Anything that is new

c   A natural means to a given end
d. Anything digital

c. Multilinear evolutionary theory
d. Unilinear evolutionary theory

5. The assertion that there is only one path through which an organism or society can evolve is
a. Universal evolutionary theory
b. Neoevolutionary theory

module 12.2

Collective Behaviour

Collective behaviour occurs when people come together to achieve a single and meaningful short-term goal that may inspire social change (Kurzman, 2008). Some sociologists prefer to use the term *collectivity* rather than *group* to highlight the strength of the bonds between the people involved. A **collectivity**, then, is a substantial number of people who join together on the basis of loosely defined norms. Collectivities generate little solidarity or loyalty, usually last only a short while, have no defined boundaries, recognize few leaders, and display only a basic division of labour among members. In **localized collectivities** the members are located in one another's immediate physical presence (think of crowds, demonstrations, and riots), while in **dispersed collectivities** they are in different places at the same time (through rumours, gossip, and fads) (Turner & Killian, 1993, as cited in Lindsey & Beach, 2003, p. 413).

LOCALIZED COLLECTIVITIES

collectivity A substantial number of people who join together on the basis of loosely defined norms.

localized collectivities Collectivities in which the members are located in one another's immediate physical presence.

dispersed collectivities Collectivities in which the members are in different places at the same time.

Crowds are unorganized collections of people who gather temporarily for a particular cause and are united by a common mood (e.g., people attending a parade) (Budilova, 2003). Since individuals are able to blend into a crowd, some members feel a level of anonymity that at times may increase their willingness to violate conventional norms. Some suggest that crowds can enable people to lose themselves and get caught up in the moment (Best, 2006, p. 9; Schweingruber & Wohlstein, 2005). For example, young women "flashed" their breasts along Calgary's "Red Mile" during the 2004 Stanley Cup playoffs (see Danielewicz, 2005). Herbert Blumer (1969) identified four basic types of crowds: casual, conventional, expressive, and acting.

A **casual crowd** is a collection of people who just happen to be in the same place at the same time—for example, people shopping at a mall. The casual crowd lacks any formal leadership or structure and is the simplest and most rudimentary form of collective behaviour (Hooper, 2001, p. 160).

A **conventional crowd** emerges from structured social events such as weddings, ethnic festivals, and hockey games. People who attend these events generally behave in ways that are appropriate to the given activity (e.g., having your face painted with team colours is acceptable at a hockey game), and they generally disperse without incident.

Expressive crowds are intended to provide participants with the opportunity to express their emotions. For example, participants in Gay Pride parades want to express their joy and pride in who they are, while people attending a funeral want to deal with their own grief as well as provide support for the family of the deceased.

When a crowd gathers with the intention to express anger and direct it outwardly at a specific person, category of people, or event, Blumer called it an **acting crowd**. A **mob** is a crowd that gathers to achieve an emotionally driven goal, confronts it, and then fades away—for example, the various demonstrations held around the world to challenge China's treatment of Tibetan monks. A relatively recent phenomenon is referred to as a **flash mob** (Srivastava, 2005), a planned gathering of large numbers of people who converge in a public or semi-public place for a brief and predetermined period of time and then disperse immediately after the event. Most of these flash mobs are coordinated via websites (e.g., www.flashmob.com) or text messaging. One unique example is a worldwide organization that arranges pillow fights: participants show up, bash each other with pillows, and then leave (www.pillowfightday.com).

A **riot** is also an acting crowd, but unlike a mob that focuses on a single person or event, a riot involves public disorder and directs its hostility toward multiple targets, moving from one to another in unpredictable ways. Riots can last for days, with participants dispersing and regrouping in response to the actions of the agents of social change. A famous riot occurred in Los Angeles in April 1992. After police were acquitted in the beating of Rodney King, a young African American, many people became outraged and took to the streets. The riot lasted for 6 days and resulted in 53 deaths, 10 000 arrests, 2300 injuries, and 1000 buildings lost to fire. The cost to the city was estimated at more than $1 billion (Davis, 2007; Matheson & Baade, 2004, p. 2691).

A fifth type of crowd, the protest crowd, was recently added to the four types originally identified by Blumer (Lindsey, Beach, & Ravelli, 2009, p. 278). **Protest crowds** are deliberately assembled by the leaders of social movements to demonstrate public support for these movements. Examples of protest crowds include the 1963 civil rights rally in Washington, DC—at which more than 250 000 people heard Martin Luther King Jr. give his famous "I have a dream" speech—and the 200 000 Mexicans who, in February 2008, protested against NAFTA's agricultural policies.

DISPERSED COLLECTIVITIES

Because people in a dispersed collectivity are not in physical proximity to each other, they are more likely to react in emotional and relatively unconventional ways to situations or messages (Lofland, 2004/1981). Sociologists define five types of dispersed collective behaviours: rumours; mass hysteria; disaster behaviour; fashion, fads, and crazes; and publics.

RUMOURS   A **rumour** is specific information passed from person to person that lacks reliable evidence to substantiate its claim or claims (Houmanfar & Johnson, 2003, p. 119). Rumours are most likely to occur when people face ambiguous situations and desperately want accurate information even though none is available (Donovan, 2007). For example, when a company is losing money, the rumour mill works overtime as workers worry about layoffs or factory closures. Rumours play an important role in the emergence and development of the other forms of dispersed collectivities (e.g., fads and mass hysteria) because they can spread rapidly through a circle of friends, a community, or even the world via the Internet.

crowd An unorganized collection of people who gather temporarily for a particular cause.

casual crowd A chance collection of individuals in the same location at the same time.

conventional crowd A collection of people who gather for a structured social event.

expressive crowd A collection of people who gather intentionally to express their emotions.

acting crowd A collection of people who gather to express anger and direct it outwardly at a specific person, category of people, or event.

mob A crowd that gathers to achieve an emotionally driven goal.

flash mob A planned gathering of large numbers of people for a brief and predetermined period of time.

riot A type of acting crowd that directs its anger toward multiple targets, moving from one to another in unpredictable ways.

protest crowd A deliberately assembled crowd to rally support for a social movement.

rumour Specific information passed from person to person that lacks reliable evidence.

gossip   Intimate and personal communication meant to be entertaining.

urban legend   A short, persistent, nonverifiable tale with an ironic or supernatural twist.

There are two types of rumours: gossip and urban legends. **Gossip** is intimate and personal communication meant to be entertaining and enjoyable, while rumours generally deal with more important matters. Simply put, rumours help to justify, explain, and provide meaning to ambiguous situations, while gossip is intended to be an enjoyable sharing of everyday information (Houmanfar & Johnson, 2003, p. 119). **Urban legends** are short, persistent, usually nonverifiable tales with an ironic or supernatural twist. For example, according to one urban legend, spider eggs are an ingredient for a type of chewing gum (Noymer, 2001, p. 300; Weldon, 2001, p. 282).

There are times when media report urban legends and disseminate them to the larger public. Examples include the false claims that large numbers of children are abducted by Satanists and sacrificed in their rituals (Richardson, Best, & Bromley, 1991) and that deranged people are putting razor blades in the apples they pass out at Halloween. When rumours like these are reported in the media, they can inspire mass hysteria (Lindsey, Beach, & Ravelli, 2009, p. 280).

mass hysteria   Occurs when people react to a real or imagined event with irrational or frantic fear.

MASS HYSTERIA   **Mass hysteria** occurs when people react to a real or imagined event with irrational or frantic fear. One of the most famous cases of mass hysteria was Orson Welles' "The War of the Worlds" radio broadcast on October 30, 1938. The play, presented in the form of a newscast, was broadcast across the United States and depicted a Martian invasion. Princeton University psychologist Hadley Cantril (1940) estimated that more than 1 million listeners were frightened or disturbed by what they thought was a real broadcast. However, subsequent research by sociologists David Miller (1985) and William Sims Bainbridge (1987) concluded that there was scant evidence of substantial or widespread panic. The fact that the fictional program led some people to fear for their lives nonetheless demonstrates that people are influenced by the emotions and behaviours of others.

disaster   An unexpected event that causes extensive damage to people, animals, and property.

DISASTER BEHAVIOUR   **Disasters** are usually unexpected events that cause extensive damage to people, animals, and property, and include floods, earthquakes, hurricanes, and other natural or human disasters. Some researchers estimate that in the past 10 years, disasters have affected more than 3 billion people, killed more than 750 000, and caused more than US$600 billion in damages (Birkmann, 2006, as cited in Mayunga, 2007, p. 1).

At times, large disasters can result in a breakdown of traditional socio-political guidelines that can leave people feeling overwhelmed, demoralized, and depressed (Boin & McConnell, 2007, p. 51; Knudsen, Roman, Johnson, & Ducharme, 2005, p. 260). However, people are also very resilient, and most survivors return to normal lives (Vineburgh, Ursano, & Fullerton, 2005, p. 213).

fashion   A social pattern that outwardly expresses an individual's identity as being "with it."

fad   A short-lived but enthusiastically embraced new cultural element.

For a review of fads from 2008, go to **www.people.com/people/archive/article/0,,20252039,00.html.**

FASHION, FADS, AND CRAZES   **Fashion** refers to a social pattern that appeals to a large number of people—for example, what people wear, the music they listen to, and the colour and style of their cellphones. To be considered fashionable is to pursue items that partly establish a personal identity as an outward expression of confidence and being "with it."

A **fad** is a short-lived but enthusiastically embraced new cultural element. While many consider the contemporary attraction to tattoos to be a fad, the fact that they are largely permanent led Kosut (2006) to refer to them as "ironic fads," in that they cannot be discarded as easily as a pair of leg warmers once they go out of style. According to Lofland (1973), there are four distinct types of fads: *object fads* (cellphones, pet rocks, pogs), *idea fads* (astrology, UFOs, the occult), *activity fads* (Botox injections, tongue piercing, bungee jumping), and *personality fads* (Elvis, Oprah, Jarome Iginla) (Lindsey, Beach, & Ravelli, 2009, p. 280).

A **craze** is similar to a fad but usually represents a more intense emotional connection to the phenomenon at hand. For example, fans of the band the Grateful Dead are referred to as "Deadheads" (see www.dead.net), some of whom spend a lot of time and energy following anything to do with the band. Other examples of ongoing crazes are fans of *Star Trek* (called "trekkies," see www.startrek.com) or those of the Beatles (a phenomenon referred to as Beatlemania).

craze A widespread emotional connection to a cultural phenomenon.

PUBLICS   A **public** is defined as an accumulation of people who have a defined political interest for meeting and who are organized by a common mood but not necessarily in direct contact with other members (Budilova, 2003, p. 18; Lindsey & Beach, 2003, p. 417). This collective experience is intended to establish a new norm or law, policy, or practice that would guide people's behaviour and actions (e.g., public hearings on changes to legislation on dangerous offenders; Attallah, 2002, pp. 103–104). Collective behaviour researchers view a public as an enduring collectivity that maintains an interest in a particular issue for an extended period of time. When a public becomes organized enough to convey its point of view actively to decision-makers, it becomes either an interest group or a social movement (Greenberg & Page, 2007).

public An accumulation of people who have a defined political interest for meeting and who are organized by a common mood.

SOCIOLOGICAL APPROACHES TO COLLECTIVE BEHAVIOUR

Our review of localized and dispersed collectivities highlighted several examples of collective behaviours—things that people do when they are in groups that they generally do not do on their own. Sociologists have developed three primary theories that attempt to explain the influence of a group on an individual: contagion, convergence, and emergent norm theories.

CONTAGION THEORY   French sociologist Gustave Le Bon (1841–1931) was the first to apply social psychology principles to understand why people behave differently when they are in groups than when they are alone. The theory's basic assumption is that the group exerts a powerful influence on the individual (Terrier, 2006, p. 290). Le Bon argued that when people gather in crowds, an individual loses his or her conscious personality and has it replaced by an uncivilized and potentially barbaric "collective mind" (Waddington & King, 2005, p. 491). Le Bon (1895) believed that the irrationality of the crowd was contagious and created a type of excitement that was similar to a hypnotic effect (Zvi, 2006, p. 185). For the collective mind to emerge, three complementary factors are required: *anonymity* (people have to feel that they are lost within the group), *suggestibility* (anonymity makes people more suggestible to the collective will), and *contagion* (With the other two factors present, it becomes increasingly likely that "mindless" emotional activity will spread through the group.) (Waddington & King, 2005, p. 491).

Le Bon's ideas influenced a great many writers at the time, including Émile Durkheim (Terrier, 2006, p. 290) and Sigmund Freud (Zvi, 2006, p. 185). However, these ideas have been largely discounted by contemporary researchers, who have found little evidence to suggest that people do in fact "lose themselves" to the group (Kimmel, 1990, p. 68; McPhail, 1991).

CONVERGENCE THEORY   Convergence theory argues that the group is not the source of negative, irrational behaviour but instead that such behaviour appeals to a particular type of person. When like-minded people converge, they are more likely to manifest the type of behaviour they were looking for in the first place. For example, football matches in

European football hooliganism shows how people may behave very differently in groups than when they are alone.

Europe have been marred for decades by hooligans who intentionally go to games to get into fights and participate in violent behaviour (Frosdick & Newton, 2006, p. 410; Stott & Pearson, 2006, p. 242).

Convergence theory certainly helps to explain why some people take part in actions while in a group that they would not do on their own (e.g., rarely do people go to football matches on their own and look to start a fight). However, the theory fails to explain why some people are drawn to those activities while others are not.

EMERGENT NORM THEORY Emergent norm theory is a symbolic interactionist approach in which aggressive or anti-social behaviours are viewed as resulting from an adjustment to new norms that emerge within a given group and in certain situations (Mancini, Fruggeri, & Panari, 2006, p. 211). In most situations, these changing social norms arise in ambiguous situations wherein individuals turn to others for cues on how to behave or what course of action to take (Uhl-Bien & Pillai, 2007, p. 201). For example, most reality television shows involve challenging situations in which one contestant offers a plan of action that others can accept or reject. In these ambiguous situations, such early decisions often become the new norms of behaviour (Aguirre, Wenger, & Vigo, 1998, p. 302). In a classic symbolic-interactionist interpretation, the new norms are the result of ongoing interaction between members of the group. Those who choose to follow the new norms stay with the group while those who do not generally leave the group, which acts to reinforce the display of unity among group members (McPhail & Wohlstein, 1983).

Emergent norm theory, as proposed by its pioneers, Ralph Turner and Lewis Killian (1993), views crowd behaviour as neither irrational (as contagion theory asserts) nor deliberate (as convergence theory argues), but rather as the result of dynamic exchanges between participants. In other words, the group's actions are influenced by existing norms and values but are open to new norms should the group believe they are necessary. Emergent norm theory, then, offers an attractive middle-of-the road perspective. However, critics point out that the theory has limited ability to predict how groups will behave because there are so many variables at work (e.g., time of day, weather, backgrounds of people involved, preceding events that may inspire tension or fear among the group) (Ward, 1980, p. 19).

What do you know about **Collective Behaviour**?

Multiple-choice questions (circle your answer)

1. **Collectivities in which the members are located in each other's immediate physical presence are called**
   a. Localized collectivities
   b. Communal collectivities
   c. Dispersed collectivities
   d. Casual collectivities

2. **A chance collection of individuals in the same location at the same time is called a(n)**
   a. Casual crowd
   b. Conventional crowd
   c. Expressive crowd
   d. Acting crowd

3. **A planned gathering of large numbers of people for a brief and predetermined period of time is called a(n)**
   a. Mob
   b. Acting crowd
   c. Flash mob
   d. Expressive crowd

4. **Intimate and personal communication meant to be entertaining is called**
   a. A rumour
   b. Gossip
   c An urban legend
   d. Hysteria

5. **_____ theory's basic assumption is that the group exerts a powerful influence on the individual.**
   a. Contagion
   b. Convergence
   c. Emergent norm
   d. Symbolic interactionist

Answers: a, a, c, b, a

module 12.3

Social Movements

Social movements are the most highly structured, rational, and enduring form of collective behaviour. Most social movements are established to stimulate change. They usually begin as small groups of people who possess little social power and who seek legitimacy, recognition, and change from existing social institutions such as government, political parties, and civic leaders. Social movements are perhaps the most important variety of collective behaviour, as they can lead to profound social change (Carroll & Ratner, 2007, p. 43). Doherty (2002, p. 7, as cited in Fagan, 2004, p. 20) defines four characteristics of those who participate in social movements:

1. They have a shared common identity.
2. They act at least partly outside of traditional political institutions and use protest as one of their primary forms of action.

Think about Social Movements

1 Think about social movements. Have you ever been involved in a social movement such as the environmental movement or educational reform? How would you define a *social movement*?

2 Think about an issue that is important to you. What do you think you could do to make a change? How do you think social movements get started?

informal social movement
A social movement that emerges to challenge a specific local issue.

To learn more about the environmental movement in Canada, go to Greenpeace's site at **www.greenpeace.org/ canada/en/.**

formal social movement
A large, well-integrated, and established organization with bureaucratic procedures.

3. They rely on non-institutionalized networks of interaction.
4. They reject or challenge dominant forms of power.

Corbett (2006) proposes that social movements generally fall into two forms: informal, grassroots groups and formal or institutional groups.

Informal social movements generally emerge in opposition to a specific local issue, be it a *direct hazard* (e.g., changes to a community's drinking water infrastructure), a *plan* (e.g., a proposal to construct a nearby dam or nuclear power plant), or a broader *concern or threat* (e.g., a proposal to ban the domestic use of pesticides). The most common form of informal social movements is environmental groups that promote more responsible and sustainable lifestyle choices. These grassroots movements generally originate with one or more charismatic leaders, who can range from ordinary citizens to members of the intellectual or social elite (Corbett, 2006, p. 286). What these informal groups lack in resources (money, paid staff, office space) they make up for in passion and commitment. Members of informal social groups usually have a personal stake in the issues at hand, whereas members of larger, more formal social movement organizations may not.

Formal social movements are large organizations that have existed for a long time, and as such have elaborate structures and procedures (Corbett, 2006, p. 287). Formal social movements exercise bureaucratic procedures, but they do not operate within a society's existing power structures (e.g., government or business) (Laverack, 2004, p. 8)—although they may lobby these structures to further their own interests. These groups—for example, Greenpeace or pro-choice organizations—are well integrated within society, well known to the public, and a mainstay of regular media coverage.

Sociologists refer to well-established social movements as social movement organizations (SMOs). Each has its own way of achieving its goals, but also shares the methods of many other organizations. In fact, SMOs often influence, inspire, and complement each other's activities (Van Dyke, Dixon, & Carlon, 2007, p. 194).

TYPES OF SOCIAL MOVEMENTS

Social movements are classified according to a number of criteria:

■ *Level of change* (e.g., a local movement targeting domestic pesticide use versus a national organization fighting the proliferation of genetically modified foods) (Turner & Killian, 1993)

■ *Direction of change*, whereby some movements are seen as progressive and in line with public opinion (e.g., groups advocating the use of alternative fuels) while others wish to resist or reverse current trends (e.g., groups who oppose recent legislation allowing same-sex marriages) (Turner & Killian, 1993)

■ *Speed of change*, whereby some movements seek immediate change (e.g., seal hunt protesters) and others work for gradual change (e.g., women's suffrage movement) (Ng, 2007, p. 107)

■ *Target of change*, whereby some movements focus on individual behaviours (e.g., local recycling programs) while others are interested in society-wide change (e.g., legislative changes to the legal drinking age) (Johnson, 2008; Lindsey & Beach, 2003, p. 421)

Combining these various features results in four different types of social movements: revolutionary, reformist, reactionary, and religious.

revolutionary movement
A social movement that seeks a complete reorganization of society.

REVOLUTIONARY MOVEMENTS   **Revolutionary movements** are the most extreme form of social change because they seek a complete reorganization of society (Karagiannis, 2005, p. 140). These movements typically emerge when previous efforts to bring about change have failed or proven inadequate. Revolutionary movements can be both peaceful

CANADIAN SOCIETY IN FOCUS

Mothers Against Drunk Driving (MADD)

Of the 3226 people killed in motor vehicle accidents in 2006, a whopping 1210 involved alcohol. Further, estimates suggest that each year more than 71 000 Canadians are injured and more than 235 000 vehicles are damaged in incidents involving alcohol (MADD, 2008a). Mothers Against Drunk Driving (MADD) is a charitable, grassroots organization established in 1990 to help stop impaired driving in Canada. It aggressively promotes public education initiatives on the effects of drinking and driving, and more than 750 000 people have seen the group's multimedia presentations (MADD, 2008b).

Researchers at Dalhousie University and the Canadian Centre for Addiction and Mental Health conducted a study on Canadian drinking and driving trends between 1962 and 1996. The researchers found that during the study period, drunk driving was the leading cause of criminal-related deaths in Canada, and that almost half of all traffic fatalities involved someone who was impaired. Still, alcohol-related traffic fatalities have declined in Canada over the past 25 years, owing in part to better safety equipment in cars, breathalyzer and seat belt laws, and educational initiatives by grassroots organizations like MADD (Asbridge, Mann, Flam-Zalcman, & Stoduto, 2004, p. 450).

In fact, the study found that the largest factor in the decline of drinking and driving fatalities has been changes to public policy inspired by such social movement organizations (Asbridge, Mann, Flam-Zalcman, & Stoduto, 2004, p. 450). As Ross (1984, as cited in Asbridge, Mann, Flam-Zalcman, & Stoduto, 2004, p. 457) puts it, "Although [MADD's] membership is small, the movement—abetted by its powerful allies—has been remarkably successful in publicizing its viewpoint and in obtaining implementation of the policies it advocates."

Robert Mann, the study's co-author, states, "Our research concludes that, more than any other single factor, MADD Canada's work has reduced impaired driving fatalities in our country. . . . Our data suggest that MADD Canada's activities translate directly into lives saved" (as cited in MADD Canada, 2004). To date, MADD research suggests that its efforts saved more than 30 000 lives between 1982 and 2006 in Canada (MADD, 2008c).

MADD ad campaign highlights the danger of mixing alcohol and water sports.

(the recent struggles by the Québécois for greater sovereignty) and violent (the "Saffron Revolution" in Myanmar, where Buddhist monks have led many demonstrations against the oppressive military dictatorship). Such movements can be perceived by authoritarian regimes as attempts to undermine their rule and be deemed subversive and something to be crushed.

reformist movement
A social movement that works within the existing social structure to improve society.

REFORMIST MOVEMENTS   **Reformist movements**, in contrast, work within the existing social structure to improve society by addressing specific issues. The American civil rights movement did not propose to reorder society but instead to confirm the rights of every American. In Canada, Mothers Against Drunk Drivers (MADD) does not lobby to abolish alcohol but rather to educate the public on the effects of drinking and driving and to promote responsible drinking.

reactionary movement
A social movement that emerges when groups resist an event or decision they feel they cannot tolerate.

REACTIONARY MOVEMENTS   **Reactionary movements** are often inspired when people feel that society is moving in a direction they cannot tolerate or when there is an event or decision that they feel must be challenged. For example, when Dr. Henry Morgentaler was awarded the Order of Canada in July 2008 for his efforts to legalize abortion in Canada, many questioned the decision on moral and religious grounds, and some former recipients of the Order even returned their awards in protest (Pedwell, 2008). Often, the intent of these movements is to reverse the direction they feel society is travelling in and return to an earlier time. These movements appeal to people who are uncomfortable with the way things currently are and fear what the future might hold. Other Canadian examples of reactionary movements are the Aryan Nations, the Heritage Front, Canadian Liberty Net, some pro-life groups, and the Church of the Creator.

religious movement
A social movement grounded in a spiritual or supernatural belief system.

RELIGIOUS MOVEMENTS   Some argue that successful social movements, whether celebrated (e.g., civil rights) or denounced (e.g., Nazism), all begin with driven individuals who have deeply held convictions (Shields, 2007, p. 112). **Religious movements** (also referred to as *expressive movements*) are grounded in spiritual or supernatural belief systems that are thought to inspire some form of inner change. Some researchers argue that these movements are most likely to emerge as a reaction to the effects of modernization. In essence, then, they are similar to reactionary movements but based on religious views of contemporary and future social change (Coreno, 2002, p. 336). Contemporary examples of religious movements that have emerged partially in protest of social change are the Church of Scientology, Soka Gakkai, Heaven's Gate, the Moonies, and Hare Krishna (Barone, 2007, p. 118; Bruce & Voas, 2007, p. 5; Clarke, 2008).

LIFE CYCLE OF SOCIAL MOVEMENTS

While there are many varieties of social movements, a number of sociologists point out that virtually all of them progress through a life cycle of four stages (Blumer, 1969; Mauss, 1975; Spector & Kitsuse, 1977).

EMERGENCE/INCIPIENCE   During this initial stage, the movement is unorganized and does not have clear leadership or direction. Rather than having a defined set of issues or remedies, a segment of society feels dissatisfied or disillusioned with the current state of affairs.

COALESCENCE   As the movement matures, it begins to define itself and develop a strategy to achieve its goals. During this stage, the movement starts to gain some momentum and to attract new members. It begins to establish a formal organization in order to develop a strategy for change and to communicate its concerns to the larger society. The movement also may form alliances with other groups that share similar perspectives in the hope of expanding the reach and influence of both organizations.

BUREAUCRATIZATION/INSTITUTIONALIZATION   For a movement to have an influence on social change, it must incorporate some bureaucratic organization to manage its affairs. Usually, this involves hiring a paid staff (a change from earlier stages, when much of the work is completed by volunteers), establishing a formal hierarchy of paid leaders, and moving to a full-time office space. As the organization grows, there is increasing pressure to attract donations and grants to ensure that employees and operating expenses are paid. As the movement grows and gains stature, it becomes increasingly respectable, which usually means that its tactics become less confrontational over time.

DECLINE   Although some social movements can last for a very long time, most are temporary. At times, movements are successful and actually lead to social change; otherwise, the movement collapses from internal or external pressures (Gamson, 1990).

To qualify as a success, a social movement must have its recommendations implemented by those in positions of authority (Johnson, 2008). When this happens, the movement largely becomes part of the system, and is referred to as an **interest group** that advocates for change from within the establishment (Piven & Cloward, 1977). Conversely, when the movement maintains its conflict with the establishment (Della Porta, 1995), there is potential for it to be infiltrated and destroyed from within. However, the most common reasons for a social movement's decline are the fragmentation of ideas, power struggles among its leaders (Frey, Dietz, & Kalof, 1992), or the loss of the original charismatic leader.

interest group
An established lobby group that works within the system to promote change.

SOCIOLOGICAL APPROACHES TO SOCIAL MOVEMENTS

Sociologists offer a number of theories to explain when social movements are most likely to emerge and why people are attracted to join them.

RELATIVE DEPRIVATION THEORY   Relative deprivation theory suggests that the origin of many social movements resides in the discontent of those who are dissatisfied with their present condition. Sociologists appreciate that people's reactions to their objective circumstances, such as how well they are doing financially, often depend on their subjective comparison to those around them (Walker & Smith, 2002, p. 1). For example, some people would never think of getting a large-screen television until their neighbours begin to buy them. Feelings of deprivation can also arise when groups (based on racial, ethnic, sexual, or physical differences) perceive that they are not being treated fairly by the society around them (Leach, Iyer, & Pedersen, 2007; Morrison, 1971).

Yet critics of relative deprivation theory point out that some of the poorest and most deprived in society rarely complain or participate in any social movement (Johnson & Klandermans, 1995). While some deprivation is certainly relative, absolute deprivation, of course, also exists. Moreover, relative definitions of deprivation are difficult to measure (Ringen, 2006, pp. 125–126). For these reasons, relative deprivation theory is no longer as popular as it was in the 1960s.

VALUE-ADDED THEORY   In 1963, functionalist Neil Smelser defined a new, and very influential, theory of collective behaviour (Moser, 2007, p. 126). His value-added theory holds that six conditions must be met before a social movement can begin (Waddington & King, 2005, p. 494).

Condition 1: Structural Conduciveness   Smelser suggests that social movements emerge when people can identify who or what is responsible for social problems (Anker, 2008). By having a clear target for their action, social movements are more likely able to focus their

The Oka crisis in 1990 was the culmination of a long-standing dispute over land rights between Aboriginal peoples and government.

efforts. For example, in March 1990, the Mohawks at Kanesatake, west of Montreal, set up a roadblock to bring attention to their land dispute with the municipality of Oka, which was preparing to build a golf course on an Aboriginal burial site (Pertusati, 1997). For the Mohawks, it was clear that the target of their roadblock was all levels of government, which they believed were both responsible for their situation and necessary to help resolve it.

Condition 2: Structural Strain   Structural strain exists when society can no longer meet people's expectations and little appears to have been done to fix the problem. Structural strain disturbs the smooth, predictable functioning of the social system. In this sense, the Oka blockade was merely another expression of anger over the way that Aboriginal peoples have been treated in this country (Lindsey, Beach, & Ravelli, 2009, p. 274).

Condition 3: Growth and Spread of a Generalized Belief   Smelser's third condition is a clear statement of the causes of and solutions to a given problem. For people to rally around a cause, they must be confident that they understand how the movement plans to solve the problem. The generalized belief that developed in Oka after the blockade held that police brutality, poverty, and the general lack of opportunities available to members of the community were the inevitable consequences of white racism.

Condition 4: Precipitating Incident   Frustration may simmer for years until a specific incident occurs that galvanizes the need for immediate and collective action. The spark that ignited the Oka conflict was the pending construction of the golf course.

Condition 5: Mobilization for Action   Smelser's fifth condition is the readiness to take action, which can involve demonstrations and rallies. In the case of the Oka conflict, the mobilization for action occurred when the Mohawks began to set up road blockades.

Condition 6: Social Control   The final condition for a social movement to occur is the involvement of a society's formal social control agents, which can include police officers, the military, elected officials, and civic leaders. Their response to the situation can either incite greater conflict, as seen at Oka, or bring everyone together to develop strategies to address the concern.

Smelser's value-added theory provides a valuable explanation of the conditions necessary for social movements to occur, but it fails to explore the roots of the tensions. While it is easy to explain the Oka conflict as the expression of discontent with land claims and the treatment of Aboriginal peoples, the value-added theory provides little insight into what role mass media play, for example, in the emergence or maintenance of social movements.

RESOURCE MOBILIZATION THEORY   Resource mobilization theory investigates how members of social movements gather and use resources to meet their needs. To be successful, all social movements must secure money (for salaries, promotional materials, and so forth), time (for both paid staff and volunteers), and assistance from outside agencies, politicians, and media (Johnson, 2008, p. 986; McCarthy & Zald, 1977). Resource mobilization theorists suggest that successful movements are those that can effectively acquire and manage these key resources (Gamson, 1990).

While rudimentary resources (such as office space, computers, and photocopiers) may be fairly easy to secure, the greater challenge lies in finding people with the right balance of passion, skills, and abilities to assume leadership roles within the organization. A social movement may be led by a charismatic leader early on, but as the movement matures and grows it requires more bureaucratic organization.

The primary criticism of resource mobilization theory is that by placing so much emphasis on resources, it diminishes the importance of the movement's actual focus. The resources of contemporary environmental groups, for example, while certainly benefitting their cause, do not detract from the great strides achieved by average people who believe in the cause (Buechler, 1993; Donnelly & Kimble, 2006).

NEW SOCIAL MOVEMENT THEORY   New social movement theory originated during the social uprisings of the 1960s. New social movements, including environmental, peace, feminist, gay, and civil rights initiatives, were seen as distinct from old social movements, such as trade union and labour movements, and as representing a distinctly North American approach (Walter, 2007, p. 250). Whereas resource mobilization theory views social activists as exercising variations of rational choice (by using funds wisely or by engaging political parties with whom the movement has the greatest likelihood of success), new social movement theory holds that forms of action are motivated by collective identity found in the culture, ideology, and politics of post-industrial society (Carroll, 1997; Holford, 1995; Mayo, 2005, as cited in Walter, 2007, p. 250).

A defining feature of new social movements is that they are more globally focused than were earlier movements. Today, global warming, environmental destruction, and the loss of biodiversity are challenges that resonate with people around the world. In contrast to earlier movements inspired by the working class, new social movements are increasingly inspired by middle-class interests (Hilton, 2007, p. 123; Macionis & Gerber, 2008, p. 617).

Critics of new social movement theory, however, point out that while this approach adds an important cultural context to social movements, it does not adequately account for the very real power and influence exerted by the political economy (Walter, 2007).

As we have seen, social movements may be important sources of social change. By promoting or resisting certain ideas, they are able to inspire debate and discussion about the future and about the kind of society we want to live in.

What do you know about **Social Movements**?

Multiple-choice questions (circle your answer)

1. A _____ movement seeks a complete reorganization of society.
   a. Revolutionary
   b. Reformist
   c. Reactionary
   d. Religious

2. A _____ movement works within the existing social structure to improve society.
   a. Revolutionary
   b. Reformist
   c. Reactionary
   d. Religious

3. **What other term is used with *bureaucratization* to describe the life cycle of a social movement?**
   a. Emergence
   b. Incipience
   c. Coalescence
   d. Institutionalization

4. **Who developed the value-added theory of social movements?**
   a. Doug McAdam
   b. Neil Smelser

   c   Harold Blumer
   d. Ralph Turner and Lewis Killian

5. **When a society can no longer meet people's expectations and little appears to have been done to fix the problem, then, according to Smelser _____ exists.**
   a. Structural conduciveness
   b. Structural strain
   c. Value-added problems
   d. Relative deprivation

Answers: a, b, d, b, b

module 12.4

The Future

Think about the Future

1 Think about the future. How would you predict the way in which post-secondary education will change over the next 50 years?

2 Think about global climate change. How would you arrive at a viable solution to the problem?

How do you imagine our world will be in 10, 20, or 30 years? Will war, global warming, and world poverty still dominate the daily news? Or will we be living in peace and harmony with one another and nature?

Futurology is the study of the future. It is multidisciplinary, meaning that it relies on the expertise of people from a wide range of fields. Sociology and sociologists are well represented in the field of futurology, but so too are economists, climatologists, government and business leaders, and those from many other disciplines. The purpose of futurology is to give us a picture of what is ahead.

PREDICTING THE FUTURE

futurology   The study of the future.

extrapolation   Predicting the future by examining what is going on in the present and comparing that with what has happened in the past.

How do futurologists predict the future? They have developed a number of sophisticated methods to provide future scenarios. One way to predict the future is to examine what is going on in the present and compare that with what has happened in the past. This method of predicting the future is called **extrapolation**. By examining trends in areas such as the economy, demographics, technology, and collective behaviours such as fads, fashions, or social movements, futurologists can envision the world several years into the future. For example, in Canada the proportion of seniors as compared with other age groups is growing significantly (see Chapter 11). Based on current trends, we can predict that Canada's population will continue to age.

The problem with extrapolation is that it is limited to short-term forecasting (Helmer & Gordon, 1979). By focusing on one trend in isolation, we do not take into account how other social, natural, or technological factors may interact with it. For instance, if we consider a technological change alone, it is difficult for us to predict all of its unintended consequences. Did we predict an increase in car accidents because of the introduction of cellphones or the need to ban them from change rooms or the potential health risks they pose? It is very difficult to predict all of the ways that a new technology will alter our social and physical worlds.

Thus, long-range forecasting—predicting 10, 20, or 50 years into the future—requires more in-depth methods. These methods use a variety of correlational studies to examine the connections between a variety of variables. But further, they also tend to rely more on our intuition and our ability to take a more holistic approach to our understanding of change (Helmer & Gordon, 1979). A variety of methods are used by futurologists.

Long-range forecasts can be based on correlations. This method entails defining a variable to be forecast and then comparing it with another variable to determine their relationship. One way of making correlations is through the leader–follower method. For example, in technological forecasting, we can make predictions about advances in a particular technology by examining changes in the leading technology. If we want to predict how automobile engines are going to change, we would examine changes in race-car engines. If we want to predict how automobile sound systems are going to change, we would examine changes in home entertainment technology.

Long-range forecasts can also be made by the **Delphi method**. This method entails surveying experts from a wide range of fields to produce insights and predictions based on trends in their respective fields. This information is compiled to discover correlated or influential patterns that cross over from one field to another. The result is a form of scenario building.

Computer-simulated modelling is another method of long-range forecasting that uses extrapolations and correlations to predict future trends.

Figure 12–1 lists the top 10 forecasts for 2009 and beyond presented in *Outlook 2009*, a publication of the World Future Society.

FIVE SCENARIOS OF THE FUTURE

James Robertson (1978, 1983) argues in his book *The Sane Alternative* that all visions of the future fit into one of five scenarios:

1. **Business-as-usual scenario.** This view holds that the future will be much like the past and the present. There will continue to be changes and issues of concern, as there always have been, but we should not concern ourselves too much. For the most part, people that hold this view believe that the world in the future will not be much different from the world today.
2. **Disaster scenario.** This view predicts that we are heading for catastrophic changes. Nuclear war, famine, poverty, pandemics, and global warming are all disaster scenario concerns.
3. **Authoritarian control (AC).** People that hold this view also see the threat of disaster as very real. They believe that the best way to avert disaster is through some form of authoritarian government control.
4. **Hyper-expansionist (HE) scenario.** This view of the future also assumes that we are headed for disaster. However, people that hold this view believe that all disasters can be avoided through the development of new technologies. They consider that technology can solve all problems.
5. **Sane, humane, ecological (SHE) scenario.** People that hold this view also believe that disaster is likely, but they do not believe that government or technology have all the answers. Rather, they believe that we should change direction. They believe that the key to the future is balance—balance within ourselves, from one person to another, and with nature.

To learn more about the future, go to **www.wfs.org**.

Delphi method Predicting the future by surveying experts from a wide range of fields to produce insights and predictions based on trends in their respective fields.

business-as-usual scenario The view holds that the future will be much like the past and the present.

disaster scenario The view predicts that we are heading for catastrophic changes.

authoritarian control (AC) The view that the best way to avert disaster is through some form of authoritarian government control.

hyper-expansionist (HE) scenario The view that all disasters can be avoided through the development of new technologies.

sane, humane, ecological (SHE) scenario The view that the key to the future is balance—balance within ourselves, from one person to another, and with nature; it calls for a change in direction.

FIGURE 12–1 **Top 10 Forecasts for 2009 and Beyond**

1. "Everything you say and do will be recorded by 2030." By the late 2010s all human communication will be recorded by invisible nanodevices. Humans will have nanoimplants. All conversation and activity will be recorded and recoverable.

2. "Bioviolence will become a greater threat as the technology becomes more accessible. Emerging scientific disciplines (notably genomics, nanotechnology, and other microsciences) could pave the way for a bioatttack." Viruses, bacteria, and nanopollution present our greatest long-term risks.

3. "The car's days as the king of the road may soon be over." Government restrictions on car ownership, improved wireless communication that reduces the need to travel, and flying delivery drones that replace trucks could all contribute to a reduction in the number of cars on the road.

4. "Careers, and the college majors for preparing for them, are becoming more specialized." There is a growing demand for niche disciplines such as nanotechnology,

5. "There may not be world law in the foreseeable future, but the world's legal systems will be networked." The Global Legal Information Network (GLIN) is growing. By 2010 it will include 100 countries. This database will provide greater understanding and cooperation among countries.

6. "Professional knowledge will become obsolete almost as quickly as it's acquired." Most professions will require continuous instruction and retraining.

7. "The race for biomedical and genetic enhancement will—in the twenty-first century—be what the space race was in the previous century." Money is already being invested in the fields of biomedical and genetic enhancement.

8. "Urbanization will hit 60% by 2030." The movement to urbanization is likely to exacerbate existing environmental and socio-economic problems.

9. "The Middle East will become more secular while religious influence in China will grow." Support for religious government in places like Iraq is declining, while in places like China globalization seems to be having an opposite effect.

10. "Access to electricity will reach 83% of the world by 2030." In 1970, 40 percent of the world's population had access to electricity. By 2000, that number had reached 73 percent. Access to electricity is linked to a rising standard of living.

Source: World Future Society. (2008). Ten forecasts for 2009 and beyond. *Outlook 2009.* Retrieved July 21, 2009, from http://www.wfs.org/foresight/index3.htm.

If we consider science-fiction film and literature, we are most likely to see disaster scenarios (e.g., *The Day After Tomorrow*, 2004), authoritarian control scenarios (e.g., *Gattaca*, 1997), or hyper-expansionist scenarios (e.g., *Armageddon*, 1998). However, we can see evidence of the other scenarios present in our everyday thinking and behaviour.

In the section that follows, we will apply the five scenarios to the issue of global climate change.

APPLYING THE FIVE SCENARIOS TO GLOBAL CLIMATE CHANGE   Perhaps the most well-known current environmental challenge is global climate change. While many use the phrase *global warming*, the more accurate term is *global climate change*, because even though the planet is warming up, the more pressing concern is the effect that this change is having on global weather patterns (Bell, 2004, p. 5).

The Earth's temperature is regulated by the greenhouse effect (Schneider, 2008, p. 31). This term reflects the fact that the Earth is similar to a greenhouse in that the atmosphere absorbs and traps heat over the Earth just as the glass panes in a greenhouse do. As short-wave radiation from the sun passes through the Earth's atmosphere, it is absorbed by land and

The film "The Day After Tomorrow" presents a disaster scenario of the planet's future based on projections of global climate change.

water and warms the planet. Part of the absorbed energy is then re-radiated to the atmosphere in the form of long-wave infrared radiation. Very little of this radiation escapes into space because it is trapped by gases in the atmosphere called *greenhouse gases* (notably carbon dioxide, methane, nitrous oxide, and water vapour). These gases act as a blanket and over time have increased the earth's temperature.

While greenhouse gases naturally vary over time, research has shown that they are higher today than at any point in the past 800 000 years (CNRS, 2008). This latest increase is assumed to be the result of industrialization and population growth.

Today, media reports of global climate change tend to focus on *disaster* scenarios. It is now generally accepted that higher temperatures threaten the world's boreal forests as well as increase the risk of fire; decrease the availability of fresh water; increase the frequency of severe weather systems, including hurricanes; and enable tropical diseases to move northward, where populations have little or no immunity to them (Environment Canada, 2007d). There are those that believe global climate change marks the end of humanity.

However, while some see us as ultimately doomed, others see global climate change either as a challenge or an opportunity. For instance, in spite of warnings that climate change will be catastrophic and change the world forever, industries engaged in the extraction of natural resources such as oil and precious metals look at climate change as an opportunity. Companies that take a *business-as-usual* approach are currently exploring the far north and staking claims on territories that they predict will be available to them as the northern polar ice cap melts (Brett, 2007; Krauss, Myers, Revkin, & Romero, 2005; Walton, 2009).

Some believe that the best way to deal with global climate change is to have more government controls. In fact, there appears to be a resurgence of authoritarianism around the world (Petrou, 2009). The Socialist Party of Canada adhered to an authoritarian control approach to address the issue of global climate change during the 2008 federal election campaign. In its platform, the party proposed greater governmental control to combat climate change (Angus, 2008):

- Government expropriation of any company that did not comply with tight government established emission control guidelines
- Public ownership of all power industries
- Phasing out of the use of fossil fuels
- The elimination of military spending
- The retooling of auto plants to focus on building mass transit vehicles, and other green technologies

- Expansion of all public transit
- Free public transit
- Limiting the number of cars that a family can own

Hyper-expansionist approaches to global climate change abound. From applying new technologies to control floodwaters and hurricane damage in the Netherlands and New Orleans (de Jong, 2006) to searching for new sources of energy for vehicles (e.g., ethanol fuel) to making homes and vehicles more energy efficient, each approach focuses on a belief that technology can solve the problem.

Others consider that the issue of global climate change requires a new way of seeing the world and our place in it. The *sane, humane, ecological* approach requires such a shift in thinking. Polls suggest that a change in thinking is occurring because most Canadians are now committed to the idea of doing their part to fight climate change (CBC News, 2007ab). A recent example of a SHE approach in action is the One Million Acts of Green project initiated by George Stroumboulopoulos. It is a simple program that encourages people to think globally by acting locally. By committing to one small change in their lives, one small act of green, each person can make a difference. As stated on the website, "Together we can make an impact. Together we can make our lives, our communities, and our environment greener." The project is a good example of the emerging field of ecological or environmental citizenry. Environmental citizenry connects people's feelings of citizenry within a larger community and their responsibility to act as stewards of the environment (see Latta, 2007). Although the SHE scenario involves greater directional change than that asked of participants in the One Million Acts of Green project, the project is nonetheless a move in a SHE direction.

Robertson's five scenarios of the future are applicable to the study of change in other areas as well, including mass media, communications, transportation, and health care.

To find out more about the One Million Acts of Green project, go to **http://green.cbc.ca.**

SOCIOLOGY, THE ENVIRONMENT, AND SOCIAL CHANGE

As the world has changed from the time of Comte, Marx, and Durkheim, so too has sociology. We have witnessed the development of new theoretical models (e.g., queer theory, post-structuralism) and emerging fields of study (e.g., mass media, globalization, and technology). Environmental sociology is an emerging field of study that provides an excellent example of how the discipline has adapted to our changing world. It reflects not only an issue (the environment) that is having a profound effect on our social behaviour, but also the importance of following an interdisciplinary approach to gain a greater depth of understanding of human behaviour. Working with those in other disciplines, in this case ecologists, sociologists are able to better understand the relationship between nature and human behaviour in an increasingly more complex and rapidly changing world.

environmental sociology The study of the interaction between human society and the physical environment.

Environmental sociology is the study of the interaction between human society and the physical environment (Dunlap, 2002, p. 331). It is a field that emerged after the 1970 Earth Day demonstrations (Hannigan, 2006, p. 1), when sociologists recognized a shift in social consciousness and the beginning of a new social movement.

new environmental paradigm The view that human societies and the natural environment interact with each other and that human actions do affect nature.

From these early beginnings, sociologists began to connect with the work of ecologists—those that study how living organisms interact with the environment—to develop a new understanding of the role that human interactions play within an ecosystem. The result is the development of a **new environmental paradigm**. This paradigm emphasizes that human societies and the natural environment interact with each other and that human actions do affect nature (Dunlap, 2002, p. 334; Manoli, Johnson, & Dunlap, 2007, p. 4).

new ecological paradigm The view that modern industrial society is beginning to exceed the limits of the environment.

Building on the new environmental paradigm, sociologists have introduced a **new ecological paradigm**, which emphasizes that modern industrial society is beginning to exceed

WHY SHOULD WE CARE?

Reconsidering Waste

Think about getting ready for school this morning. Did you shave with a disposable razor? How many Q-tips did you use? Did you have to open a new deodorant and throw away your old one? When you left for school, did you drive? Once there, did you buy a coffee? A muffin? Just think about how much waste you have already created (disposable razor, Q-tip, deodorant, pollution from your car's exhaust, Styrofoam coffee cup, paper bag for the muffin). Today, people are attracted to disposable products because of their convenience—few products today require any maintenance; when something no longer works, we just throw it away and rarely think about where it goes. The consequences of this convenience are filling our landfills and incineration plants across the country and around the world.

In a documentary entitled *Waste = Food* (2006), director Rob van Hattum presents an optimistic view of the future and our ability to manage the world's rapidly growing landfill sites. The documentary highlights the potential of designing products to be more eco-effective in that they become fuel for other machines or organisms at the end of their life cycle (e.g., your disposable razor becomes a nutrient-rich food for other organisms as it decomposes). Van Hattum (2006) believes that these new technologies could lead to changes equal to those brought about by the Industrial Revolution.

Though this approach is innovative for future products, we still have much work to do with the waste that is already in landfills around the world and that in some cases is making people sick. When organic material decomposes in landfills, it releases chemicals that can leak into groundwater and cause many ailments, including respiratory conditions and cancers. Also, when biodegradable waste breaks down, it releases methane (a greenhouse gas) that contributes to global climate change. When plastics and textiles are incinerated, they release nitrous oxide, another greenhouse gas. Carbon dioxide is also produced when garbage trucks collect waste and take it to landfills or incineration plants (Kallman, 2008).

Today, Canadian landfills account for 25 percent of human-made methane gas and 25 megatonnes of CO_2 (the equivalent of driving 5.5 million cars). Some Canadian landfills are starting to use landfill gas to generate electricity and heat, a technology that will hopefully continue to expand (Environment Canada, 2007c).

So the next time you get ready for school, consider using an electric razor, taking the bus or riding your bike, and carrying your own coffee mug.

This article is also a peerScholar assignment in MySocLab.

the limits of the environment (Dunlap, 2002, p. 334; Manoli, Johnson, & Dunlap, 2007, p. 4). This paradigm was intended to cut across boundaries within sociology and present a less anthropocentric (human-oriented) and a more ecocentric view, wherein humans are only one part of a global ecosystem (Hannigan, 2006, p. 13). In sum, then, environmental sociology can be thought of as a conscious endeavour to overcome the anthropocentrism of our past (Stoddart, 2008).

Environmental sociologists tackle the key themes that we have examined throughout this book—capitalism, racism, and sexism. They have demonstrated that the dominant ideologies in our society are intertwined with our approach to nature.

For instance, the **dominant social paradigm** based on capitalism views economic growth and large hierarchical societies as positive. This ideology also legitimates the

dominant social paradigm The capitalist view supported by an ideology that legitimates the domination of nature for the material benefit of humans.

environmental racism
A form of discrimination
against minority groups
and people from poor
countries who are
subjected to a dispropor-
tionate share of environ-
mental hazards and
polluting industries.

ecofeminism   A combi-
nation of feminist think-
ing and ecological
thought.

domination of nature for the material benefit of humans. The expansion of the tar sands project in Alberta in spite of the evidence of significant environmental impacts (Sierra Club, 2008) is a good example of the value our society places on capitalism. The **alternative environmental paradigm** challenges this position and advocates smaller, nonhierarchical societies that use science and technology not to dominate the environment but instead to achieve harmony with it. Table 12–2 shows that the two paradigms propose very different views of human society and its relationship to the natural environment.

Environmental racism is a form of discrimination against minority groups and people from poor countries who are subjected to a disproportionate share of environmental hazards (e.g., toxic waste) and polluting industries (e.g., chemical plants) (Dodds & Hopwood, 2006, p. 269; Westra, 1999, p. 103). Many instances of environmental racism exist in Canada. For example, landfill sites are often located near Aboriginal communities (Bain Lindsay, 2006).

Sexism can also be seen in our approach to the environment. **Ecofeminism** combines feminist thinking with ecological thought. Ecofeminists argue that the oppression of women and the exploitation of nature are both products of a masculine orientation to the social and physical worlds. The hyper-expansionist view discussed above is the type of masculine-oriented thinking that ecofeminists oppose. The belief that we can fix society's problems by creating new technologies is a male orientation.

Environmental sociology is but one way in which sociology has changed. It reflects a growing trend toward interdisciplinary approaches to understanding both our social and physical worlds. As we face the challenges of this new century, sociology can provide leadership in developing a sane, humane, and ecological future.

TABLE 12–2 **Competing Social Paradigms**

	Dominant Social Paradigm	Alternative Environmental Paradigm
Core Values	Material (economic growth)	Non-material (self-actualization)
	Natural environment valued as resource	Natural environment intrinsically valued
	Domination over nature	Harmony with nature
Economy	Market forces	Public interest
	Risk and reward	Safety
	Reward for achievement	Incomes related to need
	Differentials	Egalitarian
	Individual self-help	Collective/social provisions
Polity	Authoritative structures (experts influential)	Participative structures (citizen/worker involvement)
	Hierarchical	Non-hierarchical
	Law and order	Liberation
Society	Centralized	Decentralized
	Large-scale	Small-scale
	Associational	Communal
	Ordered	Flexible
Nature	Ample reserves	Earth's limited resources
	Nature hostile/neutral	Nature benign
	Environment controllable	Nature delicately balanced
Knowledge	Confidence in science and technology	Limits to knowledge
	Rationality of means	Rationality of ends
	Separation of fact/value, thought/feeling	Integration of fact/value, thought/feeling

Source: Cotgrove, S., & Duff, A. (1980). Environmentalism, middle-class radicalism, and politics. *Sociological Review, 28* (2), p. 341. Reprinted with permission.

What do you know about **the Future**?

Multiple-choice questions (circle your answer)

1. **Examining technological advances in race-car engines to predict how the automotive industry might change their engines in the future is called the**
   a. Delphi method
   b. Leader-follower method
   c. Technological extrapolation method
   d. Alpha method

2. **The development of electric, hydrogen, or hybrid cars best represents which scenario of the future?**
   a. Business as usual
   b. Authoritarian control
   c. Hyper-expansionist
   d. Sane, humane, ecological

3. **Which scenario of the future views greater government control as the best possible solution to society's problems?**
   a. Business as usual

   b. Authoritarian control
   c. Hyper-expansionist
   d. Sane, humane, ecological

4. **Environmental sociology emerged in the**
   a. 1950s
   b. 1960s
   c. 1970s
   d. 1980s

5. **Locating landfill sites near Aboriginal communities is an example of**
   a. Environmental racism
   b. Anthropocentrism
   c Ecofeminism
   d. The new ecological paradigm

Answers: b, c, b, c, a

Summary

1. *Social change* refers to changes in the typical features of a society (e.g., norms and values) over time.
2. *Collective behaviours* occur when people come together to achieve a single, meaningful, short-term goal that may result in social change.
3. *Social movements* involve groups and individuals whose organized efforts bring about or resist social change.
4. Inspirations for social change include technology, the physical environment, demographic shifts, economic competition, war, ideas, governments, individuals, and social movements.
5. Functionalists explain social change through *equilibrium theory*, which holds that changes in one part of society require changes in others in order to restore balance and harmony.
6. Conflict theorists view social change as coming about necessarily through active revolt against oppression and exploitation.
7. Evolutionary theorists hold that all societies have an internal drive that inspires them to adapt to their environment in order to better compete for survival.
8. Cyclical theorists argue that social change occurs not in a defined direction, but rather through ebbs and flows in a series of endless cycles.

module 12.2 COLLECTIVE BEHAVIOUR

9. A *collectivity* is a substantial number of people who join together on the basis of loosely defined norms.

10. Members of localized collectivities, or *crowds*, are bonded through their immediate physical presence. There are several types of crowds: casual crowds, conventional crowds, acting crowds, mobs, flash mobs, riots, and protest crowds.

11. Dispersed collectivities do not share physical proximity and are instead bonded through their emotional responses—including rumours; mass hysteria; disaster behaviour; fashion, fads, and crazes; and publics—to situations and messages.

12. Contagion theorists argue that the irrationality of crowds is contagious and results in a "collective mind."

13. Convergence theorists contend that the source of crowd behaviour lies not in the group but rather in the individuals who comprise it.

14. Emergent norm theorists view crowd behaviour as neither irrational nor deliberate, but rather as the result of dynamic exchanges between participants.

module 12.3 SOCIAL MOVEMENTS

15. Social movements are the most highly structured, rational, and enduring form of collective behaviour.

16. Social movements can either be formal or informal in nature. *Informal social movements* generally emerge in opposition to a specific local issue. They would be considered grassroots initiatives. *Formal social movements* are large, well-integrated, and established organizations with bureaucratic procedures.

17. *Revolutionary movements*, whether peaceful or violent, seek a complete reorganization of society.

18. *Reformist movements* address specific issues by working within existing social structures.

19. *Reactionary movements* form in response to a movement, event, or decision that is deemed intolerable.

20. *Religious movements* are grounded in a spiritual or supernatural belief system thought to inspire a form of inner change.

21. *Relative deprivation theory* asserts that many social movements arise from people discontented with their present condition, a discontent that is relative to those around them.

22. *Value-added theory* holds that six conditions must be met before a social movement can begin.

23. *Resource mobilization theory* contends that successful social movements must be able to acquire and manage key resources.

24. *New social movement theory* holds that forms of action are motivated by collective identity found in the culture, ideology, and the politics of post-industrial society.

module 12.4 THE FUTURE

25. Futurologists make predictions about the future using a number of sophisticated methods including extrapolation, the Delphi method, and computer-simulated modelling.

26. All views of the future fit into one of five scenarios: business-as-usual; disaster; authoritarian control; hyper-expansionist; and sane, humane, ecological.

27. Environmental sociology is a relatively new field in sociology that examines the connection between human society and the natural environment. It challenges society to view the world from an ecological perspective, proposing a balance between humans and between humans and nature.

Key Terms

acting crowd   365
alternative environmental
   paradigm   382
authoritarian control (AC)   377
business-as-usual scenario   377
casual crowd   365
collective behaviours   358
collectivity   364
conventional crowd   365
craze   367
crowd   365
Delphi method   377
digital immigrants   359
digital natives   359
disaster   366
disaster scenario   377
dispersed collectivities   364
dominant social paradigm   381
ecofeminism   382
environmental racism   382
environmental sociology   380

equilibrium theory   362
exponential growth   359
expressive crowd   365
extrapolation   376
fad   366
fashion   366
flash mob   365
formal social movement   370
futurology   376
gossip   366
hyper-expansionist (HE)
   scenario   377
ideational culture   363
informal social movement   370
innovation   359
interest group   373
localized collectivities   364
Luddites   360
mass hysteria   366
mob   365
neoevolutionary theory   363

new ecological paradigm   380
new environmental paradigm   380
protest crowd   365
public   367
reactionary movement   372
reformist movement   372
religious movement   372
revolutionary movement   370
riot   365
rumour   365
sane, humane, ecological
   (SHE) scenario   377
saturation   359
sensate culture   363
social change   358
social movements   358
technology   360
unilinear evolutionary theory   362
universal evolutionary theory   362
urban legend   366
vested interests   359

Test Yourself

1. Changes in the typical features of a society (e.g., norms and values) over time are called
a. Social change
b. Collective behaviours
c. Social movements
d. Innovation

2. Veblen's term to describe why privileged members resist change is
a. Luddites
b. Privileged interests
c. Veblen interests
d. Vested interests

3. The term used to refer to someone who is resistant to new technology is
a. Luddite
b. Technophile
c. Anti-tech
d. Veblenite

4. The equilibrium theory of change belongs to which perspective?
a. Conflict theory
b. Feminist theory
c. Symbolic interactionist theory
d. Functionalism

5. The idea behind _____ is that social change occurs in a cycle like the changing seasons of the year.
a. Equilibrium theory
b. Multilinear evolutionary theory
c. Ideational theory
d. Cyclical theory

6. Collectivities in which members are in different places at the same time are called
a. Localized collectivities
b. Urban collectivities
c. Dispersed collectivities
d. Casual collectivities

7. A collection of people who gather for a structured social event are called
   a. Casual crowd
   b. Conventional crowd
   c. Expressive crowd
   d. Acting crowd

8. _____ crowds are deliberately assembled by the leaders of social movements to demonstrate public support for these movements.
   a. Protest
   b. Acting
   c. Conventional
   d. Expressive

9. A widespread emotional connection to a cultural phenomena is called
   a. A fad
   b. Hysteria
   c. A craze
   d. Mass hysteria

10. _____ theory argues that crowd behavior occurs because like-minded people come together to make it happen.
    a. Contagion
    b. Convergence
    c. Emergent norm
    d. Symbolic interactionist

11. A(n) _____ social movement is one that is a large, well-integrated, established organization with bureaucratic procedures.
    a. Formal
    b. Revolutionary
    c. Reformist
    d. Informal

12. What is the first stage in the life cycle of a social movement?
    a. Emergence/incipience
    b. Coalescence
    c. Bureaucratization
    d. Institutionalization

13. _____ suggests that the origin of many social movements resides in the discontent of those who are dissatisfied with their present condition.
    a. Relative deprivation theory
    b. Value-added theory
    c. Resource mobilization theory
    d. Absolute deprivation theory

14. _____ investigates how members of social movements gather and use resources to meet their needs.
    a. Value-added theory
    b. New social movement theory
    c. Relative deprivation theory
    d. Resource mobilization theory

15. Which theory on social movements is more globally focused?
    a. Resource mobilization theory
    b. New social movement theory
    c. Value-added theory
    d. Relative deprivation theory

16. The view that the best way to avoid disasters is to develop new technologies is called the
    a. Business-as-usual scenario
    b. Authoritarian control scenario
    c. Hyper-expansionist scenario
    d. Sane, humane, ecological scenario

17. The One Million Acts of Green project is an example of which future scenario?
    a. Business-as-usual
    b. Authoritarian control
    c. Hyper-expansionist
    d. Sane, humane, ecological

18. *Anthropocentric* can be defined as
    a. Human oriented
    b. Nature oriented
    c. An anthropological approach to the environment
    d. Environmentally conscious

19. Which of the following traits is not an aspect of the alternative environmental paradigm?
    a. Incomes related to need
    b. Decentralization
    c. Nonhierarchical
    d. Natural environment as a resource

20. Which of the following statements is false?
    a. *Global climate change* is a more accurate term than *global warming*.
    b. The level of greenhouse gases are at their highest levels in 800 000 years.
    c. Ecofeminists argue that our environmental problems are in part a result of a masculine orientation to the social and natural worlds.
    d. The dominant social paradigm advocates that the Earth's resources are limited.

Log in to MySocLab for a host of resources that will help you save time and improve your grade. MySocLab contains cutting-edge learning tools such as study plans, practice tests, videos, audio segments, quizzes, and more—all designed to help you better understand the learning ob-jectives for this chapter. Along with your eBook, MySocLab for *Sociology for Everyone* can be found at **www.mysoclab.com**.

module 12.1
WHAT IS SOCIAL CHANGE?

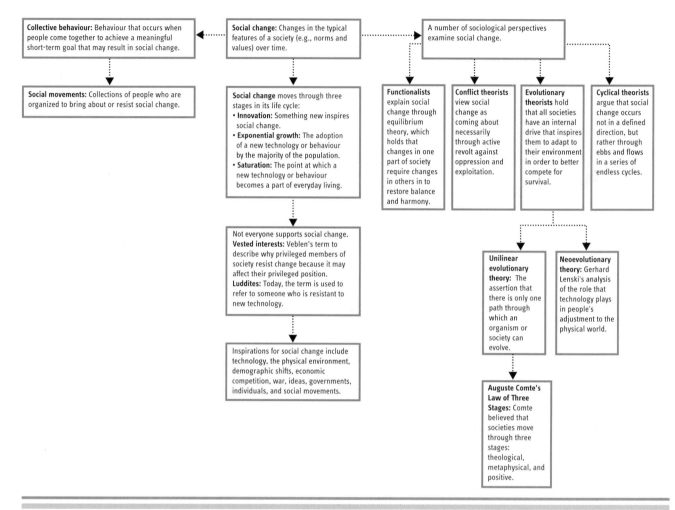

Collective behaviour: Behaviour that occurs when people come together to achieve a meaningful short-term goal that may result in social change.

Social change: Changes in the typical features of a society (e.g., norms and values) over time.

A number of sociological perspectives examine social change.

Social movements: Collections of people who are organized to bring about or resist social change.

Social change moves through three stages in its life cycle:
• **Innovation:** Something new inspires social change.
• **Exponential growth:** The adoption of a new technology or behaviour by the majority of the population.
• **Saturation:** The point at which a new technology or behaviour becomes a part of everyday living.

Functionalists explain social change through equilibrium theory, which holds that changes in one part of society require changes in others in to restore balance and harmony.

Conflict theorists view social change as coming about necessarily through active revolt against oppression and exploitation.

Evolutionary theorists hold that all societies have an internal drive that inspires them to adapt to their environment in order to better compete for survival.

Cyclical theorists argue that social change occurs not in a defined direction, but rather through ebbs and flows in a series of endless cycles.

Not everyone supports social change.
Vested interests: Veblen's term to describe why privileged members of society resist change because it may affect their privileged position.
Luddites: Today, the term is used to refer to someone who is resistant to new technology.

Unilinear evolutionary theory: The assertion that there is only one path through which an organism or society can evolve.

Neoevolutionary theory: Gerhard Lenski's analysis of the role that technology plays in people's adjustment to the physical world.

Inspirations for social change include technology, the physical environment, demographic shifts, economic competition, war, ideas, governments, individuals, and social movements.

Auguste Comte's Law of Three Stages: Comte believed that societies move through three stages: theological, metaphysical, and positive.

module 12.2
COLLECTIVE BEHAVIOUR

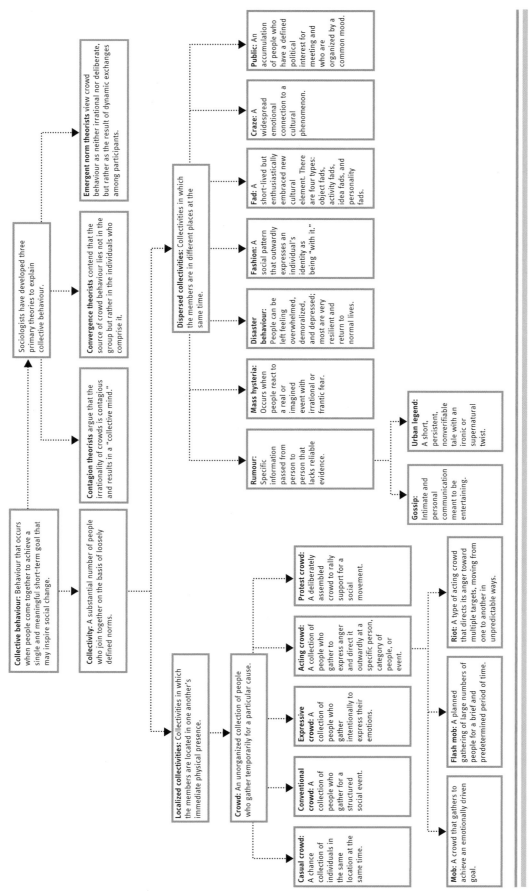

Collective behaviour: Behaviour that occurs when people come together to achieve a single and meaningful short-term goal that may inspire social change.

Sociologists have developed three primary theories to explain collective behaviour.

Emergent norm theorists view crowd behaviour as neither irrational nor deliberate, but rather as the result of dynamic exchanges among participants.

Convergence theorists contend that the source of crowd behaviour lies not in the group but rather in the individuals who comprise it.

Contagion theorists argue that the irrationality of crowds is contagious and results in a "collective mind."

Collectivity: A substantial number of people who join together on the basis of loosely defined norms.

Dispersed collectivities: Collectivities in which the members are in different places at the same time.

Public: An accumulation of people who have a defined political interest for meeting and who are organized by a common mood.

Craze: A widespread emotional connection to a cultural phenomenon.

Fad: A short-lived but enthusiastically embraced new cultural element. There are four types: object fads, activity fads, idea fads, and personality fads.

Fashion: A social pattern that outwardly expresses an individual's identity as being "with it."

Disaster behaviour: People can be left feeling overwhelmed, demoralized, and depressed; most are very resilient and return to normal lives.

Mass hysteria: Occurs when people react to a real or imagined event with irrational or frantic fear.

Rumour: Specific information passed from person to person that lacks reliable evidence.

Urban legend: A short, persistent, nonverifiable tale with an ironic or supernatural twist.

Gossip: Intimate and personal communication meant to be entertaining.

Localized collectivities: Collectivities in which the members are located in one another's immediate physical presence.

Crowd: An unorganized collection of people who gather temporarily for a particular cause.

Protest crowd: A deliberately assembled crowd to rally support for a social movement.

Acting crowd: A collection of people who gather to express anger and direct it outwardly at a specific person, category of people, or event.

Expressive crowd: A collection of people who gather intentionally to express their emotions.

Conventional crowd: A collection of people who gather for a structured social event.

Casual crowd: A chance collection of individuals in the same location at the same time.

Riot: A type of acting crowd that directs its anger toward multiple targets, moving from one to another in unpredictable ways.

Flash mob: A planned gathering of large numbers of people for a brief and predetermined period of time.

Mob: A crowd that gathers to achieve an emotionally driven goal.

module 12.3
SOCIAL MOVEMENTS

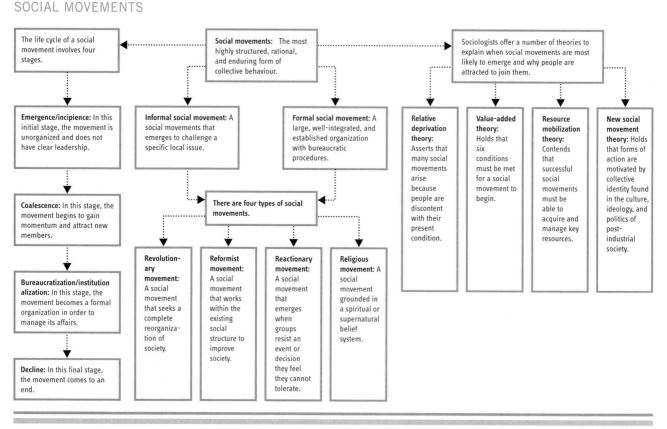

The life cycle of a social movement involves four stages.

Social movements: The most highly structured, rational, and enduring form of collective behaviour.

Sociologists offer a number of theories to explain when social movements are most likely to emerge and why people are attracted to join them.

Emergence/incipience: In this initial stage, the movement is unorganized and does not have clear leadership.

Informal social movement: A social movements that emerges to challenge a specific local issue.

Formal social movement: A large, well-integrated, and established organization with bureaucratic procedures.

Relative deprivation theory: Asserts that many social movements arise because people are discontent with their present condition.

Value-added theory: Holds that six conditions must be met for a social movement to begin.

Resource mobilization theory: Contends that successful social movements must be able to acquire and manage key resources.

New social movement theory: Holds that forms of action are motivated by collective identity found in the culture, ideology, and politics of post-industrial society.

Coalescence: In this stage, the movement begins to gain momentum and attract new members.

There are four types of social movements.

Bureaucratization/institutionalization: In this stage, the movement becomes a formal organization in order to manage its affairs.

Revolutionary movement: A social movement that seeks a complete reorganization of society.

Reformist movement: A social movement that works within the existing social structure to improve society.

Reactionary movement: A social movement that emerges when groups resist an event or decision they feel they cannot tolerate.

Religious movement: A social movement grounded in a spiritual or supernatural belief system.

Decline: In this final stage, the movement comes to an end.

module 12.4
THE FUTURE

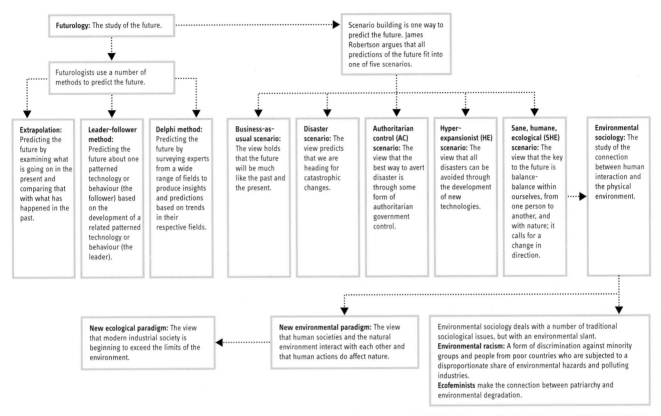

Futurology: The study of the future.

Scenario building is one way to predict the future. James Robertson argues that all predictions of the future fit into one of five scenarios.

Futurologists use a number of methods to predict the future.

Extrapolation: Predicting the future by examining what is going on in the present and comparing that with what has happened in the past.

Leader-follower method: Predicting the future about one patterned technology or behaviour (the follower) based on the development of a related patterned technology or behaviour (the leader).

Delphi method: Predicting the future by surveying experts from a wide range of fields to produce insights and predictions based on trends in their respective fields.

Business-as-usual scenario: The view holds that the future will be much like the past and the present.

Disaster scenario: The view predicts that we are heading for catastrophic changes.

Authoritarian control (AC) scenario: The view that the best way to avert disaster is through some form of authoritarian government control.

Hyper-expansionist (HE) scenario: The view that all disasters can be avoided through the development of new technologies.

Sane, humane, ecological (SHE) scenario: The view that the key to the future is balance-balance within ourselves, from one person to another, and with nature; it calls for a change in direction.

Environmental sociology: The study of the connection between human interaction and the physical environment.

New ecological paradigm: The view that modern industrial society is beginning to exceed the limits of the environment.

New environmental paradigm: The view that human societies and the natural environment interact with each other and that human actions do affect nature.

Environmental sociology deals with a number of traditional sociological issues, but with an environmental slant.
Environmental racism: A form of discrimination against minority groups and people from poor countries who are subjected to a disproportionate share of environmental hazards and polluting industries.
Ecofeminists make the connection between patriarchy and environmental degradation.

References

Aaron, P.G. & Joshi, R.M. (2006). Written language is as natural as spoken language: A biolinguistic perspective. *Reading Psychology, 27*(4), 263–311. doi:10.1080/0270271 0600846803

Abbott, P., Wallace, C., & Tyler, M. (2005). *An introduction to sociology: Feminist perspectives* (3rd ed.). London: Routledge.

ABC. (2007). *Primetime: The science of evil.*

Abelson, R., Friquegnon, M., & Lockwood, M. (Eds.). (1977). *The philosophical imagination: An introduction to philosophy.* New York: St. Martin's Press.

Abourezk, J. (1974). A brief history of the Middle East conflict. *The Link, 7*(2).

Abrams, P. (1968). *The origins of British sociology: 1834–1914.* Chicago: University of Chicago Press.

Abu-Lughod, J.L. (1989). *Before European hegemony: The world system A.D. 1250–1350.* New York: Oxford University Press.

Ackman, D. (2001). "How big is porn?" *Forbes.com.* Retrieved 29/5/2009, from http://www.forbes.com/2001/05/25/0524porn.htm

Adbusters. (2008). *Adbusters Culturejammer headquarters.* Retrieved 5/11/2008, from http://www.adbusters.org/home/

Adler, P.A. (1996). Preadolescent clique stratification and the hierarchy of identity. *Sociological Inquiry, 66*(2), 111–142.

Adler, R., Rolls, J., Proctor, R., & Towne, N. (2009). *Looking out/looking in* (brief Canadian ed.). Toronto: Nelson Education.

Adu-Febiri, F. (2006). The destiny of cultural diversity in a globalized world. *Review of Human Factor Studies, 12*(1), 30–64.

Agarwal, G. (2007). Obesity registers. *CMAJ: Canadian Medical Association Journal Supplement, 176*(1), 65-65. doi:10.1503/cmaj.1060166

Age of Enlightenment. (2007). *Age of Enlightenment—MSN encarta.* Retrieved 3/11/2008, from http://encarta.msn.com/encyclopedia_761571679/Age_of_Enlightenment.html

Agnew, R. (1985). Social control theory and delinquency: A longitudinal test. *Criminology, 23,* 47–62.

Agriculture and Agri-Food Canada. (2007). *Canada's fish and seafood industry.* Retrieved 04/02/2008, from http://atn-riae.agr.ca/seafood/industry-e.htm

Aguirre, B.E., Wenger, D., & Vigo, G. (1998). A test of the emergent norm theory of collective behavior. *Sociological Forum, 13*(2), 301–320. Retrieved from http://library.mtroyal.ca:2048/login?url= http://search.ebscohost.com/loginaspx?direct =true&AuthType=ip,url,cookie,uid&db=a9h&AN= 847808&site=ehost-live

Ahmad, W. & Bradby, H. (2008). Ethnicity and health. *Current Sociology, 56*(1), 47. Retrieved from http://proquest.umi.com/pqdweb?did=

1409330941&Fmt=7&clientId=65345&RQT=309&VName=PQD

Aiken, C.F. (1908). *The Catholic encyclopedia: Confucianism* (Volume IV ed.). New York: Robert Appleton Company. Retrieved from http://www.newadvent.org/cathen/04223b.htm

Akers, R. & Sellers, C. (2004). *Criminological theories: Introduction, evaluation and application.* Los Angeles: Roxbury.

Alasuutari, P. & Alasuutari, P. (1992). I'm ashamed to admit it but I have watched *Dallas*, the moral hierarchy of television programmes. *Media, Culture and Society, 14,* 561–582.

Alberta Learning Information Service. (2006). *Prevent family violence.* Retrieved from http://www.alis.gov.ab.ca/tips/archive.asp?EK=7759

The Alberta Pioneer Railway Association. (2007). *History of the telegraph.* Retrieved 03/05/2008, from http://www.railwaymuseum.ab.ca/?q=node/44

Albrecht, G.L. (1992). *The disability business: Rehabilitation in America.* Newbury Park, CA: Sage Publications, Ltd.

Alexander, J.C. (1998). *Neofunctionalism and after.* Malden, MA: Blackwell.

Allen, L. (2007). Denying the sexual subject: Schools' regulation of student sexuality. *British Educational Research Journal, 33*(2), 221–234.

Allen, M.P. (1989). *The founding fortunes: A new anatomy of the super-rich families in America.* New York: E.P. Dutton.

Allen, T. (2007). Katrina: Race, class and poverty: Reflections and analysis. *Journal of Black Studies, 37*(4), 466–468.

Alliance for Equality of Blind Canadians. (2008). *AEBC supports reinstatement of court challenges Program.* Retrieved 28/01/2008, from http://www.blindCanadians.ca/reports/index.php?ReportID=39

Alliance for equality of blind Canadians/L'alliance pour l'égalitÉdes personnes aveugles du Canada (AEBC)— reports. Retrieved 28/01/2008, from http://www.blindCanadians.ca/reports/index.php?ReportID=39

Almeida, P. (2006). Social movement unionism, social movement partyism and policy outcomes: Health care privatization in el Salvador. In H. Johnston, & P. Almeida (Eds.), *Latin American social movements: Globalization, democratization and transnational networks* (pp. 57–76). Lanham, MD: Rowman and Littlefield Publishers, Inc.

Al-Shehab, A.J. (2008). Gender and racial representation in children's television programming in Kuwait: Implications for education. *Social Behavior & Personality: An International Journal, 36*(1), 49–63. Retrieved from http://library.mtroyal.ca:2048/login?url= http://library.mtroyal.ca:2924/login.aspx?direct=true&AuthType=ip,url,cookie,uid&db=a9h&AN=30104108&site=ehost-live

Altemeyer, R. (1981). *Right-wing authoritarianism.* Winnipeg: University of Manitoba Press.

Altheide, D.L. (2003). *The mass media.* (pp. 657–684). Walnut Creek, CA: Altamira Press.

Ambert, A. (2005). *Contemporary family trends—divorce: Facts, causes, and consequences.* Ottawa, ON: The Vanier Institute of the Family.

Ambrose, D. (2006). 30,000 BC: Painting animality. *Angelaki: Journal of the Theoretical Humanities, 11*(2), 137–152. doi:10.1080/09697250601029309

American Association for the Advancement of Science. (2008). *AAAS—AAAS news release.* Retrieved 3/9/2008, from http://www.aaas.org/news/releases/2002/1106id2.shtml

American Association of University Professors. (2005). *AAUP: Faculty association speaks out on three top issues.* Retrieved 3/9/2008, from http://www.aaup.org/AAUP/newsroom/prarchives/2005/AMResolutions.htm

American Civil Liberties Union. (2003). *USA Patriot Act.* Retrieved 1/30/2008, from http://www.aclu.org/safefree/resources/17343res 20031114.html

American Sociological Association. *Departmental listings for 1999.* Retrieved 10/02/2002, from www.asanet.org/pubs/dod.html

Ammerman, N.T. (1997). Organized religion in a voluntaristic society. *Sociology of Religion, 58*(3), 203–215.

Anapol, D. (1997). *Polyamory: The new love without limits: Secrets of sustainable intimate relationships.* San Rafael: Internet Resource Center.

Andersen, M.L. & Francis, H.T. (2006). *Sociology: Understanding a diverse society.* (4th ed.). Belmont, CA: Thomson Wadsworth.

Anderson, K. (1991). *Chain her by one foot: The subjugation of women in 17th century new france.* New York: Routledge.

Anderson, S., Cavanagh, J., & Lee, T. (2005). *Field guide to the global economy.* New York: New Press.

Angus, I. (2008). Canada's election and the climate crisis: Five parties, no solutions. *New Socialist: Ideas for Radical Change.* Retrieved 22/2/2009, from http://www.newsocialist.org/index.php?id=1702

Anheier, H.K. (2005). *Nonprofit organizations: Theory, management, policy.* New York: Routledge, Inc.

Anker, J. (2008). Organizing homeless people: Exploring the emergence of a user organization in Denmark . *Critical Social Policy, 28*(1), 27–50. Retrieved from http://library.mtroyal.ca:2048/login?url=http://search.ebscohost.com/login.aspx?direct=true&AuthType=ip,url,cookie,uid&db=a9h&AN=28842183&site=ehost-live

Appadurai, A. (1996). *Modernity at large: Cultural dimensions of globalization.* Minneapolis, MN: University of Minnesota Press.

Applebaum, B. (2005). In the name of morality: Moral responsibility, whiteness and social justice education. *Journal of Moral Education, 34*(3), 277–290.

Armstrong, P. (2004). Gender relations. In L. Tepperman, & J. Curtis (Eds.), *Sociology* (pp. 380–401). Toronto: Oxford University Press.

Armstrong, P. & Armstrong, H. (1994). *The double ghetto: Canadian women and their segregated work.* Toronto, ON: McClelland and Stewart.

Arnett, K. & Fortune, T. (2004). Strategies for helping underperforming immersion learners succeed. *ACIE Newsletter, 7* (3), 1–8.

Aronson, E. & Mills, J. (1959). The effect of severity of initiation on liking for a group. *Journal of Abnormal and Social Psychology, 59,* 177–181.

Arsenault, N., Anderson, G., & Swedburg, R. (1998). Understanding older adults in education: Decision-making. *Educational Gerontology, 24*(2), 101. Retrieved from http://library.mtroyal.ca:2048/login?url=http://search.ebscohost.com/login.aspx?direct=true&AuthType=ip,url,cookie,uid&db=a9h&AN=443551&site=ehost-live

Asbridge, M., Mann, R.E., Flam-Zalcman, R., & Stoduto, G. (2004). The criminalization of impaired driving in Canada: Assessing the deterrent impact of Canada's first per se law. *Journal of Studies on Alcohol, 65*(4), 450–459.

Assembly of First Nations. (2007). *Assembly of first nations—Assembly of first nations—the story.* Retrieved 20/12/2007, from http://www.afn.ca/article.asp?id=59

Associated Press. (2007). World's oldest newspaper goes digital. *Editor & Publisher, 2008*(February 5, 2007), 02/05/2008.

Atchley, R.C. (1999). *Continuity and adaptation in aging: Creating positive experiences.* Baltimore, Maryland: Johns Hopkins University.

Atkinson, A.B., Rainwater, L., & Smeedling, T.M. (1995). *Income distribution in OECD countries: Evidence from the Luxembourg income study (LIS).* Social Policies Study No. 18. Paris: Organization for Economic Cooperation & Development.

Atkinson, M. (2004). Tattooing and civilizing process: Body modification as self-control. *Canadian Review of Sociology and Anthropology, 41*(2), 125–146.

Attallah, P. (2002). The audience. In P. Attallah, & L.R. Shade (Eds.), *Mediascapes: New patterns in Canadian communication* (pp. 90–106). Scarborough, ON: Thomson Nelson.

Attwood, F. (2007). Sluts and riot grrrls: Female identity and sexual agency. *Journal of Gender Studies, 16*(3), 233–247.

Aubin, B. & Gatehouse, J. (2007, March 5). Do immigrants need rules? The debate rages on. *Maclean's.*

Aucoin, D. (2005). *Finding their religion—the Boston globe.* Retrieved 3/12/2008, from http://www.boston.com/news/globe/living/articles/2005/04/13/finding_their_religion/?page=1

Auletta, K. (1982). *The underclass.* New York: Random House.

Austin, Z. (2005). Mentorship and mitigation of culture shock: Foreign-trained pharmacists in Canada. *Mentoring & Tutoring: Partnership in Learning, 13*(1), 133–149.

Authoritarian Personality. (n.d.). *Authoritarian personality (hypnotic world psychology).* Retrieved 16/01/2008, from http://psychology.hypnoticworld.com/influence_personality/authoritarian_personality.php

Avery, J. (2003). *Information theory and evolution.* New Jersey, NJ: World Scientific.

Aylward, C. (1999). *Canadian critical race theory: Racism and the law.* Halifax: Fernwood.

Azadi, Sousan [with Angela Ferrante]. (1987). *Out of Iran: A woman's escape from the ayatollahs.* Toronto, ON: McCelland-Bantam, Inc.

Babad, E.Y., Birnbaum, M., & Benne, K.D. (1983). *The social self: Group influences on personal identity.* Beverly Hills, CA: Sage Publications, Ltd.

Babbie, E. (1994). *What is society?.* Thousand Oaks, CA: Pine Forge Press.

Babbie, E. (2008). *The basics of social research.* Belmont: Thomson Wadsworth.

Babooram, A. & Wang, J. (2008). *Recycling in Canada.* Retrieved 24/07/2008, from http://www.statcan.ca/english/freepub/16-002-XIE/2007001/article/10174-en.htm

Badiali, M. (2006). *Investing in oil sands: Alberta's dirty secret is out. . . .* Retrieved 7/28/2008, from http://www.dailywealth.com/archive/2006/jan/investing-in-oil.asp

Baer, H. (2008). Global warming as a by-product of the capitalist treadmill of production and consumption—the need for an alternative global system. *Australian Journal of Anthropology, 19*(1), 58–62. Retrieved from http://library.mtroyal.ca:2048/login?url= http://search.ebscohost.com/login.aspx?direct=true&AuthType=ip,url,cookie,uid&db=a9h&AN=31341365&site=ehost-live

Bagguley, P. & Mann, K. (1992). Idle thieving bastards? Scholarly representation of the 'underclass'. *Work, Employment and Society, 6,* 113–126.

Bain Lindsay, H. (2006). *Race and waste in Nova Scotia.* Retrieved 27/07/2008, from http://www.dominionpaper.ca/environment/2006/12/07/race_and_w.html

Bainbridge, W.S. (1987). Collective behavior and social movements. In R. Stark (Ed.), *Sociology* (2nd ed., pp. 544–576). Belmont, CA: Wadsworth.

Bainbridge, W.S. (2007). Converging technologies and human destiny. *Journal of Medicine & Philosophy, 32*(3), 197–216. doi:10.1080/03605310701396968

Baker, G.R., Norton, P.G., Flintoft, V., Blais, R., Brown, A., Cox, J., et al. (2004). The Canadian adverse effects study: The incidence of adverse effects in Canadian hospitals. *Canadian Medical Association Journal, 170*(11), 1678–1686.

Baker, M. (2001). Paid and unpaid work: How do families divide their labour? In M. Baker (Ed.), *Families: Changing trends in Canada* (4th ed., pp. 96–115). Toronto: McGraw-Hill Ryerson.

Baker, M. (2005). *Families: Changing trends in Canada* (5th ed.). Toronto: McGraw-Hill Ryerson.

Baker, P. (1998). Clinton perjury allegations. *Washington Post.* Retrieved from http://www.washingtonpost.com/wp-srv/politics/special/clinton/stories/gperjury092498.htm

Balikci, A. (1970). *The Netsilik Eskimo.* Garden City, New York: The American Museum of Natural History.

Bampton, R. & Christopher Cowton. (2002). The E-interview. *Forum Qualitative Sozialforschung/Forum: Qualitative Social Research, 3*(2). Retrieved from http://www.qualitative-research.net/fqs/fws-eng.htm

Bandura, A. (1977). *Social learning theory.* New York: General Learning Press.

Baran, P. (1957). *The political economy of growth.* New York: Monthly Review Press.

Baran, S.J. & Davis, D.K. (2009). *Mass communication theory: Foundations, ferment, and future* (5th ed.). Belmont, CA: Thomson Wadsworth.

Barash, D.P. (2007). The DNA of religious faith. *Chronicle of Higher Education, 53*(33), B6–B10. Retrieved from http://library.mtroyal.ca:2048/login?url=http://search.ebscohost.com/login.aspx?direct=true&AuthType=ip,url,cookie,uid&db=a9h&AN=25307516&site=ehost-live

Barker, L. (2006). Teaching evolutionary psychology: An interview with David M. Buss. *Teaching of Psychology, 33*(1), 69–76.

Barker, M. (2005). This is my partner, and this is my . . . partner's partner: Constructing a polyamorous identity in a monogamous world. *Journal of Constructivist Psychology, 18*(1), 75–88.

Barlow, M. (2002). *Water incorporated; the commodification of the world's water—globalization—global policy forum.* Retrieved 8/5/2008, from http://www.globalpolicy.org/globaliz/special/2002/0305water.htm

Barlow, M. (2006). Globalization harms the world's cultures. In L.I. Gerdes (Ed.), *Globalization opposing viewpoints* (pp. 42–48). New York: Thompson/Gale.

Barness, L.A. (2007). Obesity in children. *Fetal & Pediatric Pathology, 26*(2), 75–85. doi:10.1080/15513810701448755

Barnett, B.M. (2004). Introduction: The life, career, and social thought of Gerhard Lenski—Scholar, teacher, mentor, leader. *Sociological Theory, 22*(2), 163–193. doi:10.1111/j.0735-2751.2004.00210.x

Barone, C. (2007). A neo-Durkheimian analysis of a new religious movement: The case of Soka Gakkai in Italy. *Theory & Society, 36*(2), 117–140. doi:10.1007/s11186-007-9023-3

Barrera, A. (2008). Globalization's shifting economic and moral terrain: Contesting marketplace mores. *Theological Studies, 69*(2), 290–308. Retrieved from http://library.mtroyal.ca:2048/login?url=http://search.ebscohost.com/login.aspx?direct=true&AuthType=ip,url,cookie,uid&db=a9h&AN=32140358&site=ehost-live

Barron, S. (2006). Street youth, strain theory and crime. *Journal of Criminal Justice, 34,* 209–223.

Bartos, O.J. (1996). Postmodernism, postindustrialism, and the future. *Sociological Quarterly, 37*(2), 307. Retrieved from http://proquest.umi.com/pqdweb?did=9711432 &Fmt=7&clientId=65345&RQT=309& VName=PQD

Basen, G., Eichler, M., & Lippman, A. (Eds.). (1993). *Misconceptions. the social construction of choice and the new reproductive and genetic technologies (vol. 1).* Hull: Voyageur.

Basen, G., Eichler, M., & Lippman, A. (Eds.). (1994). *Misconceptions. the social construction of choice and the new reproductive and genetic technologies (vol. 2).* Maple Pond: Voyageur.

Basok, T. (2007). *Canada's temporary migration program: A model despite flaws.* Retrieved 03/30, from http://www.migrationinformation.org/Feature/display.cfm?id=650

Basow, S. (1992). *Gender stereotypes and roles* (3rd ed.). Pacific Grove, California: Brooks/Cole Publishing.

Bassett, E. & O'Riordan, K. (2002). Ethics of internet research: Contesting the human subjects research model. *Ethics and Information Technology, 4*(3), 233–247.

Bathum, M.E. & Bauman, L.C. (2007). A sense of community among immigrant Latinas. *Family & Community Health, 30*(3), 167–177.

Bauch, H. (2007). *Should we sell our water to the US?* Retrieved 07/08/2008, from http://www.Canada.com/montrealgazette/features/waterunlimited/story.html?id=24ca3d1d-fb73-4233-903b-ccd07dc00827

Baudrillard, J. (1983). *Simulations.* New York: Semiotext(e).

Bauerlein, M. (2007). *The dumbest generation.* New York: Tarcher/Penguin.

Bauman, Z. (1989). *Modernity and the holocaust.* Cambridge, UK: Polity Press.

BBC. (n.d.). *Buddhism: The dalai lama.* Retrieved 09/03/2008, from http://www.bbc.co.uk/religion/religions/buddhism/people/dalailama_1.shtml

BBC World. (2007). *Q&A: Sudan's Darfur conflict.* Retrieved 22/01/2008, from http://news.bbc.co.uk/2/hi/africa/3496731.stm

BC Health Coalition. (2005). *Health care privatization in BC.* Retrieved 07/11/2008, from http://www.bchealthcoalition.ca/./images/PDF/Privatization/privatization%2520fact%2520sheet%2520%2520feb.%252025format2.pdf

BC Work Futures. (2005). *BC work futures for trades & technical occupations.* Retrieved 4/2/2008, from http://handson.workfutures.bc.ca/profiles/profile.cfm?noc=8241& lang=en&site=txt

Beagan, B.L. (2005). Everyday classism in medical school: Experiencing marginality and resistance. *Medical Education, 39,* 777–784.

Beale, A.V. & Hall, K.R. (2007). Cyberbullying: What school administrators (and parents) can do. *Clearing House, 81*(1), 8–12. Retrieved from http://library.mtroyal.ca:2048/login?url= http://library.mtroyal.ca:2924/login.aspx?direct=true&AuthType=ip,url,cookie,uid&db=a9h&AN=27957591&site=ehost-live

Bealinger, A.A. (2006). Preface. *Foreign aid: Control, corrupt, contain?* (pp. 1–4). New York: Novinka Books.

Beaty, L.A. & Alexeyev, E.B. (2008). The problem of school bullies: What the research tells us. *Adolescence, 43*(169), 1–11. Retrieved from http://library.mtroyal.ca:2048/login?url=http://library.mtroyal.ca:2924/login.aspx?direct=true&AuthType=ip,url,cookie,uid&db=a9h&AN=31526118&site=ehost-live

Beaujot, R. (2000). *Earning and caring in Canadian families.* Peterborough: Broadview Press.

Beccaria, C. (1764 [1963]). *On crimes and punishments.* Indianapolis: Bobbs-Merrill.

Becker, H. (1952). Social class variations in the teacher-pupil relationship. *Journal of Educational Sociology, 25,* 451–465.

Becker, H. (1963). *Outsiders: Studies in the sociology of deviance.* London: Free Press of Glencoe.

Becker, M. (2007). World social forum. *Peace & Change, 32*(2), 203–220. doi:10.1111/j.1468-0130.2007.00427.x

Bedard, G. (2000). Deconstructing whiteness: Pedagogical implications for anti-racism education. In G.J.S. Dei, & A. Calliste (Eds.), *Power, knowledge and anti-racism education: A critical reader* (pp. 41–56). Halifax: Fernwood Publishing.

Bedell, D. (2001). *Unlikely innovators: Many online technologies were first perfected by the adult industry.* Retrieved 30/08/2008, from http://www.adultwebmasterschool.com/news/adulttech.htm

Beech, H. (2002, July 1). With women so scarce, what can men do? *Time,,* 8.

Beecher, H. (1966). Ethics and clinical research. *New England Journal of Medicine, 274*(24), 1354–1360.

Beer, D. & Burrows, R. (2007). Sociology and, of and in web 2.0: Some initial considerations. http://www.socresonline.org.uk/12/5/17.html *Sociological Research Online, 12*(5), 12/05/2008.

Beerkens, E. & Derwende, M. (2007). The paradox in international cooperation: Institutionally embedded universities in a global environment. *Higher Education, 53*(1), 61–79. doi:10.1007/s10734-005-7695-z

Beetham, D. (1996). *Bureaucracy* (2nd ed.). Minneapolis, MN: University of Minnesota Press.

Behrouzi, M. (2005). *Democracy as the political empowerment of the people: The betrayal of an Ideal.* Lanham, MD: Lexington Books.

Bell, D. (1973). *The coming of the postindustrial age.* New York: Basic.

Bell, M.M., & Carolan, M.S. (2004). *An invitation to environmental sociology* (2nd ed.). Thousand Oaks, CA: Pine Forge Press.

Bellah, R., Madsen, R., Sullivan, W.M., Swidler, A., & Tipton, S.M. (1996). *Habits of the heart: Individualism and commitment in American life.* (2nd ed.). Berkeley, CA: University of California Press.

Bellah, R.N. (1975). *The broken covenant: American civil religion in time of trial.* Chicago: University of Chicago Press.

Bellis, M. (2008). *The invention of radio.* Retrieved 04/05/2008, from http://inventors.about.com/od/rstartinventions/a/radio.htm

Bengtson, V.L. (2001). Beyond the nuclear family: The increasing importance of multigenerational bonds. *Journal of Marriage & Family, 63*(1), 1.

Bentham, J. (1838 [1962]). In John Bowring (Ed.), *The works of jeremy bentham.* Russell and Russell: New York.

Bentley, C.S. (2008). The great information equalizer. *New American (08856540), 24*(8), 41–42. Retrieved from http://library.mtroyal.ca:2048/login?url=http://search.ebscohost.com/login.aspx?direct=true&AuthType=ip,url,cookie,uid&db=a9h&AN=31686042&site= ehost-live

Beres, M.A. (2007). 'Spontaneous' sexual consent: An analysis of sexual consent literature. *Feminism & Psychology, 17*(1), 93–108.

Bereska, T. (2008). *Deviance, conformity, and social control* (4th ed.). Toronto: Pearson.

Bergin, T. & Erman, M. (2008). *Rising oil prices power enormous Exxon profits.* Retrieved 01/08/2008, from http://www.Canada.com/vancouversun/news/business/story.html?id=f27e3320-da0a-4264-a6fa-d85c843ec677

Berko, R., Rosenfeld, L., & Samovar, L. (1994). *Connecting: A cultural sensitive approach to interpersonal communication competency.* Toronto: Harcourt Brace College Publishers.

Berkowitz, P. (2005). The court, the constitution, and the culture of freedom. *Policy Review, 132,* 3–25.

Berkowitz, P. & Eisenkraft, H. (2007, February). Critics call for more data but universities say they already issue more reports than ever and are accountable to the public. *University Affairs,* pp. 29–30.

Bermanis, S., Canetti-Nisim, D., & Pedahzur, A. (2004). Religious fundamentalism and the extreme right-wing camp in israel. *Patterns of Prejudice, 38*(2), 159–176. Retrieved from http://library.mtroyal.ca:2048/login?url=http://search.ebscohost.com/login.aspx?direct=true&AuthType=ip,url,cookie,uid&db=a9h&AN=13133229&site=ehost-live

Bernburg, J., Kohn, M., & Rivera, C. (2006). Official labeling, criminal embeddedness and subsequent delinquency: A longitudinal test of labelling theory. *Journal of Research in Crime and Delinquency, 43*(1), 67–88.

Bernd, S. & Brown, R. (2000). Perceived intragroup homogeneity in minority-majority contexts. In C. Stangor (Ed.), *Stereotypes and prejudice: Key readings* (pp. 326–337). New York: Psychology Press.

Berndt, T.J. & Keefe, K. (1995). Friends' influence on adolescents' adjustment to school. *Child Development, 66*(5), 1312–1329.

Bernstein, H. (2006). Studying development/development studies. *African Studies, 65*(1), 45–62. doi:10.1080/00020180600771733

Berry, D. (2004). Internet research: Privacy, ethics and alienation: An open source approach. *Internet Research, 14*(4), 323–332.

Bessenoff, G.R. (2006). Can the media affect us? Social comparison, self-discrepancy, and the thin ideal. *Psychology of Women Quarterly, 30*(3), 239–251. doi:10.1111/j.1471-6402.2006.00292.x

Best, J. (2006). Blumer's dilemma: The critic as a tragic figure. *American Sociologist, 37*(3), 5–14. Retrieved from http://library.mtroyal.ca:2048/login?url=http://search.ebscohost.com/login.aspx?direct=true&AuthType=ip,url,cookie,uid&db=a9h&AN=23815021&site=ehost-live

Bevington, D. & Dixon, C. (2005). Movement-relevant theory: Rethinking social movement scholarship and activism. *Social Movement Studies, 4*(3), 185–208. doi:10.1080/14742830500329838

Bhabha, H. (1994). *The location of culture.* New York: Routledge.

Bhambra, G.K. (2007). Sociology and postcolonialism: Another 'missing' revolution? *Sociology, 41*(5), 871–884.

Bibby, R. (1995). *The bibby report: Social trends Canadian style.* New York: Stoddart Pub.

Bibby, R.W. (2002). *The resilience and renaissance of roman Catholicism in Canada.* Unpublished manuscript.

Bibby, R.W. (2006a). *The boomer factor: What Canada's most famous generation is leaving behind.* Toronto, ON: Bastion Books.

Bibby, R.W. (2006b). *The comeback of organized religion in Canada.* Unpublished manuscript.

Bibby, R.W. (2008). *Research of Reginald W. Bibby.* Retrieved 3/10/2008, from http://www.reginaldbibby.com/

Billboard Liberation Front. (2008). *The billboard liberation front.* Retrieved 5/11/2008, from http://www.billboardliberation.com/

Birch, K. (2007). The totalitarian corporation? *Totalitarian Movements & Political Religions, 8*(1), 153–161. doi:10.1080/14690760601121739

Birchard, K. (2004). Women make gains in getting Canadian research chairs. *Chronicle of Higher Education* pp. A38.

Bird, D. & O'Connell, J. (2006). Behavioral ecology and archaeology. *Journal of Archaeological Research, 14*(2), 143–188. Retrieved from http://library.mtroyal.ca:2048/login?url=http://library.mtroyal.ca:2924/login.aspx?direct=true&AuthType=ip,url,cookie,uid&db=a9h&AN=21844837&site=ehost-live

Birkmann, J. (Ed.). (2006). *Measuring vulnerability to natural hazards: Towards resilience societies.* New York: United Nations University.

Bittman, M., England, P., Sayer, L., Fohlbre, N., & Matheson, G. (2003). When does gender trump money? *American Journal of Sociology, 190*(1), 186–214.

Black, E. (n.d.). *War against the weak.* Retrieved 8/18/2007, from http://www.waragainsttheweak.com/

Blacks Academy. *Theories of poverty: The culture of poverty.* Retrieved 13/12/2007, from http://www.blacksacademy.net/content/3253.html

Blank, R.M., Card, D., Levy, F., & Medoff, J.L. (1993). Poverty, income distribution, and growth: Are they still connected? *Brookings Papers on Economic Activity, 1993*(2), 285–339.

Blauner, R. (1972). *Racial oppression in America.* New York: Harper & Row.

Block, J.L. (2008). Issues for DSM-V: Internet addiction. *American Journal of Psychiatry, 165*(3), 306–307. doi:10.1176/ appi.ajp.2007.07101556

Bloomquist, E. (2000). *Responsible non-monogamy: A brief introduction to polyamory.* Retrieved 10/7 from http://www.iresource.org/pamphlets/non-monogamy.html

Blumenberg, W. (1998). *Karl Marx : An illustrated biography* [Karl Marx in Selbstzeugnissn und Bilddokumenten]. (Rev. ed.). London: New Left Books.

Blumer, H. (1969). Collective behavior. In A.M. Lee (Ed.), *Principles of sociology* (3rd ed., pp. 65–121). New York: Barnes & Noble.

Boe, R. (2002). Future deomographic trends may help Canada's aboriginal youth. *Forum on Corrections Research, 14*(3), 13–16.

Boehnke, K., Kindervater, A., Baier, D., & Rippl, S. (2007). Social change as a source of macrosocial stress: Does it enhance nationalistic attitudes? *European Societies, 9*(1), 65–90. doi:10.1080/14616690601079440

Boeree, G. (2006). *Sigmund Freud.* Retrieved 6/11/2007, from http://webspace .ship.edu/cgboer/freud.html

Bogardus, E. (1925). Measuring social distance. *Journal of Applied Sociology, 9*, 299–308.

Bogardus, E. (1967). *A forty year racial distance study.* Los Angeles: University of Southern California Press.

Boin, A. & McConnell, A. (2007). Preparing for critical infrastructure breakdowns: The limits of crisis management and the need for resilience. *Journal of Contingencies & Crisis Management, 15*(1), 50–59. doi:10.1111/j.1468-5973.2007. 00504.x

Bolender, J. (2003). The genealogy of the moral modules. *Minds & Machines, 13*(2), 233–255.

Bolgomolny, A. (n.d.). *Is mathematics beautiful?* Retrieved 10/10/2007, from http://www.cut-the-knot.org/manifesto/beauty.shtml

Bonger, W. (1916). *Criminality and economic conditions.* Boston: Little, Brown.

Bonner, K. (1998). Reflexivity, sociology and the rural–urban distinction in Marx, Tonnies and Weber. *Canadian Journal of Sociology & Anthropology, 35*(2), 165–189.

Booker, K.C. (2007). Perceptions of classroom belongingness among African American college students. *College Student Journal, 41*(1), 178–186.

Bordo, S. (1998). Pills and power tools. *Men and Masculinities, 1*(1), 87–90.

Botanical Society of America. (2008). *Statement on evolution, botanical society of America.* Retrieved 3/9/2008, from http://library.mtroyal.ca:4136/outreach/evolution.php

Bottomore, T.B., Harris, L., & Miliband, R. (Eds.). (1991). *A dictionary of Marxist thought* (2nd ed.). Malden, MA: Blackwell Publishing Limited.

Bouchard, B. & Zhao, J. (2000). University education: Recent trends in participation, accessibility and returns. *Education Quarterly Review, 6*(4), 24–32.

Bourdieu, P. (1973). Cultural reproduction and social reproduction. In R. Brown (Ed.), *Knowledge, education and cultural change* (pp. 71–112). London: Tavistock.

Bourdieu, P. (1984). *Distinction.* London: Routledge.

Bourdieu, P. (1991). *Language and symbolic power.* Cambridge: Polity Press.

Bourgeault, R. (1983). The Indian, the Metis and the fur trade: Class, sexism and racism in the transition from "communism" to capitalism. *Studies in Political Economy, 12*, 45–80.

Bourzac, K. (2005). *Photo essay: Dirty oil.* Retrieved 8/9/2008, from http://www.technologyreview.com/Energy/16059/

Bowles, S. & Gintis, H. (1976). *Schooling in capitalist America: Educational reform and the contradictions of economic life.* New York: Basic Books.

Boxer, M.J. (2007). Rethinking the socialist construction and international career of the concept "bourgeois feminism." *American Historical Review, 112*(1), 131–158.

Boyd, D. (2007). *Viewing American class divisions through Facebook and MySpace.* Retrieved 11/05/2008, from htstp://www.danah.org/papers/essays/ClassDivisions.html

Boyd, M. & Myles, J. (1991). Gender, power and postindustrialism. *Canadian Review of Sociology & Anthropology, 28*(4), 407–436.

Bradford, N. (2007). Placing social policy? reflections on Canada's new deal for cities and communities. *Canadian Journal of Urban Research, 16*(2), 1–26. Retrieved from http://library.mtroyal.ca:2048/login?url=http://search.ebscohost.com/login.aspx?direct=true&Auth Type=ip,url,cookie,uid&db=a9h&AN=31934353&site=ehost-live

Bradshaw, Y.W. (1988). Reassessing economic dependency and uneven development: The Kenyan experience. *American Sociological Review, 53*(5), 693–708.

Brady, D. & Denniston, R. (2006). Economic globalization, industrialization and deindustrialization in affluent democracies. *Social Forces, 85*(1), 297. Retrieved from http://proquest.umi.com/pqdweb?did=1139918031&Fmt=7&clientId=65345&RQT=309&VName=PQD

Brady, S. & Mathews, K. (2006). Effects of media violence on health-related outcomes among young men. *Archives of Pediatric and Adolescent Medicine.* Retrieved 17/5/2009, from http://archpedi.ama-assn.org/cgi/ search?fulltext= tv+and+violence

Brecher, J. & Costello, T. (2006). Globalization and the race to the bottom. In J.M. Charon & L.G. Vigilant (Eds.), *Social problems: Readings with four questions* (pp. 127–135). Belmont, CA: Thomson Wadsworth.

Brem, M. (2006). *Migrant workers in Canada: A review of the Canadian seasonal agricultural workers program* (Policy Brief). Ottawa: The North-South Institute.

Bresalier, M., Gillis, L., McClure, C., McCoy, L., Mykhalovskiy, E., Taylor, D., et al. (2002). *Making* care visible: Antiretroviral therapy and the health work of people living with HIV/AIDS. Toronto: Making Care Visible Working Group.

Brest, P. & Vandenberg, A. (1987). Politics, feminism, and the constitution: The anti-pornography movement in Minneapolis. Stanford Law Review, 39(3), 607–661.

Breton, R. (2005). Ethnic relations in Canada: Institutional dynamics [edited and with an introduction by Jeffrey G. Reitz]. Montreal: McGill-Queen's University Press.

Brett, P. (2007). Global warming opens Arctic seabed to the search for oil and gas International Herald Tribune. Retrieved 10/2/2009, from http://www.iht.com/bin/printfriendly.php?id=8110116

Brickell, C. (2006). A symbolic interactionist history of sexuality? Rethinking History, 10(3), 415–432.

British Museum. (n.d.). The rosetta stone. Retrieved 01/05/2008, from http://www.Britishmuseum.org/explore/highlights/highlight_ objects/aes/t/the_rosetta_stone.aspx

Britt, B. (2003). Manufactured consent or purloined dissent? Radical Society: Review of Culture & Politics, 30(1), 47–60. doi:10.1080/1476085032000125529

Brizendine, L. (2006). The female brain. New York: Broadway Books.

Broadway, M. (2007). Meatpacking and the transformation of rural communities: A comparison of Brooks, Alberta and Garden City, Kansas. Rural Sociology, 72(4), 560–582. Retrieved from http://library.mtroyal.ca:2048/login?url=http://search.ebscohost.com/login.aspx?direct=true&AuthType=ip,url,cookie,uid&db=a9h&AN=28097521&site=ehost-live

Brock University. (2008). Sociology department. Retrieved 07/08/2008, from http://www.brocku.ca/sociology/facultylist. php#anaisla

Brockman, J. (2001). Gender in the legal profession: Fitting or breaking the mold. Vancouver: University of British Columbia Press.

Brod, H.B. (2005). Pornography and alienation of male sexuality. In T.L. Steele (Ed.), Sex, self and society: The social context of sexuality. California: Wadsworth.

Bronfen, E. (2006). Reality check: Image affects and cultural memory. Differences: A Journal of Feminist Cultural Studies, 17(1), 20–46. doi:10.1215/10407391-2005-003

Brown, A. (2007). Perestroika and the end of the cold war. Cold War History, 7(1), 1–17. doi:10.1080/14682740701197631

Brown, A.R. (2008). Popular music cultures, media and youth consumption: Towards an integration of structure, culture and agency. Sociology Compass, 2(2), 388–408.

Brown, S. (2008, September 11). Groups call for inquiry into First Nations representation on juries. North Bay Nugget.

Brown, S.K. & Bean, F.D. (2006). New migrants, new models of assimilation. Retrieved 1/23/2008, from http://www.cri.uci.edu/pdf/NewImmigrantsNewModelsOfAssimilation_082306.pdf

Brownfield, D. (2003). Differential association and gang membership. Journal of Gang Research, 11(1), 1–12.

Bruce, S. & Voas, D. (2007). Religious toleration and organisational typologies. Journal of Contemporary Religion, 22(1), 1–17. doi:10.1080/13537900601114388

Bruckerhoff, J.J. (2008). Giving nature constitutional protection: A less anthropocentric interpretation of environmental rights. Texas Law Review, 86(3), 615–646. Retrieved from http://library.mtroyal.ca:2048/login?url=http://search.ebscohost.com/login.aspx?direct=true&AuthType=ip,url,cookie,uid&db=a9h&AN=31179726&site=ehost-live

Bryant, B. (1957). Future perfect: A guide to personality and popularity for the junior miss. New York, NY: The Bobbs-Merrill Company, Inc.

Brym, R. & Fox, B.J. (1989). From culture to power: The sociology of English Canada. Toronto: Oxford University Press.

Brym, R. & Saint-Pierre, C. (1997). Canadian sociology. Contemporary Sociology, 26(5), 543–546.

Brzozowski, J. (2004). Family violence in Canada: A statistical profile 2004 (No. 85-224-XIE). Ottawa: Statistics Canada.

Buch-Hansen, M., Oksen, P., & Prabudhanitisarn, S. (2006). Rethinking natural resource habitat in Thailand. Journal of Political Ecology, 13, 48–59.

Budgeon, S. & Roseneil, S. (2004). Editors' introduction: Beyond the conventional family. Current Sociology, 52(2), 127–134.

Budilova, E.A. (2003). Social-psychological problems in Russian science in the second half of the nineteenth century and early twentieth century. Journal of Russian & East European Psychology, 41(1), 5. Retrieved from http://library.mtroyal.ca:2048/login?url=http://search.ebscohost.com/login.aspx?direct= true&AuthType=ip,url,cookie,uid&db=a9h&AN=10457527&site=ehost-live

Buechler, S.M. (1993). Beyond resource mobilization? Emerging trends in social movement theory. Sociological Quarterly, 34(2), 217–235.

Bullard, R.D. (1990). Dumping in Dixie: Race, class, and environmental quality. Boulder, CO: Westview Press.

Burke, B. (2005). Antonio Gramsci, schooling and education, the encyclopedia of informal education. Retrieved from http://www.infed.org/thinkers/et-gram.htm

Bursey, J., Daechsel, H., Hinshelwood, A. & Murphy, C. (n.d.). The archaeology of Ontario: First people of North America. Retrieved 23/1/2008, from http://www.ontarioarchaeology.on.ca/summary/first.htm

Burtch, B. (1992). The sociology of law: Critical approaches to social control. Toronto: Harcourt Brace.

Bushman, B. & Huesmann, R. (2006). Short-term and long-term effects of violent media on aggression in children and adults. Archives of Pediatric and Adolescent Medicine. Retrieved 17/5/2009, from http://archpedi.ama.org/cgi/search?fulltext=tv+and+violence

Butler, J. (1997). Excitable speech: A politics of the performative. New York: Routledge.

Buunk, A.P., Zurriaga, R., & González, P. (2006). Social comparison, coping and depression in people with spinal cord injury. Psychology & Health, 21(6), 791–807. doi:10.1080/14768320500444117

Cabezas, A.L. (2006). The eroticization of labor in Cuba's all-inclusive resorts: Performing race, class and gender in the new tourist economy. Social Identities, 12(5), 507–521. Retrieved from http://library.mtroyal.ca:2048/login?url=http://search.ebscohost.com/login.aspx?direct=true&AuthType=ip,url,cookie,uid&db=a9h&AN=22373124&site=ehost-live

Cable News Network. (2005). Mideast: Land of conflict. Retrieved 3/13/2008, from http://www.cnn.com/SPECIALS/2003/mideast/

Cady Stanton, E. (1895). The woman's bible. New York: European Publishing Company.

CAEFS. (2004). CAEFS' fact sheets: Human and fiscal costs of prison. Retrieved 9/13/2008, from http://dawn.thot.net/election2004/issues32.htm

CAEFS. (2008). Criminalized and imprisoned women. Retrieved 9/13/2008, from http://www.elizabethfry.ca/eweek08/pdf/crmwomen.pdf

Calasanti, T., Slevin, K. F., & King, N. (2006). Ageism and feminism: From "et cetera" to center. NWSA Journal, 18(1), 13–30. Retrieved from http://library.mtroyal.ca:2048/login?url=http://search.ebscohost.com/login.aspx?direct= true&AuthType=ip,url,cookie,uid&db=a9h&AN=20712362&site=ehost-live

Calomiris, C.W. (2007). A raw deal: Reconsidering the Great Depression. Foreign Affairs [H.W.Wilson—SSA], 86(5), 141. Retrieved from http://proquest.umi.com/pqdweb?did=138272 1281&Fmt= 7&clientId=65345&RQT=309&VName=PQD

Camiscioli, E. (2001). Producing citizens, reproducing the "French race": Immigration, demography, and pronatalism in early twentieth-century France. Gender and History, 13(3), 593–621.

Campanella, R. (2007). An ethnic geography of New Orleans. The Journal of American History, December, 704–715.

Campbell, A. (2005). Keeping the "lady" safe: The regulation of femininity through crime prevention literature. Critical Criminology, 13(2), 119–140.

Campbell, S. (2008). Nursing the planet. Primary Health Care, 18(3), 41–48. Retrieved from http://library.mtroyal.ca:2048/login?url=http://search.ebscohost.com/login.aspx?direct=true&AuthType=ip,url,cookie,uid&db=a9h&AN=31697372&site=ehost-live

Canada and globalization. Retrieved 3/10/2008, from http://www.david-kilgour.com/secstate/globali3.htms

Canada in the making—specific events & topics. Retrieved 22/1/2008, from http://Canadiana.org/citm/specifique/deportation_e.html

Canada Revenue Agency. (2008a). Corporation tax rates. Retrieved 01/04/2008, from http://www.cra-arc.gc.ca/tax/business/topics/corporations/rates-e.html

Canada Revenue Agency. (2008b). What are the income tax rates in Canada? Retrieved 01/04/2008, from http://www.cra-arc.gc.ca/tax/individuals/faq/taxrates-e.html

Canadian Association of Food Banks. (2007a). *Canadian association of food banks.* Retrieved 19/12/2007, from http://www.cafb-acba.ca/english/index.html

Canadian Association of Food Banks. (2007b). *Hunger count 2007.* Toronto: Canadian Association of Food Banks.

Canadian Business. (2007). *The rich 100: The rich list | after hours | gotta do it | Canadian business online.* Retrieved 18/12/2007, from http://www.anadian-business.com/after_hours/lifestyle_activities/article.jsp?content=20061204_83955_83955&gclid=CNPV3b2vhpACFQoCYAod8QUGrQ

Canadian Centre for Justice Statistics. (2003). *Crime statistics in Canada.* Ottawa: Statistics Canada.

Canadian Centre for Justice Statistics. (2006). *Crime statistics in Canada.* Cat. No. 85-002-XIE Vol 27, no. 5. Ottawa: Statistics Canada.

Canadian Council of Human Resources Associations. (n.d.). *HR profession defined.* Retrieved 28/03/2008, from http://www.cchra.ca/Web/profession/content.aspx?f=29754

Canadian Council on Learning. (2007a). Learning to know: Participation in post-secondary education. Retrieved from http://www.ccl-cca.ca/NR/rdonlyres/CAC7D2C5-DA8A-4E4B-BO52-F06662BD8ED8/0/Participation InPostSecondaryEducationEn.pdf

Canadian Council on Learning. (2007b). *Lessons in learning: Canada slow to overcome limits for disabled learners.* Retrieved27/06/2008, from http://www.ccl-cca.ca/CCL/Reports/LessonsInLearning/LinL20070222_Slow_overcome_limits_disabled_learners.htm

Canadian Council on Learning. (2009). *Why boys don't like to read.* Retrieved 25/07/2009, from http://www.ccl-cca.ca/CCL/Reports/LessonsInLearning/LinL20090218 Whyboysdontliketoread.htm

Canadian Council on Social Development. (1996). *The progress of Canada's children 1996.* Ottawa: Canadian Council on Social Development.

Canadian Council on Social Development. (2004). *A profile of eco-nomic security in Canada.* Retrieved 7/10/2008, from http://www.ccsd.ca.factsheets /economic_security/poverty/index.htm

Canadian Heritage. (1998). *Visible minority workers are at greater economic risk* No. 2007

Canadian Heritage. (2003). *Terms of agreement between the government of Canada and the national association of Japanese Canadians.* Retrieved 1/22/2008, from http://www.pch.gc.ca/progs/em-cr/eval/archive/2002_18/7_e.cfm

Canadian Heritage. (2004a). *Canadians and their government: A resource guide.* Retrieved 04/04/2008, from http://www.Canadianheritage.gc.ca/special/gouv-gov/section2/infobox1_e.cfm

Canadian Heritage. (2004b). *Multiculturalism — Canadian diversity: Respecting our differences.* Retrieved 05/06/2008, from http://www.pch.gc.ca/progs/multi/respect_e.cfm

Canadian Heritage. (2004c). *The top jobs.* Retrieved 04/04/2008, from http://www.Canadianheritage.gc.ca/special/gouv-gov/section2/infobox2_e.cfm

Canadian Heritage. (2005). *Multiculturalism: A Canada for all: Canada's action plan against racism—an overview.* Retrieved 1/27/2008, from http://www.Canadianheritage.gc.ca/multi/plan_action_plan/overview_vue_e.cfm

Canadian Heritage. (2007a). *Canadian multiculturalism: An inclusive citizenship.* Retrieved 1/25/2008, from http://www.pch.gc.ca/progs/multi/inclusive_e.cfm

Canadian Heritage. (2007b). *Canadian television fund.* Retrieved 02/06/2008, from http://www.Canadianheritage.gc.ca/progs/ac-ca/progs/fct-ctf/index_e.cfm

Canadian Heritage. (2007c). *Guide to the Canadian Charter of Rights and Freedoms.* Retrieved 6/27/2008, from http://www.pch.gc.ca/progs/pdp-hrp/Canada/guide/equality_e.cfm

Canadian Heritage. (2007d). *Human rights program—the Canadian Charter of Rights and Freedoms.* Retrieved 1/28/2008, from http://www.pch.gc.ca/progs/pdp-hrp/Canada/freedom_e.cfm

Canadian Heritage. (2008a). *Canada magazine fund.* Retrieved 02/06/2008, from http://www.Canadianheritage.gc.ca/progs/ac-ca/progs/fcm-cmf/index_e.cfm

Canadian Heritage. (2008b). *Publications assistance program.* Retrieved 02/06/2008, from http:/www.Canadianheritage.gc.ca/progs/ac-ca/progs/pap/index_e.cfm

Canadian Human Rights Commission. (2007). *Discrimination and harassment.* Retrieved 6/27/2008, from http://www.chrc-ccdp.ca/discrimination/federally_regulated-en.asp

Canadian Labour Congress. (n.d.). *History of labour.* Retrieved 3/29/2008, from http://Canadianlabour.ca/index.php/history_of_labour

Canadian Newspaper Association. (2006). *Canadian newspaper circulation data, 2006.* Retrieved 05/01/2008, from http://www.cna-acj.ca/Client/CNA/cna.nsf/object/CircData06/$file/CIRCULATION%20DATA%202006.pdf

Canadiana. (2008). *Canada in the making: The deportation of the Acadians, 1755–1762.* Retrieved 1/22/2008, from http://Canadiana.org/citm/specifique/deportation_e.html

Cantril, H. (1940). *The invasion from Mars: A study in the psychology of panic.* Princeton, NJ: Princeton University Press.

Cardoso, F.H. & Faletto, E. (1979). *Dependency and development in Latin America* (M.M. Urquidi Trans.). Berkeley, CA: University of California Press.

Carey, J.W. (1967). Harold Adams Innis and Marshall McLuhan. *The Antioch Review, 27*(1), 5–39.

Carleton University. (2007). *Wallace clement.* Retrieved 19/12/2007, from http://www.carleton.ca/socanth/faculty/clement.html

Carmichael, C. (2006). Violence and ethnic boundary maintenance in Bosnia in the 1990s. *Journal of Genocide Research, 8*(3), 283–293.

Carolan, M.S. (2004). Ecological modernization theory: What about consumption? *Society & Natural Resources, 17*(3), 247–260. Retrieved from http://library.mtroyal.ca:2048/login?url=

http://search.ebscohost.com/login.aspx?direct=true&AuthType=ip,url,cookie,uid&db=a9h&AN=12255240&site=ehost-live

CARP. (2005). *CARP's fight against scams & frauds: Report & recommendations.* Retrieved 6/26/2008, from http://www.carp.ca/article_display.cfm? documentID=1467& CabinetID=256& LibraryID=70&cityID=0

Carpay, J. (2006). *Health care laws challenged in Alberta courts.* Retrieved 6/30/2008, from http://www.fcpp.org/main/publication_detail.php?PubID=1526

Carroll, T. (2007). Curious conceptions: Learning to be old. *Studies in Continuing Education, 29*(1), 71–84. doi:10.1080/01580370601146338

Carroll, W.K. (2004). *Bill Carroll: Professor of sociology.* Retrieved 30/3/2008, from http://web.uvic.ca/~wcarroll/

Carroll, W.K. (2008). In Kearnes L. (Ed.), *Biography*

Carroll, W.K. & Ratner, R.S. (2007). Ambivalent allies: Social democratic regimes and social movements. *BC Studies,* (154), 41–66. Retrieved from http://library.mtroyal.ca:2048/login?url=http://library.mtroyal.ca:2924/login.aspx?direct=rue&AuthType=ip,url,cookie,uid&db=a9h&AN=27232715&site=ehost-live

Carruthers, B.G. & Babb, S. (2000). *Economy/Society: Markets, meanings, and social structure.* London, UK: Pine Forge Press.

Carstensen, L.L. (1995). Evidence for a life-span theory of socioemotional selectivity. *Current Directions in Psychological Science, 4*(5), 151–156. doi:10.1111/1467-8721.ep11512261

Carter, G.W. (2003). *J.K. Lasser's taxes made easy for your home-based business: The ultimate tax handbook for the self-employed* (5th ed.). Hoboken, NJ: John Wiley & Sons Inc.

Casper, L.M., McLanahan, S.S., & Garfinkel, I. (1994). The gender-poverty gap: What we can learn from other countries. *American Sociological Review, 59*(4), 594–605.

Cassem, N. (1988). The person confronting death. In A. Nicholi (Ed.), *The new Harvard guide to psychiatry* (pp. 728–758). Cambridge, MA: Belknap.

Castaldo, J. (2007). *The CEO poll: Business leaders on Canada's place in a global economy.* Retrieved 19/12/2007, from http://www.Canadianbusiness.com/managing/strategy/article.jsp?content=20071130_153512_6376

Castañeto, M.V. & Willemsen, E.W. (2006). Social perception of the personality of the disabled. *Social Behavior & Personality: An International Journal, 34*(10), 1217–1231. Retrieved from http://library.mtroyal.ca:2048/login?url=http://search.ebscohost.com/login.aspx?direct=true& AuthType=ip,url,cookie,uid&db=a9h& AN=23218520&site=ehost-live

Catton Jr., W.R. & Dunlap, R.E. (1978). Environmental sociology: A new paradigm. *American Sociologist, 13*(1), 41–49. Retrieved from http://library.mtroyal.ca:2048/login?url=http://search.ebscohost.com/login.aspx?direct=true&AuthType= ip,url,cookie,uid&db=a9h&AN=4945426&site=ehost-live

CAUT. (2001a). Academic freedom in jeopardy at Toronto. *CAUT Bulletin Online, 48*(5). Retrieved from http://www.caut.ca/en/bulletin/issues/2001_may/default.asp

CAUT. (2001b). *Law suit launched against U of T and CAMH in Dr. David Healy controversy*CAUT.

CAUT. (2002). *Settlement in Healy legal dispute a "vindication"* CAUT.

CAUT. (2005). *Policy statement on academic freedom*CAUT.

CAUT. (2006). *Statement on the controversy over professor Shiraz Dossa*CAUT.

CAUT. (2007a). *CAUT almanac of post-secondary education.*

CAUT. (2007b). *Issues and campaigns: David Healy*CAUT.

CAUT. (2007c). *Issues and campaigns: Dr. Nancy Olivieri*CAUT.

CBC. (1995). *Mike Harris: His political legacy.* Retrieved 25/7/2009, from http://www.cbc.ca/newsinreview/may%202002/PDFs/harris.pdf

CBC. (2004). *Marijuana use doubled over past decade: study.* Retrieved 25/1/2008, from http://www.cbc.ca/Canada/story/2004/11/24/drugstudy041124.html

CBC. (2005). *Breaking point: October 30, 1995—summary.* Retrieved 25/1/2008, from http://www.cbc.ca/breakingpoint/chapter9_0.shtml

CBC. (2007a). Black found guilty of obstruction, mail fraud. *CBC.ca.* Retrieved 15/9/2008, from http://www.cbc.ca/money/story/2007/07/13/black-verdict.html

CBC. (2007ab). Canadians willing to fork out more to help environment: polls. *CBC.ca.* Retrieved 25/7/2009, from http://www.cbc.ca/canada/toronto/story/2007/07/04/enviro-survey.html

CBC. (2007b). The Fifth Estate—failing Jeffery Baldwin. Retrieved 31/10/2007, from http://www.cbc.ca/fifth/failingjeffrey/

CBC. (2007c). Obese children will die younger than their parents: report. *CBC.ca.* Retrieved 17/7/2009, from http://www.cbc.ca/health/story/2007/03/27/obesity-child.html

CBC. (2007d). Online sexual predators on rise, US officials say. *CBC.ca.* Retrieved 10/1/2009, from http://www.cbc.ca/news/story/2007/07/25/onlinepredators.html

CBC. (2008a). Life expectancy hits 80.4 years: Statistics Canada. *CBC.ca.* Retrieved 14/12/2009, from http://www.cbc.ca/Canada/story/2008/01/14/death_stats.html

CBC. (2008b). Man, 20, found guilty of 2nd degree murder in Jane Creba shooting. Retrieved 15/7/2009, from http://www.cbc.ca/Canada/story/2008/12/07/creba-verdict.html

CBC. (2008c). Senators approve anti-spanking bill. *CBC.ca.* Retrieved 23/6/2008, from http://www.cbc.ca/Canada/story/2008/06/19/spanking-bill.html?ref=rss

CBC. (2009a). "Conrad Black denied bail by top US court". Retrieved from http://www.cbc.ca/money/stroy/2009/06/11/us-supreme-court-conrad-black.html

CBC. (2009b). Pickton loses appeal in BC court. Retrieved from http://www.cbc.ca/Canada/british-columbia/stroy/2009/06/25/bc-pickton-appeal-ruling.html

CBC Digital Archives. (2008). *Thalidomide: Bitter pills, broken promises.* Retrieved 01/07/2008, from http://archives.cbc.ca/health/public_health/topics/88/

CBC News. (2006). *CBC news in depth: Retirement.* Retrieved 12/11/2007, from http://www.cbc.ca/news/background/retirement/mandatory_retirement.html

CBC News. (2007a). *Child poverty rates unchanged in nearly 2 decades: Report.* Retrieved 2/12/2007, from http://www.cbc.ca/Canada/story/2007/11/26/child-poverty.html

CBC News. (2007b). *New copyright law on its way: Industry Canada.* Retrieved 8/5/2008, from http://www.cbc.ca/arts/music/story/2007/11/19/copyright-law.html?ref=rss

CBC News. (2008). *Retiring mandatory retirement.* Retrieved 25/62008, from http://www.cbc.ca/news/background/retirement/mandatory_retirement.html

CBC News in Depth. (2005). *Bill 101.* Retrieved 26/8/2009, from http://www.cbc.ca/news/background/bill101/

CBC News in Depth. (2008). *Canada's military.* Retrieved 10/11/2007, from http://www.cbc.ca/news/background/cdnmilitary/

CBC News in Review. (1999). *Chinese boat people: Human cargo.* Retrieved 28/1/2008, from http://www.cbc.ca/newsinreview/oct 99/Boat People/Chi-Can.html

CBC Radio Canada. (n.d.). *History—1901–1939.* Retrieved 04/05/2008, from http://www.cbc.radio-Canada.ca/history/1901-1939.shtml

CBS. (n.d.). *CBS 6 Albany: WRGB history.* Retrieved 05/05/2008, from http://www.cbs6albany.com/sections/wrgb/history/

CBS News. (2004). *Sex trial on Pitcairn Island.* Retrieved 22/2/2008, from http://www.cbsnews.com/stories/2004/09/30/world/printables646483.shtml

CBS News. (2007). *Cutting through advertising clutter, the average person may see 5,000 ads a day.* Retrieved 02/06/2008, from http://www.cbsnews.com/stories/2006/09/17/sunday/main2015684_page2.shtml

Cech, R. & Marks, M.B. (2007). edagogical tools for teaching supply and demand using lessons from transitional economies. *Social Studies, 98*(1), 3–7. Retrieved from http://library.mtroyal.ca:2048/login?url=http://search.ebscohost.com/login.aspx?direct=true& AuthType=ip,url,cookie,uid&db=a9h&AN=24660560&site=ehost-live

Centers for disease control and prevention—influenza (flu): The disease. Retrieved 30/07/2007, from http://www.cdc.gov/flu/about/disease.htm

Central Intelligence Agency. (2003). *National strategy for combating terrorism*

Central Intelligence Agency. (2008). *The world factbook—rank order—life expectancy at birth.* Retrieved 6/13/2008, from https://www.cia.gov/library/publications/the-world-factbook/rankorder/2102rank.html

Centre for Marine Biodiversity. (n.d.). *What is marine biodiversity?* Retrieved 7/29/2008, from http://www.marinebiodiversity.ca/cmb/what-is-marine-biodiversity

The Centre for Spatial Economics. (2008). *The economic cost of wait times in Canada.* Ottawa, ON: Canadian Medical Association.

Cerkovich, S., Girodano, P., & Rudolph, J. (2000). Race, crime, and the American dream. *Journal of Research in Crime and Delinquency, 37*(2), 131–170.

Cernohous, S. (2007). Wikis: Open source information communities for educators and students. *Athletic Therapy Today, 12*(3), 2–5. Retrieved from http://library.mtroyal.ca:2048/login?url=http://search.ebscohost.com/login.aspx?direct=true&AuthType=ip,url,cookie,uid&db=a9h&AN=24993180&site=ehost-live

Chagnon, N. (1983). In Chagnon N. (Ed.), *Yanomamö: The fierce people* (3rd ed.). New York: Holt, Rinehart and Winston.

Chagnon, N. (1997). *Yanomamo* (5th ed.). Fort Worth, TX: Harcourt Brace.

Chambliss, W. (1964). A sociological analysis of the law of vagrancy. *Social Problems, 12*, 67–77.

Chan, K. & McNeal, J. (2004). Chinese Children's attitudes towards television advertising: Truthfulness and liking. *International Journal of Advertising, 23*, 337–359.

Chan, W. & Rigakos, G. (2002). Risk, crime and gender. *British Journal of Criminology, 42*(4), 743–761.

Chandler, D. (1994). *The Sapir-Whorf hypothesis.* Retrieved 01/10/2007, from http://www.aber.ac.uk/media/Documents/short/whorf.html

Chang, A. (2008). *As Olympics near, smog blankets Beijing.* Retrieved 01/08/2008, from http://www.thestar.com/Sports/Olympics/article/468185

Chappell, N., McDonald, L., & Stones, M. (2008). *Aging in contemporary Canada* (2nd ed.). Toronto, ON: Pearson Education Canada, Inc.

Charbonneau, L. (2005). *In God they trust.* Retrieved 3/13/2008, from http://www.universityaffairs.ca/issues/2005/may/_print/in_god_they_trust.html

Charmaz, K. (1991). *Good days, bad days: The self in chronic illness & time.* New Brunswick, NJ: Rutgers University Press.

Cheal, D. (2002). *Sociology of family life.* New York: Palgrave.

Chen, J.C., Owusu-Ofori, S., Pai, D., Toca-McDowell, E., Wang, S. & Waters, C.K. (2003). *A study of female academic performance in mechanical engineering.* Retrieved 1/15/2008, from http://fie.engrng.pitt.edu/fie96/papers/276.pdf

Chesney-Lind, M. (1988). Girls and status offences: Is juvenile justice still sexist? *Criminal Justice Abstracts, 20*(1), 144–165.

Chesney-Lind, M. (1989). Girls, crime and woman's place: Toward a feminist model of female delinquency. *Crime and Delinquency, 35*(1), 5–30.

Chesney-Lind, M. & Sheldon, R. (1992). *Girls, delinquency and juvenile justice.* Pacific Grove: Brooks/Cole Publishing.

Chibbaro, J.S. (2007). School counselors and the cyberbully: Interventions and implications. *Professional School Counseling, 11*(1), 65–67. Retrieved from http://library.mtroyal.ca:2048/login?url=http://search.ebscohost.com/login.aspx?direct=true&AuthType=ip,url,cookie, uid& db=a9h&AN=27264345&site=ehost-live

Chilana, R.S. & Zabel, D. (2005). *Sikhism* American Library Association. Retrieved from http://library.mtroyal.ca:2048/login? url=http://search.ebscohost.com/login.aspx?direct=true&AuthType=ip,url,cookie,uid&db=a9h&AN=20290979&site=ehost-live

Childe, V.G. (1951). *Social evolution.* London, UK: Watts.

Chinese Canadian National Council. (2005). *CCNC: Chinese head tax and exclusion act.* Retrieved 1/8/2008, from http://www.ccnc.ca/redress/history.html

Chirot, D. (1977). *Social change in the twentieth century.* New York: Harcourt Brace Jovanovich, Inc.

Chirot, D. & McCauley, C. (2006). *Why not kill them all?: The logic and prevention of mass political murder.* Princeton, NJ: Princeton University Press.

Chou, C., Condron, L., & Belland, J.C. (2005). A review of the research on internet addiction. *Educational Psychology Review, 17*(4), 363–388. doi:10.1007/s10648-005-8138-1

Christensen Hughes, Julia M., & McCae, D.L. (2006). Academic misconduct within higher education in Canada. *Canadian Journal of Higher Education, 36*(2), 1–21.

Christian, J. & Abrams, D. (2004). A tale of two cities: Predicting homeless people's uptake of outreach programs in London and New York. *Basic and Applied Social Psychology, 26*(2&3), 169–182.

Chu, J. (2004). God's things and Caesar's: Jehovah's witnesses and political neutrality. *Journal of Genocide Research, 6*(3), 319–342. Retrieved from http://library.mtroyal.ca:2048/login? url=http://search.ebscohost.com/login.aspx?direct=true&AuthType=ip,url,cookie,uid&db=a9h&AN=14361184&site=ehost-live

Chunn, D. & Gavigan, S. (1995). Women, crime and criminal justice in Canada. In M. Jackson, & C. Griffiths (Eds.), *Canadian criminology: Perspectives on crime and criminality* (2nd ed., pp. 141–184). Toronto: Harcourt Brace.

Chunn, D. & Gavigan, S. (2006). Welfare law, welfare fraud, and the moral regulation of the "never deserving" poor. In A. Glasbeek (Ed.), *Moral regulation and governance in Canada: History, context, and critical issues* (pp. 327–356). Toronto: Canadian Scholars' Press.

CIDA. (2007). *Women and men working together for rural development in Rwanda.* Retrieved 7/15/2008, from http://acdi-cida.gc.ca/CIDAWEB/acdicida.nsf/En/NAT-711113816-LCG

CIDA. (2008). *CIDA in brief.* Retrieved 7/14/2008, from http://www.acdi-cida.gc.ca/cidaweb/acdicida.nsf/En/JUD-829101441-JQC

Citizen's forum on Canadian unity—Spicer commission report (1991). Retrieved 3/10/2007, from http://www.uni.ca/initiatives/spicer.html

The City of Calgary. (2007). *Affordable housing.* Retrieved 06/11, from http://www.calgary.ca/portal/server.pt/gateway/PTARGS_0_2_104_0_0_35/http:/content.calgary.ca/CCA/City%20Hall/Business% 20Units/Corporate%20Properties%20and%20Buildings/Affordable% 20Housing/Affordable%20 Housing.htm

The City of Vancouver. (2005). *Homeless action plan.* Vancouver: Vancouver City Council.

Clark, W. (2003). *Pockets of belief: Religious attendance patterns in Canada.* Canadian Social Trends (Spring) catalogue No. 11-008. Ottawa, ON: Statistics Canada.

Clarke, P.B. (Ed.) (2008). *Encyclopedia of new religious movements.* London, UK: Routledge, Taylor & Francis Group.

Clarke, T. (2008). *Turning on Canada's tap: Why we need a pan-Canadian policy and strategy now on bulk water exports to the US.* Ottawa, ON: Polaris Institute.

Clark-Kauffman, E., Duncan, G. J., & Morris, P. (2003). How welfare policies affect child and adolescent achievement. *The American Economic Review, 93*(2), 299. Retrieved from http://proquest.umi.com/pqdweb?did=355798421&Fmt=7&clientId=65345&RQT=309&VName=PQD

Clement, W. (2001). Canadian political economy's legacy for sociology. *Canadian Journal of Sociology, 26*(3), 405–420.

Clement, W. (2006). The territorial politics of welfare. *Canadian Journal of Political Science, 39*(2), 435. Retrieved from http://proquest.umi.com/pqdweb?did=1092752491&Fmt=7&clientId=65345&RQT=309&VName=PQD

Clifton, J.A. (Ed.) (1968). *Introduction to cultural anthropology—essays in the scope and methods of the science of man.* Boston, MA: Houghton Mifflin Co.

Cloward, R. (1959). Illegitimate means, anomie, and deviant behavior. *American Sociological Review, 24*(2), 164–176.

Cloward, R. & Ohlin, L. (1960). *Delinquency and opportunity: A theory of delinquent gangs.* Glencoe, IL: Free Press.

CMAJ. (2003). *Reasonable control: Gun registration in Canada* Canadian Medical Association. Retrieved from http://library.mtroyal.ca:2048/login?url=http://library.mtroyal.ca:2924/login.aspx?direct=true&AuthType=ip,url,cookie,uid&db=a9h&AN=9057470&site=ehost-live

CNRS (Centre National de la Recherche Scientifique). (2008). *Evolution of greenhouse gases over the last 800,000 years.* Retrieved 7/23/2008, from http://www2.cnrs.fr/en/1201.htm

Coder, J., Rainwater, L., & Smeeding, T. (1989). Inequality among children and elderly in ten modern nations. *American Economic Review, 79*(2), 320–324.

Codjoe, H. (2001). Fighting a "public enemy" of black academic achievement—the persistence of racism and the schooling experiences of black students in Canada. *Race Ethnicity and Education, 4*(4), 343–375.

Cohen, J.J. (2006). Professionalism in medical education, an American perspective: From evidence to accountability. *Medical Education, 40*(7), 607–617. Retrieved from http://library.mtroyal.ca:2048/login?url=http://search.ebscohost.com/login.aspx?direct=true&AuthType=ip,url,cookie,uid&db=a9h&AN=21326051&site=ehost-live

Colapinto, J. (2000). *As nature made him: The boy who was raised a girl.* New York: HarperCollins.

Colleges Ontario. (2008). *Ontario colleges: An overview.* Retrieved 10/12/2008, from http://www.collegesOntario.org/Client/CollegesOntario/Colleges_Ontario_LP4W_LND_ WebStation.nsf/resources/FACT+SHEET+1-2/$file/CO_FACT SHEET_01.pdf

Collins, J. (2006). Redefining the boundaries of work: Apparel workers and community unionism in the global economy. *Identities, 13*(1), 9–31. doi:10.1080/10702890500534304

Collins, R. (1979). *The credential society.* New York: Academic Press.

Comack, E. (2004). Feminism and criminology. In R. Linden (Ed.), *Criminology: A Canadian perspective* (5th ed., pp. 164–195). Toronto: Thomson Nelson.

Comack, E. & Brickley, S. (2007). Constituting the violence of criminalized women. *Canadian Journal of Crime and Criminal Justice, 49*(1), 1–36.

Comfort, D., Johnson, K., & Wallace, D. (2003). *Part-time work and family-friendly practices in Canadian workplaces* No.71-584-M1E, no.6, Statistics Canada.

Comte, A. (Ed.). (1975). *Auguste Comte: The foundations of sociology* (Kenneth Thompson, Ed.). New York: Wiley.

Conaghan, J. & Millns, S. (2005). Special issue: Gender, sexuality and human rights. *Feminist Legal Studies, 13*(1), 1–14.

Conference Board of Canada. (2008a). *The 2008 Ontario budget.* Retrieved 30/06/2008, from http://www.conferenceboard.ca/budget/on/default.asp

Conference Board of Canada. (2008b). *Budget du québec de 2008.* Retrieved 30/06/2008, from http://www.conferenceboard.ca/documents.asp?rnext=2480

Connell, R. (2002). Hegemonic masculinity. In S. Jackson, & S. Scott (Eds.), *Gender: A sociological reader* (pp. 60–62). New York: Routledge.

Connell, R.W. (1987). *Gender and power.* Stanford: Stanford University Press.

Conservative Party of Canada. (2008). Retrieved 24/9/2008, from http://www.conservative.ca/?section_id= 78176&tpid=3171&

Consumer Reports. (2008). *Protect yourself online.* Retrieved 10/1/2009, from http://www.consumerreports.org/cro/electronics-computers/computers-internet/interent-and-other-services/protect-yourself-online/overview/protect-yourself-online-ov.htm

Cook, N. (2006). Bazaar stories of gender, sexuality and imperial spaces in Gilgit, northern Pakistan.

ACME: An international E-Journal for Critical Geographies, 5(2), 230–257.

Cook, N. (Ed.). (2007). Gender relations in global perspective: Essential readings. Toronto: Canadian Scholars' Press Inc.

Cooley, C.H. (1902). Human nature and the social order. New York: C. Scribner's sons.

Coontz, S. (1992). The way we never were: American families and the nostalgia trap. New York: Basic Books, HarperCollins.

Corbett, J.B. (2006). Communicating nature: How we create and understand environmental messages. Washington, DC: Island Press.

Coreno, T. (2002). Fundamentalism as a class culture. Sociology of Religion, 63(3), 335–360. Retrieved from http://library.mtroyal.ca:2048/login?url=http:/ /search.ebscohost.com/login.aspx?direct=true& AuthType=ip,url,cookie,uid&db=a9h&AN=74515 98&site=ehost-live

Cornock, M. (2005). Deathly definitions. Nursing Standard, 19(41), 34. Retrieved from http:// library.mtroyal.ca:2048/login? url=http://search. ebscohost.com/login.aspx?direct=true& AuthType=ip,url,cookie,uid&db=a9h&AN=1748 0907&site=ehost-live

Coser, L. (1956). The functions of social conflict. New York: Free Press.

Coser, R. (Ed.). (1964). The family: Its structures and functions. New York: St. Martin's Press.

Cotgrove, S. & Duff, A. (1980). Environ mental-ism, middle-class radicalism and politics. Sociological Review, 28(2), 333–351. doi:10.1111/ 1467-954X.ep5467932

Cotgrove, S. & Duff, A. (1981). Environmentalism, values, and social change. British Journal of Sociology, 32(1), 92–110. Retrieved from http:// library.mtroyal.ca:2048/login?url=http://search. ebscohost.com/login.aspx? direct=true&AuthType=ip,url,cookie,uid&db=a9 h&AN=5295847&site=ehost-live

Cotgrove, S. (1976). Environmentalism and utopia. Sociological Review, 24(1), 23–42. doi:10.1111/ 1467-954X.ep5463422

Cotter, J. (2008). Groups warn of more bird deaths in oilsands ponds. Retrieved 10/08/2008, from http:// www.thestar.com/News/Canada/article/420962

Couch, C.J. (1996). Information technologies and social orders. New Brunswick (USA): Aldine-Transaction.

Couldry, N. (2004). Theorising media as practice. Social Semiotics, 14(2), 115–132. doi:10.1080/ 1035033042000238295

Council of Canadians with Disabilities. (1998). Publications: Latimer watch. Retrieved 28/06/2008, from http://www.ccdonline.ca/publications/latimer-watch/1098e.htm

Council of Europe. (2007). Council of Europe parliamentary assembly. Retrieved 3/9/2008, from http://library.mtroyal.ca:4134/Main.asp?link=/ Documents/WorkingDocs/Doc07/EDOC11297 .htm

Courtenay, W. (2000). Constructions of masculinity and their influence on men's well being: A theory of gender and health. Social Science and Medicine, 50, 1385–1401.

Cowan, J. (2008). Environmentalists take Ottawa to court over Kyoto. Retrieved 09/08/2008, from http:// www.Canada.com/topics/news/national/story. html?id =fbcb81d2-a9ab-4ebe-bd11a26fdff802a3

Cox, O.C. (1948). Caste, class, and race: A study in social dynamics. Garden City, NY: Doubleday.

Coyne, A. (1995, February 13). There is a national culture, even if no one can define it. Globe and Mail. Retrieved 21/11/2008 from http://www. andrewcoyne.com/columns/Globe/1995/ 19950213.html

Craine, S. & Coles, B. (1995). Alternative careers, youth transitions and young people's involvement in crime. Youth and Policy, 48, 6–26.

Cram, F. & Jackson, S. (2003). Disrupting the sexual double standard: Young women's talk about heterosexuality. British Journal of Social Psychology, 42, 113–127.

Cristi, M. (2001). From civil to political religion. Waterloo, ON: Wilfred Laurier Press.

Cronk, G. (2005). George Herbert Mead [Internet encyclopedia of philosophy]. Retrieved 17/09/2007, from http://www.iep.utm.edu/m/mead.htm#SH3c

Crossroads Christian Communications Inc. (2007). David and Norma-Jean Mainse. Retrieved 3/ 9/2008, from http://www. crossroads.ca/broadcas/ dmainse.htm

Croteau, D. & Hoynes, W. (2003). Media society: Industries, images, and audiences 3rd ed.). Thousand Oaks, CA: Sage Publications, Ltd.

Crouch, M. & McKenzie, H. (2006). The logic of small samples in interview-based qualitative research. Social Science Information, 45(4), 483–499.

Crowley, B. J., Hayslip Jr., B., & Hobdy, J. (2003). Psychological hardiness and adjustment to life events in adulthood. Journal of Adult Development, 10(4), 237.

CRTC. (1998). Public notice CRTC 1998-132. Retrieved 02/06/2008, from http://www.crtc.gc. ca/archive/ENG/Notices/1998/PB98-132.HTM

CRTC. (2001). The MAPL system. Retrieved 02/06/ 2008, from http://www.crtc.gc.ca/eng/iNFO_SHT/ R1.HTM

CRTC. (2004). Canadian content for radio and television. Retrieved 02/06/2008, from http://www. crtc.gc.ca/public/old_pubs_e/G11.htm

CRTC. (2007). Mandate. Retrieved 02/06/2008, from http://www.crtc.gc.ca/eng/cancon/mandate .htm

CRTC mandate. Retrieved 02/06/2008, from http:/ /www.crtc.gc.ca/eng/cancon/mandate.htm

CTV.ca. (2005). Internet use threatens to overtake TV in Canada. Retrieved 07/05/2008, from http:// www.ctv.ca/servlet/Article News/story/CTVNews/ 1123592 641078_62/?hub=Canada

Cukier, W. & Thomlinson, N. (2005). Two-tier health care, education, and policing: A comparative analysis of the discourses of privatization. Canadian Journal of Criminology & Criminal Justice, 47(1), 87–126. Retrieved from http://library.mtroyal.

ca:2048/login?url=http://search.ebscohost. com/login.aspx?direct=true&AuthType= ip,url,cookie,uid&db=a9h&AN=15808974&site= ehost-live

Cumming, E. & Henry, W.E. (1961). Growing old: The process of disengagement. New York: Basic Books.

Curran, D. & Renzetti, C. (1994). Theories of crime. Boston: Allyn and Bacon.

Currie, J. & Newson, J. (Eds.). (1998). Universities and globalization: Critical perspectives. Thousand Oaks, California: Sage.

Curtis, G. (2006). Jesus camp shuts down due to negative response (Christian Today). Retrieved 28/ 02/2008, from http://www.christiantoday.com/ article/jesus.camp.shuts.down.due.to.negative. response/8539.htm

Curtis, J., Grabb, E., & Guppy Guppy (Eds.). (2004). Social inequality in Canada: Patterns, problems and policies (Fourth ed.). Toronto: Pearson Prentice Hall.

Dalit freedom network: Abolish caste, now and forever. Retrieved 29/11/2007, from http://www. dalitnetwork.org/

Dalton, K. (1964). The premenstrual symdrome. Springfield: Charles C. Thomas.

Dalton, K. (1971). The premenstrual syndrome. Springfield: Charles C. Thomas.

Daly, K. (2000). It keeps getting faster: Changing patterns of time in families. Ottawa: Vanier Institute of the Family.

Danielewicz, I. (2005). Show us yer tits! Retrieved 06/07/2008, from http://gauntlet.ucalgary.ca/ story/5201

Danzon, P.M. (1992, Spring). Hidden overhead costs: Is Canada's system really less expensive? Health Affairs,, 21–43.

David Suzuki Foundation. (2007a). Climate change: Kyoto: Canada's emissions. Retrieved 23/ 07/2008, from http://www.davidsuzuki.org/ Climate_Change/Kyoto/Canadian_Emissions .asp

David Suzuki Foundation. (2007b). Kyoto protocol: FAQs. Retrieved 8/7/2008, from http://www. davidsuzuki.org/Climate_Change/Kyoto/FAQs.asp

Davidson, I. & McGrew, W.C. (2005). Stone tools and the uniqueness of human culture. Journal of the Royal Anthropological Institute, 11(4), 793–817.

Davies, B. (1990). The problem of desire. Social Problems, 37(4), 501–516.

Davies, Ian R.L., Sowden, P.T., Jerrett, D.T., Jerrett, T.I., & Corbett, G.G. (1998). A cross-cultural study of English and Setswana speakers on a colour triads task: A test of the Sapir-Whorf hypothesis. The British Journal of Psychology, 89, 1–15. Retrieved from http://library.mtroyal.ca:2083/pqdweb?did= 27463825&Fmt=7&clientId=65345&RQT=309& VName=PQD

Davies, J.B., Sandstöm, S., Shorrocks, A., & Wolff, E.N. (2008). The world distribution of household wealth (No. 2008/03). Helsinki, Finland: World Institute for Development Economics Research.

Davies, S. & Tanner, J. (2003). The long arm of the law: Effects of labelling on employment. *Sociology Quarterly, 44*(3), 385–404.

Davies, S. & Guppy, N. (2006). *The schooled society: An introduction to the sociology of education*. Don Mills: Oxford University Press.

Davis, D.M. (2007). The Los Angeles riots revisited: The changing face of the Los Angeles unified school district and the challenge for educators. *Educational Studies, 42*(3), 213–229. doi:10.1080/00131940701632613

Davis, K. & Moore, W.E. (1945). Some principles of stratification. *American Sociological Review, 10*, 242–249.

Dawkins, R. (2006). *The god delusion*. New York: Houghton Mifflin Company.

Dawley, A. & Faler, P. (1976). Working-class culture and politics in the industrial revolution: Sources of loyalism and rebellion. *Journal of Social History, 9*(4), 466.

DAWN. (2003). *The feminist principle of equality and inclusion*. Retrieved 25/07/2008, from http://dawn.thot.net/feminism8.html

Dawson, L. & Kass, N. (2005). Views of US researchers about informed consent in international collaborative research. *Social Science and Medicine, 61*, 1211–1222.

Dawson, L.L. (2006). *Comprehending cults: The sociology of new religious movements* (2nd ed.). Oxford: Oxford University Press.

Day, S. (2007). Book review of Sandra Harding (2006) science and social inequality: Feminist and postcolonial issues. Urbana and Chicago, Ill: University of Illinois press. *Canadian Journal of Sociology Online, 2007 (March)*, 17/12/2007.

de Vries, M. (2006). An enduring bond? Jews in the Netherlands and their ties with Judaism. *Journal of Ethnic & Migration Studies, 32*(1), 69–88. Retrieved from http://library.mtroyal.ca:2048/login?url=http://search.ebscohost.com/login.aspx?direct=true&AuthType= ip,url,cookie,uid&db=a9h&AN=18807113&site=ehost-live

Dei, G.J.S. & Calliste, A. (2000). Mapping the terrain: Power, knowledge and anti-racism education. In G.J.S. Dei & A. Calliste (Eds.), *Power, knowledge and anti-racism education: A critical reader* (pp. 11–22). Halifax: Fernwood Publishing.

Dei, G.S. (1997). Race and the production of identity in the schooling experiences of African-Canadian youth. *Discourse: Studies in the Cultural Politics of Education, 18*(2), 241–257.

Dei, G.S. (2003). Challenges for anti-racist educators in Ontario today. *Orbit, 33*(3), 2–5.

Dei, G.S. (2008). Schooling as community: Race, schooling, and the education of African youth. *Journal of Black Studies, 38*(3), 346–366.

DeKeseredy, W. (2001). Patterns of family violence. In M. Baker (Ed.), *Families: Changing trends in Canada* (4th ed., pp. 238–266). Toronto: McGraw-Hill.

Delamotte, Y. & Walker, K.F. (1976). Humanization of work and the quality of working life—trends and issues. *International Journal of Sociology, 6*(1), 8–40.

Delaney, T. (2004). *Classical social theory: Investigation and application*. Upper Saddle River, New Jersey: Prentice-Hall, Inc.

Della Porta, D. (1995). Power in movement: Social movements, collective actions and politics. *Acta Sociologica (Taylor & Francis Ltd), 38*(3), 275–278. Retrieved from http://library.mtroyal.ca:2048/login?url=http://search.ebsco host.com/login.aspx?direct=true& AuthType=ip,url,cookie,uid&db=a9h&AN=9510290767&site=ehost-live

deMarrais, K. & LeCompte, M. (1999). *The way schools work: A sociological analysis of education* (3rd ed.). New York: Longman.

Demers, S. & Bennett, C. (2007). Single sex classrooms. The Literacy and Numeracy Secretariat. Province of Ontario. Retrieved 13/5/2009, from http://www.edu.gov.ca/eng/literacynumeracy/inspire/research/Demers.pdf

D'Emillio, J. (2005). Capitalism and gay identity. In T.L. Steele (Ed.), *Sex, self, and society: The social context of sexuality*. California: Wadsworth.

Dennett, D.C. (2006). *Breaking the spell: Religion as a natural phenomenon*. New York: Viking.

Denney, D., Ellis, T., & Barn, R. (2006). Race diversity and criminal justice in Canada: A view from the UK. *Internet Journal of Criminology*. Retrieved from http://www.internetjournal ofcriminology.com

Denton, M. & Boos, L. (2007). The gender wealth gap: Structural and material constraints and implications for later life. *Journal of Women & Aging, 19* (3/4), 105. Retrieved from http://proquest.umi.com/pqdweb?did=1379694341&Fmt=7&clientId=65345&RQT=309&VName=PQD

Denzin, N. (2007). Katrina and the collapse of civil society in New Orleans. *Cultural Studies Critical Methodologies, 7*(2), 145–153.

Denzin, N.K. (1992). *Symbolic interactionism and cultural studies: The politics of interpretation*. Cambridge, MA: Blackwell.

DePalma, A. (1999). *Tough rules stand guard over Canadian culture*. Retrieved 5/15/2008, from http://www.globalpolicy.org/globaliz/cultural/Canadian.htm

Derenne, J.L. & Beresin, E.V. (2006). Body image, media, and eating disorders. *Academic Psychiatry, 30*(June), 257–261.

Desai, R.M. (2008). *The new philanthropy and development aid*. Retrieved 15/06/2008, from http://www.brookings.edu/opinions/2008/0424_development _aid_desai.aspx

Desroches, F. (1991). Tearoom trade: A law enforcement problem. *Canadian Journal of Criminology, 33*(1), 1–21.

Desyllas, M.C. (2007). A critique of the global trafficking discourse and US policy. *Journal of Sociology & Social Welfare, 34*(4), 57–79.

Devor, H. (2005). More than manly woman: How female transsexuals reject lesbian identities. In T.L. Steele (Ed.), *Sex, self and society: The social context of sexuality*. California: Wadsworth.

Dhruvarajan, V. & Vickers, J. (2002). *Gender, race and nation: A global perspective*. Toronto, ON: University of Toronto Press.

Dicum, G. (2006a). *Environmental justice and environmental racism*. Retrieved 26/07/2008, from http://environment.about.com/od/activismvolunteering/a/robert_ bullard.htm

Dicum, G. (2006b). *Meet Robert Bullard, the father of environmental justice*. Retrieved 02/08/2008, from http://www.grist.org/news/maindish/2006/03/14/dicum/

Didsbury, H. (1979). *Student handbook for the study of the future*. Washington: World Future Society.

Diehm, C. (2007). Identification with nature: What it is and why it matters. *Ethics & the Environment, 12*(2), 1–22. Retrieved from http://library.mtroyal.ca:2048/login?url=http://search.ebscohost .com/login.aspx?direct=true&AuthType=ip,url,cookie,uid&db=a9h&AN=29363016&site=ehost-live

Digital ethnography » blog archive » the history of YouTube. Retrieved 10/05/2008, from http://mediatedcultures.net/ksudigg/?p=108

Ding, Q.J. & Hesketh, T. (2006). Family size, fertility preferences, and sex ration in China in the era of the one child policy. *British Medical Journal, 333*, 371–373.

Diversity Watch. (2003). *Japanese: Ryerson University school of journalism*. Retrieved 22/01/2008, from http://www.diversitywatch.ryerson.ca/backgrounds/japanese.htm

Doane, A.W., Jr. (1997). Dominant group ethnic identity in the United States: The role of "hidden" ethnicity in intergroup relations. *Sociological Quarterly, 38*(3), 375. Retrieved from http://proquest. umi.com/pqdweb?did=14478129&Fmt=7&clientId=65345&RQT=309&VName=PQD

Dockery, T.M. & Bedeian, A.G. (1989). "Attitudes versus actions": LaPiere's (1934) classic study revisited. *Social Behavior and Personality, 17*(1), 9–16.

Dodd, N. (1999). *Social theory and modernity* [Nigel Dodd, 1999 Polity Press]. Cambridge, UK: Polity Press.

Dodds, L., & Hopwood, B. (2006). BAN waste, environmental justice and citizen participation in policy setting. *Local Environment, 11*(3), 269–286. doi:10.1080/13549830600558762

Dodge, D. (2007). *How Napster changed the world—A look back 7 years later*. Retrieved 08/05/2008, from http://dondodge.typepad.com/the_next_big_thing/2007/03/how_napster_cha.html

Doherty, B. (2002). *Ideas and action in the green movement*. London, UK: Routledge.

Dolezal, J.A. (2008). Literary activism, social justice, and the future of bioregionalism. *Ethics & the Environment, 13*(1), 1–22. Retrieved from http://library.mtroyal.ca:2048/login?url=http://search.ebscohost.com/login.aspx?direct=true &AuthType=ip,url,cookie,uid&db=a9h&AN=32132413&site=ehost-live

Dolittle, R. & Wilkes, J. (2008, November 6). Brandon Crisp found dead. *Toronto Star*. Retrieved from http://www.thestar.com/News/Ontario/article/531591

Dollard, J., Doob, L.W., Miller, N.E., Mowrer, O.W., & Sears, R.R. (1939). *Frustration and aggression*. New Haven, Connecticut: Yale University Press.

Donnelly, P.G. & Kimble, C.E. (2006). An evaluation of the effects of neighborhood mobilization on community problems. *Journal of Prevention & Intervention in the Community, 32*(1), 61–80. doi:10.1300/J005v32n01?05

Donovan, P. (2007). How idle is idle talk? One hundred years of rumor research. *Diogenes, 54*(1), 59–82.

Doucet, A. (2004). Fathers and the responsibility for children: A puzzle and a tension. *Atlantis: A Women's Studies Journal, 28*(2), 103–114.

Doucet, C. (2000). *Notes from exile: On being Acadian*. Toronto, ON: McClelland & Stewart.

Dowsett Johnston, A. & Dwyer, M. (2004). Ranking Canadian universities: Ann Dowsett Johnston and Mary Dwyer explain the methodology behind the annual Maclean's survey. *Macleans*, 38–39.

Doyle, S. (2008, April 7). Lobbyists make final preparations for high-stakes CRTC hearings. *The Hill Times*. Retrieved from http://www.thehilltimes.ca/html/index.php?display=story&full_path=2008/april/7/lobbying/&c=2

Drakich, J., Grant, K., & Stewart, P. (2002). The academy in the 21st century: Editors' introduction. *The Canadian Review of Sociology and Anthropology, 39*(3), 249–260.

Drakich, J. & Stewart, P. (2007). Years later, how are university women doing? *Academic Matters, February*, 6–9.

Driedger, L. (2003). Changing boundaries: Sorting space, class, ethnicity and race in Ontario*. *The Canadian Review of Sociology and Anthropology, 40*(5), 593–621. Retrieved fromhttp://proquest.umi.com/pqdweb? did=665943441&Fmt=7&clientId=65345&RQT=309&VName=PQD

Driscoll, C. (2004). Can behaviors be adaptations? *Philosophy of Science, 71*(1), 16–35.

Drog. (2005). The exploitation of migrant workers in Canada. Retrieved from http://www.kuro5hin.org/story/2005/1/13/114947/716

Duay, D. & Bryan, V. (2006). Senior adults' perceptions of successful aging. *Educational Gerontology, 32*(6), 423–445. doi:10.1080/03601270600685636

Dube, S.C. (1988). *Modernization and development: The search for alternative paradigms*. Tokyo: The United Nations University.

Duffy, A. & Momirov, J. (2005). Family violence: A twenty-first century issue. In N. Mandell, & A. Duffy (Eds.), *Canadian families* (3rd ed., pp. 144–175). Toronto: Thomson Nelson.

Dumme, T.J.B. (2008). Health geography: Supporting public health policy and planning. *CMAJ: Canadian Medical Association Journal, 178*(9), 1177–1180. doi:10.1503/cmaj.071783

Dunlap, R.E. (2000). The evolution of environmental sociology: A brief history and assessment of the American experience. In M. Redclift, & G. Woodgate (Eds.), *The international handbook of environmental sociology* (pp. 21–39). Cheltenham, UK: Edward Elgar Publishing Ltd.

Dunlap, R.E. (2002). Paradigms, theories and environmental sociology. In R.E. Dunlap, F.H. Buttel, P. Dickens & A. Gijswijt (Eds.), *Sociological theory and the environment: Classical foundations, contemporary insights* (pp. 329–350). Lanham, MD: Rowman and Littlefield Publishers, Inc.

duPreez, P. (1994). *Genocide: The psychology of mass murder*. New York: Marion Boyers.

Durham, M.G. (2005). Girls, media, and the negotiation of sexuality: A study of race, class and gender in adolescent peer groups. In T.L. Steele (Ed.), *Sex, self and society: The social context of sexuality*. California: Wadsworth.

Durkheim, É. (1897). *Le suicide*. Paris: Felix Alcan.

Durkheim, É. (1912[1954]). *The elementary forms of religious life*. Glencoe, IL: Free Press.

Durkheim, É. (1964[1893]). *The division of labor in society*. Glencoe, IL: Free Press.

Dyck, E. (2005). Flashback: Psychiatric experimentation with LSD in historical perspective. *Canadian Journal of Psychiatry, 50*(7), 381–388.

Dyck, N. (1997). Tutelage, resistance and co-optation in Canadian Indian administration. *The Canadian Review of Sociology and Anthropology, 34*(3), 333–348.

Dyer, G. (2004, September 30). Cultural conundrum on Pitcairn. Retrieved 25/9/2007, from http://www.gwynnedyer.net/articles/Gwynne%20Dyer%20article_%20%20Pitcairn.txt

Dyer, R. (2002). *Only entertainment* (2nd ed.). New York: Routledge, Inc.

Easton, D. & Liszt, C.A. (1997). *The ethical slut*. California: Greenery Press.

Education Quality and Accountability Office. (2008). *Ontario student achievement results, 2007–2008*. Retrieved 24/11/2008, from http://www.eqao.com/pdf_e/08/3693_ProvincialReport_08_web.pdf

Egan, D. (2006). Resistance under the black light: Exploring the use of music in two exotic dance clubs. *Journal of Contemporary Ethnography, 35*(2), 201–219.

Eichler, M. (1980). *The double standard: A feminist critique of feminist social science*. New York: St. Martine's Press.

Eichler, M. (1988a). *Canadian families today: Recent changes and their policy consequences* (2nd ed.). Toronto: Gage.

Eichler, M. (1988b). *Families in Canada today* (2nd ed.). Toronto: Gage Educational Publishing.

Eichler, M. (1991). *Non-sexist research methods: A practical guide*. New York: Routledge.

Eichler, M. (Ed.). (1995). *Change of plans towards a nonsexist city*. Toronto: Garamond.

Eichler, M. (1997). *Family shifts: Families, policies, and gender equality*. Toronto: Oxford University Press.

Eichler, M. (2001). Women pioneers in Canadian sociology: The effects of a politics of gender and a politics of knowledge. *Canadian Journal of Sociology, 26*(3), 375–403.

Eichler, M. (2008). *Marriage and divorce* The Canadian Encyclopedia. Historica Foundation.

Eichler, M., Larkin, J., & Neysmith, S. (Eds.). (2002). *Feminist utopias: Re-visioning our futures*. Toronto: Inanna Press.

Eisenstadt, E.N. (Ed.). (1968). *Max Weber: On charisma and institution building*. Chicago: University of Chicago Press.

Eisenstadt, S.N. (1966). *Modernization: Protest and change*. Englewood Cliffs, New Jersey: Prentice-Hall, Inc.

Eisenstein, E.L. (1979). *The printing press as an agent of change: Communications and cultural transformations in early-modern Europe*. Cambridge, UK: Cambridge University Press.

Elbers, C., Lanjouw, P.F., Mistiaen, J.A., Özler, B., & Simler, K. (2004). On the unequal inequality of poor communities. *The World Bank Economic Review, 18*(3), 401. Retrieved from http://proquest.umi.com/pqdweb?did=800025471&Fmt=7&clientId=65345&RQT=309&VName=PQD

Elections Canada. (2007). *Appendix 1: Evolution of the federal electoral system*. Retrieved 05/04/2008, from http://www.elections.ca/content.asp?section=gen&document=part4&dir=ces&lang=e&anchor=51&textonly=false#51

Elections Canada. (2008). *The electoral system of Canada*. Retrieved 05/04/2008, from http://www.elections.ca/content.asp?section=gen&document=part1&dir=ces&lang=e&anchor=2&textonly=false#2

Ellwood, W. (2003). *The no-nonsense guide to globalization*. Oxford OX4 1BW, UK: New Internationalist Publications Ltd.

Employment by age, sex, type of work, class of worker and province (monthly). Retrieved 26/03/2008, from http://www40.statcan.ca/l01/cst01/labr66a.htm

Enviromation. (2007). Environment minister unveils "turning the corner" green plan. *Enviromation, April 2007*(44), 334–335.

Environment Canada. (2007a). *Clean air online—CEPA 1999 section 71*. Retrieved 8/7/2008, from http://library.mtroyal.ca:2137/cleanair-airpur/Turning_the_Corner/CEPA_1999,_Sec._71-S074B0A75-1_En.htm

Environment Canada. (2007b). *The green lane: Climate change*. Retrieved 22/07/2008, from http://www.ec.gc.ca/climate/overview_science-e.html

Environment Canada. (2007c). *Landfill gas*. Retrieved 7/29/2008, from http://library.mtroyal.ca:2137/wmd-dgd/default.asp?lang=En&n=10E36DBA-1

Environment Canada. (2007d). *Water*. Retrieved 24/07/2008, from http://www.ec.gc.ca/default.asp?lang=en&n=76d556b9-1

Environment Canada. (2008a). *Federal government actions on clean air*. Retrieved 24/07/2008, from http://www.ec.gc.ca/cleanair-airpur/Federal_Government-WSADF88240-1_En.htm

Environment Canada. (2008b). *Regulatory framework for industrial greenhouse gas emissions*. Retrieved 8/7/2008, from http://library.mtroyal.ca:2137/doc/virage-corner/2008-03/541_eng.htm

Environment Canada. (2008c). *Turning the corner*. Retrieved 8/7/2008, from http://library.mtroyal.ca:2137/default.asp?lang=En&n=75038EBC-1#m10

Environmental Protection Agency. (2007). *Ecosystems and biodiversity*. Retrieved 21/07/2008, from http://www.epa.gov/climatechange/effects/eco.html

Epstein, S. (2005). A queer encounter. In T.L. Steele (Ed.), *Sex, self and society: The social context of sexuality*. California: Wadsworth.

Erikson, E.H. (1950). *Childhood and society*. New York: Norton.

Erikson, E.H. (1968). *Identity: Youth and crisis*. New York: Norton.

Eryilmaz, D. & Darn, S. (2005). *BBC British council teaching English—methodology—non-verbal communication*. Retrieved 01/10/2007, from http://www.teachingenglish.org.uk/think/methodology/nonverbal.shtml

Esmail, N. (2007). Complementary and alternative medicine in Canada: Trends in use and public attitudes, 1997–2006. Retrieved 30/08/2008, from http://www.fraserinstitute.org/commerce.web/product_files/Altmedicine.pdf

Etzkowitz, H. (1992). Inventions. In E. Borgatta, & M.L. Borgatta (Eds.), *Encyclopedia of sociology* (pp. 1001–1005). New York: Macmillan.

Evans, M. (2006). Memories, monuments, histories: The re-thinking of the Second World War since 1989. This article is based on a keynote address given to the war and memory conference, University of Sydney, 4/8/2006. *National Identities, 8*(4), 317–348.

Evans, P. (1995). *Embedded autonomy: States and industrial transformation*. Princeton, NJ: Princeton University Press.

Evans, P. & Swift, K. (2000). Single mothers and the press: Rising tides, moral panic and restructuring discourses. In S. Neysmith (Ed.), *Restructuring caring labour: Discourse, state practice and everyday life* (pp. 93–115). Toronto: Oxford University Press.

Evans-Pritchard, E.E. (1966). *Theories of primitive religion* (2nd ed.). London, UK: Oxford (Clarendon Press).

Evolution of greenhouse gases over the last 800,000 years—CNRS web site—CNRS. Retrieved 23/07/2008, from http://www2.cnrs.fr/en/1201.htm

Dubuc, N. & Thompson, M. (Producers), & Ewing, H. and Grady, R. (Directors). (2006). *Jesus camp*. [Video/DVD] Magnolia Home Entertainment.

Exxon's profits: Measuring a record windfall—US news and world report. Retrieved 13/06/2008, from http://www.usnews.com/articles/business/economy/2008/02/01/exxons-profits-measuring-a-record-windfall.html

Facebook. (2008). *World wide pillow fight club 3.0*. Retrieved 07/07/2008, from http://www.facebook.com/event.php?eid=2411934188

Fagan, A. (2004). *Environment and democracy in the Czech Republic: The environmental movement in the transition process*. Cheltenham, UK: Edward Elgar Publishing Inc.

Faith, K. & Jiwani, Y. (2002). The social construction of dangerous girls and women. In B. Schissel, & C. Brooks (Eds.), *Marginality and condemnation: An introduction to critical criminology* (pp. 83–107). Halifax: Fernwood.

Falls, J. (2008). *Social classes and social networking*. Retrieved 11/05/2008, from http://www.socialmediaexplorer.com/2008/01/23/social-classes-and-social-networking/

Fathers for Life. (2007). *Children of divorce & separation—statistics*. Retrieved 16/11/2007, from http://fathersforlife.org/divorce/chldrndiv.htm

Fausto-Sterling, A. (2009). Dualing dualisms. In A. Ferber, K. Holcomb & T. Wentling (Eds.), *Sex, gender, and sexuality: The new basics* (pp. 6–20). New York: Oxford University Press.

Feagin, J.R. & Feagin, C.B. (2008). *Racial and ethnic relations* (8th ed.). New York: Prentice-Hall, Inc.

Federal Communications Commission. (2005). *Internet: Something to share*. Retrieved 07/05/2008, from http://www.fcc.gov/omd/history/internet/something2share.html

Federman, M. (2004). *What is the meaning of the medium is the message?* Retrieved 01/06/2008, from http://individual.utoronto.ca/markfederman/article_mediumisthe message.htm

Feffer, J. (2002). Challenging globalization: An introduction. In J. Feffer (Ed.), *Living in hope: People challenging globalization* (pp. 1–22). New York: Zed Books.

Feinstein, D. (2008). *The distraction of offshore drilling*. Retrieved 29/07/2008, from http://www.latimes.com/news/opinion/commentary/la-oe-feinstein18-2008jul18,0,4078387.story

Fellegi, I.P. (1997). *On poverty and low income*. Retrieved 09/12/2007, from http://www.statcan.ca/english/research/13F0027XIE/13F0027XIE.htm

Fendler, L. & Tuckey, S.F. (2006). Whose literacy? Discursive constructions of life and objectivity. *Educational Philosophy & Theory, 38*(5), 589–606.

FeralChildren.com. A list of isolated, confined and feral children. Retrieved 11/1/2007, from http://www.feralchildren.com/en/children.php

Ferguson, H. (1986). Double-blind challenge studies of behavioral and cognitive effects of sucrose-aspartame ingestion in normal children. *Nutrition Reviews, 44*(Supplement), 144–150.

Ferguson, M. (1993). Invisible divides: Communication and identity in Canada and the US *Journal of Communication, 43*(2), 42–16.

Ferguson, S. (2004, November 22). Stressed out. *Maclean's*.

Ferrante, J. (2006). Global inequality and the challenges of reducing extreme poverty. (cover story). *Sociological Viewpoints, 22*, 5–19. Retrieved from http://library.mtroyal.ca:2048/login?url=http://search.ebscohost.com/login.aspx?direct=true&AuthType=ip,url,cookie,uid&db=a9h&AN=21435791&site=ehost-live

Ferreira, F.H.G. & Ravallion, M. (2008). *Global poverty and inequality: A review of the evidence* No. WPS4623. Washington, DC: The World Bank.

Fetchenhauer, D. & Buunk, B.P. (2005). How to explain gender differences in fear of crime: Towards an evolutionary approach. *Sexualities, Evolution & Gender, 7*(2), 95–113.

Fillion, K. (2008, January 9). How to fix boys. *Maclean's*. Retrieved 13/5/2009, from http://www.macleans.ca/culture/entertainment/article.jsp?content= 20080109_70985_70985

Financial Crimes Enforcement Network. (2003). *USA patriot act information*. Retrieved 1/30/2008, from http://www.fincen.gov/pa_main.html

Finch, J. (1989). *Family obligations and social change*. London: Polity.

FindLaw for Legal Professionals. (1987). *US Supreme Court: Edwards v. Guillard, 482 US 578 (1987)*. Retrieved 3/10/2008, from http://caselaw.lp.findlaw.com/scripts/getcase.pl?navby=CASE&court=US&vol=482&page=578

Fine, M. & Torre, M. (2006). Intimate details: Participatory action research in prison. *Action Research, 4*(3), 253–269.

Fine, S. (2001, August 27). Schools told to fix boys' low grades. *Globe and Mail*. Retrieved 13/5/2009, from http://www.globeandmail.com/series/school/fix.html

Finger, J. & Flanagan, N. (2006). *The management bible*. Cape Town, SA: Zebra Press.

Firn, D. (2004). Lilly's cialis winning share from viagra: Stakes high in US$3.2B impotence battleground. *National Post*, pp. 12.

Fischer, M.J. (2007). Settling into campus life: Differences by race/ethnicity in college involvement and outcomes. *Journal of Higher Education, 78*(2), 125–161.

Fishbein, D. (1996). Selected studies on the biology of antisocial behaviour. In J. Conklin (Ed.), *New perspectives in criminology*. Needham Heights: Allyn & Bacon.

Fishlow, A. (1995). Inequality, poverty and growth: Where we stand. *The World Bank, Washington DC*.

Fleras, A. (2009). *Unequal relations: An introduction to race, ethnic and aboriginal dynamics in Canada* (6th ed.). Toronto: Pearson.

Fleras, A. & Elliot, J. (2006). *Unequal relations: An introduction to race, ethnic and aboriginal dynamics in Canada*. Toronto: Prentice Hall.

Fontaine, K.R. & Allison, D.B. (2002). Obesity and the internet. In C.G. Fairburn, & K.D. Brownell (Eds.), *Eating disorders and obesity: A comprehensive handbook* (2nd ed., pp. 609–612). New York: The Guilford Press.

Forbes. (2001). *How big is porn?* Retrieved 10/1/2009, from http://www.forbes.com/2001/05/25/0524porn.html

Forbes. (2007). *The world's billionaires—forbes.com*. Retrieved 18/12/2007, from http://www.forbes.com/lists/2007/10/07billionaires_The-Worlds-Billionaires _Rank.html

Forbes. (2008). *The global 2000*. Retrieved 13/06/2008, from http://www.forbes.com/lists/2008/18/biz_2000 global08_The-Global-2000_Sales.html

Foreign Affairs and International Trade Canada. (2008). *Dispute settlement under the NAFTA*. Retrieved 04/03, from http://www.international.gc.ca/trade-agreements-accords-commerciaux/agr-acc/nafta-alena/settle.aspx?lang=en

Forero, O.A. & Redclift, M.R. (2007). The production and marketing of sustainable forest products: Chewing gum in Mexico. *Development in Practice, 17*(2), 196–207. doi:10.1080/09614520701195907

Foster, J.B. (1999). Marx's theory of metabolic rift: Classical foundations for environmental sociology. *American Journal of Sociology, 105*(2), 366. Retrieved from http://library.mtroyal.ca:2048/login?url=http://search.ebscohost.com/login.aspx?direct=true&AuthType=ip,url,cookie,uid&db=a9h&AN=2398089&site=ehost-live

Foster, J.B. (2007). *The imperialist world system*. Retrieved 17/06/2008, from http://www.monthly-review.org/0507jbf.htm

Fotopoulos, T. (1999). Mass media, culture, and democracy. *Democracy & Nature: The International Journal of Inclusive Democracy, 5*(1), 33. Retrieved from http://library.mtroyal.ca:2048/login?url=http://search.ebscohost.com/login.aspx?direct=true&AuthType=ip, url,cookie,uid&db=a9h&AN=6651944&site=ehost-live

Foucault, M. (1977). *Discipline and punish*. New York: Vintage.

Foucault, M. (1980). *Power/Knowledge*. New York: Pantheon Books.

Fox, C.J. & Miller, H.T. (2005). Postmodern philosophy, postmodernity, and public organization theory. In T.D. Lynch, & P.L. Cruise (Eds.), *Handbook of organization theory and management: The philosophical approach* (2nd ed., pp. 631–661). London, UK: CRC Press.

Frank, A.G. (1969). The development of under-development. *Latin america: Underdevelopment or revolution*. (pp. 3–17). London and New York: Monthly Review Press.

Frank, A.G. (1972). *Lupenbourgeoisie: Lumpendevelopment: Dependence, class, and politics in Latin America*. New York and London: Monthly Review Press.

Frank, A.G. (1998). *Reorient: Global economy in the Asian age*. Berkeley, CA: University of California Press.

Frankenberg, R. (1993). *The social construction of whiteness: White women, race matters*. London: Routledge.

Fraser, D. (2007). The Canadian response to the USA patriot act. *IEEE Security and Privacy, 5*(5), 66–68.

The Fraser Institute. (2004). *Claims for Canadian content regulations*. Retrieved 5/14/2008, from http://oldfraser.lexi.net/publications/forum/1998/august/claims.html

Frediani, A.A. (2007). Amartya Sen, the world bank, and the redress of urban poverty: A Brazilian case study. *Journal of Human Development, 8*(1), 133–152. doi:10.1080/14649880601101473

Free The Children. (n.d.). *Child labour.* Retrieved 31/10/2007, from http://www.freethechildren.org/getinvolved/geteducated/childlabour.htm

Freedom House. (2007). *Freedom house.* Retrieved 4/7/2008, from http://www.freedomhouse.org/template.cfm?page=1

Freeman, A. (2007). *Ottawa to re-evaluate foreign-aid priorities*. Retrieved 14/07/2008, from http://www.theglobeandmail.com/servlet/story/RTGAM.20071006.Aid06/BNStory/international

Freud, S. (1930[1961]). *Civilization and its discontents*. New York: W.W. Norton.

Freudenburg, W.R. (2006). environmental degradation, disproportionality, and the double diversion: Reaching out, reaching ahead, and reaching beyond. *Rural Sociology, 71*(1), 3–32. Retrieved from http://library.mtroyal.ca:2048/login?url=http://search.ebscohost.com/login.aspx? direct=true&AuthType=ip,url,cookie, uid=a9h&AN=19780047&site=ehost-live

Frey, R.S., Dietz, T., & Kalof, L. (1992). Characteristics of successful American protest groups. *American Journal of Sociology, 98*(2), 368–387.

Frideres, J.S. (1996). The royal commission on aboriginal peoples: The route to self-government. *The Canadian Journal of Native Studies, 16*(22), 247–266.

Frideres, J.S. (2002). Overcoming hurdles: Health care and aboriginal people. In B.S. Bolaria, & H.D. Dickinson (Eds.), *Health, illness, and health care in Canada* (3rd ed.). Scarboroough, ON: Nelson Canada.

Friends of Canadian Broadcasting. (2005). *Controversy over Canadian content by Mindelle Jacobs*. Retrieved 5/15/2008, from http://www.friends.ca/News/ Friends_ News/archives/articles-06280503.asp

Friesen, J. & Seguin, R. (2009, July 20). Quebec keeps open mind on euthanasia. *Globe and Mail*. Retrieved 20/7/2009 from http:www.theglobeandmail.com/news/national/quebec-keeping-open-mind-on-euthanasia/article1221516/

Frosdick, S. & Newton, R. (2006). The nature and extent of football hooliganism in England and Wales. *Soccer & Society, 7*(4), 403–422. Retrieved from http://library.mtroyal.ca:2048/login?url=http://search.ebscohost.com/login.aspx?direct=true&AuthType=ip,url,cookie,uid&db=a9h&AN=22564308&site=ehost-live

Fujiwara, S. (2007). Problems of teaching about religion in Japan: Another textbook controversy against peace? *British Journal of Religious Education, 29*(1), 45–61.

Furseth, Inger. Repstad, Pål. (2006). *An introduction to the sociology of religion: Classical and contemporary perspectives*. Abigdon: Ashgate.

Gage Encyclopedia of Childhood and Adolescence. (1998). *Feral children*. Retrieved 11/1/2007, from http://findarticles.com/p/articles/mi_g2602/is_0002/ai_2602000247

Gagné, G. (2002). *The NAFTA and the softwood lumber dispute: What kind of Canada-US partnership?*. Montréal: Centre d'études sur l'intégration et la Mondialisation.

Gagné, M., Tourigny, M., Joly, J., & Pouliot-Lapointe, J. (2007). Predictors of adult attitudes toward corporal punishment of children. *Journal of Interpersonal Violence, 22*(10), 1285–1304.

Galabuzi, G. (2006). *Canada's economic apartheid: The social exclusion of racialized groups in the new century*. Toronto, ON: Canadian Scholars' Press.

Galison, P.L. (1999). Buildings and the subject of science. In P.L. Galison & E. Thompson (Eds.), *The architecture of science*. Cambridge, MA: The MIT Press.

Galt, V. (2008, May 23). Older workers a drain? Not a chance, study finds. *Globe and Mail*, pp. B5.

Gamson, J. (2002). Publicity traps: Television talk shows and lesbian, gay, bisexual, and transgender visibility. In C. Williams, & A. Stein (Eds.), *Sexuality and gender* (pp. 311–331). Oxford: Blackwell.

Gamson, W.A. (1990). *The strategy of social protest* (2nd ed.). Belmont, CA: Wadsworth.

Gannon, M. (2005). *Crime statistics in Canada*. Statistics Canada, Catalogue no. 85-002 XIE.

Gannon, M., Mihorean, K., Beattie, K., Taylor-Butts, A., & Kong, R. (2005). *Criminal justice indicators, 2005*. Statistics Canada, Catalogue no. 85-227-XIE.

Gans, H.J. (1995). *The war against the poor: The underclass and antipoverty policy*. New York: BasicBooks.

Gans, H.J. (1999). *Popular culture and high culture: An analysis and evaluation of taste*. New York: Basic Books.

Gantsho, M.S. & Karani, P. (2007). Entrepreneurship and innovation in development finance institutions for promoting the clean development mechanism in Africa. *Development Southern Africa, 24*(2), 335–344. doi:10.1080/03768350701327269

Gardner, D. (2000). *When racial categories make no sense*. Retrieved 10/01/2008, from http://www.sinc.sunysb.edu/Stu/lmarfogl/project/race_gerdner.htm

Garland, D. (1996). The limits of the sovereign state: Strategies of crime control in contemporary society. *British Journal of Criminology, 36*(4), 445–471.

Garland, D. (2006). "Governmentality" and the problems of crime: Foucault, criminology, sociology. In A. Glasbeek (Ed.), *Moral regulation and governance in Canada: History, context, and critical issues* (pp. 357–388). Toronto: Canadian Scholars' Press.

Garland-Thomson, R. (1997). Feminist theory, the body, and the disabled figure. In L.J. Davis (Ed.), *The disabilities studies reader* (pp. 279–294). New York: Routledge, Inc.

Garner, R. (Ed.). (2000). *Social theory: Continuity and confrontation: A reader*. Peterborough, ON: Broadview Press.

Garner, R. (Ed.). (2007). *Social theory: Continuity + confrontation A reader* (2nd ed.). Peterborough: Broadview Press.

Gartner, R., Dawson, M., & Crawford, M. (1998). Woman killing: Intimate femicide in Ontario, 1974–1994. *Resources for Feminist Research, 26*(3/4), 151–173.

Gaskell, J., McLaren, A., & Novogrodsky, M. (1989). *Claiming an education: Feminism and Canadian schools*. Toronto: Our Schools Our Selves.

Gaston, K.J. (2008). Biodiversity and extinction: The importance of being common. *Progress in Physical Geography, 32*(1), 73–79. doi:10.1177/0309133308089499

Gastwirth, J., Modarres, R., & Bura, E. (2005). The use of the lorenz curve, gini index and related measures of relative inequality and uniformity in securities law. *METRON—International Journal of Statistics, 3*, 451–469.

Gatherer, D. (2006). Cultural evolution: The biological perspective. *Parallax, 12*(1), 57–68.

Gazso, A. (2004). Women's inequality in the workplace as framed in news discourse: Refracting from gender ideology*. *The Canadian Review of Sociology and Anthropology, 41*(4), 449–473. Retrieved from http://library.mtroyal.ca:2083/pqdweb?did=778900691&Fmt=7&clientId=65345&RQT=309&VName=PQD

Geertzen, J., Van Wilgen, C., Schrier, E., & Dijkstra, P. (2006). Chronic pain in rehabilitation medicine. *Disability & Rehabilitation, 28*(6), 363–367. doi:10. 1080/09638280500287437

Gentleman, J. & Park, E. (1997). Divorce in the 1990s. *Health Reports, 9*(2), 53–58.

George, S. (2008). *Globalization and war.* Retrieved 25/07/2008, from http://www.tni.org/detail_page.phtml?act_id=18042

George Weston Limited. (2007). *About us: Corporate profile.* Retrieved 18/12/2007, from http://weston.ca/en/abt_corprof.html

Gerald, G. (2007). The "down low": New jargon, sensationalism, or agent of change? In G. Herdt, & C. Howe (Eds.), *21st century sexualities: Contemporary issues in health, education, and rights* (pp. 44–46). New York: Routledge.

Gerhardt, U. (2001). Parsons's analysis of the societal community. In J.A. Trevino, & N.J. Smelser (Eds.), *Talcott parsons today: His theory and legacy in contemporary sociology* (pp. 177–222). Lanham, MD: Rowman and Littlefield Publishers, Inc.

Gerlach, C. (2006). Extremely violent societies: An alternative to the concept of genocide. *Journal of Genocide Research, 8*(4), 455–471.

Germain, A. & Kidwell, J. (2007). Not separate, still unequal: The Beijing agreement and the feminization of HIV/AIDS. *21st century sexualities: Contemporary issues in health, education, and rights* (pp. 121–123). New York: Routledge.

Gershon, R.A. (2005). The transnationals: Media corporations, international TV trade and entertainment flows. In A. Cooper-Chen (Ed.), *Global entertainment media: Content, audiences, issues* (pp. 17–38). Mahwah, NJ: Lawrence Erlbaum Associates.

getFAST.ca—*free assessment summary tool Mozilla/5.0 (windows; U; windows NT 5.1; en-GB; rv:1.8.1.12) Gecko/20080201 Firefox/2.0.0.12.* Retrieved 26/02/2008, from https://www.getfast.ca/

Gibel Azoulay, K. (2006). Reflections on 'race' and the biologization of difference. *Patterns of Prejudice, 40*(4), 353–379.

Gibson, J. L. & Howard, M.M. (2007). Russian anti-semitism and the scapegoating of Jews. *British Journal of Political Science, 37*, 193–223.

Giddens, A. (1978). *Sociology: A brief but critical introduction.* (2nd. ed.). New York: Harcourt, Brace & Jovanovich.

Giddens, A. (1997). *Sociology* (3rd ed.). London: Polity Press.

Giddens, A. (2003). *Runaway world: How globalization is reshaping our lives.* New York: Routledge.

Gilbert, D. & Kahl, J.A. (1993). *The American class structure: A new synthesis* (4th ed.). Belmont, CA: Wadsworth.

Gill, C. (2004). 'Cuz the black chick always gets it first: Dynamics of race in *Buffy the Vampire Slayer.* In E. Pohl-Weary (Ed.), *Girls who bite back: Witches, mutants, slayers and freaks* (pp. 39–55). Toronto: Sumach Press.

Gillis, A. (2007). Cheating themselves. *University Affairs* (pp. 11–15).

Gillis, C. (2008, March 10). Why our grocery bill is about to hurt. *Maclean's.*

Gillis, C. (2009, April 13). Generation tame. *Maclean's.*

Ginsburg, J.A., Doherty, R.B., Ralston Jr, F., & Senkeeto, N. (2008). Achieving a high-performance health care system with universal access: What the United States can learn from other countries. *Annals of Internal Medicine, 148*(1), 55–75. Retrieved from http://library.mtroyal.ca:2048/login?url=http://library.mtroyal.ca:2924/login.aspx?direct= true&AuthType=ip,url,cookie,uid& db=a9h&AN=28331372&site=ehost-live

Ginsberg, P. & Gekonge, M. (2004). MTV, technology, the secular trend, and HIV/AIDS: Why Kenyan parents need to learn about adolescent development. *Dialectical Anthropology, 28*(3), 353–364. doi:10.1007/s10624-004-3587-3

Gladwell, M. (2000). *The tipping point: How little things can make a big difference.* New York: Little, Brown and Company.

Glasbeek, A. (2005). *Family violence.* Unpublished manuscript.

Glasbeek, A. (2006a). "My wife has endured a torrent of abuse": Gender, safety and anti-squeegee discourses in Toronto, 1998–2000. *Windsor Yearbook of Access to Justice, 24*(1), 55–76.

Glasbeek, A. (2006b). *Moral regulation and governance in Canada: History, context and critical issues.* Toronto: Canadian Scholars' Press.

Global Initiative to End All Corporal Punishment of Children. (2007). *End all corporal punishment of children.* Retrieved 11/12/2007, from http://www.endcorporal punishment.org/

Göçmen, D. (2006). *[Marxism-thaxis] false consciousness.* Retrieved 11/9/2007, from http://www.mail-archive.com/marxismthaxis@lists.econ.utah.edu/msg03424.html

Godelier, M. (1999). *The enigma of the gift* (Nora Scott Trans.). Chicago: University of Chicago Press.

Goff, C. (2004). *Criminal justice in Canada* (3rd ed.). Scarborough: Nelson.

Goffman, E. (1959). *The presentation of self in everyday life.* New York: Anchor.

Goffman, E. (1961). *Asylums: Essays on the social situation of mental patients and other inmates.* New York: Anchor Books.

Goldberg, M. (2008). Urban child poverty. Senate Committee on Social Affairs, Science, and Technology. Retrieved 21/4/2008, from http://www.firstcallbc.org/pdfs/EconomicEquality/3-senate%20brief.pdf

Goldstein, J. (2004). *International relations* (5th ed.). New York: Pearson Longman.

Goode, E. (2001). *Deviant behaviour.* Toronto: Prentice Hall.

Goodman, E. (2003). *Nature's terror rides man-made wings.* Retrieved 9/4/2008, from http://community.seattletimes.nwsourcecom/archive/?date=20030425 &slug=goodman 25

Goodrich, P. (1993). Oedipus lex: Slips in interpretation and law. *Legal Studies, 13*(3), 381–395.

Gordon, J. & Blum, I. (2004). Shifting programs or undercutting equity? A preliminary study using three university academic calendars. In M. Reimer (Ed.), *Inside corporate U: Women in the academy speak out* (pp. 103–117). Toronto: Sumach Press.

Gordon, J.A. (2006). From liberation to human rights: Challenges for teachers of the burakumin in Japan. *Race, Ethnicity & Education, 9*(2), 183–202.

Gordon, L. (1984). Paul Willis—education, cultural production, and social reproduction. *British Journal of Sociology of Education, 5*(2), 105–115.

Gorlick, C. (2005). Divorce: Options available, constraints forced, pathways taken. In N. Mandell, & A. Duffy (Eds.), *Canadian families: Diversity, conflict and change* (3rd ed., pp. 210–238). Toronto: Thomson Nelson.

Gorman-Murray, A. (2007). Contesting domestic ideals: Queering the Australian home. *Australian Geographer, 38*(2), 195–213.

GourmetSpot.com. (n.d.). *How many people can one farmer feed?* Retrieved 27/03/2008, from http://www.gourmetspot.com/know/farmerfeeds.htm

Government of Alberta. (2008). *Budget 2008.* Retrieved 30/06/2008, from http://www.alberta.ca/budget2008/#

Government of Alberta, Employment, Immigration and Industry. (2005). *OCCinfo—rig technician.* Retrieved 4/2/2008, from http://www.alis.gov.ab.ca/occinfo/Content/RequestAction.asp?aspAction=GetHTMLProfile&format=html&occPro_ID=71018427

Government of Canada. (2003). *The Canada Health Act: Overview and options (94-4E).* Retrieved 29/06/2008, from http://www.parl.gc.ca/information/library/prbpubs/944-e.htm#chistoricaltxt

Government of Canada. (2007a). *Canadian environmental sustainability indicators 2007.* Retrieved 23/07/2008, from http://www.ec.gc.ca/environmentandresources/CESIHL 2007/CESIHL2007_e.cfm#s4

Government of Canada. (2007b). *Chinese head tax and historical recognition initiatives.* Retrieved 1/8/2008, from http://www.pch.gc.ca/progs/multi/redress-redressement/index_e.cfm

Government of Canada. (2007c). *Prizes—Social sciences and humanities research council of Canada.* Retrieved 11/11/2007, from http://www.sshrc-crsh.gc.ca/web/winning/prize/aurora_e.asp

Government of Canada. (2007d). *Understanding homelessness.* Retrieved 06/12, from http://www.sans-abri.gc.ca/about_ us/understanding_homelessness_e.asp

Government of Canada. (2008a). *Regulatory framework for industrial greenhouse gas emissions.* Retrieved 23/07/2008, from http://www.ec.gc.ca/doc/virage-corner/2008-03/541_eng.htm#targets

Government of Canada. (2008b). *Turning the corner: Canada's energy and GHG emissions projections*

(Reference Case No. 2006-2020). Ottawa, ON: Government of Canada. Retrieved from http://www.ec.gc.ca/doc/virage-corner/2008-03/pdf/prov-terr_eng.pdf

Government of Western Australia, Department of Health. (2007). *Office of aboriginal health.* Retrieved 1/27/2008, from http://www.aboriginal.health.wa.gov.au/healthinfo/index.cfm

Goyder, J. (2005). The dynamics of occupational prestige: 1975–2000. *The Canadian Review of Sociology and Anthropology, 42*(1), 1–23. Retrieved from http://proquest.umi.com/pqdweb?did=815235431&Fmt=7&clientId=65345&RQT=309&VName=PQD

Goyder, J. & Frank, K. (2007). A scale of occupational prestige in Canada, based on NOC major groups. *Canadian Journal of Sociology, 32*(1), 63–83.

Goyder, J., Guppy, N., & Thompson, M. (2003). The allocation of male and female occupational prestige in an Ontario urban area: A quarter-century replication*. *The Canadian Review of Sociology & Anthropology, 40*(4), 417–439. Retrieved from http://library.mtroyal.ca:2083/pqdweb?did=665951271&Fmt=7&clientId=65345&RQT=309&VName=PQD

Grabb, E.G. (1990). *Theories of social inequality: Classical and contemporary perspectives* (2nd ed.). Toronto, ON: Holt, Rinehart and Winston.

Gracey, H.L. (1977). Learning the student role: Kindergarten as academic boot camp. In H. Gracey, & D. Wrong (Eds.), *Readings in introductory sociology* (3rd ed.,). Boston, MA: Allyn and Bacon.

Graham, M. & Bruce, E. (2006). "Seen and not heard" sociological approaches to childhood: Black children, agency and implications for child welfare. *Journal of Sociology & Social Welfare, 33*(4), 51–67.

Gramsci, A. (1926/1937). *Selections from the prison notebooks* (1971st ed.). London: Lawrence & Wishart.

Grant, B. (1997). Disciplining students: The construction of student subjectivities. *British Journal of Sociology of Education, 18*(1), 101–114.

Grant, K.R. (2002). A conversation on th eFuture of the academy with James Turk, PhD, executive director, Canadian Association of University Teachers. *Canadian Review of Sociology & Anthropology, 39*(3), 261–274.

Grant, O. (2004). *Compassionate conservativism in a free market: A moralist justification of bankruptcy law or big business as usual?* Unpublished manuscript.

Graves, Frank L. and Jenkins, Richard W. (2002). Canadian attitudes towards productivity: Balancing standard of living and quality of life. *The Review of Economic Performance and Social Progress,* 243–258.

Gray, J. *The pros and cons of text messages.* Retrieved 07/05/2008, from http://www.helium.com/items/633125-nothing-embodies-modern-living

Gray, P.S., Holmstrom, L.L., & Karp, D.A. (2002). Why laundry, not Hegel? Social class, transition to college, and pathways to adulthood. *Symbolic Interaction, 25*(4), 437–462.

Greeley, A.M. (1972). *The denominational society: A sociological approach to religion in America.* Glenview, IL: Scott, Foresman.

Green, C. & Wilson, B. (2007). Marches on Washington and the black protest movement. *Journal of Ethnic & Cultural Diversity in Social Work, 16*(3), 199–212. doi:10.1300/J051v6n03_17

Green, M.J., Sonn, C.C., & Matsebula, J. (2007). Reviewing whiteness: Theory, research, and possibilities. *South African Journal of Psychology, 37*(3), 389–419.

Greenberg, E.S. & Page, B.I. (2007). *The struggle for democracy* (8th ed.). New York: Pearson Longman.

Greenpeace Canada. (2008). *Greenpeace activists interrupt syncrude tar sands operation.* Retrieved 8/9/2008, from http://www.greenpeace.org/Canada/en/recent/greenpeace-activists-interrupt

Greenpeace International. (2008). *Home| Greenpeace International.* Retrieved 6/16/2008, from http://www.greenpeace.org/international/

Grelland, H.H. (2006). The Sapir-Whorf hypothesis and the meaning of quantum mechanics. *AIP Conference Proceedings, 810*(1), 325–329.

Griffiths, C. & Cunningham, A. (2000). *Canadian corrections.* Toronto: Nelson.

Griffiths, C. & Verdun-Jones, S. (1994). *Canadian criminal justice* (2nd ed.). Toronto: Harcourt Brace.

Grimshaw, D., Beynon, H., Rubery, J., & Ward, K. (2002). The restructuring of career paths in large service sector organizations: 'delayering', upskilling and polarisation. *Sociological Review, 50*(1), 89–116. Retrieved from http://library.mtroyal.ca:2048/login?url=http://search.ebscohost.com/login.aspx?direct=true&AuthType=ip,url,cookie,uid&db=a9h&AN=6412541&site=ehost-live

Grindstaff, L. & West, E. (2006). Cheerleading and the gendered politics of sport. *Social Problems, 53*(4), 500–518.

Griswold, D.T. (2006). Globalization promotes democracy. In L.I. Gerdes (Ed.), *Globalization opposing viewpoints* (pp. 49–57). New York: Thompson/Gale.

Groening, M. (1987). *School is hell.* New York: Pantheon Books.

Gross, R.M. (1996). *Feminism and religion: An introduction.* Boston, MA: Beacon Press.

Gyimah, S.O., Walters, D., & Phythian, K.L. (2005). Ethnicity, immigration and housing wealth in Toronto. *Canadian Journal of Urban Research, 14*(2), 338–363. Retrieved from http://library.mtroyal.ca:2083/pqdweb?did=1014644061&Fmt=7&clientId= 65345&RQT= 309&VName=PQD

Hackler, J. (2006). *Canadian criminology: Strategies and perspectives.* Toronto: Prentice Hall.

Hadler, J. (2009, January 9). Raiding the polygamists: An Eldorado north of the border. *Time.* Retrieved from http://www.time.com/time/world/article/0,0599,1870696,00.html

Hagan, J. & Hansford-Bowles, S. (2005). From resistance to activism: The emergence and persistence of activism among American Vietnam War resisters in Canada. *Social Movement Studies, 4*(3), 231–259.

Hagan, J. & McCarthy, B. (1992). Mean streets: The theoretical significance of situational delinquency among homeless youths. *American Journal of Sociology, 98*(3), 597–627.

Hagens, N. (2008). *Unconventional oil: Tar sands and shale oil.* Retrieved 10/08/2008, from http://www.theoildrum.com/node/3839

Haggerty, K. (2004). Ethics creep: Governing Social science research in the name of ethics. *Qualitative Sociology, 27*(4), 391–414.

Haigh, R.A. (1999). Reconstructing paradise: Canada's health care system, alternative medicine and the *Charter of Rights. Health Law Journal, 7*(141), 191.

Hale, S. (1990). *Controversies in sociology.* Toronto: Copp Clark Pitman.

Haley, E. (2004). The 'captive scientist': Corporate influences over scientific research. In M. Reimer (Ed.), *Inside corporate U: Women in the academy speak out* (pp. 87–99). Toronto: Sumach Press.

Halifax Regional Municipality. (2008). *Housing and homelessness in HRM.* Retrieved 06/11, from http://www.halifax.ca/planning/homeless.html

Hall, R. & Sandler, B.R. (1986). *The campus climate revisited: Chilly climate for women faculty, administrators, and graduate students* (Project on the Status and Education of Women). Washington, DC: Association of American Colleges.

Hall, S., Held, D., Hubert, D., & Thompson, K. (Eds.). (1996). *Modernity: An introduction to modern societies.* Oxford, UK: Blackwell Publishing Limited.

Hamdad, M. (2003). *Valuing households' unpaid work in Canada, 1992 and 1998: Trends and sources of change.* Ottawa: Statistics Canada.

Hammond, I. (2005). Lessons from Ivan Illich. *Canadian Association of Radiologists Journal, 56*(1), 13–14.

Hannigan, J. (1998). *Fantasy city: Pleasure and profit in the postmodern city.* New York: Routledge.

Hannigan, J. (2006). *Environmental sociology* (2nd ed.). New York: Routledge, Taylor & Francis Group.

Harding, S. (2005). "Science and democracy": Replayed or redesigned? *Social Epistomology, 19*(1), 5–18.

Harding, S. (2006). *Science and social inequality: Feminist and postcolonial issues.* Chicago, ILL: University of Illinois Press.

Haritaworn, J., Lin, C. J., & Klesse, C. (2006). Poly/logue: A critial introduction to polyamory. *Sexualities, 9*(5), 515–529.

Harley, H. (2008). In Ravelli B. (Ed.), *Personal communication, May 27, 2008*

Harman, L. (2005). Family poverty and economic struggles. In N. Mandell, & A. Duffy (Eds.), *Canadian families: Diversity, conflict and change* (pp. 241–275). Toronto: Thomson Nelson.

Harnois, C.E. (2005). Different paths to different feminisms? Bridging multiracial feminist theory and quantitative sociological gender research. *Gender & Society, 19*(6), 809–828.

Harper, C.L. (2008). *Environment and society: Human perspectives on environmental issues* (4th ed.). Upper Saddle River, New Jersey: Pearson Prentice Hall.

Harris, K.M. (1993). Work and welfare among single mothers in poverty. *American Journal of Sociology, 99*(2), 317–352.

Harris, R., Ellicott, A., & Holmes, D. (1986). The timing of psychosocial transitions and changes in women's lives: An examination of women aged 45 to 60. *Journal of Personality and Social Psychology, 51*, 409–416.

Harris, R.G. (1999). *Determinants of Canadian productivity growth: Issues and prospects* (Discussion Paper No. 8). Ottawa: Industry Canada.

Harris, S. (2004). *The end of faith: Religion, terror and the future of reason.* New York: W.W. Norton & Company, Inc.

Harris, S. (2006). *Letter to a Christian nation.* New York: Knopf Publishing Group.

Harrison, K.D. (2007). *When languages die: The extinction of the world's languages and the erosion of human knowledge.* New York, NY: Oxford University Press.

Hartl, R.F., Novak, A.J., Rao, A.G., & Sethi, S.P. (2003). Optimal pricing of a product diffusing in rich and poor populations. *Journal of Optimization Theory and Applications, 117*(2), 349. Retrieved from http://proquest.umi.com/pqdweb?did=983551831&Fmt=7&clientId=65345&RQT=309&VName=PQD

Hartman, C. & Squires, G. (2006). *There is no such thing as a natural disaster: Race, class, and Hurricane Katrina.* New York: Routledge.

Harvey, D. (1989). *The condition of postmodernity.* London: Blackwell.

Harvey, D.L. & Reed, M.H. (1996). The culture of poverty: An ideological analysis. *Sociological Perspectives, 39*(4), 465. Retrieved from http://proquest.umi.com/pqdweb?did=10976631&Fmt=7&clientId=65345&RQT=309&VName=PQD

Hastings, P.D., McShane, K.E., Parker, R., & Ladha, F. (2007). Ready to make nice: Parental socialization of young sons' and daughters' prosocial behaviors with peers. *Journal of Genetic Psychology, 168*(2), 177–200.

Hatfield, M. (2004). Vulnerability to persistent low income. *Horizons: Policy Research Initiative, 7*(2), 19–33.

Hawthorne, S. (2007). Land, bodies, and knowledge: Biocolonialism of plants, indigenous peoples, women, and people with disabilities. *Signs: Journal of Women in Culture & Society, 32*(2), 314–323. Retrieved from http://library.mtroyal.ca:2048/login?url=http://search.ebscohost.com/login.aspx?direct=true&AuthType=ip,url,cookie,uid&db=a9h&AN=23730418&site=ehost-live

Hayden, C. (2005). Bioprospecting's representational dilemma. *Science as Culture, 14*(2), 185–200. doi:10.1080/095054305 00110994

Healey, J. F. & O'Brien, E. (Eds.). (2007). *Race, ethnicity and gender: Selected readings* (2nd ed.). Los Angeles: Pine Forge Press.

Health Canada. (2004). *Home & continuing care.* Retrieved 26/06/2008, from http://www.hc-sc.gc.ca/hcs-sss/home-domicile/index-eng.php

Health Canada. (2005). *Statistical profile on the health of First Nations in Canada.* Retrieved 28/01/2008, from http://www.hc-sc.gc.ca/fnih-spni/pubs/gen/stats_profil_e.html

Health Canada. (2006a). *2003 first ministers' accord on health care renewal.* Retrieved 29/06/2008, from http://www.hc-sc.gc.ca/hcs-sss/delivery-prestation/fptcollab/2003accord/index-eng.php

Health Canada. (2006b). *Healthy Canadians: A federal report on comparable health indicators 2006.* Retrieved 30/06/2008, from http://www.hc-sc.ca/hcs-sss/pubs/system-regime/2006-fed-comp-indicat/2006-fed-comp-indicat-3-eng.php

Health Council of Canada. (2008). *Rekindling reform: Health care renewal in Canada, 2003–2008.* Toronto, ON: Health Council.

Heclo, H. (2007). Is America a Christian nation? *Political Science Quarterly, 122*(1), 59–87.

Hedley, R.A. (2002). *Running out of control: Dilemmas of globalization.* Bloomfield, CT: Kumarian Press, Inc.

Heilman, S.C. (2000). *Defenders of the faith: Inside ultra-orthodox Jewry.* Berkeley, CA: University of California Press.

Heisz, A. (2007). *Income inequality and redistribution in Canada: 1976 to 2004* (No. 2007). Ottawa: Statistics Canada.

Helleiner, J. (1997). "Women of the itinerant class": Gender and anti-traveller racism in Ireland. *Women's Studies International Forum, 20*(2), 275–287.

Helleiner, J. (2000). *Irish travellers: Racism and the politics of culture.* Toronto: University of Toronto Press.

Hellman, C. & Huang, R. (2008). *List of known terrorist organizations.* Retrieved 14/07/2008, from http://www.cdi.org/terrorism/terrorist-groups.cfm

Helly, D. (2004). Are Muslims discriminated against in Canada since September 2001? *Canadian Ethnic Studies, 36*(1), 24–47.

Hemphill, H. & Haines, R. (1997). *Discrimination, harassment, and the failure of diversity training: What to do now?.* Westport, Connecticut: Quorum Books.

Henry, F. & Tator, C. (1994). The ideology of racism—"democratic racism." *Canadian Ethnic Studies, 26*(2), 1–14.

Herdt, G. & Howe, C. (2007). Sexual health, wellness, and medical models. In G. Herdt, & C. Howe (Eds.), *21st century sexualities: Contemporary issues in health, education, and rights* (pp. 89–91). New York: Routledge.

Herman, E.S. (1999, Winter). The threat of globalization. *New Politics, 7*(22), 13/06/2008. Retrieved from http://www.globalpolicy.org/globaliz/define/hermantk.htm

Herman, E.S. (2003). The propaganda model: A retrospective. *Against all Reason, 1*, 1–14.

Herman, E.S. & Chomsky, N. (1988). *Manufacturing consent: The political economy of the mass media.* New York: Pantheon Books.

Herzog, H. (2005). On home turf: Interview location and its social meaning. *Qualitative Sociology, 28*(1), 25–47.

Hetherington, E. & Baltes, P. (1988). Child psychology and life-span development. In E. Hetherington, R. Lerner & M. Perlmutter (Eds.), *Child development in life-span perspective.* Hillsdale, NJ: Erlbaum.

Hevesi, D. (1992). Woody Allen tells his side to a magazine. *New York Times.* Retrieved 14/5/2008, from http://query.nytimes.com/gst/fullpage.html?res+9E0CE3D61F3BF930A1575B0A964958

Hietalahti, J. & Linden, M. (2006). Socio-economic impacts of microfinance and repayment performance: A case study of the small enterprise foundation, South Africa. *Progress in Development Studies, 6*(3), 201–210.doi:10.1191/1464993406 ps138oa

Hill Collins, P. (2005). The sexual politics of black womanhood. In T.L. Steele (Ed.), *Sex, self and society: The social context of sexuality.* California: Wadsworth.

Hill Lindley, S. (2003). *"You have stept out of your place": A history of women and religion in America.* Lousiville, KY: Westminster John Knox Press.

Hiller, H.H. & Di Luzio, L. (2001). Text and context: Another "chapter" in the evolution of sociology in Canada. *Canadian Journal of Sociology, 26*(3), 487–512.

Hilton, I. (2008). The reality of global warming. *World Policy Journal, 25*(1), 1–8. Retrieved from http://library.mtroyal.ca:2048/login?url=http://search.ebscohost.com/login.aspx?direct=true&AuthType=ip,url,cookie,uid&db=a9h&AN=32695579&site=ehost-live

Hilton, M. (2007). Social activism in an age of consumption: The organized consumer movement. *Social History, 32*(2), 121–143. doi:10.1080/03071020701245751

Hinderliter, R. (2007). *The history of YouTube.* Retrieved 10/05/2008, from http://mediatedcultures.net/ksudigg/?p=108

Hine, C. (2005). Internet research and the sociology of cyber-social-scientific knowledge. *The Information Society, 21*, 239–248.

Hines, S. (2004). Transgender. In J. Eadie (Ed.), *Sexuality* (pp. 231–232). London: Arnold.

Hinton, S.E. (1967). *The outsiders.* New York: Puffin Books.

Hird, M. (2004). Pansexual. In J. Eadie (Ed.), *Sexuality: The essential glossary* (pp. 150). London: Arnold.

Historica. (n.d.). *The deportation of the Acadians.* Retrieved 22/01/2008, from http://www.histori.ca/peace/page.do?pageID=275

History News Network. (2006). *What is the difference between sunni and shiite muslims—and why does it matter?* Retrieved 09/03/2008, from http://hnn.us/articles/934.html

Hochschild, A. (1989). *The second shift: Working parents and the revolution at home.* New York: Viking/Penguin.

Hochschild, A. (1997). *The time bind: When work becomes home and home becomes work.* New York: Metropolitan Books.

Hochschild, A. (2003). *The commercialization of intimate life: Notes from home and work.* Berkeley: University of California Press.

Hodson, J. & Vannini, P. (2007). Island time: The media logic and ritual of ferry commuting on

Gabriola Island, BC. *Canadian Journal of Communication, 32*(2), 261–275. Retrieved from http://library.mtroyal.ca:2048/login?url=http://library.mtroyal.ca:2924/login.aspx?direct=true&AuthType=ip,url, cookie,uid&db=a9h&AN=25930269&site=ehost-live

Hoff Sommers, C. (1994). *Who stole feminism?*. New York: Simon & Schuster.

Hoffman, D. (2000). Mothers in the motherland: Stalinist pronatalism in its pan-European context. *Journal of Social History, 34*(1), 35–54.

Hogan, R., Perucci, C., & Behringer, A. (2005). Enduring inequality: Gender and employment income in late career. *Sociological Spectrum, 25*(1), 53–77.

Hohn, C. (1987). Population policies in advanced societies: Pronatalist and migration strategies. *European Journal of Population, 3*(3/4), 459–481.

Holford, J. (1995). Why social movements matter: Adult education theory, cognitive practice, and the creation of knowledge. *Adult Education Quarterly, 45*(2), 95–111.

Holland, J., Ramazanoglu, C., Sharpe, S., & Thomson, R. (1996). Reputations: Journeying into gendered power relations. In J. Weeks (Ed.), *Sexual cultures, communities, values and intimacy* (pp. 239–260). London: Macmillan.

Hollinger, R. (1982). Introduction. *Qualitative Sociology, 5*(2), 75.

Holmes, D. (2005). *Communication theory: Media, technology and society*. Thousand Oaks, CA: Sage Publications, Ltd.

Holstein, M.B. (2005). A normative defense of universal age-based public policy. In R.B. Hudson (Ed.), *The new politics of old age policy* (pp. 23–41). Baltimore, Maryland: Johns Hopkins University Press.

Holton, G. (2004). Robert K. Merton. *Proceedings of the American Philosophical Society, 148*(4), 506–517.

Holton, R.J. (2005). *Making globalization*. 175 Fifth Avenue, New York, NY 10010: Palgrave Macmillan.

hooks, b. (1981). *Ain't i a woman: Black women and feminism*. Boston: South End Press.

hooks, b. (1990). *Yearning: Race, gender and cultural politics*. Boston: South End Press.

Hooks, G. & Smith, C.L. (2004). The treadmill of destruction: National sacrifice areas and native Americans. *American Sociological Review, 69*(4), 558–575. Retrieved from http://library.mtroyal.ca:2048/login?url=http://search.ebscohost.com/login.aspx?direct=true&AuthType=ip,url,cookie,uid&db=a9h&AN=14774023&site=ehost-live

Hooper, M.K. (2001). Civil disorder and policing. In M.A. Dupont-Morales, M.K. Hooper, & J.H. Schmidt (Eds.), *Handbook of criminal justice administration* (pp. 159–166). New York: Marcel Dekker, Inc.

Hopkins, N., Greenwood, R. M., & Birchall, M. (2007). Minority understandings of the dynamics to intergroup contact encounters: British muslims' (sometimes ambivalent) experiences of representing their group to others. *South African Journal of Psychology, 37*(4), 679–701. Retrieved from http://library.mtroyal.ca:2048/login?url=http://search.ebscohost.com/login.aspx?direct=true&AuthType=ip,url,cookie,uid& db=a9h&AN=27615752&site=ehost-live

Horn, M. (1999). *Academic freedom in Canada: A history*. Toronto: University of Toronto Press.

Hornosty, J. (2004). Corporate challenges to academic freedom and gender equity. In M. Reimer (Ed.), *Inside corporate U: Women in the academy speak out* (pp. 43–66). Toronto: Sumach Press.

Horton, S., Baker, J., & Deakin, J.M. (2007). Stereotypes of aging: Their effects on the health of seniors in North American society. *Educational Gerontology, 33*(12), 1021–1035. doi:10.1080/03601270701700235

Houmanfar, R. & Johnson, R. (2003). Organizational implications of gossip and rumor. *Journal of Organizational Behavior Management, 23*(2), 117–138. doi:10.1300/J075v23n02_07

Howard, L. (2006). Untouchable citizens: Dalit movements and democratization in Tamil Nadu. *Contemporary Sociology, 35*(5), 521. Retrieved from http://library.mtroyal.ca:2083/pqdweb?did=1151118821&Fmt=7&clientId=65345&RQT=309&VName=PQD

HRSDC. (2007). *Looking-ahead: A 10-year outlook for the Canadian labour market (2006–2015)*. Retrieved 25/07/2008, from http://www.hrsdc.gc.ca/en/publications_resources/research/categories/labour_market_e/sp_615_10_06/page05.shtml

Hubbard, Z. (2008). *The new American slavery—national debt goes unchecked*. Retrieved 04/07/2008, from http://www.edmondsun.com/statenews/cnhinsall_story_160180921.html

Huber, J. (2008). No probe plans after natives left off jury rolls. *National Post*. Retrieved 24/9/2008, from http://www.nationalpost.com/news/Canada/story.html?id=808876

Huber, J. & Form, W.H. (1973). *Income & ideology*. New York: Free Press.

Huber, M. & Hennessy, P. (2005). *Long-Term care for older people*. Paris: Organisation for Economic Cooperation and Development.

Huemann, L.R., Moise-Titus, J., Podoloski, C., & Eron, L. (2003). *Longitudinal relations between children's exposure to television violence and their aggression and violent behaviour in young adulthood: 1977–1992*. Retrieved 17/5/2009, from http://www.apa.org/journals/releases/dev392201.pdf

Huggan, G. & Tiffin, H. (2007). Green postcolonialism. *Interventions: The International Journal of Postcolonial Studies, 9*(1), 1–11. doi:10.1080/13698010601173783

Hughes, G. & Roesler, K. *Angry farmers storm the City of Ottawa*. Retrieved 3/8/2007, from http://www.ruralcouncil.ca/angry_farmers_040408.htm

Hugoson, M. (2006). "Instant tradition": The introduction of the Swedish Easter tree. *Folklore, 117*(1), 75–86.

Human Resources and Social Development Canada. (2006a). *Advancing inclusion of people with disabilities 2006*. Retrieved 5/1/2007, from http://www.hrsdc.gc.ca/en/hip/odi/documents/advancingInclusion06/chapter3.shtml

Human Resources and Social Development Canada. (2006b). *Canada's retirement income system—simply stated*. Retrieved 25/6/2008, from http://www.hrsdc.gc.ca/en/isp/common/hrsdc/ris/simple.shtml

Human Resources and Social Development Canada. (2007). *Mandatory retirement in Canada*. Retrieved 25/06/2008, from http://www.hrsdc.gc.ca/en/lp/spila/clli/eslc/19Mandatory_Retirement.shtml

Human Resources and Social Development Canada. (2008a). *Canadians in context—households and families*. Retrieved September 3, from http://www4.hrsdc.gc.ca/indicator.jsp?indicatorid=37&lang=en

Human Resources and Social Development Canada. (2008b). *Occupations unique to primary industry*. Retrieved 04/02, from http://www5.hrsdc.gc.ca/NOC-CNP/app/checkoccupation.aspx?lc=E&code=8

Humphreys, L. (1975). *Tearoom trade: Impersonal sex in public places*. New York: Aldine.

Hunt, A. (2003). Risk and moralization in everyday life. In R. Ericson, & A. Doyle (Eds.), *Risk and morality* (pp. 165–192). Toronto: University of Toronto Press.

Hunt, A. & Curtis, B. (2006). A genealogy of the genital kiss: Oral sex in the twentieth century. *The Canadian Journal of Human Sexuality, 15*(2).

Hunt, A. & Wickham, G. (1994). *Foucault and law: Towards a sociology of law as governance*. Boulder: Pluto Press.

Hurtado, A. (1996). *The color of privilege: Three blasphemies on race and feminism*. Ann Arbor: University of Michigan Press.

Hurtado, A. (1996). *The color of privilege: Three blasphemies on race and feminism*. Ann Arbor: University of Michigan Press.

Ibister, J. (2003). *Promises not kept* (6th ed.). Bloomfield, CT: Kumarian Press.

Ietto-Gilles, G. (2003). The role of transnational corporations in the globalisation process. In J. Michie (Ed.), *The handbook of globalisation* (pp. 139–149). Cheltenham, UK: Edward Elgar Publishing Ltd.

Ilcan, S., Oliver, M., & O'connor, D. (2007). Spaces of governance: Gender and public sector restructuring in Canada. *Gender, Place & Culture: A Journal of Feminist Geography, 14*(1), 75–92. Retrieved from http://library.mtroyal.ca:2048/login?url=http://search.ebscohost.com/login.aspx?direct=true&AuthType=ip,url,cookie,uid&db=a9h&AN=24654618&site=ehost-live

IMF. (2008). *About the IMF*. Retrieved 12/06/2008, from http://www.imf.org/external/about.htm

India—water. Retrieved 05/10/2007, from http://www.world bank.org.in/WBSITE/EXTERNAL/COUNTRIES/SOUTH ASIAEXT/iNDIAEXTN/0,,content MDK:20668501~pagePK:141137~piPK:141127~theSitePK:295584,00.html

Indian and Northern Affairs Canada. (2004). *First Nations reserves—appendix 3*. Retrieved 23/01/

2008, from http://www.ainc-inac.gc.ca/pr/pub/atr/atr21_e.html

Indian and Northern Affairs Canada. (2006a). *Government of Canada announces expert panel to advise on regulatory framework to ensure safe drinking water in First Nations communities.* Retrieved 27/07/2008, from http://www.ainc-inac.gc.ca/nr/prs/m-a2006/2-02764_e.html

Indian and Northern Affairs Canada. (2006b). *Royal commission on aboriginal peoples.* Retrieved 22/04/2008, from http://www.ainc-inac.gc.ca/ch/rcap/sg/sgmm_e.html

Indian Claims Commission. (2005). *The facts on claims.* Retrieved 22/4, from http://www.indianclaims.ca/pdf/facts_ treaties_2005.pdf

Infoplease.com. (2005). *Gap between rich and poor: World income inequality.* Retrieved 12/12/2007, from http://www.infoplease.com/ipa/A0908770.html

Ingalls, R. (2006). Unmasking the brilliant disguise: Smallness, authority and the irony of a teacher's body. *Review of Education, Pedagogy & Cultural Studies, 28*(3), 239–252.

Inglehart, R. & Baker, W.E. (2000). Modernization, cultural change, and the persistence of traditional values. *American Sociological Review, 65*(1), 19. Retrieved from http://proquest.umi.com/pqdweb?did=51111067&Fmt=7&clientId=65345&RQT=309&VName=PQD

Innis, H.A. (1930/2001). *The fur trade in Canada.* Toronto, ON: University of Toronto Press.

Innis, H.A. (1940[1954]). *The cod fisheries: The history of an international economy.* Toronto, ON: University of Toronto Press.

Innis, H.A. (1951). *The bias of communication.* Toronto, ON: University of Toronto Press.

International Labour Organization. (2002). *Safety and health in the fishing industry.* Retrieved 04/02, from http://www.ilo.org/public/english/dialogue/sector/techmeet/tmfi99/tmfir2.htm#Special%20characteristics%20of%20the%20working

International Labour Organization. (2005). *Facts on child labour*

International Labour Organization. (2006). *The end of child labour: Within reach* No. I(B). Geneva, Switzerland: ILO Publications.

International Labour Organization. (2008). *Global employment trends, January 2008.* Geneva: International Labour Organization.

International Monetary Fund. (2002). Retrieved 6/5/2008, from http://www.imf.org

The invention of radio. Retrieved 04/05/2008, from http://inventors.about.com/od/rstartinventions/a/radio.htm

IN-VSEE. *The history of the light bulb.* Retrieved 12/10/2007, from http://invsee.asu.edu/Modules/lightbulb/meathist4.htm

IPC Media. (2006). *The growth of advertising clutter—magazine effectiveness.* Retrieved 02/06/2008, from http://www.magazine-engagement.co.uk/topic4/The_Growth_of_Advertising_Clutter_article_110868.html

Irving Oil. (2007). *Our history.* Retrieved 12/18/2007, from http://irvingoil.com/company/hist.asp

Isaacson, W. (1992). Soon Yi: Woody was not my father. *Time.* Retrieved 14/5/2008, from http://www.time.com/time/printout/0,8816,976382,00.html

Isaak, R.A. (2005). *The globalization gap.* New York: Prentice-Hall, Inc.

Isla, A. (2007). An ecofeminist perspective on biopiracy in Latin America. *Signs: Journal of Women in Culture & Society, 32*(2), 323–332. Retrieved from http://library.mtroyal.ca:2048/login?url=http://search.ebscohost.com/login.aspx?direct=true&AuthType=ip,url,cookie,uid&db=a9h&AN=23730419&site=ehost-live

Iyenda, G. (2007). Researching urban poverty in sub-Saharan Africa. *Development in Practice, 17*(1), 27–38. doi:10.1080/09614520601092683

Jackson, J.P. & Weidman, N.M. (2006). *Race, racism, and science : Social impact and interaction.* New Brunswick, NJ: Rutgers University Press.

Jackson, M. (1995). Search for the cause of crime: Biological and psychological perspectives. In M. Jackson & C. Griffiths (Eds.), *Canadian criminology: Perspectives on crime and criminality* (2nd ed.,). Toronto: Harcourt Brace.

Jacobs, M. (2005). *Canada has four-tiered health care.* Retrieved 30/06/2008, from http://www.edmontonsun.com/News/Columnists/Jacobs_Mindelle/2005/06/11/1081809.html

Jaffee, D. (1998). *Levels of socio-economic development theory.* Westport, CT: Praeger.

Jakobsh, D.R. (2006). Sikhism, interfaith dialogue, and women: Transformation and identity. *Journal of Contemporary Religion, 21*(2), 183–199. Retrieved from http://library.mtroyal.ca:2048/login?url=http://search.ebscohost.com/login.aspx?direct=true&AuthType=ip,url,cookie,uid&db=a9h&AN=20855126&site=ehost-live

Jarvis, D.S.L. (2005). Multinational enterprises, international relations and international business: Reconstituting intellectual boundaries for the new millennium. *Australian Journal of International Affairs, 59*(2), 201–223.doi:10.1080/103577105 00134459

Jarvis, F. & Flanagan, N. (2006). *The management bible.* Cape Town, SA: Struik.

Jedwab, J. (2007). *Shared Canadian values: Issues and symbols.* Retrieved 09/27, from http://www.acs-aec.ca/_media/polls/11882311426341.pdf

Jeffreys, S. (1998). *The idea of prostitution.* Australia: Spinifex Press.

Jenkins, J.C. & Perrow, C. (1977). Insurgency of the powerless. *American Sociological Review, 42*(2), 249–268.

Jensen, R. (2007). *Media reform should include critique of sexual-exploitation media.* Retrieved 28/05/2008, from http://www.atlanticfreepress.com/content/view/698/81/

Jersild, A.T. (1952). *In search of self.* New York: Teachers College Press.

Jezek, G. (2006). *The history of television.* Retrieved 04/05/2008, from http://www.thehistoryoftelevision.com/

Jiwani, Y. (2001). *Intersecting inequalities: Immigrant women of colour, violence and health care*The FREDA Centre for Research on Violence Against Women and Children.

Jiwani, Y. & Young, M. (2006). Missing and murdered women: Reproducing marginality in news discourse. *Canadian Journal of Communication, 31*(4), 895–917.

Johansen, D. (2007). *Bulk water removals: Canadian legislation (PRB 02-13E).* Retrieved 07/08/2008, from http://www.parl.gc.ca/information/library/PRBpubs/prb0213-e.htm

Johnson, A. (1997). The underrepresentation of minorities in the legal profession: A critical race theorist's perspective. *Michigan Law Review, 95*(4), 1005–1062.

Johnson, A.G. (2000). *The Blackwell dictionary of sociology* (2nd ed.). London, UK: Blackwell Publishers.

Johnson, C. (2007). Activists engage in cola war. *The Daily Tar Heel*

Johnson, E.W. (2008). Social movement size, organizational diversity and the making of federal law. *Social Forces, 86*(3), 967–993. Retrieved from http://library.mtroyal.ca:2048/login?url=http://search.ebscohost.com/login.aspx?direct=true&AuthType=ip,url,cookie,uid&db=a9h&AN=31673135&site=ehost-live

Johnson, H. (1987). Getting the facts straight: A statistical overview. In E. Adelbereg, & C. Currie (Eds.), *Too few to count: Canadian women in conflict with the law* (pp. 23–46). Vancouver: Press Gang.

Johnson, H. (1996). *Dangerous domains: Violence against women in Canada.* Toronto: Nelson.

Johnson, H. & Klandermans, B. (Eds.). (1995). *Social movements and culture.* Minneapolis, MN: University of Minnesota Press.

Johnson, L., Simons, R., & Conger, R. (2004). Criminal justice system involvement and continuity of youth crime: A longitudinal analysis. *Youth and Society, 36*(1), 3–29.

Johnson, T. (2008). *Beijing weather gives Olympic athletes a break.* Retrieved 18/08/2008, from http://www.mcclatchydc.com/homepage/story/48803.html

Johnston, H. & Almeida, P. (Eds.). (2006). *Latin American social movements: Globalization, democratization and transnational networks.* Lanham, MD: Rowman and Littlefield Publishers, Inc.

Jolin, A. (2002). On the backs of working prostitutes: Feminist theory and prostitution policy. In H. Pontell (Ed.), *Social deviance: Readings in theory and research* (pp. 193–202). Toronto: Prentice Hall.

Jones, G.A. & Shanahan, T. (2007). Shifting roles and approaches: Government coordination of postsecondary education in Canada from 1995–2006. *Higher Education Research and Development, 26*(1), 31–43.

Jones, K.C. (2008). *'LOL' slips into homework but formal writing still valued.* Retrieved 07/05/2008, from http://www.informationweek.com/news/internet/social_network/showArticle.jhtml?articleID=207402196

Jones, W.T. (1969). *The classical mind: A history of western philosophy.* (Second ed.) Harcourt, Brace & World, Inc.

Joshi, T.L. (1996). *Critique of Hinduism and other religions*(Suman Oak Trans.). Bombay: Popular Prakashan.

Joynt, J. & Poe, Marshall. (2004). The unfree world. *The Atlantic Monthly, 293*(2), 52–53.

Judge, T. & Cable, D. (2004). The effect of physical height on workplace success and income. *Journal of Applied Psychology, 89*(3), 428–441.

Jung, J. & Peterson, M. (2007). Body dissatisfaction and patterns of media use among preadolescent children. *Family and Consumer Sciences Research Journal, 36*(1), 40–54.

Jurajda, [[Scaron]]. & Harmgart, H. (2007). When do female occupations pay more? *Journal of Comparative Economics, 35*(1), 170–187.

Juteau, D. (2002). The citizen makes an entrée: Redefining the national community in Quebec. *Citizenship Studies, 6*(4), 441–458.

Kaiser, C., Eccleston, C., & Hagiwara, N. (2008). Post–Hurricane Katrina racialized explanations as a system threat: Implications for whites' and blacks' racial attitudes. *Social Justice Research, 21,* 192–203.

Kallman, M. (2008). *Talking trash: The world's waste management problem | Earth Trends.* Retrieved 7/27/2008, from http://earthtrends.wri.org/updates/node/314

Kamel Boulos, M. N. & Wheeler, S. (2007). The emerging Web 2.0 social software: An enabling suite of sociable technologies in health and health care education. *Health Information & Libraries Journal, 24*(1), 2–23. doi:10.1111/j.1471-1842.2007.00701.x

Kaplan, D.E. (2001). The educational crisis in American reform Judaism. *Journal of Beliefs & Values: Studies in Religion & Education, 22*(2), 183–196. Retrieved from http://library.mtroyal.ca:2048/login?url=http://search.ebscohost.com/login.aspx?direct=true&AuthType= ip,url,cookie,uid&db=a9h&AN=5402311&site=ehost-live

Karagiannis, E. (2005). Political Islam and social movement theory: The case of Hizb ut-Tahrir in Kyrgyzstan. *Religion, State & Society, 33*(2), 137–149. doi:10.1080/09637490500118638

Karger, H., Iyiani, C., & Shannon, P. (2007). The challenge of community work in a global economy. *Journal of Sociology & Social Welfare, 34*(2), 69–85. Retrieved from http://library.mtroyal.ca:2048/login?url=http://library.mtroyal.ca:2924/login.aspx?direct=true&Auth Type=ip,url,cookie,uid&db=a9h&AN=25301790&site=ehost-live

Karliner, J. (1997). *The corporate planet: Ecology and politics in the age of globalization.* San Francisco, CA: Sierra Club Books.

Kassam, A. (2007). Location identity and gender construction in a post 9/11 world: The case of the hijabi girl. *Intercultural Education, 18*(4), 355–359.

Kastenbaum, R. (1998). *Death, society, and human experience* (6th ed.). Boston, MA: Allyn & Bacon.

Katz, C. (2008). Bad elements: Katrina and the scoured landscape of social reproduction. *Gender, Place & Culture: A Journal of Feminist Geography, 15*(1), 15–29.

Katz, J.N. (2005). The invention of heterosexuality. In T.L. Steele (Ed.), *Sex, self and society: The social context of sexuality.* California: Wadsworth.

Kaya, I. (2005). *Possible Turkish water export as a tool for peace and stability in Middle East.* Retrieved 07/08/2008, from http://www.turkishweekly.net/comments.php?id=166

Kazemipur, A. & Halli, S.S. (2001). The changing colour of poverty in Canada. *The Canadian Review of Sociology and Anthropology, 38*(2), 217–238. Retrieved from http://proquest.umi.com/pqdweb?did=74099325&Fmt=7&clientId= 65345&RQT= 309&VName=PQD

Keane, C. (1998). Evaluating the influence of fear of crime as an environmental mobility restrictor on women's routine activities. *Environment and Behaviour, 30*(1), 60–74.

Kegley, C.W. & Wittkopf, E.R. (2006). *World politics: Trends and transformation.* Belmont, CA: Thomson Wadsworth.

Keister, L.A. (2007a). Average earnings by sex and work pattern. *Social Forces, 85*(3), 1195–1225.

Keister, L.A. (2007b). Upward wealth mobility: Exploring the Roman Catholic advantage. *Social Forces, 85*(3), 1195–1225.

Kellner, D. (2005). Western Marxism. In A. Harrington (Ed.), *Modern social theory: An introduction* (pp. 154–174). Oxford: Oxford University Press.

Kellner, D. (2007). *Jean Baudrillard 1929–2007.* Retrieved 29/05/2008, from http://www.ubishops.ca/baudrillard studies/obituaries_dkellner.html

Kelly, D., Pomerantz, S., & Currie, D. (2005). Skater girlhood and emphasized femininity: 'you can't land an ollie properly in heels'. *Gender & Education, 17*(3), 229–248. Retrieved from http://library.mtroyal.ca:2048/login?url=http://search.ebscohost.com/login.aspx?direct=true&AuthType=ip,url,cookie,uid&db=a9h&AN=17575613 &site=ehost-live

Kelly, D., Pomerantz, S., & Currie, D. (2006). "No boundaries"? Girls' interactive, online learning about femininities. *Youth and Society, 38*(1), 3–28.

Kendall, D., Lothian Murray, J., & Linden, R. (2007). *Sociology in our times.* Toronto: Thomson Nelson.

Kennedy, M.D. (2004). Evolution and event in history and social change: Gerhard Lenski's critical theory. *Sociological Theory, 22*(2), 315–327. doi:10.1111/j.0735-2751.2004.00220.x

Kenny, M.G. (2004). Racial science in social context. *ISIS: Journal of the History of Science in Society, 95*(3), 394–419.

Keown, J. (2000). Voluntary euthanasia and physician assisted suicide: Beyond control? *Readings in health care ethics* (Boetzkes, Elisabeth and Waluchow, Wilfrid J., Ed.), pp. 390–394. Peterborough, ON: Broadview Press.

Kessler, S. (1990). The medical construction of gender: Case management of intersexed infants. *Signs, 16*(1), 3–26.

Khanna, P. (2008). *The second world: Empires and influence in the new global order.* New York, NY: Random House.

Kiely, R. (1995). *Sociology and development: The impasse and beyond.* Abington, UK: Routledge, Taylor & Francis Group.

Kim, M.,& Chung, A. (2005). Consuming Orientalism: Images of Asian/American women in multicultural advertising. *Qualitative Sociology, 28*(1), 67–91.

Kimble, G.A., & Wertheimer, M. (1998). *Portraits of pioneers in psychology.* Washington, DC; Mahwah, NJ: American Psychological Association; Lawrence Erlbaum Associates.

Kimmel, M. (2001). Masculinity as homophobia: Fear, shame, and silence in the construction of gender identity. In T. Cohen (Ed.), *Men and masculinity* (pp. 29–41). Belmont: Wadsworth.

Kimmel, M. (2008). Excerpt from *Guyland: The perilous world where boys become men.* USA Today. Retrieved 16/12/2008, from http://www.usatoday.com/life/books/excerpts/2008-08-20-Guyland_N.htm

Kimmel, M.S. (1990). *Revolution, a sociological interpretation.* Philadelphia, PA: Temple University Press.

Kingston, A. & Köhler, N. (2006). *Canada's rich, troubled Thomson family.* Retrieved 14/07/2008, from http://www.theCanadianencyclopedia.com/index.cfm?PgNm=TCE&Params=M1ARTM0012842

Kinser, P.A. & Lewis, J.A. (2005). Understanding gender construction: Creating space for feminist health care practice and research. *Health Care for Women International, 26*(5), 422–429. doi:10.1080/07399330590933953

Kinsey Institute. (n.d.). Origin of the institute. Retrieved 28/2/2008, from http://www.kinsey-institute.org

Kinsman, G. (1987). *The regulation of desire: Sexuality in Canada.* Montreal: Black Rose Books.

Kinsman, G. (2004). National security as moral regulation: Making the normal and the deviant in the security campaigns against gay men and lesbians. In M. Webber & K. Bezanson (Eds.), *Rethinking society in the 21st century: Critical readings in sociology* (pp. 258–274). Toronto: Canadian Scholars Press.

Kinsman, G. (2006). The creation of homosexuality as a "social problem". In A. Glasbeek (Ed.), *Moral regulation and governance in Canada: History, context and critical issues* (pp. 85–116). Toronto: Canadian Scholars' Press.

Kivisto, P. (2004). *Key ideas in sociology* (2nd ed.). Thousand Oaks, CA: Pine Forge Press, an imprint of SAGE Publications, Inc.

Klandermans, B. (1994). Targeting the critical mass. *Social Psychological Quarterly, 57*(4), 360–367.

Klandermans, B. & Staggenborg, S. (2002). In Klandermans, Bert & Staggenborg, Suzanne (Ed.), *Methods of social movement research.* Minneapolis: Minnesota University Press.

Klapper, B.S. (2008). *WTO talks break down.* Retrieved 30/07/2008, from http://www.huffingtonpost.com/2008/07/29/wto-talks-break-down_n_115696.html

Kleg, M. & Yamamoto, K. (1998). As the world turns: Ethno-racial distances after 70 years. *Social Science Journal, 35*(2), 183.

Klein, N. (2007). *The shock doctrine: The rise of disaster capitalism*. Toronto, ON: Knopf Canada.

Klesse, C. (2005). Bisexual women, non-monogamy and differentialist anti-promiscuity discourses. *Sexualities, 8*(4), 445–464.

Klesse, C. (2006). Polyamory and its "others": Contesting the terms of non-monogamy. *Sexualities, 9*(5), 565–583.

Knöbl, W. (2003). Theories that won't pass away: The never-ending story of modernization theory. In G. Delanty & E.F. Isin (Eds.), *Handbook of historical sociology* (pp. 96–107). London, UK: Sage Publications, Ltd.

Knox, R. (1988, February 16). Test shows smart people's brains use nturients better. *Boston Globe,*

Knox, D., Breed, R., & Zusman, M. (2007). College men and jealousy. *College Student Journal, 41*(2), 494–498.

Knudsen, H.K., Roman, P.M., Johnson, J.A., & Ducharme, L.J. (2005). A changed America? The effects of September 11th on depressive symptoms and alcohol consumption. *Journal of Health & Social Behavior, 46*(3), 260–273. Retrieved from http://library.mtroyal.ca:2048/login?url=http://search.ebscohost.com/login.aspx?direct=true&AuthType=ip, url, cookie,uid& db=a9h& AN=18366334& site=ehost-live

Kobali, H.L. (2004). Crossing the threshold: Men's incomes, attitudes toward the provider role, and marriage timing. *Sex Roles, 51*(7), 387–395. Retrieved from http://library.mtroyal.ca:2048/login?url=http://search.ebscohost.com/login.aspx?direct=true&AuthType=ip,url,cookie,uid&db=a9h&AN=15542170&site=ehost-live

Kohen, D., Uppal, S., Guevremont, A. & Cartwright, F. (2007). *Children with disabilities and the educational system—a provincial perspective.* Retrieved 26/6/2008, from http://www.statcan.ca/english/freepub/81-004-XIE/2007001/childis.htm

Kohlberg, L. (1966). A cognitive developmental analysis of children's sex role concepts and attitudes. In E. Maccoby (Ed.), *The development of sex differences* (pp. 82–172). Stanford: Stanford University Press.

Kohn, M.H., Pelz, H., & Wayne, R.K. (2003). Locus-specific genetic differentiation at rw among warfarin-resistant rat (rattus norvegicus) populations. *Genetics, 164*(3), 1055–1070.

Kondro, W. (2002). Affirmative action needed to give women fair shot at research chairs? *Canadian Medical Association Journal, 167*(8), 910.

Kondro, W. (2003). Gender distribution of Canada research chairs. *Clinical and Investigative Medicine, 26*(1), 6–7.

Koropov, V. (2006). Models of global culture. In M. Tehranian, & J.B. Lum (Eds.), *Globalization and identity: Cultural diversity, religion and citizenship* (pp. 45–54). New Brunswick (USA): Transaction Publishers.

Kosut, M. (2006). An ironic fad: The commodification and consumption of tattoos. *Journal of Popular Culture, 39*(6), 1035–1048. doi:10.1111/j.1540-5931. 2006.00333.x

Kovach, K.A. (1996). *Comparable worth: The Canadian legislation —implementation of pay equity laws in Canada.* Retrieved 14/07/2008, from http://findarticles.com/p/articles/mi_m1038/is_n1_v39/ai_17957857/pg_1

Kramar, K. (2005). *Unwilling mothers, unwanted babies.* Vancouver: UBC Press.

Kraus, C., Meyers, S., Revkin, A., & Romero, S. (2005). As polar ice turns to water, dreams of treasure abound. *New York Times.* Retrieved 10/2/2009, from http://www.nytimes.com/2005/10/10/science/10arctic.html?ei=5090&en=9f4059694b7112

Kübler-Ross, E. (1969). *On death and dying.* New York: Macmillan.

Kumar, N., Larkin, J., & Mitchell, C. (2002). Gender, youth and HIV risk. *Canadian Women's Studies, 21*(2), 35–40.

Kuperman, A.J. (2000). Rwanda in retrospect. *Foreign Affairs, 79*(1), 94–118.

Kurzman, C. (2008). Meaning-making in social movements. *Anthropological Quarterly, 81*(1), 5–15. Retrieved from http://library.mtroyal.ca:2048/login?url=http://search.ebscohost.com/login.aspx?direct=true&AuthType=ip,url,cookie, uid&db=a9h&AN=31280285&site=ehost-live

Kutz-Flamenbaum, R.V. (2007). Code pink, raging grannies, and the missile dick chicks: Feminist performance activism in the contemporary anti-war movement. *NWSA Journal, 19*(1), 89–105. Retrieved from http://library.mtroyal.ca:2048/login?url=http://search.ebscohost.com/login.aspx?direct=true&AuthType=ip,url,cookie,uid&db=a9h&AN=24572596&site=ehost-live

Kuznets, S. (1955). Economic growth and income inequality. *The American Economic Review, 45,* 1–28.

La Prairie, C. (1990). The role of sentencing in the over-representation of aboriginal people in correctional institutions. *Canadian Journal of Criminology, 32*(3), 429–440.

La Prairie, C. (2002). Aboriginal over-representation in the criminal justice system: A tale of nine cities. *Canadian Journal of Criminology, 44*(2), 181–208.

Ladson-Billings, G. & Tate IV, W.F. (1995). Toward a critical race theory of education. In S.J. Ball (Ed.), *Sociology of education: Major themes* (pp. 322–342). New York: Routledge.

Lahiri, R. (2005). *Caste system in Hinduism: A historical and analytical approach.* Retrieved 29/11/2007, from http://www.boloji.com/hinduism/108.htm

Landman, A., Cortese, D.K., & Glantz, S. (2008). Tobacco industry sociological programs to influence public beliefs about smoking. *Social Science & Medicine, 66*(4), 970–981. doi:10.1016/j.socscimed.2007.11.007

Langlois, J.H. & Kalakanis, L. (2000). Maxims of myths of beauty? A meta-analytic and theoretical review. *Psychological Bulletin, 126*(3), 390.

Lano, K. & Parry, C. (1995). Preface. In K. Lano, & C. Parry (Eds.), *Breaking the barriers to desire* (pp. v–vi). Nottingham: Five Leaves Publications.

LaPierre, R. (1934). Attitudes versus actions. *Social Forces, 13,* 230–237.

Lapierre-Adamcyk, E., Marcil-Gratton, N., & Le Bourdais, C. (2006). A balancing act: Parents' work arrangements and family time. In K. McQuillan, & Z. Ravanera (Eds.), *Canada's changing families: Implications for individuals and society* (pp. 49–75). Toronto: University of Toronto Press.

Lareau, A. (1987). Social class differences in family–school relationships: The importance of cultural capital. *Sociology of Education, 60*(2), 73–85.

Lareau, A. (1989). *Home advantage: Social class and parental involvement in elementary education.* London: Falmer Press.

Larkin, J., Andrews, A., & Mitchell, C. (2006). Guy talk: Contesting masculinities in HIV prevention education with Canadian youth. *Sex Education, 6*(3), 207–227.

LaRochelle-Côté, S., Myles, J., & Picot, G. (2008). *Income security and stability during retirement in Canada.* (Catalogue No. 11F0019M—No.306). Ottawa, ON: Minister of Industry.

Lasch, C. (1977). *Haven in a heartless world.* New York: Basic Books.

Latimer, J. & Foss, L. (2004). *A one day snapshot of aboriginal youth in custody across Canada. Phase II.* Ottawa: Department of Justice Canada.

Latimer, J., & Foss, L. (2005). The sentencing of aboriginal and non-aboriginal youth under the YOA: A multivariate analysis. *Canadian Journal of Criminology and Criminal Justice, 47*(3), 481–500.

Latta, P.A. (2007). Citizenship and the politics of nature: The case of Chile's Alto Bío Bío. *Citizenship Studies, 11*(3), 229–246. doi:10.1080/17450100701381805

Laverack, G. (2004). *Health promotion practice: Power and empowerment.* London, UK: Sage Publications, Ltd.

Lawrence, C., Matsuda, M., Delgado, R., & Crenshaw, K. (1993). Introduction. In M. Matsuda, C. Lawrence, R. Delgado & K. Crenshaw (Eds.), *Words that wound: Critical race theory, assaultive speech and the 1st amendment* (pp. 1–15). Boulder: Westview Press.

Lax, E. (1991). Woody and Mia: A New York story. *New York Times.* Retrieved 14/5/2008, from http://query.nytimes.com.gst/fullpage.html?res=9D0Ceedd1639F937A15751C0A967958

Laxer, G. (2004). Democracy and global capitalism. In J. Curtis, E. Grabb, & N. Guppy (Eds.), *Social inequality in Canada* (4th ed., pp. 31–37). Toronto, ON: Pearson Prentice Hall.

Lazar, F. (2003). *Governance Act—Chiefs of Ontario.* Retrieved 23/01/2008, from http://www.chiefs-of-ontario.org/governance/ga_mar21-03-3.html

Lazarsfeld, P.F. & Merton, R.K. (1948). Mass communication, popular taste and organized social action. In L. Bryson (Ed.), *The communication of ideas* (pp. 95–118). New York: Harper.

Le Bon, G. (1895). *The crowd: A study of the popular mind.* London, UK: T. Fisher Unwin.

Le Goff, P. (2005). *The Canadian and American health care systems: Funding and effectiveness* (No. PRB04-61E). Ottawa, ON: Parliamentary Information and Research Service—Library of Parliament.

Leach, B. (2005). Agency and the gendered imagination: Women's actions and local culture in steelworker families. *Identities: Global Studies of Culture and Power, 12,* 1–22.

Leach, C.W., Iyer, A., & Pedersen, A. (2007). Angry opposition to government redress: When the structurally advantaged perceive themselves as relatively deprived. *British Journal of Social Psychology, 46*(1), 191–204. doi:10.1348/014466606X99360

Leacock, E. (1992). Women's status in egalitarian society. *Current Anthropology, 33*(1), 225–259. Retrieved from http://library.mtroyal.ca:2048/login?url=http://library.mtroyal.ca:2924/login.aspx? direct=true&AuthType=ip,url,cookie, uid&db=a9h&AN=5668996&site=ehost-live

League for Human Rights of Canada. (2006). *Is your child a target? A pamphlet for parents, teachers and police on the dangers of hate group recruitment in Canada.* Retrieved 1/27/2008, from http://www.media-awareness.ca/english/issues/online_hate/upload/is_Your_Child_a_Target_bnaibrith_2006_09.pdf

Leahy, S. (2007). *Canada: Losing water through NAFTA.* Retrieved 7/31/2008, from http://www.globalresearch.ca/index.php?context=va&aid=6859

Lechner, F.J. (1989). Fundamentalism revisited. *Society, 26*(2), 51–59. Retrieved from http://library.mtroyal.ca:2048/login?url=http://search.ebscohost.com/login.aspx?direct=true&AuthType=ip,url,cookie,uid&db=a9h&AN=10979232&site=ehost-live

Lee, J. (2007, November 12). Coalition pushes for legal brothel during Olympics; Ottawa's support sought for safe, prostitute-run facility that would cater to Olympic visitors. *Vancouver Sun,* pp. A1.

Lee, M. (2007). *Eroding tax fairness: Tax incidence in Canada, 1990 to 2005.* Toronto, ON: Canadian Centre for Policy Alternatives. Retrieved from http://www.policyalternatives.ca/documents/National_Office_Pubs/2007/Eroding_Tax_Fairness_web.pdf

Lee, R. B. & DeVore, I. (Eds.). (1968). *Man the hunter.* Hawthorne, NY: Aldine De Gruyter.

Lemert, E. (1951). *Social pathology.* New York: McGraw-Hill.

Lenski, G. (1966). *Power and privilege: A theory of social stratification.* New York: McGraw-Hill Book Company.

Lenski, G. (1996). Ecological-evolutionary theory and societal transformation in post-Communist Europe. *Czech Sociological Review, 4*(2), 149–156.

Lenski, G., Lenski, J., & Nolan, P. (1970). *Human societies: An introduction to macrosociology* (9th [1999] ed.). New York: McGraw-Hill, Inc.

Lenton, R., Smith, M.D., Fox, J., & Morra, N. (1999). Sexual harassment in public places: Experiences of Canadian women. *Canadian Review of Sociology & Anthropology, 36*(4), 517–540.

Leong, S. (2006). Who's the fairest of them all? Television ads for skin-whitening cosmetics in Hong Kong. *Asian Ethnicity, 7*(2), 167–181.

Lerma, A. (n.d.). *How many scientologists are there?* Retrieved 12/02/2008, from http://www.lermanet.com/howmany.htm#Canada

Levelle, M. (2008). *Exxon's profits: Measuring a record windfall.* Retrieved 13/06/2008, from http://www.usnews.com/articles/business/economy/2008/02/01/exxons-profits-measuring-a-record-windfall.html

Levin, J. & Levin, W. (1982). *The functions of discrimination and prejudice* (2nd ed.). New York: Harper & Row.

Levine, M. (2005). Globalization in the MENA and Europe: Culture, economy and the public sphere in a transnational context. *Journal of Muslim Minority Affairs, 25*(2), 145–170. doi:10.1080/136020005 00350306

Levine, R. (1987, April). The waiting game: Power has its privilege. *Psychology Today,* 24–33.

Lewis, J. (2006). "I'll scratch your back if you'll scratch mine": The role of reciprocity, power and autonomy in the strip club. *Canadian Review of Sociology & Anthropology, 43*(3), 297–311. Retrieved from http://library.mtroyal.ca:2048/login?url=http://search.ebscohost.com/login.aspx?direct=true&AuthType=ip,url,cookie,uid&db=a9h&AN=22062374&site=ehost-live

Lewis, L. (2007). Contesting the dangerous sexuality of black male youth. In G. Herdt & C. Howe (Eds.), *21st century sexualities: Contemporary issues in health, education, and rights* (pp. 24–28). New York: Routledge.

Lewis, M. (1978). *The culture of inequality.* New York: New American Library.

Lewis, O. (1998). The culture of poverty. *Society, 35*(2), 7–9. Retrieved from http://proquest.umi.com/pqdweb?did=25162980&Fmt=7&clientId=65345&RQT=309&VName=PQD

Lewis, S. (2008). In Bruce Ravelli (Ed.), *Personal communication,*

Li, P. (1992). Race and gender as bases of class fractions and their effects on earnings. *Canadian Review of Sociology and Anthropology, 29*(4), 488–510.

Library and Archives Canada. (2007). *Hot and cool—McLuhan—old messengers, new media.* Retrieved 01/06/2008, from http://www.collectionsCanada.gc.ca/innis-mcluhan/002033-2050-e.html

Library of Congress. (n.d.). *The history of the Edison cylinder phonograph.* Retrieved 30/08/2008, from http://memory.loc.gov/ammem/edhtml/edcyldr.html

Library of Congress. (1999). *Edison motion pictures.* Retrieved 03/05/2008, from http://memory.loc.gov/ammem/edhtml/edmvhm.html

Lichterman, P. (1995). Piecing together multicultural community: Cultural differences in community building among grassroots environmentalists. *Social Problems, 42*(3), 513–534.

Lim, M. (2007). *Subprime mortgage meltdown: Roots of the crisis.* Retrieved 30/07/2008, from http://opinion.inquirer.net/inquireropinion/talkofthetown/view_article.php?article_id=101568

Lindsay, C. (2008). *Are women spending more time on unpaid domestic labour in Canada than men?* Statistics Canada. Retrieved 15/12/2008, from http://www.statcan.gc.ca/pub/89-630-x/2008001/article/10705-eng.htm

Lindsey, L.L. & Beach, S. (2003). *Essentials of sociology.* Upper Saddle River, NJ: Pearson Education, Inc.

Lindsey, L.L., Beach, S., & Ravelli, B. (2009). *Core concepts in sociology: Second Canadian edition.* (2nd. ed.). Toronto, ON: Pearson Education Canada, Inc.

Link, B.G., Phelan, J.C., Miech, R., & Westin, E.L. (2008). The resources that matter: Fundamental social causes of health disparities and the challenge of intelligence*. *Journal of Health and Social Behavior, 49*(1), 72. Retrieved from http://proquest.umi.com/pqdweb?did= 1453662421&Fmt=7&clientId=6534 5&RQT=309&VName=PQD

Lipset, S.M. (1986). Historical traditions and national characteristics: A comparative analysis of Canada and the United States. *Canadian Journal of Sociology, 11*(2), 113–155.

Lipset, S.M. (1990). *Continental divide: The values and institutions of the United States and Canada.* New York, NY: Routledge, Chapman and Hall, Inc.

Lipset, S.M. (1993). Revolution and counterrevolution: The United States and Canada. In D. Taras, B. Rasporich & E. Mandel (Eds.), *A passion for identity: An introduction to Canadian studies* (pp. 150–161). Scarborough: Nelson.

Lipset, S.M. & Bendix, R. (1959). *Social mobility in industrial society.* Berkeley, CA: University of California Press.

Little, M. (1998). *"No car, no radio, no liquor permit": The moral regulation of single mothers in Ontario, 1920–1997.* Toronto: Oxford University Press.

Little, M. (2006). Manhunts and bingo blabs: The moral regulation of Ontario single mothers. In A. Glasbeek (Ed.), *Moral regulation and governance in Canada: History, context, and critical issues* (pp. 217–232). Toronto: Canadian Scholars' Press.

Little, M. & Morrison, I. (2001). The pecker detectors are back: Changes to the spousal definition in Ontario welfare policy. *Journal of Canadian Studies, 34*(2), 110–136.

Littlewood, R. (2002). Three into two: The third sex in northern Albania. *Anthropology & Medicine, 9*(1), 37–50.

Living Tongues Institute For Endangered Languages. (2007). *Living tongues institute for endangered languages.* Retrieved 10/4/2007, from http://www.livingtongues.org/index.html

Livingstong, D.W. & Sawchuk, P.H. (2000). Beyond cultural capital theory: Hidden dimensions of working class learning. *The Review of Education/Pedagogy/Cultural Studies, 22*(2), 121–146.

Llamas, Jose Manuel Coronel. (2006). Technologies of disciplinary power in action: The norm of the 'good student'. *Higher Education, 52,* 665–686.

Llobera, J.R. (2003). *An invitation to anthropology: The structure, evolution and cultural identity of human societies.* New York: Berghahn Books.

Lochhead, C. & Shalla, V. (1996). Delivering the goods: Income distribution and the precarious middle class. *Perception, 20*(1), 08/12/2007. Retrieved from http://www.ccsd.ca/perception/201/deliver.html

Lofland, J.F. (2004[1981]). Collective behavior: The elementary forms. In M. Rosenberg, & R.H. Turner (Eds.), *Social psychology: Sociological perspectives* (4th printing ed., pp. 411–446). New Brunswick (USA): Transaction Publishers.

Lofland, L. (1973). *A world of strangers*. New York: Basic Books.

Long, D. (2006). *Putting God in a box: Televised religion and the limitations of pop culture*. Retrieved 13/3, from http://www.mediasense.ca/Televised%20 Religion%20and%20the%20Limitations%20of%20Pop%20Culture.pdf

Long, T.E. & Hadden, J.K. (1983). Religious conversion and the concept of socialization: Integrating the brainwashing and drift models. *Journal for the Scientific Study of Religion, 22*(1), 1.

Loranhe, L. (2006). *The wealth trap*. Retrieved 06/03/2008, from http://www.asiatour.com/wealth-trap.htm

Lothane, Z. (2006). Mass psychology of the led and the leaders. (An earlier version of this paper was read at the conference "Prejudice and Conflict" organized by International Association for Psychoanalytic Studies, Salt Lake City, Utah, December, 2005.) *International Forum of Psychoanalysis, 15*(3), 183–192. doi:10.1080/08037060600924983

Loue, S. (2006). *Sexual partnering, sexual practices, and health*. USA: Springer.

Lowe, E. (2006). What a difference 50 years makes: Coming of age, then and now. *Transitions, 36*(1).

Lubey, K. (2006). Spectacular sex: Thought and pleasure in the encounter with pornography. *Differences: A Journal of Feminist Cultural Studies, 17*(2), 113–131. doi:10.1215/10407391-2006-005

Luddites. Retrieved 03/07/2008, from http://web.uvic.ca/philosophy/department_files/sophia/issues/sophia2002/jpetch.htm

Lueck, M. (2007). Hope for a cause as cause for hope: The need for hope in environmental sociology. *American Sociologist, 38*(3), 250–261. doi:10.1007/s12108-007-9017-7

Luffman, J. & Sussman, D. (2007). *Perspectives on labour and income (vol. 8, no.1)—the aboriginal labour force in western Canada*. Retrieved 28/01/2008, from http://www.statcan.ca/english/freepub/75-001-XIE/10107/art-2.htm

Lundell, L. (2005). *Chaoulli v. Quebec (attorney general): The Supreme Court of Canada sets the stage for fundamental health care reform*. Retrieved 30/06/2008, from http://www.hg.org/articles/article_698.html

Luxton, M. (2001). Conceptualizing 'families': Theoretical frameworks and family research. In M. Baker (Ed.), *Families: Changing trends in Canada* (4th ed., pp. 28–50). Toronto: McGraw-Hill Ryerson.

Luxton, M. & Corman, J. (2005). Families at work: Making a living. In N. Mandell, & A. Duffy (Eds.), *Canadian families: Diversity, conflict and change* (3rd ed., pp. 346–372). Toronto: Thomson Nelson.

Lynch, M. & McConatha, D. (2006). *Hyper-symbolic interactionism: Prelude to a refurbished theory of symbolic interaction or just old wine?*

Lynn, M. & Parker, L. (2006). Critical race studies in education: Examining a decade of research on US schools. *Urban Review, 38*(4), 257–290.

Macdonald, B.J. (2003). Thinking through Marx: An introduction to the political theory of Antonio Negri. *Strategies: Journal of Theory, Culture & Politics, 16*(2), 85.

MacDonald, E. & Rang, S. (2007). *Exposing Canada's chemical valley: An investigation of cumulative air pollution emissions in the Sarnia, Ontario area*. Toronto, ON: EcoJustice.ca.

Macionis, J.J. (1995). *Chapter 10: Social Stratification*. Retrieved 03/12/2007, from http://cwx.prenhall.com/bookbind/pubbooks/macionis7/chapter10/objectives/deluxe-content.html

Macionis, J.J. & Gerber, L.M. (2008). *Sociology* (6th ed.). Toronto, ON: Pearson Education Canada, Inc.

Mackie, M. (1973). Arriving at "truth" by definition: The case of stereotype inaccuracy. *Social Problems, 20*(4), 431–447.

MacKinnon, C. (2005). Pornography, civil rights and speech. In T.L. Steele (Ed.), *Sex, self and society: The social context of sexuality*. California: Wadsworth.

MacLennan, H. (1945). *Two solitudes*. Toronto, ON: Collins.

MacPhail, C. & Campbell, C. (2001). "I think condoms are good, but aai, I hate those things": Condom use among adolescents and young people in a South African township. *Social Science and Medicine, 52*(11), 1613–1627.

MacQueen, K. (2007, June 25). Polygamy: Legal in Canada. *Maclean's*.

MADD. (2008a). *Lives saved*. Retrieved 07/2008, from http://madd.ca/english/research/lives_saved.pdf

MADD. (2008b). *MADD youth*. Retrieved 15/07/2008, from http://www.maddyouth.ca/cms/page.php?2

MADD. (2008c). *The magnitude of the alcohol/drug-related crash problem in Canada overview*. Retrieved 16/07/2008, from http://madd.ca/english/research/magnitudememo.html

MADD Canada. (2004). *MADD Canada news*. Retrieved 6/24/2008, from http://www.madd.ca/english/news/pr/p041102.htm

Maich, S. (2006, October 30). Porno-graphy, gambling, lies, theft and terrorism: The Internet sucks (Where did we go wrong?). *Maclean's*.

Mair, R. (2005). *Harper's appeasing of Quebec*. Retrieved 23/04/2008, from http://thetyee.ca/Views/2005/12/26/HarperQuebec/

Malarek, V. (2003). *The Natashas : The new global sex trade*. Toronto: Viking Canada.

Malehealth. (2003). *Malehealth: Mid-life crisis*. Retrieved 11/11/2007, from http://www.malehealth.co.uk/userpage1.cfm?item_id=125

Malley-Morrison, K. & Hines, D.A. (2004). *Family violence in a cultural perspective: Defining, understanding, and combating abuse*. Thousand Oaks, CA: Sage Publications, Ltd.

Malthus, T. (1998). *An essay on the principle of population*. Retrieved 10/7, from http://www.esp.org/books/malthus/population/malthus.pdf

Mancini, T., Fruggeri, L., & Panari, C. (2006). An extension of the school moral atmosphere construct, and its association with aggressive behaviours in secondary school. *European Journal of Psychology of Education—EJPE, 21*(2), 209–228. Retrieved from http://library.mtroyal.ca:2048/login?url=http://search.ebscohost.com/login.aspx?direct=true&AuthType=ip,url,cookie,uid&db=a9h&AN=21647376&site=ehost-live

Mandell, N. & Duffy, A. (Eds.). (2005a). *Canadian families: Diversity, conflict and change* (3rd ed.). Toronto: Thomson Nelson.

Mandell, N. & Duffy, A. (2005b). Explaining family lives. In N. Mandell & A. Duffy (Eds.), *Canadian families: Diversity, conflict and change* (3rd ed., pp. 3–30). Toronto: Thomson Nelson.

Mandell, N. & Momirov, J. (2005). Family histories. In N. Mandell & A. Duffy (Eds.), *Canadian families* (3rd ed., pp. 31–63). Toronto: Thomson Nelson.

Manoli, C.C., Johnson, B., & Dunlap, R.E. (2007). Assessing children's environmental worldviews: Modifying and validating the new ecological paradigm scale for use with children. *Journal of Environmental Education, 38*(4), 3–13. Retrieved from http://library.mtroyal.ca:2048/login?url=http://search.ebscohost.com/login.aspx?direct=true&AuthType=ip,url,cookie,uid&db=a9h&AN=27718370&site=ehost-live

Marbley, A.F. (2005). African-American women's feelings on alienation from third-wave feminism: A conversation with my sisters. *Western Journal of Black Studies, 29*(3), 605–614.

Marciniak, K. (2006). Immigrant rage: Alienhood, "hygienic" identities, and the Second World. *Differences: A Journal of Feminist Cultural Studies, 17*(2), 33–63. doi:10.1215/10407391-2006-002

Marger, M. (1998). *Social inequality: Patterns and processes*. Mountain View, CA: Mayfield.

Margolis, E. & Rowe, J. (n.d.). *Manufacturing assimilation: Photographs of Indian schools in Arizona*. Retrieved 13/11/2007, from http://www.public.asu.edu/~jeremy/indianschool/paper.htm

Markle, T. (2007). *Coke part 1*. Retrieved 21/10, from http://www.theknoll.ca/php/display.php?article_id=53

Marotta, T. (2006). What made Stonewall different? *The Gay and Lesbian Review, March–April*, 33–35.

Marsh, J.H. *The Canadian encyclopedia*. Retrieved 9/10/2007, from http://www.theCanadianencyclopedia.com/index.cfm?PgNm=ArchivedFeatures&Params=A2126

Marshall, G. (2008). *Naomi Klein: No logo: Ad nauseum | book reviews | SpikeMagazine.com*. Retrieved 5/11/2008, from http://www.spikemagazine.com/0400nologo.php

Marshall, G., Rose, D., Vogler, C., & Newby, H. (1985). Class, citizenship, and distributional conflict in modern Britain. *British Journal of Sociology,*

36(2), 259. Retrieved from http://library.mtroyal. ca:2048/login?url=http://search.ebscohost .com/ login.aspx?direct=true&AuthType=ip,url,cookie, uid&db=a9h&AN=5304796&site=ehost-live

Marshall, K. (2006). Converging gender roles. *Perspectives on Labour and Income, 7*(7). Retrieved 15/12/2008, from http://www.statscan.gc.ca/pub/ 75-001-x/107061/9268_eng.htm

Marshall, S. (1984). Keep us on the pedestal: Women against feminism in twentieth-century America. In J. Freeman (Ed.), *Women: A feminist perspective* (3rd ed., pp. 568–581). Mountain View, CA: Mayfield.

Marsman, H.J. (2003). *Women in Ugarit and Israel: Their social and religious position in the context of the ancient near east.* Leiden: Brill.

Martin, D. (2005). Secularisation and the future of Christianity. *Journal of Contemporary Religion, 20*(2), 145–160. Retrieved from http://library.mtroyal. ca:2048/login?url=http://search.ebscohost.com/ login.aspx?direct=true&AuthType=ip,url,cookie, uid&db=a9h&AN=17018793&site=ehost-live

Martin, E. (2009). The egg and the sperm: How science has constructed a romance based on stereotypical male–female roles. In A. Ferber, K. Holcomb, & T. Wentling (Eds.), *Sex, gender, and sexuality: The new basics* (pp. 248–254). New York: Oxford University Press.

Martin, K., Vieraitis, L., & Britto, S. (2006). Gender equality and women's absolute status. *Violence Against Women, 12*(4), 321–339.

Martinelli, A. (2005). *Global modernization: Rethinking the project of modernity.* London, UK: Sage Publications, Ltd.

Martino, W. & Frank, B. (2006). The tyranny of surveillance: Male teachers and the policing of masculinities in a single sex school. *Gender and Education, 18*(1), 17–33.

Martinson, D.L. (2005). Pornography and deceptive advertising: What is the role of government in a free society? *Social Studies, 96*(1), 30–33. Retrieved from http://library.mtroyal.ca:2048/ login?url=http://search.ebscohost.com/login. aspx?direct=true&AuthType=ip,url,cookie, uid&db=a9h&AN=16429291&site=ehost-live

Marty. (2008). *What is a rigpig?* Retrieved 4/2/ 2008, from http://www.rigpig.com.au/index. php?option=com_content&task=view&id=15&I temid=1

Marx, K. & Engels, F. (1846). *The German ideology* (1964 ed.). London: Lawrence & Wishart.

Marx, K. & Engels, F. (1964). *On religion.* New York: Schocken Books (Updated Scholars Press Reprint).

Masko, A.L. (2005). "I think about it all the time": A 12-year-old girl's internal crisis with racism and the effects on her mental health. *Urban Review, 37*(4), 329–350.

Mason, C. (2007). Reproducing the souls of white folk. *Hypatia, 22*(2), 98–121.

Mason, M. & Goulden, M. (2004). Do babies matter: Closing the baby gap. *Academe, 90*(6), 3–7.

Matheson, C. & Endicott, L. (1998). Lesbian and bisexual identity: Discourse on difference. *Atlantis, 23*(1), 38–47.

Matheson, V.A., & Baade, R.A. (2004). Race and riots: A note on the economic impact of the Rodney King riots. *Urban Studies, 41*(13), 2691–2696. doi:10.1080/0042098042000294628

Matsumura, M. & Mead, L. (2007). *10 significant court decisions regarding evolution/creationism.* Retrieved 13/03/2008, from http://www.ncseweb. org/resources/articles/5690_10_ significant_court_ decisions _2_15_2001.asp

Matthews, B. & Beaman, L. (2007). *Exploring gender in Canada: A multi-dimensional approach.* Toronto: Pearson Prentice Hall.

Matthews, B.J. (2005). The body beautiful: Adolescent girls and images of beauty. In B. Ravelli (Ed.), *Exploring Canadian sociology: A reader* (pp. 39–50). Toronto, ON: Pearson Education Canada, Inc.

Mauss, A.L. (1975). *Social problems as social movements.* Philadelphia, PA: Lippincott.

Mayer, A. (1960). Russell Woods: Change without conflict. A case study of neighborhood transition in Detroit. In N. Glazer, & D. McIntire (Eds.), *Studies in housing and minority groups.* Berkeley, CA: University of California Press.

Mayer, S. (1997). *What money can't buy.* Cambridge, MA: Harvard University Press.

Mayerowitz, S. (2008, April 18). Major BlackBerry outage leaves millions without email. *ABC News.* Retrieved 17/5/2009, from http:// abcnews.go.com.Buisness/story?id=3052158

Mayo, M. (2005). *Global citizens: Social movements and the challenge of globalization.* London, UK: Zed Books.

Mayunga, J.S. (2007). *Understanding and applying the concept of community disaster resilience: A capital-based approach.* Retrieved July 8, 2008, from http://www.ehs.unu.edu/file.php?id=296

Mazur, A. (1993). Signs of status in bridal portraits. *Sociological Forum, 8* (June), 273–283.

Mazzarella, W. (2004). Culture, globalization, mediation. *Annual Review of Anthropology, 33,* 345. Retrieved from http://proquest.umi.com/pqdweb? did=749594031&Fmt=7& clientId=65345&RQT= 309&VName=PQD

McAdam, D. (1999). *Political process and the development of black insurgency, 1930–1970* (2nd ed.). Chicago, IL: University of Chicago Press.

McAdam, D. & Paulsen, R. (1994). Specifying the relationship between social ties and activism. *American Journal of Sociology, 99*(3), 640–667.

McCabe, D. (1998). *Listening to the voices for change.* Retrieved 6/29/2008, from http://reporter-archive.mcgill.ca/Rep/r3017/staggenborg.html

McCarney, J. (2005). *Ideology and false consciousness by Joseph.* Retrieved 11/09/2007, from http:// marxmyths.org/joseph-mccarney/article.htm

McCarthy, J.D., & Zald, M.N. (1977). Resource mobilization & social movements: A partial theory. *American Journal of Sociology, 82*(6), 1212–1241.

McCarthy, W. (2007). *What's love got to do with it? Adolescent romantic relationships and crime.*

McCarty, T.L., Romero, M.E., & Zepeda, O. (2006). Reclaiming the gift: Indigenous youth counter-narratives on native language loss and revitalization. *American Indian Quarterly, 30*(1), 28–48.

McCormick, C. (1995). Contemporary sociological thought. In M. Jackson & C. Griffiths (Eds.), *Canadian criminology: Perspectives on crime and criminality* (2nd ed., pp. 123–140). Toronto: Harcourt Brace.

McCormick, C. *Daily Gleaner,* June 24.

McDaniel, S. & Tepperman, L. (2002). *Close relations: An introduction to the sociology of families* (Brief edition ed.). Toronto: Prentice Hall.

McDermott, E. (2004). Telling lesbian stories: Interviewing and the class dynamics of "talk". *Women's Studies International Forum, 27,* 177–187.

McGee, J.D. (1977). The contribution of A.A. Campbell Swinton, F.R.S., to television *Notes and Records of the Royal Society of London, 32*(1), 91–105.

McGill University. (2008). *Suzanne Staggenborg.* Retrieved 6/29/2008, from http://www.mcgill. ca/sociology/faculty/staggenborg/

McGrath, A. (2005). *Introduction to queer theory.* Unpublished manuscript.

McHugh, N.A. (2007). *Feminist philosophies A-Z.* Edinburgh: Edinburgh University Press.

McIntire, C.T. (2006). Transcending dichotomies in history and religion. *History & Theory, 45*(4), 80–92. Retrieved from http://library.mtroyal.ca:2048/ login?url=http://library.mtroyal.ca:2924/login. aspx?direct=true&AuthType=ip,url,cookie,uid& db=a9h&AN=22930670&site=ehost-live

McIntyre, L.J. (2006). *The practical skeptic: Core concepts in sociology* (3rd ed.). Montreal, Que.; Boston, MA: McGraw-Hill Higher Education.

McKay, A. (2004a). Sexual health education in the schools: Questions and answers. *The Canadian Journal of Human Sexuality, 13*(3–4), 129–141.

McKay, A. (2004b). Oral sex among teenagers: Research, discourse and eduation. *The Canadian Journal of Human Sexuality, 13*(3–4), 201–203.

McKay, I. (1998). Changing the subject(s) of the 'history of Canadian sociology': The case of Colin McKay and Spencerian Marxism, 1890–1940. *Canadian Journal of Sociology, 23*(4), 389–426.

McKinney, D.W. (1973). *The authoritarian personality studies.* The Hague, Netherlands: Mouton.

McKinney, S.J. (2004). *Jewish education and formation in Glasgow: A case study* Routledge. Retrieved from http://library.mtroyal.ca:2048/login?url= http://search.ebscohost.com/login.aspx?direct =true&AuthType=ip,url,cookie,uid&db=a9h&A N=13310130&site=ehost-live

McLaren, P. & Farahmandpur, R. (2000). Reconsidering Marx in post-Marxist times: A requiem for postmodernism? *Educational Researcher, 29*(3), 25–33.

McLeod, K. (1992). Multiculturalism and multicultural education in Canada: Human right and human rights education. In K. Moodley (Ed.), *Beyond multicultural education: International perspectives* (pp. 215–242). Calgary: Detselig Enterprises.

McLuhan, E. (n.d.). *FAQS—Marshall McLuhan.* Retrieved 07/06/2007, from http://www. marshallmcluhan.com/faqs.html

McLuhan, M. (1960). *Explorations in communication*. Boston: Beacon Press.

McLuhan, M. (1962). *The Gutenberg galaxy : The making of typographic man*. Toronto: University of Toronto Press.

McLuhan, M. (1964). *Understanding media*. New York: McGraw-Hill.

McLuhan, M. (1967a). *The mechanical bride: Folklore of industrial man*. S.L.

McLuhan, M. (1967b). *The medium is the message*. New York: Bantam Books.

McLuhan, M. & Fiore, Q. (1968). *War and peace in the global village*. Toronto; New York: McGraw-Hill.

McLuhan, M., Hutchon, K., & McLuhan, E. (1977). *City as classroom: Understanding language and media*. Agincourt, ON: Book Society of Canada.

McMaster University. (2004). *Michael Atkinson, dept of sociology, McMaster University*. Retrieved 11/11/2007, from http://socserv2.mcmaster.ca/sociology/atkinson.htm

McMullin, J. (2004). *Understanding inequality: Intersections of class, age, gender, ethnicity, and race in Canada*. Toronto: Oxford University Press.

McPhail, C. (1991). *The myth of the madding crowd*. New York: Aldine deGruyter.

McPhail, C. & Wohlstein, R.T. (1983). Individual and collective behaviors within gatherings, demonstrations and riots. *Annual Review of Sociology, 9*, 579–600.

McQueen, C. (2005). *Humanitarian intervention and safety zones: Iraq, Bosnia and Rwanda*. New York, NY: Palgrave MacMillan.

Mead, G.H. (1934). *Mind, self and society from the standpoint of a social behaviorist*. Chicago: University of Chicago Press.

Meaghan, D. (2004). College 'equity' centres and women's studies faculty: Regulation of feminism? In M. Reimer (Ed.), *Inside corporate U: Women in the academy speak out* (pp. 177–197). Toronto: Sumach Press.

Measor, L. (2006). Condom use: A culture of resistance. *Sex Education, 6*(4), 393–402.

Media Awareness Network. (2007). *Beauty and body image in the media*. Retrieved 05/10/2007, from http://www.media-awareness.ca/english/issues/stereotyping/women_and_girls/women_beauty.cfm

Medicard Finance. (2003). *Plastic surgery statistics*. Retrieved 10/07, from http://www.plasticsurgerystatistics.com

Meenan, A.L. (2007). *Internet gaming: A hidden addiction*. American Academy of Family Physicians. Retrieved from http://library.mtroyal.ca:2048/login?url=http://search.ebscohost.com/login.aspx?direct=true&AuthType=ip,url,cookie,uid&db=a9h&AN=27084078&site=ehost-live

Melendez, R. (2007). No place to call home: Transgender persons, discrimination, and HIV. *21st century sexualities: Contemporary issues in health, education, and rights* (pp. 10–109). New York: Routledge.

Mellow, M. (2005). The work of rural professionals: Doing the gemeinschaft-gesellschaft gavotte. *Rural Sociology, 70*(1), 50–69.

Mernissi, F. (2005). The Muslim concept of active female sexuality. In T.L. Steele (Ed.), *Sex, self and society: The social context of sexuality*. California: Wadsworth.

Merrifield, R. (2007, March). Healthy weights for healthy kids. The Standing Committee on Health, Canadian Government.

Merton, R.K. (1938). Social structure and anomie. *American Sociological Review, 3*, 672–682.

Merton, R.K. (1948). Discrimination and the American creed. In R.M. MacIver (Ed.), *Discrimination and national welfare* (pp. 99–126). New York: Harper & Brothers.

Merton, R.K. (1968). *Social theory & social structure* (2nd. ed.). New York: Free Press.

Messner, M. & Montez de Oca, J. (2005). The male consumer as loser: Beer and liquor ads in mega sports media events. *Signs, 30*(3), 1879–1909.

Messner, S. & Rosenfeld, R. (1994). *Crime and the American dream*. Belmont, CA: Wadsworth Publishing.

Metzger, P. (2007). *CBC news in depth: Technology*. Retrieved 04/05/2008, from http://www.cbc.ca/news/background/tech/hd-video.html

Michael, R.T., Gagnon, J.H., Laumann, E.O., & Kolata G. (1994). *Sex in America: A definitive survey*. Boston: Little, Brown and Company.

Microcredit Summit. (n.d.). *The microcredit summit campaign*. Retrieved 14/07/2008, from http://www.microcreditsummit.org/Aboutmicrocredit.htm

Microsoft. (2008). *People make the difference*. Retrieved 26/03/2008, from http://www.microsoft.com/business/people ready/overview/default.mspx?WT.svl=1

Microsoft: Future homes to use smart appliances, interactive wallpaper. Retrieved 5/11/2008, from http://www.computerworld.com/action/article.do?command=viewArticleBasic&articleId=9003752

Mielo, G. (2004). Why Mcluhan's still hot and cool. *Et Cetera, 61*(2), 215. Retrieved from http://proquest.umi.com/pqdweb?did=678673211&Fmt=7&clientId=65345&RQT=309&VName=PQD

Milanovic, B. (2006). *Global income inequality: What it is and why it matters* (No. 3865). Washington, DC: World Bank.

Miles, R. & Brown, M. (2003). *Racism* (2nd ed.). London: Routledge.

Miliband, R. (1957). Karl Marx: Selected writings in sociology and social philosophy. *British Journal of Sociology, 8*(4), 378–379.

Millar, W.J. (2001). Patterns of use: Alternative health care providers. (Catalogue No. 82-003) *Health Reports (December), 13*(1), 30/06/2008.

Millard, J. & Grant, P. (2006). The stereotypes of black and white women in fashion magazine photographs: The pose of the model and the impression she creates. *Sex Roles, 54*(9), 659–673.

Miller, D. (1985). *Introduction to collective behavior*. Belmont, CA: Wadsworth.

Miller-Bernal, L. & Poulson, S.L. (Eds.). (2007). *Challenged by coeducation women's colleges since the 1960s*. Nashville, TN: Vanderbilt University Press.

Mills, C.W. (1959[2000]). *The sociological imagination* (Fortieth Anniversary Edition ed.). New York: Oxford University Press.

Millward, H. & Xue, G. (2007). *Local urban form measures related to land-use and development period: A case-study for Halifax, Nova Scotia*, University of Winnipeg / Institute of Urban Studies. Retrieved from http://library.mtroyal.ca:2048/login?url=http://search.ebscohost.com/login.aspx?direct=true&AuthType=ip,url,cookie,uid&db=a9h&AN=31934360&site=ehost-live

Minchin, T.J. (2006). "Just like a death": The closing of the international paper company mill in Mobile, Alabama, and the deindustrialization of the south, 2000–2005. *Alabama Review, 59*(1), 44. Retrieved from http://proquest.umi.com/pqdweb?did=1294823651&Fmt=7&clientId=65345&RQT=309&VName=PQD

MIT Center for International Studies. (2008). *Military budget*. Retrieved 05/06/2008, from http://web.mit.edu/CIS/fpi_military_spending.html

Miyake, K. (2007). How young Japanese express their emotions visually in mobile phone messages: A sociolinguistic analysis. *Japanese Studies, 27*(1), 53–72. doi:10.1080/10371390701268646

Mol, A.P.J. & Spaargaren, G. (2004). Ecological modernization and consumption: A reply. *Society & Natural Resources, 17*(3), 261–265. Retrieved from http://library.mtroyal.ca:2048/login?url=http://search.ebscohost.com/login.aspx?direct=true&AuthType=ip,url,cookie,uid&db=a9h&AN=12255245&site=ehost-live

Molnar, A. (2006). The commercial transformation of public education. *Journal of Education Policy, 21*(5), 621–640. doi:10.1080/02680930600866231

Mondello, B. (2005). *100th anniversary of first-ever US movie theater: NPR*. Retrieved 03/05/2008, from http://www.npr.org/templates/story/story.php?storyId= 4707873

Montgomery, K. (2005). Imagining the anti-racist state: Representations of racism in Canadian history textbooks. *Discourse: Studies in the Cultural Politics of Education, 26*(4), 427–442.

Moody, H.R. (2006). *Aging: Concepts and controversies* (5th ed.). Thousand Oaks, CA: Pine Forge Press.

Mookherjee, D. & Napel, S. (2007). Intergenerational mobility and macroeconomic history dependence. *Journal of Economic Theory, 137*(1), 49–78.

Moore, B.J. (1966). *Social origins of dictatorship and democracy*. Boston, MA: Beacon Press.

Moore, E. & Peniston, B.E. (2004). *Wage inequality in Oregon—still growing?* Retrieved 12/12/2007, from http://www.olmis.org/olmisj/ArticleReader?itemid=00003899&segmentid=0003&tour=0&p_date=1

Moran, E.F. (1981). Human adaptation to arctic zones. *Annual Review of Anthropology, 10*, 1–25. Retrieved from http://library.mtroyal.ca:2048/login?url=http://search.ebscohost.com/login.aspx?direct=true&AuthType=ip,url,cookie,uid&db=a9h&AN=11238159&site=ehost-live

Morck, R.K., Stangeland, D.A., & Yeung, B. (1998). *Inherited wealth, corporate control and economic growth: The Canadian disease?* Retrieved 12/7, from http://www.business.ualberta.ca/rmorck/Research%20Papers/NBER%20CCO%20Inherited%20Wealth.pdf

Morley, L. (2001). Mass higher education: Feminist pedagogy in the learning society. In P. Anderson & J. Williams (Eds.), *Identity and difference in higher education: 'outsiders within'* (pp. 28–37). Aldershot: Ashgate.

Morris, D.B. (1998). *Illness and culture in the postmodern age.* Berkeley, CA: University of California Press.

Morris, E. (2007). "Ladies" or "loudies"? Perceptions and experiences of black girls in classrooms. *Youth and Society, 38*(4), 490–515.

Morris, J. (2008). Out of New Orleans: Race, class, and researching the Katrina diaspora. *Urban Education, 43*(4), 463–487.

Morrison, D.E. (1971). Some notes toward theory on relative deprivation, social movements and social change. *American Behavioral Scientist, 14*(5), 675–690.

Morrison, I. (1998). Ontario works: A preliminary assessment. *Journal of Law and Social Policy, 13*, 1–46.

Morrison, K. (2008). *Wal-mart puts squeeze on suppliers.* Retrieved 13/06/2008, from http://www.nwaonline.net/articles/2008/06/12/business/061208walmartinflat.txt

Morrow-Howell, N., Hinterlong, J., & Sherraden, M. (Eds.). (2001). *Productive aging: Concepts and challenges.* Baltimore, Maryland: Johns Hopkins University Press.

Moser, S.C. (2007). In the long shadows of inaction: The quiet building of a climate protection movement in the United States. *Global Environmental Politics, 7*(2), 124–144. Retrieved from http://library.mtroyal.ca:2048/login?url=http://search.ebscohost.com/login.aspx?direct=true&AuthType=ip,url,cookie,uid&db=a9h&AN=24893146&site=ehost-live

Mosher, J. (2000). Managing the disentitlement of women: Glorified markets, the idealized family and the undeserving other discourses. In S. Neysmith (Ed.), *Restructuring caring labour: Discourse, state practice and everyday life* (pp. 30–51). Toronto: Oxford University Press.

Mourougane, A. (2008). *Achieving sustainability in the energy sector in Canada* (Economics Department Working Paper No. 618). Paris: OECD. Retrieved from http://www.olis.oecd.org/olis/2008doc.nsf/LinkTo/NT00003436/$FILE/JT03248408.PDF

Mukherjee, R. (2006). The ghetto fabulous aesthetic in contemporary black culture. *Cultural Studies, 20*(6), 599–629.

Mulder, M.B. (1999). On pastoralism and inequality. *Current Anthropology, 40*(3), 366–367. Retrieved from http://library.mtroyal.ca:2048/login?url=http://library.mtroyal.ca:2924/login.aspx?direct=true&AuthType=ip,url,cookie,uid&db=a9h&AN=2194267&site=ehost-live

Mulgrew, I. (2008). *Robert Latimer granted day parole.* Retrieved 11/07/2008, from http://www.nationalpost.com/news/story.html?id=338933

Muller, G.P. (2002). Explaining poverty: On the structural constraints of income mobility. *Social Indicators Research, 59*(3), 301. Retrieved from http://proquest.umi.com/pqdweb?did=204673191&Fmt=7&clientId=65345&RQT=309&VName=PQD

Multiculturalism—Canadian diversity: Respecting our differences. Retrieved 05/06/2008, from http://www.pch.gc.ca/progs/multi/respect_e.cfm

Mulvey, S. (2007). *BBC NEWS—EU attacked for 'inefficient' aid.* Retrieved 15/06/2008, from http://news.bbc.co.uk/2/hi/europe/6705773.stm

Murdoch, G. (1949). *Social structure.* New York: Macmillan.

Murdock, G.P. (1945). The common denominator of culture. *The science of man in the world crisis* (pp. 145). New York: Columbia University Press.

Murphy, B., Roberts, P. and Wolfson, M. (2007). *High income Canadians.* Ottawa: Statistics Canada.

Myhill, D. & Jones, S. (2006). 'She doesn't shout at no girls': Pupils' perceptions of gender equity in the classroom. *Cambridge Journal of Education, 36*(1), 99–113.

Myles, J. (2003). Where have all the sociologists gone? Explaining economic inequality. *Canadian Journal of Sociology, 28*(4), 551–559.

Nack, A. (2005). Identity and stigma of women and STDs. In T.L. Steele (Ed.), *Sex, self and society: The social context of sexuality* (California Trans.). Wadsworth.

Naess, A. (1988). Deep ecology and ultimate premises. *The Ecologist, 18*(4/5), 128–131.

Nagel, J. (1994). Constructing ethnicity. *Social Problems, 41*(1), 152–176.

Nakashima, R. (2008). *MySpace to allow users to share data with Yahoo, others.* Retrieved 11/05/2008, from http://www.foxnews.com/wires/2008May08/0,4670,MySpaceDataSharing,00.html

Nakhaie, M. (2002). Class, breadwinner ideology and housework among Canadian husbands. *Review of Radical Political Economics, 34*(2), 137–157.

Nakhaie, R.M. (1997). Vertical mosaic among the elites: The new imagery revisited. *Canadian Review of Sociology and Anthropology, 34*(1), 1–24.

Namaste, V. (2005). *Sex change, social change: Reflections on identity, institutions, and imperialism.* Toronto: Women's Press.

Nash, C. (2008). *Material entanglements: Queer geographies and trans experiences.* Unpublished manuscript.

National Anti-Poverty Organization. (2003). *The face of poverty in Canada: An overview.* Retrieved from http://oafb.ca/portal/images/pdfs/Poverty_Canada/Face%20of%20Poverty %20in%20Canada%202003.pdf

National Center for Education Statistics (NCES). (2005). *Total fall enrollment in degree-granting institutions, by level of enrollment, sex, attendance status, and type and control of institution: 2004.* Retrieved 28/05/2007, from http://nces.ed.gov/programs/digest/d05/tables/dt05_175.asp

National Post. (2005). *The Canadian values study: A joint project of Innovative Research Group, the Dominion Institute and the National Post.* Retrieved from http://www.innovativeresearch.ca/Canadian%20Values%20Study_Factum%20280905.pdf

National Science Teachers Association. (2005). *NSTA: Pressroom.* Retrieved 3/9/2008, from http://library.mtroyal.ca:3939/about/pressroom.aspx?id=50794

Nayebi, H. & Abdollahyan, H. (2006). Social stratification and its indices: A critique. *Critique: Critical Middle Eastern Studies, 15*(3), 249–263.

Neckerman, K.M., & Torche, F. (2007). Inequality: Causes and consequences. *Annual Review of Sociology, 33*, 335. Retrieved from http://proquest.umi.com/pqdweb?did=1320238661&Fmt=7&clientId=65345&RQT=309&VName=PQD

Neegan, E. (2005). Excuse me: Who are the First Peoples of Canada? A historical analysis of aboriginal education in Canada then and now. *International Journal of Inclusive Education, 9*(1), 3–15.

Nell, V. (1998). Why young men drive dangerously: An evolutionary perspective. *The Safety and Health Practitioner, 16*(10), 19–23.

Nelson, A. (2004). *Gender in Canada* (2nd ed.). Toronto: Pearson.

Nelson, A. (2006). *Gender in Canada* (3rd ed.). Toronto: Pearson.

Nelson, L.D. (1998). *Herbert Blumer's symbolic interactionism.* Retrieved 26/05/2007, from http://www.colorado.edu/Communication/meta-discourses/Papers/App_Papers/Nelson.htm

Nelson, T.D. (Ed.). (2004). *Ageism: Stereotyping and prejudice against older persons* (2nd ed.). Cambridge, MA: MIT Press.

Neugarten, B.L., Havighurst, R.J., & Tobin, S. (1968). Personality and patterns of aging. In B.L. Neugarten (Ed.), *Middle age and aging.* Chicago, IL: Chicago University Press.

Newbold, D. (2005). Foundation trusts: Economics in the 'postmodern hospital'. *Journal of Nursing Management, 13*(5), 439–447. doi:10.1111/j.1365-2834.2005.00587.x

Newman, D.M. (2006). *Sociology: Exploring the architecture of everyday life* (6th ed.). Thousand Oaks, CA: Pine Forge Press, an imprint of SAGE Publications, Inc.

Newman, D. & Smith, R. (1999). *Newman study site Huber.* Retrieved 07/12/2007, from http://www.pineforge.com/newman4study/resources/huber1.htm

Newman, P.C. (1998). *Titans: How the new Canadian establishment seized power.* Toronto, ON: McClelland and Stewart.

Ng, K.H. (2007). Political context, policy networks and policy change: The complexity of transition in Hong Kong. *Pacific Review, 20*(1), 101–126. doi:10.1080/09512740601133245

Nickle's Daily Oil Bulletin. (2008). Ottawa regulations: Carbon capture and storage for new oil sands plants. *Canadian Mining Journal, 129*(3), 27–28.

Nielsen, T. (2008). In Ravelli B. (Ed.), *Personal correspondence.*

Nielsen Media Research. (1994). *Report on television.* New York: A.G. Nielsen.

Noble, B. (2006). *Sons of the movement: FTMs risking incoherence on a postqueer cultural landscape*. Toronto: Women's Press.

Nolan, M. (2001). *CTV, the network that means business*. Edmonton, AB: University of Alberta.

Nolan, P. & Lenski, G. (2006). *Human societies: An introduction to macrosociology* (10th ed.). Boulder, CO: Paradigm Publishers.

NOVA. (2008). *Judgment day: Intelligent design on trial*. Retrieved 3/10/2008, from http://www.pbs.org/wgbh/nova/id/program.html#ch01

Novak, M. & Campbell, L. (2006). *Aging and society: A Canadian perspective* (5th ed.). Toronto, ON: Thomson/Nelson.

Noymer, A. (2001). The transmission and persistence of 'urban legends': Sociological application of age-structured epidemic models. *Journal of Mathematical Sociology, 25*(3), 299. Retrieved from http://library.mtroyal.ca:2048/login?url=http://search.ebscohost.com/login.aspx?direct=true&AuthType=ip,url,cookie,uid&db=a9h&AN=5512689&site=ehost-live

Nuyen, A.T. (2003). Confucianism, globalisation and the idea of universalism. *Asian Philosophy, 13*(2), 75–86. Retrieved from http://library.mtroyal.ca:2048/login?url=http://search.ebscohost.com/login.aspx?direct=true&AuthType=ip,url, cookie,uid&db=a9h&AN=11762884&site=ehost-live

Obach, B.K. (2007). Theoretical interpretations of the growth in organic agriculture: Agricultural modernization or an organic treadmill? *Society & Natural Resources, 20*(3), 229–244. doi:10.1080/08941920601117322

Oberg, K. (1960). Culture shock: Adjustments to new cultural environments. *Practical Anthropology, 7*, 177–182.

O'Brien, R. (2005). *Bodies in revolt: Gender, disability, and a workplace ethic of care*. London, UK: Routledge, Taylor & Francis Group.

Odd, A.W. (2005). *The global cold war: Third world interventions and the making of our Times*. Cambridge, UK: Cambridge University Press.

O'Dea, T.F. (1966). *The sociology of religion*. Englewood Cliffs, NJ: Prentice-Hall, Inc.

OECD. (2001). *OECD economic outlook* No. 70 (December). Paris: OECD.

OECD. (2006). *Improving water management: Recent OECD experience*. Paris: OECD. Retrieved from http://www.oecd.org/dataoecd/31/41/36216565.pdf

OECD. (2007). *Guidance manual on environmental sound management of waste*. Paris: OECD. Retrieved from http://www.oecd.org/dataoecd/23/31/39559085.pdf

OECD. (2008a). *Country statistical profiles 2008*. Retrieved 7/27/2008, from http://stats.oecd.org/wbos/viewhtml.aspx?queryname=459&querytype=view&la

OECD. (2008b). *Debt relief is down: Other ODA rises slightly*. Retrieved 15/06/2008, from http://www.oecd.org/document/8/0,3343,en_2649_34447_40381960_1_1_1,00.html

OECD. (2008c). *Factbook 2008*. Retrieved 22/07/2008, from http://titania.sourceoecd.org/vl=2294693/cl=11/nw=1/rpsv/factbook/080101-f1.htm

OECD. (2008d). *Factbook 2008–municipal waste*. Retrieved 24/07/2008, from http://oberon.sourceoecd.org/vl=4895345/cl=20/nw=1/rpsv/factbook/080202.htm

OECD. (2008e). *Health data 2008*. Retrieved 06/30/2008, from http://www.oecd.org/dataoecd/46/36/38979632.xls

OECD Observer. (2003). *News brief—July 2003 edition*. Retrieved 05/09/2008, from http://www.oecdobserver.org/news/fullstory.php/aid/1020/News_brief_-_July_2003_edition.html

OECD Observer. (2005). *GDP and GNI*. Retrieved 15/06/2008, from http://www.oecdobserver.org/news/fullstory.php/aid/1507/GDP_and_GNI.html

Ogden, L.A. (2008). 'Race' in post-universalist perspective. *Cultural Geographies, 15*(2), 155–171. Retrieved from http://library.mtroyal.ca:2048/login?url=http://search.ebscohost.com/login.aspx?direct=true&AuthType=ip,url,cookie,id&db=a9h&AN=31626321&site=ehost-live

O'Hara, P. (2002). The contemporary relevance of Thorstein Veblen's institutional–evolutionary political economy. *History of Economics Review, 35*, 78–103.

Olsen, R.E. (1978). *Karl Marx*. Boston, MA: Twayne Pubs.

Olzak, S. (2006). *The global dynamics of racial and ethnic mobilization*. Palo Alto, CA: Stanford University Press.

Omi, M. & Winant, H. (2008). *Racial formation in the new millennium*. New York: Routledge.

O'Neil, D. (2006). *Patterns of subsistence: Foraging*. Retrieved 18/05/2007, from http://anthro.palomar.edu/subsistence/sub_2.htm

O'Neil, D. (2007). *Patterns of subsistence: Pastoralism*. Retrieved 25/03/2008, from http://anthro.palomar.edu/subsistence/sub_3.htm

Ontario Health Quality Council. (2008). *Annual report summary (2008)*. Toronto, ON: Ontario Health Quality Council.

Ontario Human Rights Commission. (2008). *Education and disability: Human rights issues in Ontario's education system*. Retrieved from http://www.ohrc.on.ca/en/resources/discussion_consultation/education?page=Education-I

Ontario Ministry of Education. (1987). *The development of a policy on race and ethnocultural equity* (Provincial Advisory Committee on Race Relations' Report (Ontario Ministry of Education). Toronto: Queen's Printer.

Ontario Ministry of Education. (2008). *Safe schools*. Retrieved from http://www.edu.gov.on.ca/eng/document/nr/05.11/bg1123.html

O'Reilly, S., Knox, D., & Zusman, M.E. (2007). College student attitudes toward pornography use. *College Student Journal, 41*(2), 402–406. Retrieved from http://library.mtroyal.ca:2048/login?url=http://search.ebscohost.com/login.aspx?direct=true&AuthType=ip,url,cookie,uid&db=a9h&AN=25093215&site=ehost-live

Oringderff, J. (2004). "My way": Piloting an online focus group. *International Journal of Qualitative Methods, 3*(3), http://www.ualberta/~ijqm/backissues/3_3/html/oringderff.html.

Oromaner, M. (1975). Karl Marx: The essential writings. *Contemporary Sociology, 4*(5), 566.

Orum, A.R., Johnston, J.W.C., & Riger, S. (1999). *Changing societies: Essential sociology for our times*. Lanham, MD: Rowman and Littlefield Publishers, Inc.

Ostrander, S.A. (1984). *Women of the upper class*. Philadelphia, PA: Temple University Press.

Ottawa Citizen. (2008, February). More teen time linked to depression: Study. *Ottawa Citizen*. Retrieved 17/5/2009, from http://www.ottawacitizen.com/Life/More+Teen+time+linked+depression+study/1256819/story.html

Ou, Y. & McAdoo, H.P. (1999). The ethnic socialization of Chinese American children. In H.P. McAdoo (Ed.), *Family ethnicity: Strength in diversity* (2nd ed., pp. 252–276). Thousand Oaks, CA: Sage Publications, Ltd.

Owen Sound's Black History. (2004). *The underground rail road*. Retrieved 28/01/2008, from http://www.osblackhistory.com/underground.php

Owens, I. (2000). Maintaining diversity in information agencies: Accountability, professionalism, job performance, policies and standards. *Bulletin, 26 (April/May)*(4), 14/01/2008. Retrieved from http://www.asis.org/Bulletin/May-00/owens.html

Page, S. (2008) Rethinking immersion. *Ottawa Citizen*. Retrieved from http://www.Canada.com/ottawacitizen/story.html?id=a63b697d-81ab-441f-bc89-0e139fcf

Palamarek, M. (2008).

Palameta, B. (2004). Low income among immigrants and visible minorities. *Perspectives on Labour and Income, 5 (April)*(5), 11/12/2007.

Palmore, E.B. (2004). Research note: Ageism in Canada and the United States. *Journal of Cross-Cultural Gerontology, 19*(1), 41–46. Retrieved from http://library.mtroyal.ca:2048/login?url=http://search.ebscohost.com/login.aspx?direct=true&AuthType=ip,url,cookie,uid&db=a9h&AN=12233298&site=ehost-live

Parenti, M. (1993). *Inventing Reality: The politics of news media* (2nd ed.). New York: St. Martin's Press.

Parenti, M. (2001). *Monopoly media manipulation*. Retrieved 12/05/2008, from http://www.michaelparenti.org/MonopolyMedia.html

Parenti, M. (2007). *Contrary notions: The Michael Parenti reader*. San Francisco, CA: City Lights Books.

Park, J. (2007). *Work stress and job performance*. (Catalogue No. 75-001-XIE). Ottawa, ON: Statistics Canada.

Park, M.A. (2004). *Biological anthropology* (4th ed.). Montreal, Que.; Boston, MA: McGraw-Hill.

Park, S. (2006). Adoptive maternal bodies: A queer paradigm for rethinking mothering? *Hypatia, 21*(1), 201–226.

Parker, I. (2003). The psychogenesis of the ego: Notes on freud's 'case of homosexuality in a women'. *Psychodynamic Practice, 9*(1), 71.

Parkinson, G. & Drislane, R. (2007). *Thomson Nelson Canadian dictionary for the social sciences*. Toronto, ON: Nelson.

Parks, C. (2005). *Ancestors of science: Papyrus paper technology*. Retrieved 05/01/2008, from http://nextwave.sciencemag.org/career_development/previous_issues/articles/3430/ancestors_of_science_papyrus_paper_technology/(parent)/158

Parks Canada. (2006). *New designations recognize the national historic significance of Canadian people, places and events*. Retrieved 9/29/2007, from http://news.gc.ca/web/view/en/index.jsp?articleid=259609&categoryid=9&do_as=true&view_as=search&df_as=30&mf_as=11&yf_as=2006&dt_as=30&mt_as=11&yt_as=2006&categoryid=9&do_as=true&view_as=content&df_(TRUNCATED)

Parsons, K. (2007). *Atheism: Twilight or dawn?* Retrieved 11/03/2008, from http://www.infidels.org/library/modern/keith_parsons/twilight.html

Parsons, T., Bales, R., & and Shils, E. (1962). *Working papers on the theory of action*. London: Collier-Macmillan.

Parsons, T. (1937). *The structure of social action*. New York: McGraw-Hill.

Parsons, T. (Ed.). (1947). *Max Weber: The theory of economic and social organization*. New York: The Free Press.

Parsons, T. (1951). *The social system*. Glencoe, IL: Free Press.

Parsons, T. (1955). The American family: Its relation to personality and to social structure. In T. Parsons & R. Bales (Eds.), *Family, socialization and interaction process* (pp. 3–33). New York: The Free Press.

Parsons, T. (1959). The social class as a social system: Some of its functions in American society. *Harvard Educational Review, 29*, 291–318.

Pascali, L. (2006). Two stoves, two refrigerators, due cucine: The Italian immigrant home with two kitchens. *Gender, Place & Culture: A Journal of Feminist Geography, 13*(6), 685–695. doi:10.1080/09663690601019935

Paschall, M., Kypri, K., & Saltz, R. (2006). Friday class and heavy alcohol use in a sample of New Zealand college students. *Journal of Studies on Alcohol, 67*(5), 764–769.

Pastore, R.T. (1997). *Aboriginal peoples: The Beothuks: Newfoundland and Labrador heritage*. Retrieved 22/01/2008, from http://www.heritage.nf.ca/aboriginal/beothuk.html

Patriquin, M. (2007, October 22). Canada: A nation of bigots? *Maclean's*.

Pattucci, A. (1998). *Women in science: Meeting career challenges*. Thousand Oaks: Sage.

Paul, L.J. (2004). The untenured female academic in the corporate university. In M. Reimer (Ed.), *Inside corporate U: Women in the academy speak out* (pp. 226–244). Toronto: Sumach Press.

Paulson, J. (2007). No logo. *Science & Society, 71*(3), 361–363.

Pearce, T. (2008). About Dr. Kimmel/Guyland: The perilous world where boys become men. Retrieved from http://www.guyland.net/interviews.htm

Peat, D. (2008). *3 patients die waiting for a bed: EMS*. Retrieved 30/06/2008, from http://chealth.canoe.ca/channel_health_news_details.asp?channel_id=41&relation_id=1826&news_channel_id=41&news_id=24297

Peckover, S. (2002). Supporting and policing mothers: An analysis of the disciplinary practices of health visiting. *Journal of Advanced Nursing, 38*(4), 369–377.

Pedro, K. (2008, November 5). Online addictions: Help now available for gaming addicts. *London Free Press*. Retrieved 10/1/2009, from http://www.lfpress.com/cgi-bin/publish.cgi?p=249015&s=hottopics.html

Pedwell, T. (2008). *Morgentaler to get Order of Canada*. Retrieved 10/07/2008, from http://cnews.canoe.ca/CNEWS/Politics/2008/07/01/6036816-cp.html

Pellow, D.N. (2007). *Resisting global toxics: Transnational movements for environmental justice*. Cambridge, MA: MIT Press.

Pelz, H., Rost, S., Hunerberg, M., Fregin, A., Heiberg, A., Baert, K., et al. (2005). The genetic basis of resistance to anticoagulants in rodents. *Genetics, 170*(4), 1839–1847.

Pendakur, K. & Pendakur, R. (1996). *The colour of money: Earning differentials among ethnic groups in Canada* No. Strategic Research and Analysis Publication (SRA-34B). Ottawa, ON: Department of Canadian Heritage.

Pendakur, R. (2000). *Immigrants and the labor force: Policy, regulation and impact*. Montreal/Kingston: McGill-Queen's University Press.

Pereira, J. (2003). From Canada. *Palliative Medicine, 17*(2), 167–168. doi:10.1191/0269216303pm722op

Perier, P. (1998). Le play and his followers: Over a century of achievement. *International Social Science Journal, 50*(157), 343.

Peron, J. (2006). Globalization reduces poverty in developing nations. In L.I. Gerdes (Ed.), *Globalization opposing viewpoints* (pp. 113–119). New York: Thompson/Gale.

Persaud, C. (2008). The smart-phone—what's in a name? *Marketnews, 33* (March), 44–45.

Perse, E.M. (2001). *Media effects and Society*. Mahwah, New Jersey: Lawrence Erlbaum Associates.

Pertusati, L. (1997). *In defense of Mohawk land: Ethnopolitical conflict in native North America*. Albany, NY: State University of New York Press.

Petch, J. (2002). *Luddites*. Retrieved 03/07/2008, from http://web.uvic.ca/philosophy/department_files/sophia/issues/sophia2002/jpetch.htm

Peters, J. (1999). Redefining western families. *Marriage and Family Review, 28*(3/4), 55–66.

Petrou, M. (2009, March 9). The end of democracy? *Maclean's*.

Pettett, C. (2007). Homophobia and harassment in school-age populations. In G. Herdt & C. Howe (Eds.), *21st century sexualities: Contemporary issues in health, education, and rights* (pp. 29–31). New York: Routledge.

Philipps, L. (2004). Measuring the effects of feminist legal research: Looking critically at "failure" and "success". *Osgoode Hall Law Journal, 42*(4), 603–614.

Phillips, P.C. & Phillips, E. (2000). *Women and work: Inequality in the Canadian labour market*.

Toronto, ON: Lorimer. Retrieved from http://isbndb.com/d/book/women_and_work_a28

Phillips, S. (2007). *A brief history of Facebook*. Retrieved 10/05/2008, from http://www.guardian.co.uk/technology/2007/jul/25/media.newmedia

Phonautogram—Thomas Edison—Lawrence Berkeley National Laboratory—Édouard-Léon Scott de Martinville—New York Times. Retrieved 03/05/2008, from http://www.nytimes.com/2008/03/27/arts/27soun.html

Piirimäe, P. (2006). The explanation of conflict in Hobbes's leviathan. *TRAMES: A Journal of the Humanities & Social Sciences, 10*(1), 3–21.

Pintor, R.L., Gratschew, M., & Sullivan, K. (2002). *Voter turnout rates from a comparative perspective*. Stockholm, Sweden: IDEA. Retrieved from http://www.idea.int/publications/vt/upload/Voter%20turnout.pdf

Piven, F.F. & Cloward, R.A. (1977). *Poor people's movements: Why they succeed, how they fail*. New York: Random House.

Pohl, R. (2001). *Homelessness in Canada*. Retrieved 06/11, from http://www.streetlevelconsulting.ca/homepage/

Polster, C. (2002). A break from the past: Impacts and implications of the Canada Foundation for Innovation and the Canada Research Chairs initiatives. *Canadian Review of Sociology and Anthropology, 39*(3), 275–299.

Polster, C. (2004). Intellectual property, higher education and women's inequality. In M. Reimer (Ed.), *Inside corporate U: Women in the academy speak out* (pp. 138–152). Toronto: Sumach Press.

Pope, W. (1976). *Durkheim's "suicide": A classic analyzed*. Chicago: Chicago University Press.

Porter, J. (1965). *The vertical mosaic: An analysis of social class and power in Canada*. Toronto, ON: University of Toronto Press.

Possamaï, A. & Lee, M. (2004). New religious movements and the fear of crime. *Journal of Contemporary Religion, 19*(3), 337–352. doi:10.1080/1353790042000266354

Potter, D. (2007). *Ministries aren't just for the big names anymore*. Retrieved 13/03/2008, from http://www.beliefnet.com/story/221/story_"22110_1.html

Potts, M. (2006). China's one child policy. *British Medical Journal, 333*, 361–362.

Preckel, F., Holling, H., & Vock, M. (2006). Academic underachievement: Relationship with cognitive motivation, achievement motivation, and conscientiousness. *Psychology in the Schools, 43*(3), 401–411.

Preibisch, K. & Binford, L. (2007). Interrogating racialized global labour supply: An exploration of the racial/national replacement of foreign agricultural workers in Canada*. *The Canadian Review of Sociology and Anthropology, 44*(1), 5. Retrieved from http://library.mtroyal.ca:2083/pqdweb?did=1366162351&Fmt=7&clientId=65345&RQT=309&VName=PQD

Preibisch, K.L. (2007). Local produce, foreign labor: Labor mobility programs and global trade competitiveness in Canada. *Rural Sociology, 72*(3), 418–449.

Prendergast, C. (2008). The unexceptional schizophrenic: A postmodern introduction. *Journal of Literary Disability, 2*(1), 55–62.

Prensky, M. (2001). Digital natives, digital immigrants. *On the Horizon, 9*(5), 1–5.

Prentice, A. (1977). *The school promoters: Education and social class in mid-nineteenth century Upper Canada.* Toronto: McClelland & Stewart.

Proffitt, J.M. (2007). Challenges to democratic discourse: Media concentration and the marginalization of dissent. *Review of Education, Pedagogy & Cultural Studies, 29*(1), 65–84. doi:10.1080/10714410601090696

Proulx, C. & Helms, H. (2008). Mothers' and fathers' perceptions of change and continuity in their relationships with young adult sons and daughters. *Journal of Family Issues, 29*(2), 234–261.

Province of Nova Scotia. (2003). *Halifax Gazette—Canada's first newspaper.* Retrieved 03/05/2008, from http://www.gov.ns.ca/nsarm/virtual/gazette/

Prügl, E. (2002). Toward a feminist political economics. *International Feminist Journal of Politics, 4*(1), 31–36. Retrieved from http://library.mtroyal.ca:2048/login?url=http://search.ebscohost.com/login.aspx?direct=true&AuthType=ip,url,cookie,uid&db=a9h&AN=6774876&site=ehost-live

Prüss-Üstün, A., Bos, R., Gore, F., & Bartram, J. (2008). *Safer water, better health: Costs, benefits and sustainability of interventions to protect and promote health.* Geneva: World Health Organization.

Public Health Agency of Canada. (2005). *Division of aging and seniors—no. 11—criminal victimization and fear of crime among Canadian seniors.* Retrieved 26/06/2008, from http://www.phac-aspc.gc.ca/seniors-aines/pubs/factoids/2001/no11_e.htm

Public Health Service Reports on Smoking. (1969). *Congressional Digest, 48*(6/7), 166–167.

Public Safety Canada. (2007). *Backgrounder: The long-gun registry.* Retrieved 16/06/2008, from http://www.publicsafety.gc.ca/media/nr/2007/nr20071116-2-eng.aspx

Queenan, J. (1989). The many paths to riches. *Forbes, October 23,* 148–149.

Quinion, M. (1999). *World wide words: Rule of thumb.* Retrieved 14/11/2007, from http://www.worldwidewords.org/qa/qa-rul1.htm

Raby, R. (2005). Polite, well-dressed and on time: Secondary school conduct codes and the production of docile citizens. *Canadian Review of Sociology & Anthropology, 42*(1), 71–91.

Räikkä, J. (2004). The self-fulfilling prophecies and global inequality. *Philosophy & Geography, 7*(2), 193–200.

Rajiva, M. (2006). Brown girls, white worlds: Adolescence and the making of racialized selves. *Canadian Review of Sociology & Anthropology, 43*(2), 165–183. Retrieved from http://library.mtroyal.ca:2048/login?url=http://search.ebscohost.com/login.aspx?direct=true&AuthType=ip,url,cookie,uid&db=a9h&AN=21214089&site=ehost-live

Ramage-Morin, Pamela L. (2008). *Chronic pain in Canadian seniors.* Retrieved 24/06/2008, from http://www.statcan.ca/english/freepub/82-003-XIE/2008001/article/10514/findings-en.htm

Raman, S.M. (1999). Caste in stone. *Harvard International Review, 21*(4), 30. Retrieved from http://library.mtroyal.ca:2083/pqdweb?did=47034960&Fmt=7&clientId=65345&RQT=309&VName=PQD

Ramcharan, S., de Lint, W., & Fleming, T. (2001). *The Canadian criminal justice system.* Toronto: Pearson Education Canada Inc.

Ramcharan, S., & Ramcharan, C. (2005). *Law, order and the Canadian criminal justice system.* Mississauga, ON: Canadian Educators Press.

Randeria, S. (2007). Global designs and local lifeworlds. *Interventions: The International Journal of Postcolonial Studies, 9*(1), 12–30. doi:10.1080/13698010601173791

Rasberry, C.N. (2008). Battling body image: Confessions of a health educator. *Journal of American College Health, 56*(4), 423–426. Retrieved from http://library.mtroyal.ca:2048/login?url=http://library.mtroyal.ca:2924/login.aspx?direct=true&AuthType=ip,url,cookie,uid&db=a9h&AN=31161528&site=ehost-live

Ravallion, M., Chen, S., & Sangraula, P. (2008). *Dollar a day revisited* (No. WPS4620). Washington, DC: The World Bank.

Ravanera, Z. & McQuillan, K. (2006). Introduction. In K. McQuillan, & Z. Ravanera (Eds.), *Canada's changing families: Implications for individuals and society* (pp. 3–11). Toronto: University of Toronto Press.

Ravelli, B. (1994). Health care in the United States and Canada. In R. Luhman (Ed.), *The sociological outlook: A text with readings* (4th ed., pp. 467–468). San Diego: Collegiate Press.

Ravelli, B. (2000). Culture. In M. Kanwar, & D. Swenson (Eds.), *Canadian sociology* (3rd ed., pp. 39–61). Dubuque, IA: Kendall/Hunt.

Ray, J.J. (1988). Why the F scale predicts racism: A critical review. *Political Psychology, 9*(4), 671–679.

Raymond, J.G. (2003). *Ten reasons for not legalizing prostitution and a legal response to the demand for prostitution.* Retrieved 12/13/2007, from http://www.catwinternational.org/

Rea, M.C. (2006). Polytheism and Christian belief. *Journal of Theological Studies, 57*(1), 133. Retrieved from http://proquest.umi.com/pqdweb?did=1008676081&Fmt=7& clientId=65345&RQT=309&VName=PQD

Redhead, R. (2007a). Imag(in)ing women's agency. *International Feminist Journal of Politics, 9*(2), 218–238. doi:10.1080/14616740701259879

Redhead, S. (2007b). This sporting life: The realism of the football factory. *Soccer & Society, 8*(1), 90–108. Retrieved from http://library.mtroyal.ca:2048/login?url=http://search.ebscohost.com/login.aspx?direct=true&AuthType=ip,url,cookie,uid&db=a9h&AN=23368982&site=ehost-live

Reich, R. (1991). *The work of nations: Preparing ourselves for the twenty-first century capitalism.* New York: Alfred A Knopf.

Reid, L.W., Adelman, R.M., & Jaret, C. (2007). Women, race, and ethnicity: Exploring earnings differentials in metropolitan America. *City &

Community, 6*(2), 137. Retrieved from http://proquest.umi.com/pqdweb?did=1274477011&Fmt=7&clientId=65345&RQT=309&VName=PQD

Reif, S., Whetten, K., & Thielman, N. (2007). Association of race and gender with use of antiretroviral therapy among HIV-infected individuals in the southeastern United States. *Southern Medical Journal, 100*(8), 775–781. Retrieved from http://library.mtroyal.ca:2048/login?url=http://search.ebscohost.com/login.aspx?direct=true&AuthType=ip,url,cookie,uid&db=a9h&AN=26234652&site=ehost-live

Reilly, S. (2007). Deindustrialization as public history: An exhibition at the Manitoba museum. *Urban History Review, 35*(2), 77. Retrieved from http://proquest.umi.com/pqdweb? did=1244143831&Fmt=7&clientId=65345&RQT=309& VName=PQD

Reimer, M. (2004). Will women's studies prgorams survive the corporate university? In M. Reimer (Ed.), *Inside corporate U: Women in the academy speak out* (pp. 118–137). Toronto: Sumach Press.

Reiss, A., & Roth, J. (Eds.). (1993). *Understanding and preventing violence.* Washington: National Academy Press.

ReligionFacts. (2008a). *Church of Scientology.* Retrieved 09/03/2008, from http://www.religionfacts.com/scientology/index.htm

ReligionFacts. (2008b). *Jehovah's Witnesses.* Retrieved 11/03/2008, from http://religionfacts.com/jehovahs_witnesses/index.htm

ReligionFacts. (2008c). *Overview of Judaism.* Retrieved 10/03/2008, from http://www.religionfacts.com/judaism/fastfacts/overview.htm

ReligionFacts. (2008d). *Salat: Muslim prayer.* Retrieved 09/03/2008, from http://www.religionfacts.com/islam/practices/salat-prayer.htm

Renold, E. (2007). Primary school studs: Deconstructing young boys' heterosexual masculinities. *Men and Masculinities, 9*(3), 275–297.

Renzetti, C. & Curran, D. (1999). *Women, men and society* (4th ed.). Boston: Allyn and Bacon.

Reutter, L., Veenstra, G., Stewart, M., Raphael, D., Love, R., Makwarimba, E., et al. (2006). Public attribution for poverty in Canada. *Canadian Review of Sociology and Anthropology, 43*(1), 1–22.

Reynolds, M. (2003). Where have all the boys gone? *McGill Reporter.* Retrieved 10/12/2008, from http://www.mcgill.ca/reporter/36/05/gender/

Reznick, O.I. (2006). *The secrets of medical decision making: How to avoid becoming a victim of the health care machine.* Ann Arbor, MI: Loving Healing Press.

Rhodes, R. (2005). Rethinking research ethics. *The American Journal of Bioethics, 5*(1), 7–28.

Rich, A. (2003). Compulsory heterosexuality and lesbian existence. *Journal of Women's History, 15*(3), 11–48.

Richardson, J.T. (1993). Definitions of cult: Form sociological-technical to popular-negative. *Review of Religious Research, 34*(4), 348.

Richardson, J.T., Best, J., & Bromley, D.G. (1991). Satanism as a social problem. In J.T. Richardson,

J. Best, & D.G. Bromley (Eds.), *The satanism scare* (pp. 3–17). New York: Aldine De Gruyter.

Richey, C. (Producer) & Richey, C. (Director). (1993). *In the gutter and other good places.* [Video/DVD] Ladder to the Moon Productions.

Richman, M.H. (2002). *Sacred revolutions: Durkheim and the college of sociology.* Minneapolis, MN: University of Minnesota Press.

Riddell, R. (2007). A good thing? *Does foreign aid really work?* (pp. 1–13). Cambridge: Oxford University Press.

Rieff, D. (1993). A global culture? *World Policy Journal, 10*(4), 73.

Ringen, S. (2006). *Citizens, families & reform.* New Brunswick (USA): Transaction Publishers.

Rist, R. (1970). Student social class and teacher expectations: The self-fulfilling prophecy in ghetto education. *Harvard Educational Review, 40*(3), 411–451.

Ritchie, A. & Barker, M. (2006). There aren't words for what we do or how we feel so, we have to make them up: Constructing polyamorous languages in a culture of compulsory monogamy. *Sexualities, 9*(5), 584–601.

Ritzer, G. (1992). *Contemporary sociological theory* (3rd ed.). New York: McGraw Hill, Inc.

Ritzer, G. (1996). *Classical sociological theory* (2nd ed.). Montreal, Que.; New York: McGraw-Hill.

Ritzer, G. (1998). *The McDonaldization thesis: Explorations and extensions.* London & Thousand Oaks, CA: Sage.

Ritzer, G. (2000). *Sociological theory* (5th ed.). New York: McGraw-Hill.

Ritzer, G. (2004). *The McDonaldization of society* (Revised New Century Edition ed.). Thousand Oaks, CA: Sage Publications, Ltd.

Ritzer, G. & Goodman, D. (2004). *Classical sociological theory* (4th ed.). New York: McGraw Hill, Inc.

Roach, M. (1998). Why men kill. *Discover, 19*(12), 100.

Roberts, A. (n.d.). *Extracts from Erving Goffman.* Retrieved 13/11/2007, from http://www.mdx.ac.uk/WWW/STUDY/xgof.htm

Roberts, J. (2001). *Public fear of crime and perceptions of the criminal justice system.* Ottawa: Solicitor General of Canada.

Roberts, J. & Birkenmayer, A. (1997). Sentencing in Canada: Recent statistical trends. *Canadian Journal of Criminology, 39*(4), 459–482.

Roberts, J., & Doob, A. (1997). Race, ethnicity and criminal justice in Canada. *Crime and Justice, 21*, 469–522.

Robertson, J. (1978). *The sane alternative.* St. Paul, MN: River Basin Publishing Company.

Robertson, J. (1983). *The sane alternative.* London: The author.

Robertson, R. (2002). *Women in management: Analysis of current population survey data* (No. GAO-02-156), US General Accounting Office.

Robinson, Jr. & Alonford, J. (n.d.). *Apartheid, social and political policy of racial segregation and discrimination enforced by white minority governments in South Africa from 1948 to 1994.* Retrieved 09/01/2008, from http://www.africanaencyclopedia.com/apartheid/apartheid.html

Robinson, V. (1997). My baby just cares for me: Feminism, heterosexuality, and non-monogamy. *Journal of Gender Studies, 6*(2), 143–157.

Rochlin, M. (2009). The heterosexual questionnaire. In A. Ferber, K. Holcomb & T. Wentling (Eds.), *Sex, gender and sexuality: The new basics, an anthology* (pp. 299–300). New York: Oxford University Press.

Rodriquez Rust, P. (Ed.). (2000). *Bisexuality in the United States.* New York: Columbia University Press.

Rogers Communication. (2007). *History of Rogers.* Retrieved 12/18/2007, from http://your.rogers.com/aboutrogers/historyofrogers/overview.asp?shopperID=9A3X0KG9V3XS9NWRNCNEXV602LPQ3GUC

Rokach, A., Lechcier-Kimel, R., & Safarov, A. (2006). Loneliness of people with physical disabilities. *Social Behavior & Personality: An International Journal, 34*(6), 681–699. Retrieved from http://library.mtroyal.ca:2048/login?url=http://search.ebscohost.com/login.aspx?direct=true&AuthType=ip,url,cookie,uid&db=a9h&AN=21903298&site=ehost-live

Romero, M. (2006). Racial profiling and immigration law enforcement: Rounding up of usual suspects in the Latino community. *Critical Sociology, 32*(2–3), 447–473.

Rose, D.B. (2008). Love in the time of extinctions. *Australian Journal of Anthropology, 19*(1), 81–84. Retrieved from http://library.mtroyal.ca:2048/login?url=http://search.ebscohost.com/login.aspx?direct=true&AuthType=ip,url,cookie,uid&db=a9h&AN=31341444&site=ehost-live

Rose, M. & Kelly, E. (2008). *Canadian women poets: Himani Bannerji.* Retrieved from http://www.brocku.ca/Canadian womenpoets/Bannerji.htm

Rosen, J. (2008, March 27). Researchers play tune recorded before Edison. *The New York Times.*

Rosenbaum, J. (1989). Family dysfunction and female delinquency. *Crime and Delinquency, 35*(1), 31–44.

Rosenthal, J.L. (1992). *The fruits of revolution: Property rights, litigation, and French agriculture, 1700–1860* Cambridge University Press.

Rossides, D.W. (1998). *Social theory: Its origins, history, and contemporary relevance.* Dix Hills, NY: General Hall.

Rostow, W.W. (1960). *Stages of economic growth: A non-communist manifesto.* Cambridge, UK: Cambridge University Press.

Roszak, T. (1969). *The making of a counter-culture: Reflections on the technocratic society and its youthful opposition.* New York: Doubleday.

Roth, C.F. (2002). Goods, names, and selves: Rethinking the Tsimshian potlatch. *American Ethnologist, 29*(1), 123. Retrieved from http://proquest.umi.com/pqdweb?did=128816021&Fmt=7&clientId=65345&RQT=309&VName=PQD

Rousseau, J. (2006). *A dissertation on the origin and foundation of the inequality of mankind and is it authorised by natural law* (1754). Retrieved 15/08/2007, from http://www.marxists.org/reference/subject/economics/rousseau/inequality/ch01.htm

Rowling, L., Scanlon, L., & Wever, Z. (2007). 'You don't have an identity . . . you are just lost in a crowd': Forming a student identity in the first-year transition to university. *Journal of Youth Studies, 10*(2), 223–241.

Roy, C. (2002). *The original raging grannies: Using creative and humorous protests for political education.* Retrieved 09/06/2008, from http://www.geocities.com/raginggrannies/GrannyHerstory.pdf

The Royal College of Psychiatrists. (2004). *Factsheet 17: Domestic violence* (No. 2007).

Royal Commission on the Status of Women in Canada. (2007). *Briefs to the Royal Commission on the Status of Women in Canada.* Retrieved 29/05/2007, from http://www.library.utoronto.ca/media-commons/microtext/collection/pages/carylcos.html

Rubin, L. (1994). *Families on the fault line.* New York: HarperCollins.

Rubin, L.B. (1976). *Worlds of pain: Life in the working class family.* New York: Basic.

Rubin, R.H. (2001). Alternative lifestyles revisited, or whatever happened to swingers, group marriages, and communes? *Journal of Family Issues, 22*(6), 711–726.

Rudel, T.K. & Hooper, L. (2005). Is the pace of social change accelerating? Latecomers, common languages, and rapid historical declines in fertility. *International Journal of Comparative Sociology, 46*(4), 275–296.

Rumbaut, R.G. (2004). Ages, life stages, and generational cohorts: Decomposing the immigrant first and second generations in the United States. *The International Migration Review, 38*(3), 1160. Retrieved from http://proquest.umi.com/pqdweb?did=762568041&Fmt=7&clientId=65345&RQT=309&VName=PQD

Russell, C.L. (2008). How are your person first skills? *Teaching Exceptional Children, 40*(5), 40–43. Retrieved from http://library.mtroyal.ca:2048/login?url=http://search.ebscohost.com/login.aspx?direct=true&AuthType=ip,url,cookie,uid&db=a9h&AN=32197150&site=ehost-live

Rust, P. (1995). *Bisexuality and the challenge to lesbian politics: Sex, loyalty and revolution.* New York: New York University Press.

Ryan, W. (1971). *Blaming the victim.* New York: Pantheon.

Sachs, J.D. (2005a). *The end of poverty: Economic possibilities for our time.* New York: The Penguin Press.

Sachs, J.D. (2005b). The end of poverty. *Time.* Retrieved 5/4/2009, from http://www.time.com/time/magazine/article/0,9171,1034738-5,00.html

Sachsenmaier, D. (2006). *Global history and critiques of Western perspectives.* Routledge. Retrieved from http://library.mtroyal.ca:2048/login?url=http://search.ebscohost.com/login.aspx?direct=true&AuthType=ip,url,cookie,uid&db=a9h&AN=23233532&site=ehost-live

Sadker, M. & Sadker, D. (2009). Missing in interaction. In E. Disch (Ed.), *Reconstructing gender:*

A multicultural anthology (5th ed., pp. 362–368). New York: McGraw Hill.

Saettler, P. (2004). *Evolution of American educational technology*. Charlotte, NC: Information Age Publishing.

Sahib, P.R., Koning, R., & van Witteloostuijn, A. (2006). Putting your best cyber identity forward: An analysis of "success stories" from a Russian internet marriage agency. *International Sociology, 21*(1), 61–82.

SAHRDC. (2001). *Caste, ethnicity and nationality: Japan finds plenty of space for discrimination.* Retrieved 30/11/2007, from http://www.hrdc.net/sahrdc/hrfeatures/HRF39.htm

Said, E. (1978). *Orientalism.* New York: Pantheon Books.

Salaff, J.W., Greve, A. & Ping, Lynn Xu Li. (2002). *When ties do not tie in? Can skilled Chinese immigrants find jobs outside Chinatown?* Retrieved 17/01, from http://www.chass.utoronto.ca/~salaff/Salaff-Greve-Xu-labor.pdfSalari, S. & Zhang, W. (2006). Kin keepers and good providers: Influence of gender socialization on well-being among USA birth cohorts. *Aging & Mental Health, 10*(5), 485–496.

Sallot, J. (1999, January 11). Latimer sentence too harsh, poll told. *Globe and Mail*, pp. A5.

Salzman, P.C. (2004). *Pastoralists: Equality, hierarchy and the state.* Boulder, CO: Westview Press.

Sanders, S., Graham, C., Yarber, W., Crosby, R., Dodge, B., & Milhausen, R. (2006). Women who put condoms on male partners: Correlates of condom application. *American Journal of Health Behavior, 30*(5), 460–466.

Sandland, R. (2005). Feminism and the Gender Recognition Act 2004. *Feminist Legal Studies, 13*(1), 43–66.

Sangster, J. (2006). Introduction to regulating girls and women. In A. Glasbeek (Ed.), *Moral regulation and governance in Canada: History, context, and critical issues* (pp. 31–56). Toronto: Canadian Scholars Press.

Sangster, J. (2007). Making a fur coat: Women, the labouring body, and working-class history. *International Review of Social History, 52*, 241. Retrieved from http://proquest.umi.com/pqdweb?did=1331477351&Fmt=7&clientId=65345&RQT=309&VName=PQD

Saskatchewan Job Futures. (2008). *Occupations unique to primary industry.* Retrieved 04/02, from http://www.saskjobfutures.ca/ profiles/profile_type.cfm?type=8& lang=en&site=graphic

Sassoon, A.S. (1994). Hegemony. In W. Outhwaite & T. Bottomore (Eds.), *The Blackwell dictionary of twentieth-century social thought* (pp. 255–256). Oxford: Blackwell.

Scapecchi, P. (2007). *The health cost of inaction with respect to air pollution.* Paris: OECD. Retrieved from http://www.olis.oecd.org/olis/2006doc.nsf/LinkTo/NT00009556/$FILE/JT03233269.PDF

Schaefer, R.T. (2008). *Racial and ethnic groups* (11th ed.). Upper Saddle River, NJ: Prentice-Hall, Inc.

Schippert, C. (2007). Can muscles be queer? Reconsidering the transgressive hyper-built body. *Journal of Gender Studies, 16*(2), 155–171.

Schmitz, A., Furtan, W.H., & University of Regina. Canadian Plains Research Centre. (2000). *The Canadian wheat board: Marketing in the new millennium.* Regina, SK: Canadian Plains Research Centre.

Schnaiberg, A. (1980). *The environment: From surplus to scarcity.* New York: Oxford University Press.

Schnaiberg, A. (2002). Reflections on my 25 years before the mast of the environment and technology section. *Organization & Environment, 15*(1), 30–41.

Schnaiberg, A. & Gould, K.A. (1994). *Environment and society: The enduring conflict.* New York: St. Martin's Press.

Schneider, B.E. & James, V. (2005). Social control, civil liberties and women's sexuality. In T.L. Steele (Ed.), *Sex, self and society: The social context of sexuality.* California: Wadsworth.

Schneider, T. (2008). How we know global warming is real. (cover story) *Skeptic, 14*(1), 31–37. Retrieved from http://library.mtroyal.ca:2048/login?url=http://search.ebscohost.com/login.aspx?direct=true&AuthType=ip,url,cookie,uid&db=a9h&AN=31987878&site=ehost-live

Schoenthaler, S. (2000). *Intelligence, academic performance and brain function.* California: California State University Press.

Schweingruber, D. & Wohlstein, R.T. (2005). The madding crowd goes to school: Myths about crowds in introductory sociology textbooks. *Teaching Sociology, 33*, 136–153.

Scientology. (2008). *Scientology—Church of Scientology official site.* Retrieved 12/02/2008, from http://www.scientology.org/religion/presentation/pg006.html

Scoblic, J.P. (2008). Nuclear spring. *The New Republic, 238*(7), 18–20.

Scott, E.C. & Branch, G. (2002). *"Intelligent design" not accepted by most scientists.* Retrieved 13/03/2008, from http://www.ncseweb.org/resources/articles/996_intelligent_design_not_accep_9_10_2002.asp

Scott, P. (n.d.). *A study of E-meter frequency response.* Retrieved 12/02/2008, from http://www.cs.cmu.edu/~dst/Secrets/E-Meter/freq_resp.html

Scott, R.H., III. (2007). Credit card use and abuse: A Veblenian analysis. *Journal of Economic Issues, 41*(2), 567. Retrieved from http://proquest.umi.com/pqdweb?did=1284859851&Fmt=7&clientId=65345&RQT=309&VName=PQD

Scott-Joynt, J. (2005). *What Myspace means to Murdoch.* Retrieved 10/05/2008, from http://news.bbc.co.uk/2/hi/business/4697671.stm

Segal, A.F. (2002). The Jewish tradition. W.G. Oxtoby (Ed.), (2nd ed., pp. 33–157). Don Mills, ON: Oxford University Press.

Segall, A. & Chappell, N. (2000). *Health and health care in Canada.* Toronto, ON: Prentice-Hall, Inc.

Seidman, S. (1998). Empire and knowledge: More troubles, new opportunities for sociology. In D. Clawson (Ed.), *Required reading: Sociology's most influential books* (pp. 167–172). Amherst: University of Massachusetts Press.

Seidman, S. (2008). *Contested knowledge: Social theory today* (4th ed.). Oxford: Blackwell.

Selfe, P. & Starbuck, M. (1998). *Religion.* London, UK: Hodder & Stoughton.

Sen, A. (2003). Missing women—revisited. *British Medical Journal, 327*, 1297–1298.

Service, E. (1962). *Primitive social organization: An evolutionary perspective.* New York: Random House.

Service Canada. (2008). *Occupations.* Retrieved 27/03/2008, from http://www.jobsetc.ca/category_drilldown.jsp?lang=en& category_id=125

Shaffer, L.S. (2005a). Beyond the looking glass self: Cooley's social self and its treatment in introductory textbooks. *Journal of Clinical Psychology, 61*(1), 47–65.

Shaffer, L.S. (2005b). From mirror self-recognition to the looking-glass self: Exploring the justification hypothesis. *Journal of Clinical Psychology, 61*(1), 47–65.

Shah, A. (2008). *World military spending—global issues.* Retrieved 10/11/2007, from http://www.globalissues.org/Geopolitics/ArmsTrade/Spending.asp

Shalla, V. (2004). Time warped: The flexibilization and maximization of flight attendant working time*. *The Canadian Review of Sociology and Anthropology, 41*(3), 345. Retrieved from http://proquest.umi.com/pqdweb?did=724484591&Fmt=7&clientId=65345&RQT=309&VName=PQD

Shanklin, E. (1994). *Anthropology and race.* Belmont, CA: Wadsworth.

Shanklin, E. (2000). Representations of race and racism in American anthropology. *Current Anthropology, 41*(1), 99–103.

Sharkey, P. (2007). Survival and death in New Orleans: An empirical look at the human impact of Katrina. *Journal of Black Studies, 37*(4), 482–501.

Sharma, N. (2005). Anti-trafficking rhetoric and the making of a global apartheid. *NWSA Journal, 17*(3), 88–111.

Shaw, D.J. (2002). *Canada's productivity and standard of living: Past, present and future* (No. PRB 02-23E). Ottawa: Parliamentary Research Branch.

Shecter, B. (2008). *Canwest jumps at universal TV shows.* Retrieved 14/05/2008, from http://www.nationalpost.com/related/topics/story.html?id=498627

Sheff, E. (2005). Polyamorous women, subjectivity, and power. *Journal of Contemporary Ethnography, 34*(3), 253–283.

Sheppard, R. (2006). *CBC news indepth: The 39th parliament—Harper at the helm.* Retrieved 28/01/2008, from http://www.cbc.ca/news/background/parliament39/quebecnation-history.html

Shields, J.A. (2007). Between passion and deliberation: The Christian right and democratic ideals. *Political Science Quarterly, 122*(1), 89–113. Retrieved from http://library.mtroyal.ca:2048/login?url=http://search.ebscohost.com/login.

aspx?direct=true&AuthType=ip,url,cookie,uid&db=a9h&AN=24632322&site=ehost-live

Shiva, V. (2000). *Tomorrow's biodiversity*. London, UK: Thames & Hudson.

Shiva, V. (2007). Comparative perspectives symposium: Bioprospecting/Biopiracy: Bioprospecting as sophisticated biopiracy. *Signs: Journal of Women in Culture & Society, 32*(2), 307–313. Retrieved from http://library.mtroyal.ca:2048/login?url=http://search.ebscohost.com/login.aspx?direct=true&AuthType=ip,url,cookie,uid&db=a9h&AN=23730417&site=ehost-live

Shpungin E., & Lyubansky, M. (2006). Navigating social class roles in community research. *American Journal of Community Psychology, 37*(3–4), 227–235. Retrieved from http://library.mtroyal.ca:2083/pqdweb?did=1082825441&Fmt=7&clientId=65345&RQT=309&VName=PQD

Siegal, L., & McCormick, C. (2006). *Criminology in Canada: Theories, patterns, and typologies* (3rd ed.). Toronto: Thomson Nelson.

The Sierra Club. (2008). *Tar sands industry poised to pollute Canada's largest freshwater aquifer*. Retrieved 8/9/2008, from http://www.tarsandstimeout.ca/index.php?option=com_content&task=view&id=70&Itemid=1

Sifry, D. (2007). *Sifry's alerts: The state of the live web, April 2007*. Retrieved 08/05/2008, from http://www.sifry.com/alerts/archives/000493.html

Sikhism.com. (2007). *Sikhism introduction*. Retrieved 10/03/2008, from http://www.sikhism.com/

Silversides, A. (2008). Ontario's hospitals surpass those of Quebec in C. difficile rates. *Canadian Medical Association Journal, 178*(13), 1649.

Simard, G. (2002). *The logging industry*. Retrieved 4/2/2008, from http://www.statcan.ca/english/research/25F0002MIE/25F0002MIE1999001.htm

Simmerling, M. & Schwegler, B. (2005). Beginning anew: Same principles, different direction for research ethics. *The American Journal of Bioethics, 5*(1), 44–46.

Simpson, G.E. & Yinger, M.J. (1985). *Racial and cultural minorities* (5th ed.). New York: Plenum.

Simpson, I.H., Stark, D., & Jackson, R.A. (1988). Class identification processes of married, working men and women. *American Sociological Review, 53*(2), 284–293.

Simpson, M. (2006). A paradox of sovereignty in Rousseau's social contract. *Journal of Moral Philosophy, 3*(1), 45–56.

Sinclair, S. (2003). The WTO and its GATS. In J. Michie (Ed.), *The handbook of globalization* (pp. 347–357). Cheltenham, UK: Edward Elgar Publishing.

Skelton, C. (1997). Women and education. In D. Richardson, & V. Robinson (Eds.), *Introducing women's studies: Feminist theory and practice* (2nd ed.). London: Palgrave MacMillan.

Skinner, D. (2000). McLuhan's world—and ours. *The Public Interest,* (138), 52. Retrieved from

http://proquest.umi.com/pqdweb?did=47771691&Fmt=7&clientId=65345&RQT=309&VName=PQD

Slattery, M. (2003). *Key ideas in sociology*. Cheltenham, UK: Nelson Thornes, Ltd.

Smart, C. (1989). *Feminism and the power of the law*. London: Routledge.

Smedley, A. (2007). *Race in North America: Origin and evolution of a worldview* (3rd ed.). Boulder, CO: Westview Press.

Smelser, N.J. (1963). *Theory of collective behavior*. Glencoe, IL: Free Press.

Smith, C. (Ed.). (2003). *The secular religion: Power, interests and conflict in the secularization of American public life*. Berkeley, CA: University of California Press.

Smith, C. (2007). *Is Premier Gordon Campbell's conversation on health part of a hidden agenda to introduce private health insurance?* Retrieved 30/06/2008, from http://www.straight.com/article-68136/gordon-campbell-s-conversation-on-health-one-sided

Smith, D. (1987). *The everyday world as problematic: A feminist sociology*. Boston: Northeastern University Press.

Smith, D. (1990a). *The conceptual practices of power*. Toronto: University of Toronto Press.

Smith, D. (1990b). *Texts, facts, and femininity: Exploring the relations of ruling*. London: Routledge.

Smith, D. (2000a). Comment on Hekmna's 'truth and method: Feminist standpoint theory revisited'. In C. Allen & J. Howard (Eds.), *Provoking feminisms* (pp. 59–65). Chicago: The University of Chicago Press.

Smith, D. (2000b). Sociology from women's experience: A reaffirmation. In P. Kivisto (Ed.), *Social theory: Roots and branches* (pp. 339–349). Los Angeles: Roxbury.

Smith, D. (2004). Despoiling professional autonomy: A woman's perspective. In M. Reimer (Ed.), *Inside corporate U: Women in the academy speak out* (pp. 31–42). Toronto: Sumach Press.

Smith, D. (1987). *Everyday world as problematic: A feminist sociology*. Boston, MA: Northeastern University Press.

Smith, D. (1992). Whistling women: Reflections on rage and rationality. In W. Carroll, L. Christainsen-Ruffman, R. Currie, & D. Harrison (Eds.), *Fragile truths: Twenty-five years of sociology and anthropology in Canada* (pp. 207–226). Ottawa: Carleton University Press.

Smith, D. (1999). *Writing the social: Critique, theory and investigations*. Toronto: University of Toronto Press.

Smith, D. (2004). Despoiling professional autonomy: A women's perspective. In M. Reimer (Ed.), *Inside corporate U: Women in the academy speak out* (pp. 31–42). Toronto: Sumach Press.

Smith, M. (1988). Women's fear of violent crime: An exploratory test of a feminist hypothesis. *Journal of Family Violence, 3*(1), 29–38.

Smith, M. (1993). *The Rodriguez case: A review of the Supreme Court of Canada decision on assisted suicide (BP349e)*. Retrieved 26/06/2008, from

http://dsp-psd.tpsgc.gc.ca/Collection-R/LoPBdP/BP/bp349-e.htm

Smith, M. (1998). Social movements and equality seeking: The case of gay liberation in Canada. *Canadian Journal of Political Science, 31*(2), 285–309.

Smith, P., & Alexander, J.C. (1996). Review essay: Durkheim's religious revival. *American Journal of Sociology, 102*(2), 585.

Smithsonian Institute. (2006). *Human ancestors hall: Homo sapiens*. Retrieved 26/09/2007, from http://www.mnh.si.edu/anthro/humanorigins/ha/sap.htm

Smolej, M. & Kivivuori, J. (2006). The relation between crime news and fear of violence. *Journal of Scandinavian Studies in Criminology & Crime Prevention, 7*(2), 211–227. doi:10.1080/14043850601002429

Snider, L.C. (2007). *The end of poverty by Jeffrey D Sachs (book review)*. Retrieved 15/06/2008, from http://www.cumminghome.com/business/economy/book-review-the-end-of-poverty-by-jeffrey-d-sachs.shtml

Snipp, C.M. & Hirschman, C. (2004). Assimilation in American society: Occupational achievement and earnings for ethnic minorities in the United States, 1970 to 1990. *Research in Social Stratification and Mobility, 22*, 93–117.

Snow, D.A., Soule, S.A., & Cress, D.M. (2005). Identifying the precipitants of homeless protest across 17 US cities, 1980 to 1990. *Social Forces, 83*(3), 1183–1210. Retrieved from http://library.mtroyal.ca:2048/login?url=http://search.ebscohost.com/login.aspx?direct=true&AuthType=ip,url,cookie,uid&db=a9h&AN=16832479&site=ehost-live

A sociological tour through cyberspace: Matters of theory. Retrieved 27/02/2008, from http://www.trinity.edu/mkearl/theory.html

Sociology.org. (2001). *Sociology central: Cultural universals*. Retrieved 05/10/2007, from http://www.sociology.org.uk/p2d2n2.htm

Sodikoff, G. (2004). Land and languor: Ethical imaginations of work and forest in northeast Madagascar. *History & Anthropology, 15*(4), 367–398. Retrieved from http://library.mtroyal.ca:2048/login?url=http://search.ebscohost.com/login.aspx?direct=true&AuthType=ip,url,cookie,uid&db=a9h&AN=15219039&site=ehost-live

Sommerville, C.J. (1998). Secular Society/Religious population: Out tacit rules for using the term "secularization". *Journal for the Scientific Study of Religion, 37*(2), 249.

Soukeroff, W.A. (1959). *The origin of the freedomite movement*. Retrieved 03/10/2007, from http://www.doukhobor.org/Soukeroff.htm

Soules, M. (2007). *Harold Adams Innis: The bias of communications & monopolies of power*. Retrieved 01/06/2008, from http://www.media-studies.ca/articles/innis.htm

Thesoupkitchen.ca. (2005). *The soup kitchen*. Retrieved 19/12/2007, from http://thesoupkitchen.ca/

Sparks, A. (1990). *The mind of South Africa*. New York: Knopf.

Spector, M. & Kitsuse, J. (1977). *Constructing social problems*. Menlo Park, CA: Cummings.

Srivastava, L. (2005). Mobile phones and the evolution of social behaviour. *Behaviour & Information Technology*, 24(2), 111–129. doi:10.1080/01449290512331321910

St. Denis, N. (2007). *Foreign aid strategies*. Retrieved 14/07/2008, from http://www.ffwd-weekly.com/article/news-views/international/foreign-aid-strategies/

St. Stephen's Community House. (2004). *Kensington alive*. Retrieved 9/29/2007, from http://www.ststephenshouse.com/kensingtonalive/index1.html

Stack, C.B. (1975). *All our kin: Strategies for survival in a black community*. New York: Harper & Row.

Staggenborg, S. (1991). *The pro-choice movement: Organization and activism in the abortion conflict*. New York: Oxford University Press. Retrieved from http://library.mtroyal.ca:2048/login?url=http://library.mtroyal.ca:3254/lib/mtroyalac/Doc?id=10087219

Staggenborg, S. (1998). *Gender, family, and social movements*. Thousands Oaks, CA: Sage Publications, Inc.

Staggenborg, S. (2005). *Feminism in the university*. Unpublished manuscript.

Staggenborg, S. (2008). *Social movements* Oxford University Press.

Staggenborg, S., & ebrary, I. (1991). *The pro-choice movement*. New York: Oxford University Press. Retrieved from http://library.mtroyal.ca:2048/login?url=http://site.ebrary.com/lib/mtroyalac/Doc?id=10087219

Stakelbeck, F.W. (2006). *Beijing's 'separate but unequal' tax dilemma*. Retrieved 05/09/2008, from http://www.atimes.com/atimes/China_Business/HC28Cb05.html

Stampf, O. (2007). *Global warming: Not the end of the world as we know it*. Retrieved 23/07/2008, from http://www.spiegel.de/international/germany/0,1518,481684,00.html

Stanko, E. (1997). Safety talk: Conceptualizing women's risk assessment as a technology of the soul. *Theoretical Criminology*, 1(4), 479–499.

Stark, R. & Bainbridge, W.S. (1985). *The future of religion: Secularization, revival and cult formation*. Berkeley, CA: University of California Press.

Stark, R. & Bainbridge, W.S. (1996). *Religion, deviance and social control*. New York: Routledge, Inc.

Stasiulis, D. & Ross, D. (2006). Security, flexible sovereignty, and the perils of multiple citizenship. *Citizenship Studies*, 10(3), 329–348.

Stastna, K. (2006). *The golden age of the silver screen*. Retrieved 03/05/2008, from http://www.Canada.com/montrealgazette/news/montreal/story.html?id=22268330-0af4-4443-bf95-fd0883f81775&k=47902

Statham, A. (2000). Environmental awareness and feminist progress. *NWSA Journal*, 12(2), 89. Retrieved from http://library.mtroyal.ca:2083/pqdweb?did=58675096&Fmt=7&clientId=65345&RQT=309&VName=PQD

Statistics Canada. (n.d.). *About us*.

Statistics Canada. (n.d.). *Religions in Canada*.

Statistics Canada. (2001a). *Aboriginal peoples of Canada: A demographic profile*. Retrieved 12/20/2007, from http://www12.statcan.ca/english/census01/Products/Analytic/companion/abor/Canada.cfm

Statistics Canada. (2001b). *Hate crime in Canada: An overview of issues and data sources* (Government Catalogue No. 85-551; Spring 2004). Ottawa: Statistics Canada.

Statistics Canada. (2001c). *Number and average employment income*. Retrieved 03/31, from http://www12.statcan.ca/english/census01/products/standard/themes/RetrieveProductTable.cfm?Temporal=2001&PID=57106&APATH=3&GID=355313&METH=1&PTYPE=55496&THEME=53&FOCUS=0&AID=0&PLACENAME=0&PROVINCE=0&SEARCH=0&GC=0&GK=0&VID=0&VNAMEE=&VNAMEF=&FL=0&RL=0&FREE=0

Statistics Canada. (2003a). *Canadian community health survey: Mental health and well-being*. Retrieved 27/06/2008, from http://www.statcan.ca/Daily/English/030903/d030903a.htm

Statistics Canada. (2003b). *Canadian crime statistics: 2002*. Catalogue No.85-205-XIE.

Statistics Canada. (2003c). *Earnings of Canadians: Making a living in a new economy*. Retrieved from http://www12.statscan.ca/English.census01/Products/Analytic/companion/ear/contents.Cfm

Statistics Canada. (2003d). *Ethnic diversity study: Portrait of a multicultural society*. Catalogue no. 89-593-XIE.

Statistics Canada. (2003e). Update on families. *Canadian Social Trends*, 69, 11-13.

Statistics Canada. (2004a). *Blacks in Canada: A long history by Anne Milan & Kelly Tran*. Catalogue no. 11-008. Retrieved from http://www.statcan.ca/english/freepub/11-008-XIE/2003004/articles/6802.pdf

Statistics Canada. (2004b). *Canadian community health survey*. Retrieved 27/06/2008, from http://www.statcan.ca/Daily/English/040615/d040615b.htm

Statistics Canada. (2004c). *The economy: Farming in Canada*. Retrieved 04/02/2008, from http://www43.statcan.ca/03/03b/03b_002_e.htm

Statistics Canada. (2004d). *Profile of disability in 2001 (Canadian social trends)* Catalogue No. 11-008. Ottawa, ON: Statistics Canada. Retrieved from http://www.statcan.ca/english/freepub/11-008-XIE/2003004/articles/6804.pdf

Statistics Canada. (2004e). *The sandwich generation*. Retrieved 04/02/2008, from http://www.statcan.gc.ca/daily-quotidien/040928/dq040928b-eng.htm

Statistics Canada. (2005a). *Canadian community health survey: Obesity among children and adults*. Retrieved 28/06/2008, from http://www.statcan.ca/Daily/English/050706/d050706a.htm

Statistics Canada. (2005b). *Diverging trends in unionization. The Daily, April 22*. Retrieved 28/03/2008, from http://www.statcan.ca/Daily/English/050422/d050422c.htm

Statistics Canada. (2005c). *Human activity and the environment: Solid waste*. Retrieved 24/07/2008, from http://www.statcan.ca/Daily/English/051202/d051202b.htm

Statistics Canada. (2005d). *Life expectancy at birth, by sex, by province*. Retrieved 23/7/2009, from http://www40.statcan.gc.ca/l01/cst01/health26-eng.htm?sdi=sex

Statistics Canada. (2005e). *National population health survey: Healthy aging*. Retrieved 21/1/2009, from http://www.statcan.gc.ca/daily-quotidien/050509/dq050509a-eng.htm

Statistics Canada. (2005f). *Report of the pan-Canadian education initiators program 2005—highlights*. Ottawa: Statistics Canada. Retrieved from http://www.statcan.ca/english/freepub/81-582-XIE/2006001/highlights.htm#D

Statistics Canada. (2005g). *Use of alternative health care*. Retrieved 30/06/2008, from http://www.statcan.ca/Daily/English/050315/d050315b.htm

Statistics Canada. (2006a). *2006 community profiles*. Retrieved 11/06/2007, from http://www12.statcan.ca/english/census06/data/profiles/community/Details/Page.cfm?Lang=E&Geo1=CMA&Code1=421__&Geo2=PR&Code2=24&Data=Count&SearchText=Quebec&SearchType=Begins&SearchPR=24&B1=All&Custom

Statistics Canada. (2006b). *Access to health care services*. Retrieved 30/08/2008, from http://www.statcan.ca/Daily/English/060711/d060711c.htm

Statistics Canada. (2006c). *Canada's population by age and sex. The Daily, October 26*. Retrieved 13/11/2007, from http://www.statcan.ca/Daily/English/061026/d061026b.htm

Statistics Canada. (2006d). *Canadian Internet use survey. The Daily, August 15*. Retrieved 09/11/2007, from http://library.mtroyal.ca:2069/Daily/English/060815/d060815b.htm

Statistics Canada. (2006e). *Divorces by province and territory*.

Statistics Canada. (2006f). *Education and earnings*. Retrieved 21/1/2009, from http://www.statcan.gc.ca/daily-quotidien/060623/dq060623b-eng.htm

Statistics Canada. (2006g). *Education matters: Insights on education, learning and training in Canada*. Retrieved 10/12/2007, from http://www.statcan.ca/english/freepub/81-004-XIE/2006003/backto.htm#p

Statistics Canada. (2006h). *Education matters: Profile of Canada's school principals. The Daily, June 26*. Retrieved 10/12/2008, from http://www.statcan.gc.ca/daily-quotidien/060626/dq060626a-eng.htm

Statistics Canada. (2006i). *Family income and the well-being of children. The Daily, May 11*. Retrieved 06/06/2007, from http://www.statcan.ca/Daily/English/060511/d060511c.htm

Statistics Canada. (2006j). *Inequality in wealth. The Daily, December 13*. Retrieved 06/12/2007, from http://www.statcan.ca/Daily/English/061213/d061213c.htm

Statistics Canada. (2006k). *Television viewing. The Daily, March 31.* Retrieved 07/05/2008, from http://www.statcan.ca/Daily/English/060331/d060331b.htm

Statistics Canada. (2006l). *Television viewing, by age and sex, by province.* Retrieved 09/11/2007, from http://www40.statcan.ca/l01/cst01/arts23.htm

Statistics Canada. (2006m). *University enrolment. The Daily, November 7.* Retrieved 28/05/2007, from http://library.mtroyal.ca:2069/Daily/English/061107/d061107a.htm

Statistics Canada. (2006n). *Women in Canada. The Daily, March 7.* Retrieved 15/12/2008, from http://www.statcan.gc.ca/daily-quotidien/060307/dq060307a-eng.htm

Statistics Canada. (2006o). *Women in Canada: A gender-based statistical report.* Catalogue no. 89-503-XPE. Ottawa: Minister of Industry. Retrieved from http://www.statcan.ca/freepub/89-503-XIE/0010589-503-XIE.pdf

Statistics Canada. (2007a). *Education indicators. The Daily, December 12.* Retrieved 10/12/2008, from http://www.statcan.gc.ca/daily-quotidien/071212/dq071212d-eng.htm

Statistics Canada. (2007b). *The evolving linguistic portrait, 2006 Census: The proportion of francophones and of French continue to decline.* Retrieved 28/01/2008, from http://www12.statcan.ca/english/census06/analysis/language/continue_decline.cfm

Statistics Canada. (2007c). *Family portrait: Continuity and change in Canadian families and households in 2006.* Retrieved 10/11/2007, from http://www12.statcan.ca/english/census06/analysis/famhouse/ind1.cfm

Statistics Canada. (2007d). *Family violence in Canada: A statistical profile 2007.* Catalogue No. 85-224 XIE. Ottawa, ON: Minister of Industry.

Statistics Canada. (2007e). *High-income Canadians. The Daily, September 24.* Retrieved 07/12/2007, from http://www.statcan.ca/Daily/English/070924/d070924a.htm

Statistics Canada. (2007f). *Immigration in Canada: A portrait of the foreign-born population, 2006 Census.* Retrieved 26/01/2008, from http://www12.statcan.ca/english/census06/analysis/immcit/highlights.cfm

Statistics Canada. (2007g). *Income of Canadians. The Daily, May 3, 2007.* Retrieved 09/12/2007, from http://www.statcan.ca/Daily/English/070503/d070503a.htm

Statistics Canada. (2007h). *Labour force survey.* Retrieved 29/03/2008, from http://www.statcan.ca/Daily/English/070706/d070706a.htm

Statistics Canada. (2007i). *Lower income and declines in self-rated health.* Retrieved 29/06/2008, from http://www.statcan.ca/Daily/English/070605/d070605a.htm

Statistics Canada. (2007j). *Participation and activity limitation survey.* Retrieved 27/06/2008, from http://www.statcan.ca/Daily/English/071203/d071203a.htm

Statistics Canada. (2007k). *Physically active Canadians.* Retrieved 21/1/2009, from http://www.statcan.gc.ca/daily-quotidien/070822/dq070822b-eng.htm

Statistics Canada. (2007l). *Population by mother tongue and age groups, 2006 counts, for Canada, provinces and territories: 20% sample data.* Retrieved 25/04/2008, from http://www12.statcan.ca/english/census06/data/highlights/language/Table401.cfm?Lang=E&T=401&GH=4&SC=1&S=99&O=A

Statistics Canada. (2007m). *A portrait of seniors. The Daily, February 27.* Retrieved 16/06/2008, from http://www.statcan.ca/Daily/English/070227/d070227b.htm

Statistics Canada. (2007n). *A portrait of seniors in Canada.* Retrieved 13/11/2007, from http://library.mtroyal.ca:2069/english/freepub/89-519-XIE/2006001/demographic.htm

Statistics Canada. (2007o). *Radio listening. The Daily, June 26.* Retrieved 06/05/2008, from http://www.statcan.ca/Daily/English/070626/d070626b.htm

Statistics Canada. (2007p). *Registered Retirement Savings Plan contributions.* Retrieved 24/06/2008, from http://www.statcan.ca/Daily/English/071108/d071108d.htm

Statistics Canada. (2007q). *Seniors as victims of crime.* Retrieved 26/06/2008, from http://www.statcan.ca/Daily/English/070306/d070306b.htm

Statistics Canada. (2008a). *2006 Census: Labour market activities, industry, occupation, education, language of work, place of work and mode of transportation.* Retrieved 01/07/2008, from http://library.mtroyal.ca:2069/Daily/English/080304/d080304a.htm

Statistics Canada. (2008b). *Aboriginal peoples in Canada in 2006: Inuit, Métis and First Nations, 2006 Census. The Daily, January 15.* Retrieved 23/01/2008, from http://www.statcan.ca/Daily/English/080115/d080115a.htm

Statistics Canada. (2008c). *Canada at a glance 2008—households.* Retrieved 07/05/2008, from http://www45.statcan.gc.ca/2008/cgco_2008_006-eng.htm

Statistics Canada. (2008d). *Canadian community health survey.* Retrieved 28/06/2008, from http://www.statcan.ca/Daily/English/080618/d080618a.htm

Statistics Canada. (2008e). *Canadian Internet use survey.* Retrieved 19/06/2008, from http://www.statcan.ca/Daily/English/080612/d080612b.htm

Statistics Canada. (2008f). *Composting organic waste.* Retrieved 24/07/2008, from http://www.statcan.ca/Daily/English/080327/d080327c.htm

Statistics Canada. (2008g). *Earnings and incomes of Canadians over the past quarter century, 2006 Census: Incomes of families.* Retrieved 24/06/2008, from http://www12.statcan.ca/english/census06/analysis/income/eicopqc30.cfm

Statistics Canada. (2008h). *Educational portrait of Canada, 2006 Census: National picture.* Retrieved 25/06/2008, from http://www12.statcan.ca/english/census06/analysis/education/historical.cfm

Statistics Canada. (2008i). *Electronic commerce and technology. The Daily, April 24.* Retrieved 5/1/2009, from http://www.statcan.gc.ca/daily-quotidien/080424/dq080424a-eng.htm

Statistics Canada. (2008j). *Employment by industry.* Retrieved 27/03/2008, from http://www40.statcan.ca/l01/cst01/econ40.htm

Statistics Canada. (2008k). *Female offenders, 2005. The Daily, January 24.* Retrieved http://www.statcan.ca/Daily/English/080124/d080124a.htm

Statistics Canada. (2008l). *Internet use and social and civic participation. The Daily, December 4.* Retrieved 8/1/2009, from http://www.statcan.gc.ca/internetuse.daily-quotidien/071105/dq071105a-eng.htm

Statistics Canada. (2008m). *Labour force and participation rates by sex and age group, 2003–2007,* Statistics Canada.

Statistics Canada. (2008n). *Latest release from the labour force survey.* Retrieved 29/03/2008, from http://www.statcan.ca/english/Subjects/Labour/LFS/lfs-en.htm

Statistics Canada. (2008o). *Low income cut-offs for 2007 and low income measures for 2006.* Ottawa: Minister of Industry.

Statistics Canada. (2008p). *Participation and activity limitation survey 2006: A profile of assistive technology for people with disabilities.* Retrieved 27/06/2008, from http://www.statcan.ca/english/freepub/89-628-XIE/89-628-XIE2008005.htm

Statistics Canada. (2008q). *Preliminary results of the pension satellite account, 1990 to 2007.* Retrieved 25/06/2008, from http://www.statcan.ca/english/freepub/13-605-XIE/13-605-XIE2008002.htm

Statistics Canada. (2008r). *Selected dwelling characteristics and household equipment.* Retrieved 09/11/2007, from http://library.mtroyal.ca:2567/l01/cst01/famil09c.htm

Statistics Canada. (2008s). *University enrolment.* Retrieved 10/12/2008, from http://www40.statcan.gc.ca/l01/cst01/edu54a_eng.htm

Steele, T.L. (2005). "Doing it": The social construction of S-E-X. In T.L. Steele (Ed.), *Sex, self and society: The social context of sexuality.* California: Wadsworth.

Steffen, W., Crutzen, P.J., & McNeill, J.R. (2007). The anthropocene: Are humans now overwhelming the great forces of nature? *AMBIO—A Journal of the Human Environment, 36*(8), 614–621. Retrieved from http://library.mtroyal.ca:2048/login?url=http://search.ebscohost.com/login.aspx?direct=true&AuthType=ip,url,cookie,uid&db=a9h&AN=28601278&site=ehost-live

Steger, M.B. (2002). *Globalism: The new market ideology.* Lanham, MD: Rowman and Littlefield Publishers, Inc.

Stephens, P. (1998). *Think sociologically.* Cheltenham, UK: Nelson Thornes Ltd.

Stephens, W. (1963). *The family in cross-cultural perspective.* New York: Holt Rinehart & Winston.

Stevenson, B. & Wolfers, J. (2008). *Economic growth and subjective well-being: Reassessing the easterlin paradox.* Retrieved 23/4/2008, from http://bpp.wharton.upenn.edu/jwolfers/Papers/EasterlinParadox.pdf

Stiglitz, J. (2003). *Globalization and its discontent*. New York: W.W. Norton.

Stoddart, M.C. (2008). *Anthropocentrism and environmental sociology: Re-evaluating the HEP-NEP dichotomy*. Retrieved 18/7/2008, from http://www.allacademic.com/meta/p93848_index.html

Stoett, P. (2006). *Canada, Kyoto, and the Conservatives: Thinking/moving ahead*. Retrieved 06/09/2008, from http://www.wilsoncenter.org/events/docs/paperstoett1.pdf

Stoody, C. (2006). *CBC news indepth: Softwood lumber dispute*. Retrieved 04/03, from http://www.cbc.ca/news/background/softwood_lumber/

Stott, C. & Pearson, G. (2006). Football banning orders, proportionality, and public order policing. *Howard Journal of Criminal Justice, 45*(3), 241–254. doi:10.1111/j.1468-2311.2006.00419.x

Streeten, P.P. (1995). *Thinking about development*. Cambridge, UK: Cambridge University Press.

Strinati, D. (1993). The big nothing? Contemporary culture and the emergence of postmodernism. *Innovation in Social Sciences Research, 6*(3), 359–374. Retrieved from http://library.mtroyal.ca:2048/login?url=http://search.ebscohost.com/login.aspx?direct=true&AuthType=ip,url,cookie,uid&db=a9h&AN=9707202883&site=ehost-live

Strinati, D. (2004). *An introduction to the theories of popular culture* (2nd ed.). London, UK: Routledge.

Strohschein, L.A. (2007). Prevalence of methylphenidate use among Canadian children following parental divorce. *Canadian Medical Association Journal, 176*(12), 1711–1714.

Struthers, J. (2007). *Great depression*. Retrieved 19/12/2007, from http://www.theCanadianencyclopedia.com/index.cfm?PgNm=TCE&Params=A1ARTA0003425

Stubblefield, A. (2007). *"Beyond the pale": Tainted whiteness, cognitive disability, and eugenic sterilization*. Indiana University Press. Retrieved from http://library.mtroyal.ca:2048/login?url=http://search.ebscohost.com/login.aspx?direct=true&AuthType=ip,url,cookie,uid&db=a9h&AN=24127104&site=ehost-live

Sukidi. (2006). Max Weber's remarks on Islam: The Protestant ethic among Muslim puritans. *Islam & Christian-Muslim Relations, 17* (April)(2), 195–205.

Sullivan, P. (2008). *CMA pegs air pollution's annual national toll at 21,000 deaths—and growing*. Retrieved 24/08/2008, from http://www.cma.ca/index.cfm/ci_id/10042903/la_id/1.htm

Sullum, J. (2007). Thank Deng Xiaoping for little girls. *Reason, 39*(7), 40–48.

Sumner, W.G. (1906/1960). *Folkways*. New York: New American Library.

Surridge, G. (2008). *Doubts on Thomson*. Retrieved 14/05/2008, from http://www.financialpost.com/story.html?id=477503

Suter, E., Daas, K., & Mason Bergen, K. (2008). Negotiating lesbian family identity via symbols and rituals. *Journal of Family Issues, 22*(1), 26–47.

Sutherland, E. (1940). White collar criminality. *American Sociological Review, 5*: 1–12.

Sutherland, E. (1947). *Principles of criminology* (2nd ed.). Philadelphia: J.B. Lippincott.

Sutherland, E., & Cressey, D. (1960). *Principles of criminology* (6th ed.). Philadelphia: J.B. Lippincott.

Sutherland, E., Cressey, D., & Luckenbill, D. (1992). *Principle of criminology* (11th ed.). Philadelphia: J.B. Lippincott.

Sutton, P.W. (2007). *The environment: A sociological introduction*. Cambridge, UK: Polity Press.

Swami, V., Antonakopoulos, N., Tovée, M.J., & Furnham, A. (2006). A critical test of the waist-to-hip ratio hypothesis of women's physical attractiveness in Britain and Greece. *Sex Roles, 54*(3), 201–211.

Swartz, J. & Hopkins, J. (2007). Could cell text alert have helped at Va. tech? *USA Today (April 18, 2007)*, Retrieved from http://library.mtroyal.ca:2048/login?url=http://library.mtroyal.ca:2924/login.aspx?direct=true&AuthType=ip,url,cookie,uid&db=a9h&AN=J0E299332230407&site=ehost-live

Swatos, W.H. (1973). *Encyclopedia of religion and society*. Walnut Creek, CA: Altamira Press.

Swenson, D. (1999). *Society, spirituality, and the sacred*. Peterborough, ON: Broadview Press.

Swenson, D. (2008). *Society, spirituality, and the sacred* (2nd ed.). Peterborough, ON: Broadview Press.

Swift, K. & Birmingham, M. (2000). Location, location, location: Restructuring and the everyday lives of "welfare moms". In S. Neysmith (Ed.), *Restructuring caring labour: Discourse, state practice and everyday life* (pp. 93–115). Toronto: Oxford University Press.

Swift, R. (1991). Among the believers. *Utne Reader, 45 (May/June)*, 99–104.

Symes v. Canada. (1993). 4. S.C.R. 695. http://www.hrcr.org/safrica/equality/symes_Canada.html

Syncrude. (2006). *Air quality*. Retrieved 8/9/2008, from http://sustainability.syncrude.ca/sustainability2006/environmental/air.html

Syncrude. (2008). *Syncrude responds to oil sands protest*. Retrieved 8/9/2008, from http://www.syncrude.ca/users/news_view.asp?FolderID=5690&NewsID=127

Tait, S. (2007). Television and the domestication of cosmetic surgery. *Feminist Media Studies, 7*(2), 119–135.

Tanenbaum, L. (2005). Slut! Growing up female with a bad reputation. In T.L. Steele (Ed.), *Sex, self and society: The social context of sexuality*. California: Wadsworth.

Tanner, J. (Ed.). (2003). *Sociology of art: A reader*. New York: Routledge.

Tartaro, C. & Lester, D. (2005). An application of Durkheim's theory of suicide to prison suicide rates in the United States. *Death Studies, 29*(5), 413–422.

Tarter, A. (2006). *American culture from a global perspective* American Library Association.

Tator, C. & Henry, F. (2006). *Racial profiling in Canada: Challenging the myth of 'a few bad apples'*. Toronto, ON: University of Toronto Press.

Tauli-Corpuz, V. (2007). Is biopiracy an issue for feminists in the Philippines? *Signs: Journal of Women in Culture & Society, 32*(2), 332–337. Retrieved from http://library.mtroyal.ca:2048/login?url=http://search.ebscohost.com/login.aspx?direct=true&AuthType=ip,url,cookie,uid&db=a9h&AN=23730420&site=ehost-live

Taylor, D. & Offner, C. (1975). In Anderson N. (Ed.), *The world's religions*. Grand Rapids: InterVarsity.

Taylor, J. & Clifton, R.A. (2005). Types of employment. In L.W. Roberts (Ed.), *Recent social trends in Canada 1960–2000* (pp. 189–203). Montreal, Quebec: McGill-Queens University Press.

Taylor, V.A., Rupp, L.J., & Whittier, N. (2006). *Feminist frontiers* (7th ed.). Boston, MA: McGraw-Hill.

Teaching on YouTube | open culture. Retrieved 29/04/2008, from http://www.oculture.com/2008/04/teaching_on_youtube.html

Terrier, J. (2006). The idea of a Republican tradition: Reflections on the debate concerning the intellectual foundations of the French third Republic1. *Journal of Political Ideologies, 11*(3), 289–308. doi:10.1080/13569310600923865

Thibos, M., Lavin-Loucks, D., & Martin, M. (2007). *The feminization of poverty*. Dallas, TX: The J. Mcdonald Williams Institute. Retrieved from http://www.thewilliamsinstitute.org/Portals/10/Poverty_Disparity/Feminization%20of%20Poverty.pdf

Thomas, W.I. & Thomas, D.S. (1928). *The child in America*. New York: Knopf.

Thompson Jr., E.H. (2006). Images of old men's masculinity: Still a man? *Sex Roles, 55*(9), 633–648.

Thompson, J., Baird, P., & Downie, J. (2005). The Olivieri case: Context and significance. *Ecclectica, December*. Retrieved from http://www.ecclectica.ca/issues/2005/3/index.asp?Article=2

Thompson, L. & Cupples, J. (2008). Seen and not heard? Text messaging and digital sociality. *Social & Cultural Geography, 9*(1), 95–108. doi:10.1080/14649360701789634

Thomson Corporation. (2000). *Into the new millenium: The story of the Thomson corporation*. Retrieved 18/12/2007, from http://www.thomson.com/pdf/corporate/millennia.pdf

Thorne, B. (1982). *Feminist rethinking of the family: An overview*. New York: Longman.

Thurow, L.C. (1987). A surge in inequality. *Scientific American, 265*(5), 30–37.

Tibbetts, J. (2008). *Students look overseas for cheaper tutors*. Retrieved 17/06/2008, from http://www.Canada.com/calgaryherald/news/story.html?id=a1df434e-9af5-493a-9de4-34b6d33d0e6b

Tieffer, L. (2005). In pursuit of the perfect penis. In T.L. Steele (Ed.), *Sex, self and society: The social context of sexuality*. California: Wadsworth.

Time. (2006). *Numbers*. Retrieved 01/07/2008, from http://www.time.com/time/magazine/article/0,9171,1189340,00.html

Tinker, I. (2000). Alleviating poverty: Investing in women's work. *Journal of the American Planning*

Association, 66(3), 229. Retrieved from http://proquest.umi.com/pqdweb?did=56285847&Fmt=7&clientId=65345&RQT=309&VName=PQD

Tomlinson, J. (2006). Women's work–life balance trajectories in the UK: Reformulating choice and constraint in transitions through part-time work across the life-course. *British Journal of Guidance & Counselling, 34*(3), 365–382.

Tonkiss, F. (2006). *Contemporary economic sociology: Globalization, production, inequality.* London and New York: Routledge.

Tonmyr, L., Jamieson, E., Mery, L. S., & MacMillan, H. (2005). *The relation between childhood adverse experiences and disability due to mental health problems in a community sample of women.*

Torjman, S. (1997, November). *Welfare warfare.* Retrieved 12/12, from www.caledoninst.org/Publications/PDF/welfare.pdf

Toronto District School Board. (2008). *Minutes January 29, 2008.* Unpublished manuscript.

Toronto District School Board. (2009). Oasis Alternative School. Retrieved 11/5/2009, from http://www.tdsb.on.ca/profiles/Brochure/5584.pdf

Toronto Star. (2008, May 27). Japan wants cellphone limits for kids. *Toronto Star.* Retrieved 19/5/2009, from http://www. parentcentral.ca/parent/article/431455

Tourism Saskatchewan. (2004). *Regina Multicultural Council.* Retrieved 9/29/2007, from http://www.regina multiculturalcouncil.ca/

Tran, J. (2007). Sold into slavery. *Christian Century, 124*(24), 22–26.

Travoto, F. (2004). Population and society. In L. Tepperman & J. Curtis (Eds.), *Sociology* (pp. 458–485). Toronto: Oxford University Press.

Tremblay, T. (1999). Internet censorship as 'Cybriety': Freud, McLuhan, and media pleasures. *Mosaic: A Journal for the Interdisciplinary Study of Literature, 32*(1), 167–182.

Trevino, J.A. & Smelser, N.J. (Eds.). (2001). *Talcott Parsons today: His theory and legacy in contemporary sociology* (M. Lanham Trans.). Rowman and Littlefield Publishers, Inc.

Trier, J. (2007). "Cool" engagements with YouTube: Part 1. *Journal of Adolescent & Adult Literacy, 50*(5), 408–412. Retrieved from http://library.mtroyal.ca:2048/login?url=http://search.ebscohost.com/login.aspx?direct=true& AuthType=ip,url,cookie,uid&db=a9h&AN=23913238&site=ehost-live

Trochim, W.M.K. (2006). *Two research fallacies.* Retrieved 14/01/2008, from http://www.socialresearchmethods.net/kb/fallacy.php

Trotter, E.C. & Alderson, K.G. (2007). University students' definitions of having sex, sexual partner, and virginity loss. *The Canadian Journal of Human Sexuality, 16*(1-2), 11–29.

Trounstine, P.J. & Christensen, T. (1982). *Movers and shakers: The study of community power.* New York: St. Martin's Press.

Tuchman, G. (1978). Introduction: The symbolic annihilation of women. In A. Kaplan Daniels & J. Benet (Eds.), *Hearth & home: Images of women in the mass media* (pp. 3–38). New York: Oxford University Press.

Tudiver, N. (1999). *Universities for sale: Resisting corporate control over Canadian higher education.* Toronto: Lorimer.

Tumin, M.M. (1953). Some principles of stratification: A critical analysis. *American Sociological Review, 18,* 387–393.

Turcotte, M. & Schellenberg, G. (2007). *A portrait of seniors in Canada.* Retrieved 24/06/2008, from http://www.statcan.ca/english/freepub/89-519-XIE/89-519-XIE2006001.htm

Turmel, A. (2004). Towards a historical sociology of developmental thinking: The case of generation. *Paedagogica Historica, 40*(4), 419–433.

Turner, B. (1986). *Equality.* London: Tavistock.

Turner, B.S. (1998). *Max Weber: Classic monographs (volume VII: Weber and Islam).* London, UK: Routledge.

Turner, J.H., Beeghley, L., & Powers, C.H. (2006). *The emergence of sociological theory* (5th. ed.). Belmont, CA: Wadsworth.

Turner, L. (2007). Cosmetic surgery: The new face of reality TV. *British Medical Journal, 328*(7449), 1208-none.

Turner, R.H. & Killian, L.M. (1993). *Collective behavior* (4th ed.). Upper Saddle River, New Jersey: Prentice-Hall, Inc.

Turney, L. & Pocknee, C. (2005). Virtual focus groups: New frontiers in research. *International Journal of Qualitative Methods, 4*(2). Retrieved from http://www.ualberta.ca/~ijqm/backissues/4_2/pdf/turney.pdf.

Tylor, E.B. (1883). *Primitive culture: Researches into the development of mythology, philosophy, religion, language, art and custom.* New York: Henry Holt and Company.

US Census Bureau, 2004–2005. *Self-described religious identification of adult population: 1990–2001.* Retrieved 02/12, from http://www.census.gov/prod/2004pubs/04statab/pop.pdf

Uhl-Bien, M. & Pillai, R. (2007). The romance of leadership and the social construction of followership. In B. Shamir, R. Pillai, M.C. Bligh, & M. Uhl-Bien (Eds.), *Follower-centered perspectives on leadership* (pp. 187–210). Greenwich, CN: Information Age Publishing.

Uk Heo & Sung Deuk Hahm. (2007). The political economy of US direct investment in East Asian NICs, 1966–2000. *International Interactions, 33*(2), 119–133. doi:10.1080/03050620701277723

UNAIDS. (2000). *AIDS epidemic update: December 2000.* Geneva: UNAIDS.

United Nations. (1987). *Report of the world commission on environment and development: Our common future* No. A/42/427). Geneva: United Nations.

United Nations. (1999). *Report of the independent inquiry into the actions of the United Nations during the 1994 genocide in Rwanda.*

United Nations. (2003). *World youth report.* Vienna: United Nations.

United Nations. (2006). *The world's women 2005: Progress in statistics,* No. ST/ESA/STAT/SER.K/17. New York: United Nations.

The United Nations Children's Fund (UNICEF). (2005). *The state of the world's children 2006: Excluded and invisible.* New York, NY: The United Nations Children's Fund (UNICEF).

United Nations Framework Convention on Climate Change. (2008a). *Emissions trading,* Retrieved 06/09/2008, from http://unfccc.int/kyoto_protocol/mechanisms/emissions_trading/items/2731.php

United Nations Framework Convention on Climate Change. (2008b). *Status of ratification.* Retrieved 06/09/2008, from http://unfccc.int/kyoto_protocol/status_of_ratification/items/2613.php

United Nations Office on Drugs and Crime (UNODC). (2006). *Trafficking in persons: Global patterns.* United Nations.

United Nations Permanent Forum on Indigenous Issues. (2007). *International day of the world's indigenous people.* Retrieved 1/27/2008, from http://157.150.195.10/esa/socdev/unpfii/en/news_internationalday2006.html

United States Census Bureau. (2006). *Census 2000 ability to speak English by language spoken at home (PHC-T-37).* Retrieved 10/10/2007, from http://www.census.gov/population/www/cen2000/phc-t37.html

United States Department of State. (2007). *Definitions.* Retrieved 13/12/2007, from http://www.state.gov/g/tip/c16507.htm

University of Toronto. (2000). *John Hannigan.* Retrieved 7/31/2008, from http://www.utsc.utoronto.ca/acad/bios/data/hannigan.html

Urban, H.B. (2006). Fair game: Secrecy, security, and the Church of Scientology in cold war America. *Journal of the American Academy of Religion, 74*(2), 356. Retrieved from http://proquest.umi.com/pqdweb?did=1072680751&Fmt=7&clientId=65345&RQT=309&VName=PQD

U-S-History. (n.d.). *Depression-era soup kitchens.* Retrieved 14/07/2008, from http://www.u-s-history.com/pages/h1660.html

US World News. (2007, October).

Vago, S. (2000). *Law and society* (6th ed.). Upper Saddle River: Prentice Hall.

Vago, S. & Nelson, A. (2004). *Law and society* (Canadian ed.). Toronto: Pearson.

Valladão, A.G.A. (2006). Democratic hegemony and American hegemony. *Cambridge Review of International Affairs, 19*(2), 243–260. doi:10.1080/09557570600723712

Valverde, M. (2006). Introduction to the age of light, soap and water. In A. Glasbeek (Ed.), *Moral regulation and governance in Canada: History, context, and critical issues* (pp. 117–142). Toronto: Canadian Scholars Press.

van den Hoonard, Will. (2001). Is research–ethics review a moral panic? *Canadian Review of Sociology and Anthropology, 38*(1), 19–36.

Van Der Veen, Robert J., & Van Parijs, P. (1986). A capitalist road to communism. *Theory & Society, 15*(5), 635–655. Retrieved from http://library.mtroyal.ca:2048/login?url=http://search.ebscohost.com/login.aspx?direct=true&

AuthType=ip, url,cookie,uid&db=a9h&AN=10747579&site=ehost-live

Van Dusen, L. (2006). *Intelligent design decision reflects Dr. Brian Alters' testimony*. Retrieved 13/03/2008, from http://www.Canadian-universities.net/News/Press-Releases/January_4_2006_Intelligent_design_decision_reflects_Dr_Brian_Alte.html

Van Dyke, N., Dixon, M., & Carlon, H. (2007). Manufacturing dissent: Labor revitalization, union summer and student protest. *Social Forces, 86*(1), 193–214. Retrieved from http://library.mtroyal.ca:2048/login?url=http://search.ebscohost.com/login.aspx?direct=true&AuthType=ip,url,cookie,uid&db=a9h&AN=26297700&site=ehost-live

van Hattum, R. (2006). *Waste = food (an inspiring documentary on the cradle to cradle design concept)*. Retrieved 7/27/2008, from http://video.google.nl/videoplay?docid=-3058533428492266222

Van Hoorebeek, M. (2004). Copyright infringement and potential technological prevention measures in UK universities. *Education & the Law, 16*(4), 217–248.

The Vancouver Organizing Committee for the 2010 Olympic and Paralympic Winter Games. (2007). *Vancouver 2010—ilanaaq—Vancouver 2010 Olympic winter games emblem*. Retrieved 9/29/2007, from http://www.vancouver2010.com/en/LookVancouver2010/Vancouver2010OlympicGamesEmblem

Vandegriend, B. (2006). *Why blogs are popular*. Retrieved 08/05/2008, from http://www.basilv.com/psd/blog/2006/why-blogs-are-popular

Varnhagen, C., Gushta, M., Daniels, J., Peters, T., Parmar, N., Law, D., et al. (2005). How informed is online informed consent? *Ethics & Behavior, 15*(1), 37–48.

Vause, J. (2008). *China announces emergency Olympics smog plan*. Retrieved 01/08/2008, from http://www.cnn.com/2008/WORLD/asiapcf/07/31/oly.beijing.pollution/

Veblen, T. (1899[1979]). *The theory of the leisure class*. New York: Penguin.

Veblen, T. (2004 [1919]). *The vested interests and the common man*. Whitefish, MT: Kessinger Publishing.

Veenstra, G. (2006). Neo-Marxist class position and socioeconomic status: Distinct or complementary determinants of health? *Critical Public Health, 16*(2), 111–129.

Vegreville 2007. (n.d.). *Vegreville history of Vegreville*. Retrieved 9/29/2007, from http://www.vegreville.com/main.asp?MainID=55

Venturini, B., Castelli, L., & Tomelleri, S. (2006). Not all jobs are suitable for fat people: Experimental evidence of a link between being fat and "out-of-sight" jobs. *Social Behavior & Personality: An International Journal, 34*(4), 389–398. Retrieved from http://library.mtroyal.ca:2048/login?url=http://library.mtroyal.ca:2924/login.aspx?direct=true&AuthType=ip,url,cookie,uid&db=a9h&AN=21148944&site=ehost-live

Verheyen, R. (2005). *Climate change damage and international law: Prevention duties and state responsibility*. The Netherlands: Koninklijke Brill NV.

Vineburgh, N.T., Ursano, R.J., & Fullerton, C.S. (2005). Workplace preparedness and resiliency: An integrated response to terrorism. In V. Bowie, B.S. Fisher, & C.L. Cooper (Eds.), *Workplace violence: Issues, trends, strategies* (pp. 207–216). Portland, OR: Willan Publishing.

Viruell-Fuentes, E.A. (2006). "My heart is always there": The transnational practices of first-generation Mexican immigrant and second-generation Mexican American women. *Identities, 13*(3), 335–362.

Vivian, J. & Maurin, P.J. (2009). *The media of mass communication* (5th Canadian ed.). Toronto, ON: Pearson Education Canada, Inc.

Vold, G., Bernard, T., & Snipes, J. (2002). *Theoretical criminology* (5th ed.). New York: Oxford University Press.

Volti, R. (2005). *Society and technological change* (5th ed.). New York: Worth Publishers.

Waddington, D. & King, M. (2005). The disorderly crowd: From classical psychological reductionism to socio-contextual theory—the impact on public order policing strategies. *Howard Journal of Criminal Justice, 44*(5), 490–503. doi:10.1111/j.1468-2311.2005.00393.x

Waddle, R. (2006). *Reality TV: Guilty pleasure or window to our souls?* Retrieved from http://www.archives.umc.org/interior.asp?ptid=1&mid=1284

Wade, D.T. (2007). *Social roles and long-term illness: Is it time to rehabilitate convalescence?* Sage Publications, Ltd. Retrieved from http://library.mtroyal.ca:2048/login?url=http://search.ebscohost.com/login.aspx?direct=true&AuthType=ip,url,cookie,uid&db=a9h&AN=25553584&site=ehost-live

Walby, S. (1997). *Gender transformations*. London: Routledge.

Waldrep, B.D. (2007). Lewis Sperry Chafer and the roots of nondenominational fundamentalism in the south. *Journal of Southern History, 73*(4), 807–836. Retrieved from http://library.mtroyal.ca:2048/login?url=http://search.ebscohost.com/login.aspx?direct=true&AuthType=ip,url,cookie,uid&db=a9h&AN=27375328&site=ehost-live

Walker, G. (2007). Climate change 2007: A world melting from the top down. *Nature, 446*(7137), 218-221. doi:10.1038/446718a

Walker, I. & Smith, H.J. (Eds.). (2002). *Relative deprivation: Specification, development, and integration*. Cambridge, UK: Cambridge University Press.

Walker, R.C. (2006). Interweaving Aboriginal/indigenous rights with urban citizenship: A view from the Winnipeg low-cost housing sector, Canada. *Citizenship Studies, 10*(4), 391–411.

Walks, R.A. & Bourne, L.S. (2006). Ghettos in Canada's cities? Racial segregation, ethnic enclaves and poverty concentration in Canadian urban areas. *Canadian Geographer, 50*(3), 273–297. Retrieved from http://library.mtroyal.ca:2083/pqdweb?did=1162629781&Fmt=7&clientId=65345&RQT=309&VName=PQD

Wallace, R.A. & Wolf, A. (1999). *Contemporary sociological theory: Expanding the classical tradition* (5th ed.). Upper Saddle River, NJ: Prentice-Hall, Inc.

Wallace, R.A. & Wolf, A. (2006). *Contemporary sociological theory: Expanding the classical tradition* (6th. ed.). Upper Saddle River, NJ: Prentice-Hall, Inc.

Wallerstein, I. (1976). *The modern world-system*. New York: Academic Press, Inc.

Wallerstein, I. (2004). *World-systems analysis: An introduction*. Durham, NC: Duke University Press.

Walsh, Y. (2001). Deconstructing 'brainwashing' within cults as an aid to counselling psychologists. *Counselling Psychology Quarterly, 14*(2), 119–128.

Walter, P. (2007). Adult learning in new social movements: Environmental protest and the struggle for the Clayoquot Sound rainforest. *Adult Education Quarterly, 57*(3), 248–263. Retrieved from http://library.mtroyal.ca:2048/login?url=http://search.ebscohost.com/login.aspx?direct=true&AuthType=ip,url,cookie,uid&db=a9h&AN=24957352&site=ehost-live

Walters, D., Phythian, K., & Anisef, P. (2007). The acculturation of Canadian immigrants: Determinants of ethnic identification with the host society. *The Canadian Review of Sociology and Anthropology, 44*(1), 37. Retrieved from http://library.mtroyal.ca:2083/pqdweb?did=1366162361&Fmt=7&clientId=65345&RQT=309&VName=PQD

Walton, M. (2008). Countries in tug-of-war over arctic resources. *CNN*. Retrieved 10/2/2009, from http://cnn.site.printhis.clickability.com/pt/cpt?action=cpt&title= Countries+in+tug-of-war

Wang, E.S., Chen, L.S., Lin, J.Y., & Wang, M.C. (2008). The relationship between leisure satisfaction and life satisfaction of adolescents concerning online games. *Adolescence, 43*(169), 177–184. Retrieved from http://library.mtroyal.ca:2048/login?url=http://library.mtroyal.ca:2924/login.aspx? direct=true&AuthType=ip,url,cookie,uid&db=a9h&AN=31526226&site=ehost-live

Ward, A. (n.d.). *Feral children*. Retrieved 02/11/2007, from http://www.feralchildren.com/en/index.php

Ward, D.A. (1980). Toward a normative explanation of "old fashioned revivals". *Qualitative Sociology, 3*(1), 3–22. Retrieved from http://library.mtroyal.ca:2048/login?url=http://search.ebscohost.com/login.aspx?direct=true&AuthType=ip,url,cookie,uid&db=a9h&AN=16371292&site=ehost-live

Waring, M. (1990). *If women counted*. San Francisco: Harper.

Watchtower. (2006). *Jehovah's witnesses—who are they? What do they believe?* Retrieved 11/03/2008, from http://www.watchtower.org/e/jt/index.htm?article=article_03.htm

Watkins, K. (2007). *Human development report 2007/2008: Fighting climate change: Human solidarity in a divided world*. New York: United Nations Development Programme.

Watkinson, A.M. (2006). Supreme Court of Canada stands behind corporal punishment—sort of . . . *International Social Work, 49*(4), 531–536.

Watson, J.K. (2007). Imperial mimicry, modernisation theory and the contradictions of postcolonial

South Korea. *Postcolonial Studies, 10*(2), 171–190. doi:10.1080/13688790701348565

Watson, S. (2008). *Howstuffworks "how podcasting works".* Retrieved 09/05/2008, from http://computer.howstuffworks.com/podcasting.htm/printable

Watson, T.J. (2003). *Sociology, work and industry* (4th ed.). London, UK: Routledge, Taylor & Francis Group.

Wayne Ellwood. (2003). *The no-nonsense guide to globalization.* Oxford OX4 1BW, UK: New Internationalist Publications Ltd.

Weait, M. (2005). Harm, consent and the limits of privacy. *Feminist Legal Studies, 13*(1), 97–122.

Weatherley, D. (1988). Error without trial: Psychological research on antisemitism. In W. Bergmann, & H.A. Strauss (Eds.), (pp. 87-97). Berlin: De Gruyter.

Webb, J. (2001). *Marconi: Newfoundland and Labrador heritage.* Retrieved 04/05/2008, from http://www.heritage.nf.ca/society/marconi.html

Webber, M. (2005). "Don't be so feminist": Exploring student resistance to feminist appraoches in a Canadian university. *Women's Studies International Forum, 28*, 181–194.

Webber, M. (forthcoming). Women and education. In N. Mandell (Ed.), *Feminist issues* (5th ed.). Toronto: Pearson.

Weber, M. (1946). *From Max Weber* [1922] (H. Gerth, C.W. Mills Trans.). New York: Oxford University Press.

Weber, M. (1946[1906]). Protestant sects and the spirit of capitalism. In H. Garth & C.W. Mills (Eds.), *From Max Weber* (pp. 302–322). New York: Oxford University Press.

Weber, M. (1968). *Economy and society: An outline of interpretive sociology.* New York: Bedminster Press.

Weber, M. (2005[1904]). *The Protestant ethic and the spirit of capitalism* (translation T. Parsons). London, UK: Routledge.

Weeks, J. (2003). *Sexuality* (2nd ed.). London: Routledge.

Weeks, J. (2005). *Inequality trends in some developed OECD countries.* Retrieved 11/30, from http://www.un.org/esa/desa/papers/2005/wp6_2005.pdf

Wegierski, M. (2007). Canada's identity crisis: Looking back to the mid-1990s. *Enter Stage Right.* Retrieved from http://www.enterstageright.com/archive/articles/0207/0207canident.htm

Weir, A. (2005). The global universal caregiver: Imagining women's liberation in the new millennium. *Constellations, 12*(3), 308–330.

Weiss, J. (2004). Trans studies. In J. Eadie (Ed.), *Sexuality* (pp. 230–230). London: Arnold.

Weldon, R.A. (2001). An 'urban legend' of global proportion: An analysis of nonfiction accounts of the ebola virus. *Journal of Health Communication, 6*(3), 281. Retrieved from http://library.mtroyal.ca:2048/login?url=http://search.ebscohost.com/login.aspx?direct=true&AuthType=ip,url,cookie,uid&db=a9h&AN=5762721&site=ehost-live

Wells, B. (2002). Women's voices: Explaining poverty and plenty in a rural community. *Rural Sociology, 67*(2), 234. Retrieved from http://library.mtroyal.ca:2083/pqdweb?did=126994901&Fmt=7&clientId=65345&RQT=309&VName=PQD

Wells, E. (2006). Recent trends in theorizing pre-hispanic mesoAmerican economies. *Journal of Archaeological Research, 14*(4), 265–312. doi:10.1007/s10814-006-9006-3

Welshman, J. (2006). *Underclass: A history of the excluded, 1880-2000.* London, UK: Hambledon Continuum.

Welzel, C. (2007). *A human development view on value change.* Retrieved 05/06/2008, from http://margaux.grandvinum.se/SebTest/wvs/articles/folder_published/article_base_83

West, C. & Fenstermaker, S. (2002). Doing difference. In S. Fenstermaker, & C. West (Eds.), *Doing gender, doing difference: Inequality, power and institutional change* (pp. 55–80). New York: Routledge.

Westby, D.L. (1991). *The growth of sociological theory: Human nature, knowledge, and social change.* Englewood Cliffs, NJ: Prentice-Hall, Inc.

Western, M. & Wright, E.O. (1994). The permeability of class boundaries to intergenerational mobility among men in the United States, Canada, Norway and Sweden. *American Sociological Review, 59*(4), 606. Retrieved from http://proquest.umi.com/pqdweb?did=1528774&Fmt=7&clientId=65345&RQT=309&VName=PQD

Westra, L. (1999). *Environmental racism and the First Nations of Canada: Terrorism at Oka* Blackwell Publishing Limited. Retrieved from http://library.mtroyal.ca:2048/login?url=http://search.ebscohost.com/login.aspx?direct=true&AuthType=ip,url,cookie,uid&db=a9h&AN=4370841&site=ehost-live

Westra, L. & Lawson, B.E. (Eds.). (2001). *Faces of environmental racism: Confronting issues of global justice* (2nd ed.). Lanham, MD: Rowman and Littlefield Publishers, Inc.

What is postmodernism? Retrieved 04/03/2008, from http://www.hewett.norfolk.sch.uk/curric/soc/POSTMODE/post1.htm

Wherrett, J. (1999). *Aboriginal self-government.* Retrieved 22/04/2008, from http://www.parl.gc.ca/information/library/PRBpubs/962-e.htm

White, J. (1999). Work-family stage and satisfaction with work-family balance. *Journal of Comparative Family Studies, 30*(2), 163–175.

White, J. & Klein, D. (2008). *Family theories* (3rd ed.). Los Angeles: SAGE.

White, R. & Haines, F. (2004). *Crime and criminology* (3rd ed.). Sydney: Oxford University Press.

The White House. (2001). *Text of a letter from the president.* Retrieved 06/09/2008, from http://www.whitehouse.gov/news/releases/2001/03/20010314.html

Whitehead, H. (1987). *Renunciation and reformulation: A study of conversion in an American sect.* Ithica, NY: Cornell University Press.

Whitlock, J., Lader, W., & Conterio, K. (2007). The internet and self-injury: What psychotherapists should know. *Journal of Clinical Psychology, 63*(11), 1135–1143. doi:10.1002/jclp.20420

Whitney, C. (2007). Culture, human nature, and the democratic republic of Congo, triangulated from the mid-Pacific and Iraqi Kurdistan. *Review of Human Factor Studies, 13*(1), 41–73.

Whitt, L.A. (1998). Biocolonialism and the commodification of knowledge. *Science as Culture, 7*(1), 33. Retrieved from http://library.mtroyal.ca:2048/login?url=http://search.ebscohost.com/login.aspx?direct=true&AuthType=ip,url,cookie,uid&db=a9h&AN=6870325&site=ehost-live

WHO. (2008a). *Children's environmental health.* Retrieved 24/07/2008, from http://www.who.int/ceh/risks/cehair/en/

WHO. (2008b). *Female genital mutilation.* http://www.who.int/mediacentre/factsheets/fs241/en/

Wicks, A. (2006). Older women's "ways of doing": Strategies for successful ageing. *Ageing International, 31*(4), 263–275. Retrieved from http://library.mtroyal.ca:2048/login?url=http://search.ebscohost.com/login.aspx?direct=true&AuthType=ip,url,cookie,uid&db=a9h&AN=25640364&site=ehost-live

Williams, C. (2000). Income and expenditures. *Canadian Social Trends, Winter*(59), 7–12.

Williams, C. (2005). The sandwich generation. *Canadian Social Trends, Summer*, 16–21.

Williams, S.C. & Mackey, M.C. (1999). Women's experiences of preterm labor: A feminist critique. *Health Care for Women International, 20*(1), 29–48. doi:10.1080/073993399245944

Willis, P. (1977). *Learning to labour: How working class kids get working class jobs.* Farborough: Saxon House.

Wilson, B. & Atkinson, M. (2005). Rave and straightedge, the virtual and the real. *Youth and Society, 36*(3), 276–311.

Wilson, E.O. (1975). *Sociobiology: The new synthesis.* Cambridge, MA: Harvard University Press.

Wilson, M. & Daly, M. (1994). *Spousal homicide.* Ottawa: Canadian Centre for Justice Statistics.

Wimmer, R.D., & Dominick, J.R. (2006). *Mass media research: An introduction.* Belmont, CA: Thomson Wadsworth.

Winichakul, T. (2008). Toppling democracy. *Journal of Contemporary Asia, 38*(1), 11–37. Retrieved from http://library.mtroyal.ca:2048/login?url=http://search.ebscohost.com/login.aspx?direct=true&AuthType=ip,url,cookie,uid&db=a9h&AN=29741092&site=ehost-live

Winslow, D. (1999). Rites of passage and groups bonding in the Canadian airborne. *Armed Forces and Society, 25*(3), 429–457.

Winston, B. (1998). *Media technology and society: A history: From the telegraph to the internet.* London, UK: Routledge, Inc.

Winterdyke, J. (2006). *Canadian criminology.* Toronto: Pearson.

Winterich, J. (2007). Aging, femininity, and the body: What appearance changes mean to women with age. *Gender Issues, 24*(3), 51–69. doi:10.1007/s12147-007-9045-1

Wisdom, J.P., Rees, A.M., Riley, K.J., & Weis, T.R. (2007). Adolescents' perceptions of the gendered context of depression: "tough" boys and objectified girls. *Journal of Mental Health Counseling, 29*(2), 144–162.

Wolff, A. (1994). *Strategies for working families.* Toronto: Ontario Coalition for Better Child Care.

Wolf-Wendel, L. & Ward, K. (2003). Negotiating work and family: Parenting and dual-career dilemmas. In B. Ropers-Huilman (Ed.), *Gendered futures in higher education: Critical perspectives for change* (pp. 111–134). Albany: State University of New York.

Women and men working together for rural development in Rwanda. Retrieved 15/07/2008, from http://acdi-cida.gc.ca/CIDAWEB/acdicida.nsf/En/NAT-711113816-LCG

Wong, J. (2006). Age of consent to sexual activity in Canada: Background to proposed new legislation on "age of sexual protection." *The Canadian Journal of Human Sexuality, 15*(3-4), 163–169.

Wood, L., Giles-Corti, B., & Bulsara, M. (2005). The pet connection: Pets as a conduit for social capital? *Social Science and Medicine, 61,* 1159–1173.

Woodcock, K., Rohan, M., & Campbell, L. (2007). Equitable representation of deaf people in mainstream academia: Why not? *Higher Education, 53*(3), 359–379. doi:10.1007/s10734-005-2428-x

Woodward, J. (2007). BC's native languages rapidly dying: Linguists. *The Vancouver Sun,* September 19, 2007. Retrieved from http://www.Canada.com/vancouversun/news/story.html?id=2acdcf66-acf0-470a-b029-74d096de7c23

Woody Allen's son can never forgive his father. (2005). *Female First.* Retrieved from http://www.Femalefirst.co.uk/celebrity/Woody+Allen-2269.html

World Association of Newspapers. (2005). *World's 100 largest newspapers.* Retrieved 02/05/2008, from http://www.wan-press.org/article2825.html

World Association of Newspapers. (2007). *World digital media trends, 2007: Executive summary.* Retrieved 05/01/2008, from http://www.wan-press.org/iMG/doc/Executive_Summary_wdmt.doc

World Bank. (n.d.). *India—water.* Retrieved 05/10/2007, from http://www.worldbank.org.in/WBSITE/EXTERNAL/COUNTRIES/SOUTHASIAEXT/iNDIAEXTN/0,,contentMDK: 20668501~pagePK: 141137~piPK:141127~theSitePK:295584,00.html

World Bank. (2005). *World development indicators.* Retrieved 6/5/2008, from http://devdata.worldbank.org/wdi2005/section1_1_1.htm

World Bank. (2007a). *Atlas of global development.* Washington, DC: World Bank.

World Bank. (2007b). *World development indicators 2007.* Retrieved 05/09/2008, from http://siteresources.worldbank.org/DATASTATISTICS/Resources/WDI07section4-intro.pdf

World Bank. (2008). *About us.* Retrieved 12/06/2008, from http://web.worldbank.org/WBSITE/EXTERNAL/EXTABOUTUS/0,,contentMDK: 20046292~menuPK:51123588~pagePK:0004410~piPK:36602~theSitePK:29708, 00.html

World Bank Group. (n.d.). *Youthink!* Retrieved 07/06/2007, from http://youthink.worldbank.org/issues/development/

World Commission on Environment and Development. (1987). *Our common future: The world commission on environment and development.* Oxford: Oxford University Press.

World Economic Forum (WEF). (2007). *The global gender gap report 2007.* Geneva: World Economic Forum.

World Future Society. (2008). *Top 10 forecasts for 2009 and beyond.* Retrieved from http://www.wfs.org/Sept-Oct08/Nov-Dec%20FUTURIST/topTen.htm

World Health Organization. (2006). *Obesity in Europe.* Retrieved 28/06/2008, from http://www.euro.who.int/obesity/import/20060220_1

World Health Organization. (2008). *Governance of WHO.* Retrieved 29/06/2008, from http://www.who.int/about/governance/en/

World Resources Institute. (n.d.). *Losses of biodiversity and their causes.* Retrieved 23/07/2008, from http://www.wri.org/publication/content/8184

World Tourism Organization. (1995). *WTO statement on the prevention of organized sex tourism.* Retrieved 13/12/2007, from http://www.worldtourism.org/protect_children/statements/wto_a.htm

World Trade Organization. (n.d.). *Understanding the WTO—the GATT years: From Havana to Marrakesh.* Retrieved 12/06/2008, from http://www.wto.org/english/thewto_e/whatis_e/tif_e/fact4_e.htm

World Trade Organization. (2008). *Dispute settlement.* Retrieved 03/24, from http://library.mtroyal.ca:3650/english/tratop_e/dispu_e/dispu_e.htm

Wortley, S. (1999). Northern taboo: Research on race, crime and criminal justice in Canada. *Canadian Journal of Criminology, 41*(2), 261–274.

Wortley, S. & Tanner, J. (2003). Data denials and confusion and the racial profiling debate in Toronto. *Canadian Journal of Crime and Criminal Justice, 45*(3), 367–389.

Wotherspoon, T. (2004). *The sociology of education in Canada: Critical perspectives* (2nd ed.). Toronto: Oxford University Press.

Wotherspoon, T. (2008). Education. In L. Tepperman, J. Curtis, & P. Albanese (Eds.), *Sociology: A Canadian perspective* (2nd ed., pp. 244–275). Don Mills: Oxford University Press.

Woynillowicz, D. (2008). *Want to clean up Alberta's reputation? Clean up the oil sands.* Retrieved 8/9/2008, from http://www.pembina.org/op-ed/1652

Wright, E.O. (1996). *Class counts: Comparative study in class analysis.* Cambridge, UK: Cambridge University Press.

Wrong, D.H. (1959). The functional theory of stratification: Some neglected considerations. *American Sociological Review, 24,* 772–782.

Wyndham, L. (1949). *American and cosmic man.* Garden City, NY: Doubleday and Company.

XM Radio. (2008). *XM customer promise.* Retrieved 07/05/2008, from http://www.xmradio.com/merger/news.xmc

Yao, P. (2002). The status of pleasure courtesan and literati connections in T'ang China (618–907). *Journal of Women's History, 14*(2), 1. Retrieved from http://library.mtroyal.ca:2048/login?url=http://library.mtroyal.ca:2924/login.aspx?direct=true&AuthType=ip,url,cookie,uid&db=a9h&AN=6969489&site=ehost-live

Yates, R., Yates, R., & Bain, P. (2000). *Introduction to law in Canada* (2nd ed.). Scarborough: Prentice Hall.

York University Archives and Special Collections. (n.d.). *F0461—Ruth Morris Fonds.* Retrieved 9/17/2007, from http://archivesfa.library.yorku.ca/fonds/ON00370-f0000461.htm

Young, C. (2003). Tax policy, theoretical explorations, and social realities. *Canadian Tax Journal, 51*(5), 1922–1930.

Zahoor, A. (1996). *Ibn Khaldun.* Retrieved 22/04/2008, from http://www.unhas.ac.id/~rhiza/saintis/khaldun.html

Zakaria, F. (2008). *A renegade against Greenpeace | Newsweek future of energy | newsweek.com.* Retrieved 6/29/2008, from http://www.newsweek.com/id/131753

Zheng Wu & Nan Li. (2003). Immigration and the dependency ratio of a host population. *Mathematical Population Studies, 10*(1), 21. Retrieved from http://library.mtroyal.ca:2048/login?url=http://search.ebscohost.com/login.aspx?direct=true&AuthType=ip,url,cookie,uid&db=a9h&AN=9036992&site=ehost-live

Zimbardo, P. (2008). *The Stanford prison experiment.* Retrieved July 13, 2008, from http://www.prisonexp.org

Zitzelsberger, H. (2005). *(In)visibility: Accounts of embodiment of women with physical disabilities and differences.*

Zohrabian, A. (2005). The long-term effects and economic consequences of treatments for obesity: Work in progress. *Lancet, 365*(9454), 104–105. Retrieved from http://library.mtroyal.ca:2048/login?url=http://search.ebscohost.com/login.aspx?direct=true&AuthType=ip,url,cookie,uid&db=a9h&AN=15591034&site=ehost-live

Zottarelli, L. (2008). Post-hurricane Katrina employment recovery: The interaction of race and place. *Social Science Quarterly, 89*(3), 592–607.

Zukeran, P. (2002). *Buddhism.* Retrieved 09/03/2008, from http://www.leaderu.com/orgs/probe/docs/buddhism.html

Zweigenhaft, R.L. & Domhoff, W.G. (1998). *Diversity in the power elite: Have women and minorities reached the top?.* New Haven, CT: Yale University Press.

Credits

Photo Credits

Chapter 1: Page 3, Leland Bobbe/Getty Images; Page 4, Culver Pictures Inc.; Page 5, © SW Productions/Brand X/Corbis; Page 6, Shutterstock; Page 14, Shutterstock; Page 15 (top), Helen Abell Collection, University of Guelph Library; Page 15 (bottom), Archives and Research Collections, MacOdrom Library, Carleton University; Page 18 The Canadian Press(Fred Chartrand); Page 26, Shutterstock.

Chapter 2: Page 37, 20th Century Fox/American Zoetrope/The Kobal Collection; Page 39, © Dick Hemingway; Page 46, © JUPITERIMAGES/Creatas/Alamy; Page 52, Emilie Barrucand, French ethnologist photographed in Xingu, Amazon Portrait by Marc Lécureuil; Page 58, © Dick Hemingway.

Chapter 3: Page 67, Tony Wheeler/Lonely Planet Images; Page 71, The Canadian Press (Steve White); Page 76, photosindia/Getty Images; Page 80, The Canadian Press (Everett Collection); Page 88, Shutterstock.

Chapter 4: Page 97, PM Images/Getty Images; Page 99, Shutterstock; Page 104, © SW Productions/Brand X/Corbis; Page 110, Shutterstock; Page 114, Shutterstock; Page 117, ©Greg Smith/Corbis.

Chapter 5: Page 129, Digital Vision/Getty Images; Page 132, Shutterstock; Page 141, Digital Vision/Getty Images; Page 146, © Damian P. Gadal/Alamy; Page 154, Masterfile.

Chapter 6: Page 167, © Reuters/CORBIS; Page 169, Jupiterimages; Page 178, © JUPITERIMAGES/Creatas/Alamy; Page 181, Shutterstock; Page 182, Jupiterimages.

Chapter 7: Page 193, ICP/Alamy; Page 196, The Canadian Press (Gautam Singh); Page 202, Calgary Sun/The Canadian Press(Jack Cusano); Page 207, Jupiterimages; Page 216, © Jenny Matthews/Alamy.

Chapter 8: Page 227, JUPITERIMAGES/ Polka Dot / Alamy; Page 231, © Kim Kyung-Hoon/Reuters/Corbis; Page 235, © Bubbles Photolibrary/Alamy; Page 242, Jupiterimages; Page 252, © Image Source Pink/Alamy.

Chapter 9: Page 216, © Shaun Best/Reuters/Corbis; Page 263, © Dick Hemingway; Page 274, © Corbis Super RF/Alamy; Page 276, LAC, C-046355; Page 280, The Canadian Press Hamilton Spectator(Sheryl Nadler).

Chapter 10: Page 291, Shutterstock; Page 292, The Bridgeman Art Library/Getty Images; Page 299, © Jupiterimages/Pixland/Alamy; Page 308, © Bill Aron/Photo Edit; Page 314, Jupiterimages.

Chapter 11: Page 325, Shutterstock; Page 332, The Advertising Archives; Page 339, Shutterstock; Page 345, Masterfile.

Chapter 12: Page 357, © Rick D'Elia/Corbis/Corbis; Page 359, © codepink4peace; Page 368, Bob Thomas/Getty Images; Page 374, The Canadian Press (Shaney Komulainen); Page 377, Reprinted with permission from MADD Canada (Mothers Against Drunk Driving); Page 379, © Courtesy of Twentieth Century Fox/Bureau L.A. Collection/Corbis.

Text Credits

Chapter 1: Page 9 (top), Source: Statistics Canada, The Daily (Income of Canadians) Thursday, May 3, 2007 [online]. Available: http://www.statcan.ca/Daily/English/070503/d070503a.htm; Page 9 (bottom), Source: Statistics Canada, The Daily (Income of Canadians) Thursday, May 3, 2007 [online]. Available: http://www.statcan.ca/Daily/English/070503/d070503a.htm.

Chapter 3: Page 74, National Geographic Maps / NG Stock; Page 86, Courtesy Chris Livesey.

Chapter 4: Page 98, Source: Authors: Brizendine, Louann Title: The Female Brain, 2006 Broadway Books New York; Page 99, Source: October 1998 The Safety & Health Practiioner magazine (SHP) vol 16 issue 10 www.shponline.co.uk; page 106, "Figure of Erickson's Stages Of Personality Development", from CHILDHOOD AND SOCIETY by Erik H. Erickson. Copyright 1950, © 1963 by W.W. Norton & Company, Inc., renewed © 1978, 1991 by Erik H. Erikson. Adapted and used by permission of W. W. Norton & Company, Inc.; Page 115 (top), Source: Statistics Canada: The Daily, Thursday, October 26, 2006. Canada's population by age and sex). Available: http://www.statcan.ca/Daily/English/061026/d061026b.htm; Page 115 (bottom), Source: Statistics Canada: A Portrait of Seniors in Canada. Available: http://www.statcan.ca/english/freepub/89-519-XIE/2006001/images/chart.gif; Page 116, Reprinted with the permission of Scribner, A Division of Simon & Schuster, Inc., from ON DEATH AND DYING by Elisabeth Kubler-Ross. Copyright © 1969 by Elisabeth Kubler-Ross; copyright renewed © 1997 by Elisabeth Lubler-Ross. All rights reserved.

Chapter 5: Page 137 (top), Reprinted by permission of the publisher from CRIME AND THE MAN by Earnest Albert Hooton p 57, Cambridge, Mass.: Harvard University Press, Copyright © 1939 by the President and Fellows of Harvard College, Copyright renewed 1967 by Mary C. Hooton; Page 137 (bottom), Pearson; Page 142–143, Chris McCormick, Crime Matters, Daily Gleaner, June 24, 2004; Page 147, Source: Statistics Canada. (2003). Canadian Centre for Justice Statistics, Incident-based Uniform Crime Reporting Survey. Retrieved

July 13, 2009, fromhttp://www.statcan.gc.ca/pub/85-227-x/85-227-x2002000-eng.pdf; Page 153, Source: Statistics Canada http://www.statcan.ca/Daily/English/070718/d070718b.htm; Page 154, Source: Statistics Canada http://www.statcan.ca/Daily/English/070718/d070718b.htm.

Chapter 6: Page 170, Source: Adapted from Statistics Canada, 2007 (http://www12.statcan.ca/english/census06/analysis/famhouse/tables/table1.htm; Page 179, Source: Based on data from Statistics Canada. (2007). http://www12.statcan.ca/english/census06/analysis/famhouse/tables/table1.htm; Page 182, Source: Symes v. Canada, 1993, 4 S.C.R. 695 Supreme Court of Canada.

Chapter 7: Page 198, Source: Statistics Canada. 2006. The Daily (Inequality in Wealth) Wednesday, December 13, 2006 [online]. Available: http://www.statcan.ca/Daily/English/061213/d061213c.htm (December 6, 2007); Page 200, Source: NORC General Social Surveys, 1972–1996: Cumulative Codebook. Chicago: NORC, 1996. Reprinted by permission of NORC, Chicago, IL. http://www.norc.org/Contact+Us/; Page 210, Source: Statistics Canada. 2007. Persistence of Low Income Among Non-elderly Unattached Individuals [online]. Available: http://www.statcan.ca/english/research/75F0002MIE/75F0002MIE2007005.pdf [December, 9, 2007]; Page 211 (top), Source: Statistics Canada, 2006, Chart 6.1, p.135 "Average Income of Women and Men" from http://www.statcan.ca/english/freepub/89-503-XIE/0010589-503-XIE.pdf; Page 211 (bottom), Statistics Canada. 2007. The Daily (Income of Canadians) Thursday May 3, 2007 [online]. Available: http://www.statcan.ca/Daily/English/070503/d070503a.htm [December 10, 2007]; Page 213, Source: Statistics Canada. 2006. Education Matters [online]. Available: http://www.statcan.ca/english/freepub/81-004-XIE/2006003/backto.htm December 10, 2007]; Page 215, Courtesy National Anti-Poverty Organization Source: The Face Of Poverty In Canada: An Overview [Online]. Available: http://oafb.ca/portal/images/pdfs/poverty_canada/face%20of%20poverty%20in%20canada%202003.pdf [December 11, 2007].

Chapter 8: Page 238 (top), Source: Plastic Surgery Statistics Canada, iFinance, Medicard; Page 238 (bottom), Source: Plastic Surgery Statistics Canada, iFinance, Medicard; Page 241, Source: Adapted from the Canadian Council on Social Development (2004). A Profile of Economic Security in Canada. http://www.ccsd.ca/factsheets/economic_security/poverty/index.htm; Reprinted with permission.

Chapter 9: Page 265, Source: Statistics Canada Adapted from figure entitled "Immigration has fluctuated over the century . . . " from p. 3 of http://www.statcan.ca/english/kits/pdf/social/100yr3.pdf; Page 266, Sources: Statistics Canada, censuses of population, 1981 to 2006. http://www12.statcan.ca/Framework/Images/scheme-v101/fipstc01-en.gif [January 26, 2008]; Page 270, Source: Statistics Canada Figure 8 from page 19 from: http://www.statcan.ca/english/freepub/89-593-XIE/89-593-XIE2003001.pdf; Page 271, Source: Healey & O'Brien, 2007, p.10 based on Merton, 1948; Page 281, Source: Statistics Canada. 2008. Aboriginal identity population by age groups, median age and sex, 2006 counts, for Canada, provinces and territories - 20% sample data (table). Aboriginal

Peoples Highlight Tables. 2006 Census. Statistics Canada Catalogue no. 97-558-XWE2006002. Ottawa. Released January 15, 2008.

Chapter 10: Page 294, World Association of Newspapers, 2005: World's 100 Largest Newspapers [Online]. Available: http://www.wan-press.org/article2825.html [May 02, 2008]; Canadian Newspaper Association, 2006: Canadian Newspaper Circulation Data, 2006; Page 296, Source: Statistics Canada, 2007: Radio Listening [Online]. Available: http://www.statcan.ca/Daily/English/070626/d070626b.htm [May 06, 2008]; Page 297, [May 06, 2008] Source: Statistics Canada, 2006: Television Viewing [Online]. Available: http://www.statcan.ca/Daily/English/060331/d060331b.htm.

Chapter 11: Page 306, Sources: Shaw, 2007; Shecter, 2008; Surridge, 2008 http://your.rogers.com/investorrelations/investor_overview.asp Hugh Harley, Personal Communication, May 27, 2008; Page 327 (top), Source: Turcotte, M., & Schellenberg, G. (2007). A portrait of seniors in Canada. Retrieved June 24, 2008, from http://www. statcan.ca/english/freepub/89-519-XIE/89-519-XIE2006001.htm; Page 327 (bottom). Source: Turcotte, M., & Schellenberg, G. (2007). A portrait of seniors in Canada. Retrieved June 24, 2008, from http://www. statcan.ca/english/freepub/89-519-XIE/89-519-XIE2006001.htm; Page 329, Source: Turcotte & Schellenberg, 2007. A Portrait of Seniors in Canada. Statistics Canada. Available: http://www.statcan.ca/english/freepub/89-519-XIE/2006001/charts/chart2_2_6.htm [June 24, 2008]; Page 330, Based on OECD Health Data 2008 - Frequently Requested Data, www.oecd.org/health/healthdata; Page 335, Source: Statistics Canada. (2007). Participation and activity limitation survey. Retrieved June 27, 2008, fromhttp://www.statcan.ca/Daily/English/071203/d071203a.htm; Page 336, Source: Statistics Canada, 2003: Canadian Community Health Survey: Mental health and Well-being. Available: http://www.statcan.ca/Daily/English/030903/d030903a.htm; Page 337, Source: Statistics Canada. 2005. "Canadian community Health Survey: Obesity among Children and Adults." The Daily. July 6 Catalogue no 11-001; Page 342, Source: Statistics Canada. 2004, "Joint Canada/United States Survey of Health." The Daily. June 2. Catalogue 11-001). Available: http://www.statcan.ca/Daily/English/040602/c040602b.gif [June 29, 2008]; Page 343, Source: Turcotte, Martin and Grant Schellenberg. 2007. A Portrait of Seniors in Canada. Statistics Canada) Available: http://www.statcan.ca/english/freepub/89-519-XIE/2006001/charts/chart6_1_2.htm [June 29, 2008]; Page 344, ANNALS OF INTERNAL MEDICINE. ONLINE by Ginsberg, Doherty, Ralston Jr., Senkeeto. Copyright 2008 by American College of Physicians - Journals. Reproduced with permission of American College of Physicians - Journals via Copyright Clearance Center; Page 346, Source: OECD, 2008 [Health Data 2008]. Available: http://www.oecd.org/dataoecd/46/36/38979632.xls [June 30, 2008].

Chapter 12: Page 360, Adapted from http://www.theramartens.com/thesis_website/appendix.html [July 3, 2008]. Reprinted with permission of the author; Page 377, Source: St Paul Riveer Basin Publishing Co Robertson, James (1978) "The Sane Alternative" 1983 revised edition pp. 10–23 http://www.jamesrobertson.com/book/thesanealternative.pdf; Page 378, From www.wfs.org used with permission.

Name Index

Subject Index